A Complete Guide to DB2 Universal Database

The Morgan Kaufmann Series in Data Management Systems

Series Editor, Jim Gray

A Complete Guide to DB2 Universal Database
Don Chamberlin

Universal Database Management:
A Guide to Object/Relational Technology
Cynthia Maro Saracco

Understanding SQL's Stored Procedures:
A Complete Guide to SQL/PSM
Jim Melton

Principles of Multimedia Database Systems
V. S. Subrahmanian

Principles of Database Query Processing
for Advanced Applications
Clement T. Yu and Weiyi Meng

The Object Database Standard: ODMG 2.0
R. G. G. Cattell et al.

Introduction to Advanced Database Systems
Carlo Zaniolo, Stefano Ceri, Christos
Faloutsos, Richard Snodgrass,
V. S. Subrahmanian, and Roberto Zicari

Principles of Transaction Processing
Philip A. Bernstein and Eric Newcomer

Using the New DB2: IBM's Object-Relational
Database System
Don Chamberlin

Distributed Algorithms
Nancy A. Lynch

Object-Relational DBMSs: The Next
Great Wave
Michael Stonebraker with Dorothy Moore

Active Database Systems: Triggers and Rules
for Advanced Database Processing
Edited by Jennifer Widom and
Stefano Ceri

Joe Celko's SQL for Smarties: Advanced
SQL Programming
Joe Celko

Migrating Legacy Systems: Gateways,
Interfaces, and the Incremental Approach
Michael L. Brodie and
Michael Stonebraker

Database: Principles, Programming,
and Performance
Patrick O'Neil

Database Modeling and Design:
The Fundamental Principles, Second Edition
Toby J. Teorey

Readings in Database Systems, Second Edition
Edited by Michael Stonebraker

Atomic Transactions
Nancy Lynch, Michael Merritt,
William Weihl, and Alan Fekete

Query Processing for
Advanced Database Systems
Edited by Johann Christoph Freytag,
David Maier, and Gottfried Vossen

Transaction Processing:
Concepts and Techniques
Jim Gray and Andreas Reuter

Understanding the New SQL:
A Complete Guide
Jim Melton and Alan R. Simon

Building an Object-Oriented Database System:
The Story of O_2
Edited by François Bancilhon, Claude
Delobel, and Paris Kanellakis

Database Transaction Models
for Advanced Applications
Edited by Ahmed K. Elmagarmid

A Guide to Developing Client/Server
SQL Applications
Setrag Khoshafian, Arvola Chan,
Anna Wong, and Harry K. T. Wong

The Benchmark Handbook for Database
and Transaction Processing Systems,
Second Edition
Edited by Jim Gray

Camelot and Avalon:
A Distributed Transaction Facility
Edited by Jeffrey L. Eppinger,
Lily B. Mummert, and Alfred Z. Spector

Readings in Object-Oriented
Database Systems
Edited by Stanley B. Zdonik and
David Maier

A Complete Guide to DB2 Universal Database

Don Chamberlin
IBM Almaden Research Center

MORGAN KAUFMANN PUBLISHERS, INC.
San Francisco, California

Senior Editor Diane D. Cerra
Director of Production
 and Manufacturing Yonie Overton
Production Editor Cheri Palmer
Editorial Assistant Antonia Richmond
Cover Design Ross Carron Design
Editorial Illustration (chapter openers and
 selected section heads) Duane Bibby

Technical Illustration Cherie Plumlee
Text Design Donna Davis
Composition Fog Press
Copyeditor Robert Fiske
Proofreader Sharilyn Hovind
Indexer Ty Koontz
Printer Courier Corporation

Morgan Kaufmann Publishers, Inc.
Editorial and Sales Office
340 Pine Street, Sixth Floor
San Francisco, CA 94104-3205
USA
Telephone 415 / 392-2665
Facsimile 415 / 982-2665
Email mkp@mkp.com
WWW www.mkp.com
Order toll free   800 / 745-7323

02   01   00   5   4   3

Library of Congress Cataloging-in-Publication Data

Chamberlin, D. D. (Donald Dean)
    A complete guide to DB2 universal database / Don Chamberlin.
        p. cm.
    Includes bibliographical references and index.
    ISBN 1-55860-482-0
    1. IBM Database 2.   2. Relational databases.   I. Title.
QA76.9.D3C3845 1998
005.75'85—dc21   98-16057
                                            CIP

This book is dedicated to my wife, Judy, who made it possible.

Foreword

by Donald J. Haderle
IBM Fellow and Director of Data Management Architecture and Technology
IBM Software Solutions Division

Very simply, the purpose of a database management system is to store and retrieve data with surety. Twenty-five years ago, Dr. E. F. Codd proposed the relational data model to accomplish this purpose, combining strong mathematical foundations with an intuitive, commonsense user interface. One of the most important advantages of the relational model is its data independence, which promises to make relational systems adaptable to changing sets of requirements.

The first great challenge faced by relational systems was to meet the needs of a broad range of applications, from online transaction processing to decision support, with adequate performance and reasonable cost. For the first time, the SQL-based database systems of the 1980s provided a single language to span the whole range of applications, with support for multiple views of data and independence from physical data structures. Because of the success of these systems, relational databases have become ubiquitous, and SQL has become a world standard database language.

Today, the world of database management is rapidly changing, driven by advances in processing power, storage capacity, and communications bandwidth. A new set of challenges faces today's database systems. Some of these challenges derive from the need to store and retrieve new types of very large objects with complex state and behavior, including multimedia objects and engineering designs. Today's systems also need to increase the value of stored data by capturing more of its semantic content. They need to capture business rules and enable these rules to be shared across all the applications that access common data. A new type of database system is emerging to meet these new challenges and is described by the term *object-relational system*.

With DB2 Universal Database (UDB), IBM introduces a new generation of relational database products. For the first time, a system combines object-relational functionality with parallel processing capability that scales from personal workstations to massively parallel networks. UDB provides a rich set of built-in datatypes and functions. More important, it allows users to create new datatypes and functions to meet the specialized needs of their applications, and to define constraints and triggers to encapsulate their business rules. On top of this infrastructure, UDB provides a set of *extenders* for managing multimedia datatypes such as images, audio, and video.

This book provides a good overview of DB2 Universal Database, with particular emphasis on the features that make it an object-relational system. As one of the original designers of SQL and as a member of the DB2 development team, Don Chamberlin brings to his readers a perspective on how the various features of the system fit together into a synergistic whole. Don's book provides many examples that motivate the advanced features of UDB and illustrate how they can be used to solve real problems. After reading this book, you will be well prepared to interact with UDB as an end user, application developer, or database administrator. At the same time, using UDB as an example, you will learn how relational database management systems are evolving to meet the challenges of today's new database applications.

Foreword

by Jim Gray
Microsoft Research
Series Editor, Morgan Kaufmann Series in Data Management Systems

Twenty-four years ago, Don Chamberlin designed the SEQUEL language and led its first implementation, in an experimental database system called System R. That effort spawned the SQL relational database standard, IBM's DB2 product family, and many successful software companies. Computer scientists at IBM's Almaden Research Center have been experimenting with relational database systems since the relational model was first introduced. They prototyped a distributed relational system called R* (pronounced "R-star") and an extensible relational system called Starburst. They made major contributions to data modeling, transaction management, and workflow. They have also worked closely with IBM's product divisions to help bring you IBM's DB2 product family.

Now, more than two decades later, many of these ideas have come together in a new relational product called DB2 Universal Database (UDB), developed at IBM's laboratories in Toronto, Canada, and San Jose, California. UDB shares the DB2 name but uses new technology based on the Starburst architecture developed at Almaden Research Center. UDB is portable to many hardware and software platforms, including Intel/Windows NT, Intel/OS/2, PowerPC/AIX, SPARC/Solaris, and HPPA/HPUX.

UDB is a substantial advance over traditional relational systems. It integrates object-oriented ideas with the SQL language to produce an object-relational database management system. It includes major innovations in query optimization, recursive queries, active databases, and stored procedures. It integrates technology from DB2 Parallel Edition to support parallel processing, both on symmetric multiprocessors and on massively parallel, shared-nothing platforms. UDB has also made substantial advances in usability, providing graphical user interfaces and wizards to help you perform administrative tasks.

In short, UDB is a revolutionary product from IBM. Since it is a third-generation SQL system, I think of it as Don's grandchild. Many bright people contributed to the early relational systems, but the basic design of SQL was created by Don and his colleague, Ray Boyce.

Don is a great visionary and designer, but his greatest talent is as an expositor. He writes and speaks in crystal-clear prose. He makes complex ideas simple—seemingly trivial. Unfortunately for him, when you make something simple, most people are not impressed with how complex it could have been.

Since you are reading this, you are probably wondering about object-relational systems or about DB2 Universal Database. You probably wish for a guru to guide you through the hype and smoke and mirrors. Well, this is where you should start. I have read this book three times now, and it is *great!*

No other book will explain the concepts so clearly. No other book will take you from concept to running code in as few words. No other book will skip the irrelevant details. Don is a scientist, a teacher, and a programmer. This book combines these three perspectives into a unified and very readable presentation. It teaches both the fundamental ideas and the practical techniques needed to build object-relational database applications.

If you want to use **UDB**, this is a good book to teach you the basics. It also covers advanced topics and provides examples of good programming style. If you want to learn about object-relational database systems, this book gives you a detailed tour of a real one, warts and all. Either way, it is well worth the time you will invest in it.

Contents

Preface

In the rapidly changing world of database management systems, DB2 is an established veteran, with a history dating back to 1983. In fact, DB2 has its roots in the work done at IBM's San Jose Research Laboratory in the 1970s, where the relational data model and SQL originated. DB2 Universal Database (UDB) is the latest member of the DB2 product family. As its name suggests, UDB supports many different types of applications, on many different kinds of data, in many different hardware and software environments. Your investment in learning about UDB will be rewarded by a large payoff in functionality, performance, and productivity.

When you are trying to learn how to use a new system, the best kind of help is a friendly guide who can answer your questions and lead you over the rough spots. The second best kind of help is a set of working examples that you can refer to when writing programs of your own. The objective of this book is to provide both of these kinds of help to users of UDB. The book is organized around a series of practical examples, written in SQL, C, C++, and Java, and includes several complete application programs that can be used as templates for your own programs. The book also contains dozens of practical tips that are distilled from many hours of developing UDB applications.

As its title suggests, this book provides a complete guide to UDB Version 5 in all its aspects, including the interfaces that support end users, application developers, and database administrators. It is intended to be complementary to the IBM product documentation, providing a more narrative style and more explanatory material about the reasoning behind various product features and how these features are intended to be used. Occasionally, references are made to product manuals, such as the *SQL Reference* and the *Administration Guide*, where additional details can be found.

I hope you will find that this book is self-contained and accessible, whether or not you are familiar with previous versions of DB2. I have not assumed that you have any prior knowledge of SQL or of relational database terminology. The book covers elementary principles of database management as well as the advanced features of UDB, which include recursive queries, constraints, triggers, user-defined datatypes and functions, stored procedures, parallel databases, and graphical tools for database administration.

In the database industry, this is a time when the two dominant paradigms, relational and object-oriented database management, are merging into a constructive synthesis that is greater than the sum of its parts. Relational systems offer data independence, multiple views of data, and a high-level, set-oriented query language. Object-oriented systems offer rich and extensible sets of datatypes and the ability to associate semantic behavior with stored objects. The new generation of database systems that is now emerging, often called object-relational systems, combines the strengths of these two complementary approaches. Object-relational systems are an important focus of development by all major database vendors and by the committees responsible for database industry standards. UDB represents IBM's entry in the object-relational marketplace and sets the direction for the other members of the DB2 product family.

This book is a revision of my earlier book, *Using the New DB2: IBM's Object-Relational Database System* (Morgan Kaufmann, 1996), which described UDB's predecessor product, DB2 for Common Servers. Compared to the earlier book, about half of the material in this book is new or revised, including about 150 pages of completely new material. I hope that this book, like its predecessor, will provide value to two classes of readers. Users of the DB2 family of products will benefit from having a complete single-volume tutorial and reference on all aspects of UDB. At the same time, readers who have a general interest in database systems and in the emerging object-relational paradigm will find in this book a discussion of IBM's approach to this important subject, illustrated by many practical examples.

Examples on the World Wide Web

All the examples in this book are available from Morgan Kaufmann's site on the World Wide Web. To obtain the examples from a chapter of the book, use your Web browser to visit the Morgan Kaufmann homepage at `www.mkp.com`. Use the online catalog to find this book. Click on "Web Enhanced" and then on the chapter of interest. Each chapter has an instruction file and several files containing example code and expected results. You can use your browser to read the contents of these files and save them on your computer disk.

Acknowledgments

I am very grateful for the encouragement and support I have received from IBM in the preparation of this book, and especially for the help and cooperation provided by the DB2 development teams at IBM's Almaden, Santa Teresa, and Toronto laboratories. Special thanks are due to all who reviewed the manuscript and made many helpful suggestions, including (but not limited to) Keith Archer, Paul Bird, Serge Bourbonnais, Richard Burke, Mike Carey, Jyh-Herng Chow, Doug Doole, Jessica Escott, William Favero, Jim Kleewein, Gene Kligerman, Sam Lightstone, Serge Limoges, Nelson Mattos, Patrick Mac-Donald, Dale McInnis, John McPherson, Rodolphe Michel, Karen Nolk, Richard Page, Berthold Reinwald, Berni Schiefer, Richard Sidle, Rick Swagerman, Mike Swift, George Wilson, Tim Vincent, Xun Xue, and Shili Yang. Thanks also to the series editor, Jim Gray, for his guidance and support in the writing of the book, to Cheri Palmer and the staff at Morgan Kaufmann for their expert help in its production, and to Duane Bibby for his wonderful illustrations.

Introduction

U NIVERSAL DATABASE is an ambitious name. It suggests a product that is designed to be used for a variety of purposes and in a variety of environments, and that is a good description of DB2 Universal Database, which I will refer to in this book by the abbreviation UDB. Here are some of the ways in which UDB justifies its name:

- It scales all the way from a single-user database on a personal computer to terabyte databases on large multiuser platforms. To span this range, UDB supports two independent kinds of parallelism. It can exploit the power of a symmetric multiprocessor (SMP), in which several processing units share common memory and disks. It can also support a massively parallel "shared nothing" configuration, in which a database is partitioned among many independent machines connected by a network or a high-speed switch, providing large capacity, high performance, and modular growth. For very high-performance applications, the individual machines in a shared-nothing configuration can be symmetric multiprocessors. The scalability of UDB allows it to meet the performance requirements of diverse applications and to adapt easily to changing requirements.

- It supports a large variety of hardware and software environments. UDB servers run on Windows NT, on OS/2, and on many UNIX-based systems, including AIX, Solaris, and HP-UX. In addition to the server platforms, UDB clients run on Windows 95, Windows 3.1, and Macintosh systems.

- It supports a rich set of interfaces for different kinds of users and applications. It provides easy-to-use graphical interfaces for interactive users and for database administrators. It supports the SQL database language embedded in application programming languages, including C, C++, Java, FORTRAN, COBOL, and REXX. It supports static interfaces in which SQL statements are preoptimized for high performance, and dynamic interfaces in which SQL statements are generated by running applications. It supports important industry standards, including Open Database Connectivity (ODBC) and ISO Database Language SQL (SQL92).

- It supports many kinds of nontraditional data. This is a sense in which the term *universal* is often used in the database industry. UDB includes a set of *extenders* that make it easy to develop applications that involve extensive use of text, image, audio, and video data. UDB also allows users to define their own datatypes and functions, for storage and processing of user-defined objects with complex state and behavior. By means of a feature called *table*

1

functions, data from almost any source can be made available to UDB applications and manipulated using the power of the SQL language. By combining the query power and data independence of a relational system with the flexible datatypes and user-defined semantics of an object-oriented system, UDB earns its place in the new generation of *object-relational* database systems.

1.1 ABOUT THIS BOOK

The goal of this book is to provide a comprehensive and easy-to-read guide to UDB, written for end users, application developers, and database administrators. The book includes many examples that help to explain and motivate UDB features, and that can serve as templates for developing real applications. It also includes occasional references to IBM manuals where further details can be found on a particular subject. The book is organized as follows:

Chapter 1 provides a general overview of UDB and a summary of the different ways in which the product can be used. The chapter also includes a brief historical perspective on the SQL language and a discussion of how early decisions in its development have influenced UDB and other relational systems.

Chapter 2 describes the basics of SQL as a query language and as a language for data definition and manipulation. It includes discussions of normalization, transactions, and authorization. For experienced users of relational database systems, much of this material will be a review.

Chapter 3 discusses facilities for interactive users. The major emphasis of this chapter is on the new graphical tools introduced by UDB. In addition to interactive queries and updates, these tools allow users to create database scripts and schedule them for execution, to maintain an online history of backups and other significant events, and to browse through online help and other documentation.

Chapter 4 discusses how to create database applications using SQL embedded in C and C++ programs. The techniques described in this chapter for optimizing SQL statements in advance of their use provide the highest-performance database access supported by UDB.

Chapter 5 focuses on some of the features that make SQL a powerful query language. This chapter will show you how to write recursive queries and how you can use a subquery anywhere that a scalar value or a table is expected. This chapter also introduces several advanced query features that are new in UDB, including outer join, table functions, and specialized grouping operators for online analytical processing (OLAP) applications.

Chapter 6 introduces the object-oriented features of UDB, including support for large objects, user-defined datatypes, and user-defined functions. The chapter includes an example that shows how you can use these features to define your own classes of objects with complex state and behavior, store these objects in your database, and invoke their behavior in SQL queries.

Chapter 7 describes the language features that give active semantics to UDB data. These features, which include constraints and triggers, can be used to protect the integrity of your data and to enforce the policies of your business. This chapter includes a comprehensive example that illustrates the use of constraints and triggers as well as user-defined datatypes and functions.

Chapter 8 describes the UDB interfaces that support dynamic applications. Dynamic applications are applications that need to execute SQL statements generated "on the fly"—that is, statements that are not known at the time the application is compiled. An example of a dynamic application is an interactive query interface, which must be able to execute user-generated SQL statements and display their results. UDB supports three interfaces for dynamic applications: *Call Level Interface* (CLI), *Java Database Connectivity* (JDBC), and *Embedded Dynamic SQL.*

Chapter 9 describes how to write stored procedures. A stored procedure is a program that is installed and executed on a server machine but can be invoked from a separate client machine. By using stored procedures containing SQL statements, you can localize much of your application logic on the database server and minimize the network traffic between client and server.

Chapter 10 provides an overview of database administration and of the tools provided for UDB administrators. The tasks discussed in this chapter include creating and configuring databases, managing physical space, managing database backup and recovery, bulk loading data, monitoring and tuning the performance of the database, and examining the access plans of individual SQL statements. Chapter 10 also discusses the kinds of parallelism supported by UDB, and how a parallel database system can be reconfigured to meet changing requirements.

The book concludes with six appendices:

- Appendix A lists the special registers such as CURRENT TIME and CURRENT DATE that can be used in SQL statements.

- Appendix B lists all the built-in functions supported by UDB.

- Appendix C lists the typecodes that are used to identify datatypes when values are exchanged between the database and an application program.

- Appendix D describes the system catalog tables in which UDB maintains a description of the content of the database.

- Appendix E describes the syntax used to declare variables used for exchange of values between the database and a C or C++ program.

• Appendix F lists the IBM publications that pertain to **UDB**. These books are included in HTML form with the product, and hardcopy versions can also be ordered by the publication numbers given in Appendix F.

1.1.1 Notational Conventions

The SQL language is insensitive to upper- and lowercase letters in keywords and in the names of tables and columns. Thus the following SQL queries are equivalent:

```
SELECT AVG(SALARY) FROM EMPLOYEES;
select avg(salary) from employees;
Select Avg(Salary) From Employees;
```

The only place in SQL where upper- and lowercasing is significant is inside a quoted string. But there are two kinds of quoted strings: strings enclosed in single quotes denote data values, and strings enclosed in double quotes denote identifiers (names). The following example illustrates both kinds of quoted strings:

```
SELECT avg(salary) FROM "Employees" WHERE job = 'Typist';
```

In the example above, we are searching for data in a table named "Employees" (not "EMPLOYEES" or "employees"), and we are searching for the data value 'Typist' (not 'TYPIST' or 'typist').

Since SQL is insensitive to upper- and lowercasing except inside quoted strings, the SQL examples in this book have been written using a convention that is intended to make them consistent and easy to read. This convention is as follows:

1. SQL keywords are written in uppercase. Examples: SELECT, FROM, WHERE.

2. The names of tables and columns, when used in queries, are written in lowercase. Examples: employees, salary, job. However, when used in text outside of SQL queries, names of tables and columns are written in uppercase.

3. The names of functions are written in lowercase. This applies both to built-in functions and to new functions defined by users. Examples: avg, sum, length, substr.

4. The names of datatypes are written in lowercase with an initial capital. This applies both to built-in datatypes and to new datatypes defined by users. Examples: Integer, Varchar, Blob, Complex.

The following example illustrates this convention applied to some simple SQL statements:

```
SELECT name, salary, bonus
FROM employees
WHERE bonus > salary AND location = 'Armonk';

CREATE TABLE games
    (hometeam     Varchar(20),
     visitors     Varchar(20),
     gamedate     Date,
     homescore    Integer,
     visitorscore Integer);
```

1.1.2 Syntax Diagrams

This book makes extensive use of syntax diagrams to describe how to write SQL statements and clauses. A syntax diagram represents all the ways of constructing a valid statement or clause as a set of paths through the diagram from the starting symbol ├─ to the ending symbol ─→│. The symbol ─→ means "continued on the next line." Along a path, words appearing in uppercase (such as ORDER BY) represent words that must appear in the statement or clause, and words appearing in lowercase (such as column-name and integer) can be replaced by symbols of the user's choice (for example, specific column names or integers). "Loops" inside a syntax diagram represent parts of the path that can be used more than once. The name of the element (statement or clause) that is defined by a syntax diagram is shown on the border around the diagram. For example, the following syntax diagram defines an element named "order-by-clause," which consists of the words ORDER BY followed by a list of column names or integers separated by commas, with an optional word ASC or DESC after each column name or integer.

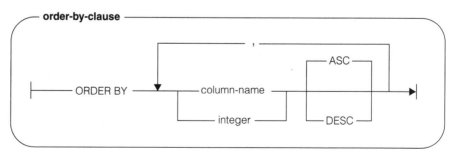

When a path fragment is printed above an empty path fragment, such as ASC in the example above, that fragment represents a default option that is effective if no other option is specified. Thus, in the example above, the ASC option is effective whenever the DESC option is not specified.

Occasionally, an SQL statement may contain a series of options that can be specified in any order. This is denoted by a sequence of bullets in the syntax diagram. The fragments between the bullets can be written in any order. For example, the following diagram represents a syntax in which a size option, a color option, and a speed option can be specified in any order.

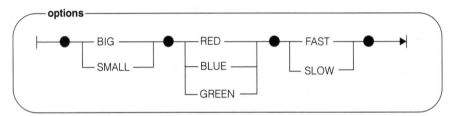

In some cases, a syntax diagram will contain some elements that are defined by lower-level syntax diagrams of their own. For example, the following diagram shows how a *search condition* can be built up from combinations of predicates and other search conditions, connected by the words AND, OR, and NOT. The elements *predicate* and *search-condition* are enclosed in small ovals to indicate that they are defined by syntax diagrams of their own. This syntax diagram is recursive, because the element named *search-condition* is used inside its own definition. (Any syntax diagram in the book can easily be found by looking for its element name in the index.)

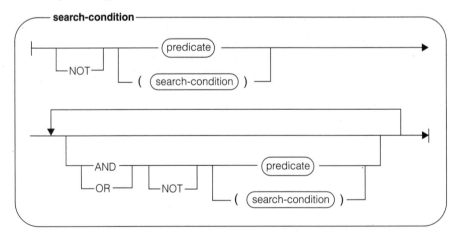

1.1.3 Examples

This book contains many examples, some written in pure SQL and some written using SQL embedded in a host programming language. The source code, sample data, and expected results for all these examples can be downloaded from the Morgan Kaufmann Web site, `http://www.mkp.com` (use the online catalog to find this book).

Although UDB supports several host programming languages, the embedded SQL examples in this book are based on the C, C++, and Java languages. These host languages were chosen because of their widespread use on the platforms supported by UDB. Details of how SQL can be embedded in other host programming languages such as FORTRAN, COBOL, and REXX can be found in the *Embedded SQL Programming Guide*.

Since UDB supports several operating system platforms, the examples in this book are designed to be platform independent except as noted. The only general exception to this rule involves filenames. OS/2 and Windows platforms generally use the "\" character as a delimiter in filenames, whereas UNIX-based platforms such as AIX generally use the "/" character for the same purpose. Filenames in this book can easily be converted from one convention to the other by replacing "/" by "\" or vice versa. For example, the UNIX filename "`/u/images/boat.gif`" is equivalent to the OS/2 filename "`\u\images\boat.gif`".

1.1.4 Tips

During the course of creating and testing the examples in this book, I often encountered small tidbits of information that I felt would be helpful to users in developing applications of their own. A lot of this information was collected the hard way: by making mistakes and figuring out why things didn't work as I expected. Whenever I felt that users would benefit from some such piece of information or advice, I included it in the form of a "Tip." To help you identify them and find them quickly, tips are printed in a special format as shown in the example below. I have tried to include in these tips the kind of information that distinguishes a veteran user from a beginner and that is usually accumulated by painful experience. I hope that reading these tips will save you the many hours it would take to find this information out for yourself.

 TIP: If you are planning to put on both socks and shoes, you should put the socks on first.

1.2 PRODUCT OVERVIEW

UDB is a versatile family of products that supports many different configurations and modes of use. In this section, we will discuss the different versions of UDB that are available and some of the ways in which they can be installed and used. We will also briefly discuss some other products that are closely related to UDB.

1.2.1 UDB Clients and Servers

A client-server computing environment consists of a set of computers connected by some kind of network, often a local-area network (LAN). A given machine in the network can act as a *server* (provider of services to other machines), or as a *client* (requester of services from other machines), or as both a client and a server. In a client-server database environment, servers generally manage databases, and clients generally run application programs and interact with users. When an application or user at a client machine needs to access data in a database, client software sends a request to the server on which the data resides. Various protocols have been developed for handling the interactions between clients and servers. Generally, these protocols are transparent to database applications and users, who may not know or care on which server the data actually resides or how it is retrieved. UDB provides both client and server software for many kinds of platforms.

UDB clients and servers can communicate with each other on local-area networks using various protocols such as APPC, TCP/IP, NetBios, and IPX/SPX (discussed in the *Quick Beginnings* books for the various platforms). In addition, UDB systems can participate in heterogeneous networks that are distributed throughout the world, using a protocol called *Distributed Relational Database Architecture* (DRDA). DRDA consists of two parts: an *Application Requestor* (AR) protocol and an *Application Server* (AS) protocol. Any client that implements the AR protocol can connect to any server that implements the AS protocol. All DB2 products, and many other systems as well, implement the DRDA protocols. Thus, for example, a user in San Francisco running UDB on Windows NT might access a database in London managed by DB2 for OS/390.

The UDB product family includes four "editions" that support increasingly complex database and user environments, and two "developer's editions" that provide tools for application program development. All the UDB editions contain the same database management engine, support the full SQL language, and provide graphical user interfaces for interactive query and database administration.

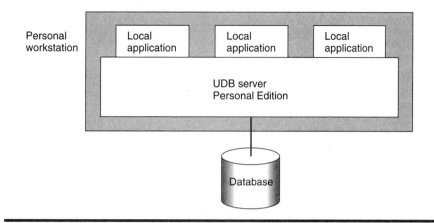

Figure 1-1: Example Configuration of UDB Personal Edition

With the exception of the Personal Edition and the Personal Developer's Edition, all versions of **UDB** are multiuser systems that support remote clients and include client software (called *Client Application Enablers*, or CAEs) for all supported platforms. The licensing terms for the multiuser versions of **UDB** depend on the number of users and the number of processors in your hardware configuration.

Personal Edition

UDB Personal Edition provides the simplest **UDB** installation. This version of **UDB** can create and administer databases, and can provide database access for one local user, running one or more applications, as illustrated in Figure 1-1. **UDB** Personal Edition is available only on Windows NT, Windows 95, and OS/2 platforms. If access to databases on host systems is required, **UDB** Personal Edition can be used in conjunction with DB2 Connect Personal Edition.

Workgroup Edition

UDB Workgroup Edition is a server that supports both local and remote users and applications. Remote clients can connect to a Workgroup Edition server, but Workgroup Edition does not provide a way for its users to connect to databases on host systems. Workgroup Edition can be installed on a symmetric multiprocessor platform containing up to four processors. Figure 1-2 illustrates a possible configuration of Workgroup Edition.

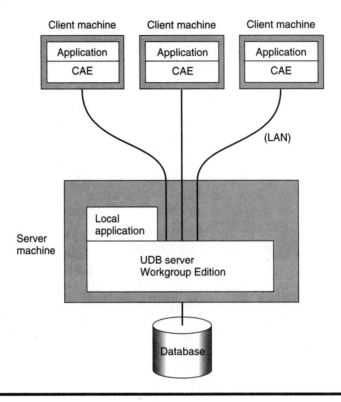

Figure 1-2: Example Configuration of UDB Workgroup Edition

Enterprise Edition

UDB Enterprise Edition provides local and remote users with access to local and remote databases. It supports more users than Workgroup Edition, and it can be installed on symmetric multiprocessor platforms with more than four processors. It implements both the AR and AS protocols, and can participate in DRDA networks with full generality, as illustrated in Figure 1-3.

Enterprise-Extended Edition

As noted earlier, all the UDB editions can take advantage of parallel processing when installed on a symmetric multiprocessor platform. UDB Enterprise-Extended Edition introduces a new dimension of parallelism that can be scaled to very large capacity and very high performance. An Enterprise-Extended Edition (EEE) database can be partitioned across multiple machines that are connected by a network or a high-speed switch. Additional machines can be added to an EEE system as application requirements grow. The individ-

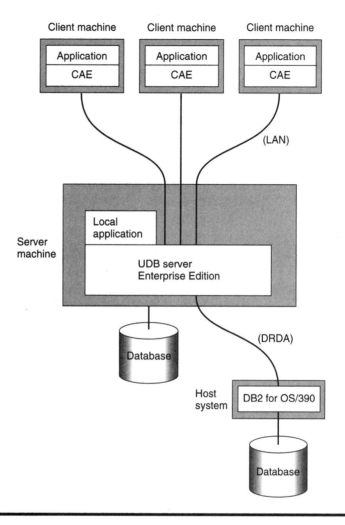

Figure 1-3: Example Configuration of UDB Enterprise Edition

ual machines participating in an EEE installation may be either uniprocessors or symmetric multiprocessors. Partitioned databases and Enterprise-Extended Edition are discussed in more detail in Section 10.2.

Personal Developer's Edition

UDB Personal Developer's Edition includes all the tools needed to develop application programs for UDB Personal Edition, including host language pre-compilers, header files, and sample application code. It is available only for Windows NT, Windows 95, and OS/2 platforms.

Universal Developer's Edition

UDB Universal Developer's Edition includes all the tools needed to develop application programs for all UDB servers, including Software Developer's Kits for Windows NT, OS/2, and UNIX platforms.

1.2.2 Related Products

This section briefly summarizes some of the other IBM software products that are complementary with or closely related to UDB.

DB2 Family of Database Managers

As mentioned earlier, UDB is the version of DB2 that is designed for personal computer and workstation platforms. In addition to UDB, the DB2 family of database managers includes DB2 for OS/390, DB2 for OS/400, and DB2 for VSE and VM. All these products are committed to compatibility with each other and with recognized industry standards (but the products are on different release cycles and may not all introduce the same features simultaneously).

DB2 Connect

DB2 Connect (formerly known as DDCS) is a communication product that enables its users to connect to any database server that implements the Distributed Relational Database Architecture (DRDA) protocol, including all servers in the DB2 product family. All the functionality of DB2 Connect is included in UDB Enterprise Edition. In addition, DB2 Connect is available separately in two versions:

- *DB2 Connect Personal Edition* provides access to remote databases for a single workstation.
- *DB2 Connect Enterprise Edition* can support a cluster of client machines on a local network, collecting their requests and forwarding them to a remote DRDA server for processing.

Net.Data

Net.Data is a toolkit that enables you to develop applications that are accessible from the World Wide Web. These applications take the form of "web macros" that dynamically generate data for display on a web page. Net.Data is used in conjunction with a web server that handles requests from web browsers for display of web pages. When a requested page contains a web macro, the web server calls Net.Data to expand the macro into some dynamic content for the page. The definition of the macro may include SQL statements that are submitted to a UDB server for processing. For example, a web page might contain a form that users can fill in to request information from a database, and the requested information might be retrieved by Net.Data and converted into HTML (hypertext markup language) for display by your web server. Net.Data itself is a common gateway interface (CGI) program that can be installed in the cgi-bin directory of your web server. Net.Data is included with all versions of UDB except the Personal Edition.

Lotus Approach

Lotus Approach provides an easy-to-use interface for interacting with UDB and other relational databases. Using Lotus Approach, you can design data *views* in many different formats, including forms, reports, worksheets, and charts. When you define a view, you can specify how the data in the view corresponds to underlying data in a UDB database. By interacting with the view, users can query and manipulate the underlying data. Approach allows users to perform searches, joins, grouping operations, and database updates without having any knowledge of SQL. Approach can also format data attractively for printing or for display on a web page. Approach runs in the Windows environment, and is included with all versions of UDB.

DB2 Extenders

UDB allows its users to define their own datatypes and functions for storing and retrieving specialized kinds of objects. In addition, it provides several toolkits called *Extenders* that contain sets of predefined datatypes and functions. Each extender helps you to manage a particular kind of data, such as text, images, audio, or video. For example, the text extender can construct a *linguistic index* that supports fast content-based retrieval of large text documents. The text extender has linguistic knowledge of 17 languages, enabling it to search for synonyms or alternative forms of words and to be insensitive to details such as hyphenation.

The text, image, audio, and video extenders are included with the Developer's Editions of UDB. Additional extenders are under development, both by IBM and by other vendors.

DB2 DataJoiner

DB2 DataJoiner is an enhanced version of DB2 Version 2 for Common Servers that enables its users to interact with data from multiple heterogeneous sources, providing an image of a single relational database. In addition to managing its own data, DB2 DataJoiner allows users to connect to databases managed by other DB2 systems; other relational systems such as Oracle, Sybase, Microsoft SQL Server, and Informix; and nonrelational systems such as IMS and VSAM. DataJoiner masks the differences among these various data sources, presenting to the client the functionality of DB2 Version 2 for Common Servers. All the data in the heterogeneous network appears to the client in the form of tables in a single relational database. DB2 DataJoiner includes an optimizer for cross-platform queries that enables an SQL query, for example, to join a table stored in a DB2 database in San Francisco with a table stored in an Oracle database in Chicago. Data manipulation statements (SELECT, INSERT, DELETE, and UPDATE) are independent of the location of the stored data, but data definition statements (such as CREATE TABLE) are less well standardized and must be written in the native language of the system on which the data is stored.

Data Propagator

Data propagator products can be used to keep databases consistent by propagating changes from one database to another. The propagation of data is accomplished by a *capture* component that captures changes on the source database, and by an *apply* component that applies equivalent changes to the target database. Included with UDB are the capture and apply components needed for propagating changes from one UDB database to another or from a UDB database to a database on DB2 for OS/390. A separate product called *DataPropagator Relational* supplies components for propagating changes among other members of the DB2 database family. IBM also offers a product called *DataPropagator Nonrelational* for synchronizing DB2 and IMS databases.

ADSTAR Distributed Storage Manager

The ADSTAR Distributed Storage Manager (ADSM) is a network-based facility for creating and managing backup copies of stored data. UDB databases can be backed up via network connections to ADSM servers running on various platforms. The backups can be invoked either explicitly or according to an automatic schedule. ADSM also provides facilities for automating policies about how long backups should be kept and for examining the list of available backups.

Intelligent Miner

Intelligent Miner is a set of applications that can search large volumes of data for unexpected patterns, such as correlations among purchases of various products. Intelligent Miner can be used with databases managed by UDB and other members of the DB2 family.

DB2 OLAP Server

Essbase is an online analytical processing (OLAP) product produced by Arbor Software Inc., that provides operations such as CUBE and ROLLUP for multidimensional analysis of large data archives. DB2 OLAP Server, a joint product of IBM and Arbor, provides Essbase functionality for data stored in UDB and other DB2 databases.

Visual Warehouse

Visual Warehouse is a data warehouse product that provides a facility for periodically extracting data from operational databases for archiving and analysis. It includes a catalog facility for storing metadata about the information assets of an enterprise.

Digital Library

Digital Library is a set of tools for maintaining and cataloging collections of digital documents in multimedia formats. It uses UDB and other DB2 products for data storage and indexing. Digital Library also provides tools for "digital watermarking" that can trace the source of an image to protect the rights of its owner.

Visual Age

Visual Age is a collection of application development environments for various programming languages, including C++, Java, BASIC, and COBOL. Visual Age supports the object-oriented programming paradigm and provides class libraries that are useful in developing user interfaces and database applications. With Visual Age, you can quickly assemble predefined components such as buttons and dialog boxes, and bind these components to functions that access DB2 databases.

1.2.3 Instances and Databases

As we have discussed, a UDB server provides database services to applications running on its own machine and on remote client machines. Multiple copies of a UDB server can run on the same physical machine. Each copy of a UDB server is called an *instance*, and has its own name, called an *instance name*. Although the instances on a given machine share code, they operate independently of each other. Each instance can have its own system administrator and its own set of configuration parameters. For example, one instance might be configured for high-volume transaction processing, while another might be configured for decision support applications.

When a UDB server is installed, two instances are created. One of these, typically named DB2DAS00, is an *administration server* used by UDB itself to manage its own internal affairs. The other, typically named DB2, is created to manage user databases. After the initial installation of UDB, additional instances can be created by a command called db2icrt. The administration server and the creation of new instances are discussed further in Section 10.5.

Each UDB instance can create and manage one or more *databases*. A database is a collection of data, organized in the form of *tables*. Each database

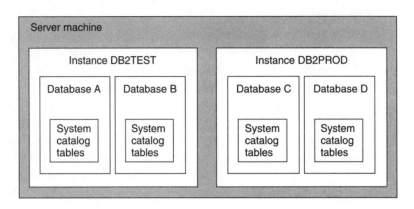

Figure 1-4: UDB Instances and Databases

belongs to a particular instance and resides on the machine where that instance is installed. Each database has a name, which is chosen at the time the database is created. Each database has a set of *system catalog tables,* which are automatically maintained by the system, containing information about the tables and other objects that are stored in the database and about users of the database and their access privileges. Information about the database can be retrieved from the system catalog tables using SQL queries. (System catalog tables are discussed in detail in Appendix D.)

Figure 1-4 shows an example of the relationships among **UDB** instances and databases. In the example, two instances named DB2TEST and DB2PROD are installed on the same server machine, and each instance manages two databases. It is possible for two databases managed by different instances to have the same database name, even if their instances are running on the same machine.

Each **UDB** client maintains a list of instances and databases with which it knows how to communicate. Installed with each **UDB** client is a graphical tool called a *Client Configuration Assistant* that can be used to add new instances and databases to the list.

Before interacting with a database, a **UDB** user or application program must establish a *connection* with that database. A connection is established by a CONNECT command, which checks to make sure that the user or application is authorized to access the given database. Under certain circumstances, it is possible for a user or application to be connected to multiple databases at the same time. (Database connections are discussed further in Section 2.7.2.)

Some **UDB** commands operate at the level of an instance rather than a database. For example, a command might change the configuration parameters of an instance, or create a new database to be managed by a given instance. Commands executed on a server machine are directed to the instance named in the environment variable DB2INSTANCE. On a client machine, an ATTACH command can be used to name the instance to which instance-level commands are to be directed.

1.2.4 Interactive Tools

The simplest and most direct way to use UDB is by using one of its interactive tools. These tools allow you to type commands and SQL statements, and display the results directly on your screen.

The oldest of the interactive tools, and one that is supported on all UDB platforms, is the *Command Line Processor*, or CLP. The CLP can be invoked from your program menu or by typing db2 at your operating system command prompt. From within a CLP session, you can execute any SQL statement or UDB command. (The details of a CLP session are described in Section 3.2.)

UDB Version 5 introduces a new suite of interactive user interfaces called *DB2 Tools*. The DB2 Tools are available on Windows and OS/2 platforms, and can be used to interact with UDB databases on any server platform. These tools are mutually complementary, and they all support consistent graphical user interfaces. Any of the tools can be invoked from your program menu, and each of them displays icons that can be used to invoke all the other tools. The individual DB2 Tools are as follows:

- The *Command Center*, much like the CLP, allows you to type commands and SQL statements and to view their results. It also allows you to create *scripts* of statements and commands for later execution, and to examine the access plans created by the system for executing your SQL statements.

- The *Script Center* allows you to manage collections of scripts, editing them and scheduling them to be executed periodically or at specific times.

- The *Journal* keeps an archival record of significant events in your system. Using the Journal, you can examine the results of scripts that were executed automatically by the Script Center. You can also see a list of all the backup copies that have been made of your database, as well as a history of recovery actions that have been executed on your system.

- The *Control Center* is a general-purpose database administration tool that enables you to control both local and remote UDB systems. The Control Center provides a hierarchic display of all the UDB instances and databases known to your machine, and their contents down to the level of individual tables. By selecting an object at any level of the hierarchy, you can obtain a menu of commands that apply to the selected object, and you can execute any command for which you hold the necessary authorization.

- The *Alert Center* displays a list of objects, such as instances, databases, or tables, that are in *alert status*. An object might be in alert status because some property of that object is outside normal bounds. The objects and properties to be monitored in this way, and the upper and lower bounds for each property, can be specified by the Control Center.

- The *Information Center* provides quick access to a wealth of information about the UDB system. It displays a list of all the UDB publications, and can launch your favorite web browser to read or search any of these publications. It also provides task-oriented help for various tasks, a list of explanations for all UDB return codes, and an index to all the sample application programs that are provided with the UDB system.

The Control Center and Alert Center are discussed further in Chapter 10. All the other DB2 Tools are discussed in Chapter 3. In the future, IBM plans to supplement the DB2 Tools with similar web-based tools that allow you to interact with UDB databases using a web browser on any platform—in fact, some of these web-based tools may be available by the time you are reading this book.

1.2.5 Application Programs

As we have seen, DB2 Tools and the CLP allow you to submit SQL statements to UDB for processing, either interactively or through a script file. But many database applications require programming language features, such as looping and branching, that are not currently supported by SQL. For this reason, UDB allows SQL statements to be embedded in various host programming languages, including C, C++, Java, BASIC, FORTRAN, COBOL, and REXX. This book discusses how database applications can be developed using SQL statements embedded in C, C++, and Java programs. A discussion of embedding SQL in the other host languages can be found in the *Embedded SQL Programming Guide*.

There are two main ways of embedding SQL statements in a host language program: *static SQL* and *dynamic SQL*. A static SQL statement is a statement that is known at the time the application is written. The form of the statement, as well as the names of the tables and columns accessed by the statement, must be known and fixed in order for the statement to be static. The only part of a static statement that can remain unknown at compile time is the specific data value to be searched for or updated, which can be represented by a variable in the host program. For example, the following static SQL statement searches for an employee whose employee number matches the C variable x, and updates that employee's salary to the value in the C variable y. The names of the table (EMPLOYEES) and columns (EMPNO and SALARY) accessed by this statement are fixed at compile time.

```
UPDATE employees SET salary = :y WHERE empno = :x
```

Static SQL statements have an important advantage: since the structure of the statement is known at compile time, the work of analyzing the statement and choosing an efficient access plan for implementing the statement can be done at compile time.[1] When the application program runs, then, its static SQL statements can be executed using the preselected access plan without further attention by the UDB optimizer. This minimizes the execution time of the application program, particularly if it invokes a given SQL statement multiple times. For this reason, static SQL statements are often used in high-performance applications that perform the same operation repeatedly, such as a banking application that updates customer accounts.

Static SQL statements exchange data with the application program by means of *host variables*, which are variables declared in the host programming language. The names of host variables must be prefixed by a colon when used inside an SQL statement. Host variables can be used to exchange both input and output values. For example, in the following SQL statement, host variable :x provides an input value (a search argument), and host variable :y retrieves an output value:

```
SELECT jobcode INTO :y FROM employees WHERE empno = :x
```

An SQL statement often returns multiple results, such as the names and addresses of all suppliers of a given part. Multiple results are delivered to a host program by means of a language feature called a *cursor*. A cursor is associated with a specific SQL statement and represents the *result set* returned by that statement, which consists of zero or more rows. Each time a FETCH statement is applied to a given cursor, it returns one row from the result set (for example, the name and address of a supplier) into the host variables named in the FETCH statement.

When an SQL statement is embedded in an application program, it is prefixed by the words EXEC SQL. All host variables that are used inside SQL statements must be declared in a special *SQL Declare Section*, which is also prefixed by the words EXEC SQL. This prefix identifies the SQL statements inside the host program and distinguishes them from host language statements.

UDB provides *precompilers* to support static SQL in several of the host programming languages, including C and C++. A precompiler finds the SQL statements embedded in your program, and for each SQL statement it generates an access plan designed to execute the statement as efficiently as possible. The

---

1. At this point, I am using the term *compile time* somewhat loosely. As you will see shortly, the database system adds a new step, called *precompilation,* to the process of preparing an application program for execution.

precompiler stores these optimized access plans in the database in the form of a *package* that is associated with your program. The SQL statements themselves are removed from the program and replaced with calls to the **UDB** runtime system, which retrieves and executes the plans in the package when you run your program.

The result of precompiling a program with embedded SQL statements is a pure host language program, which you can then compile using your favorite compiler. You can link your program to library routines or to other precompiled programs. After compiling and linking your program, you can run it in the usual way—for example, by typing its name on your operating system command line.

The details of how static SQL statements can be embedded in application programs, and how these programs can be prepared for execution, are discussed in Chapter 4.

1.2.6 Dynamic Applications

The previous section discusses static SQL statements, which are known at the time the application is written (except possibly for data values that can be obtained from host variables). Some applications, however, have a need to construct and execute new SQL statements at run time. Since these SQL statements are not written into the application, they cannot be optimized and converted to a package by the precompiler as can static SQL statements. Instead, they must be submitted to the optimizer while the application program is running, using special facilities designed for this purpose. SQL statements that are generated by a running program are called *dynamic SQL statements*, and the applications that generate them are called *dynamic applications*.

An excellent example of a dynamic application is the Command Center. The function of the Command Center is to prompt a user to enter SQL statements, which are then submitted to the system for processing. The Command Center was developed using the same dynamic SQL facilities that are available to application developers. Using these facilities, you can write interactive tools of your own, perhaps supporting a query interface that is customized for some particular application.

Another example of a dynamic application is a general-purpose bulk loader. The purpose of this program is to create tables and load them with data, under the direction of some control file. Since the bulk loader does not know in advance the name of the table to be loaded or the number and datatypes of its columns, the bulk loader cannot be written using static SQL statements. The bulk loader will need to generate and execute a CREATE TABLE statement and a suitable INSERT statement for loading the data. By making careful use of dynamic SQL facilities, the bulk loader will cause the INSERT statement to be parsed and optimized only once, even though it is executed repeatedly as rows are inserted into the new table. This is how the Import and Export utility programs described in Chapter 10 are implemented.

In general, dynamic SQL statements incur a performance penalty compared to static SQL statements because they must be parsed and optimized at run time. For this reason, dynamic SQL statements are not generally used in high-performance applications involving short, predefined transactions. For example, a reservation system for car rentals would be likely to use static SQL statements, whereas a decision-support system for long-range planning would be more likely to use dynamic SQL statements.

UDB provides three separate facilities for processing dynamic SQL statements: *Call Level Interface* (CLI), *Java Database Connectivity* (JDBC), and *Embedded Dynamic SQL*. These facilities represent three alternative approaches to the same problem. Each of them provides support for the following tasks:

- *Preparing* an SQL statement for execution by invoking the UDB optimizer to create an optimized access plan for the statement.

- *Describing* the result of an SQL statement, including the number of columns in a query result and the datatypes of the columns. This step enables the application program to allocate dynamic memory to fetch the result of a query.

- *Fetching* a result set, one row at a time, into memory locations that were allocated for this purpose.

- *Executing* an SQL statement that was previously prepared, substituting new values for some of the variables in the statement, such as the values to be inserted or updated.

The three dynamic SQL facilities are described briefly below, and are dealt with in more detail in Chapter 8.

Call Level Interface (CLI)

The Call Level Interface (CLI) is based on Microsoft's *Open Database Connectivity* (ODBC) interface, supporting ODBC 3.0, Level 1, plus certain additional features. As its name suggests, CLI is a set of function calls that can be embedded in programs to access a database. At present, CLI is supported only for the C and C++ languages (and for other languages such as BASIC that can make calls to C functions).

An important advantage of CLI is that application programs that use it do not need to be precompiled. This means that these programs can be distributed in the form of object code since there is no need to submit source code to a precompiler. An application written using CLI can also be ported to other database systems that support ODBC. In order to ensure portability, however, a CLI-based application must confine itself to SQL features that are implemented on all the database systems of interest.

If portability or object code distribution is of great importance to an application, that application can be written using CLI rather than static SQL, even though all its SQL statements are known in advance. However, a static program written using CLI gives up the advantage of having its SQL statements optimized in advance and must pay the performance cost of invoking the SQL optimizer each time it is run.

Java Database Connectivity (JDBC)

JDBC might be thought of as a CLI interface for the Java programming language. Its functionality is equivalent to that of CLI, but in keeping with its host language, it uses a more object-oriented programming style. For example, the result of a query is represented by a Java object called a ResultSet, which supports various methods for describing and fetching its values. JDBC also allows you to develop *applets*, which can be downloaded and run by any Java-enabled web browser, thus making your UDB data accessible to web-based clients throughout the world.

Embedded Dynamic SQL

Like CLI and JDBC, Embedded Dynamic SQL permits an application program to generate SQL statements at run time and submit them to UDB for processing. However, Embedded Dynamic SQL can be used with a larger collection of host languages than the other dynamic interfaces—for example, it supports FORTRAN, COBOL, and REXX.

Like static SQL, Embedded Dynamic SQL relies on the use of a precompiler—in fact, the same precompiler that is used for static SQL. For this reason, users who wish to mix together dynamic and static SQL statements in the same application, or who are familiar with the use of an SQL precompiler, may find Embedded Dynamic SQL more convenient than CLI or JDBC.

Like static SQL statements, Embedded Dynamic SQL statements must be prefixed by EXEC SQL, which enables the precompiler to distinguish them from host language statements. The precompiler replaces each Embedded Dynamic SQL statement with a call to the UDB run-time library, as it does for static SQL. In the dynamic case, however, the call does not invoke an access plan that was prepared in advance and stored in the database for later execution. Instead, the call invokes database facilities to optimize and execute an SQL statement at run time.

1.2.7 Stored Procedures

In a client-server environment, applications are often invoked from a client machine to run against a database on a server machine. If such an application contains many SQL statements, each SQL statement is sent across the network from the client to the server in a separate message. Under certain circumstances, the number of messages between client and server can be reduced and the performance of the application improved, by using a technique called a *stored procedure*. You may wish to consider using a stored procedure if your application has the following characteristics:

1. It is invoked repeatedly from a client machine but uses a database on a server machine.

2. It contains several SQL statements but does a limited amount of end-user interaction. Specifically, the application needs to gather all its input data into a set of host variables, then execute a series of SQL statements without user interaction, then deliver all its output using a set of host variables.

A stored procedure is an application program that is written according to certain conventions, then bound to a database on a server machine. A separate program, called the *client application,* is installed on a client machine. The client application must connect to the database to which the stored procedure is bound, using an SQL CONNECT statement. The client application can then invoke the stored procedure by means of an SQL statement, CALL, which names the stored procedure and provides a list of host variables that are used to exchange data with the stored procedure, in both directions. All the variables named in the CALL statement are passed to the stored procedure as inputs and can be reused by the stored procedure to return output to the client application. The CALL statement enables a client program to invoke stored procedures on a UDB server or any other database server that supports the DRDA protocol.

An SQL statement called CREATE PROCEDURE enables you to register your stored procedures in the system catalog tables of the databases to which they are bound. Although not required, this is a good practice because it enables clients to obtain a list of the stored procedures that are available in a given database.

Stored procedures are discussed in more detail in Chapter 9.

1.2.8 User Roles

As we have seen, there are many ways of interacting with a system as complex as UDB. Since the purpose of a database system is to manage shared data, it is reasonable to expect that a system like UDB will have many users and that these users will fall into several different categories. Users may vary widely in their degree of expertise and their need for access to the facilities of the system and to the data that it stores. Therefore, UDB recognizes several categories of users and has a system of authorities and privileges to control their activities. The roles in which users can interact with UDB are summarized below. The system of authorities and privileges that supports and enforces these roles is discussed further in Section 2.8.

1. *System administrator.* The role of system administrator is the most powerful user role recognized by UDB. System administrators are considered to own all the resources of the database system and are authorized to execute any system command. The *System Administration* authority applies to a UDB instance, which may include several databases. The user group that holds this authority is specified when the instance is created.

   UDB also recognizes two subsets of System Administration authority: *System Control* and *System Maintenance*. Holders of System Control authority can control the physical resources of the database system, while holders of System Maintenance authority can perform maintenance operations such as starting and stopping the server and backing up and restoring databases. However, unlike System Administration, the System Control and System Maintenance authorities do not convey the right to access or modify user data.

2. *Database administrator.* The role of database administrator applies to a specific database and carries with it the authority to create, destroy, access, and modify all objects in that database. Database administrators can also grant to other users the right to create objects and to access and modify individual objects such as tables, views, and indexes.

3. *Application developer.* One of the important user roles in UDB is that of a developer of new database applications. An application developer need not be a database administrator but, in order to be effective, must hold both some general *authorities* and some specific *privileges*.

   The *authorities* needed by application developers apply to the database as a whole and include CONNECT (the right to connect to the database), CREATETAB (the right to create tables in the database), and BINDADD (the right to bind application programs to the database). An application developer will probably need all three of these authorities.

   The *privileges* needed by application developers apply to specific objects in the database such as tables, views, and packages. In general, the creator of a new object receives a full set of privileges on the object, which the creator can then grant selectively to other users as desired. Each type of object has a certain set of privileges that are applicable to it. For example, the privileges that apply to tables include SELECT, INSERT, DELETE, UPDATE, and some other specialized privileges as described in Section 2.8.

   When a new application program is bound to a database (by a PREP or BIND command), the static SQL statements in the program are checked against the authorities and privileges of the user who is binding the program. For example, to bind a program that updates the CUSTOMERS table, a user must hold the UPDATE privilege on that table. However, once the program has been bound, users need only the EXECUTE privilege on the package in order to run it. This enables the holder of a privilege (such as UPDATE on CUSTOMERS) to *encapsulate* this privilege in a static SQL program that exercises the privilege in a specific way (perhaps updating customer addresses but not their credit ratings). The ability to run the program can then be granted to users who do not hold a generalized UPDATE privilege on CUSTOMERS. This encapsulation of privileges is one of the advantages of static SQL over dynamic SQL.

4. *End user.* The user role in UDB that requires the least level of authorization is that of the end user. In order to run an existing static SQL application, a user needs only CONNECT authority on the database and EXECUTE privilege on the application's package. In fact, if CONNECT on the database and EXECUTE on the package have been granted to PUBLIC, a user can run the application without any authorization at all.

If a user wishes to use the Command Center or a similar interface to run interactive SQL statements against the database, performing various actions such as retrieving and updating data and creating new tables, the user must hold the specific privileges that are required to perform these actions.

1.3   A BRIEF HISTORY OF SQL

Since SQL is so central to the user interface of UDB, a brief discussion of the early history of the language may be helpful in understanding how some UDB features came to be the way they are. In the discussion that follows, references to source materials are provided in square brackets. A list of these references can be found in Section 1.3.4.

Before 1970, databases were usually viewed as territories through which computer programs might "navigate," following pointers from one record to another along fixed pathways, perhaps leaving bread crumbs (sometimes called "currency status indicators") behind in case they lost their way. In 1970, Dr. E. F. Codd proposed a completely new paradigm for thinking about data, in which all meaningful relationships among data records are represented by data values rather than by hidden pointers or connections. Codd's insight made it possible to express database queries in a nonprocedural language, thus making queries independent of the structures and algorithms used in the database implementation—a concept that Codd called *data independence.* Codd's 1970 paper, "A Relational Model of Data for Large Shared Data Banks" [Codd 70], is one of the most influential and widely cited papers in all of computer science and was the basis for Codd's receiving the ACM Turing Award in 1981.

Codd's original paper noted that queries against data stored in the form of relations could be expressed either using the first-order predicate calculus or using a collection of relational operators such as join and projection. In subsequent papers, he developed these two approaches into two database access languages, which came to be known as the *relational calculus* [Codd 71a] and the *relational algebra* [Codd 71b]. Much of the early work on implementation of the relational model was focused on the operators of the relational algebra, and an algebra-based prototype was constructed at IBM's Peterlee laboratory in England [Todd 75].

1.3.1 System R

In the early 1970s, the benefits of the relational model for user productivity and data independence were reasonably well known, but important questions remained about whether a relational database system could be built to store large amounts of data in a multiuser environment with adequate performance for production use. In 1973, a project was begun at the IBM Research Laboratory in San Jose, California, to study these questions by building an industrial-strength relational prototype, which came to be known as System R [Astrahan 76]. At about the same time, a similar relational database project, known as Ingres, was formed at the University of California at Berkeley [Stonebraker 76]. The System R and Ingres projects both built successful prototypes, demonstrating that the relational model could be implemented efficiently and could support both ad hoc queries and transaction processing on production data. Both prototypes were extensively tested by experimental users, and both ultimately led to commercial products. For their work in developing the infrastructure to support the relational data model, the designers of System R and Ingres jointly received the ACM Software Systems Award in 1988.

Rather than implementing the relational algebra or calculus, the designers of System R developed a new database language, which was originally known as *Structured English Query Language*, or SEQUEL [Chamberlin 74]. The designers of SEQUEL attempted to develop a language that was easy to learn and use, basing it on familiar English keywords and avoiding potentially difficult concepts such as the division operator of the relational algebra. The SEQUEL designers also included a number of features that were not present in either of Codd's original languages, such as update operators and a grouping operator. (C. J. Date has subsequently shown how similar features could be added to the relational algebra and calculus [Date 95].) Finally, the SEQUEL designers attempted to provide a syntax that would unify several operations that had traditionally been considered separate and unrelated, including query, data manipulation, data definition (for example, definition of views), and data control (for example, constraints on data values).

The early history of the SEQUEL language is inextricable from the history of System R. The project published a series of papers on various features of the language [Boyce 73, Chamberlin 76] and its implementation [Selinger 79, Chamberlin 81]. In the late 1970s, it was discovered that the name SEQUEL conflicted with an existing trademark, so the name was shortened to SQL, or Structured Query Language. The System R prototype was used over a period of three years by experimental users in a number of locations. Summaries of the lessons learned during this period can be found in [Chamberlin 80] and [Astrahan 80].

1.3.2 Products and Standards

Although SQL was developed and prototyped at IBM, the first commercial product based on SQL was released by a small company called Relational Software, Inc., in 1979. This product was called Oracle, a name that was later adopted by the company, which is no longer small. Oracle was first implemented under the UNIX operating system on Digital PDP-11 machines and later ported to other platforms. In the same year, a relational database product based on the Ingres prototype was released, also in the UNIX environment, by a new company called Relational Technology, Inc. The Ingres product initially implemented a query language called *QUEL* and later added support for SQL.

The first commercial implementation of SQL from IBM, called *SQL/Data System,* was released in February 1981 under a System/370 operating system called DOS/VSE. This release was followed by a series of IBM products that extended support for SQL to many other operating system environments: SQL/Data System for VM/370 in 1983, DB2 for MVS (later OS/390) in 1983, OS/2 Database Manager in 1987, SQL/400 in 1988, DB2 for AIX in 1993, and DB2 for Common Servers, which supports Windows NT and various UNIX-based platforms, in 1995. DB2 Universal Database, the product described in this book, is the latest addition to the DB2 family.

During the 1980s, SQL was implemented by all major relational database suppliers and is now the world's most widely used database language. In order to promote portability among the many SQL implementations, the American National Standards Institute (ANSI) undertook a project to develop a standard specification for SQL. The result, called *Database Language SQL,* was approved as an ANSI Standard (number X3.135-1986) in October 1986. The same language was adopted by the International Organization for Standardization (ISO) as an International Standard (number 9075-1987) in June 1987 and has subsequently been accepted by the national standards organizations of Canada, the United Kingdom, France, Germany, Japan, and other countries.

SQL continues to be a focus for standardization activities. The ANSI/ISO Standard for SQL was updated in 1989 by the addition of an Integrity Enhancement feature that supports specification of constraints on data values and on relationships between tables. A much larger version of the Standard, containing many new features, was adopted by ANSI and ISO in 1992 and is often referred to as *SQL92* [ISO 92]. Addendums to this Standard were adopted in 1995 to encompass a Call Level Interface [ISO 95] and in 1996 to encompass stored procedures [ISO 96]. An even more comprehensive version of SQL, informally known as *SQL3*, is currently under development in ANSI and ISO committees.

1.3.3 Some Controversial Decisions

During the early development of SQL and System R, some decisions were made that were ultimately to generate a great deal more controversy than anyone anticipated. Chief among these were the decisions to support null values and to permit duplicate rows to occur in tables and in query results. I will devote a small amount of space here to examining the reasons for these decisions and the context in which they were made. My purpose here is historical rather than persuasive—I recognize that nulls and duplicates are religious topics, and I do not expect anyone to have a conversion experience after reading this chapter.

For the most part, the designers of System R were practical people rather than theoreticians, and this orientation was reflected in many of their decisions. To a large extent, the philosophy of the System R user interface can be expressed by three principles: (1) use common sense, (2) model the real world, and (3) trust the user. Some examples will help us to see how these principles were applied to the issues of nulls and duplicates.

Consider a database containing student records for a large university. Suppose that each student is uniquely identified by some primary key such as a social security number. One application program written for this database might print a set of mailing labels, perhaps to send a registration bulletin to all the students. The query to retrieve the students' names and addresses is a very simple one and might be written as follows:

```
SELECT name, address FROM students;
```

This query returns a large amount of data—perhaps 35,000 rows. Since neither name nor address (nor their combination) is declared to be a key, the system does not know whether the collection of names and addresses retrieved by this query contains any duplicates. If the semantics of the query language are defined in such a way that duplicates are guaranteed to be eliminated from every query result, the system will be forced to search for duplicate pairs of names and addresses, probably by making a temporary copy of all the data and sorting it. Now, sorting 35,000 records is not entirely free, even today, and in the mid-1970s, it was even more expensive. A good commonsense question to ask here is: what value is added to this query result by eliminating duplicates? The user who wrote the query probably knows that it is unlikely that two or more students with the same name will be found at the same address. And in the case that two students with identical names and addresses do exist, the writer of the program may very well choose to print a mailing label for each of them (and let them figure out who gets which label). Because of examples such as this, it was decided that SQL would make elimination of duplicate rows from query results optional, trusting the user to decide when the cost of this operation is justified. The minor issue of default behavior was decided on the basis of maximizing performance and minimizing cost—that is, the system would undertake the costly and time-consuming operation of eliminating duplicates only when asked to do so.

Of course, permitting duplicate rows in query results is not the same thing as permitting duplicate rows in tables. The System R designers were aware that a relation, as defined in Codd's groundbreaking paper, is a subset of the Cartesian product of a set of domains, and that this definition permits no duplicate rows. Certainly this formal definition of a relation is a useful one and should be supported by every database system. But the System R designers also considered it possible that some users (perhaps untutored in set theory) would appreciate a more flexible concept of a table as a container for storing information, in which duplicate rows and null values could be either permitted or not permitted according to the user's choice. As an example of an application in which duplicate rows might be meaningful, consider a table of real estate transactions that records the zip code, date, and selling price of each transaction. The designer of the table might be interested only in statistical queries, such as finding the average selling price of parcels in zip code 90210 in a given year or finding zip codes in which properties have sold for more than $1 million. Now, it might be rare, but it is certainly not impossible for two parcels in the same zip code to be sold on the same day for the same price. A reasonable commonsense question might be: should users be *required* to take precautions against storing this kind of "duplicate" data? In order to guarantee uniqueness of rows, another column would need to be added to the table, perhaps containing a parcel number. Indeed, since the very same parcel might change hands twice on the same day, it might be necessary for the application to generate a synthetic key for each transaction, and for the system to maintain some kind of index on the key to guarantee uniqueness. SQL trusts the database designer to decide whether the costs of generating and maintaining such a unique key are justified. To impose these costs on all applications regardless of their semantics seems a little heavy-handed, and seemed even more so in 1975 given the costs of storage and processing at that time.

Turning to the issue of nulls forces us to confront, head-on, the fact that databases are sometimes used to model the real world. Consider a table that records the temperature, barometric pressure, wind direction and velocity, and other weather-related data for various dates and locations. Suppose that at the weather station in Fairbanks, Alaska, on January 17, 1989, someone dropped the only barometer on the floor and broke it, and as a result the barometric pressure at that particular place and time is forever unknown. This is the kind of nasty problem that tends to happen in the real world, and it presents database designers with some unpalatable options.

One such option is to choose one of the possible values of the barometric pressure column and to dedicate it forever to representing missing information. This approach leads to at least two serious problems. The least serious of these problems is that some columns may not be able to spare a value to represent missing data since all possible values are meaningful. This situation, though certainly possible, is probably rare (if the barometric pressure in Fairbanks reaches zero, for example, representation of missing values will be the least of our problems). A much more serious problem is the fact that using a valid data value to represent missing information requires explicit defensive code to be written into *every* application that interacts with the database. For example, if zero is chosen as the representation of a missing barometric pressure, the following query will return wrong answers quietly and without any warning:

```
SELECT avg(pressure)
FROM weather
WHERE location = 'Fairbanks';
```

In order to obtain the correct answer, the query above (and every similar query in every application) would need to be rewritten as follows (assuming that zero is chosen as the representation for an unknown pressure):

```
SELECT avg(pressure)
FROM weather
WHERE location = 'Fairbanks'
AND pressure <> 0;
```

A second unpalatable option for representing missing information is to "double up" each column with an auxiliary column containing a flag that indicates whether the value in the original column is valid or missing. Needless to say, this approach significantly increases the storage required by the database and still requires defensive coding in every application program, as illustrated in the example above.

A third unpalatable option is for the database system to explicitly represent missing information by a null, or "out of band," value that is qualitatively different from, and not comparable to, a normal value. This approach leads to the three-valued logic that is part of the ANSI/ISO SQL Standard and has been implemented by UDB and by many other relational systems. It also leads to some (by now) well-documented anomalies. For example, in SQL the expression avg(salary) is not necessarily equal to the expression sum(salary) /

count(*). Furthermore, the following query, which might reasonably be supposed to return all the rows of the EMPLOYEES table, will fail to return any employees with null salaries:

```
SELECT *
FROM employees
WHERE salary > 10000
OR salary < 10000
OR salary = 10000;
```

The presence of nulls also places some limitations on query optimizers. For example, certain techniques for transforming queries into other equivalent queries are valid under two-valued logic but not under three-valued logic, so optimizers that use these techniques must observe certain limitations in the presence of nulls.

Faced with these unpalatable options, the designers of SQL fell back to the principle "trust the user." Providing support for explicit nulls and three-valued logic in the database system gives users the tools to represent missing data with minimal cost and without requiring defensive coding in every application. At the same time, supporting the NOT NULL constraint at the column level allows users to avoid the anomalies associated with null values where this is considered important. Since none of the options for representing missing information is flawless, and since users are paying the bills, it seems appropriate that users should be able to choose the approach they find least troublesome.

The concept of a null value has proved to have at least one advantage that was not anticipated in the original design of SQL. Over the years, the language has evolved in response to user needs, and additional features have been introduced. Some of these features, such as the outer join and specialized grouping operations described in Chapter 5 of this book, rely on nulls in their definition and would not have been possible without support for null values.

Before leaving the null subject, I would like to observe that nulls can sometimes give database users the flexibility they need to deal with unanticipated situations. As an example, consider a database maintained by a government agency to record information about vehicles sold in the United States. Such a database might contain a VEHICLES table with a column named MPG containing a measure of fuel efficiency in miles per gallon. Various applications might make use of this information; for example, the following query might be used to enforce standards for fleet average fuel efficiency:

```
SELECT manufacturer, avg(mpg)
FROM vehicles
GROUP BY manufacturer;
```

Imagine the problems that might be caused at this agency by the introduction of the first electric car. The MPG column is obviously inapplicable to such a vehicle, but dedicating some numeric value in this column to represent "inapplicable" would invalidate existing applications such as the average fuel efficiency query shown above. This problem may be caused by a lack of omniscience on the part of the original database designers, but this failing is unfortunately fairly common. The theoretically correct approach might be to redesign the database, perhaps adding a POWERSOURCE column and rewriting all existing applications. But programmers and database designers are not always plentiful, and problems like this are sometimes discovered on Wednesday afternoon when a final report is due on Friday. Partly because of gritty examples like this one, the designers of SQL and System R decided that nulls should be part of the bag of tools available to users to get their work done.

When the original SQL designers decided to allow users the options of handling nulls and duplicates, they viewed these features as minor conveniences, not as major departures from orthodoxy, taken at the risk of excommunication. Twenty years later, a great deal has been said, much of it rather loudly, on the issues of nulls and duplicates. E. F. Codd, originator of the relational data model, has stated that he does not consider a database system to be "fully relational" unless it supports not just one but two kinds of missing data [Codd 90]. Other well-known writers on things relational insist that the concept of nulls should be abolished altogether. In the end, I believe that the true arbiters of the null and duplicate-row issues will be users of database systems. If users find that these concepts are helpful in solving real problems, they will continue to use them. If, on the other hand, users are convinced that nulls and duplicates are harmful, they will avoid these features and scrupulously use options such as NOT NULL, PRIMARY KEY, and SELECT DISTINCT. By supporting these options, **UDB** makes it easy for users to "vote with their data."

1.3.4 References

[Astrahan 76] Astrahan, M. M., M. W. Blasgen, D. D. Chamberlin, K. P. Eswaran, J. N. Gray, P. P. Griffiths, W. F. King, R. A. Lorie, P. R. McJones, J. W. Mehl, G. R. Putzolu, I. L. Traiger, B. Wade, and V. Watson. "System R: A Relational Approach to Database Management." *ACM Transactions on Database Systems*, Vol. 1, No. 2, June 1976, 97–137.

[Astrahan 80] Astrahan, M. M., M. W. Blasgen, D. D. Chamberlin, J. N. Gray, W. F. King, B. G. Lindsay, R. A. Lorie, J. W. Mehl, T. G. Price, G. R. Putzolu, M. Schkolnick, P. G. Selinger, D. R. Slutz, I. L. Traiger, B. Wade, and R. A. Yost. "A History and Evaluation of System R." *Communications of the ACM*, Vol. 24, No. 10, October 1981, 632–646.

[Boyce 73] Boyce, R. F., and D. D. Chamberlin. *Using a Structured English Query Language as a Data Definition Facility*. IBM Research Report RJ-1318. San Jose, CA: IBM Research Laboratory, December 1973.

[Chamberlin 74] Chamberlin, D. D., and R. F. Boyce. "SEQUEL: A Structured English Query Language." *Proceedings of the ACM SIGFIDET Workshop on Data Description, Access, and Control*, 249–264. Ann Arbor, MI: ACM, May 1974. (SIGFIDET was the precursor to SIG-MOD, the ACM Special Interest Group on Management of Data.)

[Chamberlin 76] Chamberlin, D. D., M. M. Astrahan, K. P. Eswaran, P. P. Griffiths, R. A. Lorie, J. W. Mehl, P. Reisner, and B. W. Wade. "SEQUEL 2: A Unified Approach to Data Definition, Manipulation, and Control." *IBM Journal of Research and Development*, Vol. 20, No. 6, November 1976, 560–575. (Errata in Vol. 21, No. 1, January 1977.)

[Chamberlin 80] Chamberlin, D. D. "A Summary of User Experience with the SQL Data Sublanguage." *Proceedings of the International Conference on Data Bases*, 181–203. London: Heyden & Son, Ltd., July 1980.

[Chamberlin 81] Chamberlin, D. D., M. M. Astrahan, W. F. King, R. A. Lorie, J. W. Mehl, T. G. Price, M. Schkolnick, P. G. Selinger, D. R. Slutz, B. W. Wade, and R. A. Yost. "Support for Repetitive Transactions and Ad-Hoc Queries in System R." *ACM Transactions on Database Systems*, Vol. 6, No. 1, March 1981, 70–94.

[Codd 70] Codd, E. F. "A Relational Model of Data for Large Shared Data Banks." *Communications of the ACM*, Vol. 13, No. 6, June 1970, 377–387.

[Codd 71a] Codd, E. F. "A Data Base Sublanguage Founded on the Relational Calculus." *Proceedings of the 1971 ACM SIGFIDET Workshop on Data Description, Access, and Control.* New York: ACM, November 1971.

[Codd 71b] Codd, E. F. "Relational Algebra," *Database Systems*. Courant Computer Science Symposium. New York: Prentice Hall, 1971.

[Codd 90] Codd, E. F. *The Relational Model for Database Management: Version 2.* Reading, MA: Addison-Wesley, 1990.

[Date 95] Date, C. J. *Introduction to Database Systems*, sixth ed. Reading, MA: Addison-Wesley, 1995.

[ISO 92] International Organization for Standardization (ISO). *Information Technology—Database Language SQL*. Standard No. ISO/IEC 9075:1992. (ISO Documents are available from the American National Standards Institute, 11 West 42nd Street, 13th floor, New York, NY 10036, (212) 642-4900.)

[ISO 95] International Organization for Standardization (ISO). *Database Language SQL—Part 3: Call-Level Interface*. Standard No. ISO/IEC 9075-3:1995.

[ISO 96] International Organization for Standardization (ISO). *Database Language SQL—Part 4: Persistent Stored Modules*. Standard No. ISO/IEC 9075-4:1996.

[Selinger 79] Selinger, P. G., M. M. Astrahan, D. D. Chamberlin, R. A. Lorie, and T. G. Price. "Access Path Selection in a Relational Database Management System." *Proceedings of the ACM SIGMOD Conference*. New York: ACM, June 1979.

[Stonebraker 76] Stonebraker, M., G. Held., P. Kreps, and E. Wong "The Design and Implementation of Ingres." *ACM Transactions on Database Systems*, Vol. 1, No. 3, September 1976, 189–222.

[Todd 75] Todd, S. J. P. "The Peterlee Relational Test Vehicle—A System Overview," *IBM Systems Journal*, Vol. 15, No. 4, 1976.

2 Basics

Today's database applications implement a wide variety of user interfaces. Some applications present their users with forms to fill in; others provide various graphical tools for construction of database queries and updates. Somewhere below the surface of many seemingly disparate systems, however, is a common interface: SQL, the Structured Query Language. SQL has become the standard representation for queries against relational data and for interchange of these queries between clients and servers and between different database systems. Because SQL is a well-defined standard that has been implemented by many vendors, applications based on SQL are relatively portable from one system to another.

This chapter covers the basics of how to use SQL and lays the foundation on which later chapters will build to describe the advanced features of UDB. The basic tasks described in this chapter are as follows:

- Retrieving, inserting, updating, and deleting data
- Designing a database and creating tables and views
- Using the transaction concept to ensure data consistency
- Controlling access to data by using the authorization subsystem

One of the strengths of SQL is that it can be used in a variety of ways. The basic SQL statements described in this chapter can be executed interactively using one of the user interfaces described in Chapter 3. The same statements can be embedded in an application program written in some host programming language such as C or C++, using the techniques described in Chapter 4. The same SQL statements can also be generated "on the fly" by a running program, using the Dynamic SQL facilities described in Chapter 8. Many of the SQL statements described in this chapter can also be executed using database administration tools such as the Control Center, described in Chapter 10.

After reading this chapter, you will have the basic SQL skills that you will need as a UDB interactive user, application developer, and database administrator.

2.1 TABLES

In a relational database, all data is stored in *tables*, which consist of rows and columns. Each table has a name, and within a table, each column has a name. No particular ordering is maintained among the rows of a table (but rows can be retrieved in an order determined by the values in their columns).

One of the defining characteristics of a relational database is that all information in the database is represented by values that are stored in tables. No information is encoded in the form of physical structures such as indexes, pointers, connections, or orderings. Of course, all these physical structures, and others, can be used by the system to optimize its performance. But all these performance aids remain just that—internal devices that bear no essential information and are not part of the data model with which users interact.

The separation of access aids from the logical data model has several important consequences:

- Users can express their queries in a simple, high-level language that makes applications easy to develop.

- System administrators do not need to anticipate in advance exactly how the database will be used, since indexes and other structures can be added as usage patterns change without affecting existing applications.

- The system has an opportunity to choose the optimum access plan for any given query, based on the access aids that are available when the query is executed.

- The data model does not have a bias that makes some questions (those that correspond to physical access paths) easier to ask than other similar questions.

The tables that are physically stored in a database are called *base tables*. Most relational database systems, including UDB, allow users to define additional tables, called *views*, that are derived in some way from the base tables. A view might be defined to omit some data from a base table, or to combine two base tables, or to contain only summary data. In UDB, views can be defined using the same syntax that is used to write queries against base tables. (Views are discussed in more detail in Section 2.6.)

2.1.1 Example Database

In order to illustrate the use of SQL to manipulate data in tables, this chapter will use an example database consisting of four tables that might be used to manage a parts warehouse for a small company. The sample queries used in this chapter are based on these tables and have been tested using the sample data shown below.

Our sample warehouse needs to keep track of all the different kinds of parts used by the company, each of which has a unique part number. A table called PARTS is used to record information about each type of part, including its description and the quantity of that type of part that are currently on hand and on order.

PARTS

PARTNO	DESCRIPTION	QONHAND	QONORDER
P207	Gear	75	20
P209	Cam	0	10
P221	Big Bolt	650	200
P222	Small Bolt	1250	0
P231	Big Nut	0	200
P232	Small Nut	1100	0
P250	Big Gear	5	3
P285	Wheel	350	0
P295	Belt	0	25

The warehouse needs to maintain its inventory by ordering new parts when supplies get low. For this purpose, it maintains a list of suppliers, in a table named SUPPLIERS as shown on the following page.

When ordering a new supply of parts, the warehouse manager generally wants to obtain each type of part at the lowest available price. However, occasionally he receives a rush order for parts that are needed within a certain time. In order to manage the process of ordering parts, the warehouse database contains a QUOTATIONS table that lists the parts that are available from the various suppliers, as well as the price and response time in days offered by each supplier for each part.

The QUOTATIONS table records prices in an Integer column as a number of cents (for example, the number 2995 represents $29.95). SQL has a Decimal datatype that might be a more natural choice for representing prices, but Decimal data cannot be exchanged efficiently with a C program because the C language has no equivalent datatype. Representing money values in Integer form is an example of one way to deal with this problem; other techniques are discussed later in the book.

The warehouse also needs to keep track of the orders for new parts that are currently pending. This is done by means of a table named ORDERS, which records the supplier number, part number, and quantity for each order, as well as the date on which the order was placed.

SUPPLIERS

SUPPNO	NAME	ADDRESS
S51	ABC Parts Company	123 Industrial Way, Cleveland OH
S53	Parts Are We	800 River Drive, Yonkers NY
S54	Quality Parts	3820 Bayview St., Seattle WA
S58	Superfast Parts	22500 Airport Blvd., Miami FL
S59	Joe's Scrap Heap	975 Country Club Lane, Boston MA
S61	Partco Inc.	650 Stony St., Dallas TX
S99	Parts Is Parts	500 Scenic Drive, Modesto CA

QUOTATIONS

SUPPNO	PARTNO	PRICE	RESPONSETIME
S51	P207	950	45
S51	P209	1250	10
S53	P207	2995	30
S53	P285	3250	21
S54	P209	2500	18
S54	P222	75	7
S54	P285	5500	25
S54	P295	1900	14
S58	P207	?	33
S58	P221	35	10
S58	P222	20	10
S58	P231	25	10
S58	P232	10	10
S61	P207	2995	28
S61	P221	30	15
S61	P222	15	15
S61	P231	20	15
S61	P232	5	15

ORDERS

SUPPNO	PARTNO	QUANTITY	ORDERDATE
S53	P207	20	1998-6-15
S51	P209	10	1998-6-20
S61	P221	200	1998-7-01
S61	P231	200	1998-7-01
S54	P295	25	1998-6-28

2.2 NAMES AND SCHEMAS

Databases are full of things that have names. As we have seen, UDB stores all data in tables, and each table has a name. Other database objects that have names include views, indexes, functions, and triggers. A name is a string of up to 18 characters, beginning with a letter.

Normally, when you type a name, the system automatically folds all lower-case characters to uppercase. Thus, for example, the names TABLE1 and table1 and Table1 are all equivalent. If, for some reason, you wish to use a name that contains lowercase letters, blanks, or special characters, you can do so if you enclose the name in double quotes, as in "My Table". Quoted names are interpreted by the system exactly as they are written, so "My Table" and "my table" are different names. A quoted name may also be the same as an SQL keyword such as SELECT or FROM, though this can lead to some confusing queries.

If you were creating a table named PAYROLL, it would be burdensome to have to search the database to find out whether some other user has already created a table with the same name. It would be even worse if you purchased some database application that creates a PAYROLL table and were unable to use it because of a naming conflict. For these reasons, SQL has a concept called a *schema*, which is a named collection of objects such as tables and views. The name of each object needs to be unique only within its schema. For example, your database might include a schema named RESEARCH and another schema named PRODUCT, and each of these schemas might contain a table named PAYROLL. You can refer to one of the PAYROLL tables by its *qualified name*, a two-part name that includes the schema name followed by the object name, such as RESEARCH.PAYROLL.

A schema can be created explicitly by means of an SQL statement called CREATE SCHEMA. Alternatively, when you create an object in a schema that does not yet exist, the schema is implicitly created. For example, if you create a table named SCHOOL.RECORDS, a schema named SCHOOL is created if it does not already exist. If you specify only a single-part name when you create an object, the schema name is considered to be your userid. For example, if the userid SMITH is used to create a table named RECORDS, a schema named SMITH is created implicitly if it does not already exist. For this reason, it is very common for a database to contain many schemas with the same names as the users of the system.

If you create a schema explicitly, you (or some other user you designate) are considered to be the *owner* of the schema. The owner of a schema is empowered to create, alter, and drop objects within the schema, and to grant these powers to other users. A schema that is created implicitly is considered to be owned by the system—anyone can create objects in it, and these objects are then under the control of their individual owners. More information about controlling schemas and the objects that are in them can be found in Sections 2.6.7 and 2.8.5.

Schema names are limited to eight characters in length. A schema name must begin with a letter but may not begin with the letters "SYS," because these schema names are reserved for system use.[1] Like object names, schema names are folded to uppercase unless they are enclosed in double quotes, in which case they are interpreted exactly as written.

Whenever you refer to some object by an unqualified (single-part) name, the system provides an implicit schema name that is the same as the userid against which authorization is currently being checked.[2] This userid is called the *current authid*. For static SQL in an application program, the current authid is the userid of the user who bound the program. For dynamic SQL and interactive user interfaces like the Command Center, the current authid is the userid of the user who is running the program or interacting with the interface. Thus, for example, if users Smith and Jones have each created a RECORDS table in their respective schemas, user Jones can refer to his own table simply as RECORDS, but he must refer to Smith's table by its fully qualified name, SMITH.RECORDS.

In the syntax diagrams used throughout this book, since names are used so often, I will not explicitly represent the fact that the names of tables, views, and other objects can be qualified by schema names. Instead, I will use the

---

1. To avoid affecting old applications, **UDB** allows a schema implicitly created by the creation of a table, view, index, or package to have a name beginning with "SYS." This practice should be avoided by new applications.

2. Actually, for functions and datatypes, the process of resolving an implicit schema name is somewhat more complex, as we will see in Chapter 6.

diagram below to define the syntax of a name that can be used for many different kinds of objects:

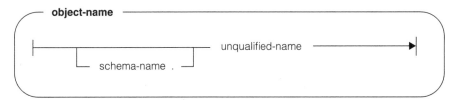

When using an object name, remember that the schema name is limited to 8 characters and the unqualified name is limited to 18 characters, and that either may be enclosed in double quotes. Object names having the above syntax may be represented in any of the following ways on syntax diagrams in this book:

alias-name

function-name

index-name

package-name

procedure-name

table-name

trigger-name

type-name

view-name

2.3 BASIC SQL DATATYPES

Each item of data stored in a UDB database has a specific datatype, such as Integer or Char(12). The datatype of a given item determines its range of values and the set of operators and functions that apply to it. Each datatype has its own internal representation. Every column of a UDB table has a datatype, specified when the table was created, that applies to all the items stored in that column. In addition to its normal values, each datatype has a special value called *null*, which represents missing or unknown information.

The datatypes that you can use in your database depend on a decision that was made at the time the database was created. The CREATE DATABASE command has options called CODESET and TERRITORY that identify the language in which data will be stored in the new database. UDB uses these options to select a *code page* for the database. For example, a database used for storing English-language data in the United States might use code page 850, but a database used for storing Japanese data might use code page 932. All data stored in the database uses the same code page. The code page determines how bit patterns are used to represent characters. In a single-byte code page such as 850, each character is represented by one byte. In a double-byte code page such as 932, on the other hand, some characters are represented by one byte and other characters are represented by two bytes. A database that uses a single-byte code page is called a *single-byte database*, and a database that uses a double-byte code page is called a *double-byte database*.

Table 2-1 shows the basic datatypes that can be used in a single-byte database.[3] Some of these datatypes have parameters, which means that when you use the datatype, you must provide some additional information such as a length or precision.

TABLE 2-1: Basic Single-Byte SQL Datatypes

Datatype	Description
Smallint	16-bit integer.
Integer	32-bit integer.
Decimal(p,s)	Decimal number with precision p and scale s. Precision is the total number of digits; scale is the number of digits to the right of the decimal point. Numeric(p,s) may be used as a synonym for Decimal(p,s). If omitted, precision defaults to 5, and scale defaults to 0.
Real	32-bit ("single-precision") floating point number.
Double	64-bit ("double-precision") floating point number. Float and Double Precision may be used as synonyms for Double.
Char(n)	Fixed-length character string of length n characters. n cannot exceed 254. If omitted, n defaults to 1.
Varchar(n)	Varying-length character string of maximum length n characters. n cannot exceed 4000. If n is greater than 254, the following operators (discussed later in this chapter) cannot be used with this datatype: GROUP BY, ORDER BY, DISTINCT, and any set operator other than UNION ALL.
Date	Consists of a year, month, and day.
Time	Consists of an hour, minute, and second.
Timestamp	Consists of a year, month, day, hour, minute, second, and microsecond.

---

3. In addition to the basic datatypes listed in Table 2-1, a single-byte database may contain *large-object* datatypes and *distinct* datatypes, both of which are discussed in Chapter 6.

TABLE 2-2: Basic Double-Byte SQL Datatypes

Datatype	Description
Graphic(n)	Fixed-length string of n double-byte characters. n cannot exceed 127.
Vargraphic(n)	Varying-length string of up to n double-byte characters. n cannot exceed 2000. If n is greater than 127, the following operators (discussed later in this chapter) cannot be used with this datatype: GROUP BY, ORDER BY, DISTINCT, and any set operator other than UNION ALL.

In a double-byte database, you can still use all the datatypes described in Table 2-1, but strings of type Char(n) and Varchar(n) may contain mixed data (mixtures of single-byte and double-byte characters). In addition, in a double-byte database, the datatypes shown in Table 2-2 may be used for pure double-byte strings.[4]

2.4 QUERIES

One of the most common and most basic tasks that a database system needs to perform is to retrieve information from the database. An SQL statement that retrieves some information is called a *query*. A query searches the tables that are stored in the database to find the answer to some question. The answer is expressed in the form of a set of rows, which is called the *result set* of the query.[5] Even if the result of a query is a single value, think of it as a result set consisting of one row and one column. Of course, the result set of a query may be empty.

The simplest form of a query in SQL scans one of the stored tables, searching for rows that satisfy some *search condition*, and for each such row selecting the values that are desired. For example, the following query finds the price and response time offered by supplier number S54 in supplying part number P209:

---

4. Large-object datatypes and distinct datatypes also exist for double-byte databases and are discussed in Chapter 6.
5. Since the result of a query may contain duplicate rows, the term *result multiset* might be more mathematically accurate, but the term *result set* is in more common usage.

```
SELECT price, responsetime
FROM   quotations
WHERE  suppno = 'S54'
AND    partno = 'P209';
```

This example illustrates the SELECT - FROM - WHERE format of a basic SQL query. The FROM clause names the table to be searched, the WHERE clause specifies a search condition that is used for finding the desired row(s), and the SELECT clause specifies the information to be retrieved from each row.

Sometimes a query contains another query inside itself. When this happens, we refer to the contained query as a *subquery*. For example, a query might use a subquery to specify some values to be used in a search condition. In general, a subquery may return multiple values, but in the special case that a subquery returns a single value, we refer to it as a *scalar subquery*. The examples that follow illustrate many uses for subqueries. (Subqueries are discussed further in Chapter 5.)

2.4.1 Expressions

One of the basic building blocks of SQL queries is the *expression*. An expression is simply a value that can be selected or computed. In the sample query above, the column names price, responsetime, suppno, and partno are expressions, as are the constants 'S54' and 'P209'. More complex expressions can be constructed by using arithmetic operators, as in qonhand+qonorder, or string concatenation, as in name || address. Expressions are used in SELECT clauses to specify the values to be retrieved and in WHERE clauses to specify the values used in the search condition. In general, an expression consists of one or more operands, connected by unary or binary operators. The operands that can be used in SQL expressions are as follows:

1. *Column names*. Examples: price, description. When a query involves more than one table, it is sometimes necessary to qualify a column name by a table name or variable to make it clear which column is being referred to. A qualified column name looks like quotations.price or x.description. When you write a multitable query, it is a good practice to qualify all the column names.

2. *Constants*. In SQL, constants can take any of the following forms:

   a. Integer constants consist simply of an optional sign and some digits. Examples: 29, -5. The datatype of an integer constant is always considered to be Integer (not Smallint).

   b. Decimal constants include a decimal point. Examples: 29.5, -3.725.

   c. Floating-point constants use an exponential notation. Examples: 1.875E5, -62E-13. The datatype of a floating-point constant is always considered to be Double (not Real).

d. Character-string constants are enclosed in single quotes. Example: 'Niagara Falls'. If it is necessary for a constant to contain a quote character, it is represented by two successive quote characters, as in 'Bobbie''s boat'. The datatype of a quoted-string constant is always considered to be Varchar (not Char).

e. String constants using double-byte character sets are enclosed in single quotes and prefixed by the letter G or N (these two prefixes are equivalent). Examples:

    G'百聞は一見にしかず'
    N'早起きは三文の徳'

The datatype of such a constant is considered to be Vargraphic. Of course, the number of bytes in a double-byte string constant must be an even number.

TIP: G-type and N-type constants can be used only inside SQL statements, never in host language code. Each host programming language has its own way to represent double-byte strings, such as the L-type constants of C and C++, which can be used in host language code but not in SQL statements.

f. Hexadecimal notation can be used in a string constant prefixed by the letter X. Examples: X'FFFF', X'12AB907F'. The letters A through F may be used in hexadecimal constants, in either upper- or lowercase. A hexadecimal constant must always have an even number of hex digits (packed two per byte). Although it contains binary data, a hexadecimal constant is considered to have the datatype Varchar. Note that the string constant '12' is a two-byte constant containing the ASCII codes for the characters "1" and "2," whereas the hex constant X'12' is a one-byte constant containing the bit pattern 00010010.

g. Dates and times can be represented using character-string constants in any of several prescribed formats. Examples:

The date December 25, 1998, can be represented in any of these ways:

    '1998-12-25'
    '12/25/1998'
    '25.12.1998'

The time 1:50 p.m. can be represented in any of these ways:

    '13.50.00' or '13.50'
    '13:50:00' or '13:50'
    '1:50 PM'

The timestamp denoting exactly 12 noon on January 5, 2001, can be represented in either of these ways:

    '2001-01-05-12.00.00.000000'
    '2001-01-05-12.00.00'

3. *Host variables.* If your SQL statement is embedded in a program written in C or some other host programming language, variables declared in the host program can be used in your SQL expressions. In order to distinguish them from column names, host variables are prefixed by a colon. Examples: :x, :deadline. (Host variables are described in more detail in Section 4.1.1.)

4. *Functions.* UDB provides a long list of functions that accept one or more arguments and compute some result. Examples: length(address) returns the length of the character string in the address column; substr(description, 1, 5) returns the first five characters of the description column.

   Certain functions operate on a collection of values derived from a column of a table, and compute a scalar result such as the average or sum of the values in the column; these are called *column functions*. (Column functions are discussed in Section 2.4.6.)

   All the built-in functions provided by UDB are listed in Appendix B. As we will see in Chapter 6, UDB allows users to create additional functions of their own.

5. *Labeled durations.* When doing arithmetic with dates and times, a length of time (called a *duration*) can be represented by a numeric expression followed by a label indicating the time units, such as 5 DAYS or 1 HOUR. The labels that can be used in this way include the singular and plural forms of the following words: YEARS, MONTHS, DAYS, HOURS, MINUTES, SECONDS, and MICROSECONDS.

   TIP: The only place where a labeled duration can be used is in an addition or subtraction where the other operand is a date, time, or timestamp. For example, suppose that you need to find out whether a date named ORDERDATE is more than ten days old. The first of the following expressions is a valid way to make this test, but the second expression is not valid because the labeled duration is not used directly in the subtraction operation:

   ```
   orderdate + 10 DAYS < CURRENT DATE    -- valid expression
   CURRENT DATE - orderdate > 10 DAYS    -- invalid expression
   ```

6. *Special registers.* UDB maintains a set of *special registers*, whose values describe the environment in which your SQL statement is being executed. For example, CURRENT DATE represents the date on which the statement is being executed, CURRENT SERVER represents the name of the database in which the statement is being executed, and USER represents the userid of the user who is connected to the database and executing the statement. (A complete list of special registers is given in Appendix A.)

7. *CASE expressions.* A CASE expression computes a value that is based on finding which of several conditions is true. The following is an example of a CASE expression whose value is a character string:

```
CASE
   WHEN weight < 100 THEN 'Light'
   WHEN weight BETWEEN 100 AND 200 THEN 'Medium'
   WHEN weight > 200 THEN 'Heavy'
END
```

(CASE expressions are discussed further in Section 5.1.)

8. *CAST expressions.* A CAST expression is used to convert a value to a desired datatype. The following is an example of a CAST expression that converts a value from the PRICE column to the datatype Decimal(8,2):

```
CAST (price AS Decimal(8,2))
```

(CAST expressions are discussed further in Section 2.4.3.)

9. *Subqueries.* A scalar subquery (that is, a subquery that returns a single value) may be used inside an expression wherever a value may be used. (Scalar subqueries are discussed further in Section 5.2.1.)

Expressions can be constructed by combining the various operands listed above, using the following operators:

1. *Arithmetic operators:* +, -, *, and /. The + and - operators can be used either as unary (prefix) operators or as binary (infix) operators. Examples:

```
qonhand + qonorder
price * qonorder
-price
```

Generally, arithmetic operators preserve the types of their operands (for example, the result of dividing two integers is still an integer, with the fractional part of the result truncated). However, floating-point arithmetic is always carried out in double precision, so if either operand is Real, the result will be Double. If either operand is null, the result of the arithmetic operator is null.

If an error (such as overflow or division by zero) occurs during processing of an arithmetic operator, the SQL statement ends immediately and generates an error code. But if you configure your database with the setting DFT_SQLMATHWARN=YES, arithmetic errors are handled differently: the expression containing the error returns a null value, processing of the SQL statement continues, and a warning code is generated. This feature is called *friendly arithmetic* because it allows some statements to run to completion when they would otherwise fail, but you should use it with caution because it can potentially lead to incorrect results. (Error and warning codes are discussed in Section 4.1.4. Database configuration parameters such as DFT_SQLMATHWARN can be examined and set by using the Control Center, which is discussed in Section 10.3.)

2. *Concatenation operator.* The || operator concatenates two strings, resulting in a new string. Example: name || address. The word concat is equivalent to the || operator, as in name concat address. If either operand is null, the result of the concatenation is null.

3. *Parentheses.* When arithmetic expressions are evaluated, unary plus and minus are applied first, followed by multiplication and division (left to right), followed by addition and subtraction (left to right). Parentheses can be used to modify this order and to introduce as many levels of nested expressions as you like.

The following are two examples of expressions:

- The number of parts available to be used weekly over the next year might be expressed as (qonorder+qonhand)/52.

- The name and address of a supplier, concatenated and limited to 50 characters, might be expressed as substr(name || address, 1, 50).

2.4.2 Datetime Arithmetic

When arithmetic operators are used with the datatypes that represent dates and times, special rules apply. In order to understand these rules, we need to discuss the concept of a *duration*. Each of the datetime datatypes (Date, Time, and Timestamp) has an associated duration. A duration is not a datatype in its own right, but simply a specialized use of the Decimal datatype, as follows:

- A *date duration* is a Decimal(8,0) number that represents the period between two Date values, in format YYYYMMDD.

- A *time duration* is a Decimal(6,0) number that represents the period between two Time values, in format HHMMSS.

- A *timestamp duration* is a Decimal(20,6) number that represents the period between two Timestamp values, in format YYYYMMDDHHMMSS.ZZZZZZ (the ZZZZZZ portion represents microseconds).

Since durations are really Decimal values, they can be used in exactly the same ways as other Decimal values (for example, they can be stored in Decimal columns and represented by Decimal constants). Durations may be positive or negative. Durations are exceptional only because they can participate in certain addition and subtraction operations with Dates, Times, and Timestamps. These operations, which are the only arithmetic operations permitted on the datetime datatypes, are shown in Table 2-3.

TABLE 2-3: Arithmetic Operations on Dates, Times, and Timestamps

First Operand Datatype	Operator	Second Operand Datatype	Result Datatype
Date	+ or –	Date duration	Date
Time	+ or –	Time duration	Time
Timestamp	+ or –	Timestamp duration	Timestamp
Date	–	Date	Date duration
Time	–	Time	Time duration
Timestamp	–	Timestamp	Timestamp duration

The following are some examples of expressions that use datetime arithmetic:

- The number of years, months, and days remaining in the century, expressed as a duration (a decimal number of form YYMMDD), can be computed as follows: `'1999-12-31' - CURRENT DATE`

- The date on which we expect an order of parts to arrive might be expressed by using a labeled duration, as follows: `orderdate + responsetime DAYS`

2.4.3 Casting

Programming languages use the term *casting* to refer to the process of changing a value from one datatype to another, as in *casting* an Integer value into the Decimal datatype. UDB supports several built-in functions, such as `decimal`, `integer`, `real`, and `date`, that have the effect of casting their operands into specific datatypes. In some cases, casting a value into a given datatype may change the value itself. For example, any Integer can be cast into a Decimal without changing its value, but casting a Decimal value into the Integer datatype may result in truncation of its fractional part.

In addition to the built-in functions that have the effect of casting, UDB supports a CAST notation, defined by the SQL92 Standard, with the following syntax:

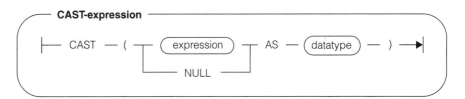

In order for a CAST to be successful, the target datatype must be well defined, including its length, scale, and precision, if any. The safest thing to do is to specify these properties explicitly, as in the following examples:

```
CAST (c1+c2 AS Decimal(8,2))
CAST (name || address AS Varchar(255))
```

If you omit the length and precision from a Decimal target datatype, it is assumed to be Decimal(5,0). A Char target datatype with no specified length is assumed to be Char(1), and a Graphic target datatype with no specified length is assumed to be Graphic(1). Other target datatypes with missing lengths result in error conditions. Of course, if the value used in a CAST expression cannot be converted to the target datatype, an error results.

If you cast a string-type value into a target datatype that has a longer length, the value will be padded with blanks. If you cast a string-type value into a target datatype that has a shorter length, the value will be truncated, and you will receive a warning message if any of the truncated characters were nonblank.

The combinations of datatypes that can be used in valid CAST expressions are summarized in Table 6-6 on page 386.

Casting is sometimes useful when a value of a particular datatype is needed as the parameter of a function. You may also occasionally cast a value into its own datatype in order to change its length, precision, or scale. For example, if a column named ELEVATION has a datatype of Decimal(8,3), you might truncate the fractional part of the values in this column by using an expression such as the following:

```
CAST(elevation AS Decimal(5,0))
```

Another use of a CAST expression is to specify the datatype of a null value. If the keyword NULL appears by itself, the system has no way of knowing whether it represents a null Integer, a null Varchar, or some other type of null value, each of which has a different representation. If you need to use NULL in a place where a typed value is required (such as in the SELECT clause of a query), you can specify the datatype of your null value by using a CAST expression, as in the following example:

```
CAST(NULL AS Varchar(20))
```

2.4.4 Search Conditions

As we saw in the simple query example on page 44, SQL statements often scan through the rows of a table, applying some search condition to find the rows that qualify for further processing. The search condition is a logical test that can be applied to each row, resulting in one of three truth values: TRUE,

FALSE, or UNKNOWN. If the search condition evaluates to TRUE, the row is accepted for further processing (for example, it might become part of the result set of a query, or it might be updated or deleted if the search condition is used in an SQL UPDATE or DELETE statement). If the search condition evaluates to FALSE or UNKNOWN, the row is not accepted for further processing.

A search condition might evaluate to UNKNOWN for a given row because the row contains a null value. For example, if the price is missing from a particular quotation, the `price` column in the row representing that quotation will contain a null value and the search condition `price > 1000` will evaluate to UNKNOWN for that row. In general, whenever a null value is used in an expression, the result of the expression is null, and whenever a null value is compared to another value (even another null value!), the result is the UNKNOWN truth value.

The logical tests that are used in search conditions are called *predicates*. UDB supports many different kinds of predicates, as shown in the syntax diagram on page 52.

All expressions used in predicates are constructed according to the rules in Section 2.4.1. The individual types of predicates supported by UDB are explained below.

1. *Simple comparison predicate.* Any two expressions may be compared, using the comparison operators =, <, <=, >, >=, and <>. The <> operator means "not equal." The expressions being compared must have compatible datatypes. (Of course, the CAST notation can be used to convert one datatype into another.) The result of a comparison predicate is UNKNOWN if either expression is null.

The meaning of > and the other comparison operators for character strings is determined by the collating sequence that was declared at database creation time.[6] Collating sequences are generally defined to be insensitive to upper- and lowercase. (For example, 'cat' < 'DOG' and 'CAT' < 'dog' are both TRUE.)

Examples:

```
price > 1000
name <> 'Safeco'
```

A string is defined to be greater than any prefix of itself. (For example, 'cat' < 'catnip' is TRUE.)

2. *BETWEEN predicate.* The meaning of expression1 BETWEEN expression2 AND expression3 is the same as the meaning of expression1 >= expression2 AND expression1 <= expression3.

---

6. However, if one of the operands comes from a table column that was created with the FOR BIT DATA property, the string comparison is done as a byte-by-byte binary comparison.

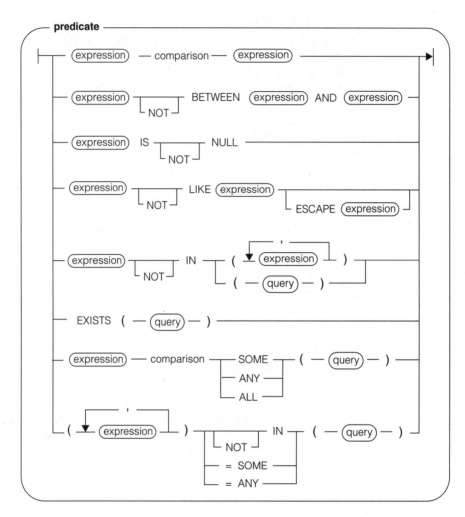

The meaning of expression1 NOT BETWEEN expression2 AND expression3 is the same as the meaning of expression1 < expression2 OR expression1 > expression3.

Example:

```
:request BETWEEN qonhand AND qonhand+qonorder
```

TIP: Note that x BETWEEN y AND z does not have the same meaning as x BETWEEN z AND y. In fact, if the value of z is greater than the value of y, the latter predicate can never be TRUE.

3. *IS NULL predicate.* The IS NULL predicate never returns the UNKNOWN truth value. If the expression used in an IS NULL predicate evaluates to null, the predicate is TRUE; otherwise, the predicate is FALSE. The meaning of

`expression1 IS NOT NULL` is the same as the meaning of `NOT (expression1 IS NULL)`.

Example:

`address IS NULL`

4. *LIKE predicate.* A LIKE predicate is a very powerful way of searching for a given pattern inside a character string. The general form of the predicate is as follows (optional phrases are indicated by square brackets):

```
match-expression [NOT] LIKE pattern-expression
    [ESCAPE escape-expression]
```

The match-expression can be of any single- or double-byte character-string datatype. The pattern-expression must be of a compatible string datatype and has certain additional restrictions: it cannot include a column name, and its length cannot exceed 4000 bytes. Typically, the pattern-expression is a short constant string.

The basic idea of a LIKE predicate is to compare the match-expression with the pattern-expression. But in performing the comparison, certain characters in the pattern-expression are considered to have special meanings:

- The underscore character (_) represents any single character.
- The percent sign (%) represents any string of zero or more characters.

Thus, for example, the following predicate is TRUE for any address that contains the words "New York":

`address LIKE '%New York%'`

Similarly, the following predicate is TRUE for any four-character part number that begins with P and ends with 2:

`partno LIKE 'P__2'`

The optional ESCAPE clause specifies a single character (called the *escape character*), which, when preceding a % or _ character in the pattern, causes the % or _ character to represent itself rather than to be interpreted as a special character. Thus, for example, the following predicate is TRUE for any description that contains the string "10% solution":

`description LIKE '%10/% solution%' ESCAPE '/'`

5. *IN predicate.* An IN predicate is useful for testing whether a given value is included in a list of values. For example, the following predicate is TRUE if the given supplier number matches any of a list of five specific values:

`suppno IN ('S51', 'S52', 'S53', 'S54', 'S55')`

The values on the right side of an IN predicate can be provided by a list of literals, as in the above example, or by a subquery that evaluates to a single column of values. For example, the following predicate is TRUE if the given supplier number matches that of any supplier number that supplies part number P221:

```
suppno IN
    (SELECT suppno
     FROM quotations
     WHERE partno = 'P221')
```

6. *EXISTS predicate.* An EXISTS predicate contains a subquery and evaluates to TRUE if the result of the subquery contains at least one row. If the subquery returns no rows, the EXISTS predicate is FALSE. An EXISTS predicate never evaluates to UNKNOWN.

In the following example, the predicate is TRUE if there exists some supplier in the QUOTATIONS table who supplies part number P221:

```
EXISTS
    (SELECT suppno
     FROM quotations
     WHERE partno = 'P221')
```

Many interesting examples of EXISTS predicates involve *correlated subqueries*, which will be discussed in Section 5.2.

7. *Quantified comparison predicate.* Like a simple comparison predicate, a quantified comparison predicate uses one of the six comparison operators =, <, <=, >, >=, and <>. Like an IN predicate, it compares a single value with a list of values returned by a subquery. The unique thing about a quantified comparison predicate is that it includes one of the keywords SOME, ANY, or ALL. The keywords SOME and ANY indicate that the predicate is TRUE if the comparison holds for at least one element in the list. The keyword ALL indicates that the predicate is TRUE if the comparison holds for all elements in the list (or if the list is empty).

The following example predicate is TRUE if the price in variable :p is less than all the prices quoted for part number P207:

```
:p < ALL
        (SELECT price
         FROM quotations
         WHERE partno = 'P207'
         AND price IS NOT NULL)
```

TIP: The phrase price IS NOT NULL guards against quotations with null prices, which would otherwise force the <ALL predicate to be always FALSE.

8. *Row predicate.* A row predicate is similar to a quantified comparison predicate, but instead of comparing a single value to the result of a subquery, it compares a *row* (a sequence of values) to the result of a subquery. The only kind of row comparison that is supported is comparison for equality. One row is equal to another row if the values of their corresponding columns are equal. A row

	AND		
	T	F	?
T	T	F	?
F	F	F	F
?	?	F	?

	OR		
	T	F	?
T	T	T	T
F	T	F	?
?	T	?	?

	NOT
T	F
F	T
?	?

Figure 2-1: Truth Tables for Three-Valued Logic

predicate with a comparison operator of = SOME, = ANY, or IN is TRUE if the row on the left side is equal[7] to at least one of the rows returned by the subquery. It is FALSE if the result of the subquery is the empty set.

The row predicate in the following example might be used when searching through the ORDERS table to find orders that are expected to have a delay of more than 20 days between order and delivery:

```
(suppno, partno) IN
        (SELECT suppno, partno
         FROM quotations
         WHERE responsetime > 20);
```

A search condition might consist of a single predicate such as `price > 1000`, or a combination of predicates connected by the logical connectives AND, OR, and NOT, such as `price < 1000 OR responsetime < 10 AND NOT suppno = 'S54'`. The truth value of the search condition for a given row is found by combining the truth values of the individual predicates, using the truth tables shown in Figure 2-1, in which "?" represents the UNKNOWN truth value.

When combining predicates to evaluate a search condition, NOT operators are applied first, followed by AND operators, and OR operators are applied last. Of course, parentheses can be used to modify the precedence of these operators. In order to provide the system with opportunities for optimization, no promises are made about the order in which predicates will be evaluated within a group of equal precedence.

---

7. "Equal" means "provably equal." If the rows being compared contain some null values, the truth value of the predicate may be UNKNOWN.

The following syntax diagram and example illustrate how predicates can be combined using AND, OR, NOT, and parentheses to form search conditions:

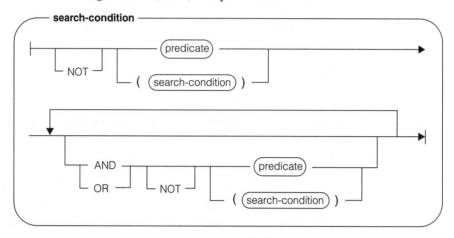

Example of a search condition on the PARTS table:

```
( partno IN ('P205', 'P207', 'P209')
  OR description LIKE '%Gear%' )
AND qonhand + qonorder <= 10
```

2.4.5 Joins

We have seen how a simple SQL query can scan a single table and select the rows that satisfy some search condition. Often, however, we need to find the answer to a question that involves a relationship among multiple tables. A query that expresses this kind of question is called a *join*.

In a join query, the FROM clause names not just one table, but a list of all the tables participating in the join, separated by commas. Conceptually, the system forms all possible combinations of rows from the tables listed in the FROM clause, and for each combination it applies the search condition. In a join query, the search condition usually specifies some relationship between the rows to be joined. For example, we might join rows from the PARTS table with rows from the QUOTATIONS table that have matching part numbers. This predicate, called a *join condition*, might be expressed as follows:

```
parts.partno = quotations.partno
```

Since more than one table in a join may have a common column name, a column name used in a join query must sometimes be prefixed by a table name to avoid ambiguity, as in the example above. Column names that are unique among the tables being joined do not require such a prefix (but qualifying all column names by table names, even when it's not required, may make the query easier to understand).

The following is an example of a join that lists the part number, description, and price of all parts supplied by supplier number S51:

```
SELECT parts.partno, parts.description, quotations.price
FROM parts, quotations
WHERE parts.partno = quotations.partno
AND quotations.suppno = 'S51';
```

If a row from one of the participating tables never satisfies the join condition (for example, a PARTS row has no matching QUOTATIONS row or vice versa), that row will not appear in the result of the join. Section 5.4 discusses techniques for expressing an alternative kind of join, called an *outer join*, that retains rows from one table that have no matching rows in the other table.

If the search condition contains no predicates that specify a relationship between the rows of the tables in the join, all possible combinations of rows from these tables will be returned, even though the rows may be completely unrelated. This type of query is called a *Cartesian product*; it is expensive to execute and rarely produces a meaningful result.

It is possible to write a query in which a table is joined to itself. The table name is repeated two or more times in the FROM clause, indicating that the join consists of combinations of two or more rows from the same table. Because the table name is not unique in such a query, each table in the FROM clause must be given a unique identifier, called a *correlation name*. A correlation name can be used anywhere in the query as a prefix to a column name that uniquely identifies the row to which the column belongs. In the following query, the QUOTATIONS table is joined to itself, using correlation names x and y. The query finds pairs of quotations for the same part in which the prices differ by more than a factor of two:

```
SELECT x.partno, x.suppno, x.price, y.suppno, y.price
FROM quotations x, quotations y
WHERE x.partno = y.partno
AND y.price > 2 * x.price;
```

Note that the example above has two join conditions, one relating the two rows by PARTNO and the other by PRICE. In general, a query may have many join conditions.

2.4.6 Column Functions

As noted earlier, a large set of functions are shipped with the UDB product. Most of these functions are *scalar functions,* such as `length` and `substr`, that take one or more scalar parameters and return a scalar result. Some of the built-in functions, however, are *column functions,*[8] which operate on a set of values and reduce it to a single scalar value. The built-in column functions are listed below and described in detail in Appendix B.

```
avg
count
count_big
grouping
max
min
stdev
sum
variance
```

When a column function is invoked with an argument expression such as qonorder+qonhand, the set of values passed to the function consists of the argument expression evaluated for each row that satisfies the search condition. This set of values is called the *argument set* of the function. For example, the following query finds the total number of bolts that are on hand or on order, including all kinds of bolts:

```
SELECT sum(qonorder + qonhand)
FROM parts
WHERE description LIKE '%Bolt%'
```

The syntax for invoking a column function is as follows:

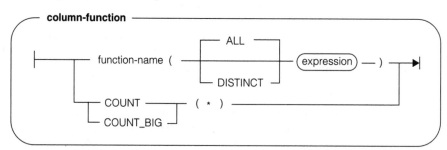

---

8. Terminology in this area is not uniform. The term *column function* is used in IBM documentation. The ANSI/ISO SQL92 Standard refers to this type of function as a *set function.* The term *aggregate function* is also used in the literature.

As shown in the diagram above, an invocation of a column function looks much like an invocation of a scalar function. The following rules apply to column functions:

1. The argument of a column function (except the grouping function) may be preceded by the keyword DISTINCT. This keyword causes duplicate values to be eliminated from the argument set before the function is applied. If DISTINCT is omitted or if ALL is specified, duplicate values are not eliminated before applying the function.

2. The argument of column functions count and count_big can be an asterisk rather than an expression. In this case, the function returns the number of rows in its argument set (that is, the number of rows that satisfy the search condition).

3. Column functions ignore null values in their argument sets. This rule is not applicable to the special functions count(*) and count_big(*), which count rows rather than individual values.

4. In general, if a column function is invoked with an empty argument set, the result of the column function is null. However, the result of invoking count or count_big with an empty argument set is zero.

The following queries illustrate applications of column functions:

- Find the maximum and minimum non-null price quotations for part number P207.

  ```
  SELECT max(price), min(price)
  FROM quotations
  WHERE partno = 'P207';
  ```

- Find the number of quotations for part number P207, regardless of whether the price quoted (or any other column, apart from PARTNO) is null.

  ```
  SELECT count(*)
  FROM quotations
  WHERE partno = 'P207';
  ```

- Find the number of quotations for part number P207 that have non-null prices.

  ```
  SELECT count(price)
  FROM quotations
  WHERE partno = 'P207';
  ```

- Find the number of different non-null prices that have been quoted for part number P207.

  ```
  SELECT count(DISTINCT price)
  FROM quotations
  WHERE partno = 'P207';
  ```

2.4.7 Grouping

As we have seen, column functions operate on sets of values and return scalar results. Rather than applying a column function to a whole table, it is sometimes desirable to divide a table into groups of related rows and to apply a column function to each group separately. This can be accomplished by a feature of SQL called *grouping*.

Grouping permits a table to be conceptually divided into groups of rows with matching values for one or more expressions (called *grouping expressions*), which are listed in a GROUP BY clause. When a query contains a GROUP BY clause, each row in the result set represents one group, and the expressions in the SELECT clause apply to the group as a whole—so each expression must include either a column function or a grouping expression.

In the simplest grouping queries, the GROUP BY clause contains one grouping expression that is simply a column of the table. For example, the following query finds the maximum, minimum, and average quoted price for each part:

```
SELECT partno, max(price), min(price), avg(price)
FROM quotations
GROUP BY partno;
```

For the purpose of forming groups, the null value is considered to be a value like any other. Thus, if a table is grouped by PARTNO as in the example above, all the rows having a null value for PARTNO will be in the same group.

A GROUP BY clause may contain expressions, as long as the expressions contain no subqueries and the result of each expression is not longer than 254 bytes. The following example illustrates a GROUP BY clause that contains two grouping expressions. It finds the number of different part numbers that were ordered in each month for which we have records. This query also illustrates how names can be given to expressions in a SELECT clause.

```
SELECT year(orderdate) as year,
       month(orderdate) as month,
       count(DISTINCT partno) as partcount
FROM orders
GROUP BY year(orderdate), month(orderdate);
```

The WHERE clause of a query serves as a filter that is applied before groups are formed, retaining only those rows that satisfy the search condition. For example, the following query finds the average and minimum price for each part, considering only quotations that have a response time of less than 30 days:

```
SELECT partno, avg(price), min(price)
FROM quotations
WHERE responsetime < 30
GROUP BY partno;
```

It is also possible to apply a qualifying condition to the groups themselves, retaining only those groups that satisfy some condition. This is done by a HAVING clause that is written after the GROUP BY clause. The HAVING clause contains a search condition in which each predicate tests some group property involving a column function or a grouping expression. For example, the following query lists the maximum and minimum prices for various parts, considering only those parts that have at least three quotations and for which the maximum price is more than twice the minimum price:

```
SELECT partno, max(price), min(price)
FROM quotations
GROUP BY partno
HAVING count(*) >= 3
AND max(price) > 2 * min(price);
```

A query can contain both a WHERE clause and a HAVING clause. The WHERE clause is applied first as a filter on rows; then the groups are formed and the HAVING clause is applied as a filter on groups. For example, the following query finds part numbers for which we have quotations from at least two different suppliers, each with a response time of less than 30 days:

```
SELECT partno
FROM quotations
WHERE responsetime < 30
GROUP BY partno
HAVING count(DISTINCT suppno) >= 2;
```

It is possible (though unusual) for a query to have a HAVING clause but no GROUP BY clause. In this case, the entire table is treated as one group. If the search condition in the HAVING clause is true for the table as a whole, the SELECT clause (which must consist only of column functions and constants) is evaluated and returned; otherwise, the query returns the empty set.

2.4.8 Query Blocks

Now that we have discussed several specific features of SQL, we are ready to put them together into a unit called a *query block*.[9] A query block is the basic unit of the SQL language that operates on one or more database tables, performing join, grouping, projection, and selection operations to distill these tables into a derived table, which can then be delivered to the user or used for further processing. The syntax of a query block is shown on the following page.

The clauses of the query block are discussed below, in the order in which they are conceptually applied. (Of course, the system is allowed to execute the query block using any method that leads to an equivalent result.)

1. The first step in processing a query block is to form a Cartesian product of all the tables named in the FROM clause. A Cartesian product consists of all possible combinations of rows taken from the respective tables. Of course, if only one table is named, the FROM clause simply generates all the rows of that table. (Remember that this is a conceptual description of query processing and does not necessarily correspond to the way a query block would really be executed. If the optimizer is smart, it will probably find some way to avoid actually computing a Cartesian product of two or more tables.)

    If any table is given a correlation name in the FROM clause, that correlation name replaces the table name for use elsewhere in the query. In other words, if the FROM clause contains the phrase `parts as x`, then in other parts of the query, the PARTNO column of this table should be referred to as `x.partno` rather than as `parts.partno`.

    The syntax diagram for a query block shown here includes the simplest form of a FROM clause, which is simply a list of table names with optional correlation names. In addition, a FROM clause may contain more complex expressions, such as a subquery that computes a temporary table, or a call to a function that returns a table. Correlation names are not restricted to table names, but can specify alternative names for columns as well. These and other advanced features of the FROM clause are described in Chapter 5 and are summarized in the syntax diagram for an *extended FROM clause* on page 229.

2. The next step is to apply the search condition in the WHERE clause as a filter to the rows generated by the FROM clause. Only those rows for which the search condition is TRUE (not UNKNOWN) survive for further processing. If no WHERE clause is provided, all the rows survive. If more than one table was named in the FROM clause, the WHERE clause will probably include some join predicates that specify the desired relationships among the tables.

---

9. Terminology in this area is not uniform. The language unit that I call a *query block* is referred to as a *subselect* in the IBM documentation and as a *query specification* in the SQL92 Standard.

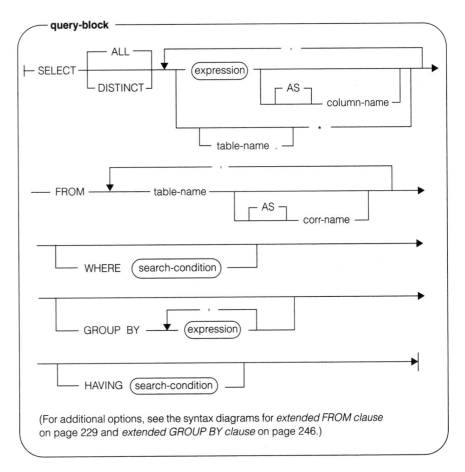

(For additional options, see the syntax diagrams for *extended FROM clause* on page 229 and *extended GROUP BY clause* on page 246.)

3. The next step is to form the surviving rows into groups according to the grouping expressions in the GROUP BY clause. Within each group, all the rows have matching values for the grouping expressions. Of course, column names used in the GROUP BY clause may be prefixed by a table name or correlation name, as in x.partno.

For the purpose of forming groups, null is considered a value. (For example, if the GROUP BY clause specifies a single column, all rows having a null value in the grouping column will be placed in the same group.)

4. After groups have been formed, the search condition in the HAVING clause is applied as a filter to the groups. Only those groups for which the search condition is TRUE are retained for further processing. If the query block has no HAVING clause, all the groups are retained. If the query block has a HAVING clause but no GROUP BY clause, the HAVING search condition applies to the whole query block, and the result of the query block is an empty table if the search condition is not TRUE.

Since a HAVING clause is testing whole groups rather than individual rows, each expression in the HAVING clause must have a well-defined value for each group. To make sure this is true, each expression in the HAVING clause must satisfy one of the following rules:

- Its outermost operator must be a column function, or
- It must contain one of the grouping expressions, and not reference any column that is not part of a grouping expression, or
- It must be a correlated reference to a column defined in a higher-level query block that contains this query block as a subquery.

5. Finally, the SELECT clause is applied to the rows or groups that have survived to this point. From these rows or groups, the SELECT clause selects the specific columns or expressions that are to be used in the final result of the query block.

If the query block contains a GROUP BY or HAVING clause, the result of the query block will contain one row per group. In this case, each expression in the SELECT clause must satisfy one of the rules listed above for expressions in the HAVING clause (that is, each expression must be a column function, or contain a grouping expression, or be correlated to a higher-level query block).

If the query block does not contain a GROUP BY or HAVING clause, the SELECT clause must satisfy one of the following rules:

- No column functions may be used. In this case, the result of the query block contains one row for each of the rows that satisfies the WHERE clause.
- Alternatively, *all* column references in the SELECT clause may appear in the arguments of column functions. In this case, the result of the query block contains exactly one row.

Each expression in the SELECT clause may be given a name that serves as its "column name" in the result of the query block. For example, the SELECT clause might contain the phrase qonorder+qonhand AS totalsupply.

An asterisk appearing in a SELECT clause means "all columns." An asterisk appearing prefixed by a table name or correlation name means "all the columns of the indicated table." For example, if the FROM clause specifies that the QUOTATIONS table is to be joined to itself by the phrase FROM quotations q1, quotations q2, then the SELECT clause might contain the phrase q1.* with the meaning, "all the columns of the row designated by the correlation name q1."

The result of the query block can be thought of as a table whose columns are the expressions in the SELECT clause and whose rows are the rows or groups that are generated and retained by the other clauses. Duplicate rows are not eliminated from the result of the query block unless the keyword DISTINCT is specified in the SELECT clause.

The following example includes all the clauses that can be used in a query block. It lists the minimum quoted price for various parts, considering only quotations that have a response time of less than 30 days, and including only parts that have at least two such quotations.

```
SELECT p.partno, min(q.price) AS lowprice
FROM parts p, quotations q
WHERE p.partno = q.partno
AND p.responsetime < 30
GROUP BY p.partno
HAVING count(*) >= 2;
```

2.4.9 Queries and Literal Tables

The result of evaluating a query block is a table, possibly containing some duplicate rows (unless SELECT DISTINCT was specified in the query block). SQL permits the results of several query blocks to be combined using the operators UNION, INTERSECT, and EXCEPT, optionally modified by the keyword ALL. The definition of these operators, applied to two tables, T1 and T2, is as follows:

- T1 UNION T2 is a table consisting of all the rows that are either in T1 or in T2, with duplicate rows eliminated.

- T1 UNION ALL T2 is a table consisting of all the rows that are either in T1 or in T2, with duplicate rows preserved. (For example, if a given row occurs three times in T1 and two times in T2, it will occur five times in T1 UNION ALL T2.)

- T1 INTERSECT T2 is a table consisting of all the rows that are common to both T1 and T2, with duplicate rows eliminated.

- T1 INTERSECT ALL T2 is a table consisting of all the rows that are in both T1 and T2. The number of occurrences of a given row in T1 INTERSECT ALL T2 is the minimum of its number of occurrences in T1 and in T2. (For example, if a given row occurs three times in T1 and two times in T2, it will occur two times in T1 INTERSECT ALL T2.)

- T1 EXCEPT T2 is a table consisting of all the rows that are in T1 but not in T2, with duplicate rows not considered significant. (For example, if a given row occurs three times in T1 and two times in T2, that row will not occur at all in T1 EXCEPT T2. If a given row occurs three times in T1 and zero times in T2, that row will occur once in T1 EXCEPT T2.)

- T1 EXCEPT ALL T2 is a table consisting of all the rows of T1 that do not have a corresponding row in T2, with duplicates considered significant. (For example, if a given row occurs three times in T1 and two times in T2, that row will occur once in T1 EXCEPT ALL T2.)

I will use the term *query* to denote an expression whose result is a table.[10] A query block is a simple form of a query. A query may also include multiple query blocks, combined by the operators UNION, INTERSECT, and EXCEPT. Of course, the partial results being combined by these operators must have the same number of columns, and the datatypes of their corresponding columns must be compatible. (The detailed rules for datatype compatibility and for determining the datatypes of the result columns are given in Section 6.6.)

When two tables are combined by UNION, INTERSECT, or EXCEPT, whenever two corresponding columns of the input tables have the same name, this name is preserved in the result column. If the corresponding columns of the input tables do not have the same name, the result column is unnamed.

In evaluating a query, INTERSECT operators take precedence over UNION and EXCEPT operators, and operators with the same precedence are executed from left to right. Of course, parentheses may be used to modify the order of execution. The syntax of a query is as follows:

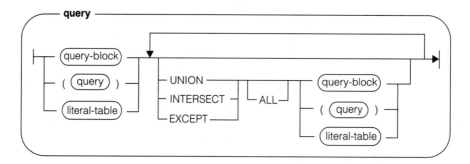

The syntax diagram above shows that the building blocks of a query are query blocks and *literal tables*. A literal table is a collection of one or more rows whose values are contained directly in the query. A literal table begins with the keyword VALUES and contains an expression (or the word NULL) for each of its column values, as shown in the syntax diagram on the following page.

Parentheses are used around each row of a literal table; however, if the literal table has only one column, the parentheses can be omitted. This potentially confusing feature is illustrated in the following examples:

---

10. Here again, terminology is not uniform. The language unit that I call a *query* is referred to as a *fullselect* in the IBM documentation and as a *query expression* in the SQL92 Standard.

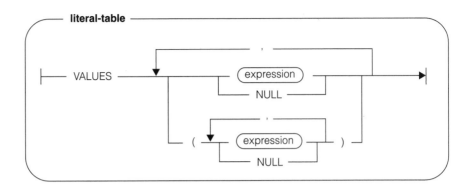

1. VALUES (`Bob`, `Carol`), (`Ted`, `Alice`), (`John`, `Mary`) is a literal table containing three rows of two columns each, as follows:

Bob	Carol
Ted	Alice
John	Mary

2. VALUES (`Bob`), (`Ted`), (`John`) is a literal table containing three rows of one column each.

3. VALUES `Bob`, `Ted`, `John` is exactly equivalent to example 2. Both examples 2 and 3 produce the following table:

Bob
Ted
John

4. VALUES (`Bob`, `Ted`, `John`) is a literal table containing one row of three columns, as follows:

Bob	Ted	John

TIP: Because of the danger of confusion between examples 3 and 4, you would be well advised to enclose each row in your literal table inside parentheses, even if the row consists of a single column.

All the values in a given column of a literal table must have compatible datatypes (for example, a column might consist of character strings or of numeric values, but not of character strings mixed with numeric values). (The detailed rules for datatype compatibility in literal tables are given in Section 6.6.) It is not permitted for *all* the values in any column of a literal table to be null, unless one of them is given an explicit datatype by a CAST expression.

Queries that use set operators and/or literal tables can sometimes express questions that would be difficult to express in other ways, as illustrated by the following examples:

- This very simple query finds all the suppliers who currently have no quotations on record.

```
    SELECT suppno
    FROM suppliers
EXCEPT
    SELECT suppno
    FROM quotations;
```

- This query lists the names and addresses of all the suppliers who can supply part number P207 for less than $10.00, including two additional suppliers who did not qualify by the normal criteria.

```
    SELECT name, address
    FROM suppliers
    WHERE suppno IN
        (SELECT suppno
         FROM quotations
         WHERE partno = 'P207'
         AND price < 1000)
UNION
    VALUES('Uncle Bill', 'P.O.Box 1117, Fresno, CA'),
          ('Repo City', '650 First St., Buffalo, NY');
```

An SQL query is a very powerful mechanism for deriving a table from tables stored in the database and from constants and host variables. A query can be used as an SQL statement in its own right, or it can be used as a subquery inside a higher-level SQL statement. For example:

- A query can be used inside a predicate, as shown in the syntax diagram for *predicate* on page 52.

- A query can be used in a FROM clause, to compute a synthetic table that is used in a higher-level statement. This usage, called a *table expression*, is discussed in Section 5.2.2.

- A query can be used in the definition of a view, as shown in the syntax diagram for *create-view-statement* on page 86.

A query, by itself, does not impose any ordering on the rows of the result set. Indeed, when a query is used as a subquery, its result set is considered to be unordered. When a query is used in a *select-statement* (see below) or in a *cursor-declaration* (see page 163), the enclosing statement can provide an ORDER BY clause that imposes an ordering on the rows of the result set before delivering them to a user or to an application program.

2.4.10 SELECT Statement

When a query is used as a top-level SQL statement, we call it a *SELECT statement*. A SELECT statement can be submitted to an interactive interface such as the Command Center, which will execute it and display the result. In addition to the normal query clauses, a SELECT statement may have two additional clauses that are meaningful only for top-level queries: an ORDER BY clause that imposes an ordering on the result set, and a FETCH FIRST clause that limits the size of the result set. The syntax of a SELECT statement is as follows:

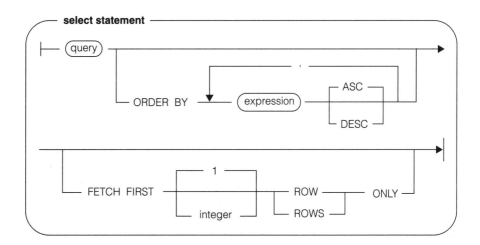

The ORDER BY clause causes the result set of a query to be ordered by the values of one or more expressions, called *sort keys*, in either ascending or descending order. If no ORDER BY clause is specified, the ordering of the result set is system-determined. Sort keys can be specified in many different ways, as shown in the following examples:

- The simplest ORDER BY clause consists simply of a column name that also appears in the SELECT clause. The following query lists all the quotations for part number P231 that have a response time of less than 30 days, in order by price from the least expensive to the most expensive.

```
SELECT suppno, price
FROM quotations
WHERE partno = 'P231'
AND responsetime < 30
ORDER BY price;
```

- A column name in the SELECT clause that is qualified by a table name or correlation name can also appear in the ORDER BY clause, just as it appears in the SELECT clause. The following example joins three tables to make a master list of the parts that are supplied by various suppliers. The rows of the result set are ordered alphabetically by the name of the supplier, and secondarily by part number.

```
SELECT s.name, q.partno, q.price, p.description
FROM suppliers s, quotations q, parts p
WHERE s.suppno = q.suppno
AND q.partno = p.partno
ORDER BY s.name, q.partno;
```

- You can also order your result set by an expression in the SELECT clause that is not a simple column name, either by repeating the expression in the ORDER BY clause or by giving the expression a name and using the name in the ORDER BY clause. The following two queries, which are equivalent, list parts in descending order by the total number of each part that is on hand or on order:

```
SELECT partno, qonorder+qonhand
FROM parts
ORDER BY qonorder+qonhand DESC;
```

```
SELECT partno, qonorder+qonhand AS totalq
FROM parts
ORDER BY totalq DESC;
```

- When a SELECT statement includes multiple query blocks, it is important to remember that the ORDER BY clause applies to the result set as a whole, not to any individual query block. You can always call for a result set to be ordered by one of its columns, simply by using the ordinal number of that column as a sort key. The following SELECT statement combines two query blocks, which list all the orders for part number P207 together with the quantity on hand for this part. The result set is delivered in descending order by its second column, which is unnamed.

```
      SELECT suppno, quantity
      FROM orders
      WHERE partno = 'P207'
   UNION ALL
      SELECT 'Stock', qonhand
      FROM parts
      WHERE partno = 'P207'
   ORDER BY 2 DESC;
```

- If you are careful, you can even order a result set by some expression that is not in the result set at all. You can do this only if the SELECT statement contains a single query block, and all the expressions in the ORDER BY clause are either in the SELECT clause or *could have been* in the SELECT clause. The following example lists all the part numbers in the QUOTATIONS table, in order by their average price, without actually including the average prices in the result set:

```
   SELECT partno
   FROM quotations
   GROUP BY partno
   ORDER BY avg(price);
```

In the example above, it is important to note that the sort key AVG(PRICE) *could have been* in the SELECT clause. It would have been an error to specify PRICE as a sort key, since PRICE would not have been valid in the SELECT clause (it would have conflicted with the GROUP BY clause since PRICE is not a group property).

The FETCH FIRST clause of a SELECT statement limits the size of the result set to N rows for some integer N. If an ORDER BY clause is specified, the result set consists of the first N rows in the specified order; otherwise, it consists of at most N rows, selected by the system.

2.4.11 VALUES Statement

If you have sharp eyes, you may have noticed that a literal table is a form of a query and that a query can stand alone as a SELECT statement. Therefore, it is possible that a SELECT statement might consist simply of a literal table. We will refer to this special case of a SELECT statement as a *VALUES statement*, since it begins with the word VALUES. If you execute a VALUES statement interactively, the system will evaluate all the expressions in your statement and display the literal table. For example, you might type the following statement:

```
   VALUES ('Carter', '1976', 'Democrat'),
          ('Reagan', '1980', 'Republican');
```

The example above is not very useful, since you had to type in all the values to be displayed. For a more useful example, suppose that you need to know the value of one of the special registers, such as CURRENT DATE or CURRENT FUNCTION PATH. It is awkward to write a SELECT statement to retrieve this value, because the special register is not contained in any table. You could choose a random table and type, for example, `SELECT CURRENT DATE FROM parts`, but this query would display the current date once for every part in the PARTS table, which is probably not what you want. The solution to the problem is to use a VALUES statement to display a "table" containing nothing but the special register that you need. For example, typing the following statement at the Command Center will cause the current date to be displayed:

```
VALUES (CURRENT DATE);
```

Another reason to use VALUES as a stand-alone SQL statement is in order to invoke a function. The built-in functions such as `substr` and `avg` are not very interesting to invoke, unless you need to use them in a query. But UDB provides a way (described in Chapter 6) for users to create new functions of their own, implemented by C programs. Such a user-defined function might interact with the outside world in some way such as sending a message or writing in a file. Suppose that someone has written a user-defined function called `placeOrder(partno, quantity)` that actually sends a message to a supplier ordering a given quantity of a given part. Since `placeOrder` is defined as an SQL function, it can be invoked from an SQL statement—perhaps in the body of a trigger that has discovered a low inventory level. But what kind of SQL statement should we use to invoke the function? The problem is similar to that of examining a special register, since the function (like the special register) does not reside in a table.

In some cases, a SELECT is the appropriate kind of statement to use for invoking a function. For example, if you wish to order 100 units of every part in the PARTS table that has less than 100 units on hand, you might write:

```
SELECT placeOrder(partno, 100)
FROM parts
WHERE qonhand < 100;
```

The statement above will result in the placing of some number of orders, between zero and the total number of rows in the PARTS table. But suppose you want to place exactly one order, for 500 units of part number P285. You need a way to call the `placeOrder` function exactly once, independently of the content of any table in the database. This is accomplished by the following VALUES statement, which you can execute interactively or embed in a program:

```
VALUES (placeOrder('P285', 500));
```

TIP: You must be very careful where you invoke a function that has side effects, such as `placeOrder` in the examples above, to make sure your function is executed a predictable number of times. In general, a function invoked in a VALUES statement will be executed exactly once, and a function invoked in the SELECT clause of a query block will be executed once for each row returned by the query block. But you should avoid calling a function with side effects in a query that involves SELECT DISTINCT, or a column function, or a join, or a set operator such as UNION, since these operations can make the number of function calls unpredictable. For the same reason, you should avoid calling a function with side effects in the WHERE or HAVING clause of any query.

2.4.12 SQLCODE and SQLSTATE

The execution of an SQL statement such as SELECT or VALUES results in two codes—SQLCODE and SQLSTATE—that indicate the success or failure of the statement and identify the type of error encountered, if any. SQLCODE is an integer code that has long been used by the DB2 product family, and SQLSTATE is a newer five-character code that is defined by the ANSI/ISO SQL Standard. In general, a zero SQLCODE denotes normal execution, a negative SQLCODE denotes an error, and a positive SQLCODE denotes a warning or condition of interest such as "no rows were found." SQLCODE and SQLSTATE are different ways of encoding the same information, but applications that use SQLSTATE will be more portable to other database systems, because SQLSTATE is defined by the SQL Standard.

If you are executing your SQL statements from an interactive interface such as the Command Center, it will display the SQLCODE and/or SQLSTATE after completion of each statement. If your SQL statements are embedded in an application program, the same return codes are returned to your program in a data structure called an SQLCA (described in Section 4.1.4).

2.5 DATA MODIFICATION

The SQL statements for modifying data are INSERT, UPDATE, and DELETE. Each of these statements makes extensive use of the building blocks already discussed, such as expressions, subqueries, and literal tables.

2.5.1 INSERT Statement

The purpose of an INSERT statement is to insert one or more rows into a table or view. The rows to be inserted can be specified as a literal table or can be derived from the database by means of a query. The syntax of an INSERT statement is as follows:

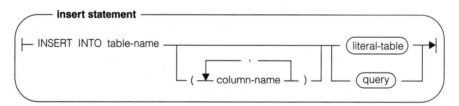

Users of SQL are familiar with the use of a VALUES clause to insert a single row into a table, as in the following example:

```
INSERT INTO quotations(suppno, partno, price, responsetime)
    VALUES ('S59', 'P227', 175, 8);
```

Since UDB allows an INSERT statement to contain a literal table, the VALUES clause in an INSERT statement is not limited to a single row, and it may contain expressions as well as constants. Furthermore, when a literal table is used in an INSERT statement, a value inside the literal table may consist simply of the word DEFAULT, indicating "the default value for the target column" (the default value of a column, if any, is determined when its table is created). Some of these features are illustrated by the following example, which inserts two rows into the ORDERS table, using a default value (the current date) for the ORDERDATE column:

```
INSERT INTO orders(suppno, partno, quantity, orderdate)
   VALUES ('S59', 'P227', 100, DEFAULT),
          ('S59', 'P231', 250, DEFAULT);
```

Columns for which no values are provided by an INSERT statement receive default values. For this reason, the INSERT statement in the following example is equivalent to the one in the previous example:

```
INSERT INTO orders(suppno, partno, quantity)
   VALUES ('S59', 'P227', 100),
          ('S59', 'P231', 250);
```

If an INSERT statement contains a query, that query is evaluated and the resulting rows are inserted into the target table. For example, if we create a table named INACTIVE with a column named SUPPNO, we might use the following statement to populate this table with all the suppliers who currently have no quotations on file:

```
INSERT INTO INACTIVE(suppno)
   SELECT suppno
   FROM suppliers
EXCEPT
   SELECT suppno
   FROM quotations;
```

If a query inside an INSERT statement contains a reference to the table into which data is being inserted, the INSERT statement is said to be *self-referencing*. The query in a self-referencing INSERT statement is completely evaluated before any rows are inserted.

The target of an INSERT statement may be either a table or a view. Inserting rows into a view has the effect of inserting rows into the table on which the view is based. Of course, the view must be updatable, and the rows being inserted must satisfy any constraints that are in effect for the table and/or the view (constraints are discussed in Section 7.1). If any error is encountered during execution of an INSERT statement (for example, some constraint is violated by the 100th row to be inserted), the statement is rolled back and no rows are inserted.

An INSERT statement may optionally list the columns of the target table for which values are provided. Omitting the column list is the same as specifying all the columns of the target table, in their natural order. Of course, if the target of the INSERT statement is a view, values can be inserted only into those columns that correspond directly to columns of the underlying table. For any column into which values can be inserted, omitting the column from the list is the same as specifying DEFAULT as the value to be inserted.

In a parallel database environment, an application program can take advantage of a feature called *buffered insert*, which improves efficiency by executing INSERT statements in "batches" rather than one at a time. If the system encounters an error while performing a buffered insert, the error is not necessarily reported to the application program in the return code for the INSERT statement that caused the error, but may instead be reported in the code for a later statement. Buffered insert is discussed further in Section 10.2.2.

2.5.2 UPDATE Statement

The purpose of an UPDATE statement is to modify the values of one or more rows in a table or view. The syntax of an UPDATE statement is as follows:[11]

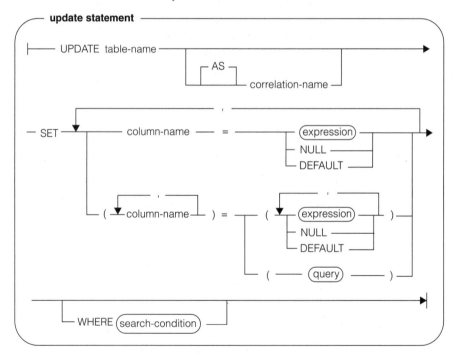

---

11. A variation of this syntax, called a *positioned UPDATE statement*, is described in Section 4.1.11.

An UPDATE statement applies its SET clause to each row of the named table for which the search condition in the WHERE clause is TRUE. If the UPDATE statement has no WHERE clause, the SET clause is applied to all the rows in the named table.

The SET clause contains one or more *assignments*. Each assignment is executed by computing the value(s) on the right-hand side of the equal sign and assigning them to the column(s) named on the left-hand side of the equal sign. The value to be assigned may be specified by an expression (possibly containing a subquery), by the keyword NULL, or by DEFAULT, which indicates that the column is to be assigned its default value. For example, the following UPDATE statement assigns new values to the PARTS row for part number P207:

```
UPDATE parts
SET description = NULL,
    qonhand = 100,
    qonorder = DEFAULT
WHERE partno = 'P207';
```

As each row is updated, all the expressions on the right-hand sides of the assignments are evaluated before any of the updates are applied. Thus, for example, the following statement could be used to interchange the values of qonorder and qonhand for a given part:

```
UPDATE parts
SET qonorder = qonhand,
    qonhand = qonorder
WHERE partno = 'P207';
```

The target of an UPDATE statement may be either a table or a view. Updating a view has the effect of updating the table on which the view is based. Of course, if the target is a view, it must be an updatable view, and the columns to be updated must correspond directly to columns of the underlying table. (Rules for defining updatable views are described in Section 2.6.5.)

It is possible that one of the updates specified by an UPDATE statement may violate some constraint, such as a check constraint or foreign key constraint (described in Section 7.1). If this or any other error is encountered during execution of an UPDATE statement, the statement is rolled back and no rows are updated.

If a subquery is used in an UPDATE statement, either in the WHERE clause or in the SET clause, that subquery is evaluated before any rows are updated. If such a subquery contains a reference to the table that is being updated, the UPDATE statement is said to be *self-referencing*. All subqueries in self-referencing UPDATE statements (even correlated subqueries!) see the table in its original state, before any updates are applied.

Whenever a subquery is used on the right-hand side of an assignment, that subquery must return at most one row. The value(s) of that row are assigned to the respective column(s) on the left-hand side of the assignment. If the subquery returns no rows, the columns on the left-hand side of the assignment are assigned null values. The use of a subquery on the right-hand side of an assignment is a powerful feature, particularly when the subquery is correlated to the table being updated, as illustrated in the following example. In this example, supplier number S53 has guaranteed to provide the lowest price and the shortest response time for all the parts that it supplies. The following UPDATE statement modifies the rows of the QUOTATIONS table to reflect this policy:

```
UPDATE quotations AS X
SET (price, responsetime) =
        (SELECT min(price), min(responsetime)
         FROM quotations
         WHERE partno = X.partno)
WHERE suppno = 'S53';
```

In a multinode parallel database system, one or more columns of a table may be designated as the *partitioning key* that controls how rows of the table are distributed among the nodes of the system. An UPDATE statement may not update a column that is part of a partitioning key. Partitioning keys are discussed further in Section 10.2.2.

2.5.3 DELETE Statement

The purpose of a DELETE statement is to delete one or more rows from a table or view. Deleting rows from a view has the effect of deleting rows from the table on which the view is based. The syntax of a DELETE statement is as follows:[12]

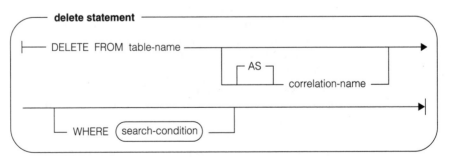

---

12. A variation of this syntax, called a *positioned DELETE statement*, is described in Section 4.1.11.

The action of a DELETE statement is simple: those rows of the named table or view for which the search condition is TRUE are deleted from the database. If the WHERE clause is omitted, all the rows of the named table or view are deleted.

If the search condition of a DELETE statement contains a subquery that references the table from which rows are being deleted, that subquery is evaluated before any rows are deleted. A DELETE statement containing such a subquery is said to be *self-referencing*.

It is possible that deletion of one of the rows specified by a DELETE statement may violate some constraint, such as a foreign key constraint (described in Section 7.1). If this or any other error is encountered during execution of a DELETE statement, the statement is rolled back and no rows are deleted.

The following example statement deletes supplier number S59 from the SUPPLIERS table:

```
DELETE FROM suppliers WHERE suppno = 'S59';
```

The use of a correlation name in a DELETE statement is a powerful feature that permits a subquery in the search condition to specify some specific property of the row that is being deleted. For example, the following statement deletes all suppliers who currently have no quotations on file:

```
DELETE FROM suppliers AS X
WHERE NOT EXISTS
    (SELECT partno
     FROM quotations
     WHERE suppno = X.suppno);
```

The use of a correlation name in UPDATE and DELETE statements is a product extension supported by UDB that is not a part of the ANSI/ISO SQL92 Standard (though it is under consideration for the future SQL3 Standard). The following statement is another example of the use of this feature. This statement deletes all the quotations whose price is more than twice the average quoted price for the same part. Note that this is a self-referencing DELETE statement, and that therefore the set of quotations to be deleted will effectively be computed before any quotations are actually deleted.

```
DELETE FROM quotations AS X
WHERE price >
    (SELECT 2 * avg(price)
     FROM quotations
     WHERE partno = X.partno);
```

2.6 DATA DEFINITION

The *data definition statements* of SQL are those statements that create and destroy database objects such as tables. Some data definition statements also alter the structure of an existing object, as in adding a column to a table. In this section, we will discuss data definition statements that operate on the following kinds of objects:

- *Tables*, which contain all the information stored in the database

- *Aliases*, which are alternative names for tables

- *Views*, which are "virtual" tables that are derived in some way from the real stored tables

- *Indexes*, which help the system to access data quickly, provide an ordering on the rows of a table, and enforce the uniqueness of the values in a table

- *Schemas*, which are collections of objects that may include tables, aliases, views, indexes, and other kinds of objects

This section also briefly discusses a subject called *normalization*, which provides some guidelines for good table design.

UDB automatically maintains a set of tables, called *catalog tables*, that contain descriptions of all the objects in the database. Data definition statements automatically cause updates to these tables. (The catalog tables are described in Appendix D.)

Data definition statements can be executed in several different ways. The easiest way is probably to use the graphical interface provided by the Control Center (described in Section 10.3). You can also execute data definition statements using an interactive SQL interface like the CLP or the Command Center (described in Section 3.1.1). You can even embed data definition statements in application programs, but this can lead to some confusing situations. As an example, consider a C program containing SQL statements to create a table and insert some data into the table. When processing this program, the precompiler will try to generate an access plan for the INSERT statement but will fail because the table does not yet exist. As a general rule, an object cannot be created and used in the same program unless you use one of the dynamic SQL techniques described in Chapter 8. To keep things simple, it is best to keep data definition statements separate from your application programs (possibly in a script file) and to execute them using an interactive interface.

2.6.1 Creating a Table

Since tables are the basic objects that are used to store information in UDB, the most fundamental data definition statement is the CREATE TABLE statement. The basic job of a CREATE TABLE statement is to specify the name of the table to be created and the names and datatypes of all its columns. In addition, the statement can optionally specify that certain columns of the table do not accept null values and that one or more columns constitute the *primary key* of the table. Primary key columns never accept null values, and the values of the primary key columns uniquely identify a row of the table.

In addition to the "basic" features described above, a CREATE TABLE statement can control the placement of the table in physical storage and can specify constraints on the data values to be stored in the table. Discussion of these CREATE TABLE features is deferred until Chapter 7. For now, I will give examples of the CREATE TABLE statements that might be used to create the tables in our sample database. Using these examples as templates and choosing datatypes from Tables 2-1 and 2-2, you can create simple tables of your own. If you want to peek ahead at the full syntax for CREATE TABLE, it can be found on page 402.

```
CREATE TABLE parts
    (partno Char(4) NOT NULL PRIMARY KEY,
     description Varchar(20),
     qonhand Integer,
     qonorder Integer);
CREATE TABLE quotations
    (suppno Char(3) NOT NULL,
     partno Char(4) NOT NULL,
     price Integer,
     responsetime Integer,
     PRIMARY KEY (suppno, partno) );
CREATE TABLE orders
    (suppno Char(3) NOT NULL,
     partno Char(4) NOT NULL,
     quantity Integer,
     orderdate Date);
CREATE TABLE suppliers
    (suppno Char(3) NOT NULL PRIMARY KEY,
     name Varchar(35),
     address Varchar(35) );
```

As you can see from the examples, a CREATE TABLE statement contains a parenthesized list of column names with a datatype specified for each column. If a column does not accept null values, the phrase NOT NULL is specified after its datatype. An optional PRIMARY KEY clause identifies the columns that constitute the primary key of the table. Every column that is identified as part of the primary key must also have a NOT NULL designation (though you might suppose that the system could figure this out for itself).

If the table name in a CREATE TABLE statement is unqualified, the new table is given a schema name equal to the current authid. A table can also be given an explicit schema name, as in the following example, which creates a table in the ACCOUNTS schema:

```
CREATE TABLE accounts.receivable
   (invoiceno Char(6) NOT NULL PRIMARY KEY,
    customername Varchar(20),
    address Varchar(50),
    amountdue Decimal(8,2) NOT NULL,
    datebilled Date NOT NULL,
    datedue Date NOT NULL);
```

If a CREATE TABLE statement references (explicitly or by default) a schema that does not yet exist, the schema is implicitly created.

When you create a table, a description of the table is stored in the system catalog table named TABLES, and descriptions of its columns are stored in the catalog table named COLUMNS.

2.6.2 Altering a Table

The ALTER TABLE statement can add a column to an existing table or increase the length of an existing column of type Varchar. When a column is added to a table, all existing rows in the table receive a default value for the new column. The ALTER TABLE statement can also be used to add or delete constraints on the values that can be stored in the table and to change certain properties of the table. As in the case of CREATE TABLE, some examples of the ALTER TABLE statement are given here, but a detailed discussion of this statement is deferred until Chapter 7, by which time you will have a better understanding of constraints. (If you want to peek ahead, the syntax for the ALTER TABLE statement is shown on page 409.)

Suppose that, after creation of the ACCOUNTS.RECEIVABLE table, our accounting department decides to add a column named STATUS to the table. This might be done by the following statement:

```
ALTER TABLE accounts.receivable
   ADD COLUMN status Varchar(18);
```

All existing rows in the ACCOUNTS.RECEIVABLE table at the time when the ALTER TABLE statement is executed receive null values for the new STATUS column, since no other default value was specified by the ALTER TABLE statement.

Later, if the accounting department finds that the Varchar(18) datatype is not long enough to contain the necessary information, the STATUS column can be enlarged by the following statement:

```
ALTER TABLE accounts.receivable
    ALTER COLUMN status SET DATA TYPE Varchar(32);
```

2.6.3 Renaming a Table

You can change the name of an existing table by using the following syntax:

Examples:

```
RENAME TABLE product.discounts TO bargains;
RENAME TABLE expenses TO budget;
```

A renamed table keeps its original schema name. Thus the second example above, if executed by user WILSON, changes the name of table WILSON.EXPENSES to WILSON.BUDGET.

When a table is renamed, any indexes defined on the table are retained, and any users who have privileges on the table retain these privileges. However, application programs (packages) that use the table become invalid and will need to be updated to use the new name.

A table cannot be renamed if it has any of the following properties:

1. It is referenced in a view definition (see Section 2.6.5).

2. It has a check constraint (see Section 7.1.4).

3. It is either a parent table or a child table in a referential integrity relationship (see Section 7.1.6).

4. It has a trigger attached to it or is referenced by a trigger (see Section 7.3).

2.6.4 Creating an Alias

Suppose that you need to develop a new application program that operates on the PARTS table. During the development process, you might need to run the program against a test table without interfering with the production data in your real parts inventory. Then, when the program is debugged and ready to go into production, you would like to easily switch the program to operate on the real PARTS table. Even after a program is in production, you may sometimes need to change the table on which the program operates, without changing the logic of the program.

Of course, you can always edit your source program and change all its table names. But this process is time consuming and prone to error. UDB provides a better way, called *aliases*, to control the table on which a program operates. An alias is simply a table name that substitutes for another table name, called the *target* of the alias. Whenever an alias is used in an SQL statement, it is equivalent to using the target name. Since an alias can be easily changed from one target to another, programs that use aliases are easily redirected from one table to another.

As an example, suppose that your database contains two tables named TEST.PARTS and PRODUCT.PARTS. You can create an alias whose target is one of these tables, as follows:

```
CREATE ALIAS parts FOR test.parts;
```

You might write an application program that contains references to the name PARTS. When you bind your program to the database, the name PARTS will be interpreted as an alias and resolved to the target table TEST.PARTS. When you are ready to put your program into production, you can redefine the target of the alias, using the following statements:

```
DROP ALIAS parts;
CREATE ALIAS parts FOR product.parts;
```

No change is necessary in the source code of your program, but before the program can begin to operate on the production table, it must be rebound. You can rebind your program explicitly, using the REBIND command, or you can allow the rebind to occur implicitly. The system knows that your program uses an alias, and when the target of that alias changes, the system will automatically rebind your program to the new target the next time it is used.

TABSCHEMA	TABNAME	TYPE	BASE_TABSCHEMA	BASE_TABNAME
JONES	T1	A	JONES	T2
S3	T3	A	JONES	T4
JONES	T5	A	S6	T6
S7	T7	A	S8	T8

Figure 2-2: Examples of Aliases in the TABLES Catalog Table

The syntax of a CREATE ALIAS statement is as follows:

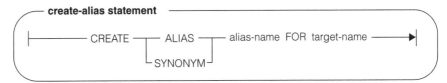

The target of an alias may be a real table, a view, or another alias. In fact, an alias can be defined even if its target does not exist at all! An alias simply declares the equivalence of the alias-name and the target-name. When an alias is referenced in an SQL statement, the target must exist and must be appropriate in the context where it is used. If the target of an alias is another alias, it is resolved through as many levels as necessary to reach a real table or view.

In a CREATE ALIAS statement, both the alias-name and the target-name may be either qualified or unqualified. Any unqualified names are given an implicit schema name equal to the current authid. Thus all the following are valid statements:

```
CREATE ALIAS t1 FOR t2;
CREATE ALIAS s3.t3 FOR t4;
CREATE ALIAS t5 FOR s6.t6;
CREATE ALIAS s7.t7 FOR s8.t8;
```

All the aliases that are currently defined are recorded in the catalog table named TABLES. Each row of TABLES that represents an alias has the code "A" in the TYPE column; it records the alias-name in columns TABSCHEMA and TABNAME, and the target-name in columns BASE_TABSCHEMA and BASE_TABNAME. Thus, if the four aliases above were defined by user Jones, they would be represented by four rows in TABLES, as shown in Figure 2-2.

2.6.5 Creating a View

One of the nice things about a relational database is that, even when they are sharing data, all users do not need to look at the data in the same way. Some users can operate directly on the real tables that are stored in the database, while other users operate on *views*, which are virtual tables derived in some way from the real tables. For example, several users may be sharing a table of data about employees. One user might see only those employees who report to her; another user might see all the employees but none of their salaries; and a third user might see only the average salary of each department. Views such as these are an aid to application development and provide a valuable degree of control over access to data.

A query returns a table that is derived in some way from data in the database, and that is exactly what a view is. SQL was perhaps the first language to exploit this fact and to make creating a view as easy as writing a query. To create a view in SQL, one needs only to write the query that defines the view and to specify the names of the columns of the view (if they cannot be derived from the query). The syntax of the CREATE VIEW statement in UDB is shown below. (See page 68 for the syntax of a query.)

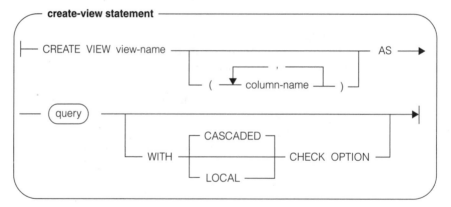

The view name in a CREATE VIEW statement may be either qualified or unqualified; if unqualified, it is given a default schema name equal to the current authid (the userid who bound the program, for static SQL, or the userid who is currently running, for dynamic SQL).

The column names of the view are listed after the view name. The list of column names can be omitted if all the column names can be derived from the query that defines the view (for example, if each column is either given a name in the SELECT clause of the query or is derived directly from a column of an underlying table). Of course, a query used in a CREATE VIEW statement cannot contain any references to host program variables, since the view definition must stand by itself, independent of any host program.

The following are some examples of views defined on our example database:

- The view FAST_QUOTES contains all the quotations whose response time is less than ten days.

  ```
  CREATE VIEW fast_quotes AS
      SELECT suppno, partno, price, responsetime
      FROM quotations
      WHERE responsetime < 10;
  ```

- The view LOW_PRICES lists the minimum price quoted for each part.

  ```
  CREATE VIEW low_prices(partno, minprice) AS
      SELECT partno, min(price)
      FROM quotations
      GROUP BY partno;
  ```

- The view OLD_ORDERS joins three tables to list all the orders that are more than two months old, including the name of the supplier and the description of the part. The column names of the view are derived from the column names of the underlying tables.

  ```
  CREATE VIEW old_orders AS
      SELECT o.partno, o.quantity, o.orderdate,
             s.name, p.description
      FROM orders AS o, suppliers AS s, parts AS p
      WHERE s.suppno = o.suppno
      AND p.partno = o.partno
      AND o.orderdate + 2 MONTHS < CURRENT DATE;
  ```

- It is often useful to define a view based on the special register USER. For example, the following view includes information from the system catalog about the tables and views that have been created by the user of the view:

  ```
  CREATE VIEW mytables AS
      SELECT tabschema, tabname
      FROM syscat.tables
      WHERE definer = USER;
  ```

- The query that defines a view need not access the database at all. The following view is based on a literal table:

  ```
  CREATE VIEW collarsizes(numeric, descriptive)    AS
      VALUES (14, 'Small'), (15, 'Medium'), (16, 'Large');
  ```

A view can be defined by a query that operates on real tables, on other views, or on some mixture of tables and views. When an SQL statement references a view, the definition of that view is "merged" into the SQL statement to form a new effective statement that is processed against the database. Since all operations on views are ultimately mapped into operations on real tables, the columns of the view inherit their characteristics (such as datatype and NOT NULL) from the columns of the underlying tables. Like real tables, the virtual tables defined by views have no intrinsic ordering of their rows, but a SELECT statement that retrieves rows from a view can contain an ORDER BY clause that specifies a desired ordering.

Read-Only Views

Because of their structure, some views are *read-only* while others are *updatable*. Read-only views can only be queried, but updatable views can also be used in INSERT, UPDATE, and DELETE statements. In general, a view is updatable if each row in the view can be uniquely mapped onto one row of a real table. This makes it possible for the system to map insertions, deletions, and updates on the view into the same operations on the underlying table. If any of the following query features is used in a view definition at the outermost level (that is, not in a subquery), the view is read-only:

- VALUES, DISTINCT, GROUP BY, HAVING, or any column function
- A join
- Any reference to a read-only view
- A call to a table function (described in Section 5.3)
- UNION, INTERSECT, or EXCEPT (except that views defined using UNION ALL can be used in UPDATE and DELETE statements if their corresponding columns have exactly the same datatypes, including lengths and default values)

Subject to the limitations above, a view name can be used in place of a table name in any SELECT, INSERT, DELETE, UPDATE, DECLARE CURSOR, or CREATE VIEW statement. In the syntax diagrams for these statements, *table-name* should be interpreted as "the name of a table or view."

Even when a view is updatable, some of its columns may not be updatable because they do not map directly onto columns of the underlying table. For example, the following statement defines an updatable view named ALLPARTS in which the PARTNO and DESCRIPTION columns are updatable but the TOTALQ column is not updatable:

```
CREATE VIEW allparts (partno, description, totalq) AS
    SELECT partno, description, qonhand + qonorder
    FROM parts;
```

When you insert, delete, or update rows of a view, you should remember that you are really operating on rows of the underlying table. For example, when you delete a row from a view, all the information in the underlying table row is deleted, including information in columns that are not visible in the view. Similarly, when you insert a row into a view, all the columns of the underlying table that are not visible in the view receive default values (if some of these columns do not have default values, you will not be able to insert a row into the view).

The definition of each view is stored in the catalog table named VIEWS. In addition, since views can be used in most of the places that tables can be used, each view is also described in the TABLES catalog table, and the columns of each view are described in the COLUMNS catalog table.

CHECK Option

Suppose that you execute the following statement, using the FAST_QUOTES view described earlier:

```
INSERT INTO fast_quotes(suppno, partno, price, responsetime)
    VALUES ('S51', 'P221', 3000, 20);
```

This is an interesting statement because it inserts a row representing a quotation with a response time of 20 days into a view whose definition includes only quotations with response times of less than 10 days. What happens to the row? The FAST_QUOTES view does not include any query features that would make it read-only, so the system is quite able to insert the specified row into the underlying QUOTATIONS table. But if the INSERT were immediately followed by a query against the FAST_QUOTES view, the new row would not be seen. This raises a question of policy: should a view support insertions and updates whose results are not visible through the view?

UDB allows the creator of each view to answer this policy question by means of a feature called the *check option*. If a view is created with the check option, each row that is inserted or updated using the view must satisfy the view definition. If any row inserted or updated by an SQL statement fails to satisfy the view definition, all the changes made by the SQL statement are rolled back and the statement has no effect. A view defined with the check option is called a *symmetric view* because everything that can be inserted into it can also be retrieved from it.

As you can see from the syntax diagram on page 86, the check option has two forms: *cascaded* and *local*. The difference between these two forms is meaningful only when a view is defined on top of another view. If a view called VIEW1 is defined by a query on another view called VIEW2, we will refer to VIEW2 as an *underlying view*. When VIEW1 is defined with a *local* check option, operations on VIEW1 must satisfy the definitions of VIEW1 and of all underlying views that also have a check option; however, they need not satisfy the definitions of underlying views that do not have a check option. On the other hand, when VIEW1 is defined with a *cascaded* check option, all operations on VIEW1 must satisfy the definitions of VIEW1 and of all underlying views, whether they have a check option or not. If a CREATE VIEW statement simply specifies WITH CHECK OPTION, the default is a cascaded check option. If no check option is specified at CREATE VIEW time, no checking is performed.

Inoperative Views

A view is defined by a query that, in general, contains references to one or more tables, views, or aliases. We will refer to the tables, views, and aliases that are used in the definition of a view V as the *underlying objects* of V. When a view is defined, the system checks the privileges of the view definer on the underlying objects and grants to the definer the appropriate privileges on the view. For example, if the view definer is authorized to perform SELECT and INSERT statements on the table that underlies a view, and if the view is not read-only because of its definition, then the definer will receive SELECT and INSERT privileges on the view as well.

It is interesting to consider what happens to a view if one of its underlying objects disappears or if the definer of the view loses a privilege on an underlying object. Since the view can no longer be used, it might seem reasonable for its definition to be dropped automatically. Sometimes, however, this policy seems more heavy-handed than necessary. For example, suppose that the definition of an alias is changed from one table to another. It seems unfortunate, and even dangerous, for this event to cause the system to completely forget about the definitions of any views that reference the alias. Similarly, if some user U temporarily loses a privilege on some table T and then regains it, it seems unfortunate for the system to forget the definitions of all views defined by user U that reference table T.

UDB has adopted a somewhat gentler policy regarding views that depend on some object or privilege that has gone away. In UDB, such a view has a special status, called *inoperative*. The definition of an inoperative view is retained in the VIEWS catalog table, with its inoperative status indicated by the column VALID = 'X'. Any SQL statement that operates on an inoperative view (except to drop it or recreate it) will result in an error message. However, a user can restore an inoperative view to normal status by retrieving its definition from the VIEWS catalog table and using this definition in a new CREATE VIEW statement. The following SQL statement can be used to retrieve from VIEWS the definitions of all inoperative views that were defined by the current user:

```
SELECT viewschema, viewname, seqno, text
FROM syscat.views
WHERE valid = 'X'
AND definer = USER
ORDER BY viewschema, viewname, seqno;
```

When a CREATE VIEW statement is executed that creates a view with the same schema name and view name as an existing inoperative view, the new view replaces the inoperative view. This is an exception to the general rule that a view cannot be defined if its name duplicates the name of a view that already exists. Since all privileges held on a view are revoked when a view becomes inoperative, the definer of the view must grant these privileges again after recreating the inoperative view. The definition of an inoperative view can be removed from the VIEWS catalog table in the usual way, by a DROP VIEW statement.

2.6.6 Creating an Index

An *index* is an access aid that can be created on a table, using one or more columns of the table as the *key columns* of the index. An index can serve the following purposes:

1. It provides a fast way to find rows of the table, based on their values in the key columns. Indexes can greatly improve the performance of queries that search for a particular column value or range of values. In some cases, all the information needed by a query may be found in the index, making it unnecessary to access the actual table.

2. An index can optionally enforce the uniqueness of its key columns, meaning that no two rows of the table are allowed to have the same values for the key columns.

3. An index always provides a logical ordering on the rows of the table, based again on the key column values. The ordering can be ascending or descending on each column. The ordering property of an index is useful in processing queries with ORDER BY and GROUP BY clauses, and in some kinds of join algorithms. Of course, you can execute a query that includes an ORDER BY or GROUP BY that is not supported by an index—the system will simply sort the data as needed to process your query.

4. An index can optionally provide a *clustering* property for a table, causing the rows of the table to be arranged in physical storage according to the ordering of their index keys. This property is useful to the optimizer in choosing an access plan. Note that all indexes provide a logical ordering, but only a clustering index provides a physical ordering for the rows of a table.

You can create as many indexes on a table as you like, using various combinations of columns as keys. However, each index carries a certain cost. Part of the cost is paid in space, since each index replicates its key values and occupies some space on disk. Another part of the cost is paid in reduced performance for insert, delete, and update operations, since each modification to a table must be reflected in all the indexes that are defined on the table. Finding the optimum set of indexes to maintain in your database is an art that you will learn by experience. Fortunately, the data independence of the relational model allows you to add and drop indexes as usage patterns change, without recoding your applications. The optimizer will find a way to process your queries, exploiting the indexes that exist at the time each query is executed.

Indexes are created by the CREATE INDEX statement, which has the following syntax:

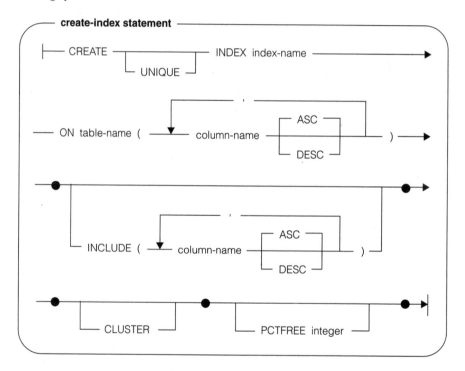

Examples:

```
CREATE INDEX i1 ON suppliers(name);
CREATE UNIQUE INDEX i2 ON quotations(partno, suppno);
CREATE INDEX i3 ON quotations(partno ASC, price DESC);
```

The keywords ASC and DESC denote ascending and descending order, respectively.

The recommended way to guarantee uniqueness of the values in a column or set of columns is to declare a primary key or unique constraint on the column(s), as described in Section 7.1. When you declare a primary key or unique constraint, the system automatically creates a unique index on the participating columns. You can tell which indexes the system is using to enforce constraints by looking at the SYSTEM_REQUIRED column of the INDEXES catalog table.

Creating your own unique index on a set of columns is similar, but not identical, to declaring a unique constraint on the same columns. Columns that have a unique constraint must be declared NOT NULL—that is, they are not allowed to contain any null values. But a unique index does not prevent its columns from containing null values. Instead, the unique index treats null like any other value. Thus, for example, if you create a unique index on a column named SERIALNO, that column will be allowed to contain no more than one null value. If you attempt to create a unique index on a set of columns that already contains nonunique values, the index creation will fail.

A CREATE INDEX statement may have an INCLUDE clause only if it also specifies the UNIQUE property. The INCLUDE clause names some additional columns whose values are stored in the index along with the key columns. Uniqueness is enforced only on the key columns, not on the additional columns in the INCLUDE clause. The extra columns increase the storage requirements of the index, but they may enable some queries to run faster by finding all the information they require in the index, making it unnecessary to access the actual table.

The CLUSTER clause declares that the index is a clustering index, which means that rows that have equal or nearly equal values of the index key will be stored near each other in physical storage. A clustering index provides a way for the system to scan over all the rows of a table while fetching a minimum number of physical pages. If an index has been identified as a clustering index, UDB attempts to preserve its clustering property when new rows are inserted into the table.

The PCTFREE clause directs the system to preserve a specified percentage of free space on each page of the index when the index is first created, to allow for future insertions and updates. The default amount of free space is 10%. This clause is a performance optimization only, since the index will continue to function, with slightly degraded performance, when its free space is exhausted.

UDB places the following limitations on indexes:

- An index may not have more than 16 key columns.

- The sum of the lengths of the key columns (including a small allowance for system overhead) may not exceed 255 bytes.

- The datatype of a key column must not be a large-object type or distinct type based on a large-object type (these types are discussed in Chapter 6).

- A column cannot appear more than once in the same index key.

- You are not allowed to create two indexes with exactly the same key (including the ordering of the columns).

- A table can have at most one clustering index.

- In a multinode parallel database system, if a table is distributed among the nodes using a partitioning key, every unique index on the table must include the partitioning key (described in Section 10.2.2).

TIP: After creating an index, you should gather the statistical information that will enable the optimizer to make best use of the index. The easiest way to do this is by selecting the indexed table in the Control Center display and invoking the *Run Statistics* action, as described in Section 10.3.7. Of course, you should not gather statistical information on a table until the table is populated with data.

2.6.7 Creating a Schema

As noted in Section 2.2, a schema can be created explicitly by a CREATE SCHEMA statement, or implicitly by creating an object whose schema name does not match any existing schema. The syntax for a CREATE SCHEMA statement is as follows:[13]

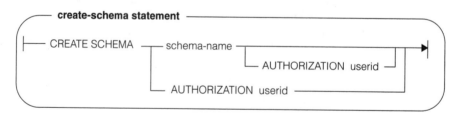

Examples:

```
CREATE SCHEMA geometry;
CREATE SCHEMA planning AUTHORIZATION citymgr;
```

---

13. In addition to the syntax shown here, UDB accepts an extended CREATE SCHEMA syntax that allows tables and other objects to be created at the same time as the schema. Since all the capabilities of this syntax are covered by other statements, it is not discussed in this book. Details of the extended syntax can be found in the *SQL Reference*.

A schema name is a single-part name of eight characters or less. Schema names beginning with "SYS" are reserved for system use. If no schema name is specified, the userid in the AUTHORIZATION clause serves as the schema name.

Since a schema can be created implicitly simply by creating an object with a given schema name, you may be wondering why anyone would use an explicit CREATE SCHEMA statement. The reason has to do with controlling access to the schema. An explicitly created schema has an *owner*, which is the userid specified in the AUTHORIZATION clause (if there is no AUTHORIZATION clause, the owner is the authid under which the CREATE SCHEMA statement was executed). The owner of a schema is authorized to create, alter, and drop objects in the schema; to drop the schema; and to grant these privileges to other users. So if you want to have complete control over your schema and all the objects in it, you should create the schema explicitly.

An implicitly created schema, on the other hand, is considered to be owned by the imaginary user SYSIBM. Any user can create objects in an implicitly created schema, and the objects in the schema are controlled by the users who created them. An implicitly created schema can be dropped only by a database administrator.

2.6.8 Dropping an Object

Tables, views, and other kinds of objects can be removed from the database by means of a DROP statement. The diagram on the following page shows the syntax for dropping various kinds of objects, both those we have discussed in this chapter and others, such as functions and triggers, which we discuss in later chapters.

Examples:

```
DROP TABLE accounts.receivable;
DROP VIEW overdue;
DROP PACKAGE payroll;
DROP SCHEMA accounts RESTRICT;
```

As usual, if an object name in a DROP statement does not have an explicit schema name, it is given an implicit schema name equal to the current authid. Of course, built-in objects such as the system catalog tables cannot be dropped.

Before you can drop a schema, all the objects in the schema must be dropped (the keyword RESTRICT in the DROP SCHEMA statement is supposed to remind you of this rule).

When you drop an object such as a table, view, or index, you may affect other objects that depend on the object you have dropped. For example, if you drop a table that is used in a view definition, that view definition will no longer be valid, and if you drop an index that is being used by a package, that

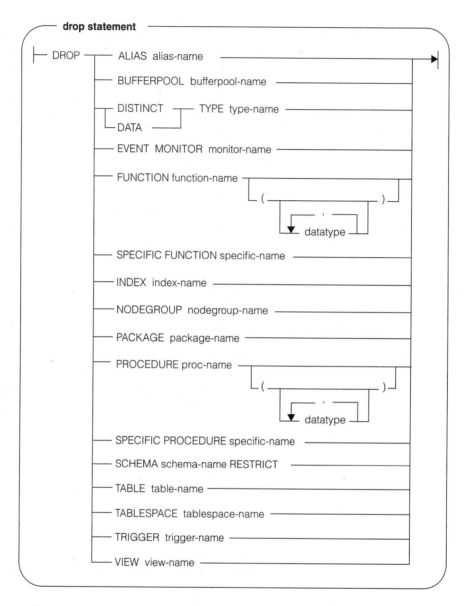

package must be rebound before it can be executed. In some cases, the system will automatically repair the dependent object (for example, a package that depends on a dropped index will automatically be rebound to use some other access plan). In other cases, dropping an object causes dependent objects to be dropped also (for example, dropping a table automatically drops all indexes defined on that table). In still other cases, you are not allowed to drop an object if other objects are depending on it. Since dependency is a complex subject that involves some types of objects not yet discussed in this book, its discussion is deferred until Chapter 7.

2.6.9 Commenting on an Object

Many of the system catalog tables that describe various objects in a UDB database contain a column named REMARKS in which you can enter an explanatory comment of up to 254 characters. Table 2-4 summarizes the types of objects that you can comment on and the names of the catalog tables in which the comments are stored. Some of these types of objects, such as constraints, datatypes, tablespaces, and triggers, are discussed in later chapters. The catalog tables—which are really views of underlying tables—are found in the SYSCAT schema. (For details about catalog tables, see Appendix D.)

Comments on various types of objects can be entered into the catalog tables by means of the COMMENT statement, shown in the syntax diagram on the following page. In each case, the text of the comment must be a string constant of no more than 254 characters. As you can see from the diagram, COMMENT ON TABLE is used to enter a comment for either a table or a view, and there is a special form of the COMMENT statement that can be used to comment on several columns of a table or view at once.

TABLE 2-4: Catalog Tables Containing Comments on Various Types of Objects

Type of Object	Catalog Table Containing Comments
Alias	TABLES
Column of a table or view	COLUMNS
Constraint	TABCONST
Datatypes	DATATYPES
Functions	FUNCTIONS
Index	INDEXES
Nodegroup	NODEGROUPS
Package	PACKAGES
Procedure	PROCEDURES
Schema	SCHEMATA
Table or view	TABLES
Tablespace	TABLESPACES
Trigger	TRIGGERS

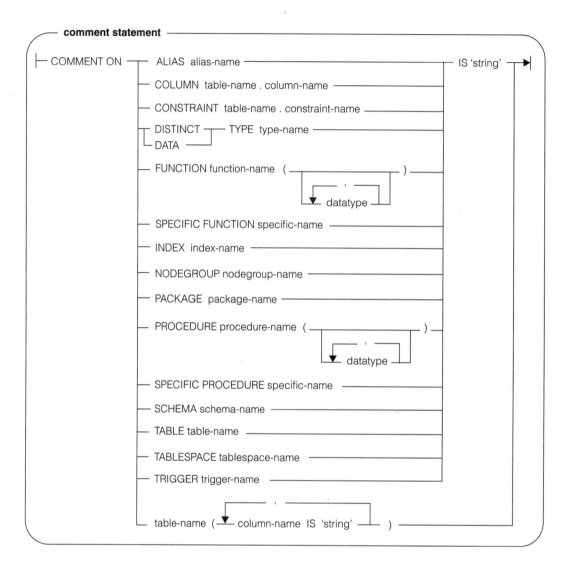

comment statement

COMMENT ON
- ALIAS alias-name
- COLUMN table-name . column-name
- CONSTRAINT table-name . constraint-name
- DISTINCT / DATA — TYPE type-name
- FUNCTION function-name (datatype ,)
- SPECIFIC FUNCTION specific-name
- INDEX index-name
- NODEGROUP nodegroup-name
- PACKAGE package-name
- PROCEDURE procedure-name (datatype ,)
- SPECIFIC PROCEDURE specific-name
- SCHEMA schema-name
- TABLE table-name
- TABLESPACE tablespace-name
- TRIGGER trigger-name

IS 'string'

- table-name (column-name IS 'string' ,)

Examples:

```
COMMENT ON PACKAGE finance.payroll
   IS 'Salary schedule effective 1-1-98';
COMMENT ON COLUMN quotations.responsetime
   IS 'Response time in days';
COMMENT ON quotations
   ( price IS 'Price in cents, 100 = one dollar',
     responsetime IS 'Response time in days' );
```

2.6.10 Normalization

Books have been written about how to arrive at a well-designed set of tables to represent a given collection of data. In fact, books have been written about just one aspect of this problem, which is called *normalization*. Normalization is the process of designing tables in such a way that each "fact" is represented exactly once. It is important to avoid multiple representations of the same fact, not only to save storage, but to avoid possible inconsistencies in the database. In this section, we present a brief introduction to the concept of normalization.

Any attempt to avoid redundant representation of facts depends crucially on what we consider to be a fact. In order to discuss this subject, we will examine a fragment of our sample database. Consider the following three columns of the PARTS table:

PARTS

PARTNO	DESCRIPTION	QONHAND
P207	Gear	75
P208	Gear	50
P281	Wheel	100
P285	Wheel	75

It is part of the semantics of this table, understood by those who use it, that part numbers uniquely identify parts. In other words, for a given part number, there can be only one description, and only one quantity on hand, at a given time. We will say that a part number *determines* the description and the quantity on hand. In our sample table, PARTNO is the only column that determines another column. For example, the DESCRIPTION column does not determine PARTNO because a description of "Gear" is associated with more than one part number.

When a column or set of columns determines another column or set of columns, we say that a *functional dependency* exists, and we describe the functional dependency using an arrow notation, as shown below:

PARTNO → { DESCRIPTION, QONHAND }

The columns on the left side of the arrow in a functional dependency are collectively called the *determinant*, and the columns on the right side of the arrow are called the *dependent*. It is important to understand that a functional dependency is a statement about the semantics of the data and that it holds for all time. In other words, the functional dependency described above doesn't just indicate that "each part number has only one description right now." Instead, it promises that "no part number will ever have more than a single description." For this reason, it is not possible to deduce functional dependencies by looking at the content of a table—the dependencies must be known *a priori*, as part of the raw material of the database design.

You are familiar with the term *primary key*, which denotes a column or set of columns that does not permit duplicate values. Since a primary key can have no duplicates, any primary key value uniquely identifies a row of the table; in other words, the primary key column(s) *determine* all the columns of the table. Actually, a table may have more than one set of columns that have the property of determining all the columns of the table. Each set of columns that has this property (and contains no column that is not essential to having this property) is called a *candidate key*, regardless of whether it is declared as a primary key. In the PARTS table in our example database, PARTNO is the only candidate key.

To continue our discussion of keys and normalization, consider the following columns of the QUOTATIONS table:

QUOTATIONS

SUPPNO	PARTNO	PRICE
S53	P207	2995
S53	P208	3250
S54	P208	4000
S54	P281	1900

In this table, given a supplier number and a part number, we can find the price (if any) offered by that supplier for that part. This means that the PRICE column is functionally dependent on the combination of the SUPPNO and PARTNO columns. We might represent this functional dependency as shown below. (Actually, since the determinant always trivially determines itself, we could include the SUPPNO and PARTNO columns on the right side of the arrow as well.)

{ SUPPNO, PARTNO } → PRICE

The QUOTATIONS table has only one candidate key—that is, only one minimal set of columns that determines all the columns of the table. This candidate key is SUPPNO and PARTNO, which is also the determinant in the functional dependency shown above.

The PARTS and QUOTATIONS tables have an important property in common: the only functional dependency that exists in each table is the dependency of all the columns of the table on the candidate key. To understand the importance of this property, let's look at a table that doesn't have the property. Consider a database design in which the contents of the PARTS and QUOTATIONS tables are combined into a single table called INVQUOTES, as shown below:

INVQUOTES

PARTNO	DESCRIPTION	QONHAND	SUPPNO	PRICE
P207	Gear	75	S53	2995
P208	Gear	50	S53	3250
P208	Gear	50	S54	4000
P281	Wheel	100	S54	1900
P285	Wheel	75	?	?

The functional dependencies in the INVQUOTES table are shown below (again, we have omitted repeating the left side of each dependency on the right side).

PARTNO → { DESCRIPTION, QONHAND }

{ PARTNO, SUPPNO } → { DESCRIPTION, QONHAND, PRICE }

A close look at the INVQUOTES table reveals that it has some obnoxious properties. For example, the fact that part number P208 is a Gear is represented twice. Indeed, this fact will be represented again (redundantly) each time a new price quote for that part is added to the table. This redundant representation of facts is both wasteful of storage and awkward when the table is updated. For example, if the description of part number P208 were to change from a Gear to a Cogwheel, it would be necessary to find and update *all* the places where this fact is represented.

The INVQUOTES table has other shortcomings as well. Since part number P285 has no price quotes at present, we have been forced to use nulls in the SUPPNO and PRICE columns for this part. This means that we can't find the number of price quotes available for a given part by simply counting the number of rows with the given part number. Worse, it means that when the first quote arrives for part number P285, we need to insert this fact into the table by updating an existing row rather than by inserting a new row. It is awkward and asymmetrical to be forced to handle the first quote for a given part differently from other quotes.

If supplier number S53 were to withdraw its quote to supply part number P207, we would be confronted with another problem. Ordinarily a quote is deleted from the table by deleting the row that represents it, but since supplier number S53 is the only supplier for part number P207, if we delete that row, we will lose the information that part number P207 is a Gear and that we have 75 of them on hand. Thus, in order to prevent loss of information, we need to treat the deletion of the last quote for a given part as another special case in which we insert null values into the SUPPNO and PRICE columns.

By now, we should be convinced that the INVQUOTES table is an example of bad table design. Our common sense tells us that the problem is caused by the redundant representation of facts. The theory of normalization is an attempt to codify our common sense into a set of rules for good table design. A number of *normal forms* have been defined as guidelines for good table design. We will discuss only one of these, named *Boyce–Codd Normal Form* (BCNF) because it was jointly defined by Raymond Boyce, coinventor of SQL, and E. F. Codd, inventor of the relational data model. BCNF can be defined, somewhat informally, as follows:

A table is in Boyce–Codd Normal Form if and only if every determinant in the table is a candidate key.

It is easy to see that the INVQUOTES table is not in BCNF because it contains a functional dependency in which the determinant is not a candidate key for the table. The offending functional dependency is as follows:

PARTNO → { DESCRIPTION, QONHAND }

This functional dependency is at the heart of what is wrong with the INVQUOTES table: it is the "fact" that is represented redundantly in multiple rows of the table. The solution to the anomalies associated with the INVQUOTES table is to break out the functional dependency whose determinant is PARTNO into a table of its own. This leads us back to the original design in which PARTS and QUOTATIONS are two separate tables, each of which is in BCNF.

In a nutshell, the process of reducing a table to BCNF involves listing the functional dependencies among the columns of each table and, if any dependencies are found in which the determinant is not a candidate key, splitting that dependency out into a table of its own. A description of some other normal forms, and a discussion of normalization in greater depth, can be found in any standard textbook on database management, such as one of the following:

- *An Introduction to Database Systems*, 6th ed. by C. J. Date (Addison-Wesley, 1995)
- *Database System Concepts*, 3rd ed. by Abraham Silberschatz, Henry F. Korth, and S. Sudarshan (McGraw-Hill, 1997)
- *A First Course in Database Systems* by Jeffrey D. Ullman and Jennifer Widom (Prentice Hall, 1997)
- *Database: Principles, Programming, Performance* by Patrick O'Neil (Morgan Kaufmann, 1994)
- *Fundamentals of Database Systems*, 2nd ed. by Ramez Elmasri and Shamkant B. Navathe (Addison-Wesley, 1994)

2.7 PROTECTING DATA CONSISTENCY

Protecting stored data is an essential function of a database system. UDB protects data in three quite different ways:

1. Protection for *data security* is provided by the authorization subsystem, which is discussed in Section 2.8. The authorization subsystem protects data against being accessed or modified by unauthorized users.

2. Protection for *data integrity* is provided by constraints and triggers, which are discussed in Chapter 7. These features protect the database against insertions, deletions, or updates that would result in invalid data values.

3. Protection for *data consistency* is provided by the concept of *transactions*, which are discussed in this section. Transactions prevent lost updates, inconsistent data values, and conflicts among multiple concurrent users.

2.7.1 Transactions

Suppose that you drive up to an automatic teller machine, insert your bank card, and instruct the machine to transfer $100 from your savings account to your checking account. Following your instructions, the machine makes two updates to the bank database: first, it subtracts $100 from your savings balance; then, it adds $100 to your checking balance. You drive to a ticket agency and write a $100 check for some concert tickets, confident that the money you transferred will cover your check.

Although you usually don't think about it, your bank's database system is protecting you against some nasty surprises. Suppose, for example, that just after the $100 was subtracted from your savings account, the power failed and your checking account was never credited. I'm sure you would prefer that the bank treat your money transfer as "all or nothing" and guarantee that if any part of the database update is done, then all parts are done. This desirable property of a database interaction is called *atomicity*.

You would also be unhappy if you discovered that, after the teller machine accepted your money transfer and printed a record of it, a power failure at the bank caused all the updates to disappear and the $100 to revert to your savings account, ultimately causing your check to bounce. You have a right to expect that, once you have received confirmation of an update, the update will not disappear. This desirable property of a database interaction is called *durability*.

Most database systems, including **UDB**, provide guarantees of atomicity and durability by using a concept called a *transaction*. A transaction is simply a set of interactions between an application and the database that the database views as a single unit of work (in fact, the **UDB** documentation uses the term *unit of work* rather than the more common term *transaction*). A transaction is implicitly begun when any data in the database is read or written. All subsequent reads and writes by the same application are considered to be part of the same transaction, until the application executes either a COMMIT statement or a ROLLBACK statement, which ends the transaction. A COMMIT statement causes all the database changes made by the transaction to become permanent, with guarantees of atomicity and durability. A ROLLBACK causes all the database changes made by the transaction to be undone and the database to be restored to its state before the transaction began. As long as a transaction is in progress and has not been committed or rolled back, the changes that it makes to the database are considered tentative and not yet reliable.

In addition to atomicity and durability, **UDB** transactions provide you with another desirable property called *isolation*. This property deals with preventing anomalies that might result from interference among multiple users who are interacting with the database at the same time. Here are some examples of possible anomalies that might result from a lack of isolation:

1. Suppose that you ask your ticket agency to list all the performances of the Metropolitan Opera for the spring season, and you get a list of four performances. You ask for tickets to all of them, but when you receive the tickets, you discover that another performance has been added and you have to pay for five tickets. This is called the *phantom row anomaly*, because a piece of data has appeared where you were told that no data existed.

2. Suppose that you ask your ticket agency for the price of tickets to a concert and are told that the price is $35. You decide to buy some tickets, but after you make your decision you discover that the price has gone up to $50. This is called the *nonrepeatable read anomaly*, because you have accessed the same piece of data twice and found different values.

3. Suppose that you scan a list of planned concerts and see that Willie Nelson will be performing in your town next summer. But when you try to buy a

ticket, you find out that the list was only tentative and that the concert was never really scheduled. This is called the *dirty read anomaly*, because you were allowed to read information before it was reliable.

4. Suppose that you ask your ticket agency if any tickets are available for a Bruce Springsteen concert, and the agency replies that one ticket is left. A short time later, I ask my agency if any tickets are left for the same concert and get the same reply. You and I both try to buy the ticket. Your agency prints a ticket and updates the available tickets to zero; then my agency does the same thing. This is called the *lost update anomaly*, because two users have updated the same piece of data and one of the updates has been lost.

Ideally, you would like to avoid all these anomalies. Unfortunately, however, there is a cost associated with this: while you are making up your mind what tickets to buy, the system must prevent all other users from buying tickets, or updating ticket prices, or changing the concert schedule. This limits the *concurrency* of the database, which is the ability of the system to provide service to multiple users at the same time. UDB allows application designers to control the trade-off between isolation and concurrency, by specifying an *isolation level* for each transaction. The following four isolation levels are supported:[14]

1. *Repeatable Read (RR).* This is the highest level of isolation, and it prevents all the anomalies described above. A transaction running with RR isolation acquires a lock on all data that it reads, preventing other transactions from updating any of this data until it has committed or rolled back. Thus, if a program reads the same piece of data twice in the same transaction with an isolation level of RR, it is guaranteed to see the same value (or absence of a value!). If an RR-level transaction reads a lot of data, the concurrency of the database can be severely limited.

2. *Read Stability (RS).* This isolation level guarantees that if a transaction reads the same row twice, it will have the same value, but it does not prevent new rows from appearing during the course of a transaction. An RS-level transaction has a smaller impact on concurrency than an RR-level transaction, and it is protected from nonrepeatable read anomalies but not from phantom row anomalies.

3. *Cursor Stability (CS).* This isolation level guarantees only that a row of a table will not change while your transaction has a cursor positioned on that row. This means that you can read data by fetching from a cursor, then update the

---

14. Terminology in this area is somewhat nonuniform. The ANSI/ISO SQL Standard recognizes the same four isolation levels as UDB, but it uses different names for them, as follows: UDB "Repeatable Read" corresponds to ANSI "Serializable"; UDB "Read Stability" corresponds to ANSI "Repeatable Read"; UDB "Cursor Stability" corresponds to ANSI "Read Committed"; and UDB "Uncommitted Read" corresponds to ANSI "Uncommitted Read."

TABLE 2-5: Anomalies Seen at Various Levels of Isolation

	Phantom	Nonrepeatable Read	Dirty Read	Lost Update
Repeatable Read (RR)	NO	NO	NO	NO
Read Stability (RS)	YES	NO	NO	NO
Cursor Stability (CS)	YES	YES	NO	NO
Uncommitted Read (UR)	YES	YES	YES	NO

current row of that cursor without danger that someone else has updated the row since you read it. If you execute the same query more than once in a CS-level transaction, you may get different answers, but at least each answer will contain data that was committed at the time you read it. CS-level transactions are protected against dirty reads and lost updates, but not against phantoms and nonrepeatable reads. Obviously, the CS level of isolation provides much less protection and has much less impact on concurrency than the levels described above.

4. *Uncommitted Read (UR).* This is the lowest level of isolation and provides the least amount of protection against the isolation anomalies. UR-level transactions have virtually no effect on concurrency. Since a UR-level transaction can read data that is in an inconsistent state (for example, it may see the debit to your savings account but not the credit to your checking account), this isolation level is usually used only in statistical surveys or other applications where perfect accuracy is not required.

Table 2-5 summarizes the isolation levels and their protection against the types of anomalies described above.[15] A YES entry indicates that the given anomaly is possible at the given isolation level.

The PREP and BIND commands for application programs have a parameter that controls the isolation level for all transactions executed by the program

---

15. Table 2-5 assumes that both of the interfering transactions are running at the given isolation level. Interactions between two transactions running at different isolation levels are somewhat more complicated. The "Lost Update" column also assumes that the transactions use positioned (cursor-based) updates. Updatable cursors always have an effective isolation level of at least CS, even in a transaction with isolation level UR.

that is being bound. The parameter consists of the word ISOLATION followed by the abbreviation of the desired level: RR, RS, CS, or UR. The default isolation level, both for application programs and for interactive sessions, is Cursor Stability (CS). During an interactive session, if no transaction is in progress and you are not connected to a database, you can change your isolation level for future transactions by a command such as the following:

```
CHANGE ISOLATION TO RS;
```

Both the Command Center and the CLP have a feature called *autocommit* that automatically ends a transaction and commits updates after each SQL statement, and in both interfaces this feature is turned on by default.

COMMIT and ROLLBACK

As noted above, a transaction is implicitly begun whenever any data is read or written, and is ended by a COMMIT or ROLLBACK statement. These statements may be embedded in an application program or executed interactively. The syntax of the COMMIT and ROLLBACK statements is shown on page 108.

COMMIT causes all database changes made by the current transaction to become permanent and visible to other transactions running at isolation level RR, RS, or CS. ROLLBACK cancels all database changes made by the current transaction and restores the rows modified by this transaction to their state before the transaction was begun. Both COMMIT and ROLLBACK cause all open cursors to be closed, except that cursors declared WITH HOLD are not closed by a COMMIT statement.

The system implements transaction semantics by acquiring and holding *locks* on the various data items that you read or write. For example, if you read a row in an RR-level transaction, the system must hold a lock that prevents any other user from updating that row until the end of your transaction. These locks are acquired automatically as your transaction runs, and you do not need to be aware of them unless your transaction gets into a *deadlock* condition in which it is unable to acquire the locks that it needs in order to proceed. In this case, your transaction will automatically be rolled back to the last commit point and you will receive a code indicating a rollback due to deadlock (SQLCODE –911, SQLSTATE 40001). Any SQL statement that reads or updates the database might result in this code.

TIP: Using short transactions with frequent COMMIT statements reduces your chance of being caught in a deadlock and rolled back.

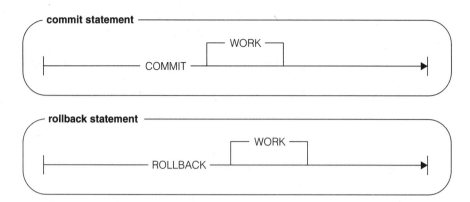

LOCK TABLE

If you know in advance that you will be reading or updating a whole table, you can save the system the overhead of acquiring many individual locks on the rows of the table by using an SQL statement that locks the whole table at once. You can lock a table in SHARE mode, which allows other transactions to read the table but prevents them from modifying it, or in EXCLUSIVE mode, which prevents other transactions from reading or modifying the table (except that UR-level transactions are allowed to read the table). If you acquire an explicit lock on a table, the lock is held until the end of the transaction in which it is acquired. The syntax for explicitly locking a table is as follows:

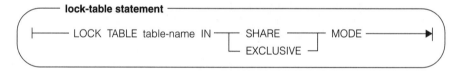

Example:

```
LOCK TABLE quotations IN SHARE MODE;
```

Locks are automatically released at the end of each transaction, except for locks that are acquired by an open cursor that was declared WITH HOLD; these locks are held until the end of the transaction in which the cursor is closed.

TIP: A good reference book for learning more about transactions is *Transaction Processing: Concepts and Techniques,* by Jim Gray and Andreas Reuter (Morgan Kaufmann, 1993).

2.7.2 Database Connections

Before leaving the topic of transactions, we need to discuss the closely related concept of a *database connection*. Before any access to data is possible, your application program or query interface must be connected to a database. In general, your application may be running on a client machine and the database may be located on a different server machine. During the course of an application program or query session, it may be necessary to connect to more than one database.

A database connection can be established explicitly by an SQL CONNECT statement, such as CONNECT TO dbase1.[16] You can also cause **UDB** to connect to a database automatically. This is done by setting the environment variable DB2DBDFT to the name of the default database you wish to use. If this environment variable is defined, **UDB** will establish an *implicit connection* to the default database at the beginning of each application or interactive session. Of course, you can override the implicit connection by using an explicit CONNECT statement.

UDB provides two types of database connections, called Type 1 and Type 2. If you are using Type 1 connections, each transaction is confined to a single database, so you must end a transaction before connecting to a new database. If you are using Type 2 connections, a transaction can connect to multiple databases, possibly on different servers, and can commit or roll back its changes to all these databases at the same time. A transaction that uses Type 2 connections is sometimes called a *distributed unit of work*. For application programs, the choice between Type 1 and Type 2 connections is made when the program is precompiled, by including the option CONNECT 1 or CONNECT 2 on the PREP command (the default is CONNECT 1). For an interactive session, the choice between Type 1 and Type 2 connections can be made by the SET CLIENT command (discussed in Section 3.3.2).

TIP: A program that contains static SQL statements must be precompiled in the database with which it interacts. Thus, a static application containing a distributed unit of work must be precompiled in multiple databases. In order to avoid errors during precompilation, split your application up into several source files, each of which accesses a single database, and precompile each source file in the database that it accesses. You can then compile the source files and link them into a single executable program. To precompile a source file in a given database, connect to that database before executing the PREP command.

---

16. Dynamic SQL programming interfaces such as ODBC and JDBC acquire database connections using function calls rather than SQL statements. These interfaces are discussed in Chapter 8.

```
        ┌ CONNECT TO dbase1;
        │
        │ ... (Reads and updates against dbase1) ...
        │
(Application is │ COMMIT;
connected to  ⟨
dbase1)      │ ... (More reads and updates against dbase1) ...
        │
        │ COMMIT;
        └
        ┌ CONNECT TO dbase2;
        │
(Application is │ ... (Reads and updates against dbase2) ...
connected to  ⟨
dbase2)      │ COMMIT;
        └ DISCONNECT ALL;
```

Figure 2-3: Example of Type 1 Connections

Figure 2-3 shows a typical sequence of statements executed by an application using Type 1 connections. Each CONNECT statement terminates the current database connection and establishes a new one. Each transaction operates on a single database and must be ended, either by COMMIT or by ROLLBACK, before a new database connection can be established. The final DISCONNECT ALL statement leaves the application unconnected to any database. Each SQL statement that accesses data is directed to the database named in the most recent CONNECT statement.

Figure 2-4 on page 112 shows a typical sequence of statements executed by an application using Type 2 connections, which permit multiple connections to be acquired within the same transaction. In the example, the application connects to dbase1, then to dbase2, and then to dbase1 again before committing its first set of updates. As before, each SQL statement is directed to the database named in the most recent CONNECT statement. However, using Type 2 connections, multiple databases can participate in the same transaction. Each COMMIT or ROLLBACK statement applies to all the modifications made by the current transaction, in all the databases to which it is connected. The database connections are retained until they are explicitly terminated by a RELEASE or DISCONNECT statement. The RELEASE statement tells the system that the connection to a specific database can be terminated at the end of the current transaction (of course, the database connection cannot be terminated before the end of the transaction, because the database may contain uncommitted updates). The statements provided by UDB for controlling database connections are described in the following sections.

CONNECT

The syntax of the CONNECT statement is as follows:

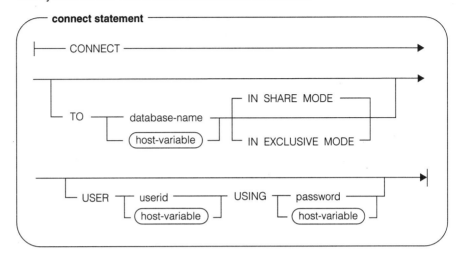

Example:

```
CONNECT TO dbase1;
```

When using Type 1 connections, the CONNECT statement terminates the previous database connection, if any. When using Type 2 connections, the CONNECT statement retains the previous connection, acquires a new connection if necessary, and directs subsequent SQL statements to the database named in the new connection.[17] An application cannot be connected to the same database more than once at the same time, even if it is using Type 2 connections (however, this restriction does not apply to CLI applications, as described in Chapter 8).

The phrase IN EXCLUSIVE MODE prevents other users from connecting to this database while you are connected to it. The default SHARE MODE makes no such restriction. As we will see in Section 2.8, you must be authorized to connect to a database, but no additional authorization is required to connect in exclusive mode. Obviously, you should think carefully before connecting to a database in exclusive mode, because you are denying other users access to

---

17. This description assumes that your application was precompiled with the option SQLRULES DB2, which is the default. If the precompile option SQLRULES STD was specified, a different syntax is used for reactivating a previously established connection. For example, rather than the statement `CONNECT TO dbase1`, you would use the statement `SET CONNECTION dbase1`. This alternative syntax is based on the SQL92 Standard.

```
                          CONNECT TO dbase1;

                          ...(Reads and updates against dbase1)...

                          CONNECT TO dbase2;

                          ...(Reads and updates against dbase2)...

                          CONNECT TO dbase1;

                          ...(Reads and updates against dbase1)...

                          COMMIT; ◄─────────────── (Commits updates against
                                                    both databases)

                          ...(Reads and updates against dbase1)...

                          CONNECT TO dbase2;

                          ...(Reads and updates against dbase2)...

                          RELEASE dbase2; ◄─────── (Indicates that dbase2 is no
                                                    longer needed after the end of
                                                    this transaction. Its connection
                                                    will be terminated at the next
                                                    COMMIT)

                          CONNECT TO dbase1;

                          ...(Reads and updates against dbase1)...

                          COMMIT; ◄─────────────── (Commits updates against
                                                    both databases and
                                                    terminates connection to
                                                    dbase2)

                          ...(Reads and updates against dbase1)...

                          COMMIT;

                          DISCONNECT ALL;
```

(Application is connected to dbase1)

(Application is connected to dbase2)

Figure 2-4: Example of Type 2 Connections

the database. If you try to connect to a database in exclusive mode when some other users are already connected to it, your CONNECT statement will fail.

The USER and USING phrases provide a userid and password that are passed to the server machine for authentication, if your database installation performs authentication on the server machine. If your installation performs authentication on the client machine, the USER and USING phrases can be omitted. The way in which authentication is done is specified at the time your database system is installed.

If the CONNECT statement has no operands (that is, it consists only of the word CONNECT), it returns information about the current database connection. If such a CONNECT statement is executed by a program, the connection information is returned in the SQLERRP field of the SQLCA structure (described in Section 4.1.4); if it is executed interactively, the connection information is displayed to the user.

CONNECT RESET

The syntax of the CONNECT RESET statement is as follows:

If your application is using Type 1 connections, CONNECT RESET commits the current transaction and ends the current connection. If your application is using Type 2 connections, CONNECT RESET retains the current connection, acquires a connection to the default database defined by the environment variable named DB2DBDFT, and directs subsequent SQL statements to the default database.

DISCONNECT

The syntax of the DISCONNECT statement is as follows:

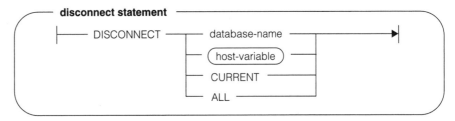

Example:

```
DISCONNECT dbase1;
```

A DISCONNECT statement can be used only when no transaction is in progress (that is, when no reading or writing of the database has taken place since the last COMMIT or ROLLBACK). It disconnects the application from a named database, or from the currently connected database, or from all databases.

RELEASE

The syntax of the RELEASE statement is as follows:

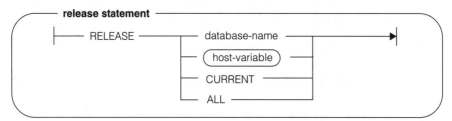

Example:

```
RELEASE dbase1;
```

A RELEASE statement is similar to a DISCONNECT statement, except that it is used inside a transaction to mark one or more database connections as ready to be terminated at the end of the current transaction. The actual connections are terminated by the next COMMIT statement (but not by a ROLLBACK statement). The connections to be terminated may be of either Type 1 or Type 2.

Precompiler Options

As noted previously, an application uses Type 2 connections if it is precompiled with the option CONNECT 2. When an application is using Type 2 connections, the exact meanings of COMMIT and ROLLBACK are determined by another precompiler option named SYNCPOINT, which can take the following values:

1. SYNCPOINT ONEPHASE (this is the default). This option means that although a transaction can connect to multiple databases, it can modify data in only one of them. If a transaction attempts to modify data in more than one database, an error will result.

2. SYNCPOINT TWOPHASE. Using this option, a transaction can modify data in all the databases to which it is connected. When the transaction ends by a COMMIT or ROLLBACK, all the changes to all the databases are committed or rolled back together. In this option, the database manager cooperates with a transaction manager that uses a two-phase commit protocol to ensure that either all the databases commit or all the databases roll back. If the transaction attempts to commit its changes but one of the databases is unable to commit successfully, all the databases will be rolled back by the transaction manager. For this purpose, UDB provides a transaction manager of its own, or can coop-

erate with another transaction manager such as CICS. For more information on transaction managers, see the *Administration Guide*.

The built-in transaction manager of UDB stores information about active transactions in a database. The database to be used for this purpose is specified in a database manager configuration parameter named TM_DATABASE. The default value for this parameter is "1ST_CONN," which causes the transaction manager to use the first database to which a connection is made in the given session.

3. SYNCPOINT NONE. Like TWOPHASE, this precompiler option allows a transaction to modify data in multiple databases and transmits a COMMIT or ROLLBACK to all the connected databases at the end of the transaction. Unlike TWOPHASE, however, this option does not employ a commit protocol to ensure that the COMMIT is successful in all the databases. With SYNCPOINT NONE, it is possible that the changes made by the transaction will be committed in some of the connected databases and will fail to commit in others. Since atomicity is one of the main properties that defines a transaction, the SYNCPOINT NONE option does not provide a true distributed transaction.

In addition to CONNECT and SYNCPOINT, two other precompiler options influence the detailed behavior of Type 2 database connections. The DISCONNECT option allows connections to be automatically terminated at the end of a transaction, and the SQLRULES option modifies the syntax of the CONNECT statement. These options, and a variation of the CONNECT statement called SET CONNECTION, are described in more detail in the *SQL Reference*.

2.8 AUTHORIZATION

As stated earlier, protecting data against unauthorized access and modification is one of the essential tasks of a database management system. UDB accomplishes this task by means of a system of *authorities* and *privileges*. In this section, we will examine the various types of authorities and privileges, and how they are created and used.

An *authority* is a general right to perform certain kinds of administrative actions. Some authorities apply at the level of a UDB instance, which may manage multiple databases. Other authorities apply to a specific database. Authorities are generally (with some exceptions) held by *groups* of users rather than by individuals. The concept of a *group* is defined and managed by the operating system on which UDB is running—for example, in AIX, users can be placed into groups by the *System Management Interface Tool* (SMIT), and in Windows NT, users and groups are managed by a tool called the *User Manager*.

A *privilege* is a specific right to perform certain kinds of actions on a specific object within a database, such as a table or view. Privileges can be held either by individual users or by groups.

2.8.1 Instance-Level Authorities

Three authorities apply at the level of a UDB instance and therefore span all the databases managed by that instance. Each of these instance-level authorities is held by a group, and the names of the groups holding these authorities are recorded in the database manager configuration file. The names of the groups holding the instance-level authorities can be seen by executing the following command:

```
GET DATABASE MANAGER CONFIGURATION;
```

The three instance-level authorities are as follows:

1. *System Administration authority.* In general, authorities and privileges are granted from one user to another, forming a treelike structure of grants. The root of this tree is the System Administration, or SYSADM, authority, which is the highest authority recognized by UDB. It is held by a group and confers on members of that group the ownership of all UDB resources and the ability to execute any UDB command, including the ability to confer or revoke all the other authorities and privileges.

   When a UDB instance is created, the group (as defined by the operating system) to which the creator of the instance belongs is given SYSADM authority for the new instance. Operating system facilities can be used to control the membership of this group. Because of the sensitive nature of SYSADM authority, you may choose to create a separate group specifically to administer each UDB instance. The name of the system administration group for each instance is recorded in the database manager configuration parameter named SYSADM_GROUP.

2. *System Control authority.* System Control, or SYSCTRL, is an instance-level authority that conveys the right to control system resources. For example, a holder of SYSCTRL authority can create and destroy databases and tablespaces (units of physical storage in which data resides).

   Although a holder of SYSCTRL controls the resources used by the database manager, SYSCTRL does not automatically include the right to read or modify the actual data that is stored in databases. Access to data requires DBADM authority or one of the more specific privileges.

   The name of the group holding SYSCTRL authority is recorded in the database manager configuration parameter named SYSCTRL_GROUP. When an instance is first created, no group is given SYSCTRL authority; it is up to the system administrators to decide whether they wish to share authority in this way. Any member of the system administration group can specify the name of the group that holds SYSCTRL authority by using the Control Center or by executing a command such as the following:

```
UPDATE DATABASE MANAGER CONFIGURATION
    USING SYSCTRL_GROUP goodguys;
```

The operations for which SYSCTRL is the minimum required authority are listed below and described in Chapter 10. In addition to these operations, holders of SYSCTRL authority can perform any operation that is available to a holder of SYSMAINT authority.

CREATE, ALTER, and DROP TABLESPACE

CATALOG and UNCATALOG for nodes and databases

CREATE and DROP DATABASE

FORCE APPLICATION

RESTORE to a new database

3. *System Maintenance authority.* System Maintenance, or SYSMAINT, is an instance-level authority that conveys the right to perform maintenance operations such as starting and stopping the DB2 server, backing up and restoring databases, and operating the database monitor. Like SYSCTRL, SYSMAINT does not include the right to read or modify the data that is stored in databases.

The name of the group holding SYSMAINT authority is recorded in the database manager configuration parameter named SYSMAINT_GROUP, which is set to null when the instance is created. Any member of the system administration group can specify the name of the SYSMAINT group by using the Control Center or a command such as the following:

```
UPDATE DATABASE MANAGER CONFIGURATION
    USING SYSMAINT_GROUP hackers;
```

The operations for which SYSMAINT is the minimum required authority are listed below and described in Chapter 10.

UPDATE DATABASE CONFIGURATION

BACKUP and RESTORE for an existing database

ROLLFORWARD

DB2START and DB2STOP

GET, RESET, and UPDATE MONITOR SWITCHES

2.8.2 Database-Level Authorities

Database-level authorities apply to a specific database rather than to a UDB instance. Each of these authorities is recorded in the catalog table named DBAUTH, in the database to which the authority applies. The user who creates a database automatically receives a full set of database-level authorities on the new database; this user can then grant database-level authorities selectively to other users or groups by means of the GRANT statement, which is discussed in Section 2.8.7. Database-level authorities are important to users who need to develop new database applications. They are as follows:

1. *Database Administration (DBADM) authority.* DBADM authority conveys the right to access and modify all the objects within a given database, including tables, indexes, views, packages, and everything else that is stored there. It also includes the right to grant any privilege on a specific object in the database to any user. A holder of DBADM can also grant the other database-level authorities (but not DBADM itself) to other users.

2. *BINDADD authority.* This authority conveys the right to create packages in the database by precompiling and/or binding application programs. The user who binds a program receives CONTROL privilege on the resulting package.

3. *CONNECT authority.* This authority conveys the right to connect to the database, using the SQL CONNECT statement.

4. *CREATETAB authority.* This authority conveys the right to create tables in the database. The creator of a table receives CONTROL privilege on the table.

5. *CREATE_NOT_FENCED authority.* This authority conveys the right to create user-defined functions that operate within the address space of the database. These functions are called *nonfenced functions.* Great care must be taken when creating a nonfenced function because the database is not protected against damage that might be caused by errors in these functions. (User-defined functions are described in Section 6.4.)

6. *IMPLICIT_SCHEMA authority.* This authority conveys the right to create a schema implicitly by creating an object with a schema name that does not match any existing schema. By default, when a database is created, IMPLICIT_SCHEMA authority is granted to PUBLIC, which means that any user can create schemas implicitly. A database administrator can change this policy by revoking IMPLICIT_SCHEMA from PUBLIC and granting it to a restricted set of users or groups.

2.8.3 Table and View Privileges

In general, privileges convey the right to perform a specific action on a specific object. For the privileges described in this section, the object to which the action applies is a table or view, or in some cases a column of a table or view.

Privileges that apply to a table or view as a whole are recorded in the catalog table named TABAUTH, and privileges that apply to a specific column are recorded in the catalog table named COLAUTH. Table and view privileges may be held by individual users and/or groups of users.

Table and view privileges are granted and revoked by means of SQL GRANT and REVOKE statements, which are described in Section 2.8.7. The privileges that apply to tables and views are as follows:

1. *CONTROL privilege*. CONTROL is like a "master" privilege—it includes all the privileges that are applicable to a given table or view. (ALTER, INDEX, and REFERENCES privileges apply only to tables; INSERT, DELETE, and UPDATE apply only to tables and updatable views.) The CONTROL privilege also includes the right to grant any applicable privilege on a table or view to other users or groups, the right to drop the table or view, and the right to update the statistics that apply to a table.

   The creator of a table automatically receives CONTROL privilege on it. The creator of a view receives CONTROL privilege on it only if they hold CONTROL privilege on all the tables on which the view is defined.

2. *ALTER privilege*. Conveys the right to change the definition of a table, using the ALTER TABLE statement; to comment on a table, using the COMMENT statement; or to attach triggers to a table, using the CREATE TRIGGER statement (described in Section 7.3).

3. *DELETE privilege*. Conveys the right to delete rows from the table or updatable view.

4. *INDEX privilege*. Conveys the right to create indexes on the table.

5. *INSERT privilege*. Conveys the right to insert rows into the table or updatable view.

6. *REFERENCES privilege*. Conveys the right to create and drop foreign key constraints in other tables, referencing this table as the parent table. (Foreign key constraints are discussed in Section 7.1.) The REFERENCES privilege may be held on the table or view as a whole, or on individual columns.

7. *SELECT privilege*. Conveys the right to retrieve data from the table or view, using the SELECT statement, or to use the table or view in a subquery.

8. *UPDATE privilege*. Conveys the right to update rows of the table or updatable view. The UPDATE privilege may be held on the table or view as a whole, or on individual columns.

In order to create a view, a user must hold SELECT or CONTROL privilege on all the tables that are used in the definition of the view. The creator of a view receives SELECT privilege on the view, and also receives CONTROL privilege on the view if they hold CONTROL privilege on all the underlying tables.

In addition, if the view is not read-only because of its definition, the definer of the view receives the same INSERT, DELETE, and UPDATE privileges on the view that they hold on the underlying table.

When a privilege on a table or view is revoked, all privileges that are derived from the revoked privilege are revoked also. For example, if a user has created a view V1 based on table T1, and that user loses the UPDATE privilege on table T1, the UPDATE privilege on view V1 will be lost also.

 TIP: Holding UPDATE privilege on a table is not exactly the same as holding column-level UPDATE privileges on all the columns of the table. If a new column is added to the table in the future, the table-level UPDATE privilege will automatically extend to the new column, but column-level UPDATE privileges will still apply to the original columns only.

2.8.4 Index Privileges

There is only one privilege that applies to indexes: the CONTROL privilege, which conveys the right to drop the index. The CONTROL privilege is automatically given to the user who creates an index. It may be held by individual users and/or groups of users. In order to grant the CONTROL privilege on an index, a user must hold SYSADM or DBADM authority. The holders of the CONTROL privilege on various indexes are recorded in the catalog table named INDEXAUTH.

2.8.5 Schema Privileges

The user who creates a schema by a CREATE SCHEMA statement receives all privileges on that schema, and the ability to grant these privileges to others. When a schema is created implicitly, CREATEIN privilege on that schema is granted to PUBLIC, but the other schema privileges are not automatically granted. Schema privileges are recorded in the catalog table named SCHEMAAUTH.

The privileges that apply to schemas are as follows:

1. *CREATEIN privilege.* Conveys the right to create objects in the schema, such as tables and views.

2. *ALTERIN privilege.* Conveys the right to comment on any object in the schema, or to alter any table in the schema.

3. *DROPIN privilege.* Conveys the right to drop any object in the schema.

2.8.6 Package Privileges

The privileges described in this section apply to packages, which are created by precompiling and/or binding an application program. The package encapsulates all the SQL statements in the program, including an optimized plan for executing each statement. All package privileges are recorded in the catalog table named PACKAGEAUTH. Package privileges may be held by individual users and/or groups of users.

Package privileges are granted and revoked by means of GRANT and REVOKE statements, which are described in Section 2.8.7. In order to grant any package privilege, a user must hold SYSADM authority, DBADM authority, or the CONTROL privilege on the package in question. The privileges that apply to packages are as follows:

1. *CONTROL privilege.* The CONTROL privilege is like a "master" privilege that includes the EXECUTE and BIND privileges, as well as the right to grant these privileges to others. It also includes the right to drop the package. The CON-TROL privilege is automatically given to the user who creates a package. In order to create a package, a user must hold all the privileges necessary to execute the SQL statements that are included in the package.

2. *EXECUTE privilege.* This privilege conveys the right to execute a package by executing the application program from which the package was bound. A user holding EXECUTE privilege on a package can execute it even if they do not hold the privileges needed to execute the individual statements inside the package. This provides a useful form of *encapsulation* of privileges. For example, the personnel manager of a company, who holds the privilege to update employee records, might create a package by binding an application program that updates salaries in a particular way. The personnel manager might then grant the EXECUTE privilege on this package to a clerk, who can then run the application even though he does not hold the general privilege to update employee records. In effect, the manager has granted to the clerk an encapsulated privilege to update salaries in a particular way, under the control of the application program.

TIP: In order to create a package that encapsulates a particular privilege, a user must hold that privilege as an individual user or as a member of PUBLIC (not as a member of a named group).

3. *BIND privilege.* This privilege conveys the right to rebind a package, using the PREP, BIND, or REBIND command. Rebinding a package may be necessary in case the package has become invalid due to changes in the database. It may also be desirable to rebind a package in order to take advantage of a new index. When a package is rebound, it is replaced by a new package based on the latest indexes, view definitions, table statistics, and other information found in the database. In order to rebind a package, a user must hold not only the BIND privilege for the package, but also the privileges needed to execute all the static SQL statements found in the package.

2.8.7 GRANT and REVOKE Statements

Database-level authorities, and all privileges, can be granted by a user to another user, or to a group, by means of the GRANT statement. Authorities and privileges can also be revoked, by means of the REVOKE statement. As shown in the syntax diagram below, the GRANT and REVOKE statements have very similar syntax:

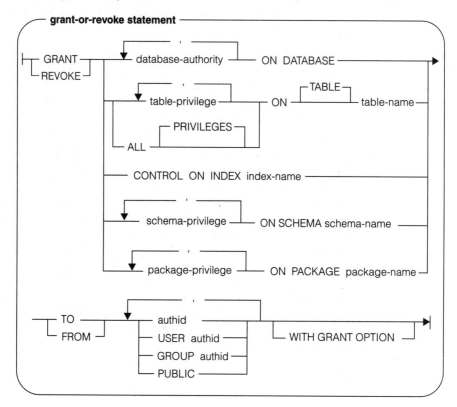

Examples:

```
GRANT DBADM ON DATABASE TO palmer;
GRANT CONNECT, CREATETAB, BINDADD ON DATABASE TO cerra;
GRANT SELECT, INSERT, DELETE, UPDATE ON test.table1
    TO tester1, tester2 WITH GRANT OPTION;
GRANT SELECT, UPDATE(address, balance)
    ON bank.accounts to GROUP tellers;
GRANT ALTERIN, CREATEIN, DROPIN ON SCHEMA science
    TO feinman, fermi, dirac;
```

TABLE 2-6: Authorizations Required to Execute GRANT and REVOKE Statements

If you hold . . .	You can grant and revoke . . .		
	DBADM	Any database-level authority or any CONTROL privilege	Specific privileges other than CONTROL
SYSADM	Yes	Yes	Yes
DBADM	No	Yes	Yes
CONTROL on a specific object	No	No	Yes, on the object for which you hold CONTROL
GRANT OPTION for a specific privilege	No	No	You can grant the privilege for which you hold GRANT OPTION, but GRANT OPTION does not imply the ability to revoke

```
GRANT BIND, EXECUTE ON PACKAGE program5 TO PUBLIC;
REVOKE ALL PRIVILEGES ON test.table1 FROM USER tester2;
REVOKE CONTROL ON INDEX i1 FROM smith, jones;
```

TIP: A convenient graphical interface for granting and revoking privileges, equivalent to the GRANT and REVOKE statements, is provided by the Control Center (described in Chapter 10).

When you grant a privilege on a schema, table, or view to another user, you can optionally include the phrase "WITH GRANT OPTION," which allows the recipient of the privilege to grant it in turn to other users (and optionally to pass along the grant option as well). As a general rule, in order to grant a privilege on an object, you must hold the CONTROL privilege on the object, or hold the grant option for the privilege you are granting, or hold the DBADM or SYSADM authority.

The ability to grant a specific privilege does not carry with it the ability to revoke the same privilege. In general, to revoke a privilege on a given object, you must hold the CONTROL privilege on the object, or DBADM or SYSADM authority. When you revoke a privilege from a user or group, that privilege is taken away, regardless of how many times (or by whom) the privilege was granted. The authorization requirements for GRANT and REVOKE statements are summarized in Table 2-6.

If you have granted a privilege to someone with the grant option, you cannot revoke only the grant option (to accomplish this purpose, you can revoke the privilege and then grant it again without the grant option).

The following rules apply to GRANT and REVOKE statements:

- Keywords must be used in the proper combinations: "GRANT . . . TO . . ." and "REVOKE . . . FROM . . ."

- The phrase "WITH GRANT OPTION" can be used only in a GRANT statement for privileges on a schema, table, or view.

- The names of the authorities and privileges that apply to each type of object can be chosen from the lists in Sections 2.8.2 through 2.8.6. For example, CONNECT authority applies only to databases, and EXECUTE privilege applies only to packages.

- The UPDATE or REFERENCES privilege can be granted on specific columns of a table or view by enclosing a list of column names in parentheses, as in the example above that grants UPDATE on the ADDRESS and BALANCE columns of the BANK.ACCOUNTS table to the group named TELLERS. If no column list is specified, the grant applies to all columns of the table or view.

- Privileges cannot be revoked on individual columns. The REVOKE statement for table privileges always applies to all the columns of the table or view. After revoking UPDATE or REFERENCES privileges on a table or view, you can grant back individual column-level privileges if you wish.

- When granting or revoking table or view privileges, the term "ALL PRIVILEGES" means "all privileges (except the CONTROL privilege) that are applicable to the given object." For example, ALL PRIVILEGES on a table includes SELECT, INSERT, DELETE, UPDATE, ALTER, INDEX, and REFERENCES, but ALL PRIVILEGES on a view includes only SELECT, INSERT, DELETE, and UPDATE.

- The authid(s) to which the grant or revoke applies are eight-character identifiers for users or groups that are known to your operating system. You need to use the keyword USER or GROUP only when referring to an authid that is defined both as a user and as a group. If an authid identifies a user or a group but not both, the system will figure out which kind of identifier it is.

- Privileges and authorities that are granted to PUBLIC can be exercised by any user, including users who have no explicit privileges or authorities, and including new userids that may be created after the grant is made. It is often useful to grant CONNECT authority to PUBLIC, allowing any user to connect to the database. DBADM authority cannot be granted to PUBLIC.

- If you try to grant several privileges in a single GRANT statement and you are not authorized to make some of the grants, those grants that you are authorized to make will be effective, and you will receive a warning that not all of your grants were effective.

- When a privilege is revoked, packages that depend on that privilege become invalid, and views and triggers that depend on that privilege become inoperative.

TIP: Granting DBADM to a user automatically grants all the other database privileges as well, such as CONNECT and CREATETAB. But revoking DBADM from a user does not revoke the other database privileges—you must revoke them individually if you so desire. Similarly, granting CONTROL on a table or view automatically grants all the other table-level privileges as well, such as SELECT and UPDATE, all with GRANT OPTION. But revoking CONTROL on a table or view does not revoke the other table privileges—these privileges, with GRANT OPTION, remain in effect until you revoke them individually or specify REVOKE ALL PRIVILEGES.

2.8.8 Authorization Checking

The userid against which authorization is checked for a given SQL statement is called the *authid* for that statement. The authid for a static SQL statement in an application program is that of the user who bound the package for that program. This enables a user who holds certain privileges to encapsulate these privileges in a package that uses the privileges only in a certain way, and to grant to other users the right to execute the package without granting the privileges on which the package is based. For dynamic SQL statements, on the other hand, the authid is always the userid of the current user. Dynamic SQL statements include all statements executed via the Call Level Interface (CLI) or Embedded Dynamic SQL facilities (described in Chapter 8), or via an interactive user interface such as the Command Center.

The time at which a privilege is checked depends on the type of the SQL statement. Authorization is checked at bind time for static SELECT, INSERT, DELETE, UPDATE, and VALUES statements, and at run time for all other types of statements. Table 2-7 summarizes the authorization-checking rules for various types of SQL statements.

TABLE 2-7: Authorization-Checking Rules for Static and Dynamic SQL Statements

Type of Statement	Static SQL	Dynamic SQL
Data manipulation statements (SELECT, INSERT, UPDATE, DELETE, and VALUES)	Checked against binder of program, at bind time	Checked against current user, at run time
All other SQL statements	Checked against binder of program, at run time	Checked against current user, at run time

Privileges that are granted to groups are not taken into account when binding a package. That is, when binding a package that contains static SQL statements, the binder of the package must hold the privileges required to execute the static SQL statements, either as an individual or as a member of PUBLIC. (The reason for this policy is that packages are owned by individuals, not by groups, and the group membership of an individual may change over time. Groups are managed by the operating system, and UDB is not informed of changes in group membership.)

Table 2-8 summarizes the privileges that are required to execute the statements and commands that are discussed in this chapter and in later chapters. The SYSADM and DBADM authorities are also sufficient to execute any statement or command in the table, even in the absence of any other authority or privilege. Certain options of the CREATE TABLE statement (Section 7.2.1), ALTER TABLE statement (Section 7.2.2), and CREATE TRIGGER statement (Section 7.3.1) require additional privileges, which are discussed in their respective sections.

TABLE 2-8: Privileges Required to Execute Various SQL Statements

In order to execute . . .	An authid must hold . . .
ALTER TABLE statement	ALTER or CONTROL privilege on the table, or ALTERIN privilege on the schema that contains the table.
BIND command	Binding a package for the first time requires BINDADD authority for the database, and either CREATEIN privilege on its schema or IMPLICIT_SCHEMA authority if the schema does not yet exist. Rebinding an existing package requires BIND privilege on the package, or ALTERIN privilege on its schema. In addition, the authid must hold all the privileges required by the static SQL statements contained in the package.
CALL statement	EXECUTE or CONTROL privilege on the package that represents the stored procedure to be called.
COMMENT statement	ALTER or CONTROL privilege on the object that is being commented on, or ALTERIN privilege on the schema that contains the object. Alternatively, you can comment on an object if you are the DEFINER or OWNER of the object (as recorded in the system catalog tables).
CONNECT statement	CONNECT authority for the database in question.
CREATE SCHEMA	Any user can explicitly create a schema as long as its schema name and owner are both equal to his or her userid. To explicitly create a schema with a different name or owner requires DBADM or SYSADM authority.

TABLE 2-8 *(Continued)*

In order to execute . . .	An authid must hold . . .
CREATE statement for an alias, distinct type, function, index, procedure, table, trigger, or view	CREATEIN privilege, to create an object in an existing schema; or IMPLICIT_SCHEMA authority to implicitly create a new schema. In addition, the following privileges are required: • To create an index requires INDEX or CONTROL privilege on the table that is being indexed. • To create a table requires CREATETAB authority on the database. • To create a trigger requires ALTER or CONTROL privilege on the table to which the trigger is attached, or ALTERIN privilege on the schema that contains this table. In addition, the creator of the trigger must hold the privileges required to execute the statements in the trigger body. • To create a view requires SELECT or CONTROL privilege on all the tables and views that are referenced in the view definition.
DELETE statement	DELETE or CONTROL privilege on the table or view from which rows are to be deleted, and SELECT or CONTROL privilege on all tables or views that are used in subqueries. In addition, if the DELETE statement is in a program that was precompiled with LANGLEVEL=SQL92E or MIA, and it contains a column reference in a search condition, SELECT or CONTROL privilege is required on the table or view from which rows are to be deleted.
DROP SCHEMA statement	In order to drop a schema, you must be the OWNER of the schema, as recorded in the SCHEMATA catalog table, and the schema must be empty.
DROP statement for any object in a schema	CONTROL privilege on the object that is being dropped, or DROPIN privilege on the schema that contains the object. Alternatively, you can drop an object if you are the DEFINER of the object, as recorded in the system catalog tables.
INSERT statement	INSERT or CONTROL privilege on the table or view into which rows are to be inserted, and SELECT or CONTROL privilege on all tables or views that are used in subqueries.
LOCK TABLE statement	SELECT or CONTROL privilege on the table to be locked.
PREP command	If the package does not yet exist, you need BINDADD authority on the database, and either CREATEIN privilege on the schema or IMPLICIT_SCHEMA authority on the database. If the package already exists, you need either BIND privilege on the package or ALTERIN privilege on its schema. In addition, you must hold all the privileges required by the static SQL statements contained in the package.
REBIND command	BIND privilege on the package, or ALTERIN privilege on its schema.
RENAME TABLE statement	CONTROL privilege on the table.

TABLE 2-8 *(Continued)*

In order to execute . . .	An authid must hold . . .
RENAME TABLE statement	CONTROL privilege on the table.
SELECT statement, including a single-row SELECT statement or a query used in a cursor declaration	SELECT or CONTROL privilege on all the tables and views referenced in the query and its subqueries.
UPDATE statement	UPDATE or CONTROL privilege on the updated table or view, or UPDATE privilege on the updated columns. SELECT or CONTROL privilege is also required on all tables and views that are used in subqueries. In addition, if the UPDATE statement is in a program that was precompiled with LANGLEVEL=SQL92E or MIA and it contains a column reference in a search condition or on the right side of a SET clause, SELECT or CONTROL privilege is required on the updated table or view.
VALUES statement, including single-row VALUES statement	SELECT or CONTROL privilege on any tables or views referenced in subqueries.

Interactive SQL

S QL was originally designed as a query language—a language that allows its users to dream up new questions, ask them quickly, and receive answers on the spot, without taking the trouble to write a computer program. The language was designed for an interactive dialog between a person and a database system, in which the user might compose each query based on the results of earlier queries. In this type of environment, the user is exploring the database and does not always know in advance where the exploration will lead. This type of ad-hoc, unplanned interaction between a person and a database is sometimes referred to as *decision support.*

One of the greatest strengths of the relational data model has always been its flexibility in decision support applications. SQL does not restrict its users to ask only questions that follow anticipated paths. All the information in the database is represented in the form of data values and is accessible via interactive queries. The SQL user does not need to understand the access aids such as indexes that are being used to process queries, and the queries do not need to be revised if changes are made to the access aids.

Since decision support is such an important application, all relational systems provide some kind of interactive interface for submitting SQL queries and updates, viewing the results, and performing other interactive tasks. For this purpose, UDB provides a set of interactive programs that are collectively called DB2 Tools. The DB2 Tools all provide similar graphical interfaces for interacting with the database.

At present, the DB2 Tools are supported only on the Windows and OS/2 platforms. Using DB2 Tools on a Windows or OS/2 machine, you can interact with a UDB database that is running on AIX or on another UNIX platform. In the future, IBM plans to supplement the DB2 Tools with similar web-based tools that allow you to interact with UDB databases using a web browser on any platform—in fact, some of these web-based tools may be available by the time you are reading this book.

An alternative to the DB2 Tools is an older interface called the Command Line Processor (CLP), which is supported on all UDB platforms. The CLP is a very simple, text-oriented interface that allows you to type SQL statements on a command line and to view the results on your display.

In this chapter, you will learn how to use the DB2 Tools and the CLP. In addition to these interfaces, you can execute SQL statements interactively using Lotus Approach and various other decision support products.

3.1 DB2 TOOLS

All the DB2 Tools can be invoked by clicking on their icons in the DB2 program folder or in a lower-level folder such as the Administration Tools folder. All the tools perform complementary tasks and present consistent graphical user interfaces, and they are all affected by a common collection of "settings" that can be controlled by clicking on the Tool Settings icon. Each of the tools presents a toolbar containing icons that represent all the other tools. By clicking on the icons in the toolbar, you can switch from one tool to another or start up a tool that is not already running. You can read the names of all the tools by moving your mouse cursor slowly over the icons in the toolbar.

In this section, we will discuss the Command Center, the Script Center, the Journal, and the Information Center. These are the main tools that are used for interactively composing and executing SQL statements and for obtaining online information. In Chapter 10, we will discuss additional database administration tools called the Control Center and the Client Configuration Assistant.

3.1.1 The Command Center

The Command Center allows you to execute individual SQL statements and to create, edit, and run *scripts* that are written in SQL. The Command Center interface contains three panels, labeled Script, Results, and Access Plan. You can view only one of these panels at a time, and you can switch to a different panel by clicking on its "tab." The Script panel is used to create and edit an SQL statement (or a script consisting of several statements); the Results panel shows you the result of executing a statement or script; and the Access Plan panel provides a graphical representation of the access plan chosen by UDB for processing an SQL statement.

The simplest way to interact with the Command Center is simply to type an SQL statement in the Script panel and to click on the Execute icon (the one that has a picture of gears on it). The Execute icon causes the Command Center to execute the SQL statement in the Script panel and to show you the result in the Results panel. You can switch back and forth between the Script panel and Results panel as often as you like, running many SQL statements and keeping a log of the results. A list of all the SQL statements you have executed is kept at the top of the Script panel, so you can easily select one of these statements, edit it, and execute it again. Figure 3-1 shows the Script panel containing one of the queries from Chapter 2, and Figure 3-2 shows the Results panel containing the result of executing this query.

In addition to SQL statements, the Command Center allows you to execute DB2 commands and operating system commands, simply by typing them in the Script panel. Any line that begins with a "!" character is sent to the

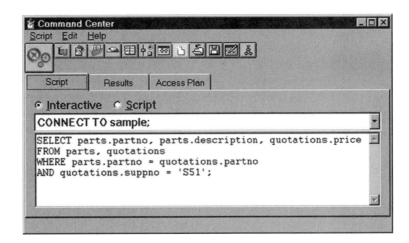

Figure 3-1: Script Panel of the Command Center

operating system for execution. The distinction between an SQL statement and a DB2 command is somewhat arbitrary. In general, SQL statements operate on data in tables, and DB2 commands (such as CREATE DATABASE, BACKUP, and RESTORE) operate on the database as a whole. In every case, the result of executing the SQL statement, DB2 command, or operating system command is displayed in the Results panel.

The Script panel has two modes, called Interactive mode and Script mode, that can be selected by clicking on "radio buttons" near the top of the panel, as shown in Figure 3-1. Interactive mode is used mainly for entering statements for immediate execution, and Script mode is used mainly for creating scripts that can be saved and executed repeatedly. You can save a script by pulling down the Script menu from the menu bar at the top of the panel, selecting the Save command, and specifying in a dialog box the path and filename where you wish the script to be stored. Using the Save dialog box, you can enter a brief description of your script and, if you wish, you can save it on a UDB system other than the one you are currently using. You can also specify a *working directory* for your script (this is the directory in which the script appears to be running, if it executes any operating system commands). I recommend choosing the "Save to Script Center" option on the Save dialog box, which allows your script to be used via the Script Center tool.

The third Command Center panel, called the Access Plan panel, is used for displaying access plans generated by the UDB optimizer. By typing an SQL statement in the Script panel and selecting "Create Access Plan" from the

Figure 3-2: Results Panel of the Command Center

Script menu, you can see the access plan that would be used to execute your statement. The access plan for the SQL statement in Figure 3-1 is shown in Figure 3-3. The plan is shown in the form of a graph that illustrates the flow of data. By using the "zoom slider" and the scroll bars, you can examine the graph at any desired level of detail. The nodes at the bottom of the graph represent tables that participate in the query (in this example, the PARTS and QUOTATIONS tables). Each node in the graph represents some operation such as scanning a table, joining two tables, or sorting an intermediate result. By double-clicking on a node in the graph, you can see more details about the node, such as its estimated cost (in arbitrary units called *timerons*) and its estimated cardinality (the number of rows that the optimizer expects to find in the intermediate result represented by the node). In Figure 3-3, we see that the optimizer has decided to perform index scans on the PARTS and QUOTATIONS tables, to sort the results into a common order by their PARTNO columns, and to perform a nested-loop join between the sorted tables. Examining the access plan for a long-running query can sometimes give you an

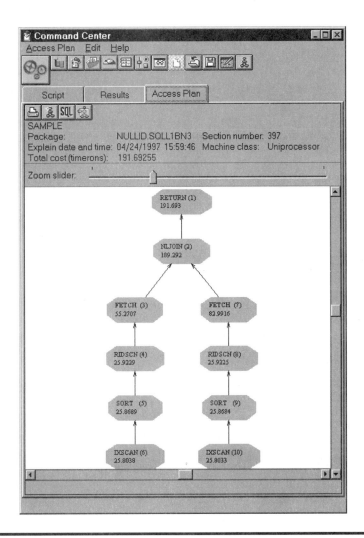

Figure 3-3: Access Plan Panel of the Command Center

idea for improving the performance of the query. For example, if you see that
the system is sorting a large table by a certain column, it might be helpful to
create an index on that column in order to avoid the sort.

The Command Center is affected by the global settings that are controlled
by clicking on the Tool Settings icon in the toolbar. It is also affected by some
settings that apply to the Command Center only and are controlled by selecting

"Options" on the Script, Results, or Access Plan menu at the top of the window. Here are some of these settings:

- You can specify whether you want the Command Center to automatically commit a transaction after each SQL statement. This feature is turned on by default.

TIP: If you want to be able to roll back your statements, or if you want to make use of transaction atomicity across multiple statements, you will need to turn off the automatic commit feature when using the Command Center.

- You can specify the *statement termination character* that is used to separate one SQL statement from another in a script. A semicolon is often used as a statement termination character (but if your script contains a CREATE TRIGGER statement, you would be wise to choose a different character, since semicolons are used inside CREATE TRIGGER). If you do not specify a statement termination character, each line in your script is treated as a separate SQL statement.

- You can specify what kind of return code you want to be displayed in the Results panel along with the result of each SQL statement. Options include the SQLCODE (a product-dependent integer code), the SQLSTATE (a five-digit code defined by the SQL Standard), and the SQLCA (a detailed data structure defined in Section 4.1.4). You can also specify whether you want warning messages to be displayed or suppressed.

TIP: When using an interactive SQL interface such as the Command Center, you can always get a list of the column names and datatypes in the result set of any query by typing DESCRIBE followed by the query. For example, the following query causes the Command Center to display the names and datatypes of all the columns in the SYSCAT.VIEWS catalog table:

```
DESCRIBE SELECT * FROM syscat.views;
```

3.1.2 The Script Center

A script is a file containing SQL statements, DB2 commands, and operating system commands. The Script Center provides a convenient way for you to create, edit, and manage scripts. It shows you a list of all the scripts that are known on a given UDB system (either your local system or a remote one). These scripts may have been created using the Script Center or the Command Center, or imported from sources other than the DB2 Tools. For each script, the Script Center displays information such as a short description of the script, the path and filename where it is stored, and the date and time when it was last modified. The Script Center is shown in Figure 3-4.

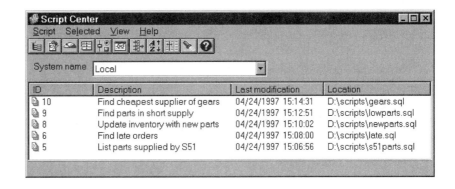

Figure 3-4: The Script Center

By right-clicking on one of the scripts in the Script Center list (or by left-clicking on the script and pulling down the Selected menu), you can perform various actions on the script such as editing it, copying it, or deleting it. You can also call for the script to be executed immediately or scheduled to be run at a designated date and time. If you schedule your script to be run later, you can also call for it to be repeated on a regular schedule, such as "every three days," or "every Friday at midnight," or "on the first and fifteenth of every month." The result of running a script can be seen using another tool called the Journal.

TIP: When you run a script using the Script Center, the system recognizes the statement termination character that was in effect when the script was saved, which may be different from the statement termination character that is currently in effect.

3.1.3 The Journal

The task of the Journal is to keep an archival record of jobs, events, and messages that take place in a UDB database. The Journal interface contains four panels named Jobs, Recovery, Alerts, and Messages, each of which can be seen by clicking on its tab. Figure 3-5 shows the Jobs panel, which can be used to see a list of pending jobs, running jobs, or completed jobs. Pending jobs are jobs that the Script Center has scheduled to be run at designated times. Figure 3-5 shows three pending jobs, one scheduled to be run weekly, one monthly, and one at a single designated date and time. By right-clicking on one of these jobs (or by pulling down the Jobs menu), you can examine the script, delete the job, run it immediately, or change or temporarily suspend its schedule.

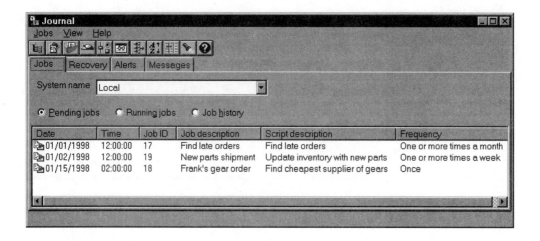

Figure 3-5: Pending Jobs Panel of the Journal

Each time a scheduled job runs, an entry is made in the Job History panel recording the date, time, job identification, and outcome of the run. By right-clicking on one of these entries (or by pulling down the Jobs menu and choosing Show Results), you can see a detailed log of what happened during the execution of the script.

The Recovery panel of the Journal keeps a list of all the backup and recovery operations that have been performed on your database. You can use this panel to find what backup copies of the database are available, or to restore the database to a specific state. Backup and recovery are described further in Section 10.6.

The Alerts panel of the Journal records all the Alert events that have been detected by the Snapshot Monitor. The Snapshot Monitor is a database administration tool that measures various performance parameters of the UDB system. A system administrator can ask the Snapshot Monitor to generate an Alert when one of these parameters reaches a designated value, such as a certain number of transactions per second. The Journal records the exact time and cause of each Alert. More details about Alerts and the Snapshot Monitor can be found in Section 10.9.

The Messages panel of the Journal displays a list of messages that have been generated by all the DB2 Tools. Each message is displayed along with its date and time in a tabular format. When you first look at the Messages panel, the column containing the actual message is very narrow, and you can see only the first few words of the messages. You can resize the columns (in the Messages

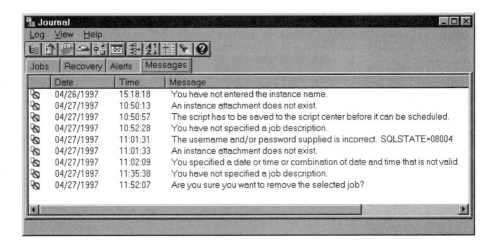

Figure 3-6: Messages Panel of the Journal

panel and in other panels displayed by the DB2 Tools) by using your mouse in the heading to drag the boundaries between the columns. In Figure 3-6, the message column has been enlarged enough that you can read the full text of the messages.

TIP: The Journal accumulates records on jobs, events, and messages, and keeps these records indefinitely. To prevent Journal records from occupying a lot of space, you should purge them occasionally. You can do this by invoking the Remove or Remove All action on the individual panels of the Journal. To select a range of records to be removed (such as all the messages you received last month), click on the first record, then shift-click on the last record in the range, then pull down the main menu and select the Remove action. SYSADM authority is required to remove job records from the Journal.

3.1.4 The Information Center

All the DB2 Tools are richly supplied with online help, which you can invoke by clicking the Help button that appears on every panel. But sometimes you may need to explore a particular subject in greater depth. This task is made easy by a tool called the Information Center. The Information Center organizes in one place all the online information that is provided by UDB. As shown in Figure 3-7, the Information Center consists of five individual panels, each of which can be seen by clicking on its tab. The contents of the panels are as follows:

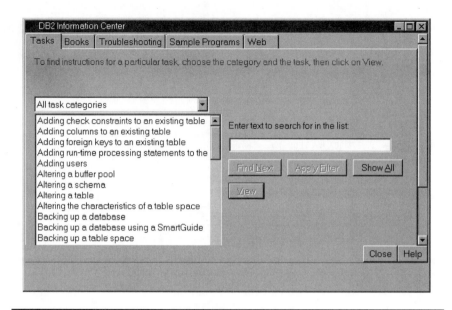

Figure 3-7: The Information Center

- The *Tasks panel* contains a list of tasks such as "Backing up a database" and "Creating a table." You can search for tasks that contain a specific word such as "Privileges." When you have selected a task, you can click on View to see the online help that is available for that task.

- The *Books panel* contains a list of all the UDB manuals that are available online. These books are distributed in HTML format on the product installation disk. By clicking on View, you can read the books using your favorite browser. If you are wondering where these books are kept, you can find them in `sqllib/doc/html`.

- The *Troubleshooting panel* can be used to find an explanation for any message that you receive from any part of UDB. If you need to know what to do about message SQL0801, or the exact meaning of SQLSTATE 22012, you can look it up on the Troubleshooting panel.

- The *Sample Programs panel* contains a list of application programs that illustrate how to use various UDB features.

- The *Web panel* uses your favorite browser to access DB2-related sites on the World Wide Web, such as the DB2 Frequently Asked Questions site maintained by IBM.

3.2 THE COMMAND LINE PROCESSOR

The Command Line Processor (CLP) is a text-oriented interface for processing SQL statements, DB2 commands, and operating system commands. It can accept input either from the keyboard or from a file, and can direct its output either to your display or to a file. It is supported on all **UDB** platforms and is compatible with earlier versions of the CLP. If you are interacting with a **UDB** database from an AIX or other UNIX workstation, the CLP is your principal interface for executing interactive SQL statements. This section describes the basics of how to use the CLP. More information about the CLP can be found in the *Command Reference*.

The CLP can be invoked by clicking on the CLP icon in the DB2 program folder, or by typing a db2 command at your operating system prompt.

TIP: Under Windows NT, **UDB** commands such as db2 are not accepted by a normal command window, but require a special DB2 command window. You can create a DB2 command window by typing db2cmd in a normal command window or by clicking on the Command Window icon in the DB2 for Windows NT program folder.

The db2 command has the following three forms:

1. If you follow the word db2 with an SQL statement or system command, the CLP will execute that statement or command and display the result. For example, to direct the CLP to connect to a database named FINANCE, you might type:

```
db2 connect to finance
```

When using the CLP in this mode, you must remember that the operating system shell is processing your input before sending it to the CLP. Therefore, if you use any characters that are considered special characters by the operating system, such as *, >, or <, you should enclose your input in single or double quotes, as in the following example:

```
db2 "select * from accounts"
```

2. If you follow the word db2 with the option -f filename, the CLP will take its input from the named file, processing all the commands in the file one after another. For example, the following command directs the CLP to process all the statements in the file named monday.clp:

```
db2 -f monday.clp
```

3. If you simply type db2 followed by neither the -f option nor a command, the CLP will go into interactive mode and will prompt you to enter SQL statements or commands, one at a time, at the keyboard. The simplest form of the db2 command is as follows:

```
db2
```

While the CLP is executing in interactive mode, it prompts you for input by means of a prompt that looks like this:

```
db2 =>
```

Any CLP input that begins with an exclamation point is interpreted as an operating system command and is directed to the operating system for execution. For example, the following line in a CLP input file would execute the operating system echo command:

```
!echo Monthly Summary
```

 TIP: When you are using the CLP to execute a series of SQL statements in a file, the !echo command can be used to generate text into the output stream, perhaps to serve as labels on the results of your queries.

The CLP will not be able to access any data until the database server has been started. The server can be started by a db2start command, which can be executed by a suitably authorized user at the CLP prompt, at the operating system prompt, or by using the Control Center (discussed in Section 10.3).

In a CLP session, you are not limited to interacting with a single database. You can connect to the database of your choice, and switch between databases, using the CONNECT statement (discussed in Section 2.7.2).

If you specify the -t option when you invoke the CLP, you must terminate each SQL statement or command with a semicolon. This option is convenient when your statements and commands span more than one input line, as is often the case. The SQL examples in this book are terminated by semicolons, as if they were entered in a CLP session with the -t option.

When you are finished with a CLP session, you can end the session by a TERMINATE command or a QUIT command. The TERMINATE command commits any transaction that is in progress, ends your database connection, if any, and ends your CLP session. The QUIT command, on the other hand, simply ends your CLP session without ending any existing transaction or database connection.

TIP: As a general rule, it is better to use TERMINATE rather than QUIT to end a CLP session. Leaving a transaction in progress between CLP sessions is a bad idea because the transaction may be holding locks that will limit access to data by other users. A database connection left active after a QUIT command can also interfere with stopping the database server or changing database configuration parameters.

3.2.1 Command Options

The -f option that directs the CLP to accept input from a file is just one of several *command options* that control the behavior of the CLP. Each of these options has a one-letter name. Some of them can be simply turned on or off, while others can be set to a particular value such as a filename. Each option has a default value that can be overridden by an explicit setting in the db2 command that starts a CLP session. In the db2 command, an option can be turned off by prefixing its letter with a + sign, or turned on by prefixing its letter with a – sign, optionally followed by a value. For example, the following command invokes the CLP with the c option turned off, the v option turned on, and the f option set to the value "infile":

```
db2 +c -v -f infile
```

During a CLP session, you can see the current settings of the command options by typing LIST COMMAND OPTIONS, and you can change the settings by using a command with the following syntax:

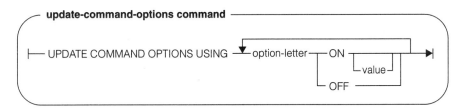

Table 3-1 summarizes the command options that are recognized by the CLP For each option, the default setting is shown in boldface type.

TABLE 3-1: CLP Command Options

Option	Value
–a	After each statement, a structure called SQLCA is displayed, containing codes that summarize the result of executing the statement.
+a	The SQLCA structure is not displayed.
–c	A COMMIT is automatically performed after each SQL statement (making your changes permanent and visible to other users).
+c	No automatic COMMIT is performed. You must execute an explicit COMMIT statement to make your changes permanent and visible to other users.
–ec	SQLCODE is displayed after each SQL statement (used mainly with +o).
–es	SQLSTATE is displayed after each SQL statement (used mainly with +o).
+e	No return code is displayed after executing an SQL statement from the operating system command line.
–f filename	The CLP takes its input from the given file. The filename may be either absolute (a path name) or relative (to the current directory).
+f	The CLP takes its input from standard input (usually your keyboard).
–l filename	All commands and SQL statements are logged in the named file, appending them to the existing content of this file, if any. Each command or statement is logged with the time of its execution (but the results of queries are not included in the log).
+l	Commands and SQL statements are not logged.
–o	Output (query results and messages) is displayed on standard output (usually your display).
+o	Output is not displayed on standard output.
–p	The CLP prompt is displayed before entry of each interactive command.
+p	No prompt is displayed.
–r filename	Results of queries are saved in the named file.
+r	Query results are not saved.
–s	If an error is encountered during execution of a statement, the CLP stops and exits to the operating system.
+s	If an error is encountered during execution of a statement, the CLP continues to the next statement.

TABLE 3-1 (*Continued*)

Option	Value
–t	The statement termination character is set to a semicolon. Input lines are concatenated until a semicolon is encountered, and the result is handled as one statement.
–td*x*	The statement termination character is set to *x*, which may be any character. For example, option -td$ indicates that input lines are to be concatenated until a $ character is encountered, and the result is to be handled as one statement. This option is useful when the semicolon character is needed for use inside an SQL statement.
+t	There is no statement termination character. Each line is considered to be a statement unless it ends with a space followed by a backslash (\).
–v	All statements and commands are echoed to standard output before they are executed.
+v	Statements and commands are not echoed.
–w	Warning messages resulting from execution of SQL statements (such as "string truncated") are displayed.
+w	Warning messages are suppressed and not displayed.
–z filename	Both query results and error messages are saved in the named file.
+z	Query results and error messages are not saved.

TIP: If you want to be able to roll back your statements, or if you want to make use of transaction atomicity across multiple statements, you will need to turn off the automatic commit feature of the CLP by using the following command:

```
UPDATE COMMAND OPTIONS USING c OFF;
```

3.3 INTERACTIVE COMMANDS

In addition to executing SQL statements, interactive tools such as the Command Center and the CLP can be used for another purpose: to execute *commands* that influence the state or behavior of a whole database or of the UDB system. The distinction between an SQL statement and a command can be subtle. The Command Center and the CLP allow you to execute commands in the same way as SQL statements: simply by typing them at the appropriate prompt. If an application program needs to execute a command, however, it must use a specialized Application Program Interface (API) rather than the EXEC SQL syntax used for SQL statements. All the available commands are described in the *Command Reference*, and their application programming interfaces are described in the *API Reference*.

Many of the commands supported by **UDB** perform database administration functions, which can be accomplished more conveniently by using the graphical user interface of the Control Center (described in Section 10.3). In this section, we will discuss a few commands that are particularly useful during interactive sessions using the Command Center or the CLP.

3.3.1 Controlling Isolation Level

Each transaction has an *isolation level* that controls the degree to which it is protected from the effects of other transactions that may be taking place concurrently. The four isolation levels supported by **UDB** are described in Section 2.7.1. By default, the Command Center and the CLP use the isolation level called Cursor Stability. The CHANGE ISOLATION command can be used to change the isolation level of future transactions—but this command can be executed only when you are not connected to a database. For example, the following command directs the Command Center or CLP to use Repeatable Read (RR)–level isolation for future transactions:

```
CHANGE ISOLATION TO RR;
```

3.3.2 Controlling Connection Type

As described in Section 2.7.2, **UDB** supports two types of database connections: Type 1, which permits connection to only one database at a time, and Type 2, which supports distributed transactions that connect to multiple databases. The behavior of Type 2 connections is further controlled by an option called SYNCPOINT, also described in Section 2.7.2, that determines how distributed transactions are coordinated.

The Command Center and the CLP, by default, acquire Type 1 connections. However, both of these tools allow you to control the database connection type and SYNCPOINT option by means of a command called SET CLIENT. For example, the following command calls for the use of Type 2 connections with a two-phase commit protocol:

```
SET CLIENT CONNECT 2 SYNCPOINT TWOPHASE;
```

Like CHANGE ISOLATION, the SET CLIENT command can be executed only when your session is not connected to a database.

You can display the current settings of the connection type, SYNCPOINT option, and other controllable client options by means of the QUERY CLIENT command, as in the following example:

```
QUERY CLIENT;
```

TIP: When using Type 2 connections, don't forget to turn off the autocommit feature that automatically commits a transaction after executing each SQL statement—otherwise, you will not be able to execute a distributed transaction.

3.3.3 Getting Help

During a Command Center session, the easiest way to get help is to click on the Help icon or the Information Center icon at the top of the window. However, an older, more text-oriented, form of help is also available in both the Command Center and the CLP. This form of help can be obtained by using a question mark as a command, as illustrated in the following examples:

?	Displays a list of all the commands supported by UDB.
? set client	Displays the syntax of a specific command such as SET CLIENT.
? SQL0204	Displays an explanation of message SQL0204, associated with SQLCODE -204.
? 42704	Displays an explanation of SQLSTATE 42704.

3.3.4 Comments

According to the SQL92 Standard, any SQL statement can contain one or more comments, and each comment begins with two hyphens and extends to the end of the line. Comments have no effect on the processing of an SQL statement.

The Command Center and the CLP allow comments to be embedded in SQL statements and in commands. However, unlike the SQL92 Standard, both of these tools require that each comment must be on a line by itself. The following example shows an SQL statement containing two comments, only one of which is acceptable to the Command Center and the CLP:

```
SELECT suppno, price
FROM quotations
-- This comment is accepted by the Command Center
WHERE partno = 'P231'    -- This comment is not
AND responsetime < 10;
```

In the SQL examples in this book, I have taken the liberty of writing SQL92-style comments on some of the lines of SQL, wherever these comments seemed to be helpful in clarifying the examples. If you want to execute the examples using the Command Center or the CLP, you will need to modify them so that each comment is on a separate line.

Static SQL

Most database users do not understand SQL and may not even realize that they are using a database. Instead of composing their own SQL statements, these users interact with application programs that perform various tasks such as making bank deposits, approving credit cards, and reserving airline tickets. The application program presents the end user with an interface that is specific to the task at hand. Under the covers, the program is using SQL statements to interact with a database to obtain the information it presents to the user.

UDB provides two ways in which an application program can interact with a database, called *static SQL* and *dynamic SQL*. In the static SQL approach, the application developer must know exactly what SQL statements are needed and must write these SQL statements directly into the application program. The program is then processed by the UDB precompiler, which converts each SQL statement into an optimized access plan and stores the plan in the database. In the application program, the original SQL statements are replaced by calls to run-time routines that load and execute the access plans. Among all the ways of using SQL, static SQL provides the highest performance because it prepares the access plan in advance and does not need to repeat this work when the application program is running. Therefore, static SQL is very well adapted to applications that perform repetitive transactions such as buying tickets or making bank deposits. Static SQL also provides a way to "encapsulate" a program that operates on the database in some specific way, allowing users of the program to perform some desired operation without granting them a generalized ability to manipulate the database.

UDB provides static SQL interfaces for C, C++, FORTRAN, and COBOL. In this chapter, we will focus on the use of static SQL with C and C++ because of their popularity on personal computer and workstation platforms. Use of static SQL with other programming languages is discussed in the *Embedded SQL Programming Guide*.

The alternative to static SQL is dynamic SQL, in which the application program presents SQL statements to the database at run time. Dynamic SQL incurs the cost of access path selection at run time, but in exchange it gives your program the flexibility to execute SQL statements that were not known in advance. UDB provides dynamic SQL interfaces for C, C++, FORTRAN, COBOL, REXX, and Java. Dynamic SQL is discussed in Chapter 8.

4.1 USING STATIC SQL IN C PROGRAMS

Each SQL statement embedded in a C program must be prefixed by the words EXEC SQL to identify the statement to the SQL precompiler. Each SQL statement ends with a semicolon and may include more than one line. The precompiler processes all the SQL statements, replacing them with pure C statements that call the database manager. The precompiler also prepares for each SQL statement a *section*, which encapsulates a plan for executing the statement. At run time, when the C program calls the database manager to execute a given SQL statement, the database manager loads and executes one of the sections. All the sections that encapsulate the SQL statements in a given program are collectively called a *package*. The SQL precompiler produces a package for each program that it processes, and stores the packages in the database.

SQL statements embedded in C programs may contain SQL-style comments, which begin with two hyphens and extend to the end of the line. Unlike the Command Center and the CLP, the SQL precompiler does not require each comment to be on a line by itself. Outside of SQL statements, of course, comments must use the normal C syntax.

A character-string constant inside an SQL statement can be continued on the next line of your application program by using the line continuation character (a backslash), as in the following example:

```
EXEC SQL DELETE FROM parts
WHERE description LIKE '%Surplus%\
Equipment%';
```

Database applications written in C and C++ should always include the following C preprocessor statement:

```
#include <sqlenv.h>
```

The header file sqlenv.h (found in sqllib/include), and the other header files that it includes in turn, contain declarations of the structures, functions, and constants that your program will need to interact with the database.

TIP: Since the SQL precompiler is usually invoked before the C preprocessor, it is a good practice to make the SQL statements in your program independent of C preprocessor facilities such as #define and #include. If your SQL statements require material to be included from another file, you can use an INCLUDE statement that is processed by the SQL precompiler, as in the following example:

```
EXEC SQL INCLUDE 'myfile.sqc';
```

4.1.1 Host Variables

Section 2.4.1 discussed how expressions in SQL statements can be built from primitive operands such as constants and column names. One of these primitive operands is a *host variable*, which is the name of a variable declared in the program in which the SQL statement is embedded. The name of a host variable is distinguished from the name of a database column by a colon prefix. For example, the expression x+y represents the value of column x added to the value of column y, but the expression x+:y represents the value of column x added to the content of host variable y. When a variable is used to retrieve a value from the database into the host program, it is called an *output host variable*. On the other hand, when a variable is given a value by the host program and this value is used by an SQL statement, the variable is called an *input host variable*. The following examples show how input host variables can be used in data manipulation statements. Note that each statement begins with the prefix EXEC SQL to mark it for processing by the SQL precompiler.

- Insert a new row into the SUPPLIERS table from input host variables.

```
EXEC SQL
    INSERT INTO SUPPLIERS(suppno, name, address)
        VALUES (:suppno, :sname, :saddr);
```

- Update the price and response time of a specific quotation, based on values in input host variables.

```
EXEC SQL
    UPDATE quotations
    SET price = :newprice,
        responsetime = :newresponse
    WHERE suppno = :suppno
    AND partno = :partno;
```

TIP: Since database columns and host variables are not in the same name space, you can name your host variables after the columns with which they compare or exchange data. This practice can be useful in remembering how your host variables are used.

As a general rule, a host variable used in an SQL statement should be a simple identifier without any host language modifiers such as subscripts. For example, :x is a valid host variable reference, but :x[5] or :x.salary or :x->salary are not valid for use in an SQL statement. The only host language operator that can be applied to a host variable in an SQL statement is the dereference operator (such as :*x), and it may be used only if the host variable is declared to be a pointer type (see Appendix E for the syntax for declaring pointers).

TABLE 4-1: Interpretation of Indicator Variables

Indicator Value	Interpretation
(positive)	Output host variable contains a non-null string value that was truncated to fit. Indicator value is the original length of the string value before truncation. For input host variables, a positive indicator value is equivalent to a zero indicator value.
0	Host variable contains a non-null value.
-1	Host variable contains a null value. Used to represent null values fetched from the database.
-2	Applies to output host variables only. Host variable contains a null value that resulted from an arithmetic error such as an overflow. Used only if "friendly arithmetic" was turned on (database configuration parameter DFT_SQLMATHWARN = YES) at the time when your program was bound.

When exchanging values between the database and a host program, we need to solve the problem of how to represent null values. This problem arises because SQL datatypes (such as Integer) allow null values, but host programming language datatypes (such as long in C) do not. UDB (and all the other DB2 products) solve this problem by allowing each host variable to be associated with a second, auxiliary variable called an *indicator variable*. In general, a negative indicator variable represents a null value, and a zero or positive indicator variable represents a non-null value (details are shown in Table 4-1).

In an SQL expression, each host variable may optionally be followed by its indicator variable. Both variables are prefixed by colons, and the indicator variable may be identified by the keyword INDICATOR, as shown in the following syntax:

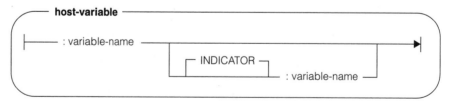

If a host variable has no indicator variable, it cannot be used to represent null values. Any attempt to retrieve a null value into such a variable will result in an error condition.

The UPDATE statement in the example above might be revised by associating indicator variables with the input variables for the new price and new response time, as shown below. This revised example allows the host program to represent null values for prices and response times.

```
EXEC SQL    -- Note price and responsetime may be null
    UPDATE quotations
    SET price = :newprice :indic1,
        responsetime = :newresponse :indic2
    WHERE suppno = :suppno
    AND partno = :partno;
```

4.1.2 The SQL Declare Section

All variables used in a C or C++ program must be declared so that they can be processed properly by the compiler. In addition, the declarations of host variables that are used in SQL statements must be marked for processing by the SQL precompiler. These requirements are met by an *SQL Declare Section*, which must contain the declarations for all host variables and indicator variables that are used in any SQL statement in the program.

As a general rule, the SQL Declare Section contains declarations written in host language syntax. Each SQL datatype is associated with a host language datatype that is used for exchanging values between host programs and the database. The C datatypes that correspond to the basic single-byte SQL datatypes are shown in Table 4-2.

TIP: Although there is no C-language equivalent for the Decimal datatype, you can exchange Decimal values with a C program by converting them either to character strings or to floating-point values. These conversions can be done by using built-in functions: the char and decimal functions can be used to convert between the Decimal and Char datatypes, and the double and decimal functions can be used to convert between the Decimal and Double datatypes. Datatype conversion is also performed automatically if you assign a database value of type Decimal to a host variable of type float or double, or vice versa.

In addition to the datatypes listed in Table 4-2, **UDB** supports some datatypes for handling large objects. Declaration of host variables for exchanging values using these datatypes involves some special considerations, which are discussed in Section 6.1.

In the structured form of a host variable for exchanging Varchar data, the length field of the structure indicates the number of bytes in the data field that are occupied by the data value. On input, the length field must be set by your program, and its value must be less than the declared length of the data field. On output, the length field is set by the system to the length of the output value (truncated if necessary to the declared length of the data field).

TABLE 4-2: C Datatypes Corresponding to Basic SQL Datatypes

SQL Datatype	C Datatype
Smallint and indicator variables	`short`
Integer	`long`
Decimal(p,s)	(no C equivalent)
Real	`float`
Double	`double`
Char(n)	`char[n+1]` (null-terminated)

Varchar(n)	`char[n+1]` (null-terminated)
	 or
	 `struct`
	 `    {`
	 `    short length;`
	 `    char data[n];`
	 `    }`

Date	`char[11]`
Time	`char[9]`
Timestamp	`char[27]`

You may have multiple SQL Declare Sections in your C program. Each Declare Section must be at some location in your program where C declarations are valid, and must be contained between the statements EXEC SQL BEGIN DECLARE SECTION and EXEC SQL END DECLARE SECTION. The SQL precompiler will remove these bracketing statements and leave the variable declarations in their original place in your C program. Each SQL Declare Section must occur before any SQL statements that use the host variables that it declares.

The variables declared in an SQL Declare Section obey the usual scoping rules when used in C statements. However, the SQL precompiler considers host variables to be global to all SQL statements in the program (compilation unit). Therefore, the name of each variable declared in an SQL Declare Section must be unique in the program.

Inside an SQL Declare Section embedded in a C program, you may use either C-style comments (which begin with /* and end with */) or SQL-style comments (which begin with - - and end with a line break).

The following is an example of an SQL Declare Section that might be embedded near the top of a C program. As you can see, inside the SQL Declare Section, the names of host variables are not prefixed by colons.

```
EXEC SQL BEGIN DECLARE SECTION;
    long qonhand, qonorder, threshold;    /* Integers   */
    char suppno[4];                       /* Char(3)    */
    char partno[5];                       /* Char(4)    */
    char orderdate[11];                   /* Date       */
    struct
        {
        short length;
        char data[50];
        } sname, saddr;                   /* Varchar(50) */
    short indic1=0, indic2=0, indic3=0;   /* Indicators */
EXEC SQL END DECLARE SECTION;
```

Inside an SQL Declare Section, declarations must obey the following rules:

- The names of host variables must not exceed 255 characters in length and must not begin with the characters EXEC or SQL.

- A declaration may include a storage class specification such as static or extern.

- Multiple variables can be declared and initialized on a single line. However, variables can be initialized only by "=" notation, not by "( )" notation, as in the following examples:
```
int x = 7;   /* OK           */
int x(7);    /* not accepted */
```

(More details about the syntax of host variable declarations can be found in Appendix E.)

4.1.3 Exchanging Double-Byte Strings

The Graphic and Vargraphic datatypes are used to store character data in which the character encodings are larger than one byte, as in the case of many Asian languages.

Two different formats are used for representing double-byte data:

- In *multibyte format* (sometimes called *DBCS format*), each character is encoded in two bytes. This format is always used inside the database for storing Graphic and Vargraphic data.

- In *wide-character format*, each character is encoded as a wchar_t, which is defined by your C compiler and which may be two or four bytes. The IBM CSet++ compiler (in the header file stddef.h) defines wchar_t as a two-byte datatype (unsigned short). Wide-character format is not used inside the database, but it is used by many C and C++ compilers. Compilers often provide libraries of functions for manipulating strings in wide-character format. The wide-character string library is declared in wstring.h and includes functions such as wstrcpy, wstrcat, wstrlen, and many others. C and C++ compilers also recognize L-type literals, such as the one below, and represent them using wide-character format.

     L"三つ子の魂百まで"

Since multibyte format is used inside the database but many compiler facilities are based on wide-character format, you may wish your graphic data to be converted from multibyte to wide-character format when it is fetched into an output variable, and to be converted from wide-character to multibyte format when it is read from an input variable. If you specify the precompiler option WCHARTYPE CONVERT, the system will perform these conversions for you automatically. If you specify the precompiler option WCHARTYPE NOCONVERT or allow this option to default, no automatic conversions will be performed, and all input and output variables will be processed in multibyte format, using two bytes per character.

The datatype that you should use in an SQL Declare Section for declaring graphic-type host variables depends on which precompiler option you choose. If you specify WCHARTYPE CONVERT, your host variables for graphic data should be declared as arrays of wchar_t. On the other hand, if you accept the default or specify WCHARTYPE NOCONVERT, your graphic host variables should be declared as arrays of sqldbchar, which is a platform-independent two-byte datatype that is defined in sql.h. The formats of the declarations to be used in the SQL Declare Section are summarized in Table 4-3.

If you precompile your program with WCHARTYPE NOCONVERT (the default), you can explicitly convert between multibyte and wide-character formats in both directions, using the C functions mbstowcs and wcstombs. For more information about double-byte data, see the *Embedded SQL Programming Guide*.

TIP: Remember that C and SQL have different ways of expressing double-byte literals (constant strings of double-byte characters). An L-type literal in C code looks like L"double-byte data" and is represented in wide-character format. An SQL double-byte literal looks like G'double-byte data' or N'double-byte data' and is represented in multibyte format. When initializing a double-byte variable in an SQL Declare Section, use an L-type literal and perform conversions as necessary.

TABLE 4-3: C Datatypes Used with Double-Byte Data

SQL Datatype	C Datatype used with WCHARTYPE NOCONVERT	C Datatype used with WCHARTYPE CONVERT
Graphic(n)	sqldbchar[n+1] (null-terminated)	wchar_t[n+1] (null-terminated)
Vargraphic(n)	sqldbchar[n+1] (null-terminated) *or* struct { short length; sqldbchar data[n]; }	wchar_t[n+1] (null-terminated) *or* struct { short length; wchar_t data[n]; }

4.1.4 Return Codes and Messages

When your application program is running, each SQL statement that is exe-cuted returns a status code and possibly some additional information. The information is returned in a structure called an SQLCA, which is declared (in the header file sqlca.h) as follows:

```
struct sqlca
   {
   unsigned char sqlcaid[8];     /* eye-catcher: "SQLCA" */
   long          sqlabc;         /* length of SQLCA      */
   long          sqlcode;        /* result code          */
   short         sqlerrml;       /* length of msg tokens */
   unsigned char sqlerrmc[70];   /* message tokens       */
   unsigned char sqlerrp[8];     /* product code         */
   long          sqlerrd[6];     /* row counts           */
   unsigned char sqlwarn[11];    /* warning flags        */
   unsigned char sqlstate[5];    /* standard result code */
   };
```

The meaning of the fields inside the SQLCA structure is as follows:

sqlcaid: Contains the string "SQLCA ".

sqlabc: Contains 136, the length in bytes of the SQLCA structure.

sqlcode: Contains a code indicating the result of executing an SQL statement. In general, zero indicates normal execution, negative codes indicate error conditions, and positive codes indicate warnings or special conditions such as "data not found." Codes returned in this field are product specific and may have different meanings for different database products. The meanings of the codes returned by UDB are documented in the *Message Reference*.

sqlerrml: Contains the actual length of the data contained in the sqlerrmc field.

sqlerrmc: Contains zero or more tokens, separated by X'FF', that provide specific information to be used with the error message that corresponds to a given return code. For example, if the return code indicates "table not found in database," the sqlerrmc field will contain the name of the table that was not found.

sqlerrp: After a successful CONNECT statement, this field contains an eight-character "signature" code that identifies the product and version. For example, SQL05000 denotes DB2 Universal Database Version 5, Release 0, Modification Level 0. When sqlcode indicates an error, sqlerrp identifies the internal UDB module that generated the error code.

sqlerrd: An array of six integers containing additional diagnostic information. The following entries in this array contain information that is meaningful to a user:

    sqlerrd[2] (the third integer in the array) contains the number of rows that were modified by an INSERT, DELETE, or UPDATE statement.

    sqlerrd[4] (the fifth integer in the array) contains the number of rows that were modified by triggers or by enforcement of foreign key constraints (discussed in Section 7.1).

    sqlerrd[5] (the sixth integer in the array) contains the node number of the node on which an error was encountered in a parallel UDB system.

sqlwarn: An array of characters, normally blank, that are set to "W" if certain warning conditions occur. The following warning conditions are defined:

    sqlwarn[0] is set to "W" if any of the other warning characters are set to "W."

    sqlwarn[1] indicates that a character-string value was truncated on retrieval.

    sqlwarn[2] indicates that some of the values passed to a column function were null (these values are ignored).

    sqlwarn[3] indicates that the number of values retrieved from the database was not equal to the number of host variables provided to receive them.

    sqlwarn[4] indicates that an UPDATE or DELETE statement does not include a WHERE clause and will therefore affect all the rows of a table.

    sqlwarn[6] indicates that the result of a date calculation was adjusted to avoid an impossible date, such as February 31.

sqlwarn[8] indicates that a string value contained a character that could not be converted to the desired code page, and was replaced by a substitute character.

sqlwarn[9] indicates that the result of a column function may be incorrect because expressions containing arithmetic errors were ignored, due to "friendly arithmetic" (database configuration DFT_SQLMATHWARN=YES).

sqlwarn[10] indicates that a code-page conversion error occurred when setting one of the fields of the SQLCA structure.

sqlstate: An array of five characters that indicates the result of executing an SQL statement. The five-character sqlstate codes are defined by the ANSI/ISO SQL92 Standard, so they are more portable from one database product to another than are the numeric codes used in sqlcode. The first two characters of the sqlstate identify an *error class* such as "syntax error," and are uniform across all SQL implementations that conform to the Standard. The last three characters of the sqlstate identify an *error subclass*, which may be implementation dependent.

The easiest way to declare an SQLCA structure in your application program is to use the following statement:

```
EXEC SQL INCLUDE SQLCA;
```

This statement includes the definition of the SQLCA structure into your program, and also declares one instance of this structure with the name sqlca. Thus, you can refer to the various parts of the structure using qualified names such as sqlca.sqlcode and sqlca.sqlstate[0]. In addition, since the field sqlca.sqlcode is used a lot, the INCLUDE SQLCA statement defines a shorthand name, SQLCODE, as equivalent to sqlca.sqlcode.

The easiest way to obtain the detailed error message that corresponds to the codes inside a given SQLCA structure is to use a utility routine named sqlaintp. This routine takes an SQLCA structure and returns a null-terminated character string containing the message associated with the codes in that structure, complete with the sqlerrmc tokens inserted into the message in the proper places, ready for display. The interface to this utility routine (declared in the header file sql.h) is as follows:

```
int sqlaintp
    (
    char *buffer,        /* message buffer              */
    short buff_size,     /* size of message buffer      */
    short line_width,    /* desired line width          */
    struct sqlca *sqlca  /* to be decoded into a message */
    );
```

The first parameter to `sqlaintp` is a pointer to a buffer that you have allocated for receiving the decoded message. The second parameter indicates the size of the buffer, and the third parameter indicates how you would like the message to be formatted (maximum number of characters between line breaks). Most messages will fit into a buffer of 512 bytes. A positive return code from `sqlaintp` indicates the length of the message, and a negative return code indicates that no message could be returned for the given codes.

TIP: Remember that you can use the "?" command interactively to display the full message associated with any given SQLCODE or SQLSTATE, as described in Section 3.3.3.

4.1.5 WHENEVER Statement

Each time your application program executes an SQL statement, a code indicating the outcome of the statement is returned in the SQLCA structure. To guard against errors, you will probably want to check the content of the SQLCA after each statement is executed. To make it easy for you to perform these checks, the SQL precompilers provide a facility called a WHENEVER statement.

Although the WHENEVER statement is prefixed by EXEC SQL like other SQL statements, it is not an executable statement. Instead, it causes the precompiler to automatically generate code in your program to check the SQLCA after each SQL statement. The generated code will cause your program either to branch to some indicated label or to continue normal execution, depending on the content of the SQLCA. The syntax of a WHENEVER statement is as follows:[1]

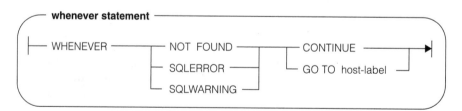

You can have as many WHENEVER statements as you like, and you can put them anywhere in your program. The behavior of your program after execution of each SQL statement is determined as follows:

---

1. The prefix EXEC SQL is omitted from this and other syntax diagrams. However, this prefix is required on all SQL statements embedded in host programs.

- If the SQL statement is successful (SQLCODE = 0), control passes to the next statement in your program.
- If the SQL statement returns SQLCODE +100, indicating that no data rows were found to satisfy your request, the previous WHENEVER NOT FOUND statement in your program (in listing order, not necessarily in execution order) is effective. This SQLCODE might be returned by a FETCH, UPDATE, or DELETE statement, or by a "single-row SELECT" statement (described in Section 4.1.10).
- If the SQL statement returns any other positive SQLCODE or any warning condition, the previous WHENEVER SQLWARNING statement in your program (again, in listing order) is effective.
- If the SQL statement returns any negative SQLCODE, indicating an error condition, the previous WHENEVER SQLERROR statement in your program (in listing order) is effective.

The WHENEVER statement that is effective, according to the rules above, will cause your program to either continue normal execution or branch to the label indicated in the GO TO clause of the WHENEVER statement. The GO TO clause simply contains a label of a host language statement, optionally prefixed by a colon. If no WHENEVER statement is effective for the condition indicated in the SQLCA structure, the default behavior is CONTINUE.

Using WHENEVER statements, you can define up to three routines for handling exceptional conditions at any given point in your program: one for errors, one for warnings, and one for "not found" conditions. Inside these handlers is a good place to call the `sqlaintp` utility routine to retrieve the message associated with the codes that are found in the SQLCA structure.

TIP: You should be extra careful if you use SQL statements inside an error-handling routine that is invoked by WHENEVER SQLERROR. If one of these SQL statements encounters an error, it can potentially put your program into an infinite loop.

The following lines of code might be embedded in a C program to define the actions desired when exceptional conditions are detected:

```
EXEC SQL WHENEVER NOTFOUND GO TO end_of_loop;
EXEC SQL WHENEVER SQLERROR GO TO print_message;
EXEC SQL WHENEVER SQLWARNING CONTINUE;
```

TIP: If you intend a WHENEVER statement to apply only to a specific part of your program (such as a function or subroutine), you must limit its scope by another WHENEVER statement at the end of the section to which it applies. Remember that WHENEVER is not an executable statement, but is interpreted by the SQL precompiler. The precompiler does not understand the scoping rules of your host language, and it assumes that each WHENEVER statement applies until another WHENEVER statement is encountered in your program listing for the same condition.

4.1.6 Cursor Declarations

INSERT, DELETE, and UPDATE statements are relatively simple to embed in application programs—they execute, possibly modifying the content of the database, and return an SQLCA structure indicating what happened. But embedded queries are more complex, because they need to return data to the application program, and the number of rows to be returned is usually not known in advance. In order to write a program that retrieves data from a database, you need a mechanism that specifies the rows to be retrieved and then fetches these rows into your program, one at a time. This mechanism is called a *cursor.*

A cursor is like a name that is associated with a query. A *cursor declaration* is used to declare the name of the cursor and to specify its associated query. Three statements, called OPEN, FETCH, and CLOSE, operate on cursors. An OPEN statement prepares the cursor for retrieval of the first row in the result set. A FETCH statement retrieves one row of the result set into some designated variables in the host program. After each FETCH statement, the cursor is said to be *positioned* on the row of the result set that was just fetched. FETCH statements are usually executed repeatedly until all the rows of the result set have been fetched (this condition is indicated by SQLCODE +100 and SQL-STATE 02000). A CLOSE statement releases any resources used by the cursor when it is no longer needed (if needed again, the cursor can be reopened).

The syntax of a cursor declaration is shown on the following page (see also "Dynamic Cursor Declaration" on page 517). A cursor declaration declares the name of the cursor (which must be different from all other cursor names in the same program), and associates it with a particular query. The syntax of a query is given on page 63. The cursor declaration does not specify where the results of the query are to be delivered—that's the job of the FETCH statement.

A query used in a cursor declaration may include some host variables. For example, the following statement associates the cursor name c1 with a query that finds parts in the PARTS table for which the quantity on order is greater than an input host variable named :threshold.

```
EXEC SQL DECLARE c1 CURSOR FOR
    SELECT partno, qonhand, qonorder
    FROM parts
    WHERE qonorder > :threshold
    ORDER BY partno;
```

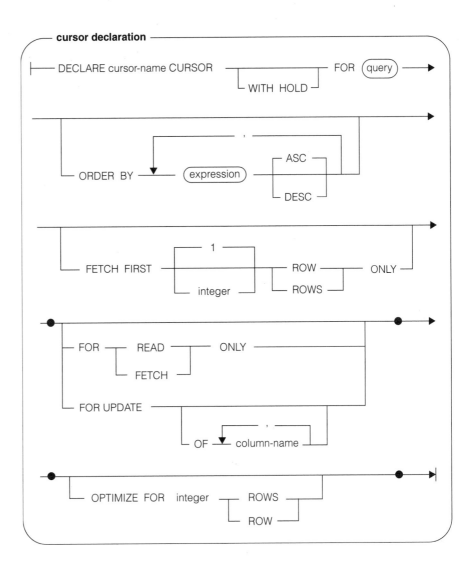

cursor declaration

DECLARE cursor-name CURSOR — [WITH HOLD] — FOR (query)

ORDER BY (expression) [ASC / DESC]

FETCH FIRST [1 / integer] [ROW / ROWS] ONLY

FOR [READ / FETCH] ONLY
FOR UPDATE OF column-name

OPTIMIZE FOR integer [ROWS / ROW]

TIP: It's bad form for a query in an application program to use the phrase SELECT * to indicate that all the columns of a table are to be retrieved. This is because, if the table is later expanded with an additional column, the program will have no host variable into which to receive the new column, and so will be unable to accept delivery of "all the columns." However, such a program will continue to run, retrieving the values of all the columns that were present when the program was bound.

A cursor declaration may contain the following optional clauses:

WITH HOLD: This clause causes the cursor to remain open after a COMMIT statement. COMMIT statements, discussed in Section 2.7.1, are used to make database changes permanent. Ordinarily, all open cursors are closed by a COMMIT statement. Cursors defined WITH HOLD remain open but release their locks (the position of the cursor becomes "before" the next row of the result set).

ORDER BY: This clause, like the ORDER BY clause in a SELECT statement, specifies the order in which the rows of the result set are to be delivered. If no ORDER BY clause is provided, the rows are delivered in a system-determined order that may not be the same from one execution to the next. (For an explanation of the ORDER BY clause, see Section 2.4.10.)

FETCH FIRST *N* ROWS ONLY: This clause, like the similar clause in a SELECT statement, limits the result set of the query to a designated number of rows.

FOR READ ONLY: This clause declares that you do not intend to use the cursor for a *positioned UPDATE* or *positioned DELETE* statement. These statements, described in Section 4.1.11, can be used to update or delete the row on which a cursor is positioned. However, if a cursor is to be used in this way, certain query processing methods are ruled out. Declaring your cursor FOR READ ONLY signals the system that it is free to use any method for process-ing the query associated with the cursor. This may result in better perfor-mance for your query. If you declare a cursor FOR READ ONLY and then use it in a positioned UPDATE or DELETE statement, an error will result.

FOR UPDATE: This clause is used to declare the columns that you plan to update by means of positioned updates that refer to this cursor. This infor-mation is useful to the query optimizer. If you specify FOR UPDATE but do not list the columns to be updated, the optimizer will assume that you may apply a positioned update to any (or all) columns of the result set. If a cur-sor definition includes a FOR UPDATE clause, it may not include an ORDER BY or FETCH FIRST clause.

OPTIMIZE FOR *N* ROWS: This clause advises the query optimizer that you expect to fetch only *N* rows of the result set associated with this cursor. This may affect the method used to process your query. If you omit this clause, the optimizer will assume that you plan to fetch the entire result set. Unlike the FETCH FIRST clause, the OPTIMIZE FOR clause does not change the actual result set that can be fetched by the cursor.

The following example declares a cursor that will be used to retrieve certain rows from the PARTS table and that may be used for a positioned update of the QONORDER column. The FOR UPDATE clause tells the optimizer that it would be a bad idea to process this query by scanning over the PARTS table using the QONORDER index, since the ordering of rows in this index may change as the column is updated.

```
EXEC SQL DECLARE c2 CURSOR FOR
    SELECT partno, qonhand, qonorder
    FROM parts
    WHERE qonhand < 100
    FOR UPDATE OF qonorder;
```

TIP: It is a good practice for all of your cursor declarations to include either a FOR UPDATE clause (if you plan to use positioned updates or deletes with the cursor) or a FOR READ ONLY clause (if you do not plan to use positioned statements). This makes your intentions explicit and gives the system the best opportunity to optimize the performance of your query.[2]

4.1.7 OPEN Statement

An OPEN statement prepares a cursor for fetching the rows in the result set. Any input variables in the query associated with the cursor are evaluated when the cursor is opened. As long as the cursor is open, it has a *position* in the result set of the query. This position may be *on* a row, or *before* or *after* a row. The OPEN statement positions the cursor before the first row of the result set.

The syntax of an OPEN statement is as follows (see also "Dynamic Open Statement" on page 517):

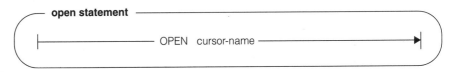

Example:

```
EXEC SQL OPEN c1;
```

---

2. If you don't follow this advice, and declare a cursor without specifying either FOR UPDATE or FOR READ ONLY, the status of your cursor depends on a precompiler option. If you precompile your program with the option LANGLEVEL MIA or LANGLEVEL SQL92E, the system will assume that your cursor can be used for a positioned update of any column (unless it is not updatable for one of the reasons listed in Section 4.1.11). If you precompile with the option LANGLEVEL SAA1 or with no LANGLEVEL option, the system will assume that your cursor is FOR READ ONLY.

4.1.8 FETCH Statement

A FETCH statement fetches the row of the result set that is next after the current position of the cursor and delivers it into the host variables listed. The cursor named in the FETCH statement must be open. If there is no row after the current position of the cursor, the FETCH statement returns SQLCODE +100 (SQLSTATE 02000), and the host variables are unchanged. The position of the cursor is advanced to be *on* the row that was just fetched.

The syntax of a FETCH statement is as follows (see also "Dynamic Fetch Statement" on page 518):

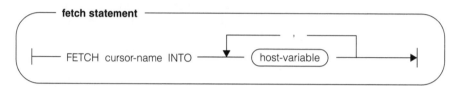

Example:

```
EXEC SQL FETCH c1
INTO :partno :indic1, :qonhand :indic2, :qonorder :indic3;
```

The host variables used in a FETCH statement must be type compatible with the values that are fetched into them (for a summary of compatibility rules, see Section 6.6). If any of the columns of the result set allow null values, the host variables associated with these columns must have indicator variables.

Depending on the access plan chosen by the optimizer, the result of the query associated with a cursor may be completely materialized and saved in a temporary table at the time when the first row is fetched, or it may be materialized one row at a time in response to individual FETCH statements. If the result is materialized in a temporary table, it will not reflect database changes that occur after the first fetch; on the other hand, if the result set is materialized as each row is fetched, it will reflect such changes. Since the optimizer reserves the right to choose how the query will be processed, whether the result is materialized at first fetch time cannot, in general, be predicted.

When character-string data is fetched into a host variable, truncation may take place if the host variable is not large enough to hold the fetched value. The sqlwarn[1] flag in the SQLCA structure and the indicator (if any) provided with the host variable are used together to provide a warning when truncation occurs, according to the following rules:[3]

---

3. These rules assume that your application has been precompiled with the option LANG-LEVEL SAA1, which is the default. An alternative set of truncation rules, invoked by the option LANGLEVEL SQL92E, is described in the *Embedded SQL Programming Guide*.

1. If the fetched value, including its null terminator, fits into the host variable (for example, a column value of type Char(5) is fetched into a host variable of type char[6]):

    The value is copied into the host variable with a null terminator.

    sqlcode is set to zero, and sqlstate is set to "00000".

    sqlwarn[1] is set to blank.

    The indicator variable, if any, is set to zero.

2. If the fetched value fits into the host variable, but there is no room for the null terminator (for example, a column value of type Char(5) is fetched into a host variable of type char[5]):

    The value is copied into the host variable with no null terminator.

    sqlcode is set to zero, and sqlstate is set to "01004".

    sqlwarn[1] is set to "N".

    The indicator variable, if any, is set to zero.

3. If the fetched value is too long to fit into the host variable (for example, a column value of type Char(5) is fetched into a host variable of type char[4]):

    The host variable is filled with as many bytes of the fetched value as will fit, not including a null terminator.

    sqlcode is set to zero, and sqlstate is set to "01004."

    sqlwarn[1] is set to "W."

    The indicator variable, if any, is set to the original length of the fetched value, before truncation.[4]

4.1.9 CLOSE Statement

A CLOSE statement closes a cursor and releases any resources that it may be holding, such as a temporary copy of the result set. If a closed cursor is later opened again, its input variables are evaluated again, its query is executed again, and the cursor is positioned before the first row of the new result set.

The syntax of a CLOSE statement is as follows:

---

4. For large-object datatypes (described in Section 6.1), the original length of the string is not returned in the indicator variable.

Example:

```
EXEC SQL CLOSE c1;
```

The optional phrase WITH RELEASE tells the system that it can release any read-locks that are associated with this cursor. This is meaningful only if you are using an isolation level of *Repeatable Read* (RR) or *Read Stability* (RS), as described in Section 2.7.1. These isolation levels cause the system to acquire locks on the rows that you fetch, to guarantee that if you close the cursor and reopen it later, the rows will be unchanged. These locks are ordinarily held until the end of a transaction, but you can release them earlier by closing a cursor WITH RELEASE.

4.1.10 Single-Row SELECT and VALUES Statements

As we have seen, the usual way to retrieve data from the database into a host program is to write a query specifying the data to be retrieved, declare a cursor for the query, open the cursor, and fetch the rows of the result set into host variables. In some cases, however, you may know that the result of your query consists of a single row. For example, if your query invokes a column function such as SUM or AVG (and does not have a GROUP BY clause), it will always return exactly one row of data. In a case like this, it seems unnecessary to declare a cursor, open it, fetch one row, and then close the cursor.

SQL provides a shortcut method for retrieving the result of a query into a list of host variables when the query is known to return no more than one row. The method is called a *single-row SELECT statement* (or, if the query consists of a literal table, a *single-row VALUES statement*).

A single-row SELECT statement is simply a query block, with an INTO clause following the SELECT clause to specify the host variables into which the result is to be delivered. The query block is executed, and if the result is a single row, the row is delivered into the host variables in the INTO clause. If the result set of the query is empty, SQLCODE +100 and SQLSTATE 02000 are returned and the host variables are unchanged. If the result set consists of more than one row, an error results.

A single-row VALUES statement is a literal table consisting of a single row, followed by an INTO clause that specifies the host variables into which the row is to be delivered. A single-row VALUES statement might be used, for example, to retrieve the current date and time into host program variables. Like a single-row SELECT, a single-row VALUES statement raises an error if the literal table contains more than one row. A literal table used in a single-row VALUES statement cannot contain a NULL column, unless the null value is given an explicit datatype by a CAST expression.

Of course, single-row SELECT and single-row VALUES statements can be used only by embedding them in host programs, prefixed by EXEC SQL. The syntaxes of the single-row statements are shown on page 170.

The following example finds the total number of gears on hand and on order, and delivers these numbers into two host variables with null indicators. If there are no rows in the PARTS table whose descriptions satisfy the LIKE predicate, the column functions will return null values.

```
EXEC SQL
    SELECT sum(qonhand), sum(qonorder)
    INTO :gearsonhand :indic1, :gearsonorder :indic2
    FROM parts
    WHERE description LIKE '%Gear%';
```

The following example retrieves the current date and time into two host variables:

```
EXEC SQL
    VALUES(CURRENT DATE, CURRENT TIME)
    INTO :today, :rightnow;
```

4.1.11 Positioned UPDATE and DELETE Statements

In addition to their use in retrieving query results into host programs, cursors can play a role in updating and deleting rows of data in the database. A special form of the UPDATE statement, called a *positioned UPDATE statement*, can be used to update exactly one row in the database, based on the position of a cursor. In a positioned update, instead of a search condition, the WHERE clause contains the phrase "CURRENT OF" followed by a cursor name. The statement updates the single row on which the named cursor is positioned. Similarly, the DELETE statement has a special form called a *positioned DELETE statement*, which names a cursor in the WHERE clause and deletes the single row on which this cursor is positioned.

Apart from their method of finding the row to be updated or deleted, positioned UPDATE and DELETE statements behave exactly the same as UPDATE and DELETE statements that contain a search condition. In fact, rather than drawing a special syntax diagram for the positioned statements, we will simply refer to the syntax diagrams for the UPDATE statement on page 76 and for the DELETE statement on page 78. To convert these diagrams into syntax diagrams for positioned UPDATE and DELETE statements, simply replace the WHERE clause with the "positioned" WHERE clause shown on page 171.

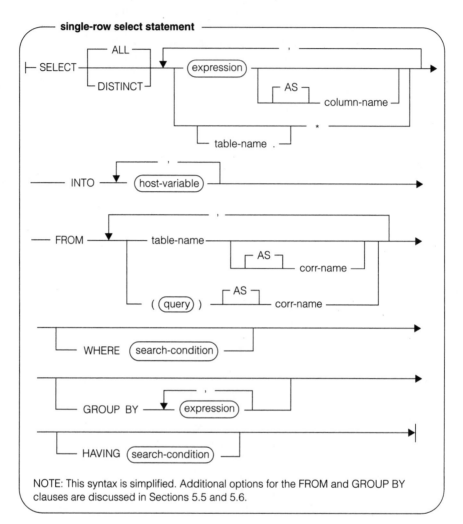

single-row select statement

NOTE: This syntax is simplified. Additional options for the FROM and GROUP BY clauses are discussed in Sections 5.5 and 5.6.

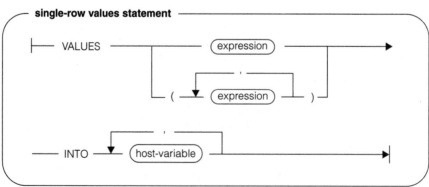

single-row values statement

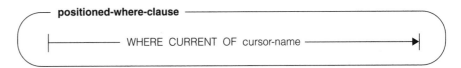

positioned-where-clause

WHERE CURRENT OF cursor-name

The following are some examples of positioned statements. (Remember that the prefix EXEC SQL is required before any statement that is embedded in a host program.)

- Update the row of the QUOTATIONS table on which the cursor C10 is positioned.

```
EXEC SQL
    UPDATE quotations
    SET price = 900,
        responsetime = 14
    WHERE CURRENT OF c10;
```

- Delete the row of the SUPPLIERS table on which the cursor C20 is positioned.

```
EXEC SQL
    DELETE FROM suppliers
    WHERE CURRENT OF c20;
```

When the row on which a cursor is positioned is deleted, the cursor's position becomes "before" the next row of the result set (or, if there is no next row, "after" the last row of the result set). Note that a positioned delete is one way (but not the only way) in which the row on which a cursor is positioned might be deleted.

In order to be used in a positioned UPDATE or DELETE statement, a cursor must meet certain requirements. Some of these requirements pertain to the cursor itself, and some pertain to the query that is associated with the cursor (in its DECLARE CURSOR statement), which we will refer to as the *cursor query*. The purpose of these requirements is to make sure that the current row of the cursor uniquely identifies a row in the database that can be updated or deleted. The requirements are as follows:

1. The cursor query must have exactly one table or view in its FROM clause, and this must be the same table or view that is named in the positioned UPDATE or DELETE statement. If it is a view, it must not be a read-only view (defined in Section 2.6.5).

2. The cursor query may not contain any of the following features, which make it impossible to identify a unique row in the database that corresponds to the current row of the cursor:

- DISTINCT, GROUP BY, or HAVING
- A column function such as AVG, MAX, MIN, SUM, COUNT, STDEV, or VARIANCE

- A set operator such as UNION, INTERSECT, or EXCEPT, with or without the ALL option

3. The cursor declaration must not include an ORDER BY or FETCH FIRST clause.

4. The cursor declaration should include a FOR UPDATE clause.[5] In the case of a positioned update, the FOR UPDATE clause must include the names of the columns to be updated (or it may omit the column list, implicitly applying to all columns).

5. The cursor must be open and positioned on a row (i.e., a FETCH statement must have been executed on the cursor).

4.1.12 Using Cursors with Interactive SQL

Since one of the purposes of a cursor is to deliver the rows of a query result, one at a time, into host program variables, you might expect cursors to be used only in application programs with embedded SQL. Surprisingly, however, the Command Center and the CLP can be used to execute cursor declarations; OPEN, FETCH, and CLOSE statements; and positioned updates and deletes. Of course, when one of these statements is executed interactively, it is not prefixed by EXEC SQL, and it may not contain any host variables.

Using a cursor in an interactive SQL session gives you an opportunity to examine the result of a query, one row at a time, updating the rows as you examine them. It can also be useful to debug some cursor logic by running it interactively before embedding it in an application program. The following example shows a series of statements that we might execute interactively in order to examine the rows of the PARTS table and to update one of the rows after examining it:

```
DECLARE c1 CURSOR FOR
    SELECT partno, qonhand, qonorder
    FROM parts
    FOR UPDATE OF qonorder;
OPEN c1;
FETCH c1;
FETCH c1;
FETCH c1;
UPDATE parts
    SET qonorder = qonorder + 25
    WHERE CURRENT OF c1;
CLOSE c1;
```

---

5. This is a piece of friendly advice rather than an absolute requirement. If your program was precompiled with the option LANGLEVEL SQL92E or LANGLEVEL MIA, a positioned update or delete can be applied to a cursor that was not declared FOR UPDATE. However, the safest and most efficient thing to do is to declare your cursor FOR UPDATE whenever you plan to use positioned statements.

4.1.13 Compound SQL

When an application program is running on a client machine, each SQL statement ordinarily results in an exchange of messages between the client and server. To reduce message traffic and improve efficiency, UDB provides a way for a program to invoke a "bundle" of SQL statements with a single message to the server. The bundle is called a *compound SQL statement*. Compound statements can be used to improve the performance of applications that need to perform several related updates without interacting with the database during the update sequence.

Compound SQL statements always have the *static* property, which means that the values of all the input host variables in the individual SQL statements are bound before any of the statements are executed. This means that host variables cannot be used to pass information from one individual statement to another inside a compound SQL statement. The reason for this restriction is obvious: the values of host variables do not change until the end of the compound statement, because results are not returned to the client machine by the individual statements inside the compound statement. If more than one of the individual statements assigns a value to the same host variable, the host variable retains the last value that was assigned to it.

The programmer who writes a compound SQL statement must specify whether the statement is *atomic* or *not atomic*. If it is atomic, all the individual statements inside the compound statement are rolled back if any individual statement fails. If it is not atomic, then changes made by successful statements within the compound statement remain effective even if other statements in the same compound statement are not successful. Atomic compound statements are accepted by UDB servers but not by other database servers reached by DRDA connections.

The syntax of a compound SQL statement is as follows:

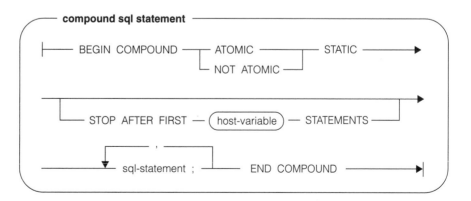

Example:

```
EXEC SQL
   BEGIN COMPOUND ATOMIC STATIC
      INSERT INTO orders(suppno, partno, quantity, orderdate)
         VALUES(:s, :p, :q, CURRENT DATE);
      UPDATE parts
         SET qonorder = qonorder + :q
         WHERE partno = :p;
   END COMPOUND;
```

Compound SQL statements can be used only in static SQL applications and may not be nested inside each other. Operations on cursors (OPEN, FETCH, CLOSE), and statements that affect database connections (CONNECT, RELEASE) are not allowed inside compound statements. A compound statement may contain a COMMIT as its last individual statement, but it may not contain a ROLLBACK.

As shown in the syntax diagram above, an application program can specify that only a certain number of the individual statements within a compound statement are to be executed, providing this number in a host variable in a STOP AFTER clause.

Like all SQL statements embedded in host programs, a compound SQL statement returns an SQLCA structure indicating its outcome. If one or more of the individual statements within the compound statement returns an error or warning condition, the errors and warnings are combined inside the SQLCA structure using a scheme described in the *SQL Reference*.

4.1.14 Example Program PARTS1: Ordering Parts

As an example of embedded SQL, we will write a C program named PARTS1 that interacts with users to process requests for parts, using the tables in our warehouse database. Our program prompts the user for a description of the parts needed. It then finds all part numbers that meet this description and, for each such part number, asks the user how many parts are needed and how soon they are needed. If the need can be met by parts that are in stock, the program simply updates its records accordingly. If, on the other hand, it is necessary to order a new supply, the program finds the supplier who can supply the parts within the required time limit at minimum cost and places an order with this supplier. After finding and processing all the parts that meet the user's description, the program prompts the user for another part description.

Steps for Example Program PARTS1: Ordering Parts

STEP 1: The program embeds the required header file `sqlenv.h`, which provides declarations for the symbols, structures, and interfaces used in embedded SQL. The file `sqlenv.h` is found in the directory `sqllib/include`, and it in turn embeds several other header files found in the same directory. In our example, we also use the statement `INCLUDE SQLCA`, which declares a structure named `sqlca` to contain return codes.

STEP 2: The SQL Declare Section contains host language declarations of all host variables used in embedded SQL statements, using the C-language datatypes listed in Table 4-2. Also at the beginning of the program, we declare a cursor named C1 to represent a query on the PARTS table. Each time this cursor is opened, it evaluates the input variable `:userdescrip` and finds all the parts that match this description (using a LIKE predicate to allow for approximate matches). Since we plan to use this cursor for a positioned update, it includes a FOR UPDATE clause.

Code for Example Program PARTS1: Ordering Parts

```c
/*
**  STEP 1: Include some header files
*/
#include <stdlib.h>
#include <string.h>
#include <stdio.h>
#include <sqlenv.h>

EXEC SQL INCLUDE SQLCA;

void main()
    {
    /*
    **  STEP 2: Declare some host variables and a cursor
    */
    EXEC SQL BEGIN DECLARE SECTION;
        char  dbname[9] = "testdb";    /* name of database                  */
        char  partno[5];               /* part number                       */
        long  qonhand;                 /* quantity on hand                  */
        long  qonorder;                /* quantity on order                 */
        long  qneeded;                 /* quantity needed                   */
        long  rneeded;                 /* response time needed (days)       */
        long  shortfall;               /* qty. needed minus qty. available  */
        long  bestprice;               /* best qualifying price for part    */
        short priceIndicator;          /* -1 (null) if no qualifying quotes */
        char  bestsuppno[4];           /* supplier no. with best price      */
        char  userdescrip[21];         /* user's description of part        */
        char  actualdescrip[21];       /* actual description of part        */
        char  msgbuffer[500];          /* buffer for DB2 error message      */
        short moreToDo = 1;            /* 1 until program is ready to exit  */
    EXEC SQL END DECLARE SECTION;

    EXEC SQL DECLARE C1 CURSOR FOR
        SELECT partno, description, qonhand, qonorder
        FROM parts
        WHERE description LIKE '%' || :userdescrip || '%'
        FOR UPDATE OF qonhand, qonorder;
```

STEP 3:   The WHENEVER statement specifies the label to which control will pass in the event of an unexpected return code from an SQL statement. After establishing this error handler, we are ready to connect to the PARTS database and to prompt the user for a description of the first part needed.

STEP 4:   The while-loop will execute as long as the user keeps responding to the prompt with more part descriptions. Each time the user enters a new part description, we open cursor C1 and fetch the first part that meets the new description. We use a LIKE predicate in searching for part descriptions, so if the user enters "Wheel," we might find parts with descriptions such as "Small Wheel," "Red Wheel," and "Wheel Cover." If no matching part is found, the FETCH statement returns SQLSTATE 02000.

STEP 5:   For each part that matches the user's description, we prompt the user for the number needed and the deadline. We then compute the "shortfall": the amount by which the number of parts needed exceeds the number of parts that are on hand. If there is no shortfall, we simply update the PARTS table (using a positioned update) to indicate that the requested parts have been removed from the warehouse. A more sophisticated version of the program might try to meet the user's needs from orders that have already been placed for the desired part but that have not yet arrived, taking into account the expected delivery times of these orders.

```
/*
**   STEP 3: Establish an error-handler and connect to the database
*/
EXEC SQL WHENEVER SQLERROR GO TO badnews;

EXEC SQL CONNECT TO :dbname;

printf("\nEnter one-word description of parts needed:");
scanf("%s", userdescrip);

/*
**   STEP 4: For each description entered by the user, open the
**   cursor and fetch the matching parts
*/
while (moreToDo)
   {
   EXEC SQL OPEN C1;

   EXEC SQL FETCH C1
       INTO :partno, :actualdescrip, :qonhand, :qonorder;

   if (!strncmp(sqlca.sqlstate, "02000", 5))
       {
       printf("Sorry, no parts meet that description.\n");
       }

   /*
   **   STEP 5: For each matching part, prompt the user for how
   **   many are needed and how soon
   */
   while(strncmp(sqlca.sqlstate, "02000", 5))
       {
       printf("\nPart number %s is a %s.\n", partno, actualdescrip);
       printf("Enter quantity needed and how soon (in days): ");
       scanf("%d %d", &qneeded, &rneeded);

       if (qneeded > 0)
          {
          shortfall = qneeded - qonhand;
          if (shortfall <= 0)
             {
             EXEC SQL
                UPDATE parts
                SET qonhand = qonhand - :qneeded
                WHERE CURRENT OF C1;
```

STEP 6:   If the parts on hand are not enough to meet the user's needs, we need to place an order for more parts. In this step, we find the minimum price in the QUOTA-TIONS table from any supplier who can supply the kind of part needed within the designated time. If no qualifying quotation exists (the minimum price is null), we print a message and prompt the user for another part description.

STEP 7:   At this point, we know that we need to place an order for parts, and we know the lowest price that meets our requirements. It is time to generate the order. One complication remains: it's possible that the lowest price might be avail-able from more than one supplier. In this step, we arbitrarily choose the sup-plier with the lowest supplier number, among all the suppliers who are tied for lowest price. We print a message indicating the order to be placed, and we insert a record of this order into the ORDERS table. We also update the PARTS table (using a positioned update) to reflect the new parts that are on order.

As an exercise for the reader, how could the SELECT statement in Step 7 be modified so that, if several qualifying quotations are tied for lowest price, the statement chooses the quotation with the fastest response time? (Remember that more than one quotation might be tied for both lowest price and fastest response.)

```
              printf("\nYour request has been filled from inventory.\n");
              }

      else
          {
          /*
          **   STEP 6: Find the minimum-cost supplier
          */
          EXEC SQL
              SELECT min(price) into :bestprice :priceIndicator
              FROM quotations
              WHERE partno = :partno
              AND responsetime <= :rneeded;

          if (priceIndicator < 0)
              {
              printf("\nSorry, no supplier can fill your request.\n");
              }
          else
              {
              /*
              **   STEP 7: Generate an order and update the database
              */
              EXEC SQL
                SELECT min(suppno) into :bestsuppno
                FROM quotations
                WHERE partno = :partno
                AND price = :bestprice
                AND responsetime <= :rneeded;

              printf("Place an order with supplier  %s ", bestsuppno);
              printf("for part %s, quantity %d\n", partno, shortfall);
              EXEC SQL
                INSERT INTO orders
                VALUES(:bestsuppno, :partno, :shortfall, CURRENT DATE);

              EXEC SQL
                UPDATE parts
                SET qonorder = qonorder + :shortfall
                WHERE CURRENT OF C1;
              }    /* end of case where a good quotation is found */

          }    /* end of case where an order is needed */

      }    /* end of case where qneeded > 0 */
```

STEP 8:   After processing all the rows returned by cursor C1 (that is, all the parts that meet the user's description), we close the cursor and commit our database changes, making them permanent. We then prompt the user for another part description and provide the opportunity to exit from the program.

STEP 9:   The label `badnews` identifies the handler for unexpected return codes from SQL statements. This handler uses the `sqlaintp` utility routine to retrieve the message associated with the failing SQL statement, and then prints the message. For example, if the PARTS1 package were to be deleted from the database for some reason, the program would print the following message:

```
Unexpected return code from DB2.
Message: SQL0805N  Package "YOURNAME.PARTS1" was not found.
SQLSTATE=51002
```

```
            EXEC SQL FETCH C1
                INTO :partno, :actualdescrip, :qonhand, :qonorder;

            }   /* end of loop while matching parts are found */

        /*
        **  STEP 8: Close the cursor, commit the updates, and prompt
        **  the user for a new part description
        */
        EXEC SQL CLOSE C1;

        EXEC SQL COMMIT;

        printf("\nEnter description of next part, or Q to quit: ");
        scanf("%s", userdescrip);
        if (!strcmp(userdescrip, "Q"))
            {
            moreToDo = 0;
            printf("Goodbye, come back soon!\n");
            }

        }   /*  end of loop while more to do */

    EXEC SQL CONNECT RESET;
    return;

badnews:
    /*
    **  STEP 9: Handler for bad return codes.
    **  Retrieves and prints an error message.
    */
    printf("Unexpected return code from DB2.\n");
    sqlaintp(msgbuffer, 500, 70, &sqlca);
    printf("Message: %s\n", msgbuffer);
    return;

    }       /*  end of main */
```

4.2 USING STATIC SQL IN C++ PROGRAMS

Since C++ is a superset of C, all the techniques used to embed SQL statements in C programs can be used in C++ programs also. In fact, the same precompiler (invoked by the same PREP command) is used to process both C and C++ programs with embedded SQL statements. The convention for filename extensions used by the UDB precompiler is shown in Table 4-4.

When you declare a C++ class, you can declare the data members of the class as host variables by including them in an SQL Declare Section inside the class definition. You can then write SQL statements inside the member functions of the class, using the host variables that are data members of that class. Each time such a host variable is used in an SQL statement, it is implicitly qualified by the "this" pointer that identifies the object whose member function is being executed.

The use of SQL statements in the member functions of a C++ class is illustrated by the example C++ program named PARTS2. This program defines a class named Request. Each instance of the Request class represents a request for a certain number of parts with a given part number. Since the member functions of the Request class need to interact with the database, the data members of the Request class (partno and qneeded) are placed inside an SQL Declare Section.

The Request class has a member function named howSoon(), which returns an integer indicating how soon the request can be satisfied. If the desired parts are already on hand, howSoon() returns zero. If the parts can be ordered, howSoon() returns the minimum response time for the given part available from any supplier. If the part number is unknown or no quotations exist for it, howSoon() returns –1. In order to compute its return value, how-Soon() contains two SQL statements that query the PARTS and QUOTATIONS

TABLE 4-4: Filename Convention for C and C++ Programs

File	Extension Under OS/2 and Windows	Extension Under UNIX Platforms
C program with embedded SQL (input to precompiler)	.sqc	.sqc
Pure C program (output of precompiler)	.c	.c
C++ program with embedded SQL (input to precompiler)	.sqx	.sqC
Pure C++ program (output of precompiler)	.cxx	.C

tables. The howSoon( ) member function uses the data members of the Request class (implicitly qualified by the "this" pointer) as host variables, and also declares some additional host variables in an SQL Declare Section of its own.

The Request class also has another member function named howMuch( ), which returns an integer indicating the minimum cost of the requested parts (zero if they are already on hand, –1 if no price quotations are available for the given part number). Like the howSoon( ) function, howMuch( ) has its own SQL Declare Section and contains SQL statements that query the PARTS and QUOTATIONS tables using data members of the Request class as host variables. Note that the minimum time returned by the howSoon( ) member function and the minimum cost returned by the howMuch( ) member function may not be available simultaneously, since they may represent quotes from different suppliers.

The example illustrates how a main program can create objects and invoke their member functions. It also illustrates how a global SQL error handler can be shared by a main program and by several member functions.

Example C++ Program PARTS2: Processing Requests for Parts

```cpp
#include <stdlib.h>
#include <string.h>
#include <sqlenv.h>
#include <iostream.h>

EXEC SQL INCLUDE SQLCA;

void handler(int n)
    {
    // Retrieves and prints error messages from DB2
    char msgbuffer[500];
    cout << endl << "Unexpected DB2 return code at point " << n << endl;
    sqlaintp(msgbuffer, 500, 70, &sqlca);
    cout << "Message: " << msgbuffer << endl;
    }

class Request
    {
    private:
        EXEC SQL BEGIN DECLARE SECTION;
            char partno[5];        // part number of part needed
            long qneeded;          // quantity of part needed
        EXEC SQL END DECLARE SECTION;
```

```
public:                          // methods

    Request (char *p, long q)    // constructor method
        {
        strncpy(partno, p, 5);
        qneeded = q;
        }

    long howSoon()               // minimum time to get parts
        {
        EXEC SQL BEGIN DECLARE SECTION;
            long qonhand1, mintime;
            short qtyind1, timeind;
        EXEC SQL END DECLARE SECTION;

        EXEC SQL
            SELECT qonhand INTO :qonhand1 :qtyind1
            FROM parts WHERE partno = :partno;
        if (SQLCODE == 0 && qtyind1 == 0 && qonhand1 >= qneeded)
            return 0;

        EXEC SQL
            SELECT min(responsetime) INTO :mintime :timeind
            FROM quotations
            WHERE partno = :partno
            AND responsetime IS NOT NULL;
        if (SQLCODE < 0) handler(1);
        if (SQLCODE < 0 || timeind < 0) return -1;
        else return mintime;
        }                // end of howSoon method

    long howMuch()               // minimum cost of parts
        {
        EXEC SQL BEGIN DECLARE SECTION;
            long qonhand2, minprice;
            short qtyind2, priceind;
        EXEC SQL END DECLARE SECTION;

        EXEC SQL
            SELECT qonhand INTO :qonhand2 :qtyind2
            FROM parts WHERE partno = :partno;
        if (SQLCODE == 0 && qtyind2 == 0 && qonhand2 >= qneeded)
            return 0;
```

```
            EXEC SQL
                SELECT min(price) into :minprice :priceind
                FROM quotations
                WHERE partno = :partno AND price IS NOT NULL;
            if (SQLCODE < 0) handler(2);
            if (SQLCODE < 0 || priceind < 0) return -1;
            else return minprice * qneeded;
            }           // end of howMuch method

    };                  // end of class Request

void main()
    {
    long time, cost, qty;
    char pno[5];
    Request *req;

    EXEC SQL CONNECT TO testdb;
    if (SQLCODE < 0) handler(3);

    while (cin >> pno >> qty)
        {
        // Create a new Request object
        req = new Request(pno, qty);

        // Invoke the howSoon and howMuch methods
        // of the Request object
        time = req->howSoon();
        cost = req->howMuch();
        cout << endl << "Request for " << qty
            << " units of part " << pno << endl;
        if (time < 0) cout << "No time information is available."
                        << endl;
        else cout << "Minimum time is " << time << " days."
                << endl;
        if (cost < 0) cout << "No cost information is available."
                        << endl;
        else cout << "Minimum cost is " << cost << " cents."
                << endl;

        // Delete the Request object and commit to release locks
        delete req;
        EXEC SQL COMMIT;
        if (SQLCODE < 0) handler(4);
        }   // end of input loop
```

```
EXEC SQL CONNECT RESET;
if (SQLCODE < 0) handler(5);

}      // end of main()
```

4.3 BUILDING AN APPLICATION PROGRAM

The process of preparing an application program to run on UDB is called *building* the application. To build an application, you will need to use the Software Developer's Kit (SDK), either on a server machine or on a client machine. The building process consists of several steps, as illustrated by Figure 4-1. In this section, we will discuss these steps, assuming that we are starting with a C program that contains embedded SQL statements, in a file named myprog.sqc (similar steps apply to C++ and other host languages).

1. In order to install a program for use with a particular database, it is first necessary to connect to the database. If our example program is designed to work with a database named TESTDB, we might connect to this database by typing the following statement at the Command Center:

   ```
   CONNECT TO testdb;
   ```

2. The next step is to invoke the UDB precompiler to scan the program for embedded SQL statements and to generate an optimized access plan for each statement. This might be done by typing the following command at the Command Center:

   ```
   PREP myprog.sqc;
   ```

   The PREP command is discussed further in Section 4.3.1. When invoked with no options, as in the example above, it scans a source program and produces an optimized access plan for each static SQL statement in the program (for some types of SQL statements, such as data definition statements, no real optimization is involved). The access plan for each statement is called a *section*, and the collection of all the sections, called a *package*, is stored in the currently connected database. The precompiler also generates a pure C-language file containing a copy of the source program in which the SQL statements have been replaced by calls that will cause UDB to retrieve and execute the plans contained in the package.

   The process of generating a compilable C program from an embedded-SQL source file is called *precompilation*, and the process of generating a package containing access plans for a program is called *binding* the program. By default, the PREP command performs both precompilation and binding (but

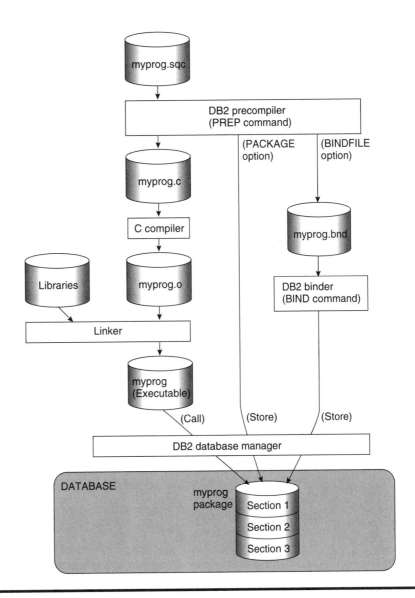

Figure 4-1: Building an Application Program Named MYPROG

you can separate these processes if you so choose). During binding, all the names of tables and other objects in SQL statements are resolved to specific objects in the database. If an SQL statement contains a syntactic error, or if the program attempts to access an object that does not exist or that you are not authorized to access, binding is unsuccessful and an error message is generated.

If you choose the BINDFILE option of the PREP command, the precompiler will generate an additional file, called a *bind file*, containing all the SQL statements and other information needed to generate a package for your program. A package can then be generated from the bind file and stored in the database by another command called BIND. The advantage of creating a bind file is that it can be used later to *rebind* your program without invoking the precompiler. Each time a program is rebound, the UDB optimizer chooses an optimal access plan for each SQL statement, based on the currently available indexes and other database conditions. The name of the bind file for our example program is `myprog.bnd`.

3. After precompiling a program, the next step is to compile the resulting C program and to link it with other programs and library functions to make an executable file. An application may consist of several source files, each containing its own embedded SQL statements. The files can be precompiled and compiled separately and then linked together. Of course, exactly one of the files must contain a `main()` function.

Since the file generated by the precompiler is a pure C program, it can be compiled and linked by the same methods that you usually use for handling C programs. The specific commands for these tasks depend on your compiler and operating system. Examples of commands for compiling and linking application programs using various compilers and operating systems are given in the manuals *Building Applications for UNIX Environments* and *Building Applications for Windows and OS/2 Environments*.

Remember that you must never modify the C program that was generated by the precompiler. If you need to modify your application, modify the `.sqc` file and repeat the PREP command.

4. After the program has been precompiled, compiled, and linked, it is ready to run. Like any other application, it can be invoked simply by typing its name on the operating system command line, as follows:

```
myprog
```

The running program executes the calls that were generated by the precompiler, which cause the UDB run-time system to retrieve the package from the database and to execute the access plans contained in its sections.

UDB provides a set of command files that can be used to simplify the process of building your application programs. Even if these files don't meet your needs exactly, they can serve as useful templates for the compiling and linking commands that you will need to use. The command files are different for every platform and compiler. They are found in the directories under `sqllib/samples` (for example, the files for building C and C++ applications are found in `sqllib/samples/c` and in `sqllib/samples/cpp`). Here are the names of some of these command files:

- `bldmsemb.bat` is used with the Microsoft Visual C++ compiler on Windows NT and Windows 95.
- `bldvaemb.bat` is used with the IBM Visual Age compiler on Windows and OS/2.
- `bldxlc` is used with the IBM XLC compiler on AIX.
- `bldcset` is used with the IBM CSet++ compiler on AIX.
- `bldcc` is used with the C and C++ compilers on HP-UX and Solaris platforms.

Before using one of these command files, you may need to edit it in the following ways:

1. The command files were designed for building the UDB sample applications, which use an error-checking utility program named `util`. If your application does not depend on this program, you can delete references to `util.c` and `util.o` from the command files.

2. The command files make some assumptions about where certain libraries are installed on your machine. For example, the `bldmsemb.bat` file assumes that the UDB library of include files is found in `%DB2PATH%\include`. If these assumptions are not correct, you may need to edit the compile and link commands.

More details about building UDB applications can be found in the IBM publications, *Building Applications for Windows and OS/2 Environments* and *Building Applications for UNIX Environments*.

4.3.1 Precompiling a Program

The UDB precompiler is invoked by the PRECOMPILE (sometimes called PREP) command. Although PREP is a command rather than an SQL statement, it can be invoked from the Command Center or the CLP, much like an SQL statement. The syntax of a PREP command is as follows:

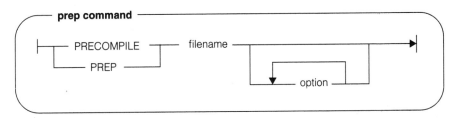

As we have seen, the PREP command creates a package containing an optimized access plan for each embedded SQL statement in a program, and may also produce a bind file that contains the original SQL statements.

In order to precompile a program, you must be connected to a database. If you are precompiling the program for the first time, you must hold BINDADD authority on the database, and CREATEIN privilege on the schema in which the package will be stored (or IMPLICIT_SCHEMA authority on the database if this schema does not yet exist). If you are precompiling a program that already has a package, you must hold BIND privilege on the package or ALTERIN privilege on the schema that contains the package. In addition, you must hold the privileges necessary to execute all the SQL statements contained in the program. These privileges must have been granted to you individually or to PUBLIC—not to a group of which you are a member.[6]

The PREP command has a great many options, which are documented in the *Command Reference*. Most of the options consist of an option name followed by an option value. I will summarize some of the more useful options here:

- The BINDFILE option causes the precompiler to create a bind file and to forego creation of a package unless the PACKAGE option is also specified.

- The BLOCKING option controls whether the result sets of queries are returned from the server machine to the client machine one row at a time or in blocks of several rows. Returning blocks of rows improves performance by reducing the number of messages exchanged between server and client, but it leads to problems when cursors are used for positioned updates and deletes (as in DELETE FROM table1 WHERE CURRENT OF cursor1). By default, the system performs blocking of rows for any cursor that is never used for a positioned update or delete. But if your program prepares and executes some dynamic SQL statements, the system cannot be sure that you will not prepare and execute a positioned update or delete on some cursor. If you wish to make a promise that your program will not dynamically prepare and execute any positioned updates or deletes, you can do so by specifying BLOCKING ALL; this promise allows the system to perform blocking of rows in some cases when it would not otherwise do so.

- The COLLECTION option specifies the name of the database schema in which the package will be created. The default schema name is the userid under which the PREP command is executed.

- The CONNECT 1 option specifies that the program will use Type 1 connections (connecting to only one database in each transaction), while CONNECT 2 specifies that the program will use Type 2 connections (connecting to multi-

---

6. The reason for this rule is that **UDB** does not continuously monitor your membership in groups and has no way to invalidate your package if you drop out of a privileged group.

ple databases in the same transaction). (Type 1 and Type 2 connections are discussed in Section 2.7.2.)

- The DATETIME option specifies the preferred format for dates and times that are generated by the package (such as the value of the CURRENT DATE and CURRENT TIME special registers). The format is specified by a three-letter code such as USA (American standard), EUR (European standard), or JIS (Japanese standard).

- The DEGREE option specifies the degree of intra-partition parallelism (number of concurrent processes on each machine) to be used in executing the SQL statements in the program. The value of the DEGREE option can be an integer between 1 and 32767, or the word ANY (which allows the system to choose its own degree of intra-partition parallelism). The default value for DEGREE is controlled by the database configuration parameter named DFT_DEGREE, which in turn has a default value of 1.

- The EXPLSNAP option controls the gathering of "Explain snapshot" information that can be used with the Control Center to display the access plans generated by the optimizer, as discussed in Section 10.8.4. EXPLSNAP YES causes snapshot information to be gathered for each static SQL statement in the program.

- The FUNCPATH option specifies a list of schemas that are to be searched, in order, when resolving function names and datatype names in static SQL statements in the program. The default function path consists of the schemas SYSIBM and SYSFUN, followed by the userid under which the program is being precompiled. (Function paths are discussed in Section 6.3).

- The ISOLATION option specifies the level of isolation required by the program, in the form of a two-letter code (RR = Repeatable Read, RS = Read Stability, CS = Cursor Stability, UR = Uncommitted Read). (Isolation levels are discussed in Section 2.7.1.)

- The MESSAGES option allows you to specify a filename in which precompiler messages are to be saved (otherwise, these messages are directed to the standard output stream).

- The QUERYOPT option allows you to control the class of optimization techniques to be applied in choosing access plans for SQL statements in the program. Valid values for QUERYOPT include 0, 1, 2, 3, 5, 7, and 9. In general, higher values cause the optimizer to use more time and memory in choosing optimal access plans, potentially resulting in better plans and improved runtime performance. The extreme values 0 and 9 should be used with caution since they may result in suboptimal plans or long optimization times, respectively. Class 5 is a good compromise for most applications. The default value for QUERYOPT is controlled by a database configuration parameter named DFT_QUERYOPT, which in turn has a default value of 5.

TIP: Don't confuse the QUERYOPT option with the OPTLEVEL option, which has nothing to do with the optimization of SQL statements and which you probably don't want to use.

- The SYNCPOINT option is used with Type 2 connections to specify how commits and rollbacks are handled for transactions that connect to more than one database. Valid values for this option are ONEPHASE, TWOPHASE, and NONE. The default is ONEPHASE. (The SYNCPOINT option is discussed in Section 2.7.2.)

- The WCHARTYPE option controls the format in which graphical (multibyte) data is exchanged with host variables. WCHARTYPE NOCONVERT (the default) specifies that data is exchanged using two bytes per character, just as it is stored in the database, using the two-byte C type `sqldbchar`. WCHARTYPE CONVERT specifies that data is exchanged using the `wchar_t` type that is defined by your C compiler and is used with the C "wide-character" function library.

The following examples illustrate the use of the PREP command and some of its options:

- The simplest form of a PREP command simply names the program to be precompiled.

```
PREP prog1.sqc;
```

- This command precompiles a C program named `prog2`, using Repeatable Read isolation and producing both a package and a bind file. The name of the resulting package will be `business.prog2`.

```
PREP prog2.sqc BINDFILE PACKAGE
    COLLECTION business ISOLATION RR;
```

- This command precompiles a C++ program named `prog3`, specifying a European format for dates and a function path that includes the SCIENCE and MATH schemas. Precompiler messages are directed to a file named `prog3.msg` in the current directory.

```
PREP prog3.sqC DATETIME EUR MESSAGES prog3.msg
    FUNCPATH sysibm, sysfun, science, math;
```

- This command precompiles a C program named `prog4`. Because performance is very critical, the user specifies the maximum level of optimization, blocking of all cursors, and EXPLSNAP YES, which makes the access plan of each static SQL statement available for examination using the Control Center.

```
PREP prog4.sqc QUERYOPT 9 BLOCKING ALL EXPLSNAP YES;
```

- This command precompiles a C program named `prog5`. Because the program contains transactions that update multiple databases, the user specifies Type 2 connections and a two-phase commit protocol.

```
PREP prog5.sqc CONNECT 2 SYNCPOINT TWOPHASE;
```

4.3.2 Rebinding a Package

The package that is stored in the database for your program contains the best access plan that the system could find for your SQL statements at the time your program was bound. However, over time, database changes may occur that would lead to a different access plan if your program were to be bound again. These changes fall into the following general categories:

1. A package may contain access plans that make use of certain physical structures such as indexes. If an index is dropped that is used by a given package, that package is marked *invalid,* and its access plans are automatically replaced by new access plans the next time the package is invoked. This process, called *implicit rebind,* is transparent to the user except for a slight delay caused by generating the new plans and possibly for a change in the performance of the application.

   The loss of an index used by a package is not too serious, because the optimizer will always be able to find an alternative access plan that does not require the missing index. However, a package may be more severely affected if one of the tables it accesses is dropped or one of the privileges it depends on is revoked. If one of these events should occur, the system will mark the package invalid and will attempt to implicitly rebind it when it is next invoked. If the table or privilege has not been restored, the implicit rebind will fail, and the application program will receive an error code when it tries to execute an SQL statement.

2. It is also possible that, after your package is created, a new index might be created that would improve the performance of your program, or the statistics of your data might change in such a way that a different access plan would give you better performance. The system will *not* automatically detect these conditions and revise your package accordingly. If you wish your package to take advantage of the latest indexes and statistics, you must explicitly rebind it, using one of the methods described below.

3. Some of the SQL statements in your program may contain calls to scalar functions such as length or to column functions such as avg. As we will see in Chapter 6, UDB allows users to write functions of their own that can be used in SQL statements in the same way as the system-provided functions. In fact, the system allows several functions to be created with the same name but different argument datatypes, such as foo(Integer) and foo(Float). When a program is bound, a process called *function resolution* finds the actual functions that most closely match the function calls in the program and uses these functions in the access plan for the program. However, if one of the functions selected is a user-defined function, it is possible that this function may later be dropped. If this happens, the package is placed into an *inoperative* state. An inoperative package cannot be used until it is explicitly rebound, using one of

the methods described below. Explicitly rebinding a package repeats the function resolution process, possibly choosing different functions from those originally selected. For example, if the function foo(Integer) is dropped, the system might select an alternative function foo(Float) and invoke it by promoting the argument. However, the system will not perform this kind of substitution unless you explicitly rebind your package. This policy, called *conservative binding semantics*, protects you against unexpected changes in the behavior of a program.

At any time, you can rebind an existing package, causing the system to regenerate all its access plans. The following is a summary of the reasons why you might choose to rebind a package:

- To take advantage of new indexes created since your package was bound.
- To take advantage of the latest statistics gathered on database tables.
- To invoke function resolution in order to take advantage of a function that was created after your package was bound, or to rescue your package from an inoperative state due to the dropping of a user-defined function.
- To avoid the delay in invoking your application that would occur if you allowed an invalid package to be automatically rebound by the system.
- To change one or more of the options with which your package was bound, such as its isolation level.

There are three ways to explicitly rebind a package, which are summarized below. In order to use any of these methods, you must be connected to the database in which the package is bound.

1. The fastest and most straightforward way to explicitly rebind a package is by using the REBIND command. The REBIND command takes only one parameter: the name of the package to be rebound. It does not require the existence of a bind file. It operates directly on the package that is stored in the database, which contains a copy of the original SQL statements from which it was created. These statements are rebound into a new package, using exactly the same options that were in effect when the package was last bound. In the rebind process, all table and function names are resolved from scratch, and new access plans are generated for all the SQL statements in the package. A REBIND command is quite efficient and should be used when you wish to rebind a package without changing the program or its bind options.

   The following is an example of a REBIND command for the myprog program:

   ```
   REBIND myprog
   ```

2. If you created a bind file when you precompiled your program, you can use the BIND command to rebind this file. You might choose to use BIND rather than REBIND if you want to change one of the options with which your program was bound, such as its isolation level. The BIND command requires the same privileges as the PREP command, and supports most of the same options (however, the CONNECT, SYNCPOINT, and WCHARTYPE options are not supported by the BIND command; if you want to change these options, you must use the PREP command).

The following is an example of a BIND command that might be used to change the isolation level of the myprog program:

```
BIND myprog ISOLATION RS
```

3. If you make any changes to the source code of your program, you must invoke the precompiler again, as in the following example:

```
PREP myprog.sqc
```

TIP: Don't be tempted to modify the C program that was produced by the precompiler. Any changes you make to this program will be lost next time you invoke the precompiler. Any necessary changes to your source code should be made in the file that serves as input to the precompiler.

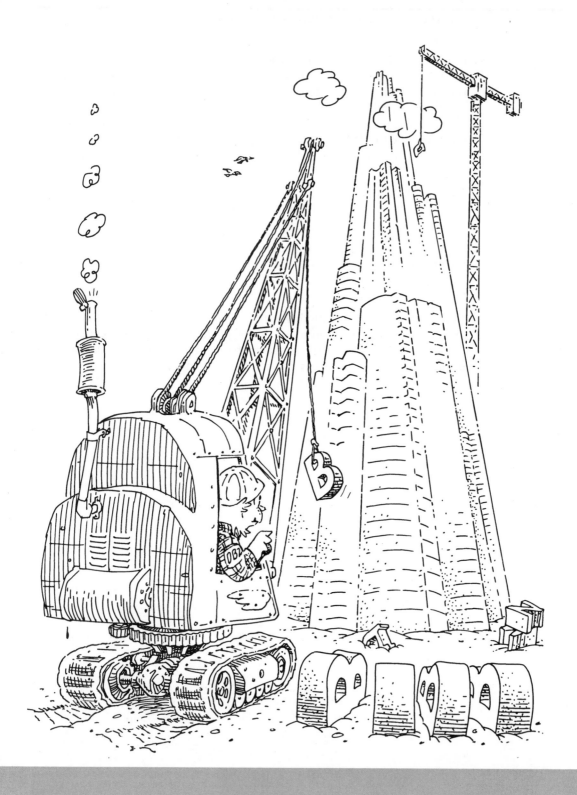

CHAPTER

5 Query Power

Have you ever wanted to know which department in your company has the highest average salary? Or how to fly from Oshkosh to Oslo in the minimum number of flights? Or what fraction of your company's accidents last year were caused by chain saws? This is the chapter in which you will learn to answer these and other important questions, each in a single SQL statement, using the query power of **UDB**.

Many of the language features introduced in this chapter involve subqueries. SQL has always supported the concept of a subquery, which is a query used inside another query to compute some intermediate result. However, the original SQL was frequently criticized because of the rules and limitations it placed on the use of subqueries. In the original SQL, for example, the table generated by a subquery did not always have column names, and a subquery could not in general be used in the same ways as a real table or view. These rules and limitations have been eliminated in the SQL92 Standard and in the **UDB** system, resulting in a new version of SQL with greatly improved orthogonality and expressive power.

One of the ways in which **UDB** earns its name as a "universal database" is through its ability to access data from many different relational and nonrelational sources. The facility called *table functions*, described in this chapter, can be used to make almost any kind of data appear to be a table that can be queried using SQL and joined to other tables in your database.

Some of the basic SQL features discussed in Chapter 2, such as joins and grouping, have been significantly enhanced in **UDB**. A new syntax called *explicit join* allows you to join tables in new ways. Another new feature, called *super groups,* allows an SQL query to group the data in a table in several different ways and provides new operations called CUBE and ROLLUP that are useful in online analytical processing (OLAP).

One of the most powerful features of **UDB** is its support for recursive queries, which involve searching the database repeatedly until some desired goal is reached. Recursive queries are used in many important database applications, such as finding all the descendants of a given person, all the components of a given assembly, or all the paths to a given destination. The **UDB** syntax for recursive queries enables you to search for all solutions to a given problem or for the optimum solution according to some criterion that you define.

The essence of a database system lies in its ability to retrieve information. The query features described in this chapter contribute greatly to the expressive power of SQL, removing several long-standing limitations of the language. UDB has been certified as compliant with the ANSI/ISO SQL92 Standard, and also supports a number of language features that are not included in SQL92. Many of these features are under consideration for inclusion in the next generation of the SQL Standard, currently known as SQL3.

5.1 CASE EXPRESSIONS

Often, a database designer will choose to conserve space by using some short encoding for the values in a database column. When retrieving values from the column, however, an application might prefer to display the actual meanings of the values rather than their short codes. This is a simple example of what can be accomplished using a powerful language feature called a *CASE expression.*

5.1.1 Simple Form

A CASE expression evaluates to a scalar value and can be used wherever you can use an expression such as x + y or foo(x). CASE is often used in a SELECT clause, in a WHERE clause, or in the SET clause of an UPDATE statement. In its simplest form, a CASE expression evaluates to one of several *result expressions,* depending on the value of a *test expression.*

To illustrate the simple form of the CASE expression, consider the following table that contains a list of military officers:

OFFICERS

NAME	STATUS	RANK	TITLE

The STATUS column is an integer code that represents various possibilities, such as "Active," "Reserve," and "Retired." The following query might be used to list the officers together with the descriptive text represented by their status codes:

```
SELECT name,
    CASE status
        WHEN 1 THEN 'Active Duty'
        WHEN 2 THEN 'Reserve'
```

```
            WHEN 3 THEN 'Special Assignment'
            WHEN 4 THEN 'Retired'
            ELSE 'Unknown'
         END AS status
      FROM officers;
```

The syntax of the simple form of a CASE expression is as follows:

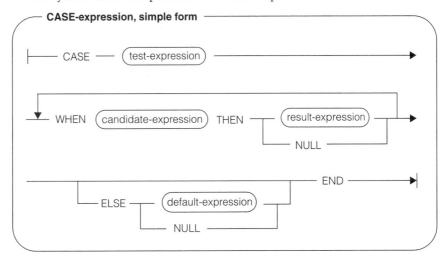

In this syntax diagram, the symbols *test-expression*, *candidate-expression*, *result-expression*, and *default-expression* all represent general expressions, constructed according to the rules described in Section 2.4.1.

The value of a simple CASE expression is the value of the first result expression whose corresponding candidate expression is equal to the test expression. If the test expression does not match any of the candidate expressions, the value of the CASE expression is the default expression, or NULL if no default has been specified. When writing a CASE expression, you must make sure that the datatypes of all the candidate expressions are compatible with the datatype of the test expression and that the datatypes of all the result expressions and the default expression are compatible with each other.

As another example of a simple CASE expression, consider a motor vehicle application that needs to compute license fees for various kinds of vehicles. The application is based on the following table:

VEHICLES

LICENSE	RENEWAL_DATE	TYPE	WEIGHT	NWHEELS

Suppose that, according to the law, fees for cars are based on their weight, fees for trucks are based on their number of wheels, and motorcycles are charged a flat fee. The following query might perform the proper fee computation for each vehicle due for renewal, based on its type:

```
SELECT license,
    CASE type
        WHEN 'Car' THEN 0.05 * weight
        WHEN 'Truck' THEN 25.00 * nwheels
        WHEN 'Motorcycle' THEN 35.00
        ELSE NULL
    END AS fee
FROM vehicles
WHERE year(renewal_date) <= 1997;
```

5.1.2 General Form

The CASE expression also has a more general form, which consists of a set of search conditions, each paired with a result expression. The search conditions can contain any kind of predicate, or even multiple predicates connected by AND, OR, and NOT. The value of the CASE expression is the result expression corresponding to the first search condition that evaluates to TRUE. If none of the search conditions is TRUE, the value of the CASE expression is the default expression, or NULL if no default is provided. The syntax of this form of CASE expression is as follows:

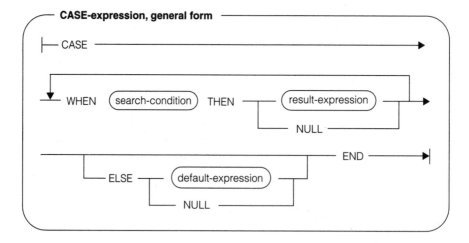

The syntax of a search condition is given on page 56. As in the simple form of CASE, *result-expression* and *default-expression* represent general expressions constructed according to the rules described in Section 2.4.1.

As an example of the general form of a CASE expression, suppose that a certain county maintains a list of properties within the county, using the following table:

PROPERTIES

PARCELNO	CITY	AREA	TAXRATE

If the property tax rate for the county changes to a system based on the area of each property, the tax rate column might be updated as follows:

```
UPDATE properties
SET taxrate =
    CASE
        WHEN area < 10000 THEN .05
        WHEN area < 20000 THEN .07
        ELSE .09
    END;
```

A CASE expression can be used to avoid dividing by zero when computing some result. Suppose that a company keeps records on all its machines in the following table:

MACHINES

SERIALNO	TYPE	YEAR	HOURS_USED	ACCIDENTS

The following query computes the average accident rate for each type of machine in the database, taking care not to divide by zero in case there are machines that have never been used:

```
SELECT type,
    CASE
        WHEN sum(hours_used) > 0
            THEN sum(accidents)/sum(hours_used)
        ELSE NULL
    END AS accident_rate
FROM machines
GROUP BY type;
```

CASE expressions make certain types of queries easy to write and efficient to execute that would otherwise be very difficult or costly. For example, using the MACHINES table, suppose that we want to know the fraction of all accidents that involve machines of type "chain saw." Using a CASE expression, we can find the answer to this question in a single pass over the MACHINES table by writing the following query:

```
SELECT sum(CASE
                WHEN type = 'chain saw' THEN accidents
                ELSE 0e0
            END) / sum(accidents)
    FROM machines;
```

TIP: The constant 0e0 in this example is a floating-point zero. We use a floating-point zero rather than an integer zero to force the computation to be done in floating point. If the constant were expressed as 0, the computation would be done in integer arithmetic, and, since the result is a fraction, it would be rounded to zero.

CASE expressions can sometimes be used to compute simple functions. You might choose to use a CASE expression rather than a function call to improve the portability of your application or to avoid the overhead of calling an external function. For example, the absolute value function, which is provided by UDB in the SYSFUN schema, can be simulated by a CASE expression. The expression abs(x) is equivalent to the following expression:

```
CASE
    WHEN x >= 0 THEN x
    ELSE -x
END
```

As an example of the use of CASE to compute absolute values, suppose that I am looking for a college and I think the ideal size for a college is about 8,000 students. My database contains the following table:

COLLEGES

NAME	STATE	ENROLLMENT

The following query lists all the colleges in Colorado and Utah, in order by how close their enrollment is to 8,000 (that is, the college whose enrollment is closest to 8,000 is first on the list):

```
SELECT name, enrollment,
    CASE
        WHEN enrollment >= 8000 THEN enrollment - 8000
        ELSE 8000 - enrollment
    END AS difference
FROM colleges
WHERE state IN ('CO', 'UT')
ORDER BY difference;
```

We will end our discussion of CASE with an example of how one CASE expression can be nested inside another. Suppose that our database contains a table of new hires and their starting dates, as shown below:

HIRES

```
NAME    STARTDATE
```

Our legal department has decided that each employee will receive vested rights in the company pension plan on the last day of the month that contains that employee's fifth service anniversary. The following query computes the month, day, and year on which each of the new hires will receive vested rights (note the use of the built-in function mod to detect leap years):

```
SELECT  name,
        month(startdate) AS vestmonth,
        CASE
            WHEN month(startdate) IN (4, 6, 9, 11) THEN 30
            WHEN month(startdate) = 2 THEN
                CASE
                    WHEN mod(year(startdate)+5, 4) = 0 THEN 29
                    ELSE 28
                END
            ELSE 31
        END as vestday,
        year(startdate) + 5 AS vestyear
FROM hires;
```

TIP: UDB imposes one limitation on the use of CASE expressions. If a CASE expression is used in a SELECT clause, in a VALUES clause (literal table), in an IN-predicate, or in a GROUP BY or ORDER BY clause, then no search condition in that CASE expression may contain a subquery whose result is a table. It may seem arbitrary, but that's the rule.

5.1.3 RAISE_ERROR Function

UDB supports a built-in function named `raise_error` that is particularly useful inside CASE expressions. The `raise_error` function, as its name implies, aborts the processing of the current SQL statement and raises an error condition. It rolls back all database changes caused by the current SQL statement but leaves the current transaction in progress, so the user or application program can still choose to commit or roll back the other statements in the transaction.

The `raise_error` function takes two character-string parameters: an SQL-STATE and a message string. The SQLSTATE must be a string of exactly five uppercase letters or digits. The SQLSTATE specified in the call to `raise_error` is returned to the application program in the SQLCA structure, along with an SQLCODE of –438. In choosing an SQLSTATE to represent a user-defined error condition, you should avoid values that have been reserved by IBM or by the SQL92 Standard. You can easily avoid conflicts by choosing an SQLSTATE whose first character is a digit between 7 and 9 or a letter between I and Z, inclusive.[1] The second parameter of `raise_error` is a message string of up to 70 characters, which is returned to the application program in the SQLERRMC field of the SQLCA structure.

To illustrate the use of `raise_error` inside a CASE statement, we will return to the PROPERTIES table used in the previous section. A recent election has raised the tax rate for some of the cities in our county. The PROPERTIES table can be updated to reflect the new tax rates by the following statement, which returns SQLSTATE 70007 if an unexpected city is encountered in the table:

```
UPDATE properties
SET taxrate =
    CASE city
        WHEN 'San Jose' THEN taxrate
        WHEN 'Santa Clara' THEN taxrate + .005
        WHEN 'Campbell' THEN taxrate + .005
        WHEN 'Los Gatos' THEN taxrate + .008
        ELSE raise_error('70007',
            'Parcel ' || parcelno || ' has unknown city')
    END;
```

---

1. Certain other values for SQLSTATE are also permitted and are described in the *DB2 SQL Reference*.

TIP: A `raise_error` function is compatible with any datatype. For example, a `raise_error` function can be used inside a CASE expression whose result expressions are of type Integer, Varchar, or any other datatype. But if you use a `raise_error` function in a way that requires it to have a datatype of its own (for example, in a CASE expression where *every* result expression is a call to `raise_error`), you must provide an explicit datatype by a CAST expression such as `CAST(raise_error('77777', 'Bad News') AS Integer)`. The actual value returned by `raise_error` is the null value.

5.1.4 NULLIF and COALESCE Functions

Among the built-in scalar functions of UDB, there are two functions that behave like special kinds of CASE expressions: `nullif` and `coalesce`. The `nullif` function is a shorthand notation for a CASE expression that returns a null value if its first parameter is equal to its second parameter; otherwise, it returns its first parameter. This function is sometimes useful in cases where a designated value such as –1 has been used as a do-it-yourself encoding for null values. For example, `nullif(salary, -1)` is a shorthand notation for the following expression:

```
CASE
    WHEN salary = -1 THEN NULL
    ELSE salary
END
```

The `coalesce` function takes a variable number of parameters and returns the first of its parameters that has a non-null value (if all parameters are null, the result is null). All the parameters passed in a given call to `coalesce` must have compatible (but not necessarily identical) datatypes (for example, the parameters might have various numeric datatypes such as Integer, Decimal, and Double). The datatype of the result of a call to `coalesce` is the "greatest" of the input datatypes (that is, the datatype to which all the input datatypes can be promoted). For example, if we call `coalesce(x, y, z)`, where x is a null Integer, y is the Decimal value 5.7, and z is a null value of type Double, the result will have datatype Double and value 5.7. (For a more complete description of how datatypes are handled by the `coalesce` function, see Section 6.6.2.)

As an example of the use of `coalesce`, consider the OFFICERS table introduced in Section 5.1.1, which has columns RANK and TITLE. The following query might be used to print the names and ranks of all the officers in certain status categories, substituting title for rank when rank is null:

```
SELECT name, coalesce(rank, title) AS rank_or_title
FROM officers
WHERE status IN (1, 2, 3);
```

In this query, the expression coalesce(rank, title) might be considered to be a shorthand for the following CASE expression:

```
CASE
    WHEN rank IS NOT NULL THEN rank
    ELSE title
END
```

The coalesce function can also be called by the name value, for compatibility with earlier DB2 products. For example, the expression value(rank, title) is equivalent to the expression coalesce(rank, title).

TIP: It is important not to confuse the value function with the VALUES keyword that is used to construct a literal table, as discussed in Section 2.4.9. Because of the danger of confusion between value and VALUES, and because the function name coalesce is used in the SQL92 Standard, you would be wise to use the name coalesce rather than value in your function calls.

5.2   SUBQUERIES

Since SQL was first introduced, it has had the concept of a *subquery:* a query enclosed in parentheses and used inside some outer-level SQL statement. A subquery may consist of a simple query block or a more complex query, perhaps containing a join, a set operation such as UNION, or even a subquery of its own. In general, the result of a subquery is a table, but a subquery that computes a single value is an important special case. The result of a subquery is used during execution of the outer-level statement in which the subquery is embedded. Under certain circumstances, a subquery may need to be evaluated more than once during execution of the outer-level statement.

To explore the use of subqueries, we will use a database of employees and departments containing the following tables:

EMP

NAME	DEPTNO	JOB	MANAGER	RATING	SALARY	BONUS	STARTDATE

DEPT

DEPTNO	DEPTNAME	BUDGET	LOCATION

Suppose that we need to find the names and salaries of all the employees who work in Menlo Park. This could be accomplished by the following query:

```
SELECT name, salary
FROM   emp
WHERE  deptno IN
  (SELECT deptno
   FROM   dept
   WHERE  location = 'Menlo Park');
```

This query contains a subquery that finds all the departments located in Menlo Park, and this set is then used in the outer-level query to find all the employees who work in these departments. In this example, the subquery can be completely evaluated before the outer-level query is begun. However, there is another kind of subquery, called a *correlated subquery*, that is evaluated once for every row of the table used in the outer-level query. You can tell that a subquery is correlated because it contains an identifier, called a *correlation name*, that represents a row of the outer-level query. The correlation name is defined in the FROM clause of the outer-level query, optionally preceded by the keyword AS. The following is an example of a correlated subquery, using correlation name x, that finds employees whose salary is more than 10% of their department budget:

```
SELECT name, salary
FROM   emp AS x
WHERE  salary >
  (SELECT 0.1 * budget
   FROM   dept
   WHERE  deptno = x.deptno);
```

You might think of this query as being processed as follows: "For each row x in the EMP table, evaluate the subquery to find the budget of x's department, then compare one-tenth of this budget to x's salary." (Of course, the optimizer reserves the right to process this query in some other equivalent way.)

In the last example, the subquery returns a single value, called a *scalar* (in this case, one-tenth of a department budget). In the previous example, the subquery returned a set of values of the same datatype (department numbers), which we might think of as a table consisting of a single column. A subquery might also return a table consisting of many rows and columns, as in the following example of a subquery inside an INSERT statement:

```
CREATE TABLE artists(name Varchar(30),
                     deptno Char(3),
                     salary Decimal(8,2));
INSERT INTO artists
    (SELECT name, deptno, salary
     FROM    emp
     WHERE   job = 'Artist');
```

In general, the user who writes a subquery must make sure that its result fits properly into the context of the statement in which it is used; otherwise, an error will result.

Whenever a column name is used in an SQL statement, the system must *resolve* the name to a column of a particular table. Subqueries introduce some complications into the rules for resolving names. If a column name appears in a subquery, the system attempts to interpret it as a column of one of the tables in the FROM clause of the subquery. If none of these tables has a column with the given name, the system looks at the next higher-level query block that contains the subquery and attempts to resolve the column name among the tables in its FROM clause. This process continues through successively higher-level query blocks until a table is found that contains a column with the given name. Of course, a correlation name can be used to force the resolution of the column to a particular table. If a column name cannot be resolved unambiguously, an error results. The following example repeats the query that finds employees whose salary is more than 10% of their department budget, writing the query in a different way this time to illustrate the resolution of column names. In the subquery inside this example, BUDGET is interpreted as a column of DEPT, but SALARY is interpreted as a column of EMP (since the table in the FROM clause of the subquery has no SALARY column).

```
SELECT name, salary
FROM   emp
WHERE  deptno IN
```

```
(SELECT deptno
 FROM   dept
 WHERE  salary > 0.1 * budget);
```

The rules governing subqueries in UDB follow two important principles of language design, called *orthogonality* and *closure*. Before continuing our discussion of subqueries, we will briefly consider these principles and their implications.

The principle of orthogonality states that the features of a language should be independent of each other and should interact in regular and predictable ways. The original rules governing usage of subqueries in SQL have been rightly criticized by Chris Date, Hugh Darwen, and others as lacking orthogonality. For example, in the original SQL, a subquery that returns a table was not allowed to be used in place of a table name in the FROM clause of a query. Orthogonality suggests that a subquery that returns a table should be usable wherever a table is expected, and that a subquery that returns a scalar should be usable wherever a scalar is expected. Indeed, these are the rules for subqueries in the SQL92 Standard, and they have been implemented in UDB, as we will see in the following sections.

The principle of closure states that the objects that are computed by expressions in a language should be the same types of objects that serve as input to those expressions. For example, the familiar arithmetic operators +, –, *, and / have the closure property because they operate on numbers and they produce numbers as their result (actually, the division operator violates closure if its second operand is zero). Closure is an important property, because it allows the result of one operator to be used as input to another operator. We will need this property if we wish to make general use of subqueries inside SQL statements.

The basic objects on which SQL operates are tables with named columns. In order for the closure property to hold, the result of an SQL query should also be a table with named columns. In general, the result of an SQL query is a table, but some of the columns of the table may have no obvious name, since they may contain some computed result like avg(salary) or salary + bonus. UDB allows you to assign column names to the result of a query by using the keyword AS in the SELECT list of the query. For example, the following query produces a table with two columns named NAME and PAY:

```
SELECT name, salary + bonus AS pay
FROM emp
WHERE job = 'Programmer';
```

Ordinarily, column names are case insensitive (that is, folded to uppercase) and contain no blanks. If you wish, however, you may name your output columns using *delimited identifiers,* which are strings enclosed in double quotes. Delimited identifiers are case sensitive and may contain blanks or SQL keywords. For example, you might make the previous example more descriptive by writing it as follows:

```
SELECT name AS "Employee Name",
       salary + bonus AS "Total Pay"
FROM emp
WHERE job = 'Programmer';
```

A subtle point to remember when you generate your own column names is that these names apply to the result of a query block, and therefore cannot be used inside the same query block in which they are defined. For example, the query block above defines "Total Pay" as the name of one of its result columns. This name can be used in an outer-level query, or even in an ORDER BY clause, which is not considered to be part of the query block. However, it may not be used inside the query block itself. For example, if you wish to form groups based on some expression such as salary + bonus, you must use the actual expression in the GROUP BY clause.

If a query includes more than one query block combined by a set operator such as UNION, the result of the query can be assigned column names by assigning the same column names to each participating query block. The following example produces a combined listing of employees and departments, with column names NAME and COST. The ORDER BY clause operates on the result of the UNION rather than on an individual query block, ordering the resulting rows in descending order by cost.

```
SELECT name, salary + bonus AS cost
FROM emp
UNION
SELECT deptname AS name, budget AS cost
FROM dept
ORDER BY cost DESC;
```

The naming of output columns in a SELECT list is useful both in outer-level queries and in subqueries. As we have seen, generated column names in outer-level queries are useful for ordering output and for making more descriptive output labels. In a subquery, generated column names are important for preserving the closure property so that the result of the subquery can be used in an outer query just as if it were a table.

5.2.1 Scalar Subqueries

An *expression* represents a scalar value, constructed from primitive parts such as column names, constants, host variables, functions, and special registers, as described in Section 2.4.1. In UDB, wherever an expression can be used, you can also use a subquery that returns a scalar value (that is, one row with exactly one column). When a subquery is used in a place where a scalar is expected, it is called a *scalar subquery*. If a scalar subquery returns more than one row or more than one column, an error results. If a scalar subquery returns zero rows, its result is interpreted as the null value (no error results in this case, unless the context where the scalar subquery is used does not permit null values for some reason).

The following example uses two scalar subqueries inside a comparison predicate to find the names and locations of departments in which the average bonus is greater than the average salary:

```
SELECT d.deptname, d.location
FROM    dept AS d
WHERE (SELECT avg(bonus)
        FROM    emp
        WHERE   deptno = d.deptno)
     > (SELECT avg(salary)
        FROM    emp
        WHERE   deptno = d.deptno)
```

Scalar subqueries are often used in SELECT clauses, as illustrated by the next example, which lists the department numbers, names, and maximum salaries of all the departments located in Sausalito.

```
SELECT d.deptno, d.deptname,
            (SELECT max(salary)
             FROM    emp
             WHERE   deptno = d.deptno) AS maxpay
FROM    dept AS d
WHERE   d.location = 'Sausalito';
```

In this example, any department in Sausalito that has no employees will appear in the result set with a null value for its maximum salary. Note that this is different from the example below, which expresses a similar query as a join. In the join formulation of the query, departments in Sausalito that have no employees do not appear in the result set at all.

```
SELECT d.deptno, d.deptname, max(e.salary) AS maxpay
FROM dept AS d, emp AS e
WHERE d.deptno = e.deptno
AND d.location = 'Sausalito'
GROUP BY d.deptno, d.deptname;
```

In our next example, we assume the existence of the following table, which contains planned pay raises for employees based on their job and rating:

SALARYPLAN

```
JOB  RATING  RAISE
```

Using the SALARYPLAN table, we will update the salaries of employees in department no. A74 by applying the appropriate pay raises. This is done by using a scalar subquery in the SET clause of an UPDATE statement.

```
UPDATE emp AS e
SET salary = salary + (SELECT raise FROM salaryplan p
                              WHERE p.job = e.job
                              AND p.rating = e.rating)
WHERE deptno = 'A74';
```

It is interesting to consider what the UPDATE statement above will do if some employee has a job and/or rating that is not found in the SALARYPLAN table. The scalar subquery will return no result, which will be interpreted as a null value; when this null value is added to the employee's current salary, the salary will become null! If this is not the behavior we desire, we can guard against it by modifying the UPDATE statement as follows:

```
UPDATE emp AS e
SET salary = salary +
                coalesce((SELECT raise FROM salaryplan p
                        WHERE p.job = e.job
                        AND p.rating = e.rating), 0)
WHERE deptno = 'A74';
```

The following points should be clear from the examples above:

1. Interesting uses of scalar subqueries often involve correlation names.

2. Scalar subqueries pose many challenges for attractive indentation of your SQL code.

5.2.2 Table Expressions

In all of the examples above, the subquery was used in place of a scalar value. But we know that a subquery can also return a table consisting of many rows and columns. Such a subquery is called a *table expression*, and it can be used in a FROM clause where the name of a table is expected.

The FROM clause of a SELECT statement lists the table(s) on which the query operates. Each table listed in the FROM clause can optionally be given a correlation name, which serves as the name of the table within the current query. We have seen how correlation names are used in correlated subqueries. They are also useful in cases where it is necessary to join a table to itself, as in the famous query "Find employees who earn more than their managers." In this query, we join the EMP table to itself as though it were two different tables named e and m.

```
SELECT  e.name, e.salary, m.name, m.salary
FROM    emp AS e, emp AS m
WHERE   e.manager = m.name
AND     e.salary > m.salary
```

UDB allows a table expression (subquery) to be used in place of a table name in a FROM clause. The table expression participates in the query just as though it were a real table in the database. The table expression must be enclosed in parentheses and followed by an AS clause that gives it a table name. The column names of the virtual table can be specified either in the AS clause along with the table name or in the SELECT clause of the subquery itself.

Suppose that, for the purpose of a particular query on the EMP table, we would like to consider only employees whose job is "Plumber," to treat the SALARY and BONUS columns as though they were combined into a single column named PAY, and to treat the STARTDATE column as though it contained only a year rather than an actual date. In other words, we would like to write a query against a table expression derived from EMP that has the following structure:

PLUMBERS

NAME	PAY	STARTYEAR

The following query uses such a table expression to list the name, combined pay, and starting year of all plumbers whose combined pay is less than $42,000 and who started work before 1990. Note how the table expression is given both a table name (PLUMBERS) and a set of column names (NAME, PAY, STARTYEAR).

```
SELECT name, pay, startyear
FROM (SELECT name, salary + bonus, year(startdate)
      FROM emp
      WHERE job = 'Plumber')
      AS plumbers(name, pay, startyear)
WHERE pay < 42000 AND startyear < 1990;
```

In the example above, it was not really necessary to use a table expression, since the predicates and column definitions in the subquery could have been moved to the outer-level query. However, in some cases, table expressions allow you to express queries that could not have been expressed otherwise. Such cases often involve grouping in the table expression.

Suppose that the personnel manager of our company is analyzing the distribution of performance ratings in the company. As part of this analysis, she uses a table expression that computes the minimum and maximum rating given to employees in each department. The result of the table expression has the following structure:

RATINGSTATS

DEPTNO	MINRATING	MAXRATING

Ratings are numbers between 1 and 10, and the personnel manager wants to find departments in which the difference between the highest and the lowest rating is greater than 4. These departments can be found by the following query, which defines and uses the RATINGSTATS table expression:

```
SELECT deptno, minrating, maxrating
FROM (SELECT deptno, min(rating), max(rating)
      FROM emp
      GROUP BY deptno)
      AS ratingstats(deptno, minrating, maxrating)
WHERE maxrating - minrating > 4;
```

This query could have been expressed without using a table expression, by moving the GROUP BY to the outer query block and changing the WHERE clause into a HAVING clause. But if the outer query block needs to do some further grouping, the table expression becomes essential to the query. As an example of such a query, suppose that the personnel manager wants to find, for each rating value, the number of departments that have that value as their maximum rating. This query can be expressed as follows, using the same RATINGSTATS table expression defined above:

```
SELECT maxrating, count(*) AS n_depts
FROM (SELECT deptno, min(rating), max(rating)
      FROM emp
      GROUP BY deptno)
      AS ratingstats(deptno, minrating, maxrating)
GROUP BY maxrating;
```

In this query, since grouping is done both in the table expression and in the outer query block, the table expression is essential. The result of the query might look something like this:

MAXRATING	N_DEPTS
8	2
9	1
10	1

We have seen how a subquery can be correlated to a table in an outer query block, causing the subquery to be evaluated once for each row of the correlated table. It is also possible for a subquery used in a table expression to be correlated to another table that occurs earlier in the same FROM clause. As an example of this powerful feature, we will define a table expression that computes the headcount and total pay for a given department. The result of the table expression will be a virtual table with the following structure:

STATS

HEADCOUNT	TOTALPAY

The following query computes the headcount and total pay of all departments located in Sausalito:

```
SELECT deptno, headcount, totalpay
FROM dept AS d,
     TABLE(SELECT count(*), sum(salary) + sum(bonus)
           FROM emp AS e
           WHERE e.deptno = d.deptno)
     AS stats(headcount, totalpay)
WHERE location = 'Sausalito';
```

You may be wondering why the table expression in this example is preceded by the word TABLE. Actually, the word TABLE may optionally be placed in front of *any* table expression, but it is *required* if the table expression is correlated to something outside itself. It may seem strange, but that's the rule.

In the result of the query above, as you might expect, departments located in Sausalito that have no employees appear with zero for HEADCOUNT and null for TOTALPAY. It is interesting to consider some alternative ways in which this query might have been written. The main alternatives are as follows (actually writing these queries is left as an exercise for the reader):

1. The headcount and total pay could have been computed by two separate correlated scalar subqueries in the outermost SELECT clause. This formulation gives the same result as the one above, but is more awkward to write, and one suspects that it may not perform as well.

2. The DEPT and EMP tables could have been joined and then grouped by DEPTNO. The disadvantage of this formulation is that departments located in Sausalito that have no employees do not appear in the result at all. To make sure that these departments appear in the query result, the join could be replaced by a left outer join (to be discussed in Section 5.4), but in this formulation a Sausalito department with no employees will appear to have a headcount of 1!

TIP: It may be worth mentioning why we wrote sum(salary) + sum(bonus) in the examples above rather than sum(salary + bonus). The reason has to do with null values. If an employee has, for example, a well-defined salary but a null bonus, we want the salary of that employee to participate in our computation. The expression sum(salary) + sum(bonus) computes the two sums independently, taking into account all non-null salaries and bonuses. The expression sum(salary + bonus), on the other hand, includes an employee's salary and bonus in the sum only if both salary and bonus are non-null.

5.3 TABLE FUNCTIONS

In the previous section, we discussed how a subquery can be used in a FROM clause to generate a table. UDB also provides another way in which virtual tables can be generated, called *table functions*. A table function is a user-defined function, written in a host programming language, that returns a table. We will learn how to create a table function in Section 6.4.8. Table functions are very powerful because they can make data that is really stored outside your database appear to be a table inside your database. Since table functions are written in a programming language such as C, they can perform operating system calls, read data from files, or even access data across a network. This enables you to bring the power of SQL to bear on querying data from a variety of sources. For example, you might write a table function that returns a list of the users who are currently logged on to your computer system. Since this list appears to UDB in the form of a one-column table, you could write a query that joins the user list to some database table, perhaps to find the telephone numbers of users who are currently logged on and who are SQL experts.

To create an example of a table function, imagine that we are working for an office supply chain with stores in several cities. Our chain uses a point-of-sale system that records every item sold, using some proprietary format. For planning purposes, we would like to access this data using UDB so that we can execute SQL queries against the data and join it to tables in our UDB database. Using the techniques described in Section 6.4.8, we create a table function named SALES that takes the name of a store as a parameter and returns a table containing all the sales records from that store. The result of the SALES function is a table with the following columns:

SALEDATE	PRODUCT	QUANTITY	PRICE

We can use a table function such as SALES in the FROM clause of a query, just as we used table expressions in Section 5.2.2. The call to the table function is wrapped in parentheses, preceded by the word TABLE, and followed by a correlation name that serves as the name of the table returned by the function. For example, the following query finds the average price of staplers sold by the Boulder store in 1997:

```
SELECT avg(price) AS avgprice
FROM TABLE(sales('Boulder')) AS sales
WHERE product = 'Stapler'
AND year(saledate) = 1997;
```

Since the SALES function makes our point-of-sale data appear like a table to UDB, we can easily process it using SQL operations such as grouping. For example, the following query lists the total revenue of the Denver store for each month in 1997:

```
SELECT month(saledate) AS month,
       sum(quantity * price) AS revenue
FROM TABLE(sales('Denver')) AS sales
WHERE year(saledate) = 1997
GROUP BY month(saledate);
```

Using a table function, it is possible to join a table in a UDB database to a virtual table that is outside the database. As an example, suppose that our database contains a SALESPLAN table that specifies, for each year, store, and product, the planned monthly sales. The following entry in the SALESPLAN table might indicate that during 1997, the Denver store is expected to sell 20 staplers per month:

SALESPLAN

YEAR	STORE	PRODUCT	MONTHLY_UNITS
1997	Denver	Stapler	20

The following example query joins the SALESPLAN table to the virtual table returned by the SALES table function, to find months in 1997 in which a store exceeded its sales plan for some item by at least 50%. For each such case, the query finds the month, store, product, planned sales, and actual units sold.

```
SELECT month(sales.saledate) AS month,
       plan.store,
       plan.product,
       plan.monthly_units AS units_planned,
       sum(sales.quantity) AS units_sold
FROM salesplan AS plan, TABLE(sales(plan.store)) AS sales
WHERE plan.year = 1997
AND plan.product = sales.product
AND plan.year = year(sales.saledate)
GROUP BY month(sales.saledate),
         plan.store, plan.product, plan.monthly_units
HAVING sum(sales.quantity) >= 1.5 * plan.monthly_units;
```

Notice that in the FROM clause in the example above, the first of the tables to be joined is given the correlation name PLAN. This correlation name is then used, later in the FROM clause, to form the parameter of the table function call. This is very similar to the way correlation names were used inside table expressions in Section 5.2.2. The result of the query might look something like this:

MONTH	STORE	PRODUCT	UNITS_PLANNED	UNITS_SOLD
1	Boulder	Stapler	20	30
8	Boulder	Stapler	20	40
8	Denver	Pencil	100	500
9	Denver	Stapler	20	30
12	Denver	Pen	50	130

TIP: In the example above, we want the output data to be grouped by month, store, and product. It might seem sufficient for the GROUP BY clause to consist of the expressions `month(sales.saledate)`, `plan.store`, and `plan.product`. However, the query will not run unless `plan.monthly_units` is also included in the GROUP BY clause, because `plan.monthly_units` appears in the SELECT clause, and the system has no way to know that its value is uniquely determined by the other columns in the GROUP BY clause.

5.4 EXPLICIT JOINS

Imagine that we are responsible for a university database containing the following tables:

TEACHERS

NAME	RANK
Barnes	Full Prof.
Baxter	Assoc. Prof.
Glenn	Assist. Prof.
Redding	Assoc. Prof.
Walker	Full Prof.

CLASSES

QUARTER	SUBJECT	TEACHER	ENROLLMENT
Fall 97	English 280	Baxter	30
Fall 97	Math 101	Glenn	40
Fall 97	Biology 580	Redding	33
Fall 97	German 130	Staff	31
Winter 97	French 140	Barnes	(null)
Winter 97	Latin 237	Glenn	20
Winter 97	Physics 405	Redding	28

From time to time, the registrar at our university might need to print a master list of all the teachers (including their ranks) and the courses they teach (including their enrollments). This can be done by joining the TEACHERS and CLASSES tables, as in the following query:

```
SELECT t.name, t.rank, c.subject, c.enrollment
FROM teachers AS t, classes AS c
WHERE t.name = c.teacher;
```

As we learned in Section 2.4.5, this query pairs rows from the TEACHERS table with rows from the CLASSES table. The WHERE clause specifies which of those pairs of rows actually participate in the join—namely, pairs in which the NAME value in the teacher row matches the TEACHER value in the class row. A predicate that specifies the relationship between two tables in a join is called a *join condition*.

SQL also provides an alternative syntax called an *explicit join* that may make it easier for you to visualize what is happening in a join query. In this alternative syntax, the tables to be joined are connected by the keyword JOIN and followed by an ON clause that specifies the join condition. The explicit join, including the join condition, is conceptually inside the FROM clause of a query. The explicit join produces a *joined table* that is then operated on by the other clauses of the query, such as the WHERE, GROUP BY, and HAVING clauses. The following query, which is exactly equivalent to the one above, illustrates the explicit join syntax:

```
SELECT t.name, t.rank, c.subject, c.enrollment
FROM teachers AS t JOIN classes AS c ON t.name = c.teacher;
```

The two join queries that we have just discussed are both examples of conventional, or *inner,* joins, and they both produce the following result:

NAME	RANK	SUBJECT	ENROLLMENT
Barnes	Full Prof.	French 140	(null)
Baxter	Assoc. Prof.	English 280	30
Glenn	Assist. Prof.	Math 101	40
Glenn	Assist. Prof.	Latin 237	20
Redding	Assoc. Prof.	Biology 580	33
Redding	Assoc. Prof.	Physics 405	28

Looking at the query result shown above, we see that it does not include any teachers (such as Prof. Walker) who are not scheduled to teach a class, or any classes (such as German 130) that do not have an assigned teacher who matches one of the names in the TEACHERS table. But the university administration might reasonably wish either or both of these kinds of data to be included in the master list. This type of requirement gives rise to a kind of query called an *outer join.*

An outer join always involves a join of two tables, which we will refer to as the *left table* and the *right table.* An outer join is different from a conventional join because it includes rows that have no "partners"—that is, rows from the left table that have no matching rows in the right table, or vice versa. There are three kinds of outer-join queries:

1. A *left outer join* includes rows from the left table that have no matching values in the right table, such as teachers who are not teaching any classes. These rows are given null values in place of the missing right-table data.

2. A *right outer join* includes rows from the right table that have no matching values in the left table, such as classes that have no teacher. These rows are given null values in place of the missing left-table data.

3. A *full outer join* includes both kinds of rows. In our example, it would include both teachers who have no classes and classes that have no teachers, supplemented by null values in place of the missing data.

Left and right outer joins can be expressed in SQL simply by replacing the word JOIN with LEFT OUTER JOIN, RIGHT OUTER JOIN, or FULL OUTER JOIN in the explicit join syntax that we have already discussed. The following example applies a full outer join to our university database:

```
SELECT t.name, t.rank, c.subject, c.enrollment
FROM teachers AS t FULL OUTER JOIN classes AS c
     ON t.name = c.teacher;
```

Result:

NAME	RANK	SUBJECT	ENROLLMENT	
Barnes	Full Prof.	French 140	(null)	
Baxter	Assoc. Prof.	English 280	30	
Glenn	Assist. Prof.	Math 101	40	
Glenn	Assist. Prof.	Latin 237	20	
Redding	Assoc. Prof.	Biology 580	33	
Redding	Assoc. Prof.	Physics 405	28	
Walker	Full Prof.	(null)	(null)	← (LOJ)
(null)	(null)	German 130	31	← (ROJ)

As you can see, the result of the full outer join is the same as the result of the inner join, augmented by some additional rows. The row labeled LOJ is a left-table row that has no right-table partner, and the row labeled ROJ is a right-table row that has no left-table partner. In both cases, nulls have been substituted for the missing data. If the query had specified LEFT OUTER JOIN in place of FULL OUTER JOIN, the row labeled LOJ would appear in the result set, but the row labeled ROJ would not. Similarly, if the query had specified RIGHT OUTER JOIN, the result set would include row ROJ but not row LOJ.

When you use the explicit join syntax, you have a choice of two places in which you can write predicates to filter out uninteresting rows: the ON clause and the WHERE clause. Both of these clauses contain a search condition that consists of one or more predicates connected by AND, OR, and NOT. The WHERE clause and the ON clause have exactly the same syntax, except that the ON clause is not allowed to contain any subqueries. However, a predicate in the ON clause will not in general have the same effect as the same predicate in the WHERE clause. To understand this, you must first understand the steps involved in processing an explicit join, which are as follows:[2]

---

2. Of course, these steps are only the *conceptual* algorithm used for processing an explicit join—the optimizer reserves the right to use another algorithm that leads to the same result.

1. A set of row pairs is formed, consisting of a Cartesian product of the left table and the right table of the explicit join, in which every left row is paired with every right row.

2. The ON clause of the explicit join is applied to this set of row pairs, filtering out all row pairs that do not satisfy its search condition.

3. If the explicit join is a left outer join, each left-table row that is not represented in the filtered set of row pairs is added back, with null values for the right table. Similarly, if the join is a right outer join, each right-table row that is not represented in the filtered set of row pairs is added back, with null values for the left table. Of course, if the join is a full outer join, both unrepresented left-table rows and unrepresented right-table rows are added. The filtered and augmented set of row pairs then becomes the result of the explicit join.

4. The query in which the explicit join is embedded treats the result of the explicit join as a table that is processed in the usual way. The table generated by the explicit join may be joined to other tables, using either explicit or implicit join syntax. Any predicates in the WHERE clause are applied to the result of the explicit join (after the set of row pairs has been filtered by the ON clause and enhanced with missing rows). Other parts of the query such as the GROUP BY and HAVING clauses also treat the result of the explicit join just as though it were a normal table.

The implications of these rules can best be illustrated by some examples. Suppose that our university registrar needs to print a master list of classes being offered in the fall quarter of 1997. By using a left outer join of the TEACHERS and CLASSES tables, the registrar intends to include those teachers who are not teaching any class in fall 1997 (with null values for the columns derived from CLASSES). Since the registrar is interested only in fall 1997 classes, she includes the predicate QUARTER = 'Fall 97'. But should this predicate be included in the ON clause or in the WHERE clause?

If the predicate QUARTER = 'Fall 97' is included in the ON clause, it is applied *before* the result of the outer join is augmented by unmatched rows from the TEACHERS table. Then each teacher who has no fall 1997 class is added to the join result, with null CLASSES data. This query and its result are shown below. Note that all the teachers are on the list, including Professor Barnes, who has no classes in fall 1997, and Professor Walker, who has no classes at all.

```
SELECT t.name, t.rank, c.subject, c.enrollment
FROM teachers AS t LEFT OUTER JOIN classes AS c
    ON t.name = c.teacher AND c.quarter = 'Fall 97';
```

Result:

NAME	RANK	SUBJECT	ENROLLMENT
Barnes	Full Prof.	(null)	(null)
Baxter	Assoc. Prof.	English 280	30
Glenn	Assist. Prof.	Math 101	40
Redding	Assoc. Prof.	Biology 580	33
Walker	Full Prof.	(null)	(null)

The result shown above is probably what the registrar intended. If, however, she had included the filtering predicate in the WHERE clause instead of in the ON clause, she would have received the following result:

```
SELECT t.name, t.rank, c.subject, c.enrollment
FROM teachers AS t LEFT OUTER JOIN classes AS c
     ON t.name = c.teacher
WHERE c.quarter = 'Fall 97';
```

Result:

NAME	RANK	SUBJECT	ENROLLMENT
Baxter	Assoc. Prof.	English 280	30
Glenn	Assist. Prof.	Math 101	40
Redding	Assoc. Prof.	Biology 580	33

In this example, the left outer join included Professors Barnes and Walker, but the WHERE clause filtered them out again because they had no fall 1997 classes, effectively undoing the work of the left outer join. These examples illustrate the importance of placing your predicates with care when you use explicit join syntax.

An outer join is always performed on exactly two tables. If you need to combine three or more tables by outer joins, you will need more than one step—for example, you might outer join the first table to the second table, then outer join the result to the third table. A query may contain more than one outer join, and the order in which these joins are performed can be controlled by parentheses. In fact, parentheses are important in such a case because the result of the query can be affected by the ordering of the outer joins. For a simple example of this phenomenon, consider the following three tables:

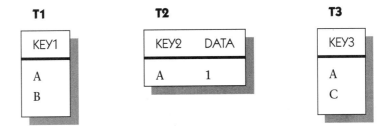

The following query left outer joins T1 and T2, then right outer joins the result to T3:

```
SELECT key1, key2, key3, data
FROM (t1 LEFT OUTER JOIN t2 ON key1 = key2)
     RIGHT OUTER JOIN t3 ON key2 = key3;
```

Result:

KEY1	KEY2	KEY3	DATA
A	A	A	1
(null)	(null)	C	(null)

The following query performs the same outer joins in the opposite order, with a different result:

```
SELECT key1, key2, key3, data
FROM t1 LEFT OUTER JOIN
     (t2 RIGHT OUTER JOIN t3 ON key2 = key3)
     ON key1 = key2;
```

Result:

KEY1	KEY2	KEY3	DATA
A	A	A	1
B	(null)	(null)	(null)

5.5 EXTENDED FROM CLAUSE

In Section 2.4.8, we learned that a FROM clause is used to list the tables that participate in a query block, optionally giving a new name called a correlation name to each table. In Sections 5.2 through 5.4, we learned that a FROM clause can contain more than a simple list of table names and view names. In general, a FROM clause consists of a list of *table references*, each of which either names an existing table or specifies how a virtual table can be materialized. During processing of a query block, all the tables represented by these table references are (conceptually) materialized and formed into a giant Cartesian product. This Cartesian product is then processed by the other clauses in the query block, such as the WHERE, GROUP BY, HAVING, and SELECT clauses.

The syntax diagrams on the following pages show that four kinds of table references can be used in a FROM clause:

1. The simplest kind of table reference is simply the name of a table or view, optionally followed by a correlation clause that provides a local name for the table (and possibly renames its columns as well).

2. Another kind of table reference is a query, called a table expression, from which a table can be derived. If the table expression is correlated to something outside itself, it must be enclosed in parentheses and preceded by the word TABLE. A table expression is always followed by a correlation clause that names the derived table (and possibly also its columns).

3. A table reference can also be a table function that takes zero or more parameters and returns a table. Like a table expression, a table function is always followed by a correlation clause that gives a name to the table (and optionally to the columns) returned by the function.

4. The fourth kind of table reference is an explicit join. The operands of the explicit join are in turn table references, of any of the four kinds. When a table reference contains more than one explicit join, parentheses can be used to specify the order in which the joins are to be performed. An explicit join is never followed by a correlation clause, since each operand of the explicit join can have a correlation clause of its own.

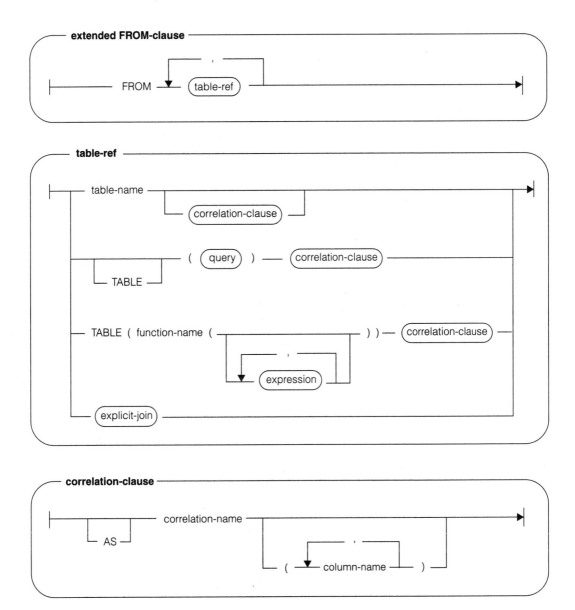

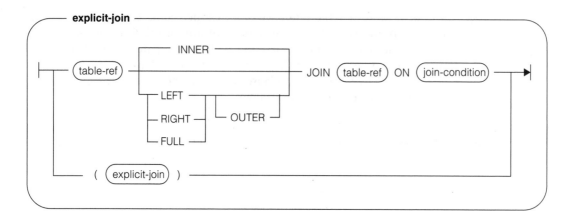

The join condition in the ON clause of an explicit join specifies the criterion for joining the rows that result from the table references on the left and right side of the join. A join condition is syntactically the same as a search condition (see syntax on page 56), with the following additional restrictions:

1. A join condition may not contain any subqueries.

2. All the columns referenced in a join condition must be columns of the tables that are being joined.

If a table reference has a correlation name, that correlation name serves as its table name throughout the query block. Similarly, if a table reference has a correlation clause that includes column names, the clause must provide names for all the columns of the table reference, and these column names must be used throughout the query block, replacing the natural names of the columns.

The fact that all the different kinds of table references can be mixed inside a FROM clause gives you a great deal of flexibility in writing queries. To illustrate this flexibility, the following example query uses a table expression, a table function, and an explicit join. The query finds months in 1997 in which a store exceeded its sales plan for some item by at least 50%, and is equivalent to the query on page 220.

```
SELECT month(sales.saledate) AS month,
       plan.store,
       plan.product,
       plan.monthly_units AS units_planned,
       sum(sales.quantity) AS units_sold
FROM  (SELECT year, store, product, monthly_units
       FROM salesplan
       WHERE year = 1997) AS plan
```

```
        JOIN TABLE(sales(plan.store)) AS sales
            ON plan.product = sales.product
            AND plan.year = year(sales.saledate)
    GROUP BY month(sales.saledate),
            plan.store, plan.product, plan.monthly_units
    HAVING sum(sales.quantity) >= 1.5 * plan.monthly_units;
```

5.6 SUPER GROUPS

The GROUP BY feature of SQL, described in Section 2.4.7, allows you to organize a table into groups of rows and to compute some properties of each group, such as the number of rows in the group or the average value of a column or expression. In this section, I will describe a new feature of UDB called *super groups* that allows you to perform more than one kind of grouping in a single query. This feature is often useful if you have a large collection of data points that span several dimensions, such as time, location, and type of measurement, and you need to analyze the data to see how it varies in each dimension. This general type of analysis is sometimes referred to as *online analytical processing*, or *OLAP*.

To illustrate the queries in this section, I will use the census database shown in the table on the following page. To help you understand the queries that follow, I have shown the rows of the census table in order by state, county, and city; of course, the table itself has no intrinsic ordering. Note that the table contains some null values—some birthdates and incomes are unknown, and some people, possibly living in rural areas, have a null value for CITY.

The simplest kind of grouping query that might be applied to the CENSUS table is one that organizes the table into groups according to the values of one of its columns, as in the following example, which finds the average income in each state:

```
SELECT state, avg(income) AS avg_income
FROM census
GROUP BY state;
```

Result:

STATE	AVG_INCOME
FL	35940
TX	36085

CENSUS

NAME	CITY	COUNTY	STATE	BIRTHDATE	SEX	INCOME
Joe	Miami	Dade	FL	8/20/55	M	32100
Chen	Miami	Dade	FL	6/05/57	M	40200
Bob	Hialeah	Dade	FL	3/21/57	M	33500
Karen	Hialeah	Dade	FL	8/23/55	F	43900
Jim	(null)	Dade	FL	10/24/56	M	29600
Joan	(null)	Dade	FL	11/15/56	F	36300
Dave	Orlando	Orange	FL	9/25/57	M	38000
Linda	Orlando	Orange	FL	5/13/55	F	46700
Jeff	Taft	Orange	FL	2/08/57	M	32600
Pat	Taft	Orange	FL	10/30/57	F	26500
Sam	Baytown	Harris	TX	3/02/55	M	28500
Bill	Baytown	Harris	TX	12/21/56	M	32800
Mary	Houston	Harris	TX	(null)	F	44700
Susan	Houston	Harris	TX	4/30/55	F	(null)
Alex	Houston	Harris	TX	7/11/57	M	30900
John	Austin	Travis	TX	1/06/56	M	38400
Fred	Austin	Travis	TX	10/25/56	M	42500
Anne	(null)	Travis	TX	8/17/55	F	34800

When writing this query, you might wish to compute the overall average income in the entire census in addition to the average income in each state. The most efficient way for UDB to obtain this information is to make a single pass over the census data, computing the average income by states and the overall average at the same time. To allow you to ask this kind of question in the most convenient and efficient way, UDB allows you to write a query that specifies more than one kind of grouping. For this purpose, three new phrases have been added to the GROUP BY clause: ROLLUP, CUBE, and GROUPING SETS.

5.6.1 ROLLUP

ROLLUP is used whenever you need to analyze a collection of data in a single dimension, but at more than one level of detail. Finding average income by state as well as overall average income is a good example. Using the ROLLUP feature, this query could be written as follows:

```
SELECT state, avg(income) AS avg_income
FROM census
GROUP BY ROLLUP(state);
```

Result:

STATE	AVG_INCOME
FL	35940
TX	36085
(null)	36000

One or more expressions, called *grouping expressions,* can be specified inside the ROLLUP clause (in the example above, there is a single grouping expression: STATE). The system first groups the data by all the grouping expressions, then by all but the last grouping expression, then by all but the last two, and so on. After grouping by only the first grouping expression, the system makes one final grouping that consists of the whole table.[3] In the example above, the group that represents the whole CENSUS table is shown with a null value in the STATE column.

To see the true power of ROLLUP, we need a more complex query. The following example asks the system to find the total population and average income in each city, county, and state, and in the census as a whole:

```
SELECT state, county, city,
       count(*) AS population,
       avg(income) AS avg_income
FROM census
GROUP BY ROLLUP(state, county, city);
```

---

3. I do not mean to imply that this is the actual sequence in which the grouping computations are performed—in fact, all the grouping computations are performed simultaneously in a single pass over the table.

Result:

STATE	COUNTY	CITY	POPULATION	AVG_INCOME
FL	Dade	Hialeah	2	38700
FL	Dade	Miami	2	36150
FL	Dade	(null)	2	32950
FL	Orange	Orlando	2	42350
FL	Orange	Taft	2	29550
TX	Harris	Baytown	2	30650
TX	Harris	Houston	3	37800
TX	Travis	Austin	2	40450
TX	Travis	(null)	1	34800
FL	Dade	(null)	6	35933
FL	Orange	(null)	4	35950
TX	Harris	(null)	5	34225
TX	Travis	(null)	3	38566
FL	(null)	(null)	10	35940
TX	(null)	(null)	8	36085
(null)	(null)	(null)	18	36000

Since the example query above did not include an ORDER BY clause, no ordering is guaranteed among the rows of the result set. But I have taken the liberty of displaying the result in an order that helps us to understand how it was computed. First, we see nine rows that group the census data by STATE, COUNTY, and CITY; then four rows that group the data by STATE and COUNTY with null values for CITY; then two rows that group by STATE with null values for COUNTY and CITY; then one final row that represents the whole census and has null values for STATE, COUNTY, and CITY.

 TIP: The order of the expressions inside the ROLLUP is important! If one kind of group is logically contained inside another (such as COUNTY inside STATE), make sure you list the most inclusive group first (STATE before COUNTY).

In the example above, a single query has computed four different levels of grouping, which would have required four separate queries without using the

ROLLUP feature. The ROLLUP feature has provided a big payoff in both convenience and efficiency. However, if we examine the query result closely, we notice something disturbing. The problem is illustrated by the following two rows in the query result:

STATE	COUNTY	CITY	POPULATION	AVG_INCOME
FL	Dade	(null)	2	32950
FL	Dade	(null)	6	35933

The first of these rows represents a group at the (STATE, COUNTY, CITY) level, containing the people who live in Dade County, Florida, in rural areas outside of any city (you can see from the CENSUS table that there are two such people, Jim and Joan). The second row, on the other hand, represents a group at the (STATE, COUNTY) level, representing all the people who live in Dade County, Florida, regardless of their city (in the CENSUS table, there are six such people). Thus we might say that the null value in the first row represents "no city," while the null value in the second row represents "all cities." It's clear that we need some way to distinguish these cases by indicating the level of grouping that applies to each row. Fortunately, **UDB** provides a function named grouping precisely for this purpose.

The grouping function is intended for use in queries that perform more than one type of grouping. The argument of the function is one of the grouping columns, and the function returns 1 if the designated column has been merged into a higher-level group. Thus, for those special rows in which a null CITY value represents "all cities," the value of grouping(city) is 1; however, for ordinary rows, the value of grouping(city) is 0.

The grouping function can be used in several ways. When an application program executes a ROLLUP query, it should probably apply the grouping function to each column in the ROLLUP, and fetch the results into host variables for use in interpreting the rows of the query result. Whenever a grouping function returns 1, its argument column contains a null value that should be interpreted as "all values."

When a query is retrieving values for display, the grouping function can be used in a CASE expression that specifies a special string to represent "all values." You can use any string you like for this purpose, but of course you will want to choose a string that can easily be distinguished from a valid data value. In the following example query, CASE expressions are used to display the string "(-all-)" instead of a null value whenever the grouping function indicates that the null represents "all values."

```
SELECT CASE grouping(state)
          WHEN 1 THEN '(-all-)' ELSE state END AS state,
       CASE grouping(county)
          WHEN 1 THEN '(-all-)' ELSE county END AS county,
       CASE grouping(city)
          WHEN 1 THEN '(-all-)' ELSE city END AS city,
       count(*) AS pop,
       avg(income) AS avg_income
FROM census
GROUP BY ROLLUP(state, county, city);
```

Result:

STATE	COUNTY	CITY	POP	AVG_INCOME
FL	Dade	Hialeah	2	38700
FL	Dade	Miami	2	36150
FL	Dade	(null)	2	32950
FL	Orange	Orlando	2	42350
FL	Orange	Taft	2	29550
TX	Harris	Baytown	2	30650
TX	Harris	Houston	3	37800
TX	Travis	Austin	2	40450
TX	Travis	(null)	1	34800
FL	Dade	(-all-)	6	35933
FL	Orange	(-all-)	4	35950
TX	Harris	(-all-)	5	34225
TX	Travis	(-all-)	3	38566
FL	(-all-)	(-all-)	10	35940
TX	(-all-)	(-all-)	8	36085
(-all-)	(-all-)	(-all-)	18	36000

In this query result, the row that represents the group of people in Dade county with null cities is easy to distinguish from the row that represents the group of all people in Dade county, regardless of city.[4]

You may be wondering how WHERE and HAVING clauses can be used in a ROLLUP query. The answer is that these clauses are used in the usual way and that they apply to groups at all levels of grouping. For example, the following query might be used to find the female population and average female income for each city, county, and state that has at least two females in the census:

```
SELECT CASE grouping(state)
          WHEN 1 THEN '(-all-)' ELSE state END AS state,
       CASE grouping(county)
          WHEN 1 THEN '(-all-)' ELSE county END AS county,
       CASE grouping(city)
          WHEN 1 THEN '(-all-)' ELSE city END AS city,
       count(*) AS f_pop,
       avg(income) AS avg_f_income
FROM census
WHERE sex = 'F'
GROUP BY ROLLUP(state, county, city)
HAVING count(*) >= 2;
```

Result:

STATE	COUNTY	CITY	F_POP	AVG_F_INCOME
TX	Harris	Houston	2	44700
FL	Dade	(-all-)	2	40100
FL	Orange	(-all-)	2	36600
TX	Harris	(-all-)	2	44700
FL	(-all-)	(-all-)	4	38350
TX	(-all-)	(-all-)	3	39750
(-all-)	(-all-)	(-all-)	7	38816

---

4. In all the query results in this section, I show the summary rows at the end of the result set to help visualize the meaning of the query. The actual ordering of the summary rows in the result set is unpredictable unless ORDER BY is specified; then it depends on the string that is chosen to represent "all values."

We can see from the query result that our census data contains two or more females in only one city (Houston); in three counties (Dade, Orange, and Harris); in two states (Florida and Texas); and in the table as a whole.

5.6.2 CUBE

The examples in the previous section showed how the ROLLUP operator is useful for grouping data at various levels of detail in one dimension (in the examples, the dimension was geography). The CUBE operator, on the other hand, is used to analyze data by forming it into groups in more than one dimension.

When analyzing the data in the CENSUS table, we might be interested in the effects of sex and birthdate on income. Since sex and birthdate are independent variables, there are four possible ways in which they might be used to form the census data into groups, as shown in the following list:

1. Group by sex and birthdate (typical group: females born in 1955).
2. Group by sex only (typical group: females of all birthdates).
3. Group by birthdate only (typical group: persons of all sexes born in 1955).
4. Treat the table as a single group containing all sexes and birthdates.

The CUBE operator asks the system to group by a list of expressions in all possible ways. For example, if you specify GROUP BY CUBE(sex, year(birth-date)), the system will form groups in all four of the ways listed, as shown in the following query:

```
SELECT sex,
       year(birthdate) AS birth_year,
       max(income) AS max_income
FROM census
GROUP BY CUBE(sex, year(birthdate));
```

Result:

SEX	BIRTH_YEAR	MAX_INCOME
F	1955	46700
F	1956	36300
F	1957	26500
F	(null)	44700
M	1955	32100
M	1956	42500
M	1957	40200
F	(null)	46700
M	(null)	42500
(null)	1955	46700
(null)	1956	42500
(null)	1957	40200
(null)	(null)	44700
(null)	(null)	46700

When looking at a row in the result of a CUBE query, you may find it difficult to tell what kind of group the row represents. For example, in the result set shown above, there are two rows with null values in both the SEX and BIRTH_YEAR columns. One of these rows represents the group that contains both sexes and an unknown birth year, and the other represents the group that contains both sexes and all birth years. In order to distinguish these groups, it is once again necessary to use the grouping function.

In a CUBE query, the grouping function can be applied to any of the columns or expressions used inside the CUBE operator. As in a ROLLUP query, whenever a null value of a grouping expression has the special meaning "all values," the grouping function returns 1. For example, if grouping(sex) = 1, a null value in the SEX column represents "all sexes" (this might be found in a row where the data is grouped by birth year rather than by sex). We can use the grouping function inside CASE expressions to display some word or symbol of our choice to represent the special meaning "all values." The following example uses "(-all-)" for this purpose, enabling us to distinguish between the group of all females and the group of females with unknown birthdates. Compare the result of this query with the result of the previous example shown on page 238.

```
SELECT CASE grouping(sex)
          WHEN 1 THEN '(-all-)' ELSE sex END AS sex,
       CASE grouping(year(birthdate))
          WHEN 1 THEN '(-all-)'
          ELSE char(year(birthdate)) END AS birth_year,
       max(income) AS max_income
FROM census
GROUP BY CUBE(sex, year(birthdate));
```

TIP: Inside a CASE expression, all the possible values for the expression must have compatible types. In this example, it was necessary to use the char function inside a CASE, to convert year(birthdate) from an integer to a character string so that its type would be compatible with the string "(-all-)."

Result:

SEX	BIRTH_YEAR	MAX_INCOME
F	1955	46700
F	1956	36300
F	1957	26500
F	(null)	44700
M	1955	32100
M	1956	42500
M	1957	40200
F	(-all-)	46700
M	(-all-)	42500
(-all-)	1955	46700
(-all-)	1956	42500
(-all-)	1957	40200
(-all-)	(null)	44700
(-all-)	(-all-)	46700

The term CUBE is intended to suggest that a query is analyzing data in more than one dimension. In the previous example, analysis was performed in two dimensions (sex and birthdate), so this query might more accurately be described as a square rather than a cube. The CUBE operator, applied in n dimensions, will generate 2^n different kinds of groups. Thus, GROUP BY CUBE(sex, year(birthdate)) produced a two-dimensional result containing four kinds of groups, whereas GROUP BY CUBE(state, sex, year(birthdate)) would produce a three-dimensional result containing eight kinds of groups. The HAVING clause, if any, would be applied in the usual way to each of the groups in the query result.

The following example is a three-dimensional query (a true cube!) that groups the census data in all possible ways by state, sex, and birth year. It displays the number of persons in each group and the average income of each group, but only for groups that have at least four members.

```
SELECT CASE grouping(state)
          WHEN 1 THEN '(-all-)' ELSE state END AS state,
       CASE grouping(sex)
          WHEN 1 THEN '(-all-)' ELSE sex END AS sex,
       CASE grouping(year(birthdate))
          WHEN 1 THEN '(-all-)'
          ELSE char(year(birthdate)) END AS birth_year,
       count(*) AS count,
       avg(income) AS avg_income
FROM census
GROUP BY CUBE(state, sex, year(birthdate))
HAVING count(*) >= 4;
```

Result:

STATE	SEX	BIRTH_YEAR	COUNT	AVG_INCOME
FL	M	1957	4	36075
FL	F	(-all-)	4	38350
FL	M	(-all-)	6	34333
TX	M	(-all-)	5	34620
FL	(-all-)	1957	5	34160
FL	(-all-)	(-all-)	10	35940
TX	(-all-)	(-all-)	8	36085
(-all-)	F	1955	4	41800
(-all-)	M	1956	4	35825
(-all-)	M	1957	5	35040
(-all-)	F	(-all-)	7	38816
(-all-)	M	(-all-)	11	34463
(-all-)	(-all-)	1955	6	37200
(-all-)	(-all-)	1956	5	35920
(-all-)	(-all-)	1957	6	33616
(-all-)	(-all-)	(-all-)	18	36000

In the result set above, we can see at least one example of each of the eight kinds of groups that are generated by the CUBE operator in three dimensions. However, out of all the groups that are formed by state, sex, and birth year, we see that only one group (males born in Florida in 1957) has at least four members. Other kinds of groups are similarly filtered by the HAVING clause until only 16 groups remain in the final result.

5.6.3 GROUPING SETS

Sections 5.6.1 and 5.6.2 have described how the ROLLUP and CUBE operators can be used in a GROUP BY clause to perform detailed analysis of data in one dimension or in many dimensions. UDB also supports some other kinds of special grouping. For example, you may wish to analyze your data in one dimension without doing a full ROLLUP, or to analyze multiple dimensions without forming a full CUBE, or simply to call for certain kinds of grouping that happen to strike your fancy. UDB allows you to specify exactly the kinds of groups you want by means of an operator called GROUPING SETS.

To use GROUPING SETS, simply make a list of exactly the kinds of groups that you wish the system to form. If some of the grouping criteria include more than one column or expression, enclose those grouping criteria in parentheses. You may use empty parentheses ( ) to indicate a single group that spans the whole table. The following example query forms the census data into groups by state and sex, then forms another set of groups by birth year, and finally forms one big group consisting of the whole CENSUS table. For each group, it displays the number of persons in the group and the average income of the group. As before, this query uses the grouping function to display a special string whenever a null value has the special meaning "all values."

```
SELECT CASE grouping(state)
          WHEN 1 THEN '(-all-)' ELSE state END AS state,
       CASE grouping(sex)
          WHEN 1 THEN '(-all-)' ELSE sex END AS sex,
       CASE grouping(year(birthdate))
          WHEN 1 THEN '(-all-)'
          ELSE char(year(birthdate)) END AS birth_year,
       count(*) AS count,
       avg(income) AS avg_income
FROM census
GROUP BY GROUPING SETS ((state, sex), year(birthdate), ( ));
```

Result:

STATE	SEX	BIRTH_YEAR	COUNT	AVG_INCOME
FL	F	(-all-)	4	38350
FL	M	(-all-)	6	34333
TX	F	(-all-)	3	39750
TX	M	(-all-)	5	34620
(-all-)	(-all-)	1955	6	37200
(-all-)	(-all-)	1956	5	35920
(-all-)	(-all-)	1957	6	33616
(-all-)	(-all-)	(null)	1	44700
(-all-)	(-all-)	(-all-)	18	36000

The total number of groups in this query result is the *sum* of the number of groups produced by each of the three grouping sets: (STATE, SEX) produces four groups, YEAR(BIRTHDATE) produces four groups, and the empty grouping set ( ) produces one group that represents the whole table, for a total of nine groups.

5.6.4 Multiple Grouping Specifications

We have now seen how a GROUP BY clause can specify grouping by individual columns or expressions, or perform a one-dimensional analysis using ROLLUP or a multidimensional analysis using CUBE, or create an arbitrary collection of groups using GROUPING SETS. There is one more thing to learn: how these features can be combined and used together in the same GROUP BY clause. A GROUP BY clause can contain several *grouping specifications*, separated by commas. Each grouping specification may use any of the features we have discussed. The total number of groups produced by the GROUP BY clause is the *product* of the number of groups produced by each grouping specification. For example, if GROUP BY STATE produces three groups and GROUP BY SEX produces two groups, then GROUP BY STATE, SEX produces six groups; similarly, if GROUP BY ROLLUP(STATE, COUNTY) produces seven

groups and GROUP BY SEX produces two groups, then GROUP BY ROLL-
UP(STATE, COUNTY), SEX produces fourteen groups, as shown in the following example:

```
SELECT CASE grouping(state)
          WHEN 1 THEN '(-all-)' ELSE state END AS state,
       CASE grouping(county)
          WHEN 1 THEN '(-all-)' ELSE county END AS county,
       sex,
       count(*) AS pop,
       avg(income) AS avg_income
FROM census
GROUP BY ROLLUP(state, county), sex;
```

Result:

STATE	COUNTY	SEX	POP	AVG_INCOME
FL	Dade	F	2	40100
FL	Dade	M	4	33850
FL	Orange	F	2	36600
FL	Orange	M	2	35300
FL	(-all-)	F	4	38350
FL	(-all-)	M	6	34333
TX	Harris	F	2	44700
TX	Harris	M	3	30733
TX	Travis	F	1	34800
TX	Travis	M	2	40450
TX	(-all-)	F	3	39750
TX	(-all-)	M	5	34620
(-all-)	(-all-)	F	7	38816
(-all-)	(-all-)	M	11	34463

The syntax diagram below shows how various kinds of grouping specifications can be used in a GROUP BY clause. UDB also supports certain combinations of grouping methods that have been omitted from this syntax diagram for simplicity (for example, you can use ROLLUP and CUBE inside the GROUPING SETS operator). For details of these combinations, see the *SQL Reference*.

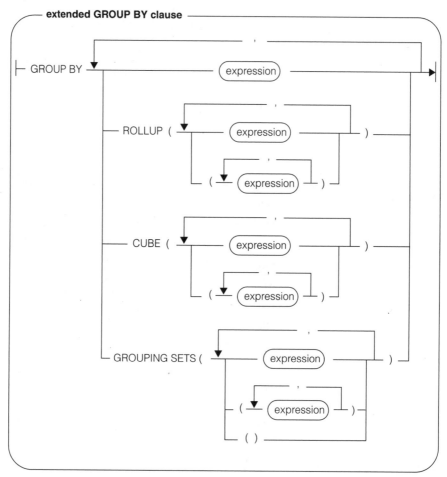

5.7 COMMON TABLE EXPRESSIONS

Suppose that, using the database of employees and departments introduced in Section 5.2, we need to find the department that has the highest total pay. This query is difficult because it involves two levels of aggregation: first, we need the sum function to combine individual employees' pay into totals by department; then, we need the max function to find the greatest of all the department totals. One way to express such a query is by creating a view and then writing a query that uses the view, as shown in the following example:

```
CREATE VIEW payroll(deptno, totalpay) AS
    SELECT deptno, sum(salary) + sum(bonus)
    FROM emp
    GROUP BY deptno;

SELECT deptno
FROM payroll
WHERE totalpay =
    (SELECT max(totalpay)
     FROM payroll);
```

It is awkward to be forced to create a view in order to express a query. We are required to think of a name that does not conflict with the names of existing views, and we must remember to drop the view when we no longer need it. The database system is forced to do some work to enter the view into the system catalog tables, even if it is needed only for processing a single query. It would be both more elegant and more efficient if we could express the query above in a single statement without defining a view.

Examining the SELECT statement above, we see that it uses the PAYROLL view in two places. We might consider replacing each of these references to PAYROLL with a table expression whose definition is the same as that of the view. This would result in the following query:

```
SELECT deptno
FROM (SELECT deptno, sum(salary) + sum(bonus) AS totalpay
      FROM emp
      GROUP BY deptno) AS payroll1
WHERE totalpay =
  (SELECT max(totalpay)
   FROM (SELECT deptno, sum(salary) + sum(bonus) AS totalpay
         FROM emp
         GROUP BY deptno) AS payroll2);
```

This query, while it is valid, has some disadvantages. First, it seems inelegant to repeat the same table expression twice in the same query. Even worse, each of the table expressions will be evaluated independently, which is inefficient and may lead to inconsistencies if some other user is updating the EMP table during the time when our query is running (if the isolation level of our query is not RR). What we would really like to do is to define the table expression once, give it a name, and use the name as often as we like in a query, without creating a permanent view. This is exactly the function that is provided in **UDB** by a feature called *common table expressions*.

A common table expression takes the form of a WITH clause at the beginning of an SQL statement. The syntax of the WITH clause is similar to that of a view definition, as shown below.

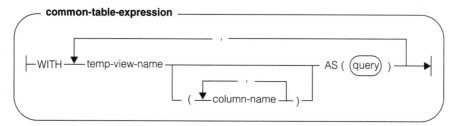

A common table expression defines one or more temporary views that are effective only during the processing of the current SQL statement. The temporary views defined in the WITH clause can be used as often as you like inside the statement. Regardless of how often you use them, each temporary view will be evaluated only once, so there is no possibility of your SQL statement seeing inconsistent data. Using a common table expression, we can rewrite our query that finds the department with the greatest total pay as follows:

```
WITH payroll(deptno, totalpay) AS
  (SELECT deptno, sum(salary) + sum(bonus)
   FROM emp
   GROUP BY deptno)
SELECT deptno
FROM payroll
WHERE totalpay =
  (SELECT max(totalpay)
   FROM payroll);
```

Queries that need to perform multiple levels of aggregation occur surprisingly often. Here's another example that finds the department(s) with the most employees also handled nicely by a common table expression:

```
WITH staff(deptno, headcount) AS
   (SELECT deptno, count(*) FROM emp GROUP BY deptno)
SELECT deptno, headcount
FROM    staff
WHERE   headcount =
   (SELECT max(headcount) FROM staff);
```

As we have seen, a common table expression behaves like a view that is defined only for the duration of a single SQL statement, saving both the user and the system the work of creating and dropping an actual view. A common table expression also has another advantage over an actual view: its definition can contain a reference to a host program variable. A real view definition can never contain a host variable, because the view is not limited to being used by a specific program. A common table expression, however, is used only within a specific SQL statement, and if that SQL statement is embedded in a program, then it has access to the host language variables declared in that program. To illustrate this, we will modify the previous example to find the department(s) with the most employees whose jobs match the job contained in program variable x:

```
WITH staff(deptno, headcount) AS
   (SELECT deptno, count(*)
    FROM emp
    WHERE job = :x
    GROUP BY deptno)
SELECT deptno, headcount
FROM staff
WHERE headcount =
   (SELECT max(headcount) from staff);
```

Common table expressions are used mainly in queries that need to use the same table expression more than once. It's even possible to write a query that joins a table expression to itself. This is done by using a common table expression and giving it a different correlation name each time it is used, as in the following example. This example finds pairs of departments in which the average salary of one department is more than twice the average salary of the other.

```
WITH deptavg(deptno, avgsal) AS
   (SELECT deptno, avg(salary)
    FROM emp
    GROUP BY deptno)
```

```
SELECT d1.deptno, d1.avgsal, d2.deptno, d2.avgsal
FROM deptavg AS d1, deptavg AS d2
WHERE d1.avgsal > 2 * d2.avgsal;
```

We have seen that a view can be defined using either a SELECT clause or a VALUES clause. This rule applies not only to permanent views but also to temporary views defined using common table expressions. In the following example, we define a common table expression (temporary view) named VITAL, which contains a list of pairs of departments and jobs that are vital to our company; the example then joins this temporary view to the EMP table to find the names of employees whose department number and job are found on the list.

```
WITH vital(deptno, job) AS
    (VALUES('A29', 'Machinist'),
           ('J16', 'Fork Lift Operator'),
           ('M07', 'Welder'))
SELECT e.name
FROM emp e, vital v
WHERE e.deptno = v.deptno
AND e.job = v.job;
```

A common table expression (WITH clause) can be used only in the following places:

1. In a top-level query (SELECT statement), as in all the examples above.

2. In a SELECT nested immediately inside a CREATE VIEW statement. Thus, the query in the previous example could be turned into a permanent view named VITALEMP as follows:

```
CREATE VIEW vitalemp(name) AS
    WITH vital(deptno, job) AS
        (VALUES('A29', 'Machinist'),
               ('J16', 'Fork Lift Operator'),
               ('M07', 'Welder'))
    SELECT e.name
    FROM emp e, vital v
    WHERE e.deptno = v.deptno
    AND e.job = v.job;
```

3. In a SELECT nested immediately inside an INSERT statement. Thus, the results of the query above could be inserted into an existing table named VITALEMP, as follows:

```
INSERT INTO vitalemp(name)
    WITH vital(deptno, job) AS
        (VALUES('A29', 'Machinist'),
               ('J16', 'Fork Lift Operator'),
               ('M07', 'Welder'))
    SELECT e.name
    FROM emp e, vital v
    WHERE e.deptno = v.deptno
    AND e.job = v.job;
```

TIP: A WITH clause is not allowed in a single-row SELECT statement. Therefore, if you embed a query in an application program and that query uses a common table expression, you must use a cursor to fetch the result of the query, even if you know that the result consists of a single row.

5.8 RECURSION

Section 5.7 showed how a common table expression (WITH clause) can be used to define a temporary view for use inside a single SQL statement. Common table expressions have another powerful feature, called *recursion*, that we have not yet discussed. A common table expression is *recursive* if it uses itself in its own definition. Recursion is very powerful, because it allows certain kinds of questions to be expressed in a single SQL statement that would otherwise require the use of a host program. Recursive queries can also be tricky to write and have the possibility of placing the system into a loop, so you will need to carefully follow certain rules when using recursion.

I will begin with a simple example. Suppose that we have a table of federal employees, with the following structure:

FEDEMP

NAME	SALARY	MANAGER

Suppose that we wish to find the names and salaries of employees in the FEDEMP table whose manager is Hoover and whose salary is greater than $100,000. This is easily done by the following (nonrecursive) query:

```
SELECT name, salary
FROM fedemp
WHERE manager = 'Hoover'
AND salary > 100000;
```

The problem becomes harder if we wish to find the employees who earn more than $100,000 and who have Hoover anywhere in their management chain. To express this question, we need a recursive query. A recursive query can be written by following these rules:

1. Define a common table expression using a WITH clause. The common table expression computes a temporary view, which in our example will be named AGENTS. The common table expression must be defined as a UNION ALL (not a regular UNION, and not any other set operation) between two parts:

   a. The first part of the UNION ALL, called the *initial subquery*, is a conventional subquery that does not involve recursion. In processing a recursive query, the system evaluates the initial subquery first. In our example, the initial subquery finds all the employees who report directly to Hoover.

   b. The second part of the UNION ALL, called the *recursive subquery*, is a subquery that adds more rows to the temporary view, based somehow on the rows that are already there. In writing the recursive subquery, you must be careful to define how the new rows are related to the old rows, and you must make sure that the query has a way to stop when it has found all the necessary rows. In our example, the recursive subquery adds to the AGENTS view the employees who are managed by employees who are already in the view. The system will stop adding new rows to the view when it reaches the set of employees who are not managers. The recursive subquery is subject to the following rules:

   - It may not contain any column function, SELECT DISTINCT, GROUP BY, or HAVING clause.
   - It may contain a reference to the common table expression in which it is embedded, but it may not contain a lower-level subquery that has such a reference.
   - Each column of the recursive subquery must be assignment-compatible with (and not longer than) the corresponding column of the initial subquery.

TIP: You may need to cast one or more columns of the initial subquery to match the datatypes and lengths of the corresponding columns of the recursive subquery. Try this technique if your recursive query fails with SQLCODE –344 or SQLSTATE 42825.

2. After the WITH clause has defined a temporary view, use the view in a SELECT statement to express the original question. In our example, the temporary view named AGENTS consists of all employees who have Hoover anywhere in their management chain, and the query that follows it selects those employees in the view whose salary is greater than $100,000.

The query that solves our problem may be written as follows:

```
WITH agents(name, salary) AS
    ((SELECT name, salary        -- Initial Subquery
      FROM   fedemp
      WHERE  manager = 'Hoover')
    UNION ALL
     (SELECT f.name, f.salary   -- Recursive Subquery
      FROM   agents AS a, fedemp AS f
      WHERE  f.manager = a.name))
    SELECT name                  -- Final Query
    FROM   agents
    WHERE  salary > 100000;
```

In visualizing the processing of this query, it is important to realize that each time the recursive subquery is executed, when it reads the temporary view AGENTS, it sees only the rows that were added to this view by the previous iteration of the recursive subquery. Thus, for example, the first evaluation of the recursive subquery adds to AGENTS all the employees whose manager-once-removed is Hoover, the second evaluation adds those employees whose manager-twice-removed is Hoover, and so on. The system keeps on evaluating the recursive subquery until no more rows are added to the temporary view. As you will see, it is necessary to be careful to make sure the system does not keep looping forever.

In Section 5.7, we learned that common table expressions (WITH clauses) can be used in queries, view definitions, and INSERT statements. WITH clauses that involve recursion can be used in exactly the same ways. If a recursive query is used inside a CREATE VIEW statement, it defines a recursive view. Similarly, if a recursive query is used in an INSERT statement, its result is inserted into the target table. Use of recursion inside an INSERT statement can be a powerful technique for generating synthetic tables. For example, suppose that I would like to generate a table named NUMBERS with columns named COUNTER and RANDOM. The COUNTER column will contain all the integers from 1 to 1,000, and the RANDOM column will contain random integers between 1 and 1,000. This table can be created and populated by the following statements (note the use of recursion in the INSERT statement):

```
CREATE TABLE numbers (counter Integer, random Integer);
INSERT INTO numbers(counter, random)
    WITH temp(n) AS
        (VALUES(1)                    -- Initial Subquery
      UNION ALL
        SELECT n+1 FROM temp          -- Recursive Subquery
        WHERE n < 1000)
    SELECT n, integer(rand()*1000)
    FROM temp;
```

Synthetic data generated by recursive INSERT statements has many uses. For example, the data generated by the example above might be used as input to a statistical experiment requiring 1,000 random integers. With some creative use of the char and translate functions, you can generate random string data as well.

5.8.1 Recursion with Computation

In the example of searching for federal employees, the problem was simply one of exploring a hierarchy (all the employees below Hoover) and printing all the rows that satisfy some condition (salary greater than $100,000). There is a more interesting class of problems that perform some computation while recursively exploring a data space. I will illustrate this class of problems with a classic recursive example called the "parts explosion problem."

Suppose that an aircraft manufacturer maintains a table of all the parts used in a certain kind of airplane and the subparts from which each part is assembled. A fragment of the data in this table is shown below. By looking at the data, we can see that each wing has one aileron, each aileron has two hinges, each hinge has four rivets, and so on.

COMPONENTS

PART	SUBPART	QTY
wing	strut	5
wing	aileron	1
wing	landing gear	1
wing	rivet	100
strut	rivet	10
aileron	hinge	2
aileron	rivet	5
landing gear	hinge	3
landing gear	rivet	8
hinge	rivet	4

Another way of looking at this data is to draw a graph in which each node represents some part used in the airplane. The nodes are connected by lines that are labeled with numbers, representing how many of each kind of subpart are needed to assemble each part. By looking at the graphical representation of this data in Figure 5-1, we see that the components database is not a strict hierarchy, as was the employee database in the previous example. For example, hinges are used in both ailerons and landing gear, and many parts use rivets. The mathematical name for this kind of data is a *directed acyclic graph*. The term *acyclic* means that the graph has no cycles (no part is a component of itself).

Suppose that, due to a national rivet shortage, we receive an urgent question from top management: what is the total number of rivets used in a wing? This question requires us to recursively explore all the components used in a wing to discover how many rivets are used at each level of the assembly. But we cannot simply add up the number of rivets used at each level—we must also take into account how many times each subassembly is used in a wing. For example, a hinge needs four rivets, but a wing needs five hinges (two in the aileron and three in the landing gear).

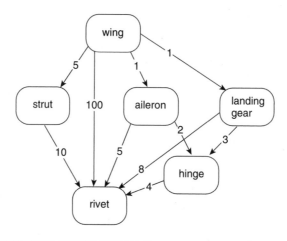

Figure 5-1: Graphical Representation of Parts and Components

To write our recursive query, we will follow the same rules used in the previous example. We begin by writing a common table expression, or temporary view, consisting of an initial subquery and a recursive subquery connected by UNION ALL. The name of the temporary view is WINGPARTS, and each row in the view describes some component of a wing and the quantity of that component used for some specific purpose in the wing (for example, the number of hinges used in the landing gear). The initial subquery lists the parts that are directly used in assembling the wing, and the recursive subquery lists the parts that are used in lower-level subassemblies inside the wing. The acyclic nature of the database provides us with a stopping rule, since the recursion will stop when it gets to primitive parts like rivets that have no subparts.

The initial WITH clause of our query, which defines the temporary view that we need, may be written as follows:

```
WITH wingparts(subpart, qty) AS
   ((SELECT subpart, qty                 -- Initial
     FROM components                      -- Subquery
     WHERE part = 'wing')
   UNION ALL
    (SELECT c.subpart, w.qty * c.qty      -- Recursive
     FROM wingparts w, components c       -- Subquery
     WHERE w.subpart = c.part));
```

We might visualize the temporary view WINGPARTS as shown in the table below. The solid lines through the table have no significance other than to help us visualize "first-generation subparts," "second-generation subparts," "third-generation subparts," and so on.

WINGPARTS

SUBPART	QTY	
strut	5	(direct usage)
aileron	1	(direct usage)
landing gear	1	(direct usage)
rivet	100	(direct usage)
rivet	50	(from struts)
hinge	2	(from aileron)
rivet	5	(from aileron)
hinge	3	(from landing gear)
rivet	8	(from landing gear)
rivet	8	(from aileron hinges)
rivet	12	(from landing gear hinges)

Note that a subpart such as a rivet may appear multiple times in the view, and that each row represents the total number of that subpart needed for some particular usage. For example, one row indicates a usage of 50 rivets due to 5 struts with 10 rivets each. Note also that the elimination of duplicate rows from this temporary view would be quite harmful to our computation!

Using the temporary view defined above, it is easy to write queries to solve the rivet problem and to answer other similar questions. Shown below are two queries that use the WINGPARTS expression, and the result of each (remember that WINGPARTS must be defined separately in each query).

1. Find the total number of rivets used in a wing.

```
WITH wingparts(subpart, qty) AS
   ((SELECT subpart, qty              -- Initial
     FROM components                  -- Subquery
     WHERE part = 'wing')
```

```
     UNION ALL
       (SELECT c.subpart, w.qty * c.qty        -- Recursive
        FROM wingparts w, components c          -- Subquery
        WHERE w.subpart = c.part))
   SELECT sum(qty) AS qty
   FROM wingparts
   WHERE subpart = 'rivet';
```

Result:

QTY
183

2. List all the subparts used to assemble a wing, with the total number of each.

```
   WITH wingparts(subpart, qty) AS
     ((SELECT subpart, qty                     -- Initial
       FROM components                         -- Subquery
       WHERE part = 'wing')
      UNION ALL
       (SELECT c.subpart, w.qty * c.qty        -- Recursive
        FROM wingparts w, components c          -- Subquery
        WHERE w.subpart = c.part))
   SELECT subpart, sum(qty) AS qty
   FROM wingparts
   GROUP BY subpart;
```

Result:

SUBPART	QTY
strut	5
aileron	1
landing gear	1
hinge	5
rivet	183

5.8.2 Recursive Searching

An important class of computer applications involves searching for a solution (usually the *best* solution according to some criterion) to a problem. Searching applications are often recursive, and I will illustrate such an application by searching a database of airline flights.

Suppose that a client has arrived at our travel agency and requested that we find for her the least expensive way to fly from San Francisco to New York. Because of membership in a frequent flyer club, our client wishes to travel only on HyFlier Airlines, which has the route map shown in Figure 5-2 (numbers represent the cost of a one-way flight).

We can see by looking at the route map that this database is not an acyclic graph as in the previous example. The data contains cycles, which make it possible to fly around in circles indefinitely. As we will see, it is necessary to be alert to this cyclic property in order to provide our query with a "stopping rule."

The data in the HyFlier route map might be represented in a relational database by the following table:

FLIGHTS

FLIGHTNO	ORIGIN	DESTINATION	COST
HY120	DFW	JFK	225
HY130	DFW	LAX	200
HY140	DFW	ORD	100
HY150	DFW	SFO	300
HY210	JFK	DFW	225
HY240	JFK	ORD	250
HY310	LAX	DFW	200
HY350	LAX	SFO	50
HY410	ORD	DFW	100
HY420	ORD	JFK	250
HY450	ORD	SFO	275
HY510	SFO	DFW	300
HY530	SFO	LAX	50
HY540	SFO	ORD	275

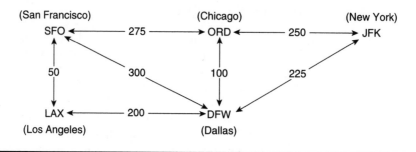

Figure 5-2: Airline Route Map

For our initial attempt to solve the client's problem, we will write a recursive query that finds ways to fly from San Francisco (SFO) to New York (JFK). The example query below uses the same template as the previous recursive examples. It defines a temporary view called TRIPS that consists of a UNION ALL between an initial subquery and a recursive subquery. The initial subquery finds all the cities that can be reached from San Francisco in a single flight. The recursive subquery finds all the cities that can in turn be reached from these cities, and, for each city reached, it records the route and the total cost. Finally, from the set of trips computed by the recursive view, we write a query that selects the trips ending in New York.

Our first try at writing a recursive query for this problem might be as follows:

```
WITH trips(destination, route, totalcost) AS
  ((SELECT destination, destination, cost      -- Initial
    FROM flights                               -- Subquery
    WHERE origin = 'SFO')
   UNION ALL
   (SELECT f.destination,                      -- Recursive
           t.route || ',' || f.destination,    -- Subquery
           t.totalcost + f.cost
    FROM trips t, flights f
    WHERE t.destination = f.origin))
  SELECT route, totalcost                      -- Final
  FROM trips                                   -- Query
  WHERE destination = 'JFK';
```

Unfortunately, the "first try" query above has two problems. The first problem is that it violates the rule that the columns of the recursive subquery must not be longer than the corresponding columns of the initial subquery. The second column selected by the initial subquery is destination, which we will assume to have datatype Char(3). The second column selected by the recursive subquery is an expression, t.route || ',' || f.destination, which is a character string that grows longer on each invocation of the recursive subquery. The system needs some advice from us about how long this column can grow, so that it can assign the proper datatype to the second column of the temporary view. Let's allow the column to grow to a length of 20 characters, allowing plenty of room for interesting routes. By casting the second column to the datatype Varchar(20) in both the initial subquery and the recursive subquery, we can comply with the length rule and also give the system the information it needs about the correct length for this column. The changes we need to make are as follows:

- In the initial subquery, replace the second destination column by CAST(destination AS Varchar(20)).
- In the recursive subquery, replace t.route || ',' || f.destination by CAST(t.route || ',' || f.destination as Varchar(20)).

The second problem with our "first try" query is more serious: the query will not stop until the system runs out of resources. The reason the query will not stop on its own is that it does not specify how far a given trip should be explored before it becomes no longer interesting. For example, in processing the query above, the system might consider a trip that flies from San Francisco to Dallas, then to Chicago, then to San Francisco again, then to Los Angeles, then back to San Francisco again, and so on, indefinitely. In order to rule out such trips, we need to think carefully about how we decide that a given trip has been explored far enough that no further extensions should be added to it.

Suppose that you are explaining to another person how to put flight segments together to find the cheapest trip from San Francisco to New York, building up various candidate trips by adding one flight at a time. You might use the following rules to decide whether it is reasonable to add a given flight segment to a given trip:

1. Don't consider any flight segments whose destination is San Francisco, because that is where we started.

2. Don't consider any flight segments whose origin is New York, because that is our final destination.

3. Don't consider any trips that have more than three flight segments.

These commonsense rules are fairly easy to add to our recursive query. In the example below, we add the stopping rules and also add the requirement that among all the trips to New York, we wish to choose the least expensive.

```
WITH trips(destination, route, nsegs, totalcost) AS
   ((SELECT destination,                -- Initial subquery
           CAST(destination AS Varchar(20)),
           1,
           cost
     FROM flights
     WHERE origin = 'SFO')
    UNION ALL
    (SELECT f.destination,               -- Recursive subquery
           CAST(t.route || ',' || f.destination
                                AS Varchar(20)),
           t.nsegs + 1,
           t.totalcost + f.cost
     FROM trips t, flights f
     WHERE t.destination = f.origin
     AND f.destination <> 'SFO'          -- Stopping rule 1
     AND f.origin <> 'JFK'               -- Stopping rule 2
     AND t.nsegs < 3 ))                  -- Stopping rule 3
SELECT route, totalcost                  -- Final query
FROM trips
WHERE destination = 'JFK'
AND totalcost =                          -- Find minimum cost
   (SELECT min(totalcost)
    FROM trips
    WHERE destination = 'JFK');
```

This query may seem intimidating, but it is really quite simple. To see how it works, we will first look at how the system might evaluate the temporary view named TRIPS. First, the system places into TRIPS all the flights that originate in San Francisco. Then, it constructs new trips by adding flights to existing trips, subject to the constraints that no trip can go back to San Francisco, continue beyond New York, or contain more than three flights. Each new trip is constructed from an old trip by adding one to the number of flight segments, concatenating the new destination onto the trip's route, and adding the new flight cost to the trip cost. The resulting table will contain some strange trips. For example, a valid trip might consist of flights from San Francisco to Los Angeles, then to Dallas, then back to Los Angeles again—not a promising start for a trip to New York. We might like to add some more commonsense rules for constructing trips, such as "Don't add any flight segment that goes to a city that we have already visited on this trip." But this rule can't

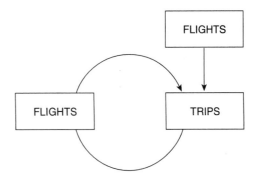

Figure 5-3: A Recursive Computation

be expressed without using a lower-level subquery inside the recursive sub-query, which is not allowed, so we will have to get along without it. The tem-porary view TRIPS constructed during the processing of this query might be visualized as shown on the following page.

We might visualize a recursive computation by a graph like the one in Fig-ure 5-3, which shows how the temporary view TRIPS is computed by starting with some flights selected by the initial subquery and then adding additional flights by repeatedly executing the recursive subquery.

After evaluating the TRIPS view, the system proceeds to evaluate the main SELECT statement in the query on page 262, which searches the TRIPS view for trips whose destination is JFK and whose total cost is equal to the mini-mum total cost of any trip to JFK. In our example database, the result of this query is the single row shown below:

ROUTE	TOTALCOST
LAX, DFW, JFK	475

TRIPS

DESTINATION	ROUTE	NSEGS	TOTALCOST
DFW	DFW	1	300
ORD	ORD	1	275
LAX	LAX	1	50
JFK	DFW, JFK	2	525
LAX	DFW, LAX	2	500
ORD	DFW, ORD	2	400
DFW	LAX, DFW	2	250
DFW	ORD, DFW	2	375
JFK	ORD, JFK	2	525
DFW	DFW, LAX, DFW	3	700
DFW	DFW, ORD, DFW	3	500
JFK	DFW, ORD, JFK	3	650
LAX	LAX, DFW, LAX	3	450
JFK	LAX, DFW, JFK	3	475
ORD	LAX, DFW, ORD	3	350
LAX	ORD, DFW, LAX	3	575
JFK	ORD, DFW, JFK	3	600
ORD	ORD, DFW, ORD	3	475

If our client is unhappy that the cheapest trip to New York involves three flights, it is easy to modify our query to select the "best" trip according to a different criterion. For example, to find the trip(s) that reach New York with the minimum number of flights, we would simply replace the part of our statement labeled "Final query" with the following:

```
SELECT route, totalcost          -- Final query
FROM trips
WHERE destination = 'JFK'
AND nsegs =                      -- Find fewest flights
   (SELECT min(nsegs)
    FROM trips
    WHERE destination = 'JFK');
```

In our example database, the result of our query would then include the following two trips, which are tied for the minimum number of flights:

ROUTE	TOTALCOST
DFW, JFK	525
ORD, JFK	525

One of the strengths of the **UDB** approach to recursion is that it is not limited to a single initial subquery or a single recursive subquery. You are allowed to write a query that contains more than one initial subquery and more than one recursive subquery, as long as all the subqueries are connected by UNION ALL and follow the rules that we have discussed. This technique gives you great power to solve complex recursive problems.

To illustrate the use of multiple recursive subqueries, we will consider an extension to the airline route problem discussed above. Suppose that, in addition to HyFlier Airlines, our client is willing to consider trip segments on her favorite railroad, FastTrack Railways. The route map for FastTrack is represented in our database by a table with the following structure:

TRAINS

TRAINNO ORIGIN DESTINATION COST

Our client now asks us to find the minimum-cost trip from San Francisco to New York, in which the segments of the trip can be either by plane or by train. Our basic approach to solving this problem will be the same as before, but we will use two initial subqueries: one to find flights originating in San Francisco and another to find train trips originating in San Francisco. We will also use two recursive subqueries: one to add additional flights to possible trips and another to add additional trains to possible trips. We might visualize the resulting computation by the graph in Figure 5-4.

The query that performs the computation in Figure 5-4 is very similar to the query that corresponds to Figure 5-3. In addition to two initial and two recursive subqueries, this query adds another new feature: it computes a "plan" for each trip by concatenating a string of flight numbers and train numbers. This plan is needed, for example, so that our client will know whether to travel from Dallas to Chicago by air or by rail. The resulting query is as follows:

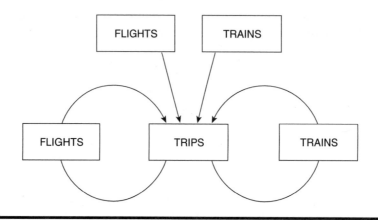

Figure 5-4: A Computation with Multiple Recursive Subqueries

```
WITH trips(destination, route, plan, nsegs, totalcost) AS
  ( (SELECT destination,              -- Initial subquery #1
            CAST(destination AS Varchar(20)),
            CAST(flightno AS Varchar(20)),
            1,
            cost
     FROM flights
     WHERE origin = 'SFO')
  UNION ALL
    (SELECT destination,              -- Initial subquery #2
            CAST(destination AS Varchar(20)),
            CAST(trainno AS Varchar(20)),
            1,
            cost
     FROM trains
     WHERE origin = 'SFO')
  UNION ALL
    (SELECT f.destination,            -- Recursive subquery #1
            CAST(t.route || ',' || f.destination
                                    AS Varchar(20)),
            CAST(t.plan || ',' || f.flightno
                                    AS Varchar(20)),
            t.nsegs + 1,
            t.totalcost + f.cost
```

```
            FROM trips t, flights f
            WHERE t.destination = f.origin
            AND f.destination <> 'SFO'      -- Stopping rule 1
            AND f.origin <> 'JFK'           -- Stopping rule 2
            AND t.nsegs < 3 )               -- Stopping rule 3
          UNION ALL
            (SELECT x.destination,          -- Recursive subquery #2
                    CAST(t.route || ',' || x.destination
                                     AS Varchar(20)),
                    CAST(t.plan || ',' || x.trainno
                                     AS Varchar(20)),
                    t.nsegs + 1,
                    t.totalcost + x.cost
            FROM trips t, trains x
            WHERE t.destination = x.origin
            AND x.destination <> 'SFO'      -- Stopping rule 1
            AND x.origin <> 'JFK'           -- Stopping rule 2
            AND t.nsegs < 3 )               -- Stopping rule 3
          )                                 -- End of WITH clause
        SELECT route, plan, totalcost       -- Final query
        FROM trips
        WHERE destination = 'JFK'
        AND totalcost =
           (SELECT min(totalcost)           -- Find minimum cost
            FROM trips
            WHERE destination = 'JFK');
```

Recursive queries are very powerful and not hard to write after you learn the rules. In writing your own recursive queries, you will stay out of trouble if you remember these guidelines:

1. Begin your query with a table expression that is a UNION ALL of one or more initial subqueries and one or more recursive subqueries.

2. Each initial subquery must be nonrecursive (its definition must not depend on the table expression in which it is embedded).

3. A recursive subquery may make use of the table expression in which it is embedded (but it may not include any lower-level subqueries that do so).

4. A recursive subquery may not contain any column function, SELECT DISTINCT, GROUP BY, or HAVING.

5. The columns of the recursive subqueries must be assignment-compatible with (and not longer than) the corresponding columns of the initial subqueries.

6. The recursive subqueries must specify how each new row is computed from the rows that already exist. If the data contains cycles, the recursive subqueries must also include a stopping rule to make sure the query terminates (such as a limit on the number of iterations).

7. Write your final query, making use of the recursive table expression and adding any additional predicates that are needed (for example, to find the best of several solutions).

TIP: When you run a recursive query, you may receive a warning message, "A recursive common table expression may contain an infinite loop" (SQLCODE +347, SQLSTATE 01605). This message will not interfere with the correct processing of your query (unless, of course, it actually contains an infinite loop). The system is simply warning you that recursive queries sometimes need stopping rules. Since the system is not very good at predicting whether a given query will terminate, you may receive this warning even though you have provided a correct stopping rule. Try not to be annoyed by this; the system has your best interests at heart.

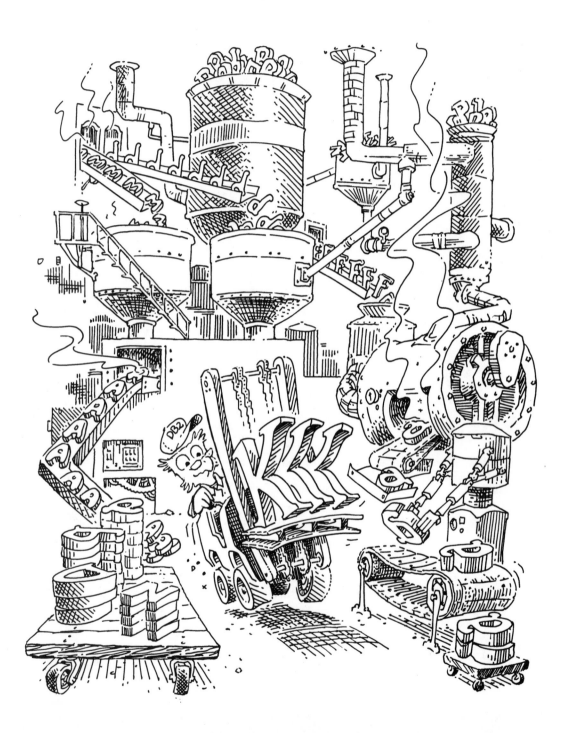

6 Datatypes and Functions

A recurring criticism of traditional database systems has been their poverty of datatypes and functions. The first relational systems typically provided only a few built-in datatypes, such as integers and strings, and a few built-in functions, such as `substr` and `avg`. These datatypes and functions are useful for storing and processing small objects with simple behavior, such as bank balances. Increasingly, however, database applications are requiring the storage and manipulation of objects that are very large (such as images, drawings, audio, and video) and/or have complex behavior (such as the components of an engineering design).

In the past few years, a number of object-oriented database systems have been developed to support the growing requirement for storage of large and complex objects. These systems typically provide their users with facilities to define new datatypes by combining simple datatypes together into complex structures. Users can also define complex behavior for objects by writing new functions in some programming language and associating these new functions with their new datatypes.

Relational database systems are based on the principle that users should access data by means of a high-level language, such as SQL, that is independent of the physical access paths or algorithms used to retrieve and manipulate the data. This principle, called *data independence*, allows the system to automatically choose the best access plan for a given query, even though such a query may not have been anticipated in the database design. Data independence also enables system administrators to add and drop indexes and other access aids in response to changing usage patterns without impacting running applications (except by affecting their performance). Another aspect of data independence is support for multiple views of data—for example, an application might be given a data view that contains salary values averaged by job code without exposing individual salaries.

The principle of data independence is as important today as ever. Furthermore, there is a growing realization that the traditional advantages of relational systems are not in any way incompatible with a rich and extensible system of datatypes and functions. In fact, a new generation of database systems called *object-relational* systems is beginning to appear, combining a high-level query language and multiple views of data with ability to define new datatypes and functions for storage and manipulation of complex objects. Compared with conventional relational systems, object-relational systems increase the value of stored data by capturing more of its semantic meaning. Part of this semantic meaning is carried in the definitions of datatypes and functions, created by users to model the objects in their application domain. Another important part of the semantic meaning of data is carried in a set of constraints and triggers that protect the integrity of the data and implement its active behavior.

The ANSI/ISO SQL Standard has recognized the importance of the trend toward capturing data semantics by the various kinds of constraints that can be specified in SQL92 and by several features that are under consideration for SQL3, including triggers, user-defined datatypes and functions, and inheritance.

In the design of UDB, IBM has included many features for capturing data semantics and has set a clear direction for the product to evolve toward support for the object-oriented paradigm. For modeling complex objects, UDB provides an extended set of built-in datatypes and also allows users to define new datatypes and functions of their own. These facilities are described in this chapter. UDB also provides an extensive set of facilities for representing the semantics of data objects using constraints and triggers, which are described in Chapter 7. Many UDB features, including user-defined datatypes, functions, and triggers, are under consideration by ANSI and ISO but are not yet formally a part of the SQL Standard.

UDB is an important step in the evolution of DB2 toward support for object-oriented functionality, and we can expect this evolution to continue. A future step in the same direction might involve indexes and other access paths based on user-defined functions. Other possible future steps are represented by object-oriented SQL extensions currently being discussed by ANSI and ISO committees, such as abstract datatypes, inheritance, and collection types.

6.1 LARGE OBJECTS

Today's multimedia applications depend on storage of many types of large data objects, such as scanned documents, medical images, and audio messages. Early versions of DB2 provided datatypes called Long Varchar and Long Vargraphic for the storage of objects up to 32K bytes in size, with certain limitations (for example, only certain types of predicates could be applied to these datatypes). UDB provides an improved facility for storing much larger objects, consisting of three datatypes with the following names:

1. *Blob* (*Binary Large Object*). The Blob datatype can contain up to two gigabytes (2^{31}–1 bytes) of binary data. Blobs cannot be assigned to or compared with values of any other datatype.

2. *Clob* (*Character Large Object*). The Clob datatype can contain up to two gigabytes (2^{31}–1 bytes) of single-byte character data. Like other character-string datatypes, a Clob has a code page associated with it (indicating, for example, that its contents are encoded using the Swedish character set). Clobs can be assigned to and compared with values of other character-string datatypes (Char, Varchar, and Long Varchar).

3. *Dbclob* (*Double-Byte Character Large Object*). The Dbclob datatype can contain up to one gigacharacter (two gigabytes, or 2^{31}–2 bytes) of double-byte character data. You can use this datatype only if your database was configured for double-byte data at database creation time. A Dbclob is associated with a double-byte code page such as Japanese. Dbclobs can be assigned to or compared with values of other double-byte string datatypes (Graphic, Vargraphic, and Long Vargraphic).

These three new datatypes are referred to generically as *Large Objects* (LOBs). Although the older Long Varchar and Long Vargraphic datatypes are still supported, this book focuses mainly on the new LOB datatypes, because we expect that they will be the preferred datatypes for new applications. The capabilities of the new LOB datatypes are a superset of the capabilities of Long Varchar and Long Vargraphic.

The design of the new LOB datatypes is based on the fact that it is quite expensive to move large objects from one place to another in memory. For this reason, every effort has been made to minimize this kind of movement. In addition to their large size, the LOB datatypes are distinguished from conventional datatypes by the following special features:

1. When a LOB is stored in a table, the table entry is actually a descriptor that points to the LOB value, which is stored elsewhere. Users can configure their databases with separate units of physical storage called *tablespaces* for holding LOB values so that they will not interfere with the clustering of tables. (Tablespaces are described in more detail in Section 10.1.)

2. LOBs can be manipulated in user programs by means of *locators*, which represent the value of a LOB without actually containing the LOB data. By manipulating these locators, application programs can defer and sometimes even avoid actually materializing the LOB in the program.

3. By means of a feature called a *file reference*, programs can input LOB data directly into the database from a file, or fetch LOB data directly from the database into a file, without passing the data through memory buffers in the application program.

4. For each LOB-type column in a table, the creator of the table can specify independently whether changes to that column are to be recorded in the system log. A user might choose to turn off logging for a LOB-type column to improve performance and to avoid the possibility of log overflow. Columns that are not logged are still guaranteed transaction semantics, and updates to these columns can be committed or rolled back in the usual way. However, if a column is not logged, it cannot participate in forward recovery (reexecution of completed transactions after a media failure). (Forward recovery is discussed in Section 10.6.)

6.1.1 Creating LOB Columns

To store LOB data in a database, you simply create a table having a column of one of the LOB datatypes, using the familiar CREATE TABLE and ALTER TABLE statements. Some examples of these statements were given in Section 2.6, and their complete syntax is discussed in Section 7.2. A CREATE TABLE or ALTER TABLE statement might define a LOB-type column using the following syntax:

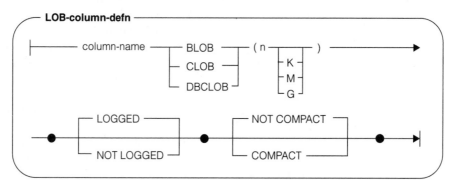

The following are some examples of statements that create tables or add columns to tables using the syntax above:

```
CREATE TABLE phonemail
   (origin     Varchar(18),
    addressee  Varchar(18),
    arrival    Timestamp,
    message    Blob(10M) NOT LOGGED COMPACT);    -- audio

CREATE TABLE graduates
   (name       Varchar(30),
    address    Varchar(200),
    degree     Varchar(50),
```

```
            grad_date  Date,
            photo      Blob(5M) NOT LOGGED COMPACT,      -- image
            thesis     Clob(500K) NOT LOGGED COMPACT);   -- text

        CREATE TABLE design
            (partno       Char(18),
             last_updated Timestamp,
             updated_by   Varchar(30),
             drawing      Blob(2M) LOGGED);           -- CGM graphics

        ALTER TABLE student ADD COLUMN transcript Clob(5K) LOGGED;
```

All the LOB datatypes are varying-length types, like Varchar and Vargraphic. When declaring a column of a LOB datatype, you must declare its maximum length, which can be anywhere in the range from one byte to two gigabytes. The maximum length can be declared as a simple integer representing a number of bytes (double-byte characters, in the case of a Dbclob), or as an integer followed by one of the following suffixes:

K: kilobytes (2^{10} or 1,024 bytes)

M: megabytes (2^{20} or 1,048,576 bytes)

G: gigabytes (2^{30} or 1,073,741,824 bytes; 2G is interpreted as $2^{31}-1$)

You may be wondering why it is necessary to declare the maximum length of the data to be stored in a LOB-type column. Actually, this information may be helpful for two reasons:

1. When you fetch data from a column into your application program, you will need to allocate a buffer big enough to hold the data. If you know that the data is limited to, say, 50K bytes, you can allocate just the right amount of memory.

2. Inside each row that contains a LOB-type value is a descriptor that points at the actual data. The maximum length of this descriptor depends on the maximum length of the data; it varies from 72 bytes for a LOB of less than 1K up to 316 bytes for a LOB of maximum size 2G. In any given table, the total size of all the columns, including the descriptors of the LOB columns, cannot exceed 4,005 bytes. So, if you know that the data in a given column will never be larger than a certain limit, you can improve clustering and leave room for more columns by declaring the maximum size.

Of course, if neither of these considerations is important to you, you can declare all of your LOB-type columns to have a maximum length of 2G, retaining the maximum flexibility for storing large objects.

When creating a LOB-type column, you have two choices to make that do not apply to columns of other datatypes. These choices are as follows:

1. *COMPACT or NOT COMPACT.* This option allows you to control a space-time trade-off in storage of the LOB data in your column. If you specify COMPACT, the LOB data will occupy minimum space on disk, but there may be a performance penalty for any update that increases the size of a LOB. If you specify NOT COMPACT, some extra space will be allocated to allow the LOB values room to grow. The default is NOT COMPACT.

2. *LOGGED or NOT LOGGED.* This option allows you to control whether updates to your column are recorded in the system log. In making this decision, you will need to consider the size of your LOB data, how valuable it is, and how easily it can be reconstructed.

   If you choose LOGGED (the default), the LOB data in this column is treated exactly like all other data. Whenever the column is updated, the new value is recorded in the system log. This provides the maximum protection for the data, but for obvious reasons it is costly both in terms of time and disk space. In fact, since the maximum size of the log is currently limited to 2 gigabytes, and a single LOB value can occupy this much space, it is not practical to choose the LOGGED option for very large LOB columns. It is an error to specify LOGGED for a column larger than one gigabyte, and it is probably unwise to specify LOGGED for columns larger than ten megabytes.

   If you choose NOT LOGGED for a column, changes to the column are not recorded in the system log, but another part of the recovery system, called *shadowing*, remains in effect. When an update is applied to a NOT LOGGED column, both the new pages and the original ("shadow") pages are retained until the end of the transaction. Shadowing enforces transaction consistency for your data (that is, the COMMIT and ROLLBACK statements apply to shadowed data, and when you invoke the RESTART command after a failure, your shadowed data will be restored to a transaction-consistent state).

   The feature that you forego by specifying NOT LOGGED for a column is the ability, after a media failure, to reapply all the changes that have been made to that column since the last media backup. A media backup can be made by the BACKUP command, and the database can be restored from a media backup by the RESTORE command. After restoring the database from a media backup, all committed transactions can be reapplied by the ROLLFORWARD command. This process, called *forward recovery*, relies on the system log and is effective only for logged columns. If a column was created with the NOT LOGGED option, any updated values in this column will be lost (set to binary zeros) during the execution of ROLLFORWARD. (The commands for backup and recovery of databases are discussed further in Section 10.6.)

6.1.2 Declaring Large-Object Variables in C and C++

When you write an application program for UDB, you will probably need to declare some variables that exchange values with the database, either for input or for output. These variables must be declared in a special part of your program called the *SQL Declare Section*, as described in Section 4.1.2. Each SQL datatype (except Decimal) has a corresponding C-language datatype that you can use in the SQL Declare Section to declare variables for exchanging values of that datatype (for example, the C datatype corresponding to the SQL Integer datatype is long). The C-language datatypes corresponding to the basic SQL datatypes are summarized in Table 4-2. The C-language structures shown in Tables 4-2 and 4-3 for exchanging values of type Varchar and Vargraphic can also be used with the old-style large-object datatypes Long Varchar and Long Vargraphic.

Declarations of variables to exchange LOB-type values require some new syntax in the SQL Declare Section. Rather than pure host language syntax, these declarations use a new syntax that is recognized and translated by the SQL precompiler. When declaring such a variable, you should use the phrase SQL TYPE IS followed by a LOB-type just as you would write it in a CREATE TABLE statement, such as CLOB(32K) or BLOB(1M). The type name is then followed by the name of the variable you are declaring. The precompiler automatically translates your declaration into a declaration of the proper host language datatype for exchanging the kind of data you specified. The examples in Table 6-1 illustrate the LOB datatypes you can use inside an SQL Declare Section and the corresponding C-language declarations that are generated by the precompiler. Of course, the variable names x, y, and z and the lengths shown here are only examples that would be replaced by lengths and variable names of your choice.

As in the case of Graphic and Vargraphic, the C datatype used to exchange Dbclob-type data is influenced by the WCHARTYPE option of the precompiler. If you specify WCHARTYPE NOCONVERT (or accept the default), the precompiler will translate your Dbclob declaration into an array of type sqldbchar, which is a two-byte datatype defined in sql.h. On the other hand, if you invoke the precompiler with the option WCHARTYPE CONVERT, your Dbclob declaration will be translated to an array of type wchar_t, which is defined by your C compiler and used in conjunction with various C-language functions for manipulating wide-character strings.

You are allowed to specify a C storage class such as static or extern on your declaration, and you may also use the C notations * (indicating a pointer) and & (indicating a reference). You may declare multiple variables in a single statement, and you may mix LOB-type declarations with other declarations in the same SQL Declare Section. (Additional details about declarations of LOB-type host variables can be found in Appendix E.)

TABLE 6-1: Declarations Generated by the C Precompiler for LOB Datatypes

If you write . . .	The C precompiler will generate . . .
`SQL TYPE IS BLOB(1K) x;`	```struct x_t\n {\n unsigned long length;\n char data[1024];\n } x;```
`SQL TYPE IS CLOB(1M) y;`	```struct y_t\n {\n unsigned long length;\n char data[1048576];\n } y;```

`SQL TYPE IS DBCLOB(1K) z;`	If you specify WCHARTYPE NOCONVERT:
	```struct z_t\n {\n unsigned long length;\n sqldbchar data[1024];\n } z;```
	
	If you specify WCHARTYPE CONVERT:
	```struct z_t\n {\n unsigned long length;\n wchar_t data[1024];\n } z;```

UDB provides macros named `SQL_BLOB_INIT`, `SQL_CLOB_INIT`, and `SQL_DBCLOB_INIT` for initializing variables of LOB datatypes. These macros take a string and use it to initialize both the length and data parts of a LOB structure. Use of the initializing macros is illustrated in the following example:

```
EXEC SQL BEGIN DECLARE SECTION;
   static SQL TYPE IS CLOB(100K)
              *p1, c1 = SQL_CLOB_INIT("Hello");
EXEC SQL END DECLARE SECTION;
```

The precompiler will translate this code into the following C declarations:

```
static struct
    {
    unsigned long length;
    char data[102400];
    } *p1, c1 = SQL_CLOB_INIT("Hello");
```

Note that in the example above, 100K bytes of memory have been allocated for variable c1, but variable p1 is only a pointer (its data buffer must be allocated separately). The C compiler will expand the macro used to initialize variable c1 as follows:

```
c1 = {sizeof("Hello")-1, "Hello"}
```

You may be wondering why special syntax is used for the declaration of LOB-type host variables, rather than allowing you to write your own host language declarations as you do for other datatypes. There are two reasons for this change:

1. UDB recognizes the convenient K, M, and G length-notations, translating them into numbers that are acceptable to C. For example, 100K is translated into 102400.

2. You may have noticed that Blob and Clob SQL datatypes share the same host language datatype. The special syntax in the declaration tells the database system whether your variable should be treated as a Blob or as a Clob.

You can use your LOB-type variables for exchanging data with the database in the usual way. If an indicator variable is used with an output LOB-type variable, the indicator variable will be set negative if the output value is null. However, if a LOB-type output value is truncated because the length of the output variable is too short (indicated by SQLSTATE 01004), the indicator variable is *not* set to the original length of the output value (as in the case of other string datatypes).

I will illustrate the use of LOB-type host variables by a simple application program named MOVIE. This program operates on a table with the following structure:

MOVIES

```
TITLE   CAST   REVIEW
```

The TITLE and CAST columns of the MOVIES table have datatype Varchar(100), and the REVIEW column has datatype Clob(50K). The MOVIE application program exchanges data with the REVIEW column using two Clob-type host variables named `review` and `newreview`.

First, the program places a new movie review in the `newreview` variable, taking care to set both the length and data fields of the structure. It then uses `newreview` as an input variable in an SQL UPDATE statement, adding the new review to the database.

Next, the program declares a cursor and uses it to retrieve all the reviews in the database for movies starring Steve McQueen. The reviews are retreived into the output variable `review`. Since Clob-type data does not include a null terminator, the program must use the length field of the `review` structure to indicate the length of each review and must generate its own null terminator before printing each review.

Example Program MOVIE: Processing Movie Reviews

```c
#include <stdio.h>
#include <string.h>
#include <sqlenv.h>

void main()
   {
   EXEC SQL INCLUDE SQLCA;

   EXEC SQL BEGIN DECLARE SECTION;
       char dbname[9] = "moviedb";        /* name of database            */
       char msgbuffer[500];               /* buffer for DB2 error message */
       char title[100];                   /* for Varchar data            */
       char cast[100];                    /* for Varchar data            */
       SQL TYPE is CLOB(50K) review;      /* output Clob structure       */
       SQL TYPE is CLOB(50K) newreview;   /* input Clob structure        */
       short indicator1, indicator2;      /* indicator variables         */
   EXEC SQL END DECLARE SECTION;

   EXEC SQL WHENEVER SQLERROR GO TO badnews;

   EXEC SQL CONNECT TO :dbname;

   strcpy (newreview.data, "Bullet is a pretty good movie.");
   newreview.length = strlen(newreview.data);
```

```
   indicator1 = 0;

   EXEC SQL
      UPDATE movies
      SET review = :newreview :indicator1
      WHERE title = 'Bullet';

   EXEC SQL COMMIT;

   EXEC SQL DECLARE c1 CURSOR FOR
      SELECT title, review
      FROM movies
      WHERE cast LIKE '%Steve McQueen%';

   EXEC SQL WHENEVER NOT FOUND GO TO close_c1;

   EXEC SQL OPEN c1;

   while (1)
      {
      EXEC SQL FETCH c1 INTO :title, :review :indicator2;

      /* Provide your own null terminator */
      review.data[review.length] = '\0';

      printf("\nTitle: %s\n", title);
      if (indicator2 < 0)
         printf("No review available\n");
      else
         printf("%s\n", review.data);
      }

close_c1:
   EXEC SQL CLOSE c1;
   return;

badnews:
   printf("Unexpected return code from DB2.\n");
   sqlaintp(msgbuffer, 500, 70, &sqlca);
   printf("Message: %s\n", msgbuffer);
   }       /* End of main */
```

6.1.3 Locators

A very powerful feature of the new LOB datatypes, which distinguishes them from Long Varchars and other implementations of large objects, is the concept of a *locator*. Locators arose out of the observation that it is quite expensive to move large objects back and forth between the database and an application program. If a program is manipulating large objects, it is desirable to defer the actual movement of bits from the database into the program as long as possible and to move only those bits that are really needed. If the program is able to specify exactly what manipulations it needs to do, it may be possible in many cases to perform the manipulations entirely in the database without ever delivering the large object to the application program.

A locator is a value that can be used in an application program to represent the value of a large object without actually containing the bytes of the large object. By manipulating locators, a program can perform operations on large objects while these objects remain inside the database system. In this way, the program can often avoid allocating the storage to hold a large object and paying the cost of moving the large object between the database and the application.

A locator variable is a variable that is declared in the SQL Declare Section of an application program to hold a locator. In each host programming language, there is a datatype designated for locator variables. For example, in C, the datatype of a locator variable is long. However, not just any long variable in the SQL Declare Section can be used as a locator variable. Locator variables must be distinguished from long variables used for input and output of Integer data; furthermore, Clob locator variables must be distinguished from Blob locator variables and from Dbclob locator variables.

A special syntax is used to notify the precompiler of the intended use of a locator variable. Inside an SQL Declare Section, any of the following phrases will be recognized by the precompiler and translated into the datatype used for locators in your host language:

```
SQL TYPE IS BLOB_LOCATOR
SQL TYPE IS CLOB_LOCATOR
SQL TYPE IS DBCLOB_LOCATOR
```

For example, in the SQL Declare Section of a C program, the declaration

```
extern SQL TYPE IS CLOB_LOCATOR loc1, loc2, loc3;
```

would be translated by the precompiler as follows:

```
extern long loc1, loc2, loc3;
```

Locator variables can be used in any SQL statement wherever an input or output variable of a LOB datatype can be used. If a LOB-type value is fetched into a locator variable, the variable is set to contain a locator that represents the LOB value. This variable can then be used in SQL statements exactly as though it contained the actual LOB value. For example, it can be used as an input variable in an SQL UPDATE statement or passed as an argument to a LOB function such as `posstr`. Whenever a locator variable is used in an SQL statement, the database system operates on the LOB-type value that is represented by that locator. The LOB-type value itself is held inside the database server and is not transferred into the application program.

In order to understand the power of locators, it is important to remember the following:

1. A locator represents a constant value. There is no way to change the value of the object that a locator represents (but, of course, it is possible to use the locator to compute another object with a different value, represented by a different locator).

2. Inside the database server, each locator corresponds to a *recipe* for assembling a LOB-type value from fragments that are stored in various places. Whenever possible, manipulations of LOBs are performed, not by manipulating the actual data, but by manipulating the recipes. For example, if two large objects are to be concatenated, a new recipe is created that includes copies of the recipes for the two original objects (which may, in turn, contain fragments copied from earlier recipes). The concatenation operation is performed entirely by manipulating the recipes rather than by touching the actual content of the large objects. If the result of the concatenation is fetched into a locator variable, the variable gets a new locator representing the new recipe.

3. The actual content of a large object is moved on only two occasions: when the object is assigned to a host language variable of a LOB datatype (not a locator datatype), or when the object is assigned to a column of a database table. Intermediate results of large-object expressions (for example, the results of `concat` and `substr` operations) are never materialized until the final assignment.

Locator variables are often used as arguments of functions that manipulate strings. This is the most efficient way to manipulate large-object data because it postpones actual movement of the data as long as possible. Shown below are some examples of functions that are useful for manipulating LOB-type data (for details of these and other functions, see Appendix B). Since all the locators are host language variables, their names are prefixed by colons.

- Two strings can be concatenated by the `concat` function or by the | | operator. In the following examples, we concatenate two large objects that are represented by locators.

```
concat(:clobloc1, :clobloc2)
:clobloc1 || :clobloc2
```

- The `length` function returns the length of its argument. This example finds the length of a large object.

```
length(:clobloc1)
```

- The `posstr` function returns the starting position of the first instance of a pattern inside a string. This function is particularly useful for finding a pattern inside a large object and can be used with either character-string or binary data. This example finds the location of the word "Experience" within a large object represented by a locator named `resumeloc`.

```
posstr(:resumeloc, 'Experience')
```

- The `substr` function returns a substring of its argument. This function is very useful for snipping a relevant part out of a large object. This example returns a substring of length 200 characters, beginning at character offset 1,200 within the large object represented by `clobloc1`.

```
substr(:clobloc1, 1200, 200)
```

Since locator variables can be used both as input and as output variables, it is possible (and often useful) to compute one locator from another without any reference to a database table. For example, suppose that locator variable `loc1` contains a locator that represents a Clob value. You may wish to find, in this Clob value, the 100-byte substring beginning with the first occurrence of "Rosebud." Since the actual Clob value resides in the database server, you need the help of the database system. But you do not need to access any particular table in the database (indeed, the value represented by the locator in variable `loc1` may not be stored in any table). This is a good application for a VALUES statement, which might create a new locator for the desired value in variable `loc2`, as follows:

```
EXEC SQL VALUES
    substr(:loc1, posstr(:loc1, 'Rosebud'), 100) INTO :loc2;
```

Once a locator has been fetched into a locator variable, it remains valid until the end of the transaction in which it was fetched. The value represented by the locator will never change, even if the underlying columns from which it was computed are updated or deleted. However, there is a way in which you can notify the system that you are no longer using a locator, so that the system can release the resources represented by that locator. This is done by a new SQL statement, FREE LOCATOR, which has the following syntax:

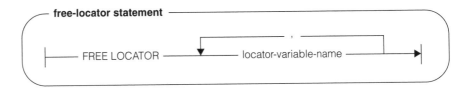

Example:

```
EXEC SQL FREE LOCATOR :loc1, :loc2;
```

It is advisable to use the FREE LOCATOR statement if you are fetching locators inside a loop and, after completing each iteration of the loop, you have no further use for the locator fetched during that iteration. Before fetching another locator into your locator variable, free the previous locator so that the database system no longer needs to keep track of it. The system cannot free a locator automatically when you fetch another locator into the same variable, because it does not know whether you have made a copy of the locator in another variable.

The following example illustrates how an application program can manipulate large objects by operating on their locators without ever "taking delivery" on the actual underlying data. Suppose we have a table that describes a set of plays used by a repertory company, with the following columns:

PLAYS

TITLE	TYPE	AUTHOR	TEXT

The TEXT column is a Clob containing the actual text of the play. The following program might be used to scan through the text of a play, replacing each instance of the word "colour" with "color," without ever reading any of the actual text into the application program (in practice, the program would need to search more carefully for various combinations of upper- and lowercase). Note how the program creates a series of locators that represent partial results, freeing each locator when it is no longer needed.

Example Program PLAY: Revising a Play

```
#include <stdio.h>
#include <string.h>
#include <sqlenv.h>
```

```
void main()
  {
  EXEC SQL INCLUDE SQLCA;

  EXEC SQL BEGIN DECLARE SECTION;
      char dbname[9] = "playdb";           /* name of database          */
      char msgbuffer[500];                 /* buffer for DB2 error message */
      SQL TYPE IS CLOB_LOCATOR loc1, loc2;
      long n;
  EXEC SQL END DECLARE SECTION;

  EXEC SQL WHENEVER SQLERROR GO TO badnews;

  EXEC SQL CONNECT TO :dbname;

  EXEC SQL SELECT text into :loc1
           FROM plays
           WHERE title = 'As You Like It';

  EXEC SQL VALUES posstr(:loc1, 'colour') INTO :n;

  while (n > 0)
      {
      EXEC SQL VALUES substr(:loc1, 1, :n-1) || 'color'
                          || substr(:loc1, :n+6) INTO :loc2;
      /*
      ** Free the old locator and keep the new one.
      */
      EXEC SQL FREE LOCATOR :loc1;
      loc1 = loc2;
      EXEC SQL VALUES posstr(:loc1, 'colour') INTO :n;
      }
  /*
  ** No data moved yet; only a series of locators has been created.
  */

  EXEC SQL UPDATE plays SET text = :loc1
           WHERE title = 'As You Like It';
  /*
  ** Now the new text is assembled according to the final recipe
  ** and assigned to the database table.
  */
```

```
EXEC SQL COMMIT;
return;

badnews:
    printf("Unexpected return code from DB2.\n");
    sqlaintp(msgbuffer, 500, 70, &sqlca);
    printf("Message: %s\n", msgbuffer);
    }    /* End of main */
```

The example program computes, using locator variable loc1, a recipe for replacing all instances of "colour" with "color" in the text of the play. Each time the body of the while-loop is executed, one more instance of the text replacement is added to the recipe. But no data is ever delivered into the application program and no bits are actually moved until the final statement, which applies the recipe to update the table in the database.

 TIP: Remember that the statement FREE LOCATOR <variable> applies to the locator that is contained in the variable, not to the variable itself. If you have made copies of a locator, freeing any one of the copies frees (and invalidates) all the copies. Thus, for example, it would be a mistake to write EXEC SQL FREE LOCATOR :loc2 after the statement loc1 = loc2 in the example program.

6.1.4 File References

In many cases, a LOB-type value may be so large that you would prefer to move it directly from a file into the database, or from the database into a file, without allocating memory buffers to hold it in your application program. This is made possible by a special declaration, called a *file reference declaration*, in the SQL Declare Section of your program. A file reference is a structure that contains the name of a file and certain other information about how the file is to be used to exchange large objects with the database. Inside the SQL Declare Section, special syntax is used to identify a variable as a file reference and to indicate whether the file will be used to exchange values of datatype Blob, Clob, or Dbclob. In place of a datatype, any of the following phrases are recognized by the precompiler and translated into the appropriate structure used for representing a file reference in your host language:

```
SQL TYPE IS BLOB_FILE
SQL TYPE IS CLOB_FILE
SQL TYPE IS DBCLOB_FILE
```

For example, in the SQL Declare Section of a C program, the declaration

```
SQL TYPE IS CLOB_FILE f1;
```

would be translated by the precompiler as follows (I have added the comments for clarity):

```
struct
  {
    unsigned long name_length;   /* length of filename    */
    unsigned long data_length;   /* length of data in file */
    unsigned long file_options;  /* denote usage of file  */
    char          name[255];     /* filename              */
  } f1;
```

After declaring a file reference in your SQL Declare Section, it is your job to fill in the name of the file and its intended usage. The name of the file, denoted by the name and name_length fields of the structure, may be either an absolute path name such as /u/clinton/games/marbles.txt or a relative path name such as games/marbles.txt. The filename represents the name of a file on the client machine (not on the database server), and relative paths are appended to the current path of the client process. The intended usage of the file is denoted by the file_options field, which you must set to one of the codes shown in Table 6-2. The C-language declarations of these codes and of the file reference structure (named sqlfile) can be found in the header file sqllib/include/sql.h.

After you have declared a file reference variable in your SQL Declare Section and filled in the appropriate fields of the reference structure, you can use the file reference variable in an SQL statement exactly as though it were a LOB-type variable. If you have set file_options to SQL_FILE_READ, you can use the file reference variable in an input role such as in a predicate, an INSERT statement, the SET clause of an UPDATE statement, or the argument of a function. If you have set file_options to SQL_FILE_CREATE, SQL_FILE_OVERWRITE, or SQL_FILE_APPEND codes, you can use the file reference variable in an output role such as SELECT INTO or FETCH INTO. If you use a file reference variable in an output role, the system will write a LOB-type value into the designated file and will set the data_length field of the file reference structure to the length of the file after output, in bytes. A file reference variable can be used together with an indicator variable, which is used to denote null values in the usual way.

When you use a Dbclob file reference as an input or output variable to exchange double-byte strings, the data is always exchanged in multibyte format (not wide-character format). In other words, Dbclob file references always use the format specified by the precompiler option WCHARTYPE NOCONVERT.

TABLE 6-2: File Option Codes for LOB File References

Code	Meaning
SQL_FILE_READ (numeric value = 2)	The content of the file is treated as an input LOB-type value.
SQL_FILE_CREATE (numeric value = 8)	A new file is created with the given name and used to receive a LOB-type output value. If the file already exists, an error results.
SQL_FILE_OVERWRITE (numeric value = 16)	An output LOB-type value is fetched into the named file, replacing its previous content. If the file does not exist, it is created.
SQL_FILE_APPEND (numeric value = 32)	An output LOB-type value is appended to the named file. If the file does not exist, it is created.

As an example of a file reference variable used for output, we will write a piece of code to fetch a student's photograph from a database table into a file. Suppose that our database contains a table with the following structure:

STUDENTS

```
STUDENTNO   NAME   POSITION   PHOTO
```

If the PHOTO column has datatype Blob(1M), the following code fragment might be used to search the table for a student whose position is "President," and to fetch that student's photograph into a file named president.photo:

```
EXEC SQL BEGIN DECLARE SECTION;
   SQL TYPE IS BLOB_FILE photoFile;
   short ind;
EXEC SQL END DECLARE SECTION;

strcpy(photoFile.name, "president.photo");
photoFile.name_length = strlen(photoFile.name);
photoFile.file_options = SQL_FILE_OVERWRITE;

EXEC SQL SELECT photo INTO :photoFile :ind
   FROM students WHERE position = 'President';
```

After execution of the statements above, SQLSTATE will be set to "00000," if a Blob was successfully written into the designated file; "02000," if no student was found with a position of "President"; or "21000," if more than one student was found with that position. If the PHOTO column of the selected student was null, the ind variable will be negative. If a Blob was written into the file, photoFile.data_length will be set to the length of the file.

As an example of a file reference variable used for input, we will write a program fragment to update a database of advertising copy. Suppose that our database contains a table named ADVERTISING with a column named COPY of datatype Clob(200K). Our legal department has advised us to attach a disclaimer to all advertising copy for our "Speedster" product. The disclaimer is contained in a file named speedlimit.txt. The following code fragment might be used to attach this disclaimer to all the appropriate entries in the ADVERTISING table:

```
EXEC SQL BEGIN DECLARE SECTION;
    SQL TYPE IS CLOB_FILE disclaimer;
EXEC SQL END DECLARE SECTION;

strcpy(disclaimer.name, "speedlimit.txt");
disclaimer.name_length = strlen(disclaimer.name);
disclaimer.file_options = SQL_FILE_READ;

EXEC SQL UPDATE advertising
        SET copy = copy || :disclaimer
        WHERE copy LIKE '%Speedster%';
```

It is important to note that both of these examples exchange potentially large amounts of data with the database without allocating any memory buffers for transferring the data.

6.1.5 Limitations of LOB Datatypes

Certain limitations apply to the use of LOB-type data, regardless of whether it is represented by a locator, a file reference, or a conventional variable. These limitations are summarized below. All the limitations (except the last one) apply to the older Long Varchar and Long Vargraphic datatypes as well as to LOBs.

1. LOB-type data cannot be used in predicates that perform direct comparisons. This includes predicates that use operators =, <>, <, <=, >, >=, IN, or BETWEEN.

Rather than using a direct comparison, many applications search for LOB-type data using a LIKE predicate,[1] as in the following examples:

```
... WHERE clob1 LIKE '%Gilligan%'
... WHERE clob1 LIKE :hostvar2
```

2. LOB-type columns cannot be used in any context that requires comparing two column values for equality or for ordering. This includes SELECT DISTINCT, COUNT(DISTINCT), GROUP BY, ORDER BY, PRIMARY KEY, and FOREIGN KEY.

3. LOB-type columns cannot be used with any column function such as `max` or `min`.

4. LOB-type columns cannot be combined by a set operator such as INTERSECT, EXCEPT, or UNION (other than UNION ALL).

5. Clob-type data cannot be compared or assigned to Dates, Times, or Timestamps (even though other character-string datatypes can be compared and assigned to datetime datatypes). Furthermore, Clobs cannot be passed as arguments to functions that expect a character-string encoding of a Date or Time, such as `date`, `time`, `timestamp`, `day`, `hour`, `month`, and `year`.

6. Indexes cannot be created on LOB-type columns.

7. LOB-type data cannot be exchanged between client (Application Requestor) and server (Application Server) machines using the DRDA (Distributed Relational Database Architecture) protocol. This means that if you are connected to a database that resides on a DRDA server, you will not be able to exchange any LOB values with that database (unless you cast the values into some other datatype).

 TIP: If the actual length of a LOB is less than 4,000 bytes, you can get around most of these restrictions by casting the LOB into a Varchar or Vargraphic datatype.

---

1. The first operand of a LIKE predicate may have a LOB datatype. The second operand (the pattern) may not have a LOB datatype unless the first operand is a Blob; in this case, the pattern may be a Blob if its length is 4,000 bytes or less.

6.1.6 Example Program SCHOLAR: Processing Scholarship Applications

As a final example of the power of LOB datatypes, locators, and file references, we will write a program to process student scholarship applications. Suppose that all the scholarship applications we have received have been entered into a table with the following structure:

APPLICANTS

NAME	DATERECEIVED	STATUS	APPLICATION

APPLICATION is a column of datatype Clob(100K), in which our data entry department has recorded each application in a predefined format. Each application consists of several parts. One part is the student's transcript, recorded in a standard 1,000-byte format beginning with the characters "*TRAN-SCRIPT*." In a later part of the application is an essay, beginning with the characters "*ESSAY*" and continuing until the end of the application.

The task of our program is to search through all the applications received in 1997 whose status is "OK." Among these applications, we need to find the one with the "best" transcript, and we need to retrieve that transcript and its accompanying essay into a file. To help in this process, we will assume the existence of a C function that can compare two transcripts in our standard format and decide which is "better." This function is assumed to have the following interface:

```
int compareTranscripts (char *t1, char *t2);
/* returns 1 if first transcript is better, else returns 2 */
```

Naturally, we prefer to fetch only the minimum data that is needed for processing each application. Even though an application can contain up to 100K bytes and may include a photograph and several supporting letters, we will locate and fetch only the 1,000-byte transcript from each application. After choosing the best transcript, we will copy the corresponding essay directly into a file without allocating any memory buffers for it in our application. To accomplish these objectives, we will use locators, file references, and some LOB functions such as posstr and substr. The storage used by our program to hold application data is limited to two 1,000-byte buffers, one to hold a transcript being considered and another to hold the best transcript seen so far. Note how the program frees each locator when it is no longer needed.

Example Program SCHOLAR: Processing Scholarship Applications

```c
#include <stdio.h>
#include <string.h>
#include <sqlenv.h>

int compareTranscripts(char *t1, char *t2);

int main()
    {
    EXEC SQL BEGIN DECLARE SECTION;
        char dbname[9] = "testdb";
        char candidate[30], winner[30];
        long transPosn, essayPosn;
        char thisTranscript[1000], bestTranscript[1000];
        SQL TYPE IS CLOB_LOCATOR loc1, bestLoc;
        SQL TYPE IS CLOB_FILE winningFile;
        char msgbuffer[500];
    EXEC SQL END DECLARE SECTION;

    EXEC SQL INCLUDE SQLCA;

    int justStarting = 1;

    EXEC SQL DECLARE c1 CURSOR FOR
        SELECT name, application FROM applicants
        WHERE year(datereceived) = 1997 AND status = 'OK';

    EXEC SQL WHENEVER SQLERROR GOTO errorExit;

    EXEC SQL CONNECT TO :dbname;

    EXEC SQL OPEN c1;

    while (1)
      {
        EXEC SQL FETCH c1 INTO :candidate, :loc1;      /* Next application */
        if (SQLCODE == 100) break;                     /* No more appl'ns  */
```

```
/*
** Fetch the transcript portion of this application
*/
EXEC SQL
   VALUES(posstr(:loc1, '*TRANSCRIPT*')) INTO :transPosn;

EXEC SQL
   VALUES(substr(:loc1, :transPosn, 1000)) INTO :thisTranscript;

if (justStarting == 1)
  {
   /*
   ** First transcript we've looked at is automatically best so far
   */
   memcpy(bestTranscript, thisTranscript, 1000);
   bestLoc = loc1;
   justStarting = 0;
   strcpy(winner, candidate);
  }
else
  {
   if (compareTranscripts(bestTranscript, thisTranscript) == 2)
     {
      /*
      ** The current transcript replaces the previous best one
      */
      memcpy(bestTranscript, thisTranscript, 1000);
      EXEC SQL FREE LOCATOR :bestLoc;
      bestLoc = loc1;
      strcpy(winner, candidate);
     }
   else
     {
      /*
      ** Don't need this locator anymore.
      */
      EXEC SQL FREE LOCATOR :loc1;
     }
  }
}        /* End of while-loop over applications */

EXEC SQL CLOSE c1;
```

```
    if (justStarting == 1)
       printf("No qualifying applications were found.\n");
    else
       {
       /*
       ** Find the position of the essay in the winning application
       */
       EXEC SQL VALUES(posstr(:bestLoc, '*ESSAY*')) INTO :essayPosn;

       /*
       ** Prepare the file reference for fetching the winning application
       */
       strcpy(winningFile.name, "winner.txt");
       winningFile.name_length = strlen(winningFile.name);
       winningFile.file_options = SQL_FILE_OVERWRITE;

       /*
       ** Copy winning transcript and essay into file
       */
       EXEC SQL VALUES(:bestTranscript || substr(:bestLoc, :essayPosn))
                   INTO :winningFile;

       printf("The winner is %s\n", winner);
       }

    EXEC SQL COMMIT;
    return 0;

errorExit:
    printf ("Unexpected return code from DB2.\n");
    sqlaintp(msgbuffer, 500, 70, &sqlca);
    printf ("Message: %s\n", msgbuffer);

    EXEC SQL COMMIT;
    return -1;

    }       /* end of main() */
```

After execution of this program, if at least one qualifying application was found, the "best" transcript and the essay that accompanies it can be found in the file named winner.txt in the directory from which the program was executed.

6.2 DISTINCT TYPES

Each data value stored in UDB has a specific datatype that determines its representation and the operations that apply to it. The built-in datatypes of UDB include the basic datatypes listed in Tables 2-1 and 2-2, plus the large-object datatypes discussed in Section 6.1 (Long Varchar, Long Vargraphic, Blob, Clob, and Dbclob).

In building a database, you may decide to use one of the built-in datatypes in a specialized way; for example, you may use the Integer datatype to represent ages, or the Decimal(8,2) datatype to represent amounts of money, or the Double data-type to represent geometric angles. When you do this, you may have certain rules in mind about the kinds of computations that make sense on your data. For example, it may make sense to add or subtract two amounts of money, but it may not make sense to multiply two amounts of money, and it almost surely makes no sense to add or compare an age to an amount of money.

UDB provides a way for you to declare such specialized usages of datatypes and the rules that go with them. The system then enforces the rules, by performing only the kinds of computations and comparisons that you have declared to be reasonable for your data. For example, if you were to write a query that involves adding an age to an amount of money, the query would fail with an error message. In other words, the system guarantees the *type-safety* of your queries.

6.2.1 Creating Distinct Types

The way to declare a specialized use of data in UDB is to create a new datatype of your own, called a *distinct type*, to supplement the system's built-in datatypes. Each distinct type shares a common internal representation with one of the built-in datatypes, called its *source type*. Despite this common representation, the distinct type is considered to be a separate datatype, distinct from all others (hence the name). The following example statements create distinct types named Sex, Money, Geometry.Angle, and Video, which take their internal representations from various built-in datatypes:

```
CREATE DISTINCT TYPE Sex AS Char(1) WITH COMPARISONS;
CREATE DISTINCT TYPE Money AS Decimal(8,2) WITH COMPARISONS;
```

```
CREATE DISTINCT TYPE Geometry.Angle
               AS Double WITH COMPARISONS;
CREATE DISTINCT TYPE Video AS Blob(100M);
```

An instance of a distinct type is considered comparable only with another instance of the same distinct type. For example, if M1 is a column of type Money and D1 is a column of type Decimal(8,2), then m1 + d1 and m1 > d1 are not valid expressions—an SQL statement containing such an expression would fail with an error message.

The phrase WITH COMPARISONS serves as a reminder that instances of the new distinct type can be compared with each other, using six comparison operators: =, <, <=, >, >=, and <>. The meanings of the comparison operators applied to instances of the distinct type are the same as if they were applied to instances of the source type. Furthermore, since the system automatically knows how to compare instances of a distinct type, you can apply the language elements ORDER BY, GROUP BY, and DISTINCT to columns of a distinct type, and you can create a unique or nonunique index on a column of a distinct type. However, since comparisons, indexes, ORDER BY, GROUP BY, and DISTINCT are not supported for LOB datatypes, neither are they supported for distinct types based on LOB datatypes (and when you create such a distinct type, you should omit the phrase WITH COMPARISONS).

The syntax of a CREATE DISTINCT TYPE statement is as follows:

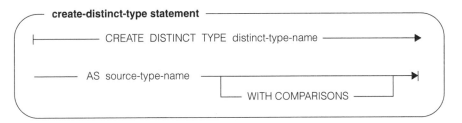

create-distinct-type statement

CREATE DISTINCT TYPE distinct-type-name

AS source-type-name

WITH COMPARISONS

The following facts are important to remember about the CREATE DISTINCT TYPE statement:

- The distinct-type name may be qualified by a schema name. The schema name may not begin with the letters SYS. If the schema name is omitted, it defaults to the userid of the user who is creating the distinct type. Whenever you are using a distinct type, you should add the schema name of the distinct type to your function path (discussed in Section 6.3).

- The distinct-type name must not be the same as the name of any built-in datatype or any other distinct type in the same schema. The name BOOLEAN is also prohibited as the name of a distinct type—it is reserved for a possible future built-in datatype.

- The source-type name must be the name of a built-in datatype. If it is qualified by a schema name, the schema name must be SYSIBM.

- If the source type takes a length or precision and scale (such as Char(n) or Decimal(p,s)), the values of these parameters must be fixed. If you omit the length of a Char type, it is assumed to be Char(1); if you omit the precision and scale of a Decimal type, it is assumed to be Decimal(5,0).

- The distinct-type name must not include any specification of length or precision and scale (since these are inherited from the source type).

- No authorization is required to execute a CREATE DISTINCT TYPE statement, unless a schema name is specified that is different from the current authid; in this case, either SYSADM or DBADM authority is required.

- The phrase WITH COMPARISONS is required if the source type is not a large-object datatype; if the source type is Blob, Clob, Dbclob, Long Varchar, or Long Vargraphic, the phrase WITH COMPARISONS is tolerated with a warning message even though comparisons are not supported.

Each distinct type is recorded in a system catalog table called DATATYPES, which has the following columns (among others):

TYPESCHEMA, TYPENAME: The name of the distinct type.

SOURCESCHEMA, SOURCENAME: The name of the source type on which the distinct type is based.

REMARKS: A descriptive comment, usually supplied by the user who created the distinct type.

You can place a comment in the REMARKS column of the DATATYPES catalog table by using the COMMENT statement described in Section 2.6.9. Here's an example:

```
COMMENT ON DISTINCT TYPE Money
    IS 'Signed dollar amounts less than $1 million';
```

After you have created a distinct type, you can use it in a CREATE TABLE or ALTER TABLE statement just as you would use a built-in datatype, as in the following examples. Note that since column names and datatype names are not in the same name space, a column is allowed to have the same name as its datatype.

```
CREATE TABLE employees
    (empno  Char(5),
     deptno Char(3),
     name   Varchar(20),
```

```
sex     Sex,
salary Money);

ALTER TABLE employees
    ADD bonus Money;
```

If you have a distinct type that is no longer needed, you can drop it by using the DROP statement described in Section 2.6.8. But before dropping a distinct type, you should make sure that it is not used in any table or view or as a parameter of any function. (For more information about finding objects that depend on a distinct type, see Section 7.5.2.) Here are some examples of statements that drop distinct types:

```
DROP DISTINCT TYPE Video;
DROP DISTINCT TYPE Geometry.Angle;
```

Of course, the built-in datatypes (which are in the SYSIBM schema) cannot be dropped.

6.2.2 Casting Functions

When you create a distinct type, two casting functions are automatically created to convert between the distinct type and its source type. For example, if you create a distinct type Age based on Integer, the system automatically generates casting functions named age(Integer) and integer(Age). Using these casting functions, you can freely convert a distinct-type value to its source type and vice versa. For example, if AGE1 and AGE2 are columns of type Age, which is based on Integer, and no "+" operator is defined for the Age datatype, the expression age1 + age2 would be an error, but the expression age(integer(age1) + integer(age2)) would be correct. This expression would be your way of telling the SQL compiler, "I know what I'm doing, and I want to add together these two Ages as though they were Integers." The casting functions between distinct types and their source types are very efficient (in fact, you might say they cost nothing), because the source type and the distinct type share the same representation, so no real work is needed to convert from one to the other.

The name of the casting function that converts a source-type value into a distinct type is the same as the name of the distinct type, and the casting function is created in the same schema as the distinct type. For example, if the distinct type Age in the COMPANY schema is based on Integer, its casting function (also in the COMPANY schema) is as follows:

```
age(Integer) returns Age
```

The age casting function in this example can be invoked on any value that can be promoted to Integer datatype by the normal rules of argument promotion (described in Section 6.6.1). For example, if C1 is a Smallint column and C2 is a Double column, age(c1) is valid (because Smallint is promotable to Integer), but age(c2) is not valid (because Double is not promotable to Integer).[2]

The name of the casting function that converts a distinct-type value into its source type is derived from the name of the source type, as shown in Table 6-3. This casting function is also generated in the same schema as the distinct type. For example, if Money in the COMPANY schema is based on Decimal(8,2), it has a system-generated casting function named decimal, also in the COMPANY schema, that takes Money as a parameter and returns Decimal(8,2).

When a distinct type is based on a datatype such as Char or Varchar that has a length parameter, the distinct type specifies (explicitly or by default) a fixed length, and the casting functions convert between instances of the distinct type and instances of the source type with the specified length. For example, suppose the distinct type Address is defined, based on Char(32). The following casting functions are automatically generated:

```
address(Char(32)) returns Address
char(Address) returns Char(32)
```

If a source-type value with a different length, such as Char(20) or Char(50), is passed to a casting function, its length is adjusted according to the rules for assignment to a host variable (for example, Char(20) would be padded with blanks to Char(32), and Char(50) would be truncated to Char(32) with a warning message). Similar rules apply to the casting functions for distinct types based on Decimal datatypes, which have a fixed precision and scale.

The casting functions that are created along with a distinct type can be invoked either by their names (like any other function) or by using a CAST expression. For example, if the distinct type Money is defined on the source type Decimal(8,2), either of the following expressions could be used to cast a Decimal constant into the Money type:

---

2. If a distinct type is defined on Smallint, casting functions are automatically created to cast both Smallint and Integer values into the distinct type. This is necessary because constants such as 25 and -9 are always considered to be of type Integer. Suppose, for example, that Hatsize is a distinct type based on Smallint. Then the expression hatsize(8) could be used to convert a constant Integer into a Hatsize even though Integer is not the source type. For similar reasons, a Double value can be cast into a distinct type based on Real (since floating-point constants are considered to be of type Double); a Varchar value can be cast into a distinct type based on Char (since character constants are considered to be of type Varchar), and a Vargraphic value can be cast into a distinct type based on Graphic (because double-byte constants are considered to be of type Vargraphic).

TABLE 6-3: Names of System-Generated Casting Functions

Source Type	Casting Function
Smallint	`smallint`
Integer	`integer`
Decimal(p,s) or Numeric(p,s)	`decimal`
Real	`real`
Double	`double`
Char(n)	`char`
Varchar(n)	`varchar`
Long Varchar	`long_varchar`
Clob(n)	`clob`
Graphic(n)	`graphic`
Vargraphic(n)	`vargraphic`
Long Vargraphic	`long_vargraphic`
Dbclob(n)	`dbclob`
Blob(n)	`blob`
Date	`date`
Time	`time`
Timestamp	`timestamp`

```
money(1234.50)
CAST(1234.50 AS Money)
```

Similarly, if SALARY is a database column of type Money, either of the following expressions could be used to cast a salary value into the Decimal type:

```
decimal(salary)
CAST(salary AS Decimal(8,2))
```

The CAST notation can also be used to convert a distinct-type value into a form of its source type that has a different length and/or precision and scale. For example, consider the following expression:

```
CAST(salary AS Decimal(10,4))
```

This expression invokes the casting function decimal(salary), resulting in a value of type Decimal(8,2), then adjusts the precision and scale of the result to conform to the desired type Decimal(10,4).

6.2.3 Using Distinct Types

Distinct types are useful tools for protecting the type-safety of a program. They can be used to make sure that different types of data are not combined in ways that do not make sense, such as comparing a Height to a Weight, even though both Height and Weight may be based on floating-point numbers.

It is important to remember that, although casting functions are automatically defined between each distinct type and its source type, you must invoke these casting functions explicitly if you wish to compare a distinct-type value with a source-type value. Furthermore, constants are always considered to have built-in types—for example, 21 is considered to be an Integer, and 'Green' is considered to be a Varchar(5). Therefore, to compare a distinct-type value to a constant, you must perform an explicit cast. For example, if MYAGE is a column of type Age, the expression myage > 21 is a type error, but myage > age(21) is correct, as is integer(myage) > 21.

When a distinct type is created, the only operations that are automatically defined on it are casting between the distinct type and its source type in both directions, and comparisons between two values of the distinct type (provided the source type is not a large-object datatype). Other operations that may apply to the source type, such as arithmetic operators, are not automatically inherited by the distinct type. It is probably not very useful to define a distinct type whose only operations are casting and comparison. Therefore, UDB provides a way for you to enhance the semantics of your distinct type, either by inheriting some of the operations of the source type or by defining new operations of your own.

In order to understand the behavior of a distinct type, it is important to realize that the system considers all arithmetic operators such as + and * to be *functions*. For example, the + operator for Integers is considered to be a function (named "+") that takes two Integers as arguments and returns another Integer (the sum of its arguments). You can even use a functional notation to invoke an arithmetic operator—just remember to enclose the name of the function in double quotes (this tells the system that the symbol "+" is being used as a name). For example, the following two queries are exactly equivalent:

```
SELECT qonhand + qonorder
FROM parts WHERE partno = 'P207';

SELECT "+"(qonhand, qonorder)
FROM parts WHERE partno = 'P207';
```

The built-in datatypes of UDB come with a collection of built-in functions that operate on them. Some of these functions implement operators such as the arithmetic operators on numeric datatypes and the concatenate (||) operator on string datatypes. Other built-in functions include scalar functions, such as length and substr, and column functions, such as sum and avg. After creating a distinct type, you can specify that the distinct type inherits some or all of the functions that operate on its source type. This is done by creating new functions, called *sourced functions*, that operate on the distinct type and duplicate the semantics of built-in functions that operate on the source type. For example, you might specify that your distinct type Weight inherits the arithmetic operators + and -, and the column functions sum and avg, from its source type Real. By selectively inheriting the semantics of the source type, you can make sure that programs do not perform operations that make no sense, such as multiplying two weights, even though the underlying source type supports multiplication.

You can also go beyond mere inheritance of source-type functions and give your distinct type some semantics of its own. This is done by creating some *external functions*, written in a host programming language, that operate on your distinct type. Since you implement these functions yourself, they can do anything you want. If you use an operator such as "+" as the name of your external function, you can invoke your function using infix notation (such as weight1 + weight2). In this way, you can define specialized meanings for arithmetic operations on your distinct type. But you are not limited to the existing operators—you can create an external function with any name and behavior that you like. For example, you might create a function named complement(Angle) that returns another Angle, or a function named zipcode(Address) that returns Char(5). (The process of creating sourced functions and external functions is discussed in Section 6.4.)

6.2.4 Assigning Distinct Types

We use the term *assignment* for the process of giving a new value to an entry in a database table or to a host variable. We refer to the database entry or host variable that is receiving the new value as the *target* of the assignment. In SQL, assignment can occur in the following ways:

1. An entry in a table can be assigned a new value by an UPDATE statement, as in:

```
UPDATE employees SET bonus = 1250.00 WHERE empno = '12345';
```

2. A new row can be inserted into a table, assigning new values to each of its columns, as in:

```
EXEC SQL
    INSERT INTO budget
    VALUES('Supersonic Wind Tunnel', 1996, :funds, :mgr);
```

3. A query (or FETCH statement) can deliver a value into a host variable, as in:
```
EXEC SQL
    SELECT bonus INTO :bonus
    FROM employees WHERE empno = '12345';
```

4. An assignment statement (SET statement) can be used in the body of a trigger. (Triggers and assignment statements are discussed in Section 7.3.)

In all these cases, the target is receiving a new value that is computed from an expression that may contain database columns and/or host language variables. If the datatype of the target is the same as the datatype of the value that is being assigned to it, the assignment is straightforward. The built-in datatypes have a set of rules for what happens when a value is assigned to a target of a different datatype, which might be summarized as follows:

1. Numeric datatypes (Smallint, Integer, Decimal, and Double) may be assigned freely to one another (however, loss of precision or a run-time error condition may occur if the source value cannot be represented in the target datatype).

2. Character-string datatypes (Char, Varchar, Long Varchar, and Clob) may be assigned freely to one another (however, padding, truncation, or a run-time error condition may occur, depending on the relative lengths of the source and the target).

3. Graphic-string datatypes (Graphic, Vargraphic, Long Vargraphic, and Dbclob) may be assigned freely to one another (again, various run-time exceptions may occur, depending on their lengths).

4. A Char or Varchar containing a valid representation of a Date may be assigned to a Date target and vice versa. Similarly, a Char or Varchar containing a valid representation of a Time may be assigned to a Time target and vice versa, and a Char or Varchar containing a valid representation of a Timestamp may be assigned to a Timestamp target and vice versa.

Some extension to these rules is necessary to cover assignments involving distinct types. Since each distinct type is generally considered to be comparable only to itself, one approach might be to require an explicit casting function to be invoked whenever a distinct type is assigned to or from another datatype. The problem with this "strict typing" approach lies with host variables. Since the host programming languages such as C and COBOL have no way to declare variables of distinct types, all host variables have built-in types. (More precisely, they have the programming language datatypes that correspond to built-in types; for example, the C datatype long corresponds to the built-in type Integer.) So when a distinct-type data value is fetched into (or inserted from) a host variable, the strict typing approach would require the programmer to use an explicit casting function. This rule would cause some serious problems for certain kinds of applications. For example, consider a program that is prompting its user for ad hoc SQL queries, executing them, and displaying the results. Suppose the user types the query SELECT * FROM students. The program needs to fetch values from the STUDENTS table into host variables for display, but if these values have distinct types, it is very difficult to insert casting functions into the query.

In order to make applications easier to develop, UDB automatically invokes a casting function when a distinct-type value is assigned to a source-type target and vice versa. The details of this policy are as follows:

1. A value of a built-in datatype can be assigned to a column of some distinct type DT only if the datatype of the value is the source type of DT or is promotable to the source type of DT (promotion rules are described in Section 6.6.1). For example, a column of type Money that is based on Decimal(8,2) can be assigned a value of type Money, Decimal, or Integer, since Integer is promotable to Decimal, but it may not be assigned a value of type Double, since Double is not promotable to Decimal. The system automatically invokes the appropriate casting function to carry out the assignment.

2. A value of a distinct type DT can be assigned to a database column of built-in type only if the type of the target column is the source type of DT. For example, a column of type Decimal(8,2) (or even Decimal with a different precision and scale) can be assigned a value of type Money. Once again, the system automatically invokes the appropriate casting function.

3. If a value of a distinct type DT is being assigned to a host variable, the assignment is carried out in a two-step process. In Step 1, the value is converted from DT to the source type of DT, using the system-provided casting function. In Step 2, the resulting value is assigned to the host variable, using the normal assignment rules for built-in types. The reason for separating these steps is that, in general, Step 1 is carried out at the server machine, and Step 2 is carried out at the client machine. Thus, for example, a Money value might be assigned to a host variable of type double by first casting Money to Decimal(8,2) and then assigning the Decimal(8,2) value to the double variable, which is permitted by the assignment rules. As in the previous cases, the system performs the type conversions automatically.

For some more examples of automatic casting on assignment, consider a geometry application. Suppose that Angle is a distinct type with a source type of Double, TRIANGLES is a table having a column named VERTEX of type Angle, and :v is a host language variable of type Double. Then, all the following examples are valid assignments:

```
EXEC SQL
    SELECT vertex INTO :v FROM triangles WHERE color = 'Red';
    /* Assignment to host variable; calls double(Angle) */
```

```
EXEC SQL
    INSERT INTO triangles(color, vertex) VALUES ('Blue', :v);
    /* Assignment to Angle column; calls angle(Double)  */

UPDATE triangles SET vertex = 45.5 WHERE color = 'Green';
    /* Assignment to Angle column; calls angle(Double)  */
    /* Decimal constant 45.5 is promoted to Double,      */
    /* then cast to Angle by calling function            */
```

6.3 FUNCTION PATH

Before proceeding any further with our discussion of user-defined datatypes and functions, we need to discuss the concept of *function path*. Since UDB allows users to create their own datatypes and functions, it is possible that multiple datatypes and/or functions may be created with the same name. For example, you might develop or purchase a specialized set of datatypes and functions for solving tax problems and keep them in a schema named TAX97. At the same time, you might develop, or purchase from another source, another set of datatypes and functions for managing investments and install them in a schema named INVEST. These two schemas might each contain a datatype named Money or a function named monthlyPayment.

If you call a function using a name such as monthlyPayment(x,y) that does not include a schema name, and multiple functions with this name that all accept the parameter types of your call exist in different schemas, the system must decide which function you intend to invoke. The same problem can occur with datatype names. The process of choosing a specific function or datatype to satisfy a given reference is called *function resolution* or *type resolution*.

You can always include an explicit schema name when you refer to a function or datatype, as in tax97.Money or invest.monthlyPayment. But there are some reasons why you might prefer to use unqualified names, including the following:

1. Fully qualified names are long and hard to remember.

2. It's better for applications not to depend on the schemas in which their datatypes and functions are installed. For example, if you replace your TAX97 package with a new upward-compatible package named TAX98, you would prefer not to have to edit all of your existing applications and change the schema name of every datatype and function from TAX97 to TAX98.

The mechanism provided in UDB for resolving datatypes and functions without requiring fully qualified names is the function path. Despite its name, the function path applies to datatypes as well as to functions. It is a sequence of schema names that will be searched, in order, whenever an unqualified (that is, schemaless) datatype name or function name is encountered. An unqualified datatype name resolves to the first matching datatype that is found on the path. The process of resolving an unqualified function name is somewhat more complex because it involves the *signature* of the function—that is, the datatypes of its parameters. (Function resolution is discussed in more detail in Section 6.4.3.)

For static SQL statements, the function path is determined by an optional FUNCPATH parameter on the PREP or BIND command that bound the application program, which specifies the list of schemas on the path. For example, the following command might be used to precompile a program named NAVIGATE with a particular function path:

```
PREP navigate FUNCPATH maps, geometry, sysibm
```

Schema names used in the FUNCPATH parameter are automatically folded to uppercase by the system unless they are enclosed in double quotes. The default function path for static SQL is SYSIBM, followed by SYSFUN, followed by the userid under which the program is being precompiled or bound. SYSIBM and SYSFUN are the schemas containing all the built-in functions, and SYSIBM is the first schema on the default path in order to minimize the time spent by the SQL compiler in searching for built-in functions.

 TIP: In the FUNCPATH parameter of a PREP or BIND command, USER is not recognized as a keyword representing the current userid. If you want to specify your own userid as a schema name in the function path for PREP or BIND, you must spell it out explicitly.

6.3.1 SET CURRENT FUNCTION PATH Statement

For dynamic SQL (including CLI), the function path is taken from a special register called CURRENT FUNCTION PATH. When a program begins to execute, the initial value of CURRENT FUNCTION PATH is SYSIBM, followed by SYSFUN, followed by the content of the USER special register (the userid of the user who is running the program). During execution of a program, the current function path register can be changed by an SQL statement with the following syntax:

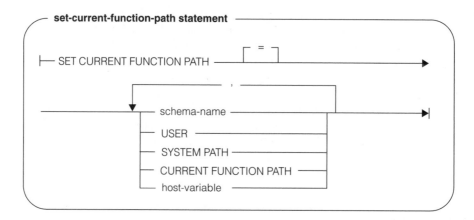

A SET CURRENT FUNCTION PATH statement can be either static or dynamic. In either case, it affects only the resolution of names in dynamic SQL statements that are executed after the SET CURRENT FUNCTION PATH is executed.

In a SET CURRENT FUNCTION PATH statement, schema names need not be enclosed in quotes unless they contain blanks or special characters or are the same as keywords. Schema names not enclosed in quotes are folded to uppercase (however, the content of a host variable is not folded to uppercase). The keywords that can be included in the path specification are interpreted as follows:

- USER represents the userid of the user who is running the program (not necessarily the same as the user who precompiled or bound the program).

- SYSTEM PATH represents the pair of schemas SYSIBM and SYSFUN (the part of the default path that contains system-provided functions).

- CURRENT FUNCTION PATH represents the function path that was in effect before the SET CURRENT FUNCTION PATH statement was executed. This is useful, for example, if you wish to keep the path intact and add a new schema to the end of it.

The following are examples of SET CURRENT FUNCTION PATH statements:

```
SET CURRENT FUNCTION PATH = USER, tax97, SYSTEM PATH;
SET CURRENT FUNCTION PATH = chem, physics, user;
SET CURRENT FUNCTION PATH = CURRENT FUNCTION PATH, maps;
```

TIP: A SET CURRENT FUNCTION PATH statement does not modify the database and therefore is not subject to rollback. For example, if you set your function path to a new value and then roll back your transaction, your function path will still retain the new value.

Like all special registers, the current function path can be examined using an SQL statement such as the following:

```
VALUES(CURRENT FUNCTION PATH);
```

The result of this VALUES statement is the current function path with each schema name enclosed in double quotes. For example, if the first SET CURRENT FUNCTION PATH statement above had been executed by user HILLARY, the result of the VALUES statement above would be "HILLARY", "TAX97", "SYSIBM", "SYSFUN".

TIP: Remember that a SET CURRENT FUNCTION PATH inside an application program does not affect the resolution of datatypes or function calls in *static* SQL statements. However, it may affect the resolution of datatypes and function calls in *dynamic* statements executed by this program.

Since all the built-in datatypes and many important functions are found in the SYSIBM schema, UDB would be very hard to use if SYSIBM were not on your function path. For this reason, every function path is required to include SYSIBM. If you specify a path that does not include SYSIBM, either in a PREP or BIND command or in a SET CURRENT FUNCTION PATH statement, the system will implicitly add SYSIBM to the beginning of the path, before the other schemas. (Placing SYSIBM at the beginning of the path allows applications that use only built-in functions to avoid any performance degradation that might be caused by searching for user-defined functions with the same name.) Of course, if you specify SYSIBM on your path in some position other than the first schema, the system will respect your wishes. The string returned by VALUES(CURRENT FUNCTION PATH) does not include the implicit SYSIBM schema (if any) that was added to your path.

The function path is used for resolving references to datatypes and functions, but not for resolving references to other objects such as tables, views, indexes, and aliases. Unqualified names of objects other than functions and datatypes have an implicit qualifier equal to the userid who bound the program (for static SQL) or the userid who is running the program (for dynamic SQL). For example, the unqualified table name RESULTS, in a static SQL statement in a program bound by user SMITH, is interpreted as SMITH.RESULTS, independently of the function path.

TIP: Whenever you are manipulating objects of a distinct type, the schema name of the distinct type should be on your function path, because the comparison operators of the distinct type are considered to be functions that are in the same schema as the distinct type. Thus, for example, if you have created a distinct type named Weight in the VEHICLES schema, a comparison of two Weight values such as `weight1 = weight2` is valid only if the VEHICLES schema is on your function path.

6.4 USER-DEFINED FUNCTIONS

In a UDB system, the functions that are available for use in SQL statements fall into the following general categories:

1. *Built-in functions*. Some functions are built into the code of the UDB system. These functions are found in the SYSIBM schema, and include the following:
   - Arithmetic and string operators: `+`, `-`, `*`, `/`, `||`
   - Scalar functions: `substr`, `concat`, `length`, `days`, and so on
   - Column functions: `avg`, `count`, `min`, `max`, `stdev`, `sum`, `variance`

   In addition to the built-in functions in the SYSIBM schema, many other functions are shipped with UDB, in the SYSFUN schema. Although these functions are shipped with the system, they are not implemented directly by system code. Instead, they are implemented as preinstalled external functions, using the same facilities that are available to users to define functions of their own. In practice, as long as both SYSIBM and SYSFUN are on your function path, there is no distinction in usage between the SYSIBM and SYSFUN functions.

2. *System-generated functions*. These functions are automatically generated when a distinct type is created and are found in the same schema as the distinct type. System-generated functions include casting functions and comparison operators for the distinct type.

3. *User-defined functions*. These functions are created explicitly by users, using a statement called CREATE FUNCTION, which names the new function and specifies its semantics. User-defined functions can be further classified into the following subcategories:

   a. *Sourced functions*. A sourced function duplicates the semantics of another function, called its *source function*. A sourced function can be an operator, a scalar function, or a column function. Sourced functions are particularly useful for allowing a distinct type to selectively inherit the semantics of its source type.

b. *External scalar functions.* An external scalar function is a function that is written by a user in a host programming language and that returns a scalar value. External scalar functions can be written in C or Java.[3] The CREATE FUNCTION statement for an external scalar function tells the system where to find the code that implements the function. If the name of an external scalar function matches the name of an operator (such as "+"), the function can be called using operator notation (such as x + y). An external scalar function may not be a column function, and it may not contain any SQL statements. In other words, an external scalar function may perform any computation you like on the parameters that are passed to it, but it may not access or modify the database.

c. *External table functions.* As discussed in Section 5.3, a user-defined function can return a table rather than a scalar value. Like an external scalar function, an external table function is written by a user in C or Java, and may not contain any embedded SQL statements. The program that implements an external table function must return one row of the result table each time it is called, and must indicate the end of the result table by a special return code.

System-generated functions and user-defined functions are always created in a specific database and can be used only in that database. Within their database, system-generated and user-defined functions can be used in the same ways as built-in functions. System-generated and user-defined functions are available to all users of the database and can be used without any specific authorization.

Creation of a user-defined function requires CREATEIN privilege on its schema, or IMPLICIT_SCHEMA authority on the database if the schema does not yet exist. In addition, if the function has the NOT FENCED property (described in Section 6.4.2), a database-level authority called CREATE_NOT_FENCED is required.

A CREATE FUNCTION statement may be embedded in an application program or executed via an interactive query interface. However, if a CREATE FUNCTION statement is embedded in a program, static SQL statements in that program cannot call the newly created function, since when the program is first bound, the new function will not yet exist (that is, the function will not exist until the program has been executed).

---

3. External functions can also be written in programming languages such as C++ that follow the C linkage conventions. Using IBM's VisualAge for Basic, an external function can be written in BASIC and provided with a "wrapper" function that enables it to be called using C linkage conventions. DB2 for Windows NT also allows a method of an OLE Automation Object to be defined as an external function. All the external function examples in this chapter are written in C.

Like many modern programming languages, SQL supports the concept of *function overloading*. This means that several functions may be defined that have the same name, as long as they are in different schemas or take different types of parameters. For example, you can define a function square(Integer) that returns Integer and another function square(Double) that returns Double. When a function call such as square(x) is encountered, the system automatically invokes the proper function for the datatype of the argument. It is easy to see that the built-in functions of UDB are already overloaded, since scalar functions such as length and operators such as + can be applied to many different datatypes. We will sometimes find it necessary to use the term *function family* to refer to a set of functions that share a common name, and *function instance* to refer to one of the functions within a function family.

When you create a new function, you may be starting a new function family or adding a function instance to an existing function family. In either case, you must make sure that your new function has a unique *signature*. The signature of a function is the combination of its fully qualified name and all its parameter types. For example, if a function square(Double) already exists, you will not be allowed to create another square(Double) function in the same schema.

In addition to its name, which it shares with all other functions in the same family, each user-defined function instance has another name called its *specific name*. The specific name of each function instance is unique within its schema. For example, in the MATH schema, we might create a function square(Integer) with a specific name of square1 and another function square(Double) with a specific name of square2. Specific names are used only to identify a function instance in cases where no arguments are present, such as in dropping a function, commenting on a function, or naming a function as the source of another function. When you invoke a function, you must always use its family name (not its specific name). The function resolution process (to be described later) will resolve the family name to a function instance based on the datatypes of the arguments and the function path.

Every user-defined and system-generated function is described in a system catalog table called FUNCTIONS, which has the following columns:

- FUNCSCHEMA, FUNCNAME: Qualified name of the user-defined function.
- SPECIFICNAME: Specific name of the function (useful for dropping a function instance from an overloaded function family).
- ORIGIN: A one-letter code that identifies the origin of the function as one of the following:
    B: built-in
    S: system-generated
    U: user-defined, sourced
    E: user-defined, external

- TYPE: A one-letter code that identifies the type of the function as one of the following:
  S: scalar function (such as `length`)
  C: column function (such as `avg`)
  T: table function (applies only to external functions)
- Various other columns that specify the properties of the function, including the name of the source (for a sourced function) or the name of the file that contains the implementation (for an external function).

Another catalog table, named FUNCPARMS, describes the datatypes of the parameters and the result of each system-generated or user-defined function. This catalog table has one row for each parameter of each function, and an additional row for the result type. For a table function, FUNCPARMS contains one row for each column of the result table. (Details of the FUNCTIONS and FUNCPARMS catalog tables are given in Appendix D.)

6.4.1 Creating a Sourced Function

A sourced function is a new function that is based on some other function that already exists, called the source function. When the new function is invoked, its arguments are cast into the parameter types of the source function; the source function is then invoked; and finally, the result of the source function is cast into the result type of the new function.

The process of executing a sourced function is illustrated in Figure 6-1. In this example, Weight is a distinct type based on the built-in Double datatype.

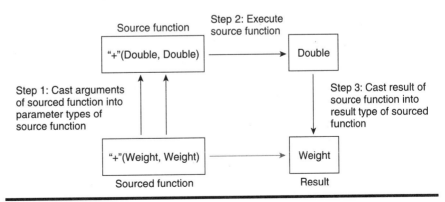

Figure 6-1: Executing a Sourced Function

Since it makes sense to add two Weights, the definer of the distinct type has created a function "+"(Weight, Weight) sourced on the built-in function "+"(Double, Double). This causes the Weight type to inherit the semantics of addition from the Double type. When two Weights are added, the system converts them to Double values, adds them together, and converts the result back into a Weight. (Remember that these "conversions" take no time because Weight and Double have the same representation.)

The syntax of a CREATE FUNCTION statement to create a sourced function is as follows:

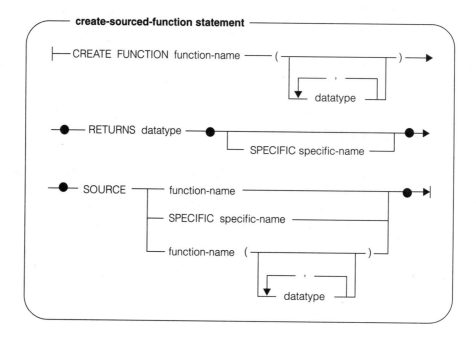

The parts of the CREATE FUNCTION statement for a sourced function are as follows:

1. *Function-name.* This is the name by which the function will be invoked. It may include a schema name, but the schema name may not begin with the letters SYS. If the schema name is omitted, it defaults to the current authid.

A function name may be an arithmetic operator such as "+" or "*", but when defining such a function you must enclose the function name in double quotes. If the name of a function is the same as an infix operator such as "+", the function can be called using infix notation (such as weight1 + weight2).

Comparison operators such as "=" and ">" may not be used as the names of functions. SQL keywords that might occur within a predicate (such as AND, OR, NOT, EXISTS, and BETWEEN) are also not valid function names.

2. (*datatype,* . . .). This part of the CREATE FUNCTION statement lists the datatypes of the function parameters. A function may take from 0 to 90 parameters. The parentheses must be present even if there are no parameters. The parameter types may be either built-in datatypes or user-defined (distinct) types.

If one of the parameter types takes an attribute such as length or scale/precision, you can either specify the attribute exactly—as in Decimal(8,3)—or use empty parentheses in place of the attribute—as in Decimal( ). Empty parentheses mean "same as the corresponding parameter of the source function." For example, creating a new function named foo(Char( )) with a source function bar(Char(5)) effectively specifies the signature of the new function to be foo(Char(5)).

When checking the signature of a function for uniqueness, the system ignores the length, precision, and scale of the function parameters. Thus, for example, schema1.foo(char(10)) and schema1.foo(char(20)) are considered duplicate signatures and cannot both exist.

TIP: When defining the datatypes of your function parameters, be careful to distinguish between empty parentheses, which mean "same as source function," and omitted parentheses, which result in a default value for the missing attribute. For example, if the signature of the new function is specified as foo(Char), its parameter is assumed to have a length of 1, regardless of the parameter of the source function.

3. *RETURNS clause.* This clause specifies the return type of the new function. If the return type takes an attribute such as length or scale/precision, you can either specify the attribute exactly—as in Decimal(8,3)—or use empty parentheses in place of the attribute—as in Decimal( ). Empty parentheses mean "same as the return type of the source function." If the source function returns a datatype of indefinite length, the new function will do the same. In the following example, the parameters and result of both the source function and the new function have indefinite lengths:

```
CREATE FUNCTION "+"(Varchar( ), Varchar( )) RETURNS Varchar( )
    SOURCE concat(Varchar( ), Varchar( ));
```

4. *SPECIFIC clause.* This clause gives a specific name to the new function instance being created. The purpose of the specific name is to provide a unique way to identify a function instance even though several function instances can have the same function name.

The specific name must be unique within its schema. If you do not specify a specific name for your function, the system will generate one automatically. The specific name is recorded in the SPECIFICNAME column of the FUNC-TIONS catalog table, and can be used to drop the function, to comment on it, or to use it as the source of another function. However, a function can never be invoked by its specific name, but only by its function name.

There is no need to specify a schema for the specific name, since the specific name of a function is implicitly qualified by the same schema as the function name. Since function names and specific names are in different name spaces, the function name and specific name of a function instance can be identical.

5. *SOURCE clause.* This clause identifies your new function as a sourced function and specifies the existing function that will serve as its "source." The source function can be either built-in or user-defined and can be an operator such as "+"; a scalar function such as `substr`; or a column function such as `avg`; however, it cannot be a table function. The source function can be identified in one of three ways:

a. By its function name, with no parameters. This method applies only if the source function is user-defined and only if its name is unique within its schema. You can provide a schema name or omit it, causing the system to search through the function path to find the first schema that contains a function with the given name. If the name of the source function is an operator such as "+" or an SQL keyword, it must be enclosed in double quotes.

b. By its specific name. This method applies only if the source function is user-defined, since built-in functions do not have specific names. You can look up the specific name of any user-defined function in the SPECIFIC column of the FUNCTIONS catalog table. You can provide a specific name that is qualified by a schema name, such as `geometry.cosine`, or you can omit the schema name, causing the system to search through the function path until it finds a function with the given specific name.

c. By its signature (its function name together with the datatypes of its parameters). This is the only way to identify a source function that is a built-in function. As usual, you can provide an explicit schema name or omit the schema name and let the system search for the function on the function path. The rules for identifying a source function by its signature are as follows:

- The system searches for a source function whose parameter types exactly match the datatypes that you specify, without any promotion of types. For example, if you specify SOURCE `foo(Integer)`, the function `foo(Double)` will not qualify, even though Integer is promotable to Double.

- If the signature includes a datatype that has an attribute such as length or scale/precision, you can either specify the attribute exactly—for example, Decimal(8,3)—or use empty parentheses in place of the attribute—for example, Decimal( ). Empty parentheses match any length or scale/precision. For example, SOURCE `length(Char())` searches for a source function named `length` that takes a Char parameter of any length (as does the built-in `length` function).

TIP: Empty parentheses are not equivalent to omitted parentheses. For example, SOURCE length(Char) searches for a source function that takes a Char parameter of default length, which is Char(1). This SOURCE clause would fail to find the system's built-in length function. In a SOURCE clause, it is a good rule to always use empty parentheses (never omitted parentheses) for all lengths, precisions, and scales.

After the system has found a source function that matches your SOURCE clause, it applies a *castability test* to the source function. The test requires that each parameter of your new function be castable into the corresponding parameter of the source function and that the result type of the source function be castable into the result type of your new function, as illustrated in Figure 6-1. The most common case is that the parameters and/or result of the new function are distinct types, and the corresponding parameters and/or result of the source function are the source types of those distinct types. If the function identified by your SOURCE clause fails the castability test (for example, its result type is not castable into the result type of the new function), the CREATE FUNCTION statement fails.[4]

The reason for the castability test is obvious: it ensures that the system has a way to do the conversions that it needs to do when the function is called. For example, in Figure 6-1, the system needs to cast the two Weight parameters into Double values and to cast the Double result back into a Weight. Since the cast functions weight(Double) and double(Weight) were created when the Weight datatype was created, the castability test is satisfied.

The most common use of sourced functions is to allow a distinct type to selectively inherit some of the functions and operators that apply to its source type. As an example, suppose that a distinct type Money has been defined, based on the built-in datatype Decimal(8,2). The Decimal datatype has arithmetic operators +, -, *, and /. We might wish to specify that the Decimal operators + and - are inherited by the Money datatype. This would be done by the following statements:

```
CREATE FUNCTION "+"(Money, Money) RETURNS Money
   SOURCE "+"(Decimal(), Decimal());
CREATE FUNCTION "-"(Money, Money) RETURNS Money
   SOURCE "-"(Decimal(), Decimal());
```

If SALARY and BONUS are two database columns of type Money, the functions above allow us to write expressions such as salary + bonus and salary -

---

4. The precise meaning of "castable" is explained in Section 6.6.4.

bonus. Of course, since the operators * and / are still undefined for Money, salary * bonus is not a valid expression.

Here are some things to notice about the CREATE FUNCTION statements in the example above:

- The operators "+" and "-" are enclosed in quotes to indicate that they are being used as function names.

- The empty parentheses after Decimal mean "any precision and scale." In other words, the source function operates on Decimal input parameters of any precision and scale. Of course, the newly created function operates only on input parameters of type Money, which has a well-defined precision and scale.

If it is meaningful to use arithmetic operators between your distinct type and its source type (or some other datatype), you must define these operators explicitly. For example, suppose that you wish to be able to multiply Money values by Integers to make new Money values. This can be accomplished by creating a sourced function, as follows:

```
CREATE FUNCTION "*"(Money, Integer) RETURNS Money
    SOURCE "*"(Decimal(), Integer);
```

This function enables you to write expressions such as money(111.11) * 2. Of course, if you want to write expressions such as 2 * money(111.11), you must define another sourced function with the signature "*"(Integer, Money).

The built-in column functions avg, count, min, max, stdev, sum, and variance do not apply to distinct types unless they are made to do so by means of sourced functions. For example, the following statement causes the Money datatype to inherit the semantics of the avg function from the underlying Decimal datatype:

```
CREATE FUNCTION avg(Money) RETURNS Money
    SOURCE avg(Decimal());
```

Creation of this function makes the following query valid when the SALARY column is of type Money:

```
SELECT deptno, avg(salary) FROM employees GROUP BY deptno;
```

A new function will be a column function if its source function is a column function. This is independent of the name given to the new function, which may or may not be the same as the name of the source function. It is even possible (though confusing and not recommended) to create a function sourced on a function with a quite different name, as in the following example:

```
CREATE FUNCTION sum(Money, Money) RETURNS Money
    SOURCE "+"(Decimal(), Decimal());
```

In this example, the name sum, which ordinarily denotes a column function, is assigned the semantics of ordinary decimal addition when applied to the Money datatype. Thus the expression sum(salary, bonus) would be a valid expression with the same meaning as salary + bonus, but sum(salary) would be invalid (unless a unary sum(Money) function is defined separately).

We have illustrated how sourced functions are used for selectively applying to a distinct type the semantics of its source type. However, it is possible to create a new function sourced on any existing function you like, either built-in or user-defined, as long as the argument types of the new function are castable to the argument types of the source function and the result type of the source function is castable to the result type of the new function. For example, the following statement might be used to give a new name to integer addition:

```
CREATE FUNCTION add(Integer, Integer) RETURNS Integer
    SOURCE "+"(Integer, Integer);
```

This statement indicates that, if x and y are of type Integer, the expression add(x,y) has the same meaning as the expression x + y. Of course, the new function name add is not recognized as an infix operator, so x add y would not be a valid expression.

6.4.2 Creating an External Scalar Function

An external function is a function whose implementation is written in some host programming language. The ability to create your own external functions is a very powerful feature of UDB. Using this feature, you can enhance the usefulness of the built-in datatypes by adding new functions that operate on them, and you can define whatever behavior you wish for your distinct types.

By defining external functions and installing them in your database, you can share these functions among all of your database applications, avoiding the necessity to duplicate the code in each application. External functions can be used wherever built-in functions can be used.

This section describes how to create an external function that returns a scalar value (external table functions are described in Section 6.4.8). External scalar functions can provide an important performance advantage when used in predicates, because they are executed at the server machine. If a function can be applied to a candidate row at the server machine, it can often eliminate the row from consideration before transmitting it to the client machine, reducing the amount of data that must be passed from server to client.

The syntax of a CREATE FUNCTION statement to create an external scalar function is as follows:

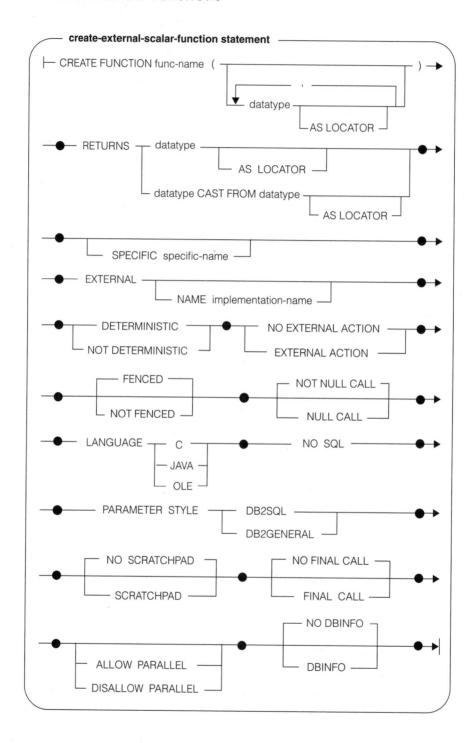

The parts of the CREATE FUNCTION statement for an external scalar function are as follows:

1. *Func-name.* This is the name by which the function will be invoked. It may include a schema name, as in `geometry.tangent`. The schema name may not begin with the letters SYS. If the schema name is omitted, it defaults to the current authid.

   As in the case of sourced functions, the name of an external function may be an arithmetic operator such as "+" but not a comparison operator such as ">" or a keyword used in predicates such as AND, OR, NOT, EXISTS, or BETWEEN. It is also wise to avoid using a datatype name as the name of a function, since it might be confused with the system-generated casting function for that datatype (a user-defined function is *not* considered a casting function by the system just because its name and result type match some datatype).

2. *(datatype, . . .).* This part of the CREATE FUNCTION statement lists the datatypes of the function parameters. A function may take from 0 to 90 parameters. The parentheses must be present even if there are no parameters. The parameter types may be either built-in datatypes or user-defined (distinct) types.

   If any parameter of an external function is a string type, its maximum length must be specified explicitly—for example, Char(12), Varchar(25), or Blob(32K). When checking the signature of an external function for uniqueness, the system ignores the length attributes of the function parameters. Thus, for example, `schema1.reverse(Varchar(10))` and `schema1.reverse(Varchar(20))` are considered duplicate signatures and cannot both exist.

   As each parameter is passed to the C program that implements the external function, it is converted from an SQL datatype to the corresponding C datatype. A list of the C datatypes corresponding to each of the SQL datatypes is given in Table 6-5 on page 334. None of the parameters of an external function may be of type Decimal, because there is no way to pass a Decimal value to a C program. If you need to pass Decimal data to an external function, you can do so by first changing its datatype to Char or Double, using the built-in cast functions `char(Decimal)` or `double(Decimal)`.

   If a function parameter is declared to have a distinct type, it is converted to its source type before being passed to the external function. For example, if Zipcode is a distinct type based on Char(5), a Zipcode parameter is passed to the program that implements the function as though its SQL datatype were Char(5). For this reason, no function parameter may have a distinct type that is based on a Decimal datatype.

   If the type of a function parameter is one of the LOB types (Blob, Clob, or Dbclob), or a distinct type that is sourced on a LOB type, you can choose to pass the parameter to the function either directly or in the form of a locator. For example, if you declare the type of a parameter as Clob(1M), the value of the parameter will be materialized in a one-megabyte buffer and a pointer to the buffer will be passed to the function. On the other hand, if you declare the type of the parameter to be Clob(1M) AS LOCATOR, the system will not allocate a large buffer for materializing the parameter—instead, it will pass to the function a locator that represents the parameter value. The function can use this locator to materialize the parameter value in small pieces, using special function calls described in Section 6.4.6. Passing LOB-type parameters to external functions in the form of locators is an efficient technique, but it can be used only with unfenced functions.

TIP: It is not advisable to define a function having a parameter of type Smallint, Real, fixed-length Char, or fixed-length Graphic, because constants and host variables are never interpreted as having these datatypes. For example, the constant 5 is considered to be an Integer, not a Smallint; the constant 5e3 is considered to be a Double, not a Real; and the constant 'abc' is considered to have datatype Varchar, not Char. Therefore, if you create a function with a parameter of type Smallint, Real, Char, or Graphic, an explicit cast will be required every time you pass a constant or host variable to your function, as in foo(Smallint(5)). Your function will be much more useful if its parameter type is Integer, Double, Varchar, or Vargraphic.

3. *RETURNS clause.* This clause specifies the result type of your function. The result type can be either a built-in or a user-defined datatype. If it is a string type, its maximum length must be specified explicitly.

Of course, since your external function is implemented by a C program, the actual value returned by the C program will have one of the C datatypes shown in Table 6-5 and will be converted into the corresponding SQL datatype as though it were an input host variable.

If the result of your external function is declared to have a distinct type, it is returned by a two-step process that is the reverse of the process used to pass a distinct-type parameter to an external function. The value returned by the C program is converted from a C datatype into an SQL datatype as though it were an input host variable; this SQL datatype is then cast into the desired distinct type using the system-provided casting function. For example, if the declared return type of your function is Zipcode, the C program would return a C datatype of null-terminated char[6], which would be converted into the SQL datatype of Char(5) and then into the distinct type Zipcode. All these conversions are done automatically, using system-provided casting functions.

If you wish the result type of your function to be different from the datatype returned by the C program that implements the function, you can specify an additional conversion by using a CAST FROM clause. For example, suppose that you want to write an external function named grade_level (Clob(10K)), which examines a piece of text and returns an estimate of its reading difficulty expressed as a Decimal(3,1). The C program that implements your function has no way to return a Decimal value, since there is no C datatype in Table 6-5 that corresponds to Decimal. But the C program can return a Double value, which could then be converted into a Decimal(3,1) by the system. You could call for this conversion to be done by the following statement:

```
CREATE FUNCTION grade_level(Clob(10K))
RETURNS Decimal(3,1) CAST FROM Double EXTERNAL ... ;
```

If your function is unfenced and its return type is a LOB type or a distinct type sourced on a LOB type, the function can return its value either directly or in the form of a locator. For example, if you specify RETURNS Clob(1M), the system will allocate a one-megabyte buffer for the return value and will pass to the function the address of the buffer. On the other hand, if you specify RETURNS Clob(1M) AS LOCATOR, the system will not allocate a buffer for the return value. Instead, it is the responsibility of the function to create and return a locator that represents the return value, using the function calls that are provided for this purpose and described in Section 6.4.6.

4. *SPECIFIC clause.* This clause gives a specific name to the new function instance being created. Like a sourced function, an external function can have a specific name that uniquely identifies it among all the function instances with the same function name. The specific name can be used to drop the function, to comment on it, or to specify it as the source of another function, but it is never used to invoke the function. Functions are always invoked by their function name, which selects a function instance by means of the function resolution process described in Section 6.4.3.

5. *EXTERNAL clause.* This clause identifies your function as an external function and tells the system how to find the C function that serves as its implementation. This C function must be compiled, linked, and placed in a directory on the server machine, from which it can be dynamically loaded by the database system when needed.

The most complete form of an EXTERNAL clause gives the full path name of the binary file that implements your function, followed by a "!", followed by the name of the proper entry point in that file. For example, the following clause tells the system that your function is implemented by the payment entry point in the file /u/dbfns/bin/mortgage:

```
EXTERNAL NAME '/u/dbfns/bin/mortgage!payment'
```

If no path name is specified, the system looks for your function in the sqllib/function directory associated with your database. Thus, if you put the mortgage binary file in sqllib/function, you can shorten the phrase above as follows:

```
EXTERNAL NAME 'mortgage!payment'
```

If you specify a default entry point when you link your function, you can omit the entry point from the EXTERNAL clause, which can then use a simple identifier to name the implementation file, as in the following example:

```
EXTERNAL NAME mortgage
```

In fact, if you specify no implementation name at all but only the keyword EXTERNAL, the system will use the function name as the implementation name, and will look for a file with this name in the default function directory and invoke its default entry point.

TIP: If you specify a filename or entry point in the EXTERNAL clause, it must exactly match the name of your executable file or entry point, including upper- and lowercase.

6. *DETERMINISTIC clause.* You must declare your function either DETERMINIS-TIC or NOT DETERMINISTIC. NOT DETERMINISTIC means that your function might return different results from two calls with the same parameters. A useful example of a nondeterministic function is a random-number generator such as the system-provided function rand, which returns a random floating-point number between 0 and 1.

The database optimizer takes some extra precautions in processing queries that contain nondeterministic functions. For example, it will never perform a query transformation that might result in an additional call to a nondeter-ministic function.

The word DETERMINISTIC is part of the draft SQL3 Standard. For compatibil-ity with earlier versions of DB2, UDB accepts the keyword VARIANT as a syn-onym for NOT DETERMINISTIC, and NOT VARIANT as a synonym for DETERMINISTIC.

7. *EXTERNAL ACTION clause.* This clause is also mandatory, and it specifies whether your function performs some action that affects the world outside the database. For example, you might write a function that sends mail to someone, writes into a file, or sets off an alarm. Of course, you want the num-ber of invocations of such a function to be predictable—for example, if the function is used once in a SELECT list, it should be invoked exactly once for each row returned by the query. The EXTERNAL ACTION clause alerts the database optimizer to the existence of these functions, so that it will not mod-ify a query in a way that changes the number of calls to such a function.

TIP: In addition to using the EXTERNAL ACTION clause, you must be careful where you invoke a function with side effects in order to make sure it is exe-cuted a predictable number of times. As a general rule, it is safe to invoke such a function in a VALUES statement or in the SELECT clause of a query that does not involve DISTINCT, a column function, a join, or a set operator such as UNION.

8. *FENCED or NOT FENCED.* The FENCED option specifies that your function must always be run in an address space that is separate from the database. This option causes a performance penalty due to process-switching when the function is called, but it protects the integrity of the database against accidental or malicious damage that might be caused by the function. This clause is optional, and the default is FENCED.

An unfenced function runs in the same address space as the database and can damage the integrity of your data. In order to create an unfenced function, you must possess either SYSADM or DBADM authority, or a database-level authority called CREATE_NOT_FENCED, which can be granted only by someone with SYSADM or DBADM authority, as described in Section 2.8.2. You can see who has been authorized to create unfenced functions by looking in the NOFENCEAUTH column of the DBAUTH catalog table.

It is strongly suggested that you run your functions in fenced mode until they are very well tested. You may wish to declare a function as FENCED at first and later convert it to NOT FENCED when you have confidence that it is working correctly. To do this, you must drop the function and recreate it with a new CREATE FUNCTION statement.

9. *NULL CALL or NOT NULL CALL.* This clause controls what happens when your function is invoked with a null value as one of its arguments. Many functions follow the convention that, if any argument is null, the function returns a null value. If your function follows this convention, you can specify NOT NULL CALL. In this case, the system will never pass a null argument to your function; instead, if a null argument is detected, the system will automatically consider the result of the function to be null. This convention makes your function easier to write, because it does not need to test its input parameters for nulls. It also improves performance by avoiding a function call whenever an argument is null. Of course, a function can still return a null value, even if it is created with a NOT NULL CALL specification.

This clause is optional, and its default is NOT NULL CALL.

TIP: If you are writing a function mainly to cause some side effect such as logging events in a file, you will probably want to specify NULL CALL rather than accepting the default of NOT NULL CALL.

10. *LANGUAGE clause.* This mandatory clause specifies the programming language in which your function is implemented, which determines the linkage convention used by UDB for invoking the function. The options are C, JAVA, and OLE. (Java functions are discussed in Section 6.4.10, and OLE functions are discussed in Section 6.4.11.)

TIP: If your function implementation is written in C++, you should specify LANGUAGE C, and you should also specify `extern "C"` as part of your function declaration in the implementation file.

11. *PARAMETER STYLE clause.* This mandatory clause identifies the conventions that are used for passing parameters to your external function. These conventions, which are described in Section 6.4.4, deal with issues such as how null values are represented and how error conditions are reported. With LANGUAGE C or OLE, you should specify PARAMETER STYLE DB2SQL, and with LANGUAGE JAVA, you should specify PARAMETER STYLE DB2GENERAL.

12. *NO SQL.* This mandatory clause specifies that your external function contains no SQL statements. At present, external functions are not allowed to access the database.

13. *SCRATCHPAD clause.* If a function is created with the SCRATCHPAD option, that function is provided with a "scratchpad" area in memory that it can use to preserve information from one function invocation to the next. Scratchpad functions are discussed in Section 6.4.7. The default is NO SCRATCHPAD.

14. *FINAL CALL clause.* When a function is used in an SQL statement, the function may be called multiple times during the processing of the statement, depending on how it is used. For example, a function used in a WHERE clause might be called once for each row of the table being queried. If the function is created with the FINAL CALL option, the function is called one extra time (the "final call") at the end of processing the SQL statement. A special parameter is passed to the function body to distinguish the final call from the other calls. The final call can be used for "cleanup" purposes, such as freeing memory allocated by the function body. The FINAL CALL option is often used with the SCRATCHPAD option and is also discussed in Section 6.4.7. The default is NO FINAL CALL.

15. *PARALLEL clause.* This optional clause tells the system whether it is safe to execute the function in parallel on multiple processors. For example, if you write a query that uses the function `excessive(salary)` in a predicate, the system might process some rows on node A and other rows on node B, and both nodes A and B might invoke the `excessive` function. If you specify DISALLOW PARALLEL, however, the system will be required to collect all the rows on a single node and process them one after another. The usual reason for disallowing parallel execution of a function is that one invocation of the function needs to pass along information to the next invocation, using a scratchpad. By default, parallel execution of a function is allowed unless the function has one of the following properties: SCRATCHPAD, FINAL CALL, NOT DETERMINISTIC, or EXTERNAL ACTION.

16. *DBINFO clause.* This optional clause causes UDB to pass an extra parameter to the function, containing a pointer to a data structure containing information such as the name of the current database, the current authid, and the name of the table and column (if any) that is being modified by the current statement. None of the examples in this book require a DBINFO clause. You can find a detailed specification of the DBINFO data structure in the *Embedded SQL Programming Guide.*

If a sourced function is defined whose source is an external function, the DETERMINISTIC, EXTERNAL ACTION, FENCED, NULL CALL, and other properties of the external function are inherited by the sourced function.

 TIP: If your CREATE FUNCTION statement was not successful, check for missing clauses. All the following clauses are required on a CREATE FUNCTION statement for an external function:

```
RETURNS
EXTERNAL
DETERMINISTIC or NOT DETERMINISTIC
EXTERNAL ACTION or NO EXTERNAL ACTION
LANGUAGE
PARAMETER STYLE DB2SQL
NO SQL
```

At this point, you may be wondering why the CREATE FUNCTION statement has so many mandatory clauses. For example, why should you be required to specify NO SQL when external functions can never contain SQL statements? A similar question might be asked about the CREATE DISTINCT TYPE statement, which requires the phrase WITH COMPARISONS, even though there is no way to create a distinct type on a non-LOB source type without comparison functions. In both cases, the answer has to do with standards. At the time when UDB was being designed, discussions were underway in ANSI and ISO committees about adding user-defined datatypes and functions to the SQL Standard. Since these discussions were still in progress, it was impossible to predict exactly what the standard syntax would eventually look like. For example, the standards committees might settle on a parameter-passing convention that is different from that adopted by UDB. For this reason, the designers of UDB decided to include in the CREATE FUNCTION and CREATE TYPE statements some required phrases that identify the parameter-passing convention and other details of the UDB implementation. These phrases protect your applications against any change in default behavior that might be required by a future version of the SQL Standard.

The CREATE FUNCTION statement in the following example creates an external function that computes a person's normal weight, based on sex and height. Sex might be a distinct type based on Char(1), and Height might be a distinct type based on Double. The function returns a value of type Weight, which might be a distinct type based on Double.

```
CREATE FUNCTION medical.normalWeight(Sex, Height)
   RETURNS Weight
   EXTERNAL NAME 'medical!nweight'
```

```
DETERMINISTIC
NO EXTERNAL ACTION
LANGUAGE C
PARAMETER STYLE DB2SQL
NO SQL;
```

An external function can be used in an SQL statement in exactly the same way as a built-in function. No special authorization is required to call an external function, even if it was created by another user.

For an example of how the `normalWeight` function created above might be used, suppose that our database contains the following table:

PATIENTS

SOCSECNO	NAME	SEX	HEIGHT	WEIGHT

Suppose that the SEX, HEIGHT, and WEIGHT columns of the PATIENTS table have datatypes of Sex, Height, and Weight, respectively. Suppose further that the following sourced function has been defined that allows us to multiply a floating-point value times a Weight to get another Weight:

```
CREATE FUNCTION "*"(Double, Weight) RETURNS Weight
    SOURCE sysibm."*"(Double, Double);
```

The following query might be used to find all the patients in the table whose weight is less than 80% of their normal weight:

```
SELECT name, weight,
        medical.normalWeight(sex, height) AS normal
FROM patients
WHERE weight < 0.8 * medical.normalWeight(sex, height);
```

6.4.3 Function Resolution

When a function is called in an SQL statement, the function may be referred to either by its fully qualified name (such as `medical.normalWeight`) or by its unqualified name (such as `normalWeight`). If an unqualified name is used, UDB automatically searches through the schemas on your function path to find an applicable function. A function is considered applicable to a given call if its function name matches the call and if the arguments of the call are "promotable" to the parameters of the function. This means that the datatype of

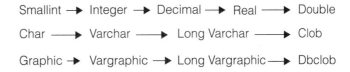

Figure 6-2: Valid Datatype Promotions for Function Arguments

each function parameter either must match the datatype of the corresponding call argument or must be found by starting with the call-argument type and moving to the right along one of the promotion paths shown in Figure 6-2.

The built-in datatypes Blob, Date, Time, and Timestamp, and any user-defined datatypes, do not appear in any of the promotion paths in Figure 6-2, and therefore they require an exact match between call-argument type and function-parameter type. The length, precision, and scale of a datatype are not considered in finding an applicable function, but after the function has been selected, the length, precision, and/or scale of the call arguments are converted to those of the function parameters. For example, if column C3 has a datatype of Char(3), and user-defined function udf.foo has a parameter of datatype Char(5), then the call foo(c3) might invoke udf.foo after padding the value of C3 with blanks to a length of five characters.

If you call a function by its unqualified name, it is possible that more than one applicable function may be found on the function path. Even if you qualify the function name by a schema name, it is possible that more than one applicable function may be found in the given schema. In either case, the system chooses the "best" applicable function, considering the parameters from left to right and using the path as a tiebreaker. This process is called *function resolution*. Conceptually, the function resolution process consists of the following steps:

1. First, find the set of all applicable functions. Each of these functions has the correct function name and number of parameters, and all the call-argument types are promotable to the corresponding function-parameter types, and the schema of the function is either on the path or named in the function call.

2. Next, consider each call argument, from left to right. For each argument, eliminate all the functions that are not the "best available" match for that argument. In this context, "best" means "farthest to the left on the promotion diagram in Figure 6-2." For example, if the call is foo(Integer, Date), and the applicable functions are foo(Decimal, Date) and foo(Double, Date), then the function foo(Decimal, Date) has a "better" match for the first argument, so foo(Double, Date) is eliminated from further consideration. Remember that length, precision, and scale of function arguments are ignored during function resolution.

3. After considering all the arguments, if more than one function remains, all the remaining functions must have the same set of parameter types and must therefore be in different schemas. In this case, select the function whose schema is earliest on the path.

4. The result type of a function is not considered during the function resolution process. However, after a function call has been resolved, if the result type of the selected function is not appropriate for the context of the function call, an error results. For example, an error will result if a table function is called where a scalar function is expected, or vice versa.

TIP: During function resolution, a host language variable such as char x[11] is always interpreted as having datatype Varchar, not Char or Date. Thus, in resolving the function call foo(:x), the system will look for a function foo(Varchar), not foo(Char) or foo(Date). If you wish your host variable to be interpreted as a Char or Date, you must use an explicit cast, as in foo(char(:x)) or foo(date(:x)).

As a general rule, function calls in static data manipulation statements are resolved when their program is bound, whereas function calls in dynamic statements are resolved at run time. The details are given in Table 6-4 (note the similarities between Table 6-4 and Table 2-7).

When a program is bound, all of its function calls that occur in static data manipulation statements are resolved, as shown in Table 6-4. After the pro-

TABLE 6-4: Function Resolution Rules for Static and Dynamic SQL Statements

Type of Statement	Static SQL	Dynamic SQL
Data manipulation statements (SELECT, INSERT, UPDATE, DELETE, and VALUES)	Functions resolved at bind time, using path specified as PREP or BIND option	Functions resolved at run time, using CURRENT FUNCTION PATH special register
All other SQL statements	Functions resolved at run time, using path specified as PREP or BIND option	Functions resolved at run time, using CURRENT FUNCTION PATH special register

gram is bound, the system guarantees that it will continue using the same function instances, even if a better-matching function instance is created and even if the program is automatically rebound (for example, when an index is dropped). However, if you explicitly rebind your program by using a BIND or REBIND command, the function resolution process will start over from scratch, and the best applicable function at that time will be selected. If the function instance to which a program has been bound is dropped, the program goes into an "inoperative" state in which it cannot be used until it is explicitly rebound. This policy, called *conservative binding semantics*, guarantees that once your program is bound, its behavior will not change without an explicit action on your part (an explicit rebind).

TIP: SQLCODE –440 (SQLSTATE 42884) indicates that the system was unable to find any applicable function for one of your function calls. If you receive this code, check your current function path to make sure that it includes the schema containing the desired function. Next, check the arguments of your function call to make sure their datatypes match (or are promotable to) the datatypes of the function parameters.

6.4.4 Implementing an External Scalar Function

Suppose you wish to define an external function, written in C, that takes n parameters and returns a scalar result. The actual function body that you write in C will need more than n parameters. Some of these C parameters will be used to indicate whether null values are being passed to the external function, one C parameter will be used for returning the result of the function, and other C parameters will be used for special purposes such as returning error codes.

We will illustrate the conventions[5] for exchanging parameters and results with external functions by writing an example function named addWeeks, which takes a Date and an Integer that represents a number of weeks and returns a new Date computed by adding the given number of weeks to the given Date. This might be a useful function, since UDB does not recognize a constant such as "5 WEEKS" as a valid duration. Since dates are not a native datatype in C, this example will give us an opportunity to see how conversion is done between SQL datatypes and C datatypes. For complete generality, we will write our function to accept and process null values rather than using the simpler NOT NULL CALL convention.

---

5. The parameter conventions described in this section are called PARAMETER STYLE DB2SQL and are used with functions written in C and C++. Functions written in Java use a different parameter convention, called PARAMETER STYLE DB2GENERAL, which is described in the *Embedded SQL Programming Guide*.

The following example shows how the addWeeks function might be used in a query that finds all the parts that have been ordered within the last four weeks:

```
SELECT partno, quantity, orderdate
FROM orders
WHERE addWeeks(orderdate, 4) > CURRENT DATE;
```

Before we can use the addWeeks function, we must register it with the database, using a CREATE FUNCTION statement such as the following:

```
CREATE FUNCTION addWeeks(Date, Integer)
    RETURNS Date
    EXTERNAL NAME 'datefns!addWeeks'
    DETERMINISTIC
    NO EXTERNAL ACTION
    NULL CALL
    LANGUAGE C
    PARAMETER STYLE DB2SQL
    NO SQL;
```

This statement registers with the database an addWeeks function that takes a Date and an Integer as parameters and returns a Date. Since this function is invoked from an SQL statement, of course its parameters and result have SQL datatypes, not C datatypes. In our example, we will refer to this function as the *SQL function,* even though we understand that it is not written in SQL.

The CREATE FUNCTION statement above promises that we will implement the SQL function by creating a C file named datefns that contains a function named addWeeks, compiling and linking this file, and placing the resulting binary file in the sqllib/function directory on our server machine. We could have placed the binary file in any desired directory on the server machine, as long as the CREATE FUNCTION statement tells the database system where to find it by a full path name. Several C functions can be contained in a single binary file, and the C functions need not have the same names as the SQL functions they support, as long as the mapping between SQL functions and C functions is declared in CREATE FUNCTION statements.

Of course, the C function that underlies our SQL function must have parameter types and result types that are recognized by the C language, not by SQL. We need a convention for mapping the parameters and result of the SQL function onto the parameters and result of the C function. All the parameters of the C function are pointers to storage that is managed by the database. If the function is declared FENCED, this storage is in an address space that is isolated from the database itself, so errors in the C function cannot damage the

```
void funcname (
            input SQL parameters,              /* IN */
            return value,                      /* OUT */
            input null indicators,             /* IN */
            return null indicator,             /* OUT */
            SQLSTATE,                          /* OUT */
            SQL function name,                 /* IN */
            specific name,                     /* IN */
            error message,                     /* OUT */
            scratchpad,                        /* IN */
            final call indicator,              /* IN */
            dbinfo pointer                     /* IN */
            ) ;
```

Figure 6-3: Parameter Conventions for External Scalar Functions

database; however, if the function is declared NOT FENCED, the C function can damage the database by storing bad data through the pointers that are passed to it as parameters. For this reason, users are strongly advised to use FENCED functions, at least until the functions have been thoroughly tested.

Figure 6-3 summarizes the parameters of a C function that serves as the implementation of an external SQL function. Each parameter is labeled "IN" (meaning that it provides input data to the function body) or "OUT" (meaning that it carries information returned by the function body).

The details of the **UDB** convention for passing parameters to a C function that implements an SQL function are as follows (assuming that N is the number of parameters of the SQL function):

1. The first N parameters of the C function are pointers to the N parameters of the SQL function, converted to their corresponding host language datatypes according to the rules for assignment of SQL datatypes to host variables. The objects pointed at are copies of the actual parameters, so the C function cannot modify its actual input parameters by using these pointers.

   If the datatype of a parameter is a distinct type, the parameter is first converted into the source type on which the distinct type is defined, then it is converted into the host language datatype that corresponds to that source type. For example, suppose that the distinct types Age and Sex are defined on the source types Integer and Char(1), respectively. If an external function avgHeight (Age, Sex) is defined, its parameters will be converted from an Age and a Sex into an Integer and a Char(1), and will then be converted into the C-language datatypes that correspond to an Integer and a Char(1), as defined in Table 6-5.

In our example, the Date and Integer parameters of the SQL function are passed to the C function using datatypes char[11] and long, respectively. The SQL datatypes that can be passed to C functions, and their corresponding C datatypes, are summarized in Table 6-5. For each of these C datatypes, there is a symbolic type name declared in the header file sqllib/include/sqludf.h, which you may prefer to use rather than spelling out the full C declaration.

TABLE 6-5: Datatypes Used for Passing Parameters to External Functions[6]

SQL Datatype	Symbolic Type Name in sqludf.h	Underlying Datatype as Seen by C Program
Smallint	SQLUDF_SMALLINT	short
Integer	SQLUDF_INTEGER	long
Decimal(p,s)	(none)	No equivalent in C. You can't pass Decimal data to an external function. As an alternative, you can convert the parameter to a Char datatype by using the char(Decimal) function, or to a Double datatype by using the double(Decimal) function.
Real	SQLUDF_REAL	float
Double	SQLUDF_DOUBLE	double
Char(n)	SQLUDF_CHAR	char[n+1] (null-terminated)
Varchar(n) (not for bit data)	SQLUDF_VARCHAR	char[n+1] (null-terminated)
Varchar(n) FOR BIT DATA	SQLUDF_VARCHAR_FBD	struct { unsigned short length; char data[n]; }

---

6. The similarities between Table 6-5 and Table C-1 in Appendix C are, of course, intentional.

TABLE 6-5 *(Continued)*

SQL Datatype	Symbolic Type Name in sqludf.h	Underlying Datatype as Seen by C Program
Long Varchar	SQLUDF_LONG	```struct { unsigned short length; char data[n]; }```
Graphic(n) and Vargraphic(n)	SQLUDF_GRAPH, SQLUDF_VARGRAPH	sqldbchar[n+1] (null-terminated)
Long Vargraphic	SQLUDF_LONGVARG	```struct { unsigned short length; sqldbchar data[n] }``` (Note: Length is denoted in two-byte units.)
Date	SQLUDF_DATE	char[11], null-terminated, in format 'yyyy-mm-dd'
Time	SQLUDF_TIME	char[9], null-terminated, in format 'hh.mm.ss'
Timestamp	SQLUDF_STAMP	char[27], null-terminated, in format 'yyyy-mm-dd-hh.mm.ss.nnnnnn'
Blob(n) and Clob(n)	SQLUDF_BLOB, SQLUDF_CLOB	```struct { unsigned long length; char data[n]; };```
Dbclob(n)	SQLUDF_DBCLOB	```struct { unsigned long length; sqldbchar data[n]; };``` (Note: Length is denoted in two-byte units.)
Locator for Blob, Clob, or Dbclob	udf_locator	unsigned long

When double-byte data (SQL datatype Graphic, Vargraphic, Long Vargraphic, or Dbclob) is exchanged with an external function, it is always exchanged in multibyte format (not wide-character format). In other words, parameters and results of external functions always use the format specified by the precompiler option WCHARTYPE NOCONVERT.

2. The next parameter of the C function is a pointer to the place where the return value should be stored. The C datatype that should be stored at this location is the C datatype that corresponds (in Table 6-5) to the declared SQL datatype of the return value, before any casting. For example, if the return value is declared as Date, the C function should store a null-terminated char[11] value in the indicated position since null-terminated char[11] is the C datatype that corresponds to the SQL datatype Date. The casting of the return value into its final datatype of Date is done by the database system; the C function need not be concerned with this process, except to provide a return value that can be validly cast into a Date. Of course, the database system has provided only enough storage to hold a return value of the declared datatype; attempting to return a longer value is one of the ways in which an unfenced function can cause a lot of trouble.

3. The next N parameters of the C function are null indicators for the N parameters of the SQL function. Each of these parameters is a pointer to a value whose C datatype is short, containing 0 if the corresponding SQL parameter is not null, or –1 if the corresponding SQL parameter is null. These parameters are always present, even if the function has been declared with the NOT NULL CALL property (of course, in such a case, all the indicator values would be zero on every call).

4. The next parameter is a pointer to the place where the C function should store the null indicator of the return value. The C datatype of this indicator is short, and it should be set to zero if the return value is not null, or to –1 if the return value is null. Even if the function has been declared with the NOT NULL CALL property, it might have a need to generate a null result, so it is important to set this indicator properly.

5. The next parameter is a pointer to the place where the C function should store the five-digit SQLSTATE generated by the function. The C datatype of the SQLSTATE is char[6], and it is initialized to 00000 with a null terminator before the C function is called. Since 00000 denotes a normal return, the C function need not set the SQLSTATE explicitly unless an error or warning is encountered. SQLSTATE codes 01H00 through 01H99 have been reserved for user-generated warning conditions, and 38600 through 38999 have been reserved for user-generated error conditions. If the C function generates one of these codes, it will be used as the SQLSTATE to be returned by the SQL statement that invoked the function. If the C function generates any SQLSTATE other than one of the reserved codes, the SQLSTATE returned by the invoking SQL statement will be 39001. Certain other SQLSTATEs can also result from invocation of a user-defined function (for example, if the C function terminates abnormally, the SQLSTATE is set to 38503).

6. The next parameter of the C function is a pointer to a storage area of type char[28], containing the fully qualified name of the SQL function (such as YOURNAME.ADDWEEKS), with a null terminator. This parameter makes it possible for several SQL functions to be implemented by the same C function, using this parameter to distinguish which SQL function is desired by each invocation.

7. The next parameter of the C function is a pointer to a storage area of type char[19], containing the specific name of the SQL function, with a null terminator. Like the previous parameter, this parameter can be useful when a single C function is used to implement several SQL functions. Remember that every user-defined function has a specific name in addition to its family name, even if the specific name is system-generated.

8. The next parameter of the C function is a pointer to a place where the C function may store up to 70 characters of message text, followed by a null terminator. If the SQLSTATE returned by the function is nonzero, this message text will be copied into the sqlerrmc field of the SQLCA control block. The sqlerrmc field consists of a series of "tokens." The first token is set to the function name, the second token to the specific name of the function, and the third token to the message text returned by the function. The message text may be truncated if necessary to fit into the sqlerrmc field.

9. The next parameter is present only if the function was defined with the SCRATCHPAD option. It is a pointer to the memory area provided for the function, to preserve information from one function invocation to the next function invocation within the same SQL statement. The datatype of the parameter is struct sqludf_scratchpad* (this structure is declared in sqllib/include/sqludf.h). Scratchpad functions are discussed in Section 6.4.7.

10. The next parameter is present only if the function was defined with the FINAL CALL option. It is a pointer to a long variable that is set equal to –1 on the first call to a function during processing of an SQL statement, to +1 on the "final call," and to 0 on all other calls to the function. The FINAL CALL option is discussed in Section 6.4.7.

11. The next parameter is present only if the function was defined with the DBINFO option. It is a pointer to a data structure, described in the *Embedded SQL Programming Guide*, that contains information such as the name of the current database, the current authid, and the name of the table and column (if any) that is being modified by the current statement.

When writing a program to implement your user-defined function, you should observe the following rules:

- Your program should be *reentrant* (that is, it should not use any static variables). This enables your function to be invoked by several different users at the same time without interference.

- If your program allocates any dynamic memory, it should free the memory before returning. The only exception to this rule is in the case of a *scratchpad function*, which may allocate memory on one invocation and free it on another.

- Your program should return to its caller by a `return` statement. It should never call the operating system `exit` function. Since all exchanging of values between the program and the database system is accomplished by parameters, the return datatype of the C function should be `void`.

- Your program should not attempt to read from the standard input stream (for example, by `scanf`) or write to the standard output stream (for example, by `printf`). These streams are not available to your program, because it is executed on the server machine in a process that is not connected to your keyboard or display. Your program may, however, read and write files on the server machine.

- If your function implementation is written in C++, you should specify `extern "C"` as part of your function declaration in the implementation file. This will ensure that your function is made available for linking by the name you gave it rather than by a "mangled" name chosen by the C++ compiler. For simplicity, avoid using an overloaded C++ function name.

 TIP: When debugging the implementation of a user-defined function, you may find it helpful for your function to write a trace of its actions in a file on the server machine. But if your function writes into a file, that file must be authorized for writing by any user; if your function creates a file, the directory in which the file is created must be authorized for writing by any user. Remember that your function is executed under a dummy process on the server machine, *not* under your own userid.

Now that we have discussed the rules for implementing an external function, we are ready to look at the implementation of the `addWeeks` function discussed at the beginning of this section. The `addWeeks` function takes a Date and an Integer as parameters, and returns a Date as a result, computed by adding the given number of weeks to the input Date. The parameters of the C function that implements `addWeeks` conform to the convention shown in Figure 6-3.

TIP: In addWeeks and the other example functions in this chapter, the symbol SQL_API_FN in the function declaration makes the function portable to multiple platforms. The value of the symbol is the string that is required to compile the function declaration on a particular platform, such as AIX or OS/2. For example, here are the definitions of SQL_API_FN on three common platforms:

On Windows NT: `__stdcall`
On OS/2: `_System`
On AIX: (empty string)

To see the definition of SQL_API_FN and other platform-dependent symbols on your system, look in `sqllib/include/sqlsystm.h`.

Example Function: addWeeks

```c
#include <stdio.h>
void SQL_API_FN addWeeks
    (
    char   *dateIn,        /* 1st input parameter, char[11], null-term. */
    long   *weeksIn,       /* 2nd input parameter, long                 */
    char   *dateOut,       /* return value, char[11], null-terminated   */
    short  *nullDateIn,    /* 1st input parameter, indicator variable   */
    short  *nullWeeksIn,   /* 2nd input parameter, indicator variable   */
    short  *nullDateOut,   /* return value, indicator variable          */
    char   *sqlstate,      /* returned SQLSTATE, char[6], null-term.    */
    char   *fnName,        /* family name of fn, char[28], null-term.   */
    char   *specificName,  /* specific name of fn, char[19], null-term. */
    char   *message        /* message area, char[70], null-terminated   */
    )

{
    /*
    ** The following array tells us how many days are in each month.
    */
    const int monthDays[] = {31, 28, 31, 30, 31, 30,
                             31, 31, 30, 31, 30, 31};
    int year, month, day, conversions, daysThisMonth;
```

```
/*
** If either input is null, return a null result.
** (This function could have specified "not null call".)
*/
if (*nullDateIn || *nullWeeksIn)
  {
  *nullDateOut = -1;
  return;
  }


/*
** Convert input date string into year, month, and day
** Return error code if conversion fails.
*/
conversions = sscanf (dateIn, "%4d-%2d-%2d", &year, &month, &day);
if (conversions != 3)
  {
  strcpy (sqlstate, "38601");
  strcpy (message, "Bad date");
  return;
  }


/*
** Check the input parameters for sanity
*/
if (year < 0 || month < 0 || month > 12
      || day < 0 || day > monthDays[month-1] || *weeksIn < 0)
  {
  strcpy (sqlstate, "38602");
  strcpy (message, "Bad input");
  return;
  }


/*
** Add up the days, then roll into months and years as needed.
*/
day = day + 7 * *weeksIn;
daysThisMonth = monthDays[month-1];
if (month == 2 && year % 4 == 0)
   daysThisMonth++;   /* leap year */
```

```
while (day > daysThisMonth)
  {
  day = day - daysThisMonth;
  month++;
  if (month > 12)
    {
    year++;
    month = 1;
    }
  daysThisMonth = monthDays[month-1];
  if (month == 2 && year % 4 == 0)
    daysThisMonth++;    /* leap year */
  }

/*
** Convert the date back into string form for output
*/
sprintf(dateOut, "%4.4d-%2.2d-%2.2d\0", year, month, day);
*nullDateOut = 0;
return;
}
```

6.4.5 Installing an External Function

The file containing the C program that implements your external function may have any name you like and may contain more than one function body. As shown in the example above, the program can include header files such as `<stdio.h>` and can call standard C functions such as `sprintf()`. Before UDB can use your external function, you must compile it, link it, and put the executable file in the appropriate directory on the database server. I will refer to this series of steps as *installing* an external function.

The process of installing an external function depends on which operating system and compiler you are using. The process is described in detail in the manual called *Building Your Applications* for your operating system. In this section, I will give a general overview of the steps that are involved.

1. Since a program may contain implementations for several external functions, the first step in installing these functions is to create a *module definition file* that lists all the entry points (functions) that are exported by your program. This file serves as input to the linker. The name and format of the module definition file required by your compiler is described in *Building Your Applications*, and some sample module definition files can be found in the directory `sqllib/samples/c`. Here are some examples:

   - Suppose that the file named `datefns.C` contains functions named `addWeeks` and `subWeeks`. If you are using the Microsoft Visual C++ compiler on Windows NT, you will need a module definition file named `datefns.def`, with the following content:

```
LIBRARY DATEFNS
EXPORTS
      addWeeks
      subWeeks
```

- On AIX, the module definition file is called an *export file*. If you plan to compile and link the `datefns.C` file on AIX using the IBM XLC compiler, you will need an export file named `datefns.exp`, with the following content:

```
#! export file for datefns
addWeeks
subWeeks
```

2. Compile and link the file containing the program that implements your function. In the directory `sqllib/samples/c`, you will find a script that you can use for this purpose. For example, on Windows NT, you can compile and link an external function using the batch file named `bldmsudf.bat` with the Microsoft Visual C++ compiler, or using the batch file named `bldvaudf.bat` with the IBM Visual Age C++ compiler. Script files with similar names (matching the pattern `bld..udf`) are provided on AIX and other platforms. Before using one of these files, you should read it and modify it as necessary, taking guidance from the comments in the file itself. For example, the `bldmsudf.bat` file is designed to compile a function written in C, but it contains comments describing the modifications that are needed if the function is written in C++.

3. Place the executable file generated in Step 2 into the appropriate directory on the server machine. After linking our program `datefns.C`, the executable file generated on Windows or OS/2 is named `datefns.dll`, and the file generated on AIX is simply named `datefns`. By default, this executable file should be placed in the directory `sqllib/function` on the server machine. If this is done, your CREATE FUNCTION statement need not include a path name (for example, it can specify EXTERNAL NAME 'datefns!addWeeks'). Alternatively, your executable file can be placed in some other directory on the server machine, and your CREATE FUNCTION statement can specify a full path name for the file (for example, EXTERNAL NAME '/usr/udflib/datefns!addWeeks'). If you are running a parallel database system on several machines, your function implementation must be accessible from all the machines in your system.

The script (such as `bldmsudf.bat`) that compiles and links your external function will copy the resulting executable file to the default directory (`sqllib/function`) on the local machine. You need to explicitly copy the file yourself only if you compiled it on some machine other than the server machine, or if you want to install it in some directory other than the default directory.

After the executable file has been copied to the appropriate directory, it should be made executable by any user. For example, under AIX, the `datefns` file can be made executable by the following command:

```
chmod a+x datefns
```

Remember that the process that executes the external function will not be running under your userid, but under a dummy userid generated by the database system.

4. "Register" your external function by executing a CREATE FUNCTION statement in each database where the function will be used. The CREATE FUNCTION statement can be executed either before or after the function is compiled and linked.

TIP: Regardless of your operating system platform, you should be very careful to protect the executable file that implements your external function against unauthorized tampering. The database does not protect this file and will execute it whenever your function is invoked. If your function implementation is replaced by another executable file, it could potentially do something harmful.

6.4.6 Using Locators with External Functions

In Section 6.1.3, we discussed the advantages of passing large objects to application programs in the form of locators. A locator is an integer that represents a value of one of the large-object types: Blob, Clob, Dbclob, or a distinct type sourced on one of these types. The value represented by the locator remains under control of UDB, so you do not need to provide a large buffer for holding it and pay the cost of transferring the value between the database and your application program.

The advantages of manipulating large objects in the form of locators apply to external functions as well as to application programs. If an external function takes a large object as a parameter or returns a large object as a result, it is much more efficient to represent the object by a locator than to copy its entire value. But external functions have a limitation that application programs do not have—they are not allowed to execute SQL statements. This means that an external function, receiving a large-object parameter in the form of a locator, cannot use an SQL statement such as `VALUES(substr(:locator, 1, 1000)) INTO :buffer` to retrieve a piece of the large object into a buffer for processing.

To make locators useful to external functions, UDB provides a special interface that can be used to manipulate large objects using locators. This interface consists of the following C functions, which I will refer to as *locator functions*:

1. `sqludf_length` retrieves the length of the value represented by a locator.

2. `sqludf_substr` retrieves a designated substring of the value represented by a locator.

3. `sqludf_create_locator` creates a new locator, representing an initially empty object. The object represented by the new locator is usually constructed one piece at a time, using `sqludf_append`.

4. `sqludf_append` appends some data from a buffer to the end of the object represented by a locator. This is how an external function might construct a large object to be returned in the form of a locator.

5. `sqludf_free_locator` allows the system to free the resources associated with a locator that is no longer needed.

All the locator functions have return codes that are zero for normal returns or nonzero in case of an error. The locator functions and the datatypes of their parameters are declared in `sqludf.h`. Their definitions are as follows:

```
extern int sqludf_length
  (
  udf_locator*     locator_p,  /* IN:  Points to a LOB locator          */
  long*            return_len  /* OUT: Returns length of LOB value       */
  );

extern int sqludf_substr
  (
  udf_locator*     locator_p,  /* IN:  Points to a LOB locator          */
  long             start,      /* IN:  Start position (first char = 1)  */
  long             length,     /* IN:  Get this many bytes               */
  unsigned char*   buffer,     /* IN:  Read into this buffer             */
  long*            return_len  /* OUT: Returns no. of bytes moved        */
  );

extern int sqludf_create_locator
  (
  int              loc_type,   /* IN:  SQL_TYP_BLOB, SQL_TYP_CLOB,
                                        or SQL_TYP_DBCLOB               */
  udf_locator**    locator_p   /* OUT: Returns pointer to a new locator  */
  );

extern int sqludf_append
  (
  udf_locator*     locator_p,  /* IN:  Points to a LOB locator          */
  unsigned char*   buffer,     /* IN:  Data to be appended to LOB        */
```

```
long            length,    /* IN:  Length of data to be appended   */
long*           return_len /* OUT: Returns LOB length after append  */
);

extern int sqludf_free_locator
   (
   udf_locator*    locator_p  /* IN: Pointer to a LOB locator          */
   );
```

Unfortunately, locator functions can be called only from an unfenced external function, which makes them relatively dangerous to use. Since an unfenced external function has the potential to damage your database, you should debug it carefully on a test database before installing it on a production database.

As an example of the use of locator functions, we will look at an external function that searches a Clob for a given word and returns each occurrence of the word along with the context in which it is found. The function is named context, and its parameters are the Clob to be searched and the target word. The function returns a new Clob containing each occurrence of the target word in the original Clob, together with the context string that immediately follows each occurrence. In this simple example, the maximum size of the target word and the amount of context to be returned are compiled into the external function as constants. Both the input Clob and the result of the function are passed in the form of locators.

The SQL statement that creates the context function is as follows:

```
CREATE FUNCTION context(Clob(1M) AS LOCATOR, Varchar(10))
    RETURNS Clob(1M) AS LOCATOR
    SPECIFIC context
    EXTERNAL NAME 'context!context'
    LANGUAGE C
    PARAMETER STYLE DB2SQL
    DETERMINISTIC
    NOT FENCED
    NO EXTERNAL ACTION
    NO SQL;
```

In the C program that implements the context function, it is desirable to avoid allocating a one-megabyte buffer to hold the entire input Clob parameter all at once. Instead, the function allocates a small buffer and fetches the Clob in overlapping chunks, searching each chunk for the target word. The overlap between chunks ensures that, whenever an occurrence of the target word is found, the whole word and its following context will be contained in the buffer. The context function creates a new locator to represent the return value, and appends each occurrence of the target word, with its trailing context and a delimiter character, to this locator. When the end of the input Clob is reached, the function simply returns the output locator.

The implementation of the context function is as follows:

Example Function: context

```c
#include <string.h>
#include <stdio.h>
#include <stdlib.h>
#include <sqlenv.h>
#include <sqludf.h>

#define CHUNKSIZE 1000
#define WORDSIZE 10
#define CONTEXTSIZE 20
#define BUFFERSIZE CHUNKSIZE+WORDSIZE+CONTEXTSIZE
#define OUTPUTMAX 1000000
#define BADNEWS "70001"

void SQL_API_FN context
   (
   udf_locator *inClobLoc,   /* IN: Locator for input Clob            */
   char   *targetWord,       /* IN: Word to search for               */
   udf_locator *outClobLoc,  /* OUT: Locator for Clob to be returned  */
   short *nullInput,         /* IN: Null indicator for param. 1       */
   short *nullTarget,        /* IN: Null indicator for param. 2       */
   short *nullOutput,        /* OUT: Null indicator for return value  */
   char   *sqlstate,         /* OUT: returned SQLSTATE, null-terminated */
   char   *fnName,           /* IN: name of function                  */
   char   *specificName,     /* IN: specific name of function         */
   char   *message           /* OUT: return message area              */
   )
   {
   char buffer[BUFFERSIZE];  /* Holds one chunk of input data         */
   long inputLength;         /* Total length of input Clob            */
   long targetWordLength;    /* Length of target word                 */
   long outputLength;        /* Total length of return Clob           */
   long inputScanned;        /* No. of input characters scanned so far */
```

```
long charsInBuffer;      /* No. of characters currently in buffer  */
long thisChunk;          /* No. of characters in current chunk     */
long thisContextLength;  /* How much context to print for this word */
long i;                  /* Iterates over characters in buffer     */
long rc;                 /* Return code from sqludf calls          */

/*
** Get length of input Clob
*/
rc = sqludf_length(inClobLoc, &inputLength);
if (rc)
   {
   strcpy(sqlstate, BADNEWS);
   sprintf(message, "sqludf_length returned %d", rc);
   return;
   }

/*
** Make sure target word is not longer than WORDSIZE
*/
targetWordLength = strlen(targetWord);
if (targetWordLength > WORDSIZE)
   {
   strcpy(sqlstate, BADNEWS);
   sprintf(message, "Sorry, the target word is too long");
   return;
   }

/*
** Create an output Clob locator
*/
rc = sqludf_create_locator(SQL_TYP_CLOB, &outClobLoc);
if (rc)
   {
   strcpy(sqlstate, BADNEWS);
   sprintf(message, "sqludf_create_locator returned %d", rc);
   return;
   }

inputScanned = 0;
outputLength = 0;
```

```
/*
** Scan until we reach the end of the input Clob
** or run out of room in the output Clob.
*/
while ( inputScanned < inputLength
        && outputLength+WORDSIZE+CONTEXTSIZE < OUTPUTMAX )
    {
    /*
    ** Read a chunk of the input Clob into the buffer.
    ** Set charsInBuffer to actual number of characters read.
    */
    rc = sqludf_substr(inClobLoc,
            inputScanned + 1,
            BUFFERSIZE,
            (unsigned char *)buffer,
            &charsInBuffer);
    if (rc)
        {
        strcpy(sqlstate, BADNEWS);
        sprintf(message, "sqludf_substr returned %d", rc);
        return;
        }

    if (charsInBuffer < CHUNKSIZE) thisChunk = charsInBuffer;
    else thisChunk = CHUNKSIZE;

    for (i=0; i<thisChunk; i++)
        {
        if (!strncmp(targetWord, &buffer[i], targetWordLength))
            {
            /*
            ** Append the target word and its context to the output Clob
            */
            if (i + targetWordLength + CONTEXTSIZE < charsInBuffer)
                thisContextLength = targetWordLength + CONTEXTSIZE;
            else thisContextLength = charsInBuffer - i;
            rc = sqludf_append(outClobLoc,
                    (unsigned char *)buffer + i,
                    thisContextLength,
                    &outputLength);
            if (rc)
                {
                strcpy(sqlstate, BADNEWS);
                sprintf(message, "sqludf_append returned %d", rc);
                return;
                }
```

```
      /*
      ** Append a "!" delimiter to mark the end of the context
      */
      rc = sqludf_append(outClobLoc,
              (unsigned char *)"!",
              1,
              &outputLength);
      if (rc)
          {
          strcpy(sqlstate, BADNEWS);
          sprintf(message, "sqludf_append returned %d", rc);
          return;
          }

      }     /* end of case where matching word is found */
  }       /* end of for loop that searches inside buffer */

inputScanned += thisChunk;
}       /* end of while loop that fetches chunks into buffer */


/*
** If no target words were found, the output Clob is initialized
** to the empty string.
*/
return;
}
```

6.4.7 Scratchpad Functions

A scratchpad function is an external function that needs to preserve some information between one function call and the next. If the phrase SCRATCH-PAD is included in the CREATE FUNCTION statement, the function body is provided with a 100-byte "scratchpad" area in which it may write any data that it chooses. The data in the scratchpad is preserved between function calls, so each invocation of the function can see the data stored by the last invocation. The data in the scratchpad is preserved only during the processing of a given SQL statement, not between SQL statements. For example, if a scratchpad function foo is used in the SQL statement SELECT foo(c1) FROM t1, the function foo is executed once for each row of table T1, and the scratchpad data is preserved across all these function invocations. But if the same SQL statement is executed a second time, it receives a new scratchpad. If a function is used multiple times in the same SQL statement, each use of the function receives its own separate scratchpad.

If a function was created with the SCRATCHPAD option, every invocation of the function is passed a parameter containing a pointer to the scratchpad area. The datatype of the parameter is `struct sqludf_scratchpad*`. The declaration of the scratchpad structure, which can be found in `sqllib/include/sqludf.h`, is as follows:

```
struct sqludf_scratchpad
    {
    unsigned long  length;     /* length of data area      */
    char           data[100];  /* initialized to binary 0s */
    };
```

As you can see in the declaration above, the scratchpad contains 100 bytes that the function implementation can use as it sees fit. If the function needs to preserve more than 100 bytes of data between invocations, it can allocate additional memory (using `malloc`) and keep a pointer to the additional memory in the scratchpad.

The scratchpad area is initialized to binary zeros before the first function call in each SQL statement. The function body can test for zeros to detect the first call, or it can use the FINAL CALL option, which causes a parameter to be passed to the function containing –1 on initial call, +1 on final call, and 0 on all other calls within an SQL statement. The "final call" is a special call made to the function body after the SQL statement has been processed.[7] If the function body needs to allocate memory, it should be written with the FINAL CALL option, and it should free the allocated memory on the final call. Since the final call takes place after processing of the SQL statement, its input and output parameters (other than the `calltype` parameter that identifies the final call) are not meaningful.

Perhaps the simplest example of a scratchpad function is a function that simply counts the number of times it has been invoked within an SQL statement. Since all the data stored by this function fits into the scratchpad, it does not need to allocate memory or to use the FINAL CALL option. The function relies on the fact that its scratchpad will be initialized to binary zeros before the first call within each SQL statement. The body of the function might be written as follows:

---

7. If the SQL statement containing the function is a query that is being processed by means of a cursor, the "final call" takes place at the time the cursor is closed (either by a CLOSE statement or by end of transaction).

```
#include <stdlib.h>
#include <sqludf.h>

void SQL_API_FN seqno
  (
    long  *returnValue,     /* return value, an integer    */
    short *returnNull,      /* return indicator variable   */
    char  *sqlstate,        /* returned SQLSTATE, char[6]  */
    char  *fnName,          /* family name of fn, char[28] */
    char  *specificName,    /* specific fn name, char[19]  */
    char  *message,         /* message area, char[70]      */
    struct sqludf_scratchpad *scratchpad   /* in sqludf.h */
  )
  {
  long *p;
  p = (long *)(scratchpad->data);  /* point at pad data  */
  *p = (*p)+1;                 /* increment counter inside pad */
  *returnValue = *p;           /* return the counter value    */
  *returnNull = 0;
  return;
  }
```

When a scratchpad function is executed in parallel on multiple nodes, each node gets its own separate scratchpad, initialized to zeros on the first call. If FINAL CALL is declared, the function gets a special "initial call" and "final call" on each participating node. The function might take advantage of the initial call to perform some computation and cache its results in the scratchpad, which does not conflict with parallel processing. However, if the function is using its scratchpad to communicate some information from one function call to the next (that is, from processing of one row to processing of the next row), the function cannot be executed in parallel. Seqno is a good example of such a function. Clearly, a function cannot successfully assign a sequence number to each row processed if every node is keeping its own count.

The seqno function is registered in the database by the following statement (assuming that the executable file has been placed in the default directory sqllib/function). Note that the function is declared to be NOT DETERMINISTIC, indicating that it does not return the same result every time it is called.

```
CREATE FUNCTION seqno() RETURNS Integer
    EXTERNAL NAME 'seqno!seqno'
    SPECIFIC seqno
    NOT DETERMINISTIC
    NO EXTERNAL ACTION
```

```
LANGUAGE C
FENCED
PARAMETER STYLE DB2SQL
NO SQL
SCRATCHPAD
DISALLOW PARALLEL;
```

You might use the `seqno` function defined above in a query to automatically generate a sequence number for each row of the result set. For example, suppose that all the candidates in a mayoral election and the dates on which they declared their candidacy are recorded in a table with the following structure:

CANDIDATES

NAME	PARTY	DECLARE_DATE

The following query will list all the candidates, with a sequence number for each indicating the order in which they entered the race:

```
SELECT seqno() AS seqno, name, party, declare_date
FROM    candidates
ORDER BY declare_date;
```

TIP: Scratchpad functions are not recommended for use inside constraints or triggers (described in Chapter 7) or inside correlated subqueries. This is because a given SQL statement may cause a constraint, trigger, or correlated subquery to be executed multiple times. The system guarantees to initialize your scratchpad only once, at the beginning of the outermost SQL statement. Scratchpad functions used inside constraints, triggers, or correlated subqueries may not be properly initialized.

As another example of an application for a scratchpad function, consider the following table of employees:

EMPLOYEES

NAME	JOB	SALARY

Suppose that you need to search this table to find the engineer with the third highest salary. This is a surprisingly difficult query to express in standard SQL. An initial attempt at writing such a query might look like this:

```
SELECT name, salary
FROM   employees e
WHERE  job = 'Engineer'
AND 2 =
   (SELECT count(*)
    FROM   employees
    WHERE  job = 'Engineer'
    AND    salary > e.salary);
```

On close inspection, this query has two serious problems. The first problem is performance: the correlated subquery will do an enormous amount of work to find the answer to such a simple question. But the more serious problem is that the query will not find the right answer if there are duplicates among the engineers' salaries. For example, consider the case when two engineers are tied for second place in the salary ordering. In this case, the query above will always return the empty set.

Another approach to this problem is to write a query that selects engineers in descending order by their salaries, and then fetch only the first three engineers in the result set. That solution is not very elegant, and it requires the database system to do lots of unnecessary work, sorting all the engineers in order by their salaries even though you will fetch only the top three. A much better solution would be to make a single scan over the engineers, somehow remembering the third highest salary seen so far as you go along. After the scan is complete, you will have the salary of the third highest-paid engineer, which you can then use to fetch all the engineers who have that salary (remember, there may be duplicates).

Implementing the "scan and remember" solution described above provides an interesting example of a user-defined function that uses the SCRATCHPAD and FINAL CALL options. We will write a general-purpose function called nthbest that can be used to find the nth largest integer in a multiset of integers (we chose the name nthbest because it is short, hoping to avoid a discussion of whether largest is necessarily best).[8]

---

8. The nthbest function in this example operates on Integer values, and we assume that salaries are represented as Integers; of course, a similar nthbest function could be written for Decimal or Money or any other datatype that supports comparison operators.

Viewed as an SQL function, nthbest will take two parameters. The first parameter is a value from the set being scanned, and the second parameter is n, the rank of the desired value within the set. The nthbest function is designed to be called repeatedly within an SQL statement, examining a set of values one at a time. The second parameter, which defines the desired rank, is meaningful only on the first call to the function within an SQL statement. Each time it is called, the nthbest function returns the nth largest value that it has seen so far; if fewer than n values have been seen, it returns null. Thus, in a series of calls to find the nth largest value, nthbest will first return n null values, followed by a nondecreasing series of values that culminates in the desired value. By using nthbest inside a max function, the final (correct) value can be isolated from the others and returned as the result of the query. For example, the third highest engineer's salary can be found by the following query:

```
SELECT  max(nthbest(salary, 3))
FROM    employees
WHERE   job = 'Engineer';
```

This query can be used as a subquery to find the actual engineer(s) who earn the third highest salary, as follows:

```
SELECT  name, salary
FROM    employees
WHERE   job = 'Engineer'
AND     salary =
    (SELECT  max(nthbest(salary,3))
     FROM    employees
     WHERE   job = 'Engineer');
```

The following SQL statement might be used to register the nthbest function in the database system as an external function. Note that the function is declared to be NOT DETERMINISTIC because two function calls with the same parameters do not always return the same result. This is often the case for scratchpad functions, because their results often depend on the state of the scratchpad as well as on their input parameters.

```
CREATE FUNCTION nthbest(Integer, Integer)
            -- candidate value, desired rank --
    RETURNS Integer
            -- value having desired rank --
    SPECIFIC nthbest
```

```
EXTERNAL NAME 'nthbest!nthbest'
NOT DETERMINISTIC
NO EXTERNAL ACTION
LANGUAGE C
FENCED
PARAMETER STYLE DB2SQL
NO SQL
SCRATCHPAD
FINAL CALL
DISALLOW PARALLEL;
```

The implementation of the nthbest function is shown in the example below. The first step in the implementation is to decide how to use the scratchpad. Since we don't know how many values we will need to store (after all, someone may ask for the 5,000th largest value), we will need to allocate memory to contain a list of the n largest values. In the scratchpad, we will record the desired rank, the number of values seen so far, and a pointer to an array of up to n values that contains a sorted list of the highest values we have seen. We declare these three variables in the form of a structure called myPad, which is overlaid on the scratchpad provided by the system.

The parameters passed to the C program that implements nthbest include a pointer to the system-provided scratchpad area and an integer indicating the type of the call (first, middle, or final). On the first call, the function tests the parameter n for validity and then allocates enough memory to hold the n largest integers encountered. On every call except the final call, the function receives a new integer value and inserts it into its proper place (if any) in the scratchpad array. If the array contains fewer than n values, the function returns null; otherwise, it returns the nth-largest value in the array (since the array is of size n, this is actually the smallest value in the array). On the final call, the function frees the memory that was allocated on the first call. Since the final call does not pass a new integer value, there is no need for the function to examine its parameters or return a result on the final call.

Example Program: nthbest

```c
#include <string.h>
#include <stdlib.h>
#include <sqludf.h>

/*
**   STEP 1: Define a structure to overlay on the scratchpad.
*/
typedef struct
    {
    long  desiredRank;      /* rank of the desired value           */
    long  valuesStored;     /* how many values are in the array    */
    long *bigValues;        /* array of the biggest values so far  */
    } myPad;

/*
**   STEP 2: Declare the parameters of the function implementation.
*/
void SQL_API_FN nthbest
    (
    long  *inValue,         /* 1st input parameter, an integer value       */
    long  *inRank,          /* 2nd input parameter, rank of desired value  */
    long  *outValue,        /* result, the value with the desired rank     */
    short *inValueNull,     /* 1st input parameter, null indicator         */
    short *inRankNull,      /* 2nd input parameter, null indicator         */
    short *outNull,         /* return value, null indicator                */
    char  *sqlstate,        /* returned SQLSTATE, char[6], null-term.      */
    char  *fnName,          /* family name of fn, char[28], null-term.     */
    char  *specificName,    /* specific name of fn, char[19], null-term.   */
    char  *message,         /* message area, char[70], null-term.          */
    struct sqludf_scratchpad *scratchpad,    /* declared in sqludf.h       */
    long  *calltype         /* -1 = first call, 0 = normal, 1 = last call  */
    )

    {
    myPad *p;               /* overlay this pointer on the scratchpad */
    long least, temp;       /* working variables                      */
    int i;                  /* loop counter                           */

    p = (myPad *)(scratchpad->data);
```

```
/*
**   STEP 3: On first call, allocate space for storing the top n values.
*/
if (*calltype == -1)   /* first call */
   {
   if (*inRankNull != 0 || *inRank <= 0)
      {
      strcpy (sqlstate, "38601");
      strcpy (message, "Bogus rank");
      return;
      }
   p -> desiredRank = *inRank;
   p -> valuesStored = 0;
   p -> bigValues = (long *)malloc(*inRank * 4);
   }


/*
**   STEP 4: On final call, free the allocated space.
*/
if (*calltype == 1)  /* last call */
   free(p->bigValues);


/*
**   STEP 5: On first or middle call, add the current value to the
**   set of stored values if it is among the n highest values seen.
*/
if (*calltype < 1)     /* first or middle call */
   {
   if (*inValueNull == 0)
      {
      least = *inValue;
      for (i = 0; i < p->valuesStored; i++)
         {
         if (p->bigValues[i] < least)
            {
            temp = least;                /* exchange */
            least = p->bigValues[i];      /* exchange */
            p->bigValues[i] = temp;       /* exchange */
            }
         }
      if (p->valuesStored < p->desiredRank)
         {
         p->valuesStored++;
         p->bigValues[p->valuesStored - 1] = least;
         }
      }
```

```
/*
**   STEP 6: Return the nth highest value seen so far
**   (or null if less than n values have been seen.)
*/
if (p->valuesStored < p->desiredRank)
    {
    *outNull = -1;              /* array not full, return null value */
    return;
    }
else
    {
    *outValue = p->bigValues[p->desiredRank - 1];
    *outNull = 0;
    return;                     /* return value having desired rank */
    }
}        /* end of first or middle call */
}
```

6.4.8 Table Functions

A table function is an external function that returns a table instead of a scalar value. Table functions are very powerful because they enable you to make almost any source of data appear to be a UDB table. All you need to do is to write a C program that collects the desired data, filters it according to some input parameters if so desired, and returns it to UDB one row at a time. The table returned by the table function can participate in joins, grouping operations, set operations such as UNION, and any other operation that could be applied to a read-only view.

In Section 5.3, we learned how to use a table function in the FROM clause of a query. In this section, we will learn how to create and implement a table function. A table function is created by a CREATE FUNCTION statement that is very similar to the statement used to create an external scalar function. Its syntax is as follows:

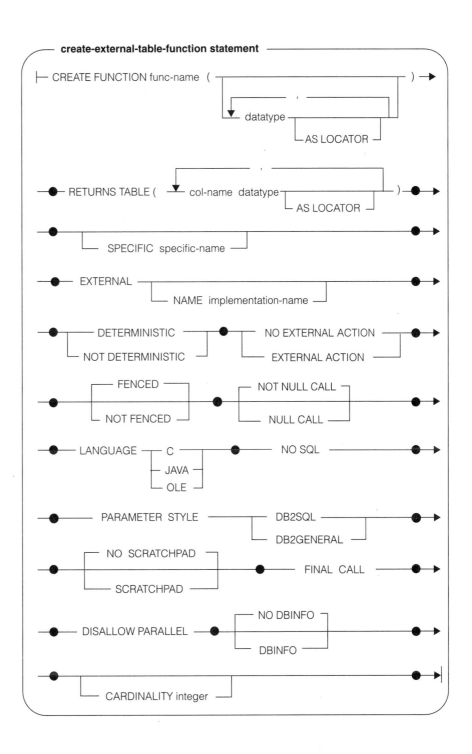

As you can see, the main difference between the CREATE FUNCTION statements for an external scalar function and a table function lies in the RETURNS clause. In the case of a table function, the RETURNS clause contains the word TABLE, and, rather than a single datatype, it specifies a column name and datatype for each of the columns of the table to be returned by the function. As in the case of a scalar function, LOB-type values can be passed to and returned by a table function either directly or in the form of locators.

Other ways in which the CREATE FUNCTION statement for a table function differs from the CREATE FUNCTION statement for an external scalar function include the following:

1. The FINAL CALL clause is required when creating a table function.

2. A table function always runs on a single node and requires a DISALLOW PARALLEL specification.

3. The meaning of NOT NULL CALL is slightly different for table functions. If a table function is called with a null argument when NOT NULL CALL has been specified, the system assumes that the result of the table function is an empty table (a table with zero rows).

4. When creating a table function, you can include a CARDINALITY clause that provides an estimate of the number of rows you expect the function to return. This estimate is used by the optimizer in making plans for executing queries that call your table function. For example, the best order in which to join several tables is strongly influenced by the expected cardinalities of the tables involved.

In Section 5.3, we discussed an example of a table function named `sales` that takes the name of a store as an input parameter and returns a four-column table containing the sales data gathered by a point-of-sale system for that store. The columns of the returned table are SALEDATE, PRODUCT, QUANTITY, and PRICE. The SQL statement used to create the `sales` function might be as follows:

```
CREATE FUNCTION sales (Varchar(20))
    RETURNS TABLE (saledate Date,
                   product  Varchar(20),
                   quantity Integer,
                   price    Integer)
    EXTERNAL NAME 'storefns.sales'
    DETERMINISTIC
    NO EXTERNAL ACTION
    LANGUAGE C
    FENCED
    PARAMETER STYLE DB2SQL
```

```
void funcname (
                   input SQL parameters,              /* IN */
                   return column parameters,          /* OUT */
                   input null indicators,             /* IN */
                   return null indicators,            /* OUT */
                   SQLSTATE,                          /* OUT */
                   SQL function name,                 /* IN */
                   specific name,                     /* IN */
                   error message,                     /* OUT */
                   scratchpad,                        /* IN */
                   final call indicator               /* IN */
                   dbinfo pointer                     /* IN */
                   ) ;
```

Figure 6-4: Parameter Conventions for Table Functions

```
NO SQL
SCRATCHPAD
FINAL CALL
DISALLOW PARALLEL;
```

The rules for writing a C program to implement a table function are also very similar to the rules for implementing an external scalar function. The parameter conventions for table functions are shown in Figure 6-4. By comparing Figures 6-3 and 6-4, we can see that the parameter conventions for table functions and external scalar functions differ only in their "return" parameters. In place of a single return value parameter and a single return null indicator, a table function has a return value parameter and a null indicator for each column in its result table. As in the case of an external scalar function, the column values returned by a table function are represented using the corresponding C datatypes listed in Table 6-5.

Table functions used in SQL statements are resolved according to the same rules used for resolution of scalar functions, and taking into account the function path. Of course, an error results if a function call that appears where a scalar function is expected resolves to a table function or vice versa.

When a table function is invoked in an SQL statement, a series of calls is made to the C program that implements the table function. The first of these is an OPEN call, with the final call indicator set to the value SQL_TF_OPEN (numeric value -1). The OPEN call allows the table function to perform preliminary actions such as opening files, allocating memory, and initializing the scratchpad. No data (except for an SQLSTATE) is returned by the OPEN call. Following the OPEN call, the system calls the table function with a series of FETCH calls, with the final call indicator set to SQL_TF_FETCH (numeric value 0). On each of these calls, the table function is expected to return one of the rows of the result table. On each call that successfully returns a row, the table function must set the SQLSTATE parameter to "00000." After all the rows of the result table have been returned, the table function indicates that there are no more rows by setting the SQLSTATE parameter to "02000." The system then calls the table function one more time, with the final call indicator set to SQL_TF_CLOSE (numeric value +1), enabling the table function to perform cleanup operations such as closing files and freeing memory. The system might also make a CLOSE call to the table function if it decides that no more rows are needed (for example, because the cursor that is fetching rows from the table function has been closed).

When writing a table function, you must make sure that your function eventually returns SQLSTATE "02000," indicating the end of the table. If your function never returns this SQLSTATE, the system will keep calling it forever, and you will need to use the facilities of your operating system to break the loop. To guard against this problem, your table function will almost certainly need to use a scratchpad to "keep its place" in the set of rows to be returned. Although a SCRATCHPAD clause is not required when creating a table function, it is very hard to write a useful table function without one.

TIP: UDB initializes the scratchpad to zeros at the beginning of each SQL statement. But within an SQL statement, your table function may receive more than one series of OPEN, FETCH, and CLOSE calls. For example, the query on page 220 calls the sales table function repeatedly to obtain the sales records of various stores. UDB does not guarantee to initialize the scratchpad on each OPEN call to a table function. To ensure correct behavior of your table function, the safe thing to do is to initialize the scratchpad explicitly on every OPEN call rather than depend on the system's initialization.

Before a table function can be used, its implementation must be compiled, linked, and installed on the **UDB** server machine. This is done using the process described in Section 6.4.5. The same tools and procedures apply to external table functions and to external scalar functions—in fact, a single file may contain implementations of some scalar functions and some table functions.

The C program that implements the sales function is shown on the following pages. In a real application, the program would collect data from some external source and present it to the database system in the form of rows. This simple example illustrates the table function interface by returning some data that is internal to the program.

Example Program: sales

```
/*
**    Implements the table function sales(store).
**
**    Returns a table with the following columns:
**        SALEDATE, PRODUCT, QUANTITY, PRICE
*/

#include <string.h>
#include <stdlib.h>
#include <sqludf.h>

#define NENTRIES 7
#define ENTRYSIZE 60

void SQL_API_FN sales
   (
   char  *store,          /* IN: name of store                         */
   char  *saledate,       /* OUT: col. 1, SALEDATE                     */
   char  *product,        /* OUT: col. 2, PRODUCT                      */
   long  *quantity,       /* OUT: col. 3, QUANTITY                     */
   long  *price,          /* OUT: col. 4, PRICE                        */
   short *storename_ind,  /* IN: null indicator for input parameter    */
   short *saledate_ind,   /* OUT: null indicator for col. 1            */
   short *product_ind,    /* OUT: null indicator for col. 2            */
   short *quantity_ind,   /* OUT: null indicator for col. 3            */
   short *price_ind,      /* OUT: null indicator for col. 4            */
   char  *sqlstate,       /* OUT: SQLSTATE, char[6] with null-term.    */
   char  *fnName,         /* IN: function name, char[28] with null-term */
   char  *specificName,   /* IN: specific name, char[19] with null-term */
   char  *message,        /* OUT: message area, char[70] with null-term */
   SQLUDF_SCRATCHPAD   *scratchpad,     /* declared in sqludf.h        */
   SQLUDF_CALL_TYPE    *calltype        /* declared in sqludf.h        */
   )
   {
   long *pad = (long *)scratchpad->data;   /* scratchpad, init. to zero */
   char data_store[15];
   char data_saledate[15];
   char data_product[15];
   long data_quantity;
   long data_price;
```

```
char data[NENTRIES][ENTRYSIZE] =
    {
    "Denver    1996-06-15  Stapler    1    1250",
    "Denver    1996-07-29  Pencil    12      35",
    "Denver    1997-01-23  Notebook   2      50",
    "Denver    1997-02-06  Stapler    2    1100",
    "Boulder   1997-01-15  Stapler    3    1500",
    "Boulder   1997-02-18  Pencil     8      40",
    "Boulder   1997-03-05  Stapler    2    1200",
    };

switch (*calltype)
    {
    case SQL_TF_OPEN:
        /*
        ** Initialize scratchpad to zeros.  Don't rely on system to
        ** initialize, since table function may be opened more than once.
        */
        *pad = 0;
        break;      /* End of case SQL_TF_OPEN */

    case SQL_TF_FETCH:
        /*
        ** Scan the data for the desired store name.
        */
        while (*pad < NENTRIES)
            {
            sscanf(data[*pad], "%s %s %s %d %d",
                   data_store, data_saledate, data_product,
                   &data_quantity, &data_price);
            (*pad)++;
            if (!strcmp(store, data_store))
                {
                /*
                ** This is the right store--return the data.
                */
                strcpy(saledate, data_saledate);
                strcpy(product, data_product);
                *quantity = data_quantity;
                *price = data_price;
                strcpy(sqlstate, "00000");
                return;
                }
            }       /* End of while loop over data */
```

```
        /*
        ** End of data reached--return "no more rows"
        */
        strcpy(sqlstate, "02000");
        break;      /* End of case SQL_TF_FETCH */

    case SQL_TF_CLOSE:
        /*
        ** Free memory that was allocated on the OPEN call.
        ** In this example, there's nothing to do.
        */
        break;      /* End of case SQL_TF_CLOSE */
    }               /* End of switch statement */
}                   /* End of function body */
```

6.4.9 Using External Functions with Distinct Types

The power of distinct types and external functions is most evident when these two features are used together. As an example of the interaction of distinct types and functions, we will define two distinct types and create external functions to convert between them.

Suppose that you work for a multinational company that produces some products in the United States and other products in France. The dimensions of the American products are recorded in feet, and the dimensions of the French products are recorded in meters. Your company has defined two distinct types, Feet and Meters, both based on the built-in Double datatype, for use in its product database. The following statements show how these distinct data-types could be used to create and populate tables containing all the American and French products, respectively:

```
CREATE DISTINCT TYPE Feet              CREATE DISTINCT TYPE Meters
   AS Double WITH COMPARISONS;            AS Double WITH COMPARISONS;

CREATE TABLE us_products               CREATE TABLE french_products
   (name Varchar(20),                     (name Varchar(20),
    size Feet);                            size Meters);

INSERT INTO us_products VALUES          INSERT INTO french_products VALUES
   ('Widget', 3),                         ('Gadget', 0.5),
   ('Wadget', 5);                         ('Gizmo', 1.5);
```

The system provides casting functions between each distinct type and its source type, but it does not provide casting functions between Feet and Meters. To make the distinct types more useful, your database administrator writes external functions to convert between Feet and Meters in both directions. The CREATE FUNCTION statements for these conversion functions, and their implementations, are shown below. The functions are created with the NOT NULL CALL feature to simplify their implementations.

```
CREATE FUNCTION feet(Meters)          CREATE FUNCTION meters(Feet)
    RETURNS Feet                          RETURNS Meters
    EXTERNAL NAME 'units!feet'            EXTERNAL NAME 'units!meters'
    DETERMINISTIC                         DETERMINISTIC
    NO EXTERNAL ACTION                    NO EXTERNAL ACTION
    NOT NULL CALL                         NOT NULL CALL
    LANGUAGE C                            LANGUAGE C
    PARAMETER STYLE DB2SQL                PARAMETER STYLE DB2SQL
    NO SQL;                               NO SQL;

void SQL_API_FN feet                  void SQL_API_FN meters
    (                                     (
    double *metersIn,                     double *feetIn,
    double *feetOut,                      double *metersOut,
    short  *nullIn,                       short  *nullIn,
    short  *nullOut,                      short  *nullOut,
    char   *sqlstate,                     char   *sqlstate,
    char   *fnName,                       char   *fnName,
    char   *specificName,                 char   *specificName,
    char   *message                       char   *message
    )                                     )
    {                                     {
    *feetOut = *metersIn * 3.28;          *metersOut = *feetIn / 3.28;
    *nullOut = 0;                         *nullOut = 0;
    }                                     }
```

Your company would like to publish two catalogs, each listing all the products and their countries of origin. The first catalog, for use in the United States, should have all its dimensions in feet, and the second catalog, for use in France, should have all its dimensions in meters. The two catalogs correspond to two views of the database that might be defined as follows:

```
CREATE VIEW                              CREATE VIEW
  us_catalog(name, size, country)          french_catalog(name, size, country)
  AS                                       AS
    SELECT name, size, 'USA'                 SELECT name, size, 'France'
    FROM us_products                         FROM french_products
  UNION ALL                                UNION ALL
    SELECT name, feet(size), 'France'        SELECT name, meters(size), 'USA'
    FROM french_products;                    FROM us_products;
```

A sales representative in France, in order to meet a customer's specifications, might issue the following query against the French catalog view to find all the products having a size less than one meter:

```
SELECT *
FROM french_catalog
WHERE size < meters(1);
```

Based on the sample data listed above, the result of this query is as follows:

NAME	SIZE	COUNTRY
Gadget	+5.00000000000000E-001	France
Widget	+9.14634146341463E-001	USA

6.4.10 Writing an External Function in Java

Writing an external function in Java is very similar to writing one in C. Of course, if you wish to use a function written in Java, a Java virtual machine must be installed on your server. You must also tell UDB where to find the Java virtual machine, and you must tell the Java virtual machine where to find the UDB class libraries that support Java external functions. This is done in two steps:

1. Set your CLASSPATH environment variable to include the paths sqllib/function and sqllib/java/db2java.zip.

2. Set the database manager configuration parameter named jdk11_path to the path name of the directory in which your Java virtual machine is installed. You can use the Control Center to set this configuration parameter, as described in Chapter 10.

To implement an external function in Java, you need to create a Java class that extends (is a subclass of) the UDF class[9] provided in the **UDB** class library. The UDF class provides many methods that you will find helpful in writing your function. The methods of the UDF class are described in the *Embedded SQL Programming Guide*. You can create a Java class that implements several external functions—each function must be implemented by a separate method. You must compile your Java class and install the resulting file in the `sqllib/ function` directory.

The CREATE FUNCTION statement for an external Java function must specify the name of the class and method that implements the function, using the syntax EXTERNAL NAME `'classname!methodname'`. It must also specify LANGUAGE JAVA and PARAMETER STYLE DB2GENERAL. As the latter phrase suggests, the conventions used for passing parameters to Java functions are slightly different from the C-language conventions illustrated in Figures 6-3 and 6-4. The main differences are as follows:

- If an SQL function has n input parameters and a scalar return value, the Java method that implements it has only n+1 parameters—n input parameters and one return parameter. Similarly, if an SQL function has n input parameters and returns a table of m columns, the Java method that implements it has n+m parameters. No parameters are needed for null indicators, because the UDF class provides an `isNull` method that can be used to test the nullness of any input parameter. A Java method can return a null value simply by not setting the value of its return parameter.

- Each SQL datatype has at least one corresponding Java datatype that can be used for exchanging parameters and results with Java external functions. Some of these corresponding datatypes are shown in Table 8-1. Java is actually more flexible than C in exchanging values with the SQL environment. The UDF class provides a collection of methods for setting the values of output parameters, using various Java datatypes. For example, a Java external function might use the statement `set(5,x)` to set its output parameter number 5 to the value of variable x. This statement might invoke one of several methods, depending on the datatype of variable x. In addition, **UDB** provides two classes, named `COM.ibm.db2.app.Blob` and `COM.ibm.db2.app.Clob`, that enable Java functions to read and write their LOB-type parameters a few bytes at a time.

- The UDF class provides methods for setting the SQLSTATE and diagnostic message to be returned by the external function. It also provides methods for reading other information such as the function name and specific name, which require separate parameters in the case of a C function. These methods simplify the calling conventions for external Java functions and keep the number of parameters to a minimum.

---

9. The full name of this class is `COM.ibm.db2.app.UDF`.

Java scratchpad functions have an important advantage over scratchpad functions written in C. When invoking an external Java function that was created with the SCRATCHPAD option, UDB keeps the Java virtual machine running between one invocation of the function and the next. As a result, a Java scratchpad function can use Java variables to preserve its state from one row to the next during the processing of a query. The use of variables is more convenient in many cases than the use of an unformatted scratchpad area.

UDB provides several examples of Java external functions in the `sqllib/samples/java` directory. Additional information about Java functions and the class libraries that support them can be found in the *Embedded SQL Programming Guide*, and on the World Wide Web at `http://www.software.ibm.com/data/db2/java`.

6.4.11 External Functions and OLE Automation

OLE (Object Linking and Embedding) Automation is an architecture, defined by Microsoft, that allows applications to expose their objects and methods for use by other applications. An object that conforms to this architecture is called an *OLE Automation Object*. OLE Automation Objects can be created by many popular Windows development environments, including Microsoft Visual Basic, Microsoft Visual C++, Powersoft PowerBuilder, Borland Delphi, and MicroFocus COBOL.

If your UDB server is running under Windows NT, you can use a CREATE FUNCTION statement to register a method of an OLE Automation Object as a user-defined function. The method can then be used in SQL statements like any external function. A function defined in this way can be either a scalar function or a table function.

To create an OLE automation external function, you need to take the following steps:

1. Using your favorite programming language and development environment, create a class that implements the `IDispatch` interface, defined in the *OLE Automation Programmer's Reference* (Microsoft Press, 1996, ISBN 1-55615-851-3). Assign a unique class identifier to your class, and register it with the Windows Registry on your NT system. Your class is now an OLE Automation Server, and client applications can create instances of it through OLE Automation.

2. Create a public method for your class that implements the function you wish to use in SQL. The input and output parameters of your method should follow the usual conventions for external functions (described in Figure 6-3 for scalar functions and Figure 6-4 for table functions). The datatypes used for exchanging parameters with OLE Automation functions depend on the language in which the function is written, as described in the *Embedded SQL Programming Guide*.

3. Register your method with UDB as a user-defined function by executing a CREATE FUNCTION statement, specifying LANGUAGE OLE and PARAMETER STYLE DB2SQL. In the EXTERNAL NAME clause, you must identify the class and method that implements your function. When your function is called by an SQL statement, an instance of your class will be created, and its method will be invoked to implement the function. If you registered your function with the SCRATCHPAD option, its implementing object will remain in existence throughout the processing of the SQL statement, enabling state information to be passed from one row to the next using the object's internal state.

More details about external functions and OLE Automation can be found in the *Embedded SQL Programming Guide*. UDB provides examples of OLE external functions written in Visual Basic and Visual C++, in directories `sqllib\samples\ole\msvb` and `sqllib\samples\ole\msvc`.

6.4.12 Dropping a Function

A user-defined function can be dropped from the system by means of a DROP FUNCTION statement, which is a variation of the DROP statement described in Section 2.6.8. The syntax of the DROP FUNCTION statement is repeated here for clarity:

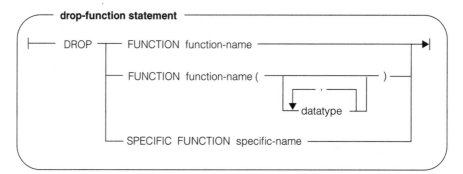

Dropping a function deletes the function from the system catalog tables, but it does not physically remove the executable file that implements the function from the directory where it resides.

As you can see from the syntax diagram above, there are three ways in which a DROP statement can identify the function instance to be dropped:

1. The function can be identified by its function name if there is only a single function instance with this name. If the schema name is omitted, it is considered to be the current authid.

Example: `DROP FUNCTION geometry.cosine;`

2. The function can be identified by its signature—that is, its name and the datatypes of all its parameters. If the schema name is omitted, it is considered to be the current authid. The function name and list of parameter types must uniquely identify a function instance. The parameter types must be an exact match for the function to be dropped, except that the length or precision/ scale of a datatype can be represented by empty parentheses, meaning "any." For example, Char() would match a Char parameter of any length, but it would not match a Varchar parameter.

Examples: DROP FUNCTION addWeeks(Date, Integer);

   DROP FUNCTION payroll.raise(Char(), Double);

TIP: Remember that Char without any parentheses denotes a Char datatype of default length, which is Char(1); similarly, Decimal without any parentheses denotes Decimal(5,0). Thus, DROP FUNCTION foo(Char()) drops a function named foo that takes a Char parameter of any length, but DROP FUNCTION foo(Char) drops a function named foo only if its parameter is Char(1).

3. The function can be identified by its specific name. This is the name given in the "specific name" clause of the CREATE FUNCTION statement when this function instance was created (or, if no specific name was supplied by the user, one was assigned by the system). Specific names are guaranteed to be unique within a schema. If the schema is omitted, it is considered to be the current authid.

Example: DROP SPECIFIC FUNCTION geometry.area1;

In order to execute a DROP FUNCTION statement, the current authid must satisfy at least one of the following conditions:

- Match the DEFINER of the function (recorded in the FUNCTIONS catalog)
- Hold the DROPIN privilege on the schema containing the function
- Hold DBADM or SYSADM authority

No one (not even a system administrator) is allowed to drop a function whose schema name is SYSIBM or SYSFUN. Similarly, no one is allowed to drop the casting and comparison functions that are automatically created by the system for each distinct type.

A function instance cannot be dropped if it is currently used in a view definition, in a constraint or trigger, or as the "source" of another function instance. In all these cases, the DROP FUNCTION statement will fail. Usage of a function instance in views, constraints, and triggers is recorded in the system catalog tables named VIEWDEP, CONSTDEP, and TRIGDEP. Usage of a function instance as the source of another function instance is recorded in the FUNCTIONS catalog table.

Usage of a function instance by a program will not cause a DROP FUNCTION statement to fail. If a function instance that is used by a program is dropped, the program's package is marked "inoperative" and cannot be used again until it is explicitly rebound. When the package is rebound, another applicable function instance will be chosen by the function resolution algorithm if one is available.

6.4.13 Commenting on a Function

Each user-defined function (but not the built-in functions) is described by an entry in the system catalog table named FUNCTIONS. Like many catalog tables, FUNCTIONS allows you to add a descriptive comment by using the COMMENT statement, described in Section 2.6.9. The syntax of the COMMENT statement as it applies to functions is repeated here for clarity:

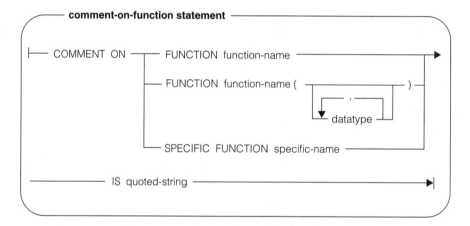

The three ways of identifying the function to which the comment applies correspond exactly to the three ways of identifying a function in a DROP FUNCTION statement. The authorization requirements for the COMMENT ON FUNCTION statement are also the same as those for DROP FUNCTION (except that ALTERIN privilege on the schema is required rather than DROPIN). The content of the quoted string in the COMMENT statement is entered into the REMARKS column of the FUNCTIONS catalog table.

Examples:

```
COMMENT ON FUNCTION addWeeks(Date, Integer) IS
    'Second operand must be positive';
COMMENT ON FUNCTION nthbest IS
    'Returns nth-largest value so far.
    Wrap in MAX() to get global nth-largest';
```

```
COMMENT ON SPECIFIC FUNCTION seqno IS
   'Counts the number of times it is called';
```

TIP: Notice that the CLP does not mind if your quoted string spans more than one line. The CLP treats line breaks within a character-string constant as though they were blanks.

6.5 STEPS TOWARD OBJECTS

The power of large objects, user-defined functions, and distinct types becomes most evident when these features are used together. Large objects provide the ability to store objects in the database that have a complex internal state. User-defined functions provide the ability to associate a complex behavior with these objects. Finally, distinct types provide the ability to combine user-defined state and behavior into a first-class datatype. Taken together, these features represent a significant step toward support of the object-oriented paradigm. As the DB2 product evolves, it might reasonably be expected to take additional steps in the same direction, such as providing support for true abstract datatypes with inheritance and polymorphism, and support for access plans based on user-defined functions.

6.5.1 Example: A Polygon Datatype

I will illustrate the synergy among large objects, user-defined functions, and distinct types by creating a datatype named Polygon. Polygons are useful in many applications, such as architecture, urban planning, VLSI design, and computer graphics.

The first step in creating a Polygon datatype is to choose a representation for Polygon data. In our example, we will represent a Polygon by an Integer that represents its degree, followed by a series of floating-point number pairs that represent the coordinates of its vertices in counterclockwise order. The Integer and the series of coordinates (of type Double) are packed together into a Blob, as illustrated in Figure 6-5. Since in UDB an Integer occupies four bytes and a Double occupies eight bytes, a Polygon of degree n can be represented by a Blob of length $16n + 4$.

The declaration of Polygon as an SQL datatype can be accomplished by the following statement:

```
CREATE DISTINCT TYPE Polygon AS Blob(16004);
```

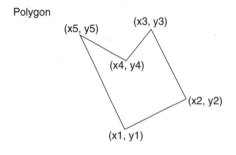

Figure 6-5: Polygon and Its Representation

Polygon

(x5, y5) (x3, y3)
(x4, y4)
(x2, y2)
(x1, y1)

Representation of polygon

5	x1	y1	x2	y2	x3	y3	x4	y4	x5	y5

Figure 6-5: A Polygon and Its Representation

This statement permits Polygons of degree up to 1,000 to be created; of course, no space is wasted if the Polygon has fewer than 1,000 sides. We do not include the phrase WITH COMPARISONS, because comparison operators are not supported on the Blob source type.

Before we can use the Polygon datatype, we need to have some way of creating an instance of a Polygon. This will be done by means of a *constructor function*, which creates a Polygon from a collection of simpler datatypes. The Polygon datatype might have many constructor functions, which create various types of Polygons from various different inputs. In this example, we will discuss one example of a Polygon constructor, which creates a three-sided Polygon (a triangle) from parameters that represent the coordinates of the vertices. The signature of this constructor function is as follows:

```
triangle(Double, Double, Double, Double, Double, Double)
    RETURNS Polygon;
```

In order for Polygon to be a useful datatype, we will need to create some functions that implement Polygon behavior. A great many such functions can be imagined, of which we will list only a few:

```
degree(Polygon) returns Integer;
area(Polygon) returns Double;
perimeter(Polygon) returns Double;
rotate(Polygon, Double) returns Polygon;
intersect(Polygon, Polygon) returns Polygon;
```

We will discuss in detail the implementation of two Polygon functions, namely, the triangle constructor and the perimeter function. Both of these functions will be implemented in a single C source file named polygon.c. We will make use of the NOT NULL CALL convention, declaring that the output of each function is null if any of its inputs are null, so that our function implementations need not be concerned with nulls. The following SQL statements are used to "register" our functions with the system (if we plan to use our functions in more than one database, we must execute the following statements while connected to each database):

```
CREATE FUNCTION
    triangle(double, double, double, double, double, double)
         --    x1,     y1,    x2,     y2,    x3,     y3
        RETURNS Polygon
        EXTERNAL NAME 'polygon!triangle'
        DETERMINISTIC
        NO EXTERNAL ACTION
        FENCED
        NOT NULL CALL
        LANGUAGE C
        NO SQL
        PARAMETER STYLE DB2SQL;

CREATE FUNCTION
    perimeter(Polygon)
        RETURNS Double
        EXTERNAL NAME 'polygon!perimeter'
        DETERMINISTIC
        NO EXTERNAL ACTION
        FENCED
        NOT NULL CALL
        LANGUAGE C
        NO SQL
        PARAMETER STYLE DB2SQL;
```

The function bodies are written using the parameter-passing conventions discussed in Section 6.4.4. The content of the implementation file, polygon.c, is shown on the following pages. This file contains the bodies of the triangle and perimeter functions, and it also contains a definition of a C structure named Pgon that can be overlaid on a Blob in order to interpret the Blob as a Polygon.

Example Program: Polygon

```c
#include <stdlib.h>      /* Standard C library        */
#include <sqludf.h>      /* UDF-related declarations  */
#include <math.h>        /* needed for sqrt function  */
#include <string.h>      /* needed for strcpy function */


/**********************************************************************
**   The following structure will be overlaid on the data area of a Blob  *
**   to represent a Polygon.                                          *
**********************************************************************/

struct Pgon
   {
   long  degree;
   double  coord[1];   /* actually an array of many coordinates */
   };


/**********************************************************************
**              CONSTRUCTOR FUNCTION FOR TRIANGLES                    *
**        Triangle(x1, y1, x2, y2, x3, y3) returns Polygon            *
**********************************************************************/

void SQL_API_FN
     triangle( double       *x1,       /* IN:  vertex 1, x-coord.  */
               double       *y1,       /* IN:  vertex 1, y-coord.  */
               double       *x2,       /* IN:  vertex 2, x-coord.  */
               double       *y2,       /* IN:  vertex 2, y-coord.  */
               double       *x3,       /* IN:  vertex 3, x-coord.  */
               double       *y3,       /* IN:  vertex 3, y-coord.  */
               SQLUDF_BLOB  *poly,     /* OUT: Polygon in a Blob   */
               short        *x1null,   /* IN:  indicator (ignored) */
               short        *x2null,   /* IN:  indicator (ignored) */
               short        *x3null,   /* IN:  indicator (ignored) */
               short        *x4null,   /* IN:  indicator (ignored) */
               short        *x5null,   /* IN:  indicator (ignored) */
               short        *x6null,   /* IN:  indicator (ignored) */
               short        *nullout,  /* OUT: indicator           */
               char         *sqlstate, /* OUT: result code         */
               char         *fnname,   /* IN:  generic fn name      */
               char         *specname, /* IN:  specific fn name     */
               char         *message   /* OUT: message text        */
             )
```

```
{
struct Pgon *p;          /* overlay a Pgon on the Blob  */
p = (struct Pgon *)(poly->data);

/*
**   Length: Blob contains Pgon structure
**           plus five additional doubles
*/
poly->length = sizeof(struct Pgon) + 5 * sizeof(double);

/*
**   Fill in the degree and the coordinates of the polygon
*/
p->degree = 3;           /* degree of a triangle is 3   */
p->coord[0] = *x1;
p->coord[1] = *y1;
p->coord[2] = *x2;
p->coord[3] = *y2;
p->coord[4] = *x3;
p->coord[5] = *y3;

*nullout = 0;            /* return null indicator       */
/*
**   No need to set sqlstate to 00000 for normal return.
*/

}       /* end of triangle function */


/************************************************************************
**                  PERIMETER FUNCTION FOR POLYGONS                    *
**                  Perimeter(Polygon) returns Double                  *
************************************************************************/

void SQL_API_FN
    perimeter(SQLUDF_BLOB    *poly,        /* IN:  Polygon in a Blob    */
              double         *perim,       /* OUT: return value         */
              short          *nullin,      /* IN:  indicator (ignored)  */
              short          *nullout,     /* OUT: indicator            */
              char           *sqlstate,    /* OUT: result code          */
              char           *fnname,      /* IN:  generic fn name       */
              char           *specname,    /* IN:  specific fn name      */
              char           *message      /* OUT: message text          */
             )
```

```
{
int     degree;                              /* degree of polygon        */
double  startx, starty;                      /* start of line segment    */
double  endx, endy;                          /* end of line segment      */
int     i;                                   /* loop counter             */
double  deltax, deltay, lengthSoFar;         /* working variables        */

struct Pgon *p;                              /* overlay Pgon on the Blob */
p = (struct Pgon *)(poly->data);

/*
**   Check the degree of the polygon for validity
*/
degree = p->degree;
if (degree < 1 || degree > 1000)
   {
   strcpy(sqlstate, "38610");                /* return abnormal sqlstate */
   strcpy(message, "Invalid degree");
   return;
   }

/*
**   Coordinates of point i are in (coord[2*i], coord[2*i+1])
**   where i ranges from 0 to degree-1.
*/
endx = p->coord[2*(degree-1)];               /* last point */
endy = p->coord[2*(degree-1)+1];             /* in polygon */
lengthSoFar = 0;
for (i=0; i<degree; i++)
   {
   startx = endx;
   starty = endy;
   endx = p->coord[2*i];
   endy = p->coord[2*i+1];
   deltax = endx - startx;
   deltay = endy - starty;
   lengthSoFar += sqrt(deltax * deltax + deltay * deltay);
   }
*perim = lengthSoFar;                         /* return value            */
*nullout = 0;                                 /* return null indicator   */
strcpy(sqlstate, "00000");                    /* return normal sqlstate  */

}       /* end of perimeter function */
```

In addition to the implementation file `polygon.c`, we need to create an export file named `polygon.exp` (under AIX) or a module definition file named `polygon.def` (under OS/2 or Windows NT). The content of these files is shown below:

```
polygon.exp                  polygon.def

#! polygon export file       LIBRARY POLYGON
triangle                     EXPORTS
perimeter                        triangle
                                 perimeter
```

To complete the definition of the Polygon object, we compile and link the `polygon.c` source file, copy the executable file to the `sqllib/function` directory, and authorize it for execution by any user, following the steps described in Section 6.4.5. Polygon is now a first-class datatype with its own behavior, which is implemented by a set of user-defined functions.

As an example of the use of Polygons, we will consider a real estate application. The following SQL statements create a table named PROPERTIES, containing a column of type Polygon, and insert two triangular parcels of property into the table:

```
CREATE TABLE properties
   (parcelno Char(6),
    owner    Varchar(32),
    parcel   Polygon);

INSERT INTO properties(parcelno, owner, parcel) VALUES
   ('123456', 'John Smith',
        triangle( 500,  600, -400, -500, 1000, -500)),
   ('123457', 'Susan Doe',
        triangle(1100, 1100, 1300, 1100, 1300, 1400));
```

The following query retrieves the parcels that have a perimeter of more than 1,000 (John's parcel qualifies, but Susan's does not):

```
SELECT owner, perimeter(parcel)
FROM   properties
WHERE  perimeter(parcel) > 1000;
```

TIP: The sample query above searches for polygons having perimeters greater than a certain value. Unless you plan ahead, this query will be slow and expensive because it must invoke an external function (`perimeter`) for each polygon in the PROPERTIES table. If this is a frequent type of query, you can make it much more efficient by precomputing the perimeter of each polygon and storing it in an additional column of the PROPERTIES table, and by creating an index on the perimeter column. Triggers can be defined to automatically compute the value of the perimeter column whenever a polygon is inserted or updated. Triggers are discussed in Chapter 7.

TIP: When writing an application program that uses a distinct type such as Polygon that is based on a LOB datatype, you may wish to use locators to avoid actually materializing large objects in your program. Since Polygon is based on Blob, for example, you can use Blob locators in your program to manipulate Polygons. However, if you wish to invoke a function that takes a Polygon as its argument, you must explicitly cast the locator to a Polygon datatype before calling the function. For example, if `loc1` is a host variable of type Blob locator, `perimeter(Polygon(:loc1))` would be a correct function call, but `perimeter(:loc1)` would fail to compile, with the error message "no function having compatible arguments was found."

6.6 DATATYPE CONVERSIONS

There are many reasons, while processing SQL statements, why it might be necessary to convert a value from one datatype into another. Now that we have discussed user-defined datatypes and functions, it may be worthwhile to summarize all the ways in which the system performs datatype conversions. There are four different ways in which datatype conversion is done by UDB, and these are summarized below.

Smallint $\rightarrow$ Integer $\rightarrow$ Decimal $\rightarrow$ Real $\longrightarrow$ Double

Char $\longrightarrow$ Varchar $\longrightarrow$ Long Varchar $\longrightarrow$ Clob

Graphic $\rightarrow$ Vargraphic $\rightarrow$ Long Vargraphic $\rightarrow$ Dbclob

Figure 6-6: Promotion of Function Arguments

6.6.1 Promotion of Function Arguments

Each function, whether built-in or user-defined, has a well-defined list of parameter types. Most of the built-in functions are really families of overloaded functions. For example, the family SYSIBM.LENGTH consists of the built-in functions length(Integer), length(Decimal), length(Char), length(Varchar), length(Date), and many other function instances. User-defined functions may also consist of overloaded families. When a function is called with a set of arguments, the best function instance is selected by the function resolution algorithm described in Section 6.4.3. Then, if the selected function is not a perfect match for the actual arguments, the arguments are promoted to match the parameter types of the function. Only built-in datatypes are promoted, and only in certain predetermined ways. Promotion of arguments is done only by moving to the right along one of the promotion paths shown in Figure 6-6. As a value is promoted, its length, precision, or scale may also be adjusted in order to fit the parameter of the chosen function.

Since the Blob, Date, Time, and Timestamp datatypes, and all distinct types, are not members of any promotion hierarchy, these datatypes are never promoted. When one of these datatypes is used as an argument of a function, the parameter of the selected function instance must be an exact match.

All combining of dissimilar datatypes by arithmetic or concatenation operators is handled by promotion. For example, if x is an Integer and y is a Double, the expression x + y is treated as a call to the function "+"(Double, Double) with promotion of the first argument.

6.6.2 UNION Semantics

The set operations UNION, INTERSECT, and EXCEPT can combine values of different datatypes. When doing so, these operations use conversion semantics similar to the promotion of arguments, but slightly more liberal. All the conversions allowed for promotion of function arguments are also allowed for the set operations, and, in addition, a Char or Varchar value containing a valid representation of a Date, Time, or Timestamp can be converted to a

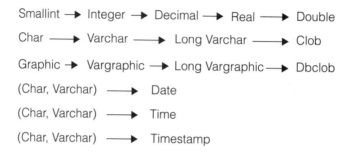

Figure 6-7: UNION Datatype Hierarchies

Date, Time, or Timestamp. The datatype conversions supported by UNION, INTERSECT, and EXCEPT are shown in Figure 6-7. As a general rule, if two datatypes T1 and T2 from the same UNION hierarchy are combined by one of the set operations, the result datatype is either T1 or T2, whichever is farther to the right in the hierarchy.[10]

When two strings are combined by a set operation, the length of the result datatype is the greater of the input lengths. For example, if a Char(50) and a Varchar(10) are combined by an INTERSECT operation, the result will be a Varchar(50), which is not the same datatype as either of the operands.

When the result of a set operation is a Decimal datatype, the result has as many digits to the right of the decimal point as either operand, and also has as many digits to the left of the decimal point as either operand. For example, if the operand types of a UNION are Decimal(8,2), which has six left-digits and two right-digits, and Decimal(7,4), which has three left-digits and four right-digits, the result of the UNION is Decimal(10,4), which has six left-digits and four right-digits. For this purpose, the Integer type is considered to have eleven digits and the Smallint type is considered to have five digits.

Since Blobs and distinct types do not participate in any of the UNION datatype hierarchies, each of these datatypes can be combined only with itself in set operations.

---

10. There is one exception to this rule: if a value of type Real is combined with a value of type Smallint, Integer, or Decimal, the result is a value of type Double.

UNION semantics for datatype conversion are also used by a few other datatype-combining operations in the SQL language. These operations are as follows:

1. Computing the result of a `coalesce` function when its operands have different datatypes. For example, if x is a Char(10) and y is a Date, then the result type of `coalesce(x, y)` is a Date, even if the value of x is returned.

2. A CASE expression whose candidate results have different datatypes. For example, consider the following expression:

```
CASE testvalue
    WHEN 1 THEN 100
    WHEN 2 THEN 200.00
    ELSE 3.0E+2
END
```

The result of this expression will be 1.0E+2, 2.0E+2, or 3.0E+2, depending on `testvalue`. The datatype of the result will always be Double, because that is the "greatest datatype" of the candidate results.

3. VALUES expressions. A VALUES expression is like a "literal table." The datatypes of the columns of this table are computed from the component parts of the VALUES expression using UNION semantics. For example, the following VALUES expression behaves like a literal table whose first column is of type Double and whose second column is of type Decimal:

```
VALUES (1, 2.0), (3E3, 4)
```

4. IN-lists. In an IN predicate, all the values in the IN-list must have types that can be combined using UNION semantics. To illustrate this rule, the first example below is a valid IN predicate, but the second is not valid:

```
length IN (1, 2.2, 3e-1)
length IN (1, 2.2, 'Three miles');
```

6.6.3 Assignment

In SQL, assignment can take place in any of the following ways:

- A column can be assigned a value by the SET clause of an UPDATE statement.
- A column can be assigned a value by an assignment (SET) statement in a before trigger (described in Section 7.3.2).
- Values can be inserted into a row by an INSERT statement.
- Values can be delivered into a host variable by a SELECT, FETCH, or VALUES statement.

The rules for assigning a value to a target of a different datatype are more liberal than the rules for argument promotion or for UNION in two respects:

1. Unlike promotions, assignment conversions are bidirectional. That is, a value can be assigned to a target of a "lower" datatype, as in assigning a Float to an Integer. Of course, precision may be lost when values are truncated, and run-time error conditions may occur if a value cannot be represented in the target datatype (for example, if a Double value is out of the range expressible by the Integer datatype).

2. Distinct-type values can be assigned to their source-type targets, and vice versa, with automatic conversion using the system-provided casting functions. When a distinct-type value is assigned to a host variable, it is first converted to its source type, and the resulting value is then assigned to the host variable.

For purposes of assignment, datatypes are treated as a collection of families with assignment in any direction supported inside each family, as shown in Figure 6-8.

6.6.4 Casting

The casting operation is invoked explicitly by the CAST expression discussed in Section 2.4.3. The following is an example of a CAST expression:

```
CAST (x AS Decimal(8,2))
```

Casting is also invoked implicitly when the arguments of a sourced function are converted to the parameter types of the source function, and the result of the source function is converted to the result type of the sourced function.

The conversions supported by casting are the most liberal of the four forms of datatype conversion. All the conversions supported by assignment are supported, along with certain additional conversions such as casting a numeric value into its character-string representation.

The rules governing castability of one datatype into another are as follows:

1. A distinct type is castable into its source type.

{ Smallint, Integer, Decimal, Real, Double }

{ Char, Varchar, Long Varchar, Clob }

{ Graphic, Vargraphic, Long Vargraphic, Dbclob }

{ (Char or Varchar representation of a Date), Date }

{ (Char or Varchar representation of a Time), Time }

{ (Char or Varchar representation of a Timestamp), Timestamp }

{ (Any distinct type), (The source type of that distinct type) }

Figure 6-8: Assignment Datatype Families

2. The source type of a distinct type is castable into the distinct type. Also, since the casting is performed by a function, any datatype that is promotable to the source type is castable into the distinct type.

3. A distinct type is never castable into another distinct type.[11]

4. Among built-in datatypes, the valid casts are listed in Table 6-6. Some of these casts may lead to run-time errors—for example, casting a Double value to the Integer datatype may cause an overflow error if the value is too large. Similarly, casting a Char or Varchar value into a numeric or datetime datatype will succeed only if the value is a valid character-string representation of the target type.

---

11. A user can create a function that converts one distinct type into another, such as the feet(Meters) and meters(Feet) examples in Section 6.4.9, but these user-defined functions are not considered to be casting functions and cannot be invoked by using the CAST notation.

TABLE 6-6: Valid Casts Between Built-In Datatypes

Cast From:	Smallint Integer Decimal	Real Double	Char	Varchar	Long Varchar Clob	Graphic	Vargraphic	Long Vargraphic Dbclob	Date	Time	Timestamp	Blob
Smallint Integer Decimal	Y	Y	Y									
Real Double	Y	Y										
Char Varchar	Y		Y	Y	Y		Y		Y	Y	Y	Y
Long Varchar Clob			Y	Y	Y							Y
Graphic Vargraphic Long Vargraphic Dbclob						Y	Y	Y				Y
Date			Y	Y					Y			
Time			Y	Y						Y		
Timestamp			Y	Y					Y	Y	Y	
Blob												Y

7

Active Data

One of the most important trends in database management is the trend toward increasing the semantic content of stored data. Since a database is a resource shared by many applications, any knowledge about data semantics that can be put into the database is knowledge that does not need to be replicated in every application. This knowledge might include rules about what values are valid for a particular column of data, how data values are related to each other, or how an action should be triggered automatically whenever a certain condition is detected. When rules like these are enforced by the database system, stored data becomes more "active," having behavior of its own that goes beyond passively accepting updates from the world outside the database. Active data is more valuable than passive data because it is richer in semantic content.

I will define an *active data feature* as a mechanism whereby an SQL statement can invoke an action that is not explicitly specified by the SQL statement. UDB includes several active data features, which I will classify into the following two broad categories:

1. *Constraints.* Constraints are rules that govern how data values can change, generally stated in a declarative way. Constraints ensure the validity of data values and may generate values automatically when necessary. Attempts to update the database in a way that violates a constraint will in general be refused. Constraints are an important part of the SQL92 Standard.

2. *Triggers.* Triggers are general-purpose automatic actions that are invoked, or "triggered," by certain events such as update of a specific table. In contrast to the declarative nature of constraints, triggers are defined by procedures, consisting of a series of SQL statements to be executed automatically whenever the triggering event is detected. Triggers are very powerful, because they are not limited to predefined actions such as rolling back an offending update. They can be used to enforce global integrity of the database or to invoke complex automatic actions, including interactions with the world outside the database such as placing an order or sending a message. A trigger facility is under consideration for inclusion in the next ANSI/ISO SQL Standard, currently known as SQL3.

This chapter describes all the active data features supported by UDB and includes a comprehensive example of a database design that uses many constraints and triggers. Also, since constraints are properties of database tables, this is the chapter in which the complete syntax of the SQL statements for creating and altering tables is described.

An active database can be very complex and richly interconnected. This chapter describes how multiple constraints and triggers interact when they are activated by the same statement. It also describes how views, triggers, constraints, programs, and other objects depend on each other and how the principle called *conservative binding semantics* prevents your views and application programs from changing their behavior unexpectedly.

7.1 CONSTRAINTS

In UDB, each constraint is associated with a specific table in the database and protects the validity of data values in that table. Constraints are associated with base tables only, not with views[1] (though, of course, a constraint on a table protects that table from invalid updates applied through a view). Most types of constraints can have names, which must be unique among all the constraints associated with a particular table. The name of a constraint is used by the system in error messages whenever the constraint is violated, and can also be used in an ALTER TABLE statement to drop the constraint. If you create a constraint and do not give it a name, the system will generate a name for the constraint automatically.

Since each constraint applies to a particular table, constraints are defined as part of a CREATE TABLE statement. After a table has been created, constraints associated with that table can be added or dropped by means of an ALTER TABLE statement. Of course, when a table is dropped, all the constraints associated with it are dropped also.

UDB includes the following six features that can be considered types of constraints, in the sense that they govern or influence the ways in which data values can be modified:

NOT NULL constraints

Column defaults

Unique constraints

Check constraints

Primary key constraints

Foreign key constraints

---

1. A view feature called the *check option*, discussed in Section 2.6.5, might be considered to be a constraint on a view.

7.1.1 NOT NULL Constraints

This very primitive form of constraint specifies that a given column of a table cannot contain a null value. Any INSERT or UPDATE statement that attempts to place a null value in the column will fail.

NOT NULL constraints may not have names. The following is an example of a CREATE TABLE statement that includes a NOT NULL constraint:

```
CREATE TABLE patients (socsecno Char(11) NOT NULL, ...);
```

If a column has a NOT NULL constraint, its entry in the COLUMNS catalog table has the value "N" in the NULLS column.

7.1.2 Column Defaults

When a column is created or added to a table, a default value can be specified for the column. The default value is generated automatically whenever a row that is inserted into the table does not include a specific value for the column. If a new column with a default value is added to a table that has some existing rows, the existing rows are given the default value for the new column.

The syntax of a default clause in a column definition is shown on page 403. The default value specified for a column can be NULL or a constant or special register that is compatible with the datatype of the column. If the datatype of the column is a Blob or a distinct type, the default value can be specified by using a casting function such as blob(X'00000000') or shoesize(8). If no explicit default value is specified for a column, its default value is determined according to the rules in Table 7-1.

In the following example of a CREATE TABLE statement, the comments indicate the default values of the four columns. The INSERT statement inserts a row that receives default values for the STATE and CITATIONS columns.

```
CREATE TABLE drivers
    (licenseno Char(8) NOT NULL,        -- No default
     state Char(2) WITH DEFAULT 'CA',   -- Default is 'CA'
     expiration Date,                   -- Default is null
     citations Smallint WITH DEFAULT);  -- Default is zero

INSERT INTO drivers(licenseno, expiration)
    VALUES ('K0123456', '1998-06-15');
```

The default value for each column can be found in the DEFAULT column of the COLUMNS catalog table.

TABLE 7-1: Default Values for Columns

If the column definition contains . . .	. . . and the datatype of the column is . . .	. . . then the default value of the column is . . .
No DEFAULT clause	(Any datatype)	Null (unless NOT NULL is specified; in this case, the column has no default).
A DEFAULT clause that specifies an explicit default value	(Any datatype)	The value specified in the DEFAULT clause.
WITH DEFAULT (but no explicit default value is specified)	Smallint, Integer, Decimal, Real, Double	Zero.
	Char, Graphic	Blanks.
	Varchar, Long Varchar, Graphic, Long Vargraphic, Clob, Dbclob, Blob	Zero-length string.
	Date	The current date when the row is inserted. When a Date column is added to a table, existing rows receive the date January 1, 0001.
	Time	The current time when the row is inserted. When a Time column is added to a table, existing rows receive the time 00:00:00.
	Timestamp	The current timestamp when the row is inserted. When a Timestamp column is added to a table, existing rows receive a timestamp containing the date January 1, 0001 and the time 00:00:00.
	A distinct type	The system-defined default value for the base datatype, cast into the distinct type.

7.1.3 Unique Constraints

A unique constraint guarantees the uniqueness of the values in a column or set of columns, called a *unique key*. All the columns in the unique key must also have NOT NULL constraints.

The following constraint might be part of the definition of a table used by a sports league. The constraint, named LEAGUERULE1, ensures that each team has at most one player in each position. If you define a constraint without specifying a name, it will receive a system-generated name.

```
CONSTRAINT leaguerule1 UNIQUE(team, position);
```

When you declare a unique constraint on a certain set of columns, UDB automatically creates a unique index on those columns to enforce the constraint. If the constraint has a name, the index is given the same name (unless an existing index is using this name, in which case the system generates another name for the index).

Since unique constraints are enforced by indexes, all the limitations of index keys apply to unique constraints as well. For example, the unique key may contain no more than 16 columns with a total length of 255 bytes or less, and may not contain any large-object columns (the full set of limitations can be found in Section 2.6.6).

Unique constraints are enforced at the end of each SQL statement. It is possible that, during processing of an UPDATE statement that updates several rows, a unique constraint might be temporarily violated. Such a statement will not be rolled back as long as the unique constraint is satisfied at the end of statement processing.

The KEYCOLUSE catalog table describes all the unique constraints that have been defined and the tables and columns to which they apply.

7.1.4 Check Constraints

Each check constraint is attached to a particular table and serves to ensure the validity of its data values. A check constraint contains a predicate (or combination of predicates connected by AND/OR) called a *check condition*. The check condition is enforced to be "not false" (that is, it must evaluate to true or unknown) for every row in the table. Whenever a row of a table is inserted or updated, the check condition is tested for the changed row, and if it is false, the insert or update is rolled back. If multiple rows are inserted or updated by a single SQL statement and a check constraint fails for any of these rows, all changes made by the SQL statement are rolled back, and the statement has no effect. When a statement is rolled back because it violates a check constraint, the current transaction remains in progress, and other statements within the transaction are not affected.

In UDB, the check condition must be some test that can be evaluated by examining a single row of the table to which the check constraint is attached. In other words, the check constraint is like a WHERE clause that refers only to the columns of a single table, with no subqueries or references to special registers. This restriction allows the check condition to be quickly evaluated whenever a row is inserted or updated.

Check constraints are attached to a table as part of a CREATE TABLE or ALTER TABLE statement. The following are examples of valid check constraints on a table with columns JOBCODE, SALARY, and BONUS:

```
CONSTRAINT check1
    CHECK (jobcode IN (10, 20, 30, 40, 50));
CONSTRAINT check2
    CHECK (salary < 100000 AND bonus <= salary);
```

The following is an example of a check constraint that is *not* valid because it cannot be tested by examining a single row:

```
CONSTRAINT check3
    CHECK (salary < (SELECT max(salary) FROM emp));
```

Although check3 in the example above is not a valid check constraint, you can accomplish its purpose by writing a trigger, as described in Section 7.3.

Each check constraint is described by a row in the CHECKS catalog table, which contains the name of the constraint, the name of the table to which it is attached, and the text of the check condition.

TIP: A check constraint may call a user-defined function, and in fact user-defined functions add greatly to the power of check constraints. However, a check constraint may not call a user-defined function that has been defined with the VARIANT, EXTERNAL ACTION, or SCRATCHPAD properties.

7.1.5 Primary Key Constraints

Each table may optionally have one primary key. A primary key is a column or combination of columns that has the combined properties of uniqueness and NOT NULL. A primary key may consist of up to 16 columns, with a combined length of up to 255 bytes. None of the columns in a primary key may have a datatype of Blob, Clob, Dbclob, Long Varchar, or Long Vargraphic. When you declare that a certain set of columns make up the primary key of a table, the system automatically maintains a unique index on that set of columns. If the primary key constraint has a name, the index is given the same name (unless an existing index is using this name, in which case the system generates another name for the index).

A primary key is similar to a unique key with two additional properties:

1. The primary key of a table serves as the default parent key for referential integrity relationships (described in the next section).

2. If a table is partitioned across nodes in a parallel database system, the first column of the primary key serves as the default partitioning key that governs the distribution of rows among the nodes.

You can find the primary key columns for a given table by looking in the COLUMNS catalog table. If a column is part of the primary key for its table, its KEYSEQ value in COLUMNS will indicate its position within the primary key. (For example, a KEYSEQ value of 2 indicates the second column in the primary key.)

Primary keys can be defined for a table as part of a CREATE TABLE statement and can be added or dropped by means of an ALTER TABLE statement. A primary key can be given a name, but there is little reason to do so, because a primary key can be dropped without reference to its name (after all, each table can have only one primary key). The following are examples of CREATE TABLE statements that specify primary keys. (Of course, each primary key specification must be contained in a separate CREATE TABLE statement, since a given table cannot have more than one primary key.)

```
CREATE TABLE patients (socsecno Char(11)
                              NOT NULL PRIMARY KEY,
                    name Varchar(15));

CREATE TABLE quotations (suppno Char(3) NOT NULL,
                    partno Char(4) NOT NULL,
                    price  Integer,
                    PRIMARY KEY (suppno, partno));
```

7.1.6 Foreign Key Constraints

A foreign key constraint specifies a relationship between two tables: the *parent table* and the *child table*. The parent table and child table may be the same table, in which case the table is said to be *self-referencing*. The relationship between the tables, sometimes called a *referential integrity* or *RI* relationship, is a 1:*n* relationship between the rows of the parent table and the rows of the child table. The relationship is based on matching values between a set of columns of the parent table, called the *parent key*, and a set of columns in the child table, called the *foreign key*. As long as the foreign key constraint is in effect, the system guarantees that, for each row in the child table with a non-null value in all of its foreign key columns, there is a row in the parent table with a matching value in the parent key. The parent key must be either a primary key or a unique key of the parent table. Of course, the foreign key and the parent key must have the same number of columns and compatible (but not necessarily identical) datatypes. None of the columns in the foreign key may have a datatype of Blob, Clob, Dbclob, Long Varchar, or Long Vargraphic.

A table may participate in multiple referential integrity relationships, both as a parent and as a child. Each relationship is created by a clause, in a CREATE TABLE or ALTER TABLE statement for the child table, that specifies the foreign key columns, the parent table, and optionally the parent key columns. If you do not specify the parent key columns, they are assumed to be the primary key columns of the parent table. You are not allowed to create an RI relationship in which the parent key and child key are exactly the same as the parent key and child key in another RI relationship.

In a CREATE TABLE or ALTER TABLE that specifies a foreign key constraint, it is advisable to give the constraint a descriptive name. If you do not specify a name, the system will generate one for you.

As we have seen, the system automatically maintains an index on each primary key. No index is maintained automatically on a foreign key, but you can create such an index, and it's probably wise to do so.

Each referential integrity relationship is recorded by a row in the REFERENCES catalog table that contains the name of the constraint, the names of the parent and child tables, and the sets of columns that comprise the parent key and foreign key. You can also find the relationships that apply to a particular column by looking in the KEYCOLUSE catalog table, which has an entry for each column that participates in a primary, unique, or foreign key.

Foreign key constraints can be illustrated by means of tables named EMP and DEPT, which participate in two referential integrity relationships. Each EMP row represents an employee, and each DEPT row represents a department. We wish to make sure that each employee is in a valid department and has a valid manager. This can be done by specifying two foreign keys for the EMP table, as shown in Figure 7-1. In one of these constraints (the one from MANAGER to EMPNO), the EMP table is self-referencing. The primary and foreign keys can be specified when the respective tables are created (as in the example) or can be added later by ALTER TABLE statements. The constraints in Figure 7-1 guarantee that each non-null DEPTNO value in EMP has a matching DEPTNO value in DEPT and that each non-null MANAGER value in EMP has a matching EMPNO value in EMP. Since we have also specified that DEPTNO and MANAGER in the EMP table are NOT NULL (note that this is not required by the foreign key constraint), we have guaranteed that every employee has both a valid department and a valid manager. (Of course, some departments may have no employees, and some employees may not be anyone's manager.)

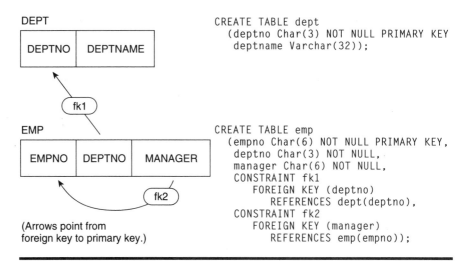

DEPT

DEPTNO	DEPTNAME

fk1

EMP

EMPNO	DEPTNO	MANAGER

fk2

(Arrows point from
foreign key to primary key.)

```
CREATE TABLE dept
    (deptno Char(3) NOT NULL PRIMARY KEY
     deptname Varchar(32));
```

```
CREATE TABLE emp
    (empno Char(6) NOT NULL PRIMARY KEY,
     deptno Char(3) NOT NULL,
     manager Char(6) NOT NULL,
     CONSTRAINT fk1
         FOREIGN KEY (deptno)
             REFERENCES dept(deptno),
     CONSTRAINT fk2
         FOREIGN KEY (manager)
             REFERENCES emp(empno));
```

Figure 7-1: Foreign Key Constraints

In the CREATE TABLE statements in Figure 7-1, the column names in the REFERENCES clauses could have been omitted, since in every case the parent key is the primary key of the parent table.

At this point, you may be wondering what happens if an SQL statement attempts to change some data value in a way that would violate a foreign key constraint. I will answer this question by listing all the ways in which the constraint could be violated and explaining what happens in each case.

1. An SQL statement could try to insert a row into the child table, with a foreign key value that matches no parent key value. Such an INSERT statement will fail, and all rows inserted by the statement will be rolled back.

2. An SQL statement could try to update a foreign key in the child table to a new value that matches no parent key value. Such an UPDATE statement will fail, and all rows updated by the statement will be rolled back.

3. An SQL statement could try to delete a row from the parent table, leaving some unmatched foreign key values in the child table. The user who created the foreign key constraint can choose among the following options to take effect in this case:

ON DELETE CASCADE: The deletion of the parent row succeeds, and all rows of the child table with matching foreign keys are deleted also.

ON DELETE SET NULL: The deletion of the parent row succeeds, and the nullable columns of all matching foreign keys in the child table are set to null. (Of course, at least one of the foreign key columns must be nullable).

ON DELETE NO ACTION: The deletion of the parent row fails, and all changes are rolled back. Constraints with this option are checked *after* all cascaded updates and deletes have taken effect.

ON DELETE RESTRICT: As in the NO ACTION option, the deletion of the parent row fails, and all changes are rolled back. However, constraints with the RESTRICT option are checked *before* cascaded updates and deletes take effect. Therefore, ON DELETE RESTRICT is slightly more restrictive than ON DELETE NO ACTION.

The default behavior of a foreign key constraint is ON DELETE NO ACTION.

4. An SQL statement could try to update the parent table, modifying a parent key value in such a way that some foreign key values in the child table would be left unmatched. The user who created the foreign key constraint can choose between the following options to take effect in this case:

ON UPDATE NO ACTION: This option requires that, after the UPDATE statement has been executed, every child row with a non-null foreign key must have *some* matching parent row—but not necessarily the same parent row as the one it had before the UPDATE statement. If this condition is not met, the UPDATE statement fails, and all changes are rolled back.

ON UPDATE RESTRICT: This option requires that, after the UPDATE statement has been executed, every child row with a non-null foreign key must have the *same* matching parent row that it had before the UPDATE statement. Therefore, ON UPDATE RESTRICT is slightly more restrictive than ON UPDATE NO ACTION. For example, an UPDATE statement that causes two rows of the parent table to exchange their parent key values might violate a RESTRICT constraint but will not violate a NO ACTION constraint. If the constraint is violated, the UPDATE statement fails, and all changes are rolled back.

The default behavior of a foreign key constraint is ON UPDATE NO ACTION.

The foreign key behaviors described above help us to understand why the UDB authorization system provides a REFERENCES privilege, by which the owner of a table can control which users are allowed to create foreign keys that reference the table. To illustrate the importance of the REFERENCES privilege, suppose that you are the owner of a table T1. If another user can create a table T2 with a foreign key that references T1, that user can find the set of parent key values that exist in T1 by inserting various child key values into T2 and noting which inserts are successful. The other user can also prevent you from deleting or updating rows in T1 by inserting matching rows into T2 and specifying a foreign key constraint with ON DELETE NO ACTION. For these reasons, users may not create foreign key constraints that reference a table unless they are granted the REFERENCES privilege by the owner of the table.

It is possible to define a chain of referential integrity relationships in which the child table of one relationship is the parent table of the next, as shown in Figure 7-2. In this way, deletion of a row from the "uppermost" parent table may cause deletions and/or updates to propagate through several related tables. For example, in Figure 7-2, deletion of a row from the DIVISION table would cause the matching rows of DEPT to be deleted, which would in turn cause matching rows of EMP to be deleted and matching foreign keys in EQUIP to be set to null. Note that, in this example, the foreign key columns do not have NOT NULL constraints. Therefore, for example, a row of the DEPT table could have a null DIVNO column, but if its DIVNO column contains a non-null value, that value must match some primary key in the DIVISION table.

A *referential cycle* is defined as a chain of RI relationships that is closed on itself, making a table its own descendant. A self-referencing table (such as the EMP table in Figure 7-1) is the simplest example of a referential cycle. Referential cycles involving more than one table are allowed in UDB only if all the DELETE rules in the cycle are CASCADE.

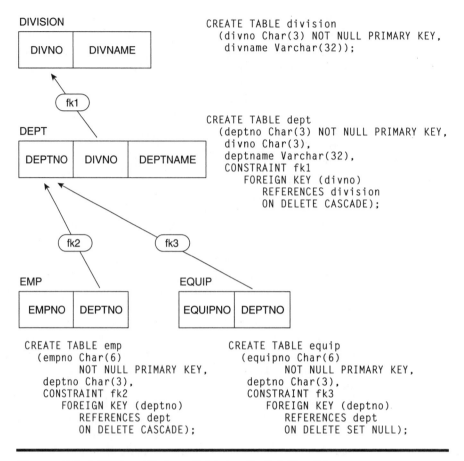

Figure 7-2: A Chain of Referential Integrity Relationships

7.2 CREATING AND DROPPING CONSTRAINTS

Since constraints always apply to a specific table, they are specified as part of the process of creating or altering that table. The basics of the statements for creating and altering tables were described in Chapter 2. This section gives more details about the UDB syntax for these statements, including the features for managing constraints.

The UDB syntax for the CREATE TABLE and ALTER TABLE statements is complex and provides many different ways for doing the same thing. Some of these alternative syntaxes are supported mainly for compatibility with previous versions of DB2 or with other products. This book describes a simplified syntax for CREATE TABLE and ALTER TABLE that provides a consistent and relatively simple way to create and name each kind of constraint. The simplified syntax gives you access to all the features of UDB and is recommended for new applications. However, since UDB is tolerant of other syntactic forms, you should consult the *SQL Reference* if you are migrating an existing application to UDB.

The CREATE TABLE statement allows you to define a constraint either as a *column constraint* or as a *table constraint.* A column constraint is a constraint that applies to a single column of a table and is defined as part of the definition of that column. For example, if an integer column named C1 is the primary key of a given table, that column might be defined by the syntax C1 INTEGER NOT NULL PRIMARY KEY. A table constraint, on the other hand, may involve more than one column of a table. For example, if the primary key of a table includes columns C1 and C2, the definition of the table might contain the following table constraint: PRIMARY KEY (C1, C2).

In the syntax diagrams on the following pages, *table-name* represents a two-part name, such as ACCOUNTS.PAYABLE. The first part of the name is a schema name, and the second part identifies the table within the schema. If the schema name is omitted, it defaults to the userid under which the statement is being compiled (for static SQL) or executed (for dynamic SQL). For example, if user SMITH creates a table named T1, the full name of the table becomes SMITH.T1.

Unlike table names, constraint names consist of a single part. Each constraint name must be unique among all the constraints attached to the same table.

7.2.1 CREATE TABLE Statement

The syntax of a CREATE TABLE statement is shown in the syntax diagrams that follow. For examples of valid CREATE TABLE statements, see the example application in Section 7.4.

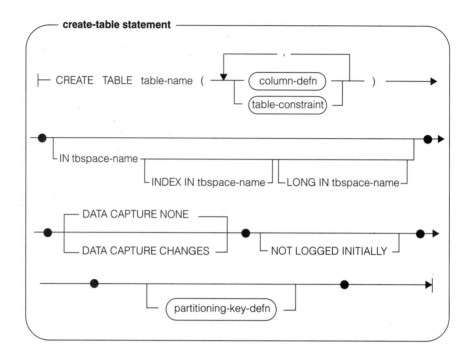

Notes:

- A table may not contain more than 500 columns.
- The sum of the column lengths in a table may not exceed 4,005 bytes.
- In the syntax diagram, *tbspace-name* represents the name of a tablespace, which is a unit of physical storage. The CREATE TABLE statement allows you to specify the tablespace in which your table will be stored and also allows you to specify separately the tablespaces to be used for indexes and large-object values in your table. You might choose to store indexes and large objects in a different tablespace from the rest of your table to increase the clustering of your data and improve performance. If you omit any tablespace specifications, the system will choose a tablespace for you. (Tablespaces are discussed in Section 10.1.)
- The clause DATA CAPTURE CHANGES is necessary if you want changes to your table to be replicated in other databases. This clause causes special entries to be made in the system log in support of data replication. If you omit this clause or specify DATA CAPTURE NONE, no special entries are made in the log when changes are made to your table.

- The clause NOT LOGGED INITIALLY means that any changes made to the table (such as inserting rows into it), in the same transaction in which the table was created, are not recorded in the recovery log. This has the consequence that the table is not protected against system failures, and cannot be used as the parent table of a referential integrity relationship, until a backup copy of the table is made (using the BACKUP command described in Section 10.6). The NOT LOGGED INITIALLY option might be used to reduce logging activity during initial loading of a large table.

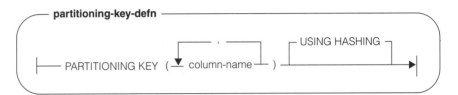

Notes:

- The concept of a *partitioning key* applies to your table only if you create the table in a tablespace that is partitioned across multiple nodes in a parallel database. If this is the case, the partitioning key controls the distribution of rows among the nodes. (Parallel databases are discussed in Section 10.2.) If you create a table in a partitioned tablespace and do not specify a partitioning key, the default partitioning key is the first column of the primary key, or (if the table has no primary key) the first column that does not have a large-object datatype.
- If your table has a partitioning key, the following restrictions apply:

    No column in the partitioning key may have a large-object datatype.

    Data in the partitioning key columns cannot be updated.

    Any primary key or unique key must contain all the columns of the partitioning key.

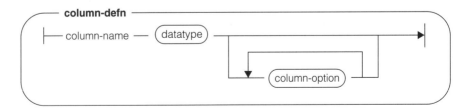

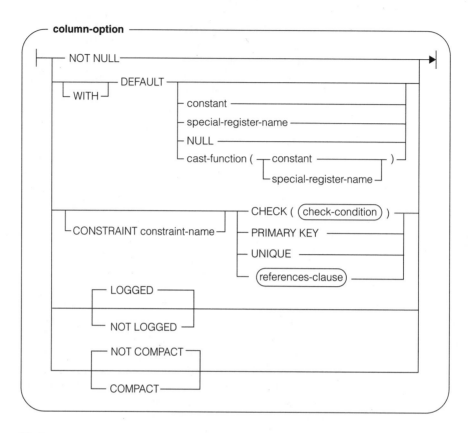

Notes:

- If no explicit default value is specified, the column default value is determined as shown in Table 7-1.

- If no name is specified for a column constraint, the system will generate a name.

- A *check condition* is any predicate, or combination of predicates connected by AND/OR, that can be evaluated by examining a single row of the table. If a check constraint is specified as a column constraint, it may contain references only to the column to which it applies. For example, CHECK (BONUS < 5000) is a valid column constraint that applies to the BONUS column. CHECK (BONUS < SALARY), on the other hand, must be specified as a table constraint, because it involves more than one column.

- If the PRIMARY KEY or UNIQUE option is specified for a column, the NOT NULL option must also be specified for that column.

- The LOGGED/NOT LOGGED and COMPACT/NOT COMPACT options apply only to columns of large-object datatypes (Blob, Clob, Dbclob, and distinct types based on these datatypes). (These options are described in Section 6.1.) The default values for these options are LOGGED and NOT COMPACT.

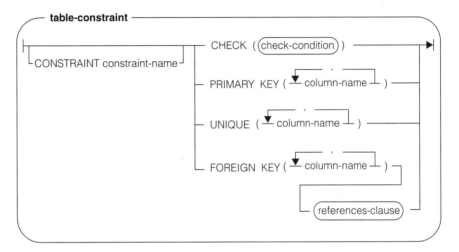

Notes:

- If no name is specified for a table constraint, the system will generate a name.

- A *check condition* is any predicate, or combination of predicates connected by AND/OR, that can be evaluated by examining a single row of the table on which the check constraint is defined.

- If a primary key or unique key is specified, all the participating columns must have been declared NOT NULL.

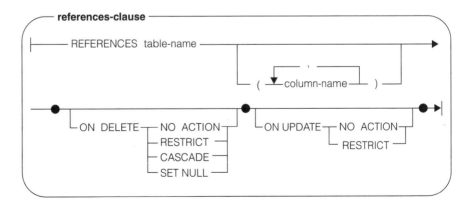

Notes:

- The REFERENCES clause names the parent table of a referential integrity relationship. If column names are specified, they must match the column names of a primary key or unique key of the parent table, which serves as the parent key of the relationship. If no column names are specified, the parent key is implicitly the primary key of the parent table.
- If a CREATE TABLE statement contains a REFERENCES clause, its authid must hold the CONTROL or REFERENCES privilege on the parent table (the REFERENCES privilege may be held on the individual columns of the parent key).
- Default actions are ON DELETE NO ACTION and ON UPDATE NO ACTION.

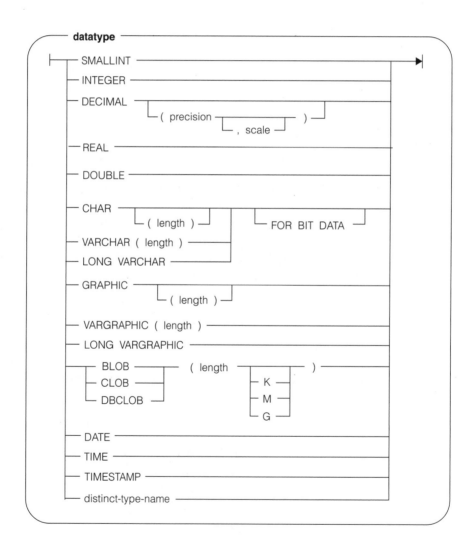

Notes:

- The maximum length of a Char, Varchar, Blob, or Clob datatype is specified in bytes; the maximum length of a Graphic, Vargraphic, or Dbclob datatype is specified in characters, each of which occupies two bytes.

- In specifying the maximum lengths of Blob and Clob datatypes, the suffixes K, M, and G represent 2^{10} bytes (1 kilobyte), 2^{20} bytes (1 megabyte), and 2^{30} bytes (1 gigabyte), respectively. In specifying the maximum length of a Dbclob datatype, these suffixes have similar meanings but refer to the maximum number of two-byte characters.

- For the Char and Graphic datatypes, the default length is 1.

- For the Decimal datatype, the precision indicates the total number of digits and the scale indicates the number of digits to the right of the decimal point. The default precision is 5, and the default scale is 0.

- The FOR BIT DATA option indicates that a character-string datatype is to be used for storing binary data and is not associated with a particular character set or code page.

- Some of the built-in datatypes have synonyms that can be used in place of their proper names. These synonyms are summarized in Table 7-2.

The system catalog tables for each database maintain a complete description of all the tables in the database, as well as the columns they contain and the constraints that apply to them. These catalog tables (which are really views of underlying tables) are found in the SYSCAT schema and are described in Appendix D. The catalog tables that describe tables, columns, and constraints are summarized in Table 7-3.

TABLE 7-2: Synonyms for Built-In Datatypes

Type Name	Synonyms
INTEGER	INT
DECIMAL	DEC, NUMERIC, NUM
REAL	FLOAT(n) where $1 \leq n \leq 24$
DOUBLE	DOUBLE PRECISION, FLOAT, FLOAT(n) where $25 \leq n \leq 53$
CHAR	CHARACTER
VARCHAR	CHARACTER VARYING, CHAR VARYING

TABLE 7-3: System Catalog Tables That Describe Tables, Columns, and Constraints

Catalog Table	Object Described
TABLES	Tables and views
COLUMNS	Columns of tables and views
TABCONST	Constraints and the tables to which they apply
CHECKS	Check constraints
COLCHECKS	Columns that participate in check constraints
REFERENCES	Referential integrity relationships (foreign key constraints)
KEYCOLUSE	Columns that participate in primary, unique, and foreign keys

7.2.2 ALTER TABLE Statement

The ALTER TABLE statement is used to add a column to an existing table, to increase the length of a Varchar column, or to add or drop some other table property such as a constraint. If the constraints that apply to a table are being changed, the authid under which the ALTER TABLE statement is being executed must hold certain privileges in addition to those listed in Table 2-8. These privileges are as follows:

- If any foreign key constraints are being added or dropped, CONTROL or REFERENCES privilege on the parent tables of these constraints (or at least column-level REFERENCES privilege on the columns that make up the parent key).

- If a primary or unique key is being dropped, CONTROL or ALTER privilege on any table that has a referential integrity relationship in which the dropped key is the parent key.

The syntax of an ALTER TABLE statement is shown on the opposite page. Some of the elements used in the ALTER TABLE syntax diagram are used also by the CREATE TABLE statement and were explained in the previous section.

Notes:

- When a column is added to a table and the column definition has the NOT NULL option, it must also have a DEFAULT clause. The default value is used for the value of the new column in the existing rows of the table.

- Adding a primary key, unique key, foreign key, or check constraint to a table causes the constraint to be checked against all existing data (unless the table is

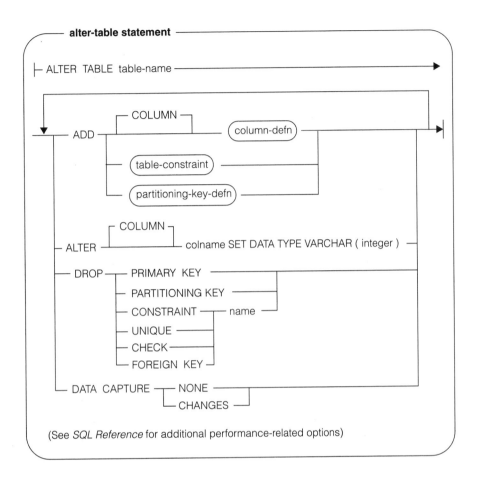

(See *SQL Reference* for additional performance-related options)

in Check Pending state); if it fails, the ALTER TABLE is rolled back. (Check Pending state is described in Section 10.7.5.)

- The ALTER COLUMN clause can be used only to increase the length of an existing column of type Varchar. The new column length must be less than 4,000, and it may not result in a violation of the maximum length of a row (4,005 bytes) or the maximum length of a unique key (255 bytes).

- The DATA CAPTURE phrase allows you to turn on and off the saving of special information in the system log in support of data replication.

- In addition to the options shown here, the ALTER TABLE allows you to change certain performance-related properties of the table, affecting (for example) the size of locks acquired on the table and the placement of its rows in physical storage. Details of these options are described in the *SQL Reference*.

The following are examples of ALTER TABLE statements:

```
ALTER TABLE equip
   ADD COLUMN description Varchar(20)
   ADD COLUMN value Decimal(8,2);
ALTER TABLE equip
   ALTER COLUMN description SET DATA TYPE Varchar(60)
   ADD CONSTRAINT check1 CHECK (value < 500000);
ALTER TABLE equip
   DROP CONSTRAINT check1;
```

TIP: If your ALTER TABLE statement has multiple ADD and DROP clauses, remember that there are no commas between the clauses.

TIP: You can add a primary key or unique key to an existing table only if all the columns in the key were declared NOT NULL when the table was created. If some of the columns in the desired key do not have the NOT NULL property (even if they do not in fact contain any nulls), you are out of luck, since there is no way to add the NOT NULL property to an existing column.

7.3 TRIGGERS

A trigger is like a genie that you can place inside the database, to wake up and do your bidding whenever a certain event takes place. You can tell your genie to wake up and execute a series of SQL statements whenever data is inserted, deleted, or updated in a specific table. Triggers are powerful tools that can be used to enforce the validity of data in ways that cannot be done by a simple constraint. They can also be used to make sure that whenever a certain action occurs in the database, another action automatically occurs. This automatic action can affect any database table or even the world outside the database. Triggers are ideal for keeping audit trails, detecting exceptional conditions, and maintaining relationships in the database.

When you create a trigger, you will need to specify the following parts:

1. *Name.* Like a table, a trigger has a two-part name that includes a schema name. The trigger name must be unique within its schema (not just within the table to which it is attached).

2. *Triggering event.* The triggering event is the event that causes the trigger to be activated. In general, a triggering event is the insertion, deletion, or update of rows in a specific table. If the triggering event is an update, it may apply to all columns of the table or only to specific named columns. A trigger is said to be *attached* to the table named in its triggering event. A trigger is always attached to a real table, not a view. (Of course, if a trigger is attached to a table, it is activated when the table is manipulated through a view defined on it.)

3. *Activation time.* The activation time of a trigger is always either *before* or *after* its triggering event takes place in the database.

   The following are some examples of triggering events and activation times:

   ```
   BEFORE INSERT ON books
   AFTER DELETE ON voters
   AFTER UPDATE ON inventory
   AFTER UPDATE OF jobcode, salary ON emp
   ```

   There is no limit on the number of triggers that can be attached to a table. Multiple triggers that have the same triggering event and activation time will be executed in the order of their creation.

4. *Granularity.* The SQL statement that caused the triggering event may insert, delete, or update multiple rows in the database. The definer of the trigger can specify whether the trigger is to be activated only once for such an SQL statement or once for each row that is modified. We will refer to this distinction as the *granularity* of the trigger, and we will refer to the two types of triggers as *statement triggers* and *row triggers*, respectively. The definition of a statement trigger contains the phrase FOR EACH STATEMENT, and the definition of a row trigger contains the phrase FOR EACH ROW. If an SQL INSERT, DELETE, or UPDATE statement operates on a table but modifies zero rows, it may activate a statement trigger but will not activate a row trigger.

   As you can see, there are three ways to classify triggers: according to their activation time (*before* or *after*), their trigger event (*insert, delete,* or *update*), and their granularity (*statement* or *row*). A trigger is sometimes referred to by one or more of its properties, as in a *before trigger,* an *after update trigger,* or a *before insert row trigger.*

   Before triggers must always be row triggers (before statement triggers are not supported by UDB).

5. *Transition variables.* When a trigger is activated, it often needs to make use of information about the specific database change that activated it. For example,

an update row trigger may need to see the data values in the updated row, both before and after the update. Similarly, a delete statement trigger may need to see all the rows that were deleted by the triggering statement. This kind of transitional information can be made available to the trigger in the form of *transition variables*. There are four kinds of transition variables:

- The *old row variable* represents the value of the modified row before the triggering event.

- The *new row variable* represents the value of the modified row after the triggering event.

- The *old table variable* represents a hypothetical read-only table containing all the modified rows as they appeared before the triggering event.

- The *new table variable* represents a hypothetical table containing all the modified rows as they appeared after the triggering event.

When defining a trigger, you can define transition variables in an optional REFERENCING clause, giving them any names you like. A trigger definition may include more than one transition variable but at most one variable of each type. In the REFERENCING clauses shown below, the first two examples define row transition variables, and the last two examples define table transition variables.

```
REFERENCING NEW AS newrow
REFERENCING OLD AS lastyear NEW AS thisyear
REFERENCING OLD_TABLE AS oldtable
REFERENCING NEW_TABLE AS arrivals
```

Row transition variables may be used in a trigger definition as though they were correlation names. Table transition variables may be used in a trigger definition as though they were table names (but only for the purpose of querying these tables, not for modifying them). Thus, using the transition variables defined in the first example above, an after update trigger might refer to salary values before and after the update as `oldrow.salary` and `newrow.salary`. Or, using the transition variable defined in the third example above, an after delete trigger might compute the number of rows that were deleted by the subquery (`SELECT count(*) FROM oldtable`).

For certain types of triggers, only some of the four possible transition variables can be used. For example, insert triggers can use new transition variables but not old transition variables, because a newly inserted row has no old value. For a similar reason, delete triggers can use old transition variables but not new transition variables. Table 7-4 summarizes the types of transition variables that are valid for each type of trigger.

It is interesting to note that old and new table transition variables can be used in an after row trigger. Even though such a trigger is executed once for each modified row, the *set* of rows to be modified is computed (and the old and new table transition variables are defined) before any of the after row triggers are executed.

6. *Trigger condition.* A trigger condition is a test that evaluates to true, false, or unknown. It may contain one or more predicates, much like a WHERE clause (though a trigger condition starts with WHEN instead of WHERE). A trigger condition can include transition variables and subqueries, as in the following examples:

```
WHEN (newrow.salary < oldrow.salary)
WHEN (newrow.salary > (SELECT max(salary)
                       FROM emp
                       WHERE jobcode = newrow.jobcode) )
WHEN (SELECT count(*) FROM oldtable) > 100
```

When the trigger is activated, the trigger body is executed only if the trigger condition is true. For example, the first trigger condition above specifies that the trigger body should be executed only if the SALARY value after the update is less than the SALARY value before the update. If no trigger condition is specified, the trigger body is executed unconditionally.

7. *Trigger body.* The trigger body consists of one or more SQL statements. Depending on the type of trigger, there may be some restrictions (which we will discuss below) on the types of statements that can be used in the trigger body. If the trigger body contains more than one SQL statement, the statements are enclosed between BEGIN ATOMIC and END, and are separated by semicolons. The word ATOMIC indicates that a trigger body behaves like an atomic compound SQL statement (discussed in Section 4.1.13). If any statement in the trigger body fails, the triggering SQL statement and all actions of

TABLE 7-4: Transition Variables Used by Various Types of Triggers

Triggering Event and Activation Time	Row Trigger Can Use . . .	Statement Trigger Can Use . . .
BEFORE INSERT	New row	(Invalid)
BEFORE UPDATE	Old row, new row	(Invalid)
BEFORE DELETE	Old row	(Invalid)
AFTER INSERT	New row New table	New table
AFTER UPDATE	Old row, new row Old table, new table	Old table, new table
AFTER DELETE	Old row Old table	Old table

all triggers activated by that statement are rolled back and an SQLCODE of −723 (SQLSTATE 09000) is returned for the triggering statement. The SQL-CODE and SQLSTATE generated by the failing statement (inside the trigger body) are also returned as part of the error message (contained in the SQL-ERRMC field of the SQLCA structure). Although the triggering statement is rolled back, the current transaction is still considered to be in progress, and the application is free to execute additional statements, commit, or roll back the transaction.

7.3.1 Creating and Dropping Triggers

The syntax of a CREATE TRIGGER statement is shown below. Remember that a trigger name is a two-part name and that its schema name (first part) defaults to the current userid.

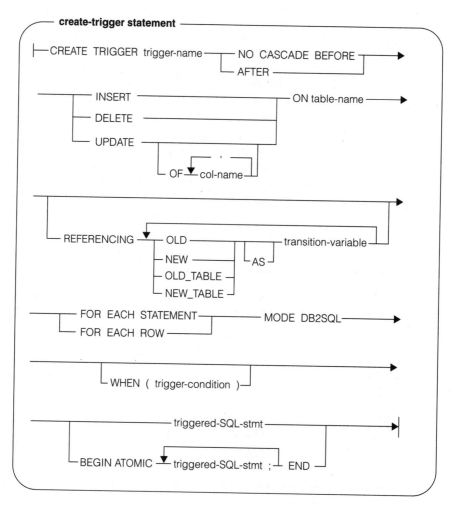

The table to which the trigger is attached (that is, the table in the ON clause) must be a real table (not a view), and it must not be a system catalog table.

The required phrase NO CASCADE in the creation of a before trigger serves as a reminder that a before trigger never activates another before trigger.

The required phrase MODE DB2SQL represents the trigger execution mode currently implemented by UDB. This phrase ensures that your existing applications will not be affected if alternative trigger execution modes are added to the product in the future.

The user who executes a CREATE TRIGGER statement must have DBADM authority, SYSADM authority, or all of the following:

- CREATEIN privilege on the schema of the trigger, or IMPLICIT_SCHEMA authority to implicitly create a new schema

- ALTER or CONTROL privilege on the table to which the trigger is attached, or ALTERIN privilege on the schema of this table

- Sufficient privileges to execute all the SQL statements in the trigger body

- SELECT privilege on the table to which the trigger is attached, if the CREATE TRIGGER statement contains any transition variables

- SELECT privilege on all the tables referenced in the trigger condition

The body of a trigger is always executed under the authority of the user who created the trigger, not the authority of the user who happened to activate it. For example, suppose that user Barney defines a trigger on insert to the PROGRAMS table, which updates a row in the BUDGET table by adding the cost of each new program. In order to define this trigger, Barney must possess UPDATE privilege on the BUDGET table. Now suppose that user Wilma inserts a new entry into the PROGRAMS table. Of course, in order to do this, Wilma must have INSERT privilege on PROGRAMS, but she need not possess UPDATE privilege on BUDGET, even though her action will cause BUDGET to be updated by activating Barney's trigger.

The definition of each trigger is recorded in the system catalog table named TRIGGERS. A descriptive comment can be added to this catalog table by using the COMMENT statement described in Section 2.6.9.

When a trigger is no longer needed, it can be dropped by using the DROP statement described in Section 2.6.8. The following is an example of a statement used to drop a trigger:

```
DROP TRIGGER emp_trig1;
```

Before continuing with our discussion of triggers, we will introduce two special SQL statements that can be used only inside the body of a trigger: the *assignment statement* and the *SIGNAL statement.*

7.3.2 Assignment Statement

Assignment statements are used only in before triggers. The usual purpose of a before trigger is to modify the behavior of an INSERT or UPDATE statement. A before trigger can accomplish this purpose by using an assignment statement to assign values to the columns of the "new row" that is about to be inserted or updated.

An assignment statement begins with the keyword SET and looks much like the SET clause of an UPDATE statement. The syntax of an assignment statement is as follows:

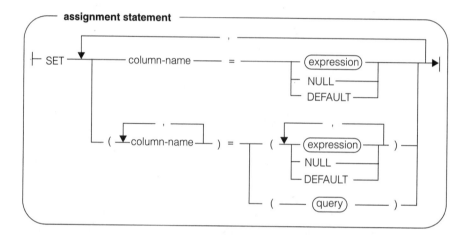

The column names on the left side of the equal sign in an assignment statement must match the names of columns in the table to which the trigger is attached. The effect of the assignment statement is to replace the values of the "new row"—that is, the row that is about to be inserted or updated—with the values on the right side of the equal sign. By modifying the values of the "new row," a before trigger can generate missing values automatically or override the values that were provided by the triggering SQL statement.

Since only the "new row" can be modified by an assignment statement, you might suppose that the system would not need any further qualification of the column names on the left side of the assignments. Nevertheless, UDB enforces the following rules:

1. Any before trigger that contains an assignment statement must define a "new row" transition variable.

2. If the trigger defines only a "new row" transition variable, column names in assignment statements (on both sides of the equal sign) may be unqualified and implicitly reference the "new row."

3. If the trigger defines both a "new row" and an "old row" transition variable, all column names in assignment statements (on both sides of the equal sign) must be qualified by a transition variable. Of course, the column names on the left side must be qualified by the "new row" variable.

The values on the right side of the equal sign in an assignment statement are the values that are being assigned to the columns of the new row. General expressions may be used, containing arithmetic operators and functions, either built-in or user-defined. The word DEFAULT represents the default value of the column being assigned. There must be a one-to-one correspondence between the values and the columns to which they are being assigned. If a subquery is used on the right side of the equal sign to generate a list of column values, the subquery must return only a single row. If an assignment statement assigns values to multiple columns, all the right-hand sides are evaluated before any of the assignments are done.

The following are examples of valid assignment statements:

```
SET newrow.startdate = CURRENT DATE;
SET deptno = 'A52', bonus = 1000;
SET newrow.perimeter = perimeter(newrow.parcel);
SET salary = (SELECT min(salary)
                FROM emp
                WHERE jobcode = newrow.jobcode);
```

The user who creates a trigger containing an assignment statement must have either SYSADM or DBADM authority or both of the following:

- UPDATE privilege for the columns referenced on the left side of the assignment statement

- SELECT privilege for the columns or tables referenced on the right side of the assignment statement (including tables referenced in subqueries)

7.3.3 SIGNAL Statement

The purpose of a SIGNAL statement is to raise an error condition and to roll back the effects of an SQL statement. A SIGNAL statement can be used in either a before trigger or an after trigger. It rolls back the effects of the triggering SQL statement[2] and also rolls back all the changes caused by triggers and

---

2. A SIGNAL statement may be executed by a trigger that was activated by another trigger or by a cascading referential integrity action. In this case, the SIGNAL statement rolls back not just the specific event that activated its trigger but also the user's original SQL statement, including all the triggers and cascading actions that it invoked.

cascading referential integrity relationships invoked by the triggering SQL statement. However, the SIGNAL statement leaves a transaction in progress, so the user or application program can still choose to commit or roll back the other statements in the transaction.

The syntax of a SIGNAL statement is as follows:

signal statement

SIGNAL SQLSTATE state (message)

The state specified in a SIGNAL statement must be expressed in the form of a character-string literal containing exactly five characters, such as '70ABC'. The five characters must all be digits or uppercase letters. In choosing an SQL-STATE to represent a user-defined error condition, you should avoid values that have been reserved by IBM or by the SQL92 Standard. You can easily avoid conflicts by choosing an SQLSTATE whose first character is a digit between 7 and 9 or a letter between I and Z, inclusive.[3] The message specified by a SIGNAL statement can be any expression that evaluates to a string of up to 70 characters.

When a SIGNAL statement is executed inside the body of a trigger, the triggering SQL statement (and all changes derived from it) are rolled back. The application that executed the triggering statement receives the SQLSTATE specified by the SIGNAL statement and an SQLCODE of –438. The message specified by the SIGNAL statement is also returned to the calling application (in the SQLERRMC field of the SQLCA structure).

The following are examples of valid SIGNAL statements:

```
SIGNAL SQLSTATE '70001' ('No such jobcode');
SIGNAL SQLSTATE 'PR099'
          ('Invalid project: ' || char(newrow.project) );
```

7.3.4 Before Triggers

As we have seen, one of the ways of classifying triggers involves before triggers, which are activated before the triggering SQL statement is executed, and after triggers, which are activated after the triggering SQL statement is executed. Although before triggers and after triggers are syntactically similar, they are quite different in purpose and in the SQL statements that can be used in

---

3. Certain other SQLSTATE values are also permitted and are described in the *SQL Reference*.

their trigger bodies. Before triggers can be thought of as a powerful form of constraint, whereas after triggers often contain more general application logic. Because of these important differences, I will discuss before triggers and after triggers separately.

I will illustrate before and after triggers by writing some sample triggers that operate on a version of the familiar table named EMP, containing employee records. In this chapter, let us assume that the EMP table contains the following columns:

EMP

EMPNO	NAME	DEPTNO	JOBCODE	PROJECT	MANAGER	SALARY	BONUS

As we have seen, before triggers are always row triggers. Before triggers are usually used to "condition" data values before they are entered into the database by an INSERT or UPDATE statement. For example, suppose that a given column of a table is subject to a NOT NULL constraint. A before trigger can be used to generate a value for that column whenever data is inserted into the table, using an algorithm that is not limited to the system-provided default value. This kind of data conditioning must be done by a before trigger rather than by an after trigger, because an after trigger would be too late. (By the time an after trigger could be activated, the insert statement would already have failed by violating the constraint.)

TIP: If a column is declared NOT NULL and its default values are generated by a before trigger, the definition of the column must also include a DEFAULT clause. The specified default value will be generated for the column and then overridden by the default value provided by the before trigger. If you specify NOT NULL but omit the DEFAULT clause, the system will not allow a row to be inserted into the table unless it contains an explicit value for the column, and the before trigger will never be activated.

Since before triggers are intended for conditioning of data that is about to be entered into the database, they are not allowed to manipulate the database itself. For this reason, only the following kinds of SQL statements are permitted in the body of a before trigger:

Assignment (SET) statements that modify the "new row"

SELECT

VALUES

SIGNAL

If your trigger needs to update the database in a more general way, using an SQL INSERT, DELETE, or UPDATE statement, you should write an after trigger rather than a before trigger. Since a before trigger never modifies the database directly, the execution of a before trigger can never activate another before trigger (this is the meaning of the required phrase NO CASCADE in the statement that creates a before trigger). However, if a before trigger modifies a column of the new row that was not modified by the original SQL statement, it may enlarge the list of after triggers that will be activated after the statement has been executed.

SELECT and VALUES statements are used in triggers mainly for invoking functions that have some side effect such as sending a message or writing into a file. Often these functions will be user-defined.

TIP: Suppose that you write a trigger that calls a function that performs some external action such as sending a message. If some statement that activates the trigger is executed and then rolled back, the database system has no way to undo the external action. Therefore, you must use such functions very carefully and provide your own mechanism to generate compensating external actions in the case of a rollback.

I will illustrate before triggers with several examples. The first example illustrates conditioning of data by automatically computing the starting salary and bonus of a newly hired employee, using a separate table of starting pay based on job code. This trigger might be used to enforce a company policy about starting pay, eliminating the necessity to embed this policy in every application program that inserts new employees. Note the use of the "new row" transition variable in the subquery.

```
CREATE TRIGGER emp_trig1
    NO CASCADE BEFORE INSERT ON emp
    REFERENCING NEW AS newrow
    FOR EACH ROW MODE DB2SQL
    SET (salary, bonus) =
      (SELECT salary, bonus
       FROM startingPay
       WHERE jobcode = newrow.jobcode);
```

It is possible for a before trigger to override the values that were provided by the triggering SQL statement. For example, the following before trigger limits salary increases to 50%. Salary increases of less than 50% are applied without modification. In this example, the assignment statement is required to use the "new row" transition variable on the left side of the equal sign (because both "old row" and "new row" transition variables are defined).

```
CREATE TRIGGER emp_trig2
    NO CASCADE BEFORE UPDATE OF salary ON emp
    REFERENCING OLD AS oldrow NEW AS newrow
    FOR EACH ROW MODE DB2SQL
    WHEN (newrow.salary > 1.5 * oldrow.salary)
    SET newrow.salary = 1.5 * oldrow.salary;
```

Of course, before triggers can be used to detect exceptional conditions and roll back SQL statements that attempt to modify the database in anomalous ways. Triggers that detect exceptional conditions are similar to check constraints but are more powerful, because they are not limited to examining the new values of a single row. The following example illustrates a trigger that prevents the deletion of any employee whose importance, as computed by a user-defined function, exceeds a given value. Triggers such as this one can be used to define and enforce corporate policies in a central way that applies to all existing and future applications.

```
CREATE TRIGGER emp_trig3
    NO CASCADE BEFORE DELETE ON emp
    REFERENCING OLD AS oldrow
    FOR EACH ROW MODE DB2SQL
    WHEN (importance(oldrow.jobcode, oldrow.project) > 20)
    SIGNAL SQLSTATE '70010' ('We need this person');
```

A before trigger can automatically generate a unique value whenever a row is inserted into a table, by using the generate_unique function. This built-in function returns a value, of type Char(13) FOR BIT DATA, that is unique on each function call. The unique value is based on the timestamp at the time of the function call. To illustrate this technique, suppose that a table named SHIPMENTS has a column named PKG_ID. Each row inserted into SHIPMENTS can be given a unique PKG_ID value by the following trigger:

```
CREATE TRIGGER shipment_trig1
    NO CASCADE BEFORE INSERT ON shipments
    REFERENCING NEW AS newrow
    FOR EACH ROW MODE DB2SQL
    SET pkg_id = generate_unique();
```

The built-in timestamp function can be applied to a value generated by the generate_unique function to convert it to UTC timestamp. Then, if desired, the local date and time can be extracted from the timestamp by adding the local time zone and using the built-in date and time functions. For example, the following query lists all shipments of more than 1,000 parts, with the date

and time of each shipment, based on the unique values generated by the trigger shown above.

```
SELECT date(timestamp(pkg_id)+CURRENT TIMEZONE) AS date,
       time(timestamp(pkg_id)+CURRENT TIMEZONE) AS time,
       part, quantity
FROM shipments WHERE quantity > 1000;
```

TIP: If you like, you can designate a column containing values generated by a
trigger, such as the PKG_ID column in the example above, to be a primary or
unique key. If you do this, you are also required to declare the column to be
NOT NULL. You must then provide some non-null value for the generated
column each time you insert a row into the table. The value you insert into
the generated column does not matter, since it will be overridden by the trigger.

7.3.5 After Triggers

Like before triggers, after triggers have triggering events, optional trigger conditions, and trigger bodies. However, after triggers differ from before triggers
in the following ways:

1. An after trigger is executed only after the triggering SQL statement, and all its
constraints, have been executed successfully. Thus, the after trigger sees the
effects not only of the triggering statement but also of all the cascaded
updates and deletions caused by any foreign key constraints that are invoked
by the triggering statement. If more than one after trigger is activated by a
given statement, each trigger can see the effects on the database that are
caused by triggers that were activated before it.

2. After triggers can have a granularity of either FOR EACH STATEMENT or FOR
EACH ROW.

3. An after trigger is not restricted to modifying the row that triggered it. An after
trigger can operate on any table in the database and can contain any of the
following kinds of SQL statements:

INSERT
DELETE
UPDATE
SELECT
VALUES
SIGNAL

Since after triggers can modify the database directly, execution of an after trigger can activate other triggers. To guard against loops, the system imposes a limit of 16 levels on the nesting of triggers.

After triggers are often used to implement some desired semantic behavior of stored data. Because there are fewer restrictions on the body of an after trigger, they are more powerful than before triggers. I will illustrate the use of after triggers with several examples.

The first example is a trigger that could be expressed either as a before trigger or as an after trigger. It enforces a policy (sadly, true only for our hypothetical company) that salaries never decrease. Furthermore, whenever an update is detected that attempts to decrease some employee's salary, the trigger invokes a user-defined function called logEvent. This example illustrates how a trigger can interact with the world outside the database. The logEvent function, which is written in C, can take some action such as writing into a file or sending a message (however, you should remember that functions are executed on the server machine, so that is where any actions will take place). In this example, assume that the logEvent function takes three parameters: a string identifying the type of event, a timestamp, and another string that provides additional details. Of course, the user who wrote the logEvent function can define its parameters and its actions in any way desired, using the techniques for defining an external function described in Chapter 6. The trigger in this example uses a VALUES statement when it needs to invoke a function without accessing a table.

```
CREATE TRIGGER emp_trig4
    AFTER UPDATE OF salary ON emp
    REFERENCING OLD AS oldrow NEW AS newrow
    FOR EACH ROW MODE DB2SQL
    WHEN (newrow.salary < oldrow.salary)
    BEGIN ATOMIC
        VALUES (logEvent('Salary decrease',
                            CURRENT TIMESTAMP, oldrow.empno));
        SIGNAL SQLSTATE '70011'
            ('Salary decrease for employee ' || oldrow.empno);
    END
```

The next after trigger example will show how two or more tables can be linked in such a way that updates to one table automatically trigger updates to another. Assume that the database contains a table named TEMPS that is updated periodically to contain the current temperature at various locations. The TEMPS table contains columns named PLACE and TEMP, and the PLACE column is the primary key. On a typical winter day, the contents of the table might look like this:

TEMPS

PLACE	TEMP
Anchorage	–15
Denver	25
Madison	8
Miami	82
San Francisco	65
Washington	35

We wish to create a trigger that will automatically maintain an auxiliary table, named EXTREMES, that keeps records of the maximum and minimum temperatures ever encountered in each place, as well as the dates on which they occurred. The structure of the auxiliary table is as follows:

EXTREMES

PLACE	HIGHTEMP	HIGHDATE	LOWTEMP	LOWDATE

First, we will create the EXTREMES table and populate it with a row for each place recorded in the TEMPS table. Each row of EXTREMES will initially have nulls for its high and low temperatures and their respective dates. The statements used to create and populate the table are as follows:

```
CREATE TABLE extremes
   (place    Varchar(20) NOT NULL,
    hightemp Integer,
    highdate Date,
    lowtemp  Integer,
    lowdate  Date,
    PRIMARY KEY (place) );
INSERT INTO extremes(place)
    SELECT place FROM temps;
```

Next, we will write a pair of triggers that inspect each update to the TEMPS table and copy the temperature and the current date into the proper cells of the EXTREMES table if a new high or low temperature occurs (or if the relevant cell of EXTREMES contains a null, indicating that no high or low temperature is yet recorded).

```
CREATE TRIGGER temps_trig1
    AFTER UPDATE ON temps
    REFERENCING NEW AS newrow
    FOR EACH ROW MODE DB2SQL
    WHEN (newrow.temp >
            (SELECT hightemp
             FROM    extremes
             WHERE   place = newrow.place)
        OR
          (SELECT hightemp
           FROM extremes
           WHERE place = newrow.place) IS NULL )
    UPDATE extremes
        SET hightemp = newrow.temp,
            highdate = CURRENT DATE
        WHERE place = newrow.place;

CREATE TRIGGER temps_trig2
    AFTER UPDATE ON temps
    REFERENCING NEW AS newrow
    FOR EACH ROW MODE DB2SQL
    WHEN (newrow.temp <
            (SELECT lowtemp
             FROM    extremes
             WHERE   place = newrow.place)
        OR
          (SELECT lowtemp
           FROM extremes
           WHERE place = newrow.place) IS NULL )
    UPDATE extremes
        SET lowtemp = newrow.temp,
            lowdate = CURRENT DATE
        WHERE place = newrow.place;
```

The triggers defined above will maintain the EXTREMES table properly when rows of the TEMPS table are updated, but we still have a problem to solve: what happens when new places are added to the TEMPS table, or when old places are deleted?

When a new place is added to the TEMPS table (by inserting a new row, since PLACE is the primary key), we can make sure the same place is added to the EXTREMES table by creating another trigger. The trigger will insert a row into EXTREMES, using the initial temperature of the new place as both the high and the low temperatures.

```
CREATE TRIGGER temps_trig3
    AFTER INSERT ON temps
    REFERENCING NEW AS newrow
    FOR EACH ROW MODE DB2SQL
    INSERT INTO extremes(place, hightemp, highdate,
                                      lowtemp, lowdate)
        VALUES(newrow.place, newrow.temp, CURRENT DATE,
                          newrow.temp, CURRENT DATE);
```

When a row is deleted from TEMPS, we could choose to keep the corresponding row in EXTREMES or to delete it. If our policy is to delete rows from EXTREMES that have no matching row in TEMPS, we can take advantage of the fact that PLACE is the primary key of TEMPS. The following foreign key constraint will ensure that when a place is deleted from TEMPS, it is also deleted from EXTREMES:

```
ALTER TABLE extremes
    ADD CONSTRAINT fk1 FOREIGN KEY(place) REFERENCES temps
        ON DELETE CASCADE;
```

After triggers are very well suited for maintaining an *audit trail*, or record of updates that have been made to the database. We will consider a very simple example of how a set of after statement triggers could be used to maintain an audit trail for a specific table. Suppose that our database contains a table called ACCOUNTS and that we wish to keep a record of all changes that are made to this table. Suppose further that, in this example, it is sufficient to record the user making the change, the type of change and when it occurred, and the number of rows that were changed. First, we create an auxiliary table named ACCOUNT_CHANGES in which the changes will be recorded. The structure of this table and the statement that is used to create it are shown below:

ACCOUNT_CHANGES

TYPE	WHEN	BYWHOM	NROWS

```
CREATE TABLE account_changes
    (type   Char(1),
     when   Timestamp,
     bywhom Char(8),
     nrows  Integer);
```

Next, we create a set of three after triggers that link the ACCOUNT_CHANGES table to the ACCOUNTS table in such a way that any changes to ACCOUNTS are automatically journalled in ACCOUNT_CHANGES. Notice that, since these triggers record aggregate changes rather than specific values, they use table transition variables rather than row transition variables. Notice also that the insert and update triggers use new table variables and that the delete trigger uses an old table variable.

```
CREATE TRIGGER account_trig1
    AFTER INSERT ON accounts
    REFERENCING NEW_TABLE AS newtable
    FOR EACH STATEMENT MODE DB2SQL
    INSERT INTO account_changes(type, when, bywhom, nrows)
        VALUES('I', CURRENT TIMESTAMP, USER,
            (SELECT COUNT(*) FROM newtable) );

CREATE TRIGGER account_trig2
    AFTER UPDATE ON accounts
    REFERENCING NEW_TABLE AS newtable
    FOR EACH STATEMENT MODE DB2SQL
    INSERT INTO account_changes(type, when, bywhom, nrows)
        VALUES('U', CURRENT TIMESTAMP, USER,
            (SELECT COUNT(*) FROM newtable) );

CREATE TRIGGER account_trig3
    AFTER DELETE ON accounts
    REFERENCING OLD_TABLE AS oldtable
    FOR EACH STATEMENT MODE DB2SQL
    INSERT INTO account_changes(type, when, bywhom, nrows)
        VALUES('D', CURRENT TIMESTAMP, USER,
            (SELECT COUNT(*) FROM oldtable) );
```

The three triggers shown above will make entries in the ACCOUNT_CHANGES table to record all INSERT, UPDATE, and DELETE statements that apply to the ACCOUNTS table, including statements that did not actually modify any rows (these will result in entries with NROWS = 0).

7.3.6 Recursive Triggers

As we have seen, a trigger body may apply some updates to the database, and these updates may in turn cause more triggers to be executed. If the updates applied by a particular trigger can cause that same trigger to be executed again, we say that the trigger is *recursive*. Great care is needed in writing recursive triggers, because they can easily lead to loops or to statements that are too complex for the system to handle.

We will illustrate recursive triggers by a simple example. Suppose that we decide to record, for each employee in our organization, the total number of other employees that the employee manages, either directly or indirectly. We will add a new column named SPAN to the EMP table for this purpose. A high-level manager might be responsible for a multilevel "tree" of employees, and the total number of employees in this tree will be recorded in the SPAN column for the manager's row in EMP. The following statement might be used to add the desired new column:

```
ALTER TABLE emp ADD COLUMN span Integer WITH DEFAULT;
```

The WITH DEFAULT clause ensures that when new employees are added to the database, they receive an initial SPAN of zero, the system-provided default value for the Integer datatype.

After setting SPAN to the correct value for all of our existing employees, we would like to create a series of triggers that will automatically maintain the SPAN column as employees are inserted, deleted, and moved from one manager to another. This might be done by the following triggers (note that we have chosen the "!" character as a statement terminator in these examples, since the semicolon is used to separate individual statements inside one of the trigger bodies):

```
CREATE TRIGGER emp_hire
   AFTER INSERT ON emp
   REFERENCING NEW AS newrow
   FOR EACH ROW MODE DB2SQL
   UPDATE emp
      SET span = span + 1
      WHERE empno = newrow.manager!

CREATE TRIGGER emp_quit
   AFTER DELETE ON emp
   REFERENCING OLD AS oldrow
   FOR EACH ROW MODE DB2SQL
   UPDATE emp
      SET span = span - 1
      WHERE empno = oldrow.manager!

CREATE TRIGGER emp_transfer
   AFTER UPDATE OF manager ON emp
   REFERENCING OLD AS oldrow NEW AS newrow
```

```
FOR EACH ROW MODE DB2SQL
BEGIN ATOMIC
    UPDATE emp
    SET span = span - 1
    WHERE empno = oldrow.manager;

    UPDATE emp
    SET span = span + 1
    WHERE empno = newrow.manager;
END!

CREATE TRIGGER emp_propagate
    AFTER UPDATE OF span ON emp
    REFERENCING OLD AS oldrow NEW AS newrow
    FOR EACH ROW MODE DB2SQL
    UPDATE emp
        SET span = span + newrow.span - oldrow.span
        WHERE empno = newrow.manager!
```

To see how this set of triggers is recursive, consider what happens when an employee transfers from one manager to another. The update of the MANAGER column activates the trigger named EMP_TRANSFER, which increases the span of the new manager and decreases the span of the old manager. The updates to the SPAN column of the new and old manager, in turn, activate the trigger named EMP_PROPAGATE, which increases the span of the new second-level manager and decreases the span of the old second-level manager. Each time the EMP_PROPAGATE trigger updates the span of a manager, it activates itself again recursively to update the span of the manager at the next level. Since the compiler doesn't know how many levels of management are represented in the database, it generates a program that can handle 16 levels of recursion; if more levels than this are encountered when the statement is executed, a run-time error (SQLSTATE 54038, SQLCODE –724) results.

The reason that recursive triggers are so tricky is that you need to avoid a situation called *multiple recursion*. Multiple recursion occurs when a recursive trigger activates itself more than once, or when a recursive trigger activates more than one other recursive trigger. Whenever UDB encounters an SQL statement that invokes a multiply recursive trigger, it will fail to compile that statement, generating an error message such as "Statement too long or too complex." To see how easy it is to fall into the trap of multiple recursion, let us modify the previous example slightly. Suppose that, instead of recording the manager of each employee, we have a table that records the mother and father of each person. The table also records the total number of descendants of each person, using the following columns:

PERSONS

NAME	MOTHER	FATHER	DESCENDANTS

We would like to write a set of triggers that is activated when a new person is inserted into the table and that automatically adds one to the DESCENDANTS column of all the new person's ancestors. Such a set of triggers might be written as follows:

```
CREATE TRIGGER new_mother
    AFTER INSERT ON persons
    REFERENCING NEW AS newrow
    FOR EACH ROW MODE DB2SQL
    UPDATE persons
        SET descendants = descendants + 1
        WHERE name = newrow.mother;

CREATE TRIGGER new_father
    AFTER INSERT ON persons
    REFERENCING NEW AS newrow
    FOR EACH ROW MODE DB2SQL
    UPDATE persons
        SET descendants = descendants + 1
        WHERE name = newrow.father;

CREATE TRIGGER maternal_ancestor
    AFTER UPDATE OF descendants ON persons
    REFERENCING OLD AS oldrow NEW AS newrow
    FOR EACH ROW MODE DB2SQL
    UPDATE persons
        SET descendants = descendants +
            newrow.descendants - oldrow.descendants
        WHERE name = newrow.mother;

CREATE TRIGGER paternal_ancestor
    AFTER UPDATE OF descendants ON persons
    REFERENCING OLD AS oldrow NEW AS newrow
    FOR EACH ROW MODE DB2SQL
    UPDATE persons
        SET descendants = descendants +
            newrow.descendants - oldrow.descendants
        WHERE name = newrow.father;
```

To see why this set of triggers is multiply recursive, consider what happens when a new person is inserted into the table. Insertion of the new person activates the NEW_MOTHER and NEW_FATHER triggers, which update the DESCENDANTS columns of the rows representing the new person's mother and father. The updates caused by these triggers, in turn, invoke the MATERNAL_ANCESTOR and PATERNAL_ANCESTOR triggers, which update the DESCENDANTS columns of the rows representing the new person's four grandparents. Each of these updates invokes both the MATERNAL_ANCESTOR and PATERNAL_ANCESTOR triggers again, causing 2^n updates to occur at the nth level of the family tree. This exponential explosion of updates is too much for the system to handle, so any INSERT statement on the PERSONS table will fail to compile.

There does exist a way in which the set of triggers above can be rewritten so that it automatically maintains the ANCESTORS column in the PERSONS table without using multiple recursion. Finding this way is left as an exercise for the reader. (Hint: the method involves combining multiple triggers into a single trigger.)

 TIP: If you attempt to compile or execute an SQL statement that invokes one or more triggers and you receive the message "The statement is too long or too complex," that is the system's way of telling you that the statement, together with all the triggers that it invokes, exceeds the resources of the compiler. Examine the statement carefully, list all the triggers that it might invoke, and make sure that none of these triggers is multiply recursive. If you are sure that no multiply recursive triggers are invoked, you can sometimes get the statement to compile by increasing the values of the database configuration parameters named APPLHEAPSZ, PCKCACHESZ, and STMTHEAP. (Database configuration parameters can be examined and set using the Control Center, which is discussed in Section 10.3.)

7.3.7 Comparing Constraints and Triggers

It is worth taking a moment at this point to consider the relative advantages of constraints and triggers for enforcing database rules. In general, it is better to use a constraint than to write a trigger that enforces the same rule, for the following reasons:

- Constraints are written in a less procedural way than triggers and give the system more opportunities for optimization.

- Constraints, unlike triggers, are enforced at the time of their creation for all existing data in the database.

- Constraints protect data against being placed into an invalid state by any kind of statement, whereas each trigger applies only to a specific kind of statement such as an update or delete.

On the other hand, triggers are more powerful than constraints and are able to enforce many rules that cannot be enforced by constraints. For example, any rule that requires knowledge of both "before" and "after" states, such as "salaries never decrease," requires the use of a trigger.

7.3.8 Interactions Among Constraints and Triggers

When using constraints and triggers, you should be aware of the order in which they will be enforced or executed during the processing of an SQL statement. A single INSERT, DELETE, or UPDATE statement may modify many rows of data. Each of these rows may be subject to a list of constraints and triggers. The sequence of events is as follows:

1. UDB executes the SQL statement "hypothetically," producing a *change list* containing old and new values for all the rows that would be modified by the statement (of course, an inserted row has no old value, and a deleted row has no new value). The changes on the change list are not yet applied to the database.

2. Before triggers that are activated by the SQL statement are executed in the order of their creation. Before triggers do not operate on the database directly, but they can modify the new values on the change list, which are waiting to be applied to the database.

3. The changes on the change list are applied to the database.

4. Constraints are checked, and all database changes for the statement are rolled back if a violation is found. Foreign key constraints with a deletion action of CASCADE or SET NULL may cause secondary database changes (for example, deletion of a row from the parent table may cause deletion or update of rows in the child table). Each of these secondary changes is executed as follows:

   a. The secondary change is executed "hypothetically," producing a change list.

   b. Before triggers activated by the secondary change are executed in their creation order, possibly modifying the new values on the change list.

   c. The change list is applied to the database and is also merged with the change list of the original SQL statement.

   d. Constraints are checked, and all database changes are rolled back if a violation is found. This sequence of events is repeated until there are no further secondary changes. At this point, the database is in a consistent state, all constraints are enforced, and all database changes have been collected on a master change list.

5. After triggers that are activated by the original SQL statement or by any of the secondary changes are now executed in their order of creation. Each after statement trigger is executed exactly once (even if no rows were modified).

Each after row trigger is executed once for each row that was modified, either by the original SQL statement or by a secondary change. The "old" and "new" transition variables for each trigger are defined by the values on the change list.

An after trigger may contain SQL statements and may update the database. Each after trigger can see the effects on the database caused by other triggers that have executed previously.

Since the body of an after trigger consists of a series of SQL statements, each of these statements may, in turn, invoke constraints and triggers of its own. Each SQL statement inside a trigger is executed independently, using the same sequence of events listed here. A consequence of this design is that the database is enforced to be in a consistent state after the execution of each individual SQL statement inside a trigger body (and, of course, after the completion of the trigger itself).

The example in Figure 7-3 may help to visualize the execution order of statements in after triggers. In this example, an original SQL statement has activated after triggers named Trigger 1 and Trigger 2 (listed in the order of their creation). Inside Trigger 1 are two SQL statements, and the first of these statements activates Trigger A and Trigger B (again, listed in the order of their creation). The execution order of the original statement and the four triggers is shown in this figure in the form of a "path."

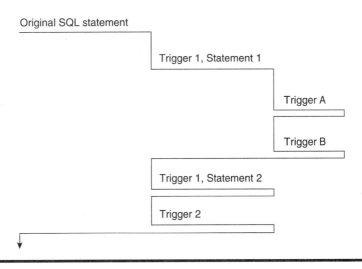

Figure 7-3: An Example of Trigger Activation Order

7.4 DESIGNING AN ACTIVE DATABASE

In this section, we will learn about the use of constraints and triggers by walking through the process of creating a database that uses many active data features as well as some user-defined datatypes and functions. Our database will serve a mail-order business that purchases items from suppliers and fills orders from customers. We will not write all the application programs needed by the business, but we will define a set of tables, constraints, and triggers that encapsulate certain policies that underlie the operation of the business.

The SQL statements that create the database for the mail-order business are shown in the STORE example program. The tables used in the STORE example are shown in Figure 7-4 and described further in the steps of the example program.

The STORE example contains SQL statements that could be placed in a file and processed using an interface such as the CLP. Some of the statements create triggers whose bodies, in turn, contain multiple SQL statements separated by semicolons. Therefore, it is necessary to choose a different delimiter character to separate the top-level SQL statements in the file. In the STORE example, we have used the "!" character for this purpose. The delimiter character for top-level SQL statements is declared to the CLP when the file is submitted for execution, as in the following command:

```
db2 -td! -f store.sql
```

TIP: The declared delimiter is interpreted by the CLP as ending an SQL statement only if it is the last character on a line. Thus, "!" can be used as a delimiter in the STORE example even though it occurs inside some of the CREATE FUNCTION statements, as long as any use of "!" inside a statement does not occur at the end of a line.

CUSTOMERS

| CUSTNO | CUSTNAME | ADDRESS | BALANCEDUE | CREDITLIMIT |

SUPPLIERS

| SUPPLIERNO | SUPPLIERNAME | ADDRESS | AMOUNTOWED |

INVENTORY

| ITEMNO | ITEMNAME | SUPPLIERNO | QUANTITYONHAND | UNITSALEPRICE |

| QUANTITYONORDER | UNITORDERPRICE | ORDERTHRESHOLD | MINIMUMORDER |

PURCHASES

| ORDERDATE | ORDERTIME | SUPPLIERNO | ITEMNO | QUANTITYORDERED |

| DATERECEIVED | QUANTITYRECEIVED | UNITPRICE |

SALES

| SALEDATE | SALETIME | CUSTNO | ITEMNO | QUANTITYSOLD | UNITPRICE | TOTALSALE |

Figure 7-4: Tables Used in the STORE Example

Steps for Example Program STORE: An Active Database

STEP 1: Before creating any tables for our business, we need to decide whether our application will need to define any distinct types. An obvious example of a specialized type of data used in business applications is Money. We have a choice of base datatypes to use for the underlying representation of Money. Perhaps the best fit is a Decimal datatype such as Decimal(8,2), but there is a problem with this datatype: since there is no equivalent of a Decimal datatype in C, we cannot pass Decimal data to a user-defined function written in C. To get around this limitation, we will define a Money datatype that uses Integer as its base datatype, and we will adopt the convention that Money is represented as an integer number of cents (for example, the integer 500 represents $5.00). Using this convention with a signed 32-bit integer as a base datatype allows us to represent amounts of money up to several millions of dollars, which will be sufficient for this application.

When we define a distinct type named Money for our business application, we also need to define the operators and functions that apply to the Money datatype. In this example, we decide that it is meaningful to add and subtract Money amounts to multiply and divide Money amounts by integers, and to find the sum or maximum of a set of Money amounts using the corresponding operators on the Integer base datatype. Other operators, such as multiplying Money by Money, will not be permitted. The SQL statements for defining the Money datatype and its operators and functions are shown in Step 1 of the example program.

STEP 2: In Step 2, we begin the process of defining our business database by creating the tables that represent our external contacts: customers and suppliers. We create a table called CUSTOMERS that records each customer's name, address, balance due, and credit limit. We also create a table called SUPPLIERS that records the name and address of each supplier, as well as the amount currently owed to that supplier by our store. The CUSTOMERS table has a CHECK constraint that requires each customer's credit limit to be greater than or equal to zero (unlike balance due, which is allowed to be negative if the customer has a credit balance).

Code for Example Program STORE: An Active Database

```
--
-- STEP 1:
--
CREATE DISTINCT TYPE Money AS Integer WITH COMPARISONS!

CREATE FUNCTION "+"(Money, Money) RETURNS Money
    SOURCE sysibm."+"(Integer, Integer)!

CREATE FUNCTION "-"(Money, Money) RETURNS Money
    SOURCE sysibm."-"(Integer, Integer)!

CREATE FUNCTION "*"(Money, Integer) RETURNS Money
    SOURCE sysibm."*"(Integer, Integer)!

CREATE FUNCTION "/"(Money, Integer) RETURNS Money
    SOURCE sysibm."/"(Integer, Integer)!

CREATE FUNCTION max(Money) RETURNS Money
    SOURCE sysibm.max(Integer)!

CREATE FUNCTION sum(Money) RETURNS Money
    SOURCE sysibm.sum(Integer)!


--
-- STEP 2:
--
CREATE TABLE customers
  (custno     Char(6) NOT NULL PRIMARY KEY,
   custname   Varchar(20),
   address    Varchar(20),
   balanceDue Money,
   creditLimit Money,
   CONSTRAINT check1
      CHECK (creditLimit >= Money(0)) )!

CREATE TABLE suppliers
  (supplierno   Char(4) NOT NULL PRIMARY KEY,
   suppliername Varchar(20),
   address      Varchar(20),
   amountOwed   Money))!
```

STEP 3:   Next, we create a table called INVENTORY to record the stock of items held in our warehouse. Each row in the INVENTORY table represents a particular type of item. In each row we record the name of the item, the quantity that is on hand and on order, and the supplier from which we order the item. We record the unit sale price and the unit order price for the item and hope that the former is larger than the latter. Our policy is to reorder a new supply of each item when its quantity on hand falls below a certain threshold, and we record the order threshold and the minimum order quantity separately for each type of item. Since we wish our database to be normalized, we do not repeat the details of the suppliers in the INVENTORY table but simply use the supplier number as a key and declare a referential integrity relationship between the INVENTORY and SUPPLIERS tables. We may need to delete a supplier from the SUPPLIERS table while some items from that supplier remain in our inventory, so we declare a delete rule of SET NULL for the RI relationship. (If a supplier is deleted, the SUPPLIERNO column in the corresponding rows of the INVENTORY table is set to null.)

STEP 4:   Next, we create a table to record the details of the purchases we have made from our suppliers. Each row in the PURCHASES table represents an order for a certain kind of item placed with a certain supplier on a certain date and time. The table has columns named ORDERDATE and ORDERTIME, which we declare to be NOT NULL WITH DEFAULT so that the date and time will be generated automatically when rows are inserted into the table.

When a shipment of merchandise arrives from a supplier, we update the corresponding row of the PURCHASES table, entering the date received and quantity received. (Since we have some business experience, we allow for the fact that the quantity received may not be the same as the quantity ordered.)

We declare referential integrity relationships between the PURCHASES table and both the SUPPLIERS and INVENTORY tables. Since we really do not want to delete a supplier or an inventory item while an order is outstanding for that item, we will accept NO ACTION semantics (the default) for the delete rules of these relationships. Before a supplier or an inventory item can be deleted, we will need to remove all corresponding rows from the PURCHASES table.

```
--
-- STEP 3:
--
CREATE TABLE inventory
   (itemno          Char(7) NOT NULL PRIMARY KEY,
    itemname        Varchar(20) NOT NULL,
    supplierno      Char(4),
    quantityOnHand  Integer,
    unitSalePrice   Money,
    quantityOnOrder Integer,
    unitOrderPrice  Money,
    orderThreshold  Integer,
    minimumOrder    Integer,
    CONSTRAINT ifk1
       FOREIGN KEY (supplierno) REFERENCES suppliers
       ON DELETE SET NULL,
    CONSTRAINT check1
       CHECK (quantityOnHand >= 0
       AND quantityOnOrder >= 0
       AND orderThreshold >= 0
       AND minimumOrder >= 0) )!


--
-- STEP 4:
--
CREATE TABLE purchases
   (orderDate        Date NOT NULL WITH DEFAULT,
    orderTime        Time NOT NULL WITH DEFAULT,
    supplierno       Char(4),
    itemno           Char(7),
    quantityOrdered  Integer,
    dateReceived     Date,
    quantityReceived Integer,
    unitPrice        Money,
    CONSTRAINT pfk1
       FOREIGN KEY (supplierno) REFERENCES suppliers,
    CONSTRAINT pfk2
       FOREIGN KEY (itemno) REFERENCES inventory,
    CONSTRAINT check1
       CHECK (quantityOrdered > 0
       AND quantityReceived >= 0),
    CONSTRAINT check2
       CHECK (dateReceived >= orderDate) )!
```

STEP 5:   In this step, we create a table to record the most important thing that happens in our business: sales. As in the PURCHASES table, we give the SALES table columns to record the date and time of each sale and declare these columns NOT NULL WITH DEFAULT so that the dates and times will be generated automatically. The SALES table also records the customer and item numbers, quantity sold, unit price, and the total monetary amount of the sale.

Since a sale involves both a customer and some type of item from our inventory, we declare referential integrity relationships between the SALES table and both the CUSTOMERS and INVENTORY tables. These relationships (foreign key constraints) will cause a transaction to be rolled back if it attempts to insert a sales record for a customer or an item that does not exist.

The five tables in our database and their referential integrity relationships (foreign keys) are shown in Figure 7-5. The labels on the arrows represent the names of foreign key constraints.

STEP 6:   After creating the tables, we are ready to create some triggers that operate on the tables. We need to design these triggers carefully, since they represent and enforce the policies of our business. A properly designed set of triggers can make applications easier to develop and can protect the integrity of our data.

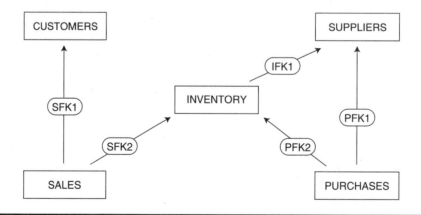

Figure 7-5: Tables and Referential Integrity Relationships in the STORE Database

```
--
-- STEP 5:
--
CREATE TABLE sales
   (saleDate      Date NOT NULL WITH DEFAULT,
    saleTime      Time NOT NULL WITH DEFAULT,
    custno        Char(6),
    itemno        Char(7),
    quantitySold  Integer,
    unitPrice     Money,
    totalSale     Money,
    CONSTRAINT sfk1
       FOREIGN KEY (custno) REFERENCES customers,
    CONSTRAINT sfk2
       FOREIGN KEY (itemno) REFERENCES inventory,
    CONSTRAINT check1
       CHECK (quantitySold > 0) )!


--
-- STEP 6:
--
CREATE TRIGGER pt1
   NO CASCADE BEFORE INSERT ON purchases
   REFERENCING NEW AS newrow FOR EACH ROW
   MODE DB2SQL
   BEGIN ATOMIC
      SET (newrow.unitPrice, newrow.supplierno) =
             (SELECT unitOrderPrice, supplierno
              FROM inventory
              WHERE itemno = newrow.itemno);
   END!


CREATE TRIGGER pt2
   AFTER INSERT ON purchases
   REFERENCING NEW AS newrow FOR EACH ROW
   MODE DB2SQL
   BEGIN ATOMIC
      UPDATE inventory
         SET quantityOnOrder = quantityOnOrder + newrow.quantityOrdered
         WHERE itemno = newrow.itemno;
   END!
```

Our first trigger, PT1, will make it easy to insert new orders into the PUR-CHASES table. We want users and application programs to be able to insert rows into PURCHASES by specifying only the item number and the quantity ordered. The ORDERDATE and ORDERTIME columns will default to the current date and time, and trigger PT1 will automatically fill in the supplier number and unit price for the desired item by looking them up in the INVENTORY table. It is necessary to copy the supplier number and unit price from INVENTORY into the new row of PURCHASES, in order to maintain a proper record of the order in case the preferred supplier or unit price of this item changes in the future. Since PT1 modifies the row that is about to be inserted, it is a before insert trigger.

Also in this step, we write an after insert trigger that propagates information from the PURCHASES table to the INVENTORY table. When a new order is inserted into PURCHASES, trigger PT2 updates the quantity on order of the corresponding item in INVENTORY.

STEP 7: When the items that we ordered finally arrive from the supplier, someone will update the DATERECEIVED and QUANTITYRECEIVED columns of the appropriate row in PURCHASES. Trigger PT3, created in this step, is an after trigger that is activated by update of the QUANTITYRECEIVED column. The trigger is designed to carry out some additional actions that are necessary when supplies are received. It performs two automatic updates: it updates the INVENTORY table to reflect the arrival of the new items, and it updates the SUPPLIERS table to reflect the amount that we owe to the supplier for the shipment (based on the actual quantity received, not the quantity ordered).

STEP 8: In this step, we create a trigger to implement our policy on reordering supplies. Whenever there is a change in the quantity on hand or the order threshold for a given item in the INVENTORY table, trigger IT1 decides whether a new supply of the item needs to be ordered. It automatically generates an order if the sum of the quantity on hand and the quantity already on order for the given item is less than the order threshold.

The process of generating an order for new supplies involves interactions with both the database and the external world. Trigger IT1 interacts with the database by inserting a row into the PURCHASES table (as we saw in Step 6, this will activate two other triggers, PT1 and PT2). Trigger IT1 also interacts with the external world by calling a function named logOrder. logOrder is a user-defined function, written in C, that does whatever is necessary to make the new order effective, such as printing a purchase order on the proper form. The trigger passes to the logOrder function all the information that it needs, including the name and address of the supplier, the item number and name, and the quantity and unit price of the order.

```
--
-- STEP 7:
--
CREATE TRIGGER pt3
  AFTER UPDATE OF quantityReceived ON purchases
  REFERENCING NEW AS newrow FOR EACH ROW
  MODE DB2SQL
  BEGIN ATOMIC
      UPDATE inventory
         SET quantityOnHand = quantityOnHand + newrow.quantityReceived,
             quantityOnOrder = quantityOnOrder - newrow.quantityReceived
         WHERE itemno = newrow.itemno;
       UPDATE suppliers
         SET amountOwed = amountOwed +
               newrow.unitPrice * newrow.quantityReceived
         WHERE supplierno = newrow.supplierno;
  END!


--
-- STEP 8:
--
CREATE FUNCTION logOrder
    (Date,  Time,  Varchar(32),  Varchar(64),
          -- order date, order time, supplier name, supplier address,
    Char(7),  Varchar(30),  Integer,  Money)
          -- item number, item name, quantity, unit price
    RETURNS Integer
          -- not used
    DETERMINISTIC
    NO SQL
    EXTERNAL ACTION
    LANGUAGE C
    FENCED
    PARAMETER STYLE DB2SQL
    EXTERNAL NAME 'storefun!logorder'!
```

The SQL statement to create the `logOrder` function is also shown in this step (of course, it must precede the creation of the trigger). The phrase EXTERNAL ACTION is included in the CREATE FUNCTION statement, because the function takes an action visible to the world outside the database. The body of the `logOrder` function must be written in C, compiled, and installed in the proper directory before the trigger can be used. The `logOrder` function is declared to return an Integer, since all user-defined functions are required to return some value; however, the return value is ignored by trigger IT1.

TIP: In a CREATE FUNCTION statement, it is helpful to give each function parameter a descriptive name, such as "Supplier address," in addition to its datatype. Since the CREATE FUNCTION syntax does not include parameter names, these names must take the form of comments. Each comment must be preceded by two hyphens and must be on a line by itself.

STEP 9: This step implements our store policy on what to do about customers who exceed their credit limit. We wish to refuse any update to the balance owed by a customer that would exceed that customer's credit limit; furthermore, we wish to print a report for review by our credit office whenever such an update is attempted. First, we create an external function called `logLimit`, which prints the credit report (the body of this function must be written separately). Next, we create a trigger named CT1, which detects credit violations, invokes the `logLimit` function, and rolls back the offending update. We need to write this trigger carefully. It would not be wise to simply roll back the update whenever the new balance due is greater than the customer's credit limit, since that rule might prevent a customer who has somehow exceeded their credit limit from making a payment. We need to include a test in the WHEN clause that compares the old and new balance due and executes the body of the trigger only if the balance due is increasing. The trigger body rolls back the update that triggered it (but not the effects of other statements in the same transaction), and it generates an SQLSTATE of 70001 and the message "Credit limit exceeded."

```
CREATE TRIGGER it1
    AFTER UPDATE OF quantityOnHand,
                    orderThreshold ON inventory
    REFERENCING NEW AS newrow FOR EACH ROW
    MODE DB2SQL
    WHEN (newrow.quantityOnHand + newrow.quantityOnOrder
            < newrow.orderThreshold)
    BEGIN ATOMIC
        INSERT INTO purchases(itemno, quantityOrdered)
            VALUES (newrow.itemno, newrow.minimumOrder);
        VALUES(logOrder(CURRENT DATE,
                        CURRENT TIME,
                        (SELECT suppliername
                            FROM suppliers
                            WHERE supplierno = newrow.supplierno),
                        (SELECT address
                            FROM suppliers
                            WHERE supplierno = newrow.supplierno),
                        newrow.itemno,
                        newrow.itemname,
                        newrow.minimumOrder,
                        newrow.unitOrderPrice ) );
    END!


--
-- STEP 9:
--
CREATE FUNCTION logLimit
    (Date,  Time,  Char(6),  Money,  Money)
            -- date, time, customer number, credit limit, amount owed
    RETURNS Integer
            -- not used
    DETERMINISTIC
    NO SQL
    EXTERNAL ACTION
    LANGUAGE C
    FENCED
    PARAMETER STYLE DB2SQL
    EXTERNAL NAME 'storefun!loglimit'!
```

We might consider implementing the credit policy in this step by means of a check constraint such as `CHECK (balanceDue < creditLimit)`. However, if expressed in this way, the constraint would prevent a customer's credit limit from being lowered to an amount less than their current balance, which our store might choose to do under certain circumstances. Also, expressing the policy in the form of a trigger gives us an opportunity to call a user-defined function that generates a credit warning report.

STEP 10: In this step, we attach some triggers to the SALES table. Trigger ST1 makes it easy to insert a new row into SALES, by automatically filling in the UNITPRICE and TOTALSALE columns of the new row (looking up the UNITPRICE value in the INVENTORY table). Thus, a new SALES row might be inserted with information only in the CUSTNO, ITEMNO, and QUANTITYSOLD columns; values for SALEDATE and SALETIME will default to the current date and time, and values for UNITPRICE and TOTALSALE will be generated by the trigger ST1.

Also in this step, we create trigger ST2, which makes sure that, whenever a sale is recorded, the customer's balance due is updated accordingly, and the items sold are subtracted from the quantity on hand in the INVENTORY table. Note that the action of this trigger might cascade to activate other triggers as well. For example, if this sale would cause a customer to exceed their credit limit, trigger CT1 will generate a warning report and roll back the statement. Similarly, if this sale results in the quantity on hand of an item falling below its order threshold, trigger IT1 will be activated and will generate a new order for the item. It is also worth noting that if the quantity sold is more than the entire quantity on hand for this item, trigger ST2 will update the quantity on hand in the INVENTORY table to a value less than zero, and the statement will be rolled back by check constraint CHECK1 in the INVENTORY table.

The order of the SQL statements in the body of trigger ST2 is important. We want to update the customer's balance due before we update the inventory table, because updating the customer's balance due results in a credit check that could roll back the statement if the customer's credit limit is exceeded. We want the credit check to be completed before we update the inventory table (which could result in placing a new order for supplies that would prove unnecessary if the customer has insufficient credit).

```
CREATE TRIGGER ct1
    AFTER UPDATE OF balanceDue ON customers
    REFERENCING OLD AS oldrow NEW AS newrow FOR EACH ROW
    MODE DB2SQL
    WHEN (newrow.balanceDue > oldrow.balanceDue
        AND newrow.balanceDue > newrow.creditLimit)
    BEGIN ATOMIC
        VALUES(logLimit(CURRENT DATE,
                        CURRENT TIME,
                        newrow.custno,
                        newrow.creditLimit,
                        newrow.balanceDue));
        SIGNAL SQLSTATE '70001' ('Credit Limit Exceeded');
    END!


--
-- STEP 10:
--
CREATE TRIGGER st1
    NO CASCADE BEFORE INSERT ON sales
    REFERENCING NEW AS newrow FOR EACH ROW
    MODE DB2SQL
    BEGIN ATOMIC
        SET (newrow.unitPrice, newrow.totalSale) =
            (SELECT unitSalePrice, unitSalePrice * newrow.quantitySold
             FROM inventory
             WHERE itemno = newrow.itemno);
    END!

CREATE TRIGGER st2
    AFTER INSERT ON sales
    REFERENCING NEW AS newrow FOR EACH ROW
    MODE DB2SQL
    BEGIN ATOMIC
        UPDATE customers
            SET balanceDue = balanceDue + newrow.totalSale
            WHERE custno = newrow.custno;
        UPDATE inventory
            SET quantityOnHand = quantityOnHand - newrow.quantitySold
            WHERE itemno = newrow.itemno;
    END!
```

STEP 11: This step is an attempt to do some automatic fine-tuning of our system for ordering new supplies. Since it takes about a month for a new order of supplies to arrive, we do not want our inventory of any item to fall below about one month's sales for that item. Therefore, whenever we find that the quantity sold of a given item in the last month is greater than the order threshold for that item, it is probably time to increase the ordering threshold and possibly the minimum order quantity as well. This policy is implemented by trigger ST3, which automatically increases both the ordering threshold and the minimum order quantity by 25% and generates a report (by calling the user-defined function logSales) that will be reviewed and approved by our purchasing manager. We show the CREATE FUNCTION statement for logSales, another function with EXTERNAL ACTION, whose C implementation must be compiled separately.

The body of trigger ST3 contains two SQL statements: the first updates the database, and the second contains several scalar subqueries that retrieve values to be passed to logSales. These SQL statements are executed sequentially, and the second statement can see the database updates made by the first statement.

```
--
-- STEP 11:
--
CREATE FUNCTION logsales
    (Date, Time, Char(7), Varchar(30),
          -- date, time, item number, item name,
    Integer, Integer, Integer)
          -- quant. sold last month, new order threshold, new order quant.
    RETURNS Integer
          -- not used
    DETERMINISTIC
    NO SQL
    EXTERNAL ACTION
    LANGUAGE C
    FENCED
    PARAMETER STYLE DB2SQL
    EXTERNAL NAME 'storefun!logsales'!

CREATE TRIGGER st3
    AFTER INSERT ON sales
    REFERENCING NEW AS newrow FOR EACH ROW
    MODE DB2SQL
    WHEN ((SELECT SUM(quantitySold)
          FROM sales
          WHERE itemno = newrow.itemno
          AND saleDate + 1 MONTH > CURRENT DATE )
          >
          (SELECT orderThreshold
          FROM inventory
          WHERE itemno = newrow.itemno) )
    BEGIN ATOMIC
       UPDATE inventory
          SET orderThreshold = orderThreshold * 1.25,
              minimumOrder = minimumOrder * 1.25
          WHERE itemno = newrow.itemno;
       VALUES (logsales(CURRENT DATE, CURRENT TIME, newrow.itemno,
                          (SELECT itemname FROM inventory
                              WHERE itemno = newrow.itemno),
                          (SELECT SUM(quantitySold) FROM sales
                              WHERE itemno = newrow.itemno
                              AND saleDate + 1 MONTH > CURRENT DATE ),
                          (SELECT orderThreshold FROM inventory
                              WHERE itemno = newrow.itemno),
                          (SELECT minimumOrder FROM inventory
                              WHERE itemno = newrow.itemno) ) );
    END!
```

STEP 12: This step represents an afterthought on the part of our marketing department. Someone in marketing wants to keep a record of the total amount of purchases by each customer in the current calendar year. This data may be used to identify big spenders for special mailings and promotional offers. We implement this last-minute addition to the database by altering the CUSTOMERS table, adding a new column to record the total sales this year, and creating the trigger ST4 to update this column whenever a new sale is recorded.

Figure 7-6 shows a graphical representation of all the triggers created in the STORE example. Each trigger is represented by an arrow with its tail on the table to which the trigger is attached and its head(s) on the table(s) that are modified by the trigger. When designing an active database, it is a good idea to draw a "trigger graph" like this one and to look for cycles. Investigate each cycle in the trigger graph to make sure that it cannot lead to a trigger invoking itself in an infinite loop. In Figure 7-6, for example, the apparent loops between triggers IT1 and PT2 and between IT1 and PT3 should be investigated, as well as the self-loops represented by CT1, ST1, and PT1. In each case, the triggers involved are written in such a way that they avoid infinite recursion.

This figure shows us that quite a complex series of actions can result from a simple database update. For example, the series of actions on page 452 might result from the insertion of a new row into the SALES table (the levels of indentation represent how the action of one trigger results in firing another trigger).

```
--
-- STEP 12:
--
ALTER TABLE customers
    ADD COLUMN salesThisYear Money!

CREATE TRIGGER st4
    AFTER INSERT ON sales
    REFERENCING NEW AS newrow FOR EACH ROW
    MODE DB2SQL
    BEGIN ATOMIC
       UPDATE customers
          SET salesThisYear =
             ( SELECT sum(totalSale)
               FROM sales
               WHERE custno = newrow.custno
               AND year(saleDate) = year(CURRENT DATE) )
          WHERE custno = newrow.custno;
    END!
```

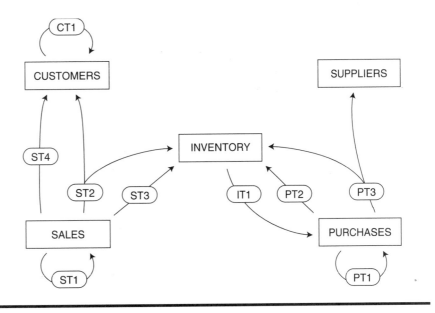

Figure 7-6: A Graph of Triggers in the STORE Database

1. ST1 conditions the new SALES row by filling in its UNITPRICE and TOTAL-SALE columns.

2. ST2 updates the CUSTOMERS table (increasing BALANCEDUE) and the INVENTORY table (decreasing QUANTITYONHAND).

   a. CT1 rolls back the statement if the customer's credit limit is exceeded.

   b. IT1 inserts a new order into PURCHASES if more supplies are needed.

      • PT1 conditions the new PURCHASES row by filling in the SUPPLIERNO and UNITPRICE columns.

      • PT2 updates the INVENTORY table (increasing QUANTITYONORDER).

3. If this sale represents a new high in monthly sales for some item, ST3 updates the INVENTORY table, increasing the THRESHOLD and MINIMUMORDER columns for this item. (If the THRESHOLD is increased to a value greater than QUANTITYONHAND, this could lead to firing triggers IT1, PT1, and PT2 again.)

4. ST4 updates the CUSTOMERS table (increasing SALESTHISYEAR).

7.5 BINDING AND DEPENDENCIES

Features of UDB such as constraints and triggers go a long way toward capturing the semantics of objects that are stored in the database. As these features are implemented, it becomes increasingly true that the behavior of an SQL statement may depend on things that are outside the statement itself, such as constraints, triggers, views, and functions. For example, if a trigger is added to a table that is updated by an SQL statement, the behavior of the SQL statement may change. This is an example of a *dependency* of one object on another. Now that this book has discussed all the kinds of objects implemented by UDB, it is time to have a general discussion of dependencies.

The example questions below illustrate some of the kinds of dependencies that can exist among various objects in a database. The questions and answers are followed by a discussion of the general rules governing dependencies.

• Suppose that you create a view on Monday, but on Tuesday one of the tables that underlies the view is dropped. What happens to the view? *Answer*: The view becomes "inoperative" and cannot be used until it is explicitly recreated.

• Suppose that you bind an application program on Wednesday, but on Thursday a new index is created that would be helpful to your program. Will the program take advantage of the new index? *Answer*: No, not until the program is rebound.

- Suppose that after you bind an application program that inserts data into a table, a check constraint is added to the table. Is your existing program subject to the new check constraint? *Answer*: Yes, its package will automatically be modified to incorporate the new constraint.

- Suppose that, after you create a trigger that encapsulates one of the rules of your business, someone tries to drop a function that is used by your trigger. What happens? *Answer*: The function cannot be dropped as long as the trigger exists.

The topic of dependencies is closely related to the topic of *binding*. Before any SQL statement (including the definition of a view, constraint, or trigger) can be used, each unqualified name used in the statement must be resolved to some specific object (table, function, and so on) in the database. We use the term *binding* to describe the process of finding the specific object that corresponds to each unqualified name in an SQL statement. For example, the unqualified table name SALARYPLAN might be bound to the specific table ADMIN.SALARYPLAN when it occurs in an application prepared under the ADMIN userid; or the unqualified function name area might be bound to the specific function geometry.area when it is used in a particular view.

After a name has been bound to a particular object, it is possible that changes may occur in the database that could potentially affect the binding. For example, after the function name area has been bound to the specific function geometry.area, another function named area could be created in a schema that is earlier in the user's function path than geometry. Or the specific function geometry.area could be dropped and no longer be available for use. We use the term *binding semantics* to describe how an object behaves after all its names have been bound. The term applies to every kind of persistent object, such as a view or program, whose definition contains an unqualified name.

7.5.1 Conservative Binding Semantics

The general approach taken by UDB to the issue of binding is called *conservative binding semantics*. This term means that, after an object is bound, its behavior will not change unpredictably. For example, if you compile an application program that invokes a user-defined function called payIncrease, you can be confident that the program will not suddenly begin using a different payIncrease function unless you take an explicit action.[4] Having stated the general principle, we will now examine the binding semantics of some specific kinds of objects.

---

4. Of course, we are assuming here that you have protected the executable file that implements your function against unauthorized tampering, using the protection features of your operating system.

The binding semantics of views are easy to describe. All the names contained in a view definition are bound to specific objects in the database at the time when the CREATE VIEW is executed. After this time, the bindings of the names never change. If a new function, alias, or other object is created later that would have been chosen if the view were rebound, the new object is ignored, even in applications that are compiled after the creation of the new object. If an object (function, table, alias, and so on) to which a view has been bound is dropped, the view becomes *inoperative*. This means that the view definition is retained in the VIEWS catalog table, but the view cannot be used until it is explicitly recreated by a new CREATE VIEW statement. The view definition is retained in order to help you recreate the view after the dropped object has been replaced with a replacement object of the same name. If a view is inoperative, creating a new view with the same name is not considered a naming conflict; instead, the inoperative view definition is replaced. The following query retrieves the names and definitions of all the inoperative views in schema S1:

```
SELECT viewname, seqno, text
FROM syscat.views
WHERE viewschema = 'S1' AND valid = 'X'
ORDER BY viewname, seqno;
```

The binding semantics of triggers are the same as those of views. Like a view, a trigger can become inoperative if some object that it depends on is dropped. The definition of an inoperative trigger is maintained in the TRIGGERS catalog table so that a user can retrieve the definition and use it in a new CREATE TRIGGER statement. The following query can be used to fetch the definitions of all inoperative triggers in schema S1:

```
SELECT trigname, text
FROM syscat.triggers
WHERE trigschema = 'S1' and valid = 'X'
ORDER BY trigname;
```

The binding semantics of programs are also conservative but are somewhat more complex than those of views and triggers. When a program is bound, a specific plan is generated for executing each SQL statement in the program, and all these plans are stored in the database in the form of a *package*. After binding a program, we do not want its behavior to change, but we do not insist that each statement always be executed using the original plan. For example, if an index that was used in the original plan for some statement is dropped, the statement can still be executed by choosing a different (but functionally equivalent) plan. Therefore, if some object that a program uses is dropped, the package for that program can become either *invalid* or *inoperative*. If an index that a package uses is dropped, the package is marked *invalid*, and the system automatically generates a new plan for executing the package the next time it is used. This process is called *implicit rebind* and is invisible to users except for performance: there may be a slight delay when the automatic rebind occurs, and the performance of the program may change due to the new access plan. On the other hand, if a function that a package uses is dropped, the package is marked *inoperative* and can no longer be executed until it is explicitly rebound. This protects the users of the application from unexpected changes in its behavior. An inoperative package can be rebound using the PREP, BIND, or REBIND command. The status of each package is stored in the PACKAGES catalog table. The following query can be used to list all the packages that are invalid or inoperative:

```
SELECT pkgschema, pkgname, valid
FROM syscat.packages
WHERE valid = 'N' OR valid = 'X';
```

TIP: When a package is implicitly rebound, the implicit rebind takes place within the scope of the first transaction executed by the package. If the first transaction is rolled back, the implicit rebind will be rolled back also. In fact, if a package always rolls back its first transaction, that package can never be implicitly rebound.

7.5.2 Types of Dependencies

The binding semantics of views, programs, and other objects are enforced by recording *dependencies* in the system catalog tables. A dependency exists whenever the definition of some object (called the *depending object*) refers to some other object (called the *underlying object*). Dependencies can be classified into four semantic categories, according to what happens when the underlying object is dropped.

R = *Restrict semantics*. As long as the dependency exists, users are not allowed to drop the underlying object.

C = *Cascade semantics*. When the underlying object is dropped, the depending object is automatically dropped also.

A = *Automatic revalidation semantics*. When the underlying object is dropped, the depending object is marked *invalid* and is automatically revalidated on its next use, selecting the best replacement for the object that was dropped.

X = *Inoperative semantics*. When the underlying object is dropped, the depending object is marked *inoperative*. An inoperative object cannot be used until a user takes some explicit action to restore it to an operative state. However, the definition of the inoperative object remains in the catalog tables as an aid to restoring the object.

TABLE 7-5: Types of Dependencies of One Object on Another

Depending Object	Underlying Object									
	Table	View	Alias	Index	Function Instance	Datatype	Constraint	Trigger	Privilege	Tablespace
Program	A(3)	A	A	A	X		A(4)	A(4)	A	
Table						R				C(5)
View	X	X	X		R				X	
Alias (6)										
Index	C									C
Function Instance					R	C				
Datatype (1)										
Constraint	C			R(7)	R		C(2)			
Trigger	X	X	X		R				X	

Table 7-5 summarizes all the kinds of dependencies that are recorded in UDB. Like the catalog tables, Table 7-5 includes only *immediate* dependencies. Of course, these dependencies may propagate; for example, if a program depends on a view, and the view depends on a privilege (held by the view definer), then loss of that privilege by the view definer will have an effect on the program even though the dependency of the program on the privilege is not recorded directly.

In Table 7-5, the codes R, C, A, and X denote the four types of dependency semantics. The numbers in parentheses refer to the following notes:

Notes:

1. Distinct types have no dependencies, because they are always based on built-in datatypes, which cannot be dropped.

2. A foreign key constraint is dependent on a primary key or unique constraint in the parent table, with Cascade semantics.

3. A program is dependent, not only on the tables that it manipulates directly, but also on tables that it manipulates indirectly through views, aliases, triggers, or foreign key constraints.

4. If a program operates on a particular table, the package generated for the program will include all the constraints and triggers that were defined on that table at the time the program was bound. If constraints or triggers are added to or deleted from that table, the program will be invalidated (and automatically rebound on next use). This type of dependency is recorded as a dependency of the program on the table, not on the individual constraints and triggers.

5. Dropping a tablespace causes all tables that are completely contained within the tablespace to be dropped. But if a table spans more than one tablespace, none of its tablespaces can be dropped as long as the table exists.

6. Aliases have no dependencies. It is permissible for an alias to be defined on a table that does not exist.

7. A unique or primary key constraint depends on the system-generated unique index that enforces the constraint.

Since all of the various kinds of dependencies are recorded in the catalog tables, you can write queries to find all the objects that depend on a given object or to find all the objects that a given object depends on. The main catalog tables that are used to record dependencies are the following:

- CONSTDEP records dependencies of constraints on other objects.
- PACKAGEDEP records dependencies of packages on other objects.
- TRIGDEP records dependencies of triggers on other objects.
- VIEWDEP records dependencies of views on other objects.

Dependencies are also recorded in certain other catalog tables that are used mainly for other purposes; for example, the COLUMNS catalog table records the datatype of each column, which represents a dependency of a table or view on a datatype.

The following are some examples of queries that might be used to find dependencies. (More information about catalog tables can be found in Appendix D.)

- Find all the objects that are depended on by the trigger named SECURITY.HIRETRIGGER:

```
SELECT bschema, bname, btype
FROM syscat.trigdep
WHERE trigschema = 'SECURITY'
AND trigname = 'HIRETRIGGER';
```

- Find all the table columns and view columns that use the distinct datatype Money:

  ```
  SELECT tabschema, tabname, colname
  FROM syscat.columns
  WHERE typename = 'MONEY';
  ```

- Find all the functions that take parameters or return results of type Money:

  ```
  SELECT DISTINCT funcschema, funcname
  FROM syscat.funcparms
  WHERE typename = 'MONEY';
  ```

 TIP: Since SQL folds all (nonquoted) names to uppercase, you should use an uppercase name when searching for an object (type, function, table, and so on) in the catalog tables unless you know that the object you are searching for was explicitly created with a (quoted) lowercase name.

8 Dynamic SQL

S QL is a language that can be used in many different ways. We have seen how static SQL statements can be embedded in programs written in a host programming language such as C. Since static SQL statements are known at precompilation time, they can be analyzed and prepared for execution by the UDB precompiler, so at run time the application program needs only to invoke a preoptimized access plan for each static SQL statement. However, it is not always possible to anticipate in advance exactly what SQL statements an application program may need to execute. Therefore, some means is needed for a program to generate SQL statements at run time and present them to the database system to be executed. This approach to processing SQL statements is called *dynamic SQL*.

In exchange for run-time flexibility, dynamic SQL applications pay a performance penalty, since their SQL statements cannot be optimized in advance. The cost of analyzing a dynamic SQL statement and choosing an optimal access plan for it is incurred when the statement is executed (however, UDB caches the access plan so that the cost of generating it is not repeated if the same statement is executed again in the same session). The performance cost of run-time optimization may be partially or fully offset by the fact that the optimizer always sees the latest available indexes and statistics when processing a dynamic SQL statement.

Another issue that you may wish to consider in choosing between static and dynamic SQL is the stability of your application. A static SQL application is encapsulated in a package whose behavior will not change without explicit action on your part. A dynamic application, on the other hand, is processed "from scratch" each time it is run, which means that its behavior may differ from one run to the next as changes are made to the database, such as the addition of new user-defined functions.

UDB provides three facilities for handling dynamic SQL statements, called the Call Level Interface (CLI), Java Database Connectivity (JDBC), and Embedded Dynamic SQL. CLI supports application programs written in C, JDBC supports Java applications, and Embedded Dynamic SQL can be used with applications written in C, FORTRAN, COBOL, or REXX. The functionalities of all the dynamic SQL facilities are similar (but not identical, as you will see). Each facility provides a way for application programs to submit dynamically computed SQL statements to the database system at run time. In each facility, the process of parsing an SQL statement and choosing an optimal access plan for it is called *preparing* the statement, and is performed by the same optimizer that is used for static SQL statements.

All the dynamic SQL facilities separate the process of preparing a statement from the process of executing it, allowing a statement to be prepared once and executed many times using different data values. This approach allows the cost of parsing and optimizing the SQL statement to be incurred only once, when the statement is prepared, rather than on each execution. For example, an UPDATE statement might be prepared to update the EMP table, assigning a new value to the SALARY column of the row whose EMPNO column matches a given value. The statement might then be executed repeatedly with several pairs of values for EMPNO and SALARY.

When a dynamic SQL statement is being prepared for execution, missing data values are represented by question marks, called *parameter markers*. Parameter markers in dynamic SQL statements play a similar role to that of host variables in static SQL statements. Before a prepared statement can be executed, real data values must be substituted for all its parameter markers. This is done by *binding* each parameter marker to a host variable, so that the value of the parameter marker is taken from the content of the variable at execution time.

TIP: Don't confuse the process of binding a parameter marker to a host variable with the process of binding an application program described in Section 4.3.

This chapter examines CLI, JDBC, and Embedded Dynamic SQL, describing how each facility can be used to prepare dynamic SQL statements for execution, to bind their parameter markers, and to execute the statements. To illustrate the use of dynamic SQL and to compare the three facilities, we will write some application programs using each of the facilities.

8.1 CALL LEVEL INTERFACE

The Call Level Interface (CLI) has several important advantages that might cause you to prefer it for some applications over Embedded Dynamic SQL or even over static SQL. These advantages can be summarized as follows:

1. CLI applications do not require a precompiler. Instead of a precompiler, CLI relies on a set of function calls that can be embedded in a C program and compiled by a conventional C compiler. By linking your program to the UDB CLI library, you have access to all the SQL facilities of the system. Since there is no need to precompile your application, you can distribute it in the form of object code. Users of your application can run it on their own databases without having access to source code and without needing to "bind" the application to each database on which it will be used.

2. CLI enables you to write portable database applications. The UDB implementation of CLI conforms to International Standard ISO/IEC 9075-3:1995 (SQL Call Level Interface). In addition, when used with an ODBC driver manager (included in your UDB installation), it implements the Open Database Connectivity[1] interface (ODBC 3.0, Level 1, plus certain additional conformance items listed in the *CLI Guide and Reference*). Therefore, applications written for UDB using the CLI interface are portable to other database systems, and many ODBC applications written for other database systems are portable to UDB. CLI programs contain no references to system-specific control blocks such as SQLCA and SQLDA.

3. CLI applications, unlike Embedded Dynamic SQL applications, can connect to the same database multiple times and can independently commit transactions in each database connection. This facility is useful in developing applications with graphical user interfaces that use multiple windows.

4. In keeping with its strategy of system independence, CLI provides a set of function calls that can be used to access system catalog tables in a standard way. Most relational systems maintain a set of catalog tables containing information about the database and its users, but the form of these catalog tables may vary from one system to another. Using CLI functions, you can access some of this catalog data in a portable way, including information about the tables and columns in the database, primary and foreign keys, and user privileges. Of course, the UDB catalog tables contain a lot of additional information that can be accessed directly by SQL statements but is not accessible via the system-independent CLI catalog functions.

5. CLI allows an application program to retrieve multiple rows from a result set with a single call, avoiding the overhead of fetching the rows one at a time. Also, an application can execute an SQL statement multiple times with a single CLI call, using an array of input variables.

6. Unlike Embedded Dynamic SQL, CLI supports *scrollable cursors*, which can be advanced forward, backward, or to an absolute position within a result set. This feature is very useful for applications that implement a graphical user interface with scroll bars.

7. CLI supports a large number of datatype conversions. For example, data of any SQL datatype can be fetched into a C variable of datatype char[]. The data is automatically converted from its SQL datatype (perhaps Double or Timestamp) into a character-string representation. Its rich set of datatype conversions makes CLI well adapted to writing programs to support interactive query interfaces.

---

1. The Open Database Connectivity (ODBC) interface is defined by Microsoft.

8. UDB supports some CLI functions (such as `SQLGetSubString()`) that make it easy to manipulate large objects in the form of locators, postponing the actual materialization of the objects as long as possible. These functions are IBM extensions (not a part of the standard ODBC interface) and are not available using Embedded Dynamic SQL.

9. Unlike Embedded Dynamic SQL, CLI supports compound SQL statements (which enable several SQL statements to be sent from client to server in a single flow, reducing execution time and network traffic).

10. Client programs written in CLI can invoke stored procedures that return multiple result sets (as described in Section 9.2.3).

A complete description of CLI is given in the *CLI Guide and Reference*. Many examples of CLI applications are provided with the UDB system and can be found in the directory `sqllib/samples/cli`.

8.1.1 Handles

In order to read and write CLI programs, you need to understand the concept of a *handle*. A handle is simply a C variable of type `long` that represents some information that is being managed for you "behind the scenes" by the CLI implementation. CLI supports the following types of handles:

1. An *environment handle* represents the global state of your application. Your CLI program will need to allocate an environment handle at the beginning and free it at the end, but otherwise it will make little use of the environment handle.

2. A *connection handle* represents the connection of your application to a particular database. Your program can be connected to multiple databases, or multiple times to the same database, using a separate connection handle for each connection. You will use connection handles to commit and roll back transactions in various databases and to control aspects of your database connections such as isolation level.

3. A *statement handle* represents the execution state of an SQL statement. Your program can allocate multiple statement handles and can reuse each one repeatedly to process many SQL statements (one at a time, of course). A statement handle is a powerful object that combines the information that a static SQL program would find in structures called SQLCA (return codes and messages), SQLDA (datatypes and bindings to host variables), and cursors (current position within a set of rows). Since all this information is represented by a statement handle, your program no longer needs to manage these (rather messy) data structures directly. Instead, your program uses CLI function calls to execute an SQL statement and to retrieve information about the statement using its handle. A statement handle can be used in the following ways:

- It can retrieve error codes and messages pertaining to the execution of the statement.
- It can find out whether the statement was a query and, if so, the datatypes of the columns in the result set.
- It can tell the system where to deliver the results of a query, and it can fetch the rows of the result set one at a time.
- Like a cursor, it can maintain a position on a "current" row in the result set and can provide a name (called a *cursor name*) that can be used by other SQL statements to update or delete the current row.

4. A *descriptor handle* represents a *descriptor* that contains information about how data is exchanged between an SQL statement and a CLI program. For example, a descriptor might contain information about the parameter markers used in an SQL statement, including their datatypes and how they are bound to variables in the host program. Another descriptor might contain information about the result set of a query, including the datatypes of its columns and how they are bound to host program variables. Since this information can also be accessed through statement handles, it is not necessary for a CLI program to operate directly on descriptor handles.

As a CLI programmer, it is your job to allocate one environment handle, one or more connection handles, and one or more statement handles, and to free these handles when they are no longer needed. You will use these handles in all the CLI function calls in your program.

8.1.2 Configuring CLI

A configuration file named db2cli.ini can be used to specify various options that control the behavior of CLI. You can specify different values for the CLI configuration options for each database to which you plan to connect. Each option also has a systemwide default that applies if the option is not included in your configuration file. Many of the configuration options can be overridden by individual CLI commands. For example, the systemwide default for the transaction isolation level is Cursor Stability (CS). A given client may have a db2cli.ini file that establishes a different default isolation level for all CLI applications run by that client. But an individual CLI application can have the last word about the isolation level of a specific database connection by using the function SQLSetConnectAttr().

The db2cli.ini file is maintained on your client machine, in the sqllib directory under Windows 95, Windows NT, or OS/2; or in the sqllib/cfg directory of a UNIX-based system, or in the sqllib\win directory under Windows 3.1.

Some of the options that can be specified in the db2cli.ini file are listed below. (For a more complete list, see the *CLI Guide and Reference*.)

CONNECTTYPE controls the type of database connections acquired by CLI applications. The systemwide default is Type 3, which permits connection to multiple databases with a separate transaction for each database.

CURSORHOLD controls whether open cursors remain open when a COMMIT statement is executed. The systemwide default is to hold cursors open across commit points. Applications that do not need this feature can improve performance by turning it off.

DB2OPTIMIZATION controls the class of optimization used in processing SQL statements by CLI applications. (Optimization classes are discussed in Section 10.8.1.)

TXNISOLATION controls the isolation level for CLI transactions. The systemwide default is Cursor Stability (CS).

8.1.3 Summary of CLI Functions

It is important to remember that CLI is not a new query language—it is simply an interface that an application program can use to submit SQL statements for processing. Your database queries and updates are still written in SQL and "wrapped" in CLI function calls. The CLI function calls handle details like connecting to the database, fetching query results into program variables, and committing or rolling back your transaction.

The following is a list of the CLI functions supported by **UDB**, organized into categories of related functions.[2] A complete description of all the parameters of these functions is beyond the scope of this book, but can be found in the *CLI Guide and Reference*. The functions marked with an asterisk in the list below are **UDB** extensions that are not a part of ODBC and that may therefore limit the portability of your application.

- Functions for allocating and freeing handles:
    SQLAllocHandle() allocates an environment, connection, statement, or descriptor handle.
    SQLFreeHandle() frees a handle.
- Functions for controlling database connections:
    SQLConnect() connects your application program to a particular database.

---

2. In addition to the functions listed here, **UDB** implements a few "deprecated functions" for compatibility with previous releases.

SQLDriverConnect() connects your application program to a particular database, optionally prompting the user for certain information such as userid and password.

SQLBrowseConnect() connects your application program to a particular database, and asks the database whether it requires any additional information to complete the connection. The additional information, if required, can be supplied by repeated calls to SQLBrowseConnect().

SQLDisconnect() closes a database connection.

SQLSetEnvAttr() controls attributes such as connection type for all database connections within the scope of an environment handle.

SQLGetEnvAttr() retrieves the current value of an attribute set by SQLSetEnvAttr().

SQLSetConnectAttr() controls attributes such as isolation level or autocommit for a specific database connection.

SQLGetConnectAttr() retrieves the current value of a database connection attribute.

SQLSetConnection()* is used to specify which database connection is used by static SQL statements embedded in a CLI program.

- Functions for preparing an SQL statement for execution and obtaining a description of the result:

SQLPrepare() prepares a statement for execution.

SQLNumResultCols() returns the number of columns in the result set if the prepared statement was a query.

SQLDescribeCol() describes a particular column in the result set.

SQLColAttribute() retrieves one specific attribute of a column in the result set, such as its name, datatype, or length.

SQLNativeSql() accepts an SQL statement and returns it, translated into the "native" form that would be sent to the database server. This translation process is used to remove local system dependencies from SQL statements. The translated statement is returned but not executed.

- Functions for handling parameter markers:

SQLNumParams() returns the number of parameter markers in a prepared SQL statement.

SQLBindParameter() binds a parameter marker to a host program variable.

SQLDescribeParam() returns the datatype, length, scale, and nullability associated with a specific parameter marker.

SQLParamData(), SQLPutData(), and SQLCancel() can be used together to send large parameter values from a CLI program to the database system, a piece at a time.

- Functions for executing an SQL statement and testing its result:

    SQLExecute() executes a statement that was previously prepared.

    SQLExecDirect() prepares and executes a statement in one step.

    SQLRowCount() returns the number of rows that were inserted, deleted, or updated by a statement, or the number of rows in the result set of a scrollable cursor.

    SQLGetDiagRec() returns the SQLSTATE, SQLCODE, and message associated with an error or warning that was encountered during processing of a statement. Multiple calls to SQLGetDiagRec() can retrieve information on multiple errors.

    SQLGetDiagField() returns a specific piece of diagnostic information, such as an SQLCODE or SQLSTATE.

    SQLGetSQLCA()[*] returns the SQLCA structure that results from processing a statement.

    SQLSetStmtAttr() controls certain attributes that govern the execution of a statement, such as the number of rows to be returned on each call to SQLFetchScroll().

    SQLGetStmtAttr() retrieves the current value of a statement attribute.

- Functions for handling the result of a query:

    SQLBindCol() tells CLI where to deliver the values for one column in the result set and what kind of type conversion to perform on the column values. If the datatype of the column is Blob, Clob, or Dbclob, SQLBindCol() can specify that the system deliver the column value in the form of a locator rather than materializing the actual value.

    SQLFetch() fetches one row of the result set into the host program locations specified by SQLBindCol().

    SQLFetchScroll() fetches multiple rows of the result set, delivering the columns into arrays at locations specified by SQLBindCol(). SQLFetchScroll() can advance a cursor forward, backward, or to an absolute position in the result set.

    SQLGetData() fetches a single column value from the current row of the result set and can be used to fetch large data values in pieces.

    SQLSetCursorName() associates a cursor name with a statement handle, for use in positioned deletes and updates. If you do not supply a cursor name for a statement handle, the system will generate one.

    SQLGetCursorName() returns the cursor name associated with a statement handle.

    SQLSetPos() positions a cursor on a specific row within a set of rows that has already been fetched.

SQLCloseCursor() closes the cursor that is associated with a statement handle, discarding the result set of the statement.

SQLMoreResults() is used to advance from one result set to the next when an SQL query has been executed multiple times using an array of input parameters. Within each result set, individual rows may be fetched using SQLFetch() or SQLFetchScroll(). SQLMoreResults() is also used to advance from one result set to the next when multiple result sets are returned by a stored procedure (as described in Section 9.2.3).

SQLFreeStmt() unbinds the parameters and columns that have been bound to a statement handle so that the handle can be used for another statement.

- Functions that are useful in handling large objects:

  SQLGetLength()[*] returns the length of a string value. This function is useful for measuring the length of a large object that is represented by a locator.

  SQLGetSubString()[*] returns a portion of a LOB-type string value that is represented by a large-object locator. The result can be either a materialized string or another locator. This function is useful for postponing the materialization of a large object as long as possible.

  SQLGetPosition()[*] returns a number representing the position of one string inside another. The string to be searched must be represented by a locator, and the string to be found may be represented by either a locator or a literal. This function is useful for searching for patterns of bits or characters within a large object.

  SQLBindFileToParam()[*] is used to bind a parameter marker in an SQL statement to a file containing a large object. The content of the file is substituted for the parameter marker when the SQL statement is executed.

  SQLBindFileToCol()[*] is used in fetching the result of a query. It directs the system to deliver the values of a particular large-object column into a file rather than into a program variable.

- Functions for managing transactions:

  SQLEndTran() can be used to commit or abort the active transaction(s) associated with a particular database connection or with all database connections. Note that in CLI, transaction commit and abort are accomplished by function calls rather than by SQL statements. Also note that the autocommit option, controlled by SQLSetConnectAttr(), automatically commits every SQL statement as soon as it is executed. The autocommit option is turned on by default, and you must turn it off if you wish to control your own transactions.

- Functions for querying the system catalog tables (each of these functions executes a query, whose result can then be retrieved using SQLFetch() and the other functions that operate on result sets):

  SQLTables() lists the names of tables (including views and aliases) that are stored in a given database.

  SQLColumns() lists the names and datatypes of the columns in a specified table.

  SQLForeignKeys() lists the names of columns used in the foreign keys of a table.

  SQLPrimaryKeys() lists the names of columns used in the primary key of a table.

  SQLSpecialColumns() lists columns that participate in either a primary key or a unique index.

  SQLStatistics() returns information about the number of rows in a table and about the indexes that are maintained on a table.

  SQLTablePrivileges() lists the privileges that you hold on various tables in the database.

  SQLColumnPrivileges() lists the privileges that you hold on various columns in the database.

  SQLProcedures() lists the stored procedures that are available for use in a given database.

  SQLProcedureColumns() lists the input and output parameters associated with a stored procedure.

- Functions for obtaining information about available databases and servers:

  SQLDataSources() lists the databases that are available for your program to use.

  SQLGetInfo() returns general information about the functionality of the database system to which the CLI program is connected.

  SQLGetFunctions() returns information about the specific CLI functions that are supported by a given database server; you can use this information to make your application more portable.

  SQLGetTypeInfo() returns information about the datatypes supported by a particular database.

- Functions that are used to operate directly on descriptors (all these operations can also be accomplished in other ways):

  SQLSetDescRec() sets the datatype and host program address that are bound to a given column or input parameter.

  SQLGetDescRec() returns the name (if any) and datatype of a column or input parameter.

SQLSetDescField() sets the value of a specific field in a descriptor, such as the datatype or length of a column or input parameter.

SQLGetDescField() returns the value of a specific field in a descriptor, such as the datatype or length of a column or input parameter.

SQLCopyDesc() copies the contents of a descriptor into another descriptor. This might be useful, for example, if data is to be fetched from one table and inserted into another table.

8.1.4 Typed Parameter Markers

As noted earlier in this chapter, a parameter marker is used to denote a data value that is not known at the time when a dynamic SQL statement is being prepared for execution. Parameter markers are represented by question marks and can be used in SQL statements executed by any of the dynamic SQL facilities. A parameter marker represents a single data value and may be used anyplace where a host variable could be used. A parameter marker may not take the place of a table name, column name, or SQL keyword. In the following dynamic SQL statement, the two question marks represent missing values for a salary and an employee number, which must be provided by binding the parameter markers to host variables before the statement is executed:

```
UPDATE employees SET salary = ? WHERE empno = ?
```

Since UDB is a strongly typed system, it needs to know the datatype of each value used in an SQL statement during compilation. If a value is represented by a constant or a host variable, the system can easily infer its datatype from the appearance of the constant or the declared datatype of the host variable. But if the value is represented by a parameter marker, inferring its datatype is more difficult. If the parameter marker is being compared to a value of a known datatype (as in the predicate empno = ?) or inserted into a column of known datatype (as in the assignment salary = ?), the system can infer its datatype from context. But in other cases, the system must rely on the user to declare the datatype of the parameter marker, using a notation called a *typed parameter marker*. The syntax of a typed parameter marker is as follows:

Although it resembles the casting notation described in Section 2.4.3, a typed parameter marker is not a true cast. Instead, it is a "promise" by the application programmer that a value of the named datatype (or a value that can be converted to that datatype) will be substituted for the parameter marker when the statement is executed.[3] The SQL compiler will rely on this promise while preparing the SQL statement for execution. Let us consider a case in which the type information in a typed parameter marker is critical to the compilation process.

Suppose that a statement being prepared for execution contains a function call with a parameter marker as one of its arguments, such as `payraise(?)`. Because UDB allows overloaded functions, a user may have defined several `payraise` functions—perhaps `payraise(Varchar(10))`, `payraise(Double)`, and `payraise(Date)`. Since function resolution is based on the datatype of the argument, the system will not be able to choose which function to invoke for `payraise(?)` and will return an error code. However, function selection will be successful if the function argument is a typed parameter marker, as in the example `payraise(CAST(? AS Double))`. In this case, the system will select the function `payraise(Double)`, relying on the user's promise that a value of datatype Double will be provided when the statement is executed. At execution time, if the parameter is bound to a host variable whose datatype corresponds to the SQL datatype Double (or to some datatype that can be converted to Double, such as Integer), the statement will execute successfully. If, on the other hand, the parameter is bound to a host variable that is incompatible with Double, the programmer's "promise" is broken and an error results.

It is a good general policy that all parameter markers used as function arguments should be typed. In earlier releases of DB2 that supported only a fixed set of built-in functions, it was sometimes possible to infer the datatype of an untyped parameter marker passed to a specific function. For example, the built-in `substr` function knows that its second argument must be an Integer. For compatibility with earlier releases, these special cases are still supported in UDB. However, it is good coding practice to use typed parameter markers when passing a parameter marker to a function, regardless of whether the function is built-in or user-defined.

8.1.5 Example Program LOADER1

We will illustrate the use of CLI and parameter markers by writing some example programs. Each of the examples will use dynamically computed SQL statements that could not be executed by a static SQL program.

---

3. If the named datatype is a distinct type, the value provided at execution time must have (or be convertible to) the base datatype of that distinct type.

The first example is a bulk loader that we will write using all three dynamic SQL facilities—CLI, JDBC, and Embedded Dynamic SQL—in order to compare the three approaches. The CLI version of this program is named LOADER1. It uses dynamic SQL to create and load a table whose name is not known at compile time. In this simple example, the names and datatypes of the columns are fixed, but in a more complex general-purpose table loader, these datatypes could be read or computed dynamically.

For this example, let us imagine that we work at a laboratory that needs to record a series of experiments in a database. Each experiment consists of a series of trials, and each trial consists of a name and a value. The data from each experiment is recorded in a file. Each file contains the name of the experiment and the number of trials, followed by the name and value of each trial in the experiment. The data from each experiment needs to be loaded into a two-column table, using the name of the experiment as the name of the table. Our loader program reads the name of the experiment and the number of trials, and creates a table to hold the data. In our example, the tables created by the loader program always have two columns—the first column has name TRIALNAME and datatype Varchar(18), and the second has name TRIALVALUE and datatype Double.

After creating the table, our loader program reads the experimental data in the form of a sequence of names and values, then loads the data into the table. The LOADER1 program reads its input data from standard input, which could be piped from a file or from another program.

Figure 8-1 shows an example of two tables that might be created and loaded by LOADER1, containing the results of two experiments named VEGETABLES and FISH.

By preparing an INSERT statement containing parameter markers and then executing it repeatedly, the LOADER1 program incurs the cost of parsing and analyzing the INSERT statement only once. The program consists of a series of steps, which are explained below and labeled in the example code.

VEGETABLES

TRIALNAME	TRIALVALUE
Eggplant	28.35
Okra	16.92
Rhubarb	14.86
Zucchini	25.07

FISH

TRIALNAME	TRIALVALUE
Carp	8.35
Flounder	6.08
Perch	5.29
Smelt	7.70

Figure 8-1: Example Tables Created by LOADER1

Steps for Example Program LOADER1: A Bulk Loader Using CLI

STEP 1: Declare variables. Since a CLI program does not pass through a precompiler, there is no need for an SQL Declare Section such as you would find in a static SQL program. We simply declare our variables using normal C syntax. To ensure the portability of our program, it is wise to use a set of datatypes that are defined in the header file sqlcli1.h rather than native C datatypes. For example, the defined type SQLHSTMT represents the C datatype used for a statement handle (probably long), and the defined type SQLDOUBLE represents the C datatype used to hold a double-precision floating-point value (probably double). The header file sqlcli1.h also includes declarations of the CLI functions that we will need to call.

TIP: The type SQLCHAR is defined in sqlcli1.h as unsigned char. Some C and C++ compilers are sensitive to the difference between the datatypes char* and unsigned char*. If you are using one of these compilers and you have declared some variables of type SQLCHAR* or SQLCHAR[], you will need to cast these variables into the char* type before using them in places where a char* is expected, such as in the arguments of C functions strcat and strlen.

TIP: Some compilers do not load floating-point routines unless your program contains an explicit reference to a floating-point number. To keep these compilers happy, the example program contains a dummy declaration double x = 1.0.

STEP 2: Allocate an environment handle. This directs CLI to set aside an area of memory that it will use to record the state of our application as long as it is running.

Code for Example Program LOADER1: A Bulk Loader Using CLI

```
#include <sqlcli1.h>
#include <stdlib.h>
#include <string.h>
#include <stdio.h>

void errorExit(SQLHENV henv, SQLHDBC hdbc, SQLHSTMT hstmt, char *place);

void main()
   {
   /*
   **   STEP 1: Declare variables
   */
   SQLHENV henv;                       /* environment handle         */
   SQLHDBC hdbc;                       /* connection handle          */
   SQLHSTMT hstmt;                     /* statement handle           */

   SQLCHAR dbname[] = "testdb";        /* name of database           */
   char qstring[80];                   /* holds an SQL statement      */
   char tablename[19];                 /* table to be created        */
   char trialname[19];                 /* name of one trial          */
   SQLINTEGER indicator1;              /* indicator for trialname    */
   SQLDOUBLE trialvalue;               /* value of one trial         */
   SQLINTEGER indicator2;              /* indicator for trialvalue   */

   SQLRETURN rc;                       /* return code                */
   SQLINTEGER ntrials;                 /* no. of trials in expt.     */
   SQLINTEGER baddata;                 /* set to 1 if bad data found */
   SQLINTEGER i;                       /* iteration variable         */
   double x = 1.0;                     /* alert compiler: using float */

   /*
   **   STEP 2: Allocate environment handle
   */
   SQLAllocHandle(SQL_HANDLE_ENV, SQL_NULL_HANDLE, &henv);
```

STEP 3: Allocate a connection handle. If we plan to have multiple database connections (to the same or different databases), we will need multiple connection handles. Each connection handle has a set of properties such as isolation level and autocommit that govern the way in which our application will connect to a database. Autocommit is a particularly important connection option, because it determines whether each SQL statement is automatically committed after execution. The default value of autocommit is ON. In this example program, since we prefer to control our own commits and rollbacks, we use `SQLSetConnectAttr()` to turn autocommit OFF.

STEP 4: Connect to the database. Using the `SQLConnect()` function, we can connect to any database in the system database directory. If the server to which we wish to connect is performing authentication, we need to provide a valid userid and password at connect time. The constant SQL_NTS is used to indicate that the database name is passed in the form of a null-terminated string.

STEP 5: Allocate a statement handle. This handle will be used to execute many SQL statements, one after another.

STEP 6: Read the name of the experiment and the number of trials.

STEP 7: Construct and execute an SQL statement to create a table. In this simple example, the name of the table is determined by the name of the experiment, and the names and datatypes of the columns are known in advance. Of course, a more complex loader program could read or compute the number of columns to be created, as well as their names and datatypes, and could construct its CREATE TABLE statement accordingly.

We construct our CREATE TABLE statement as an ordinary character string. According to our laboratory rules, the value of a trial can be null, but the name of a trial is never null, so we include the phrase NOT NULL in the definition of the TRIALNAME column. The CLI function `SQLExecDirect()` causes our dynamic CREATE TABLE statement to be prepared and executed in one step, returning a code that indicates success or failure. In case of failure, we will pass the current context (the three handles and a notation of where the error occurred) to a routine called `errorExit`, which is discussed later.

STEP 8: Prepare an INSERT statement. Now that the table has been created, we are ready to insert data into the table, using an INSERT statement for each row. But since we plan to insert many rows, we don't want each INSERT statement to be a "surprise" that the system needs to parse and analyze from scratch. It's far more efficient to prepare a "prototype" INSERT statement in which the data values are represented by parameter markers (question marks). Once prepared, the statement can be executed as many times as we like without reinvoking the system parser and optimizer. Remember that parameter markers can be used only to substitute for missing data *values*, not for table names, column names, or keywords.

```
/*
**   STEP 3: Allocate connection handle and turn off autocommit option.
**   (Warning: the default is autocommit ON.)
*/
SQLAllocHandle(SQL_HANDLE_DBC, henv, &hdbc);
SQLSetConnectAttr(hdbc, SQL_ATTR_AUTOCOMMIT, SQL_AUTOCOMMIT_OFF, 0);


/*
**   STEP 4: Connect to database
*/
rc = SQLConnect(hdbc, dbname, SQL_NTS,
                      NULL, SQL_NTS,
                      NULL, SQL_NTS);
if (rc != SQL_SUCCESS)
   errorExit(henv, hdbc, SQL_NULL_HSTMT, "Connecting to database");


/*
**   STEP 5: Allocate statement handle
*/
SQLAllocHandle(SQL_HANDLE_STMT, hdbc, &hstmt);


/*
**   STEP 6: Read name of experiment and number of trials
*/
scanf ("%18s %d\n", tablename, &ntrials);


/*
**   STEP 7: Construct and execute a CREATE TABLE statement
*/
strcpy (qstring, "CREATE TABLE ");
strcat (qstring, tablename);
strcat (qstring,
          " (trialname Varchar(18) NOT NULL, trialvalue Double)" );
rc = SQLExecDirect (hstmt, (SQLCHAR *)qstring, SQL_NTS);
if (rc != SQL_SUCCESS)
   errorExit(henv, hdbc, hstmt, "Executing Create Table");


/*
**   STEP 8: Prepare an INSERT with two parameter markers
*/
strcpy (qstring, "INSERT INTO ");
strcat (qstring, tablename);
strcat (qstring, " VALUES (?, ?)" );
rc = SQLPrepare(hstmt, (SQLCHAR *)qstring, SQL_NTS);
if (rc != SQL_SUCCESS)
   errorExit(henv, hdbc, hstmt, "Preparing Insert statement");
```

STEP 9: Bind variables to parameter markers. Before the prepared INSERT statement can be executed, it is necessary to tell the system where to find the missing data values. This is done by calls to SQLBindParameter() that associate each parameter marker with two host variable addresses: one that contains the actual data, and another "indicator" variable. The indicator variable is used to indicate a null value by the code SQL_NULL_DATA (–1). If the variable being bound to the parameter marker contains a non-null character string, the indicator variable contains the length of the string, or the code SQL_NTS (–3), which means "null-terminated string."

As part of the binding process, the SQL datatype of the parameter and the C datatype of the host variable to which it is bound must both be specified so that the system can provide any necessary conversions. Each time the prepared statement is executed, the system will take a new data value (or null) from the host variables that are bound to each of the parameter markers.

STEP 10: Read and insert the data. Now that the parameter markers are bound to variables, we can execute a loop that reads input data into the bound variables and executes the prepared INSERT statement repeatedly. We also check the input data for validity, and if it appears invalid, we set a "bad data" flag and break out of the loop. Each trial is represented by three input values, which are read by scanf: the trial name, the trial value, and a code that is set to 0 for a valid trial value or –1 for a null value. This code is used in indicator2 (the indicator variable of the TRIALVALUE column), and indicator1 (the indicator variable of the TRIALNAME column) is set to SQL_NTS to indicate a null-terminated string. The INSERT is executed by calling SQLExecute() and passing the handle of the prepared statement. The return code indicates success or failure, and we call our errorExit routine in case of failure.

```
/*
**   STEP 9: Bind host variables to the parameter markers
*/
SQLBindParameter(hstmt,
            1,                              /* first parameter marker    */
            SQL_PARAM_INPUT,                /* input parameter           */
            SQL_C_CHAR,                     /* datatype of host variable */
            SQL_VARCHAR,                    /* SQL datatype              */
            18,                             /* max length of input data  */
            0,                              /* not used in this call     */
            (SQLPOINTER)trialname,          /* address of host variable  */
            sizeof(trialname),              /* size of input buffer      */
            &indicator1 );                  /* null or length indicator  */

SQLBindParameter(hstmt,
            2,                              /* second parameter marker   */
            SQL_PARAM_INPUT,                /* input parameter           */
            SQL_C_DOUBLE,                   /* datatype of host variable */
            SQL_DOUBLE,                     /* SQL datatype              */
            0,                              /* not used in this call     */
            0,                              /* not used in this call     */
            (SQLPOINTER)&trialvalue,        /* address of host variable  */
            8,                              /* size of input buffer      */
            &indicator2 );                  /* null or length indicator  */

/*
**   STEP 10: Execute the INSERT statement for each input data record
*/
baddata = 0;
indicator1 = SQL_NTS;               /* trialname is never null */
for (i=0; i<ntrials && baddata == 0; i++)
    {
    rc = scanf("%18s %lf %d\n", trialname, &trialvalue, &indicator2);
    if (rc != 3 || (indicator2 != 0 && indicator2 != SQL_NULL_DATA))
        {
        baddata = 1;    /* bad input data */
        break;
        }
    rc = SQLExecute(hstmt);
    if (rc != SQL_SUCCESS)
        errorExit(henv, hdbc, hstmt, "Executing Insert statement");
    }
```

STEP 11: Commit or roll back. After completion of the loop, it is time to commit or roll back our transaction. If bad input data was discovered, we will roll back all database changes, including the creation of the table; otherwise, we will commit our changes. In CLI, transactions are committed or rolled back by the SQLEndTran( ) function rather than by an SQL statement. It is important to remember that we can control our own commits and rollbacks only because we turned off the autocommit option in Step 3.

STEP 12: Clean up. The orderly completion of our CLI program requires us to "clean up" by disconnecting from the database and freeing the resources represented by the statement handle, the connection handle, and the environment handle.

```
/*
**   STEP 11: Commit (or roll back if bad data was found)
*/
if (baddata)
    {
    rc = SQLEndTran(SQL_HANDLE_DBC, hdbc, SQL_ROLLBACK);
    if (rc != SQL_SUCCESS)
       errorExit(henv, hdbc, SQL_NULL_HSTMT, "Rollback due to bad data");
    printf ("Bad input data, transaction rolled back.\n");
    rc = -1;
    }
else
    {
    rc = SQLEndTran(SQL_HANDLE_DBC, hdbc, SQL_COMMIT);
    if (rc != SQL_SUCCESS)
       errorExit(henv, hdbc, SQL_NULL_HSTMT, "Commit");
    printf ("Data loaded successfully\n");
    rc = 0;
    }

/*
**   STEP 12: Clean up
*/
SQLFreeHandle(SQL_HANDLE_STMT, hstmt); /* free statement handle    */
SQLDisconnect(hdbc);                   /* disconnect from database */
SQLFreeHandle(SQL_HANDLE_DBC, hdbc);   /* free connection handle   */
SQLFreeHandle(SQL_HANDLE_ENV, henv);   /* free environment handle  */
exit(rc);

}     /* end of main */

void errorExit(SQLHENV henv, SQLHDBC hdbc, SQLHSTMT hstmt, char *place)
    {
    SQLCHAR sqlstate[SQL_SQLSTATE_SIZE + 1];
    SQLINTEGER sqlcode;
    SQLSMALLINT msglength;
    SQLCHAR msgbuffer[SQL_MAX_MESSAGE_LENGTH + 1];
    SQLSMALLINT errno;

    printf ("\nSQL error at %s, transaction rolled back.\n", place);
```

STEP 13: Analyze errors. The `errorExit` routine is called whenever the return code of a CLI function indicates that the function was not successful. This is often caused by an error in the SQL statement that the CLI function is trying to execute. For example, if the CREATE TABLE statement attempts to create a table whose name is the same as that of an existing table, the SQL statement will fail and the `SQLExecDirect()` function will return the code SQL_ERROR. The job of the `errorExit` routine is to find and print more details about why the statement failed. This is done by repeatedly calling the `SQLGetDiagRec()` function, passing the handle associated with the failed statement. Each call to `SQLGetDiagRec()` will return an SQLCODE, an SQLSTATE, and an error message. When there are no more messages to be retrieved, `SQLGetDiagRec()` will return the code SQL_NO_DATA.

STEP 14: Roll back and clean up. If an error was encountered partway through the loading process, we would like to roll back all the database changes we have made so far. This is accomplished by a call to `SQLEndTran()`, followed by calls to disconnect from the database and to free the handles.

8.1.6 Example Program QUERY1

Our second CLI example illustrates how a CLI program can interactively accept queries from a user and execute them, displaying results of various datatypes. This is the way in which interactive interfaces such as the CLP are implemented—in fact, the CLP could have been implemented as a CLI program, but for historical reasons it was implemented using Embedded Dynamic SQL instead. A true interactive query interface is quite a complex program, so we will make some simplifying assumptions for the purpose of this example. We will accept only queries whose result is a single column of datatype Double or Clob. I chose these two datatypes in order to illustrate the handling of different types of data; of course, our program could be extended to handle multiple columns and additional datatypes.

```
/*
**   STEP 13: Retrieve error codes and messages
*/
errno = 1;
sqlstate[5] = '\0';     /* Make sure it's null-terminated */
while ( SQLGetDiagRec(SQL_HANDLE_STMT, hstmt, errno,
          sqlstate, &sqlcode, msgbuffer,
          SQL_MAX_MESSAGE_LENGTH+1, &msglength) == SQL_SUCCESS )
   {
   printf("   SQLCODE = %d, SQLSTATE = %5.5s\n", sqlcode, sqlstate);
   printf("   MESSAGE: %s\n", msgbuffer);
   errno++;
   }

/*
**   STEP 14: Roll back and clean up
*/
SQLEndTran(SQL_HANDLE_DBC, hdbc, SQL_ROLLBACK);          /* rollback */
SQLDisconnect(hdbc);                          /* disconnect from database */
SQLFreeHandle(SQL_HANDLE_DBC, hdbc);   /* free connection handle   */
SQLFreeHandle(SQL_HANDLE_ENV, henv);   /* free environment handle  */
exit(-2);
}
```

The QUERY1 program prompts the user to enter an SQL statement and then executes the SQL statement and displays the result. Since the program is intended only as a query interface, it detects and rolls back any attempt to update the database. The user can cause the program to terminate by entering a null query (empty input line). The program consists of several steps, which are explained below and labeled in the example code.

The query interface application of QUERY1 is repeated in Section 8.3 as an Embedded Dynamic SQL application named QUERY3, providing a side-by-side comparison of the CLI and Embedded Dynamic interfaces.

Steps for Example Program QUERY1: A Query Interface Using CLI

STEP 1: Declare variables. As in example LOADER1, we use the types defined in sqlclil.h rather than native C datatypes to enhance the portability of our program. In this simple example, we know that all query results will consist of a single column and that its datatype will be either Double or Clob. Therefore, we declare buffers to hold results of these two datatypes. To illustrate how Clobs can be handled in CLI programs, we will first fetch Clob data in the form of a locator and then use the locator to fetch the first 10 characters of the Clob (obviously, this can be extended to fetch any desired substring). Thus, our buffers for fetching results consist of a Double, a Clob locator, an 11-character array to hold the Clob substring, and an indicator variable to represent null values.

Code for Example Program QUERY1: A Query Interface Using CLI

```c
#include <stdlib.h>
#include <string.h>
#include <stdio.h>
#include <sqlcli1.h>

void errorExit(SQLHENV henv, SQLHDBC hdbc, SQLHSTMT hstmt, char *place);

int main()
   {
   /*
   **   STEP 1: Declare variables
   */
   SQLHENV henv;                     /* environment handle                */
   SQLHDBC hdbc;                     /* connection handle                 */
   SQLHSTMT hstmt1;                  /* 1st statement handle              */
   SQLHSTMT hstmt2;                  /* 2nd statement handle              */
   SQLHSTMT hstmt3;                  /* 3rd statement handle              */
   SQLRETURN rc;                     /* return code                       */

   SQLCHAR dbname[9] = "testdb";     /* name of database                  */
   char qstring[100];                /* buffer for SQL query              */

   SQLDOUBLE  answerDouble;          /* answer buffer (if type is DOUBLE) */
   SQLINTEGER answerLocator;         /* answer locator (if type is CLOB)  */
   SQLCHAR answerString[11];         /* answer buffer (if type is CLOB)   */
   SQLINTEGER actualLength;          /* length of returned CLOB substring */
   SQLINTEGER nullindicator;         /* set to -1 if answer is null       */
   SQLINTEGER four = 4;              /* constant used in SQLBindParameter() */

   SQLSMALLINT ncols;                        /* no. of columns in result set */
   SQLCHAR colname[SQL_MAX_ID_LENGTH+1]; /* name of result column        */
   SQLSMALLINT colnamelen;                   /* actual length of column name */
   SQLSMALLINT coltype;                      /* datatype of result column    */

   SQLCHAR sqlstate[SQL_SQLSTATE_SIZE+1];              /* result sqlstate    */
   SQLINTEGER sqlcode;                                 /* result sqlcode     */
   SQLCHAR msgbuffer[SQL_MAX_MESSAGE_LENGTH+1];    /* error msg buffer */
   SQLSMALLINT msglength;                     /* actual length of error message */
   SQLSMALLINT errno;                         /* error counter              */
```

STEP 2: Allocate an environment handle and a connection handle and turn off the autocommit option. This enables us to control our own commits and rollbacks. This program is intended to be a query interface, and we will force a rollback if a user attempts to execute a statement that modifies the database.

STEP 3: Connect to the database. This call to SQLConnect() illustrates how we can check the return code after each CLI function call and invoke a routine named errorExit to retrieve and display messages in the event of an error. To save space in our example code, we will not repeat this return code check after each CLI call.

STEP 4: Allocate three statement handles. We need a separate statement handle for each statement that will be "active" at the same time. For example, hstmt1 will maintain a cursor position while hstmt2 fetches a substring and hstmt3 frees a Clob locator.

STEP 5: Get an SQL statement from the user. We prompt the user to enter a statement and read it into the qstring buffer.

```
/*
**   STEP 2: Allocate environment and connection handles.
**   Turn off autocommit option (warning: default is autocommit ON).
*/
SQLAllocHandle(SQL_HANDLE_ENV, SQL_NULL_HANDLE, &henv);
SQLAllocHandle(SQL_HANDLE_DBC, henv, &hdbc);
SQLSetConnectAttr(hdbc, SQL_ATTR_AUTOCOMMIT, SQL_AUTOCOMMIT_OFF, 0);


/*
**   STEP 3: Connect to database, test return code.
**   Similar checks for errors could be added to all CLI calls
**   but have been omitted for brevity.
*/
rc = SQLConnect(hdbc, dbname, SQL_NTS,
                      NULL, SQL_NTS,   /* provide userid, if needed   */
                      NULL, SQL_NTS);  /* provide password, if needed */
if (rc != SQL_SUCCESS)
   errorExit(henv, hdbc, SQL_NULL_HSTMT, "Connecting to database");


/*
**   STEP 4: Allocate three statement handles
*/
SQLAllocHandle(SQL_HANDLE_STMT, hdbc, &hstmt1);
SQLAllocHandle(SQL_HANDLE_STMT, hdbc, &hstmt2);
SQLAllocHandle(SQL_HANDLE_STMT, hdbc, &hstmt3);


/*
**   STEP 5: Get an SQL statement from the user
*/
printf("\nEnter a query, or empty string to quit:\n");
gets(qstring);
```

STEP 6: Execute the statement. At this point, we do not have a clue as to whether qstring contains a valid SQL statement or what kind of a statement it might be. To find the answer to these questions, we begin by examining the return code from SQLExecDirect(), which will be one of the following:

SQL_ERROR: This code indicates that qstring does not contain a valid SQL statement. We call SQLGetDiagRec() to retrieve and display the diagnostic messages, and prompt the user to enter another statement.

SQL_NO_DATA_FOUND: Surprisingly, this code does not indicate that the SQL statement was a query with an empty result set. Instead, it indicates that the statement was a valid UPDATE or DELETE statement that didn't happen to update or delete any rows. Since the database was not modified by the statement, there's no harm done, and we simply print a message and prompt the user to enter another statement.

SQL_SUCCESS or SQL_SUCCESS_WITH_INFO: These codes indicate that the SQL statement executed successfully, possibly with one or more informational messages. We print the messages, if any, and continue with our analysis of the result.

STEP 7: The next step in our analysis is to check the number of columns in the result set by calling the CLI function SQLNumResultCols(). This gives us an important clue about the SQL statement that was just executed. If the number of result columns is zero, the statement was not a query. This means that the user has successfully executed an SQL statement that was not a query, but we don't know what it was—it might even have modified the database. Since our program is a query-only interface, we will roll back the last statement and prompt the user to enter another statement.

If the number of columns in the result set is greater than one, the user will need to wait for a more sophisticated query interface than this example. We simply print a message and prompt for the next statement.

STEP 8: If the number of columns in the result set is exactly one, we know that the SQL statement was a successful one-column query. The next step is to obtain the name of the column and its datatype by calling the CLI function SQL-DescribeCol(), and to print the name of the column. We can then branch according to the datatype of the column. If the datatype of the column is a distinct type, SQLDescribeCol() retrieves the base datatype corresponding to that distinct type; the name of the distinct type can then be obtained by a call to SQLColAttributes(). Our simple example handles only a single column of type Double or Clob, but it would not be hard to extend the program to handle multiple columns of multiple datatypes.

```
while (strlen(qstring)>0)
    {
    /*
    **   STEP 6: Execute the statement and check return code
    */
    rc = SQLExecDirect (hstmt1, (SQLCHAR *)qstring, SQL_NTS);
    if (rc == SQL_NO_DATA_FOUND)
       printf("Your statement had no effect on the database.\n");
    if (rc == SQL_ERROR || rc == SQL_SUCCESS_WITH_INFO)
       {
       printf("Result of processing your SQL statement:\n");
       errno = 1;
       while ( SQLGetDiagRec(SQL_HANDLE_STMT, hstmt1, errno,
                  sqlstate, &sqlcode, msgbuffer,
                  SQL_MAX_MESSAGE_LENGTH+1, &msglength) == SQL_SUCCESS )
          {
          printf("   SQLCODE = %d, SQLSTATE = %s\n", sqlcode, sqlstate);
          printf("   MESSAGE: %s\n", msgbuffer);
          errno++;
          }
       }
    if (rc == SQL_SUCCESS || rc == SQL_SUCCESS_WITH_INFO)
       {
       /*
       **   STEP 7: Check the number of columns in the result set
       */
       rc = SQLNumResultCols(hstmt1, &ncols);
       if (ncols == 0)
          {
          printf("Your statement was not a valid query.\n");
          printf("Any updates have been rolled back.\n");
          SQLEndTran(SQL_HANDLE_DBC, hdbc, SQL_ROLLBACK);
          }
       else if (ncols > 1)
          printf("The result set has more than one column.\n");
       else
          {
          /*
          **   STEP 8: Get the column name and datatype, then
          **   print the column name
          */
          rc = SQLDescribeCol(hstmt1, 1, colname, SQL_MAX_ID_LENGTH,
                     &colnamelen, &coltype, NULL, NULL, NULL);
          printf("%s\n", colname);
          printf("------------------\n");
```

STEP 9:   If the datatype of the result column is SQL_DOUBLE, we need to fetch and display a column of double-precision floating-point numbers. In CLI, we do not need to explicitly open a cursor to fetch a result set. After a query has been executed, its statement handle automatically serves as a cursor on the result set and need not be explicitly opened.

In order to fetch answer values, we must first tell CLI where to deliver them. The SQLBindCol() function binds our buffer named answerDouble, and its indicator variable, to the first column of the result set. Then, each time we call SQLFetch(), one answer value is fetched into the answer buffer and the indicator variable. We continue fetching values and displaying them as long as we get successful return codes from SQLFetch(). If the user's SQL statement was a valid query with an empty result set, the first SQLFetch() will return a code of SQL_NO_DATA_FOUND. When we run out of results, we are ready to prompt the user for the next SQL statement.

STEP 10:   If the datatype of the result column is SQL_CLOB, we need to fetch and display a column of Clob-type data. In this example program, we demonstrate the manipulation of Clobs by first fetching each Clob in the form of a locator, then using the locator to materialize the first 10 bytes of the Clob value into a buffer. First, we bind a variable of type SQLINTEGER (and an indicator variable) to the first column of the result set and indicate by a code that we wish to retrieve values in locator form. Each call to SQLFetch() delivers the locator of the next Clob value.

```
switch(coltype)
    {
    case SQL_DOUBLE:
        /*
        **   STEP 9: Fetch a column of Double-type answers
        **   and display them
        */
        SQLBindCol(hstmt1, 1, SQL_C_DOUBLE,
                           &answerDouble, 0, &nullindicator);
        rc = SQLFetch(hstmt1);
        if (rc == SQL_NO_DATA_FOUND)
            printf("Result set is empty.\n");
        else while (rc == SQL_SUCCESS
                        || rc == SQL_SUCCESS_WITH_INFO)
            {
            if (nullindicator==SQL_NULL_DATA) printf("(Null)\n");
            else printf("%f\n", answerDouble);
            rc = SQLFetch(hstmt1);
            }
        break;        /* end of SQL_DOUBLE case */

    case SQL_CLOB:
        /*
        **   STEP 10: Fetch a column of Clob-type answers
        **   in Locator form
        */
        SQLBindCol(hstmt1, 1, SQL_C_CLOB_LOCATOR,
                           &answerLocator, 0, &nullindicator);
        rc = SQLFetch(hstmt1);
        if (rc == SQL_NO_DATA_FOUND)
            printf("Result set is empty.\n");
        else while (rc == SQL_SUCCESS
                        || rc == SQL_SUCCESS_WITH_INFO)
            {
            if (nullindicator==SQL_NULL_DATA) printf("(Null)\n");
```

STEP 11: Once we have fetched a locator, we can use it in one or more calls to `SQLGet-SubString()` to materialize any desired subset of the actual Clob value. Notice that we need to use our second statement handle for the call to `SQLGetSubString()`, because the first statement handle is still "active," maintaining a cursor position in the result set.

STEP 12: After printing the Clob value, we don't need its locator anymore, so we free it, using our third statement handle to execute a FREE LOCATOR statement. Since the parameter of the FREE LOCATOR statement is always bound to the same host variable, the call to `SQLBindParameter()` could have been taken out of the loop and executed only once at the beginning of the program (but we have left it here for clarity).

```
else   /* Clob value is not null */
   {
   /*
   **   STEP 11: For each Clob, use its locator to
   **   fetch the first 10 characters of the answer
   */
   SQLGetSubString
      (hstmt2,              /* 2nd stmt handle    */
      SQL_C_CLOB_LOCATOR,   /* source type        */
      answerLocator,        /* source locator     */
      1,                    /* starting position  */
      10,                   /* how many chars     */
      SQL_C_CHAR,           /* target type        */
      answerString,         /* target buffer      */
      11,                   /* size of buffer     */
      &actualLength,        /* returned length    */
      &nullindicator );     /* null indicator     */

   printf("%s ...\n", answerString);

   /*
   **   STEP 12: Free the Clob locator.  The
   **   SQLBindParameter could be taken out of the loop
   */
   SQLBindParameter
      (hstmt3,              /* 3rd stmt handle    */
      1,                    /* parameter number   */
      SQL_PARAM_INPUT,      /* input parameter    */
      SQL_C_CLOB_LOCATOR,   /* C type of parm     */
      SQL_CLOB_LOCATOR,     /* SQL type of parm   */
      0,                    /* not used here      */
      0,                    /* not used here      */
      &answerLocator,       /* addr. of locator   */
      0,                    /* not used here      */
      &four);               /* length of locator  */

   SQLExecDirect
      (hstmt3, (SQLCHAR *)"FREE LOCATOR ?", SQL_NTS);
   }
```

STEP 13: Using statement handle hstmt1, we now fetch the next Clob value in the form of a locator.

STEP 14: This simple example demonstrates the handling of two datatypes; obviously, it could be extended to handle other datatypes as well by adding more cases to the switch statement.

STEP 15: The call to SQLCloseCursor() closes the cursor associated with the first statement handle but retains the handle for executing another statement. We are now ready to prompt the user for another SQL statement and return to the top of the loop.

STEP 16: When the user has indicated (by entering a null line) that there are no more queries to be processed, we end our transaction, release our various handles, and exit from the program.

```
                /*
                **  STEP 13: Fetch the next Clob value in Locator form
                */
                rc = SQLFetch(hstmt1);
                }
            break;     /* end of SQL_CLOB case */

        default:
            /*
            **  STEP 14: Other datatypes could be added here
            */
            printf("Answer datatype %d is not DOUBLE or CLOB\n",
                                                    coltype);
            break;     /* end of default case */

        }              /* end of switch on coltype              */
    }              /* end of case where result set has 1 column */
}          /* end of processing a successful query          */

/*
**  STEP 15: Close the cursor and get the next query
*/
SQLCloseCursor(hstmt1);
printf("\nEnter a query, or empty string to quit:\n");
gets(qstring);
}     /* end of while-loop that processes queries */

/*
**  STEP 16: Commit the transaction and clean up
*/
printf("\nGoodbye, have a nice day.\n");

SQLEndTran(SQL_HANDLE_DBC, hdbc, SQL_COMMIT); /* commit transaction */
SQLFreeHandle(SQL_HANDLE_STMT, hstmt1); /* free statement-1 handle  */
SQLFreeHandle(SQL_HANDLE_STMT, hstmt2); /* free statement-2 handle  */
SQLDisconnect(hdbc);                    /* disconnect from database */
SQLFreeHandle(SQL_HANDLE_DBC, hdbc);    /* free connection handle   */
SQLFreeHandle(SQL_HANDLE_ENV, henv);    /* free environment handle  */
return (0);
}    /* end of main */
```

STEP 17: All of our CLI calls should check their return codes and invoke an error-handling routine if necessary (though we have omitted most of these calls for brevity). In this example, the error handler prints the place at which the error was detected; retrieves and prints all the available error codes and messages; and finally rolls back the transaction, disconnects from the database, and exits.

```
void errorExit(SQLHENV henv, SQLHDBC hdbc, SQLHSTMT hstmt, char *place)
   {
   SQLCHAR sqlstate[SQL_SQLSTATE_SIZE + 1];
   SQLINTEGER sqlcode;
   SQLSMALLINT msglength;
   SQLCHAR msgbuffer[SQL_MAX_MESSAGE_LENGTH + 1];
   SQLSMALLINT errno;

   printf ("\nSQL error at %s\n", place);

   /*
   **   STEP 17: Retrieve error codes and messages.
   **   Then roll back, clean up, and exit.
   */
   errno = 1;
   sqlstate[5] = '\0';     /* Make sure it's null-terminated */
   while ( SQLGetDiagRec(SQL_HANDLE_STMT, hstmt, errno,
             sqlstate, &sqlcode, msgbuffer,
             SQL_MAX_MESSAGE_LENGTH+1, &msglength) == SQL_SUCCESS )
      {
      printf("   SQLCODE = %d, SQLSTATE = %s\n", sqlcode, sqlstate);
      printf("   MESSAGE: %s\n", msgbuffer);
      errno++;
      }

   SQLEndTran(SQL_HANDLE_DBC, hdbc, SQL_ROLLBACK);         /* rollback */
   SQLDisconnect(hdbc);                        /* disconnect from database */
   SQLFreeHandle(SQL_HANDLE_DBC, hdbc);   /* free connection handle   */
   SQLFreeHandle(SQL_HANDLE_ENV, henv);   /* free environment handle  */
   exit(-2);
   }
```

8.2 USING DYNAMIC SQL WITH JAVA

Java Database Connectivity (JDBC) is a dynamic SQL interface for use with the Java programming language. JDBC was defined by JavaSoft, a subsidiary of Sun Microsystems, and is similar in many ways to CLI—in fact, in UDB, JDBC is implemented on top of CLI. JDBC is supported by many relational database systems and has become the de facto standard interface for accessing relational data from Java programs. The best source of information about Java and JDBC is on the World Wide Web. For example, you can find a detailed specification of the JDBC interface at `http://java.sun.com/products/jdbc`.

Since it is a dynamic interface, JDBC provides the same advantages as CLI, as well as the following additional advantages:

1. JDBC is nicely integrated into the Java language and allows you to access relational databases using an object-oriented programming style. For example, the result set of a query is represented in JDBC by a class named `ResultSet`, which implements methods such as `next` to retrieve the rows of the result set.

2. In addition to conventional applications, JDBC allows you to write Java *applets* that access your database. An applet can be invoked by any Java-enabled web browser. By writing applets, you can make your UDB data available to any machine on the World Wide Web without requiring installation of any client software other than a web browser.

Your UDB installation provides some example JDBC applications and applets in the directory `sqllib/samples/java`.

8.2.1 JDBC Applications

If you are acquainted with CLI, the process of writing a JDBC application will seem very familiar to you. JDBC provides an object-oriented interface for manipulating SQL statements and their result sets—the same kinds of objects that are manipulated in CLI by means of "handles."

A JDBC application is much like any other database application that is written in a host programming language (Java, in this case). As usual, the application runs on a client machine and the database resides on a server machine, which may or may not be the same as the client machine. As usual, the client machine must have support for the host language (in this case, a Java compiler and virtual machine), and if it needs to connect to a remote server, it must have installed the UDB Client Application Enabler (CAE). In addition, certain environment variables must be set on the client machine:

• The CLASSPATH variable, used by the Java virtual machine to search for classes, must include the library named `sqllib/java/db2java.zip`. (You may also wish to include some other class libraries.)

- On AIX and Solaris platforms, the variable LD_LIBRARY_PATH must be set to include the path sqllib/lib; similarly, on the HP-UX platform, the variable SHLIB_PATH must be set to include sqllib/lib.

Environment variables are set in different ways on different platforms. For example, on Windows NT, you can control your environment variables by clicking on Start, then Settings, then Control Panel, then System, then Environment.

Like all object-oriented interfaces, JDBC consists of a set of *classes*, which in turn implement a set of *methods*. The most important JDBC classes are Connection, Statement, and ResultSet, which are described below.

Connection

Like a CLI connection handle, a Connection represents a session with a specific database manager, interacting with a specific database, authorized against a specific user. Also, as in CLI, a Connection controls certain properties of the database interaction, such as the isolation level and whether a transaction is committed automatically after each SQL statement.

A Connection is obtained by calling the getConnection method of the DriverManager class and providing a Universal Resource Locator (URL) that identifies the database to which you wish to connect. The DriverManager class finds a JDBC driver that can connect to the desired database (since UDB's driver may not be the only JDBC driver that is installed on your machine). Once a suitable driver has been identified, a database connection is established and represented by a Connection object.

The most important methods of the Connection class are as follows:

getMetaData() returns information about the functionality of the database manager and the content of the database. This information is returned in the form of an object of type DatabaseMetaData, which has many methods of its own for retrieving specific information such as lists of table names and column names.

setTransactionIsolation(int) controls the isolation level of transactions that use this Connection.

setAutoCommit(Boolean) determines whether a transaction is automatically committed after the execution of each SQL statement in this Connection. As in CLI, the autocommit feature is turned on by default in JDBC and must be turned off explicitly for any Connection in which you need to control the boundaries of your transactions.

createStatement() creates a Statement object that can be used to execute an SQL statement. Several Statement objects can be used in the same Connection.

prepareStatement(String) prepares a specific statement for repeated execution. This method returns an object of type PreparedStatement, a subclass of Statement. The prepared statement may contain parameter markers, represented by question marks. Specific values must be bound to the parameter markers before the prepared statement is executed.

commit() commits the current transaction associated with this Connection.

rollback() rolls back the current transaction associated with this Connection.

Statement

Like a CLI statement handle, a JDBC Statement object represents one SQL statement. The statement can be executed immediately, or it can be prepared once and then executed multiple times with different parameters. The most important methods of the Statement class are as follows:

executeQuery(String) executes an SQL query and returns a ResultSet object that contains the result of the query.

executeUpdate(String) can be used to execute any SQL statement that is not a query. Despite its name, this method is not restricted to updates, but can execute other nonquery statements such as CREATE TABLE. It returns a count of the rows that were modified by the statement, if any.

setCursorName(String) defines the cursor name to be associated with the result set of this statement. Once defined, the cursor name can be used in positioned updates and deletes executed by other Statements.

execute(String) is a general-purpose method that you might use to execute an SQL statement when you do not know whether it is a query or not. This method returns a boolean that is TRUE if the statement produces a result set. Based on the result of the execute method, you can then invoke other methods such as getResultSet(), getUpdateCount(), and getMoreResults().

The Statement class has two important subclasses: PreparedStatement, which represents a statement that is prepared once for repeated execution, and CallableStatement, which represents a stored procedure. Before a PreparedStatement can be executed, values must be provided for all the parameter markers in the statement. This is done by a collection of methods that bind values of various types to the parameter markers. For each Java datatype that might be bound to a parameter of an SQL statement, the Statement class has a parameter-binding method. Here are some examples of how these methods might be used:

stmt1.setDouble(3, 28.5) binds the Double value 28.5 to the third parameter marker of the Statement object named stmt1.

`stmt1.setString(5, "Queen Elizabeth")` binds the String value "Queen Elizabeth" to the fifth parameter marker of Statement `stmt1`.

`stmt1.setNull(7, INTEGER)` binds a null value to the seventh parameter marker of Statement `stmt1`. The constant `INTEGER` is a typecode that specifies the datatype of the null value.

ResultSet

A ResultSet is an ordered set of rows that represents the result of executing an SQL query. A ResultSet maintains a *cursor position* on one of the rows of the query result, and this position can be used to define the row to be operated on by a positioned update or delete statement. When a ResultSet is first created, its cursor position is defined to be just before the first row in the set.

The methods of the ResultSet class include the following:

`getMetaData()` returns information about the size and shape of the query result, in the form of a ResultSetMetaData object, which has many methods of its own for retrieving specific information such as the number, names, and datatypes of the columns in the result set.

`next()` advances the cursor position to the next row of the result set.

The technique used in JDBC for actually fetching values into host variables is different from that of CLI and eliminates the need for null indicator variables. For each Java datatype that is compatible with an SQL datatype, the ResultSet class has a "get" method that returns the value of a column of the current row (the row on which the cursor is positioned). The column to be fetched by the "get" method can be identified either by its name or by its number. ResultSet also has a `wasNull()` method that returns a Boolean, indicating whether the last value fetched was null. The following examples illustrate how some of these methods might be used:

`result1.getDouble(3)` returns the value of the third column of the current row of the ResultSet `result1`, using the Java datatype double. If the value of this column is null, the `getDouble` method returns zero.

`result1.wasNull()` returns TRUE if the previous value fetched was null, enabling you to distinguish a real zero from a null value.

`result1.getString("address")` returns the value of the column named ADDRESS in the current row of the ResultSet `result1`, in the form of a Java String.

TIP: If you are retrieving data that may include null values, remember to call the `wasNull()` method immediately after fetching each value—after you have fetched the next value, it will be too late.

As noted above, the JDBC technique for exchanging values with the database relies on methods based on the Java datatypes (setDouble, setString, and so on for input variables, and getDouble, getString, and so on for output variables). For output, JDBC allows you a great deal of flexibility in the selection of a Java datatype to receive a given database value. For example, a numeric value might be fetched from the database by any of several methods, including getInt, getBigDecimal, and getDouble. In fact, any SQL datatype can be converted into a Java String object by the getString method.

For input, each of the JDBC "set..." methods binds a parameter marker to a value of a specific SQL datatype. You must choose a method whose SQL datatype is compatible with the way the parameter marker is used in your SQL statement.

Table 8-1 lists the SQL datatypes and their corresponding Java datatypes, and the names of methods that can be used for input and output of each datatype. The output methods listed are only examples, since each SQL datatype can be fetched by several JDBC methods. More details on input and output methods can be found in the JDBC documentation.

8.2.2 Example Program LOADER2

As an example of a JDBC application, we will rewrite the LOADER1 program that appeared as a CLI example in Section 8.1. The program (called LOADER2 this time) takes its input from a file whose name is passed to the program as an argument. The program reads the name of a table from the input file and creates a two-column table with the given name and with columns named TRIALNAME and TRIALVALUE; then it reads a series of data values and loads them into the table. As in the CLI version of the program, LOADER2 prepares an INSERT statement with two parameter markers, and then executes the statement once for each row of data to be loaded. The details of the JDBC objects and methods that accomplish these tasks are discussed further in comments in the example program.

TABLE 8-1: SQL Datatypes and Compatible Java Datatypes

SQL Datatype	Compatible Java Datatype or Class	Input Method	Example of Output Method
Smallint	short	setShort	getShort
Integer	int	setInt	getInt
Decimal	bigDecimal	setBigDecimal	getBigDecimal
Real	float	setFloat	getFloat
Double	double	setDouble	getDouble
Char	String	setString	getString
Varchar	String	setString	getString
Char or Varchar for bit data	String	setBytes	getBytes
Long Varchar	InputStream	setAsciiStream or setUnicodeStream	getAsciiStream or getUnicodeStream
Long Varchar for bit data	InputStream	setBinaryStream	getBinaryStream
Clob	InputStream	setAsciiStream or setUnicodeStream	getAsciiStream or getUnicodeStream
Graphic	byte[ ]	setString	getString
Vargraphic	byte[ ]	setString	getString
Long Vargraphic	InputStream	setAsciiStream or setUnicodeStream	getAsciiStream or getUnicodeStream
Dbclob	InputStream	setAsciiStream or setUnicodeStream	getAsciiStream or getUnicodeStream
Blob	InputStream	setBinaryStream	getBinaryStream
Date	Date	setDate	getDate
Time	Time	setTime	getTime
Timestamp	Timestamp	setTimestamp	getTimestamp

Example Program LOADER2: A Bulk Loader Application Using JDBC

```java
import java.io.*;
import java.util.*;
import java.sql.*;

public class loader2
  {

  // STEP 1: Register the JDBC driver for DB2.
  //         This code block runs before main(), and enables Java
  //         to find the driver classes for handling JDBC objects.
  static
    {
    try
      {
      Class.forName("COM.ibm.db2.jdbc.app.DB2Driver");
      // For JDK 1.1.2 on AIX or OS/2, replace the above line as follows:
      // Class.forName("COM.ibm.db2.jdbc.app.DB2Driver").newInstance();
      }
    catch (Exception e)
      {
      System.out.println("Error in registering the JDBC driver");
      e.printStackTrace();
      }
    }

  public static void main(String args[])
    {
    BufferedReader input = null;
    StringTokenizer tokens = null;
    String tablename, trialname;
    int i, ntrials;
    Double trialvalue;
    int indicator;
    boolean baddata = false;
```

```
try
  {
  // STEP 2: Create a Connection object and use it to
  //         connect to the database and turn off autocommit.
  //         (Warning: the default is autocommit ON.)
  //         The database is identified by a URL that begins
  //         with "jdbc:db2:" followed by the database name.
  String dbname = "testdb";
  String url = "jdbc:db2:" + dbname;
  Connection con = DriverManager.getConnection(url);
  con.setAutoCommit(false);

  // STEP 3: Open input file, using filename in args[0]
  input = new BufferedReader(new FileReader(args[0]));

  // STEP 4: Read first input line: name of table and no. of trials
  tokens = new StringTokenizer(input.readLine());
  tablename = tokens.nextToken();
  ntrials = Integer.parseInt(tokens.nextToken());

  // STEP 5: Create and execute an SQL CREATE TABLE statement,
  //         using a JDBC Statement object.
  Statement stmt1 = con.createStatement();
  stmt1.executeUpdate("CREATE TABLE " + tablename +
    " (trialname Varchar(18) NOT NULL, trialvalue Double)" );

  // STEP 6: Prepare an INSERT with two parameter markers,
  //         using a JDBC PreparedStatement object.
  PreparedStatement stmt2 = con.prepareStatement(
    "INSERT INTO " + tablename + " VALUES(?, ?)" );

  // STEP 7: For each input record, bind the parameter markers
  //         and execute the INSERT statement
  for (i=0; i<ntrials; i++)
    try
      {
      tokens = new StringTokenizer(input.readLine());
      // Read trialname and bind the first parameter marker
      trialname = tokens.nextToken();
      stmt2.setString(1, trialname);
```

```
               // Read trialvalue and bind the second parameter marker,
               // setting it to null if necessary
               trialvalue = Double.valueOf(tokens.nextToken());
               stmt2.setDouble(2, trialvalue.doubleValue());
               indicator = Integer.parseInt(tokens.nextToken());
               if (indicator < 0) stmt2.setNull(2, Types.DOUBLE);
               // Execute the INSERT statement
               stmt2.executeUpdate();
               }    // End of inner try-block
          catch(Exception e)
             {
             // STEP 8: If bad data is encountered,
             //          rollback the transaction
             baddata = true;
             System.out.println("Bad data, transaction rolled back");
             e.printStackTrace();
             con.rollback();
             break;
             }

        // STEP 9: Commit transaction if load was successful
        if (!baddata)
          {
          con.commit();
          System.out.println("Data loaded successfully");
          }

        // STEP 10: Close the database connection
        con.close();
        }       // End of outer try-block

     catch(Exception e)
        {
        // STEP 11: Provide a general-purpose exception handler.
        //          The printStackTrace method prints the call stack
        //          where the exception was encountered.
        System.out.println("Houston, we have a problem...");
        e.printStackTrace();
        }

   }   // End of main
 }   // End of class "Loader2"
```

8.2.3 JDBC Applets

An *applet* is a Java program that can be executed by a web browser during the process of displaying a page from the World Wide Web. The applet, in turn, can use the facilities of JDBC to connect to a database, retrieve data, and display the data as part of the web page. By writing a JDBC applet, you can make data from your UDB database available to any computer that has a Java-enabled web browser and is connected to the Internet. Of course, your JDBC applet must comply with the security restrictions placed on all applets (generally, an applet may not access or modify files on the client machine, or establish a network connection to any machine other than the one from which it was downloaded).

To illustrate the power of a JDBC applet, we will walk through the process of creating a web page that displays live data from a UDB database. Suppose that you are the manager of the parts warehouse introduced in Chapter 2 and that you would like your clients to have access to an up-to-the-minute listing of the best available price for each part in the warehouse. You can accomplish this by embedding the list of best prices on a web page.

To create a web page, you need to describe the page using a language called Hypertext Markup Language (HTML), and you must install your page on a web server. You can learn about HTML on web pages maintained by the World Wide Web Consortium at `http://www.w3.org`, and about web servers in *Web Server Technology* by Nancy Yeager and Robert McGrath (Morgan Kaufmann, 1996).

HTML is based on *tags* that label the various parts of your web page so that they can be displayed appropriately. In this section, we are mainly interested in one HTML tag, named `<applet>`. The `<applet>` tag reserves a rectangular space of a given size on your page and calls a Java program to generate the content to be displayed in the reserved space. By default, the Java program (in the form of a compiled class) is found on the web server in the same directory with the HTML file that invoked it. The following HTML example describes a web page that displays a heading (identified by the `<h2>` tag), followed by a space 400 pixels wide and 200 pixels high, in which content is generated by the Java class named `bestbuys.class`:

```
<html>
<body>
<h2>Today's Best Prices for Parts</h2>
<applet code="bestbuys.class" width=400 height=200>
</applet>
</body>
</html>
```

After registering your HTML file with a web server, you need to write and compile the Java program that generates the content for the `<applet>` tag. In our example, this program is named `bestbuys.java`, and its listing can be found later in this section. The program can be compiled using a command such as `javac bestbuys.java`, and the resulting file, named `bestbuys.class`, can be placed in the same directory as the HTML file.

One more step is necessary before your users can begin browsing the price list: you must start a JDBC server. UDB provides a JDBC server that runs on your server machine and uses one of its network ports to listen for remote machines that are using JDBC to connect to your database. The following command starts the JDBC server and tells it to listen for JDBC clients on port number 2001 (you should choose a port number larger than 1024 to avoid conflict with ports used by the operating system):

```
db2jstrt 2001
```

The process by which a web browser displays your web page and its UDB data is illustrated by Figure 8-2. It consists of the following steps:

1. A user, somewhere in the world, asks a JDK Version 1.1–enabled browser such as Netscape Communicator Version 4 or Microsoft Internet Explorer Version 4 to display your web page. The user identifies your web page by its Universal Resource Locator (URL), which includes the name of your web server and the name of the HTML file that contains your page. The browser connects to your server machine using a protocol named Hypertext Transfer Protocol (HTTP), and the web server responds by sending your HTML file back to the client machine where the browser is running.

2. The web browser interprets the tags in the HTML file and draws their content on its display. Java-enabled browsers such as the ones mentioned above contain a Java virtual machine. When the browser encounters an `<applet>` tag in an HTML file, it downloads from the server machine the Java class that is named by the `<applet>` tag—`bestbuys.class` in our example—and other Java classes, such as the DB2 JDBC driver, that were linked to this class when it

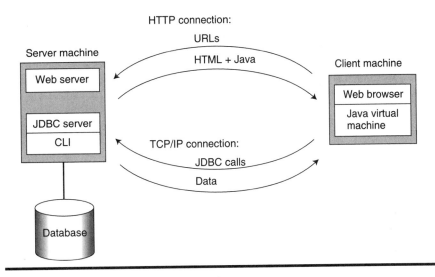

Figure 8-2: Execution of a JDBC Applet

was compiled. Using its Java virtual machine, the browser executes the methods of your class: it calls the `init()` method when the class is first downloaded, and then it calls the `paint()` method whenever it needs to draw your web page on the display—for example, when the window containing your page is uncovered.

The details of the Java applet that generates the list of "best buys" are shown in the example on the following pages. Notice that this applet has no "main" program—it merely implements the `init()` and `paint()` methods that are called by the Java virtual machine that is running inside the web browser as it displays the page.

Steps for Example Applet BESTBUYS.JAVA

STEP 1: Your Java class probably depends on other class libraries such as `java.awt` (the Abstract Windowing Toolkit) and `java.sql`. Your class references these other class libraries by `import` statements. If the referenced classes are not available on the client machine, they are downloaded over the Internet from the server machine.

STEP 2: The `init()` method is called when your Java class is first downloaded. This method, in turn, calls a method named `Class.forName()`. The purpose of this call is to register the DB2 JDBC driver (whose name is `COM.ibm.db2.jdbc.net.DB2Driver`) with the "driver manager" component of the Java virtual machine on the client. The driver manager calls on registered drivers when it needs to connect to a database (see Step 5).

STEP 3: The `paint()` method is called when the web browser wants to display your page. Its job is to generate and display the content of the 400-by-200-pixel area reserved by the `<applet>` tag. To do this, the `paint()` method will connect to your UDB database, execute a query that returns the cheapest price quotation for each different part number, and display the results.

STEP 4: In order to connect to your database, the `paint()` method must construct a URL that identifies the database. The URL consists of the characters "`jdbc:db2://`", followed by the name of your server machine and the port number on which your JDBC server is listening, followed by the local name of the database on that machine. Of course, if you execute this example code, you will need to fill in your own server machine name, port number, database name, userid, and password.

Code for Example Applet BESTBUYS.JAVA

```
// STEP 1: Import class libraries needed by this applet.
import java.sql.*;
import java.awt.*;
import java.applet.*;

public class bestbuys extends Applet
  {
  // STEP 2: The init() method is called when the applet is first
  // downloaded. It registers a JDBC driver to handle connections
  // to DB2 databases.
  public void init()
    {
    try
      {
      Class.forName("COM.ibm.db2.jdbc.net.DB2Driver");
      // For JDK 1.1.2 on AIX or OS/2, replace the above line as follows:
      // Class.forName("COM.ibm.db2.jdbc.net.DB2Driver").newInstance();
      }
    catch (Exception e)
      {
      System.out.println("Error in loading the JDBC driver");
      e.printStackTrace();
      }
    }
  // STEP 3: The paint() method generates and displays the content
  // of the <applet> tag.
  public void paint(Graphics g)
    {
    try
      {
      // STEP 4: Construct a URL to identify the database
      // Specify the name of your server machine
      String server = "yourserver.com";

      // Specify the port number your JDBC server is using
      String port = "2001";

      // Specify the name of the database you want to connect to
      String dbname = "testdb";

      // Specify a valid database userid and password
      String userid = "yourname";
      String password = "yourpw";
```

STEP 5: The call to getConnection() requests the driver manager to connect to the database identified by the given URL and to return a Connection object. The driver manager asks each registered driver whether it can obtain the desired connection. The DB2 JDBC driver (registered in Step 2) recognizes the URL because it starts with "jdbc:db2", and connects to the desired database using the given userid and password. The JDBC driver establishes its own separate connection with the server machine, using the TCP/IP protocol and the port number of the JDBC server.

STEP 6: Using the Connection object returned by the call to getConnection(), our example program creates a Statement object. It uses the executeQuery() method of the Statement to execute a query that retrieves the list of parts and minimum prices, in the form of a ResultSet.

STEP 7: Our program uses the next() and getString() methods of the ResultSet to retrieve the actual part numbers, descriptions, and prices. It then displays this data on the web page by calling the Graphics.drawstring() method, furnishing the coordinates where each line of data is to be displayed (measured from the upper left corner of the area reserved by the <applet> tag).

STEP 8: Any errors encountered during execution of the paint() method are handled by an exception handler that calls the printStackTrace() method. The resulting error messages appear on the "Java console" of the web browser. For example, if you are using Netscape Navigator, you can see the Java console by clicking Options, then Show Java Console.

```java
// STEP 5: Establish a database connection
String url = "jdbc:db2://" + server + ":" + port + "/" + dbname;
Connection con = DriverManager.getConnection(url, userid, password );

// STEP 6: Execute an SQL query
Statement stmt = con.createStatement();
String qstring =
    "SELECT p.partno, p.description, q.price "
  + "FROM company.quotations q, company.parts p, company.suppliers s "
  + "WHERE q.partno = p.partno AND q.suppno = s.suppno "
  + "AND q.price = "
  + "    (SELECT min(price) "
  + "      FROM company.quotations "
  + "      WHERE partno = q.partno)" ;
ResultSet rs = stmt.executeQuery(qstring);

// STEP 7: Display the result set
g.drawString("Part No.", 20, 25);
g.drawString("Description", 100, 25);
g.drawString("Best Price", 200, 25);
int y = 50;
while (rs.next())    // next() returns false when there are no more rows
    {
    String partno = rs.getString(1);
    String desc = rs.getString(2);
    String price = rs.getString(3);
    g.drawString(partno, 20, y);
    g.drawString(desc, 100, y);
    g.drawString(price, 200, y);
    y = y + 15;
    }
  stmt.close();
  con.close();
  }

// STEP 8: Display exceptions, if any, on the Java Console
catch( Exception e )
  {
  e.printStackTrace();
  }
}    // end of paint method
}    // end of class bestbuys
```

8.3 EMBEDDED DYNAMIC SQL

Embedded Dynamic SQL is the third facility by which SQL statements may be generated and submitted for execution at run time. It is an older interface than either CLI or JDBC, but its power is approximately the same. You might choose to use Embedded Dynamic SQL rather than one of the other dynamic interfaces for one of the following reasons:

1. It supports host programming languages other than C.

2. It is more consistent in style with static SQL, and therefore you may prefer to use it in applications that mix dynamic and static SQL statements.

3. Embedded Dynamic SQL programs tend to be somewhat more compact than equivalent CLI or JDBC programs, partly because they do not require a separate function call to bind each parameter marker.

4. Since a program that uses Embedded Dynamic SQL has a package, you can use *Execute* privilege on the package to control who is allowed to execute your program.

5. You may simply prefer the EXEC SQL notation or find it more familiar than the function calls of CLI or the method notation of JDBC.

The basic tasks to be accomplished by Embedded Dynamic SQL are the same as those of the other dynamic interfaces: to prepare an SQL statement for execution, to obtain a description of the result if the prepared statement was a query, to execute a prepared statement with real values substituted for its parameter markers, and to fetch the result of a query, one row at a time. Embedded Dynamic SQL accomplishes these tasks by means of a special set of SQL statements that can be embedded in host programs and processed by the UDB precompiler.

8.3.1 Embedded Dynamic Statements

Embedded Dynamic SQL consists of four statements: PREPARE, DESCRIBE, EXECUTE, and EXECUTE IMMEDIATE. In addition, some options are added to the OPEN and FETCH statements in support of dynamic SQL queries.

Embedded Dynamic SQL statements make heavy use of *descriptors*. A descriptor is a data structure that contains a description of the datatypes used in one row of data. A descriptor may also indicate the column names associated with a row of data and may contain pointers to the data values themselves. The data structure used for a descriptor in an Embedded Dynamic SQL statement is called an SQLDA and is described in Section 8.3.3.

PREPARE

The purpose of PREPARE is to create an access plan for an SQL statement and to translate the statement into an executable form. The syntax of a PREPARE statement is as follows:

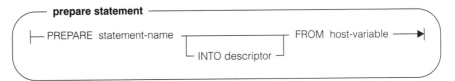

The host variable must be a character string containing an SQL statement. This statement is compiled by UDB and prepared for execution, but it is not executed. The statement name can be any identifier and is used in a later DESCRIBE, EXECUTE, or OPEN statement.

The SQL statement being prepared may not contain any host variables, but it may contain one or more parameter markers, represented by question marks, which represent values to be supplied later, when the statement is executed. The parameter markers may be given explicit datatypes by using the CAST notation as described in Section 8.1.4.

The descriptor, if provided, is used for obtaining a description of the columns of the query result, if the statement is a query. It provides an alternative to the DESCRIBE statement (described below).

Examples of PREPARE statements:

```
PREPARE s1 FROM :mystatement;
PREPARE q1 INTO :mysqlda FROM :myquery;
```

DESCRIBE

The purpose of a DESCRIBE statement is to obtain a description of the datatypes in the result set of a query that has been prepared. A DESCRIBE statement is similar to the "INTO descriptor" clause of a PREPARE statement. Its syntax is as follows:

Example:

```
DESCRIBE q1 INTO :mysqlda;
```

Unlike the other Embedded Dynamic SQL statements, DESCRIBE can be executed from an interactive interface such as the Command Center. If you type DESCRIBE followed by a query, UDB will display a list of the datatypes and column names in the result set of your query. For example, you can obtain a list of the column names and datatypes in the FUNCTIONS catalog table by executing the following query interactively:

```
DESCRIBE SELECT * FROM syscat.functions;
```

EXECUTE

The EXECUTE statement executes a previously prepared SQL statement, substituting the values in the host variable list or descriptor for the parameter markers (question marks) in the prepared statement. The host variable list (or the descriptor) must provide exactly one value for each parameter marker. The datatypes of the values provided must be compatible with the declared types of the parameter markers; if the parameter markers are untyped, the values must have datatypes appropriate for their context. The syntax of an EXECUTE statement is as follows:

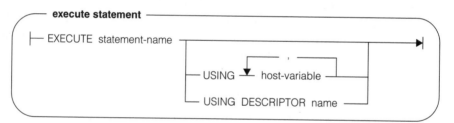

Once prepared for execution, an SQL statement can be executed repeatedly, in multiple transactions, as long as the application remains connected to the database.

If a prepared SQL statement is a SELECT or VALUES statement, it cannot be executed by an EXECUTE statement, because the EXECUTE statement provides no way to return a result set. In order to obtain the result of a dynamically prepared SELECT or VALUES statement, it is necessary to declare a cursor for the statement and to apply OPEN and FETCH statements to the cursor.

Examples of EXECUTE statements:

```
EXECUTE s1;
EXECUTE s2 USING :x, :y :yindicator, :z :zindicator;
EXECUTE s3 USING DESCRIPTOR :mysqlda;
```

EXECUTE IMMEDIATE

An EXECUTE IMMEDIATE statement prepares an SQL statement for execution and executes it immediately, combining the functions of the PREPARE and EXECUTE statements. The host variable must contain a valid SQL statement that is not a SELECT or VALUES statement and that contains no parameter markers. The syntax of an EXECUTE IMMEDIATE statement is as follows:

execute-immediate statement

EXECUTE IMMEDIATE host-variable

Example:

```
EXECUTE IMMEDIATE :mystatement;
```

Dynamic Cursor Declaration

Embedded Dynamic SQL provides a means for obtaining results of dynamically prepared queries (SELECT or VALUES statements). This is done by declaring a cursor on the result of the prepared statement and by using special options of the OPEN and FETCH statements.

A cursor can be associated with the result of a query that has been (or will be) dynamically prepared, by means of a *dynamic cursor declaration*, which has the following syntax:

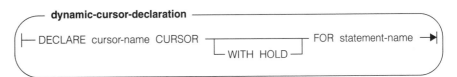

dynamic-cursor-declaration

DECLARE cursor-name CURSOR — WITH HOLD — FOR statement-name

The statement name used in a dynamic cursor declaration should also be used in a PREPARE statement. After the PREPARE statement has been executed, if the prepared statement is a query, the dynamic cursor can be used in dynamic OPEN and FETCH statements to obtain the result of the query. If WITH HOLD is specified, the cursor can remain open across transaction boundaries.

Example of a dynamic cursor declaration:

```
DECLARE c1 CURSOR FOR q1;
```

Dynamic OPEN

A dynamic OPEN statement executes a previously prepared query (SELECT or VALUES statement), substituting the values in the host variable list or descriptor for the parameter markers (question marks) in the prepared query. The host variable list (or the descriptor) must provide exactly one value for each parameter marker, and the datatypes of these values must be compatible with the declared datatypes of the parameter markers or must be appropriate in the contexts where the parameter markers are used.

The cursor named in a dynamic OPEN statement must be associated (by a dynamic cursor declaration) with a prepared query. The dynamic OPEN statement opens a cursor on the result of the prepared query and positions the cursor before the first row of the result set. Rows of the result set can then be fetched using dynamic FETCH statements.

The syntax of a dynamic OPEN statement is as follows:

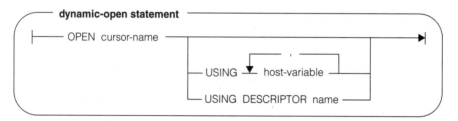

Examples:

```
OPEN c1;
OPEN c1 USING :x, :y :yindicator, :z :zindicator;
OPEN c1 USING DESCRIPTOR :mysqlda;
```

Dynamic FETCH

A dynamic FETCH statement advances the cursor to the next row of the result set and fetches it into a set of host variables or into a descriptor. The named cursor must be open, and the number of host variables (or entries in the descriptor) must match the number of columns in the result set. If the result set is empty or the cursor is positioned on or after the last row of the result set, the dynamic FETCH statement returns SQLCODE +100 (SQLSTATE 02000).

The syntax of a dynamic FETCH statement is as follows:

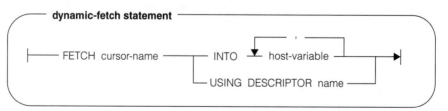

Examples:

```
FETCH c1 INTO :x :xindicator, :y :yindicator;
FETCH c1 USING DESCRIPTOR :mysqlda;
```

If a SELECT statement or a VALUES statement is executed using Embedded Dynamic SQL, that statement may not include an INTO clause. This restriction comes from the fact that, unlike static SQL, Embedded Dynamic SQL cannot handle both input and output host variables in the same statement. To illustrate the restriction, consider the following valid static SQL statement:

```
EXEC SQL SELECT salary INTO :x FROM emp WHERE name = :y;
```

In order to write an equivalent statement using Embedded Dynamic SQL, we would need to use a cursor (even though only a single result value is expected). The result would look like this:

```
EXEC SQL BEGIN DECLARE SECTION;
    char qstring[50];
EXEC SQL END DECLARE SECTION;
strcpy(qstring, "SELECT salary FROM emp WHERE name = ?");
EXEC SQL PREPARE q1 FROM :qstring;
EXEC SQL DECLARE c1 CURSOR FOR q1;
EXEC SQL OPEN c1 USING :y;
EXEC SQL FETCH c1 INTO :x;
EXEC SQL CLOSE c1;
```

8.3.2 Example Program LOADER3

Example LOADER3 is a bulk loader program, the same loader that we implemented in Section 8.1 using CLI and in Section 8.2 using JDBC. The program reads the name of a table from the input stream and creates a two-column table with the given name and with columns named TRIALNAME and TRIAL-VALUE; then it reads a series of names and values from the input stream and loads them into the table. To accomplish these tasks, LOADER3 dynamically generates a CREATE TABLE statement and executes it, then prepares an INSERT statement containing parameter markers and executes it once for each row to be loaded. The following steps explain the statements in the program listing. By comparing these steps with the corresponding steps in the earlier example programs LOADER1 and LOADER2, you can get a good understanding of the differences among the three dynamic SQL interfaces.

Steps for Example Program LOADER3: A Bulk Loader Using Embedded Dynamic SQL

STEP 1: Declare variables. Since Embedded Dynamic SQL uses a precompiler, it requires that all program variables to be used in SQL statements be declared in an SQL Declare Section.

STEP 2: Include the SQL Communication Area (SQLCA). SQLCA is a structure containing the return codes and messages that result from executing SQL statements. It is declared in the header file sqlca.h.

STEP 3: Set up an error exit. You can specify a label to which control will be transferred whenever an SQL statement fails to execute successfully. In our case, we will ask the system to branch to errorExit whenever an error is detected.

Code for Example Program LOADER3: A Bulk Loader Using Embedded Dynamic SQL

```c
#include <sqlenv.h>
#include <stdlib.h>
#include <string.h>
#include <stdio.h>

int main()
  {
  /*
  **   STEP 1: Declare variables
  */
  EXEC SQL BEGIN DECLARE SECTION;
      char dbname[9] = "testdb";     /* name of database              */
      char qstring[100]              /* holds an SQL statement         */
      char tablename[19];            /* name of experiment             */
      char trialname[19];            /* name of one trial in expt.     */
      double trialvalue;             /* value of one trial in expt.    */
      short indicator;               /* indicator variable for trialvalue */
      char  msgbuffer[500];          /* buffer for DB2 error message   */
  EXEC SQL END DECLARE SECTION;

  int rc;                            /* return code                    */
  int ntrials;                       /* no. of trials in expt.         */
  int baddata;                       /* set to 1 if bad data found     */
  int i;                             /* iteration variable             */
  double x = 1.0;                    /* alert compiler: using float    */

  /*
  **   STEP 2: Include SQLCA
  */
  EXEC SQL INCLUDE SQLCA;            /* SQL Communication Area         */

  /*
  **   STEP 3: Set up an error exit
  */
  EXEC SQL WHENEVER SQLERROR GOTO errorExit;
```

STEP 4:   Connect to the database. For this purpose, we must use a static SQL statement, since a CONNECT statement cannot be dynamically prepared. We indicate the name of the database in a program variable.

STEP 5:   Read the name of the experiment and the number of trials.

STEP 6:   Construct and execute a CREATE TABLE statement. The name of the table comes from input, and the names and datatypes of the columns are known in advance. Of course, a more general-purpose loader program could be written in which the column names and datatypes are also controlled by program input.

      The EXECUTE IMMEDIATE statement, like the SQLExecDirect() function of CLI, prepares and executes our CREATE TABLE statement in a single step.

STEP 7:   Prepare an INSERT statement containing two parameter markers (question marks). The INSERT will be executed repeatedly with different values bound to the parameter markers.

STEP 8:   Read and insert the data. The task of binding parameter markers to variables is accomplished by the USING clause on the EXECUTE statement, which lists the variables whose values are to be substituted, in order, for the parameter markers in the statement. For any parameter marker that represents a nullable value, we must provide both a program variable and a null indicator. Thus, the clause USING :trialname, :trialvalue :indicator binds variables to two parameter markers: :trialname for the first marker, and :trialvalue :indicator for the second marker.

      As in the other versions of the loader program, LOADER3 tests its input for validity, and if bad input data is encountered, it sets the baddata flag and breaks out of the input loop. Remember that if the SQL statement being executed fails for any reason, control will transfer to errorExit.

```
/*
**   STEP 4: Connect to the database
*/
EXEC SQL CONNECT TO :dbname;


/*
**   STEP 5: Read name of experiment and number of trials
*/
scanf ("%18s %d\n", tablename, &ntrials);


/*
**   STEP 6: Construct and execute a CREATE TABLE statement
*/
strcpy (qstring, "CREATE TABLE ");
strcat (qstring, tablename);
strcat (qstring,
          " (trialname Varchar(18) NOT NULL, trialvalue Double)" );
EXEC SQL EXECUTE IMMEDIATE :qstring;


/*
**   STEP 7: Prepare an INSERT with two parameter markers
*/
strcpy (qstring, "INSERT INTO ");
strcat (qstring, tablename);
strcat (qstring, " VALUES (?, ?)" );
EXEC SQL PREPARE s1 FROM :qstring;


/*
**   STEP 8: Execute the INSERT statement for each input data record
*/
baddata = 0;
for (i=0; i<ntrials; i++)
   {
   rc = scanf("%18s %lf %d\n", trialname, &trialvalue, &indicator);
   if (rc != 3 || (indicator != 0 && indicator != -1))
      {
      baddata = 1;    /* bad input data */
      break;
      }
   EXEC SQL EXECUTE s1 USING :trialname, :trialvalue :indicator;
   }
```

STEP 9:   Commit or roll back. After completion of the loop, it is time to commit or roll back our transaction. If bad input data was discovered, we will roll back all database changes, including the creation of the table; otherwise, we will commit our changes. We can use static SQL statements for these purposes.

STEP 10:   Clean up. Since Embedded Dynamic SQL has no "handles" to release as CLI does, all we need to do is disconnect from the database.

STEP 11:   Analyze errors. In this program, errorExit is not a separate procedure but simply a label for some statements that retrieve and print an error message, roll back the transaction, and exit. Note that the error-handling code executes WHENEVER SQLERROR CONTINUE before executing ROLLBACK, to avoid branching back to itself and looping in case the ROLLBACK is not successful.

```
    /*
    **   STEP 9: Commit (or roll back if bad data was found)
    */
    if (baddata)
       {
       EXEC SQL ROLLBACK;
       printf ("Bad input data, transaction rolled back.\n");
       rc = -1;
       }
    else
       {
       EXEC SQL COMMIT;
       printf ("Data loaded successfully\n");
       rc = 0;
       }

    /*
    **   STEP 10: Clean up
    */
    EXEC SQL CONNECT RESET;
    exit(rc);

errorExit:
    /*
    **   STEP 11: Handle SQL error conditions by
    **   retrieving and printing an error message
    */
    printf("\nSQL error, transaction rolled back.\n");
    sqlaintp(msgbuffer, 500, 70, &sqlca);
    printf("Message: %s\n", msgbuffer);

    EXEC SQL WHENEVER SQLERROR CONTINUE;
    EXEC SQL ROLLBACK;
    EXEC SQL CONNECT RESET;
    exit(-2);
    }    /* end of main */
```

8.3.3 The SQLDA Descriptor

Several of the Embedded Dynamic SQL statements use a *descriptor* for passing datatypes and/or values between the application program and the database. In each case, the descriptor used is a structure called an SQLDA. An SQLDA is a data structure that can describe the datatypes, lengths, and values of a variable number of data items. Such a descriptor is more flexible than a list of host variables, because it can be dynamically configured for different numbers and types of data items. This dynamic capability is important, for example, in writing a user-interface program to collect and process ad hoc queries, since the number of columns and the datatypes of the columns will be different in each query result.

Programs that need to use descriptors can embed a declaration of the SQLDA structure by means of the following statement:

```
EXEC SQL INCLUDE SQLDA;
```

This statement causes the following declarations to be included in your program:

1. A type definition for the SQLDA structure
2. Type definitions for structures named sqlvar and sqlvar2, which occur inside the SQLDA structure
3. Definition of a macro named SQLDASIZE(n), which computes the size in bytes of an SQLDA structure having n entries; this macro is useful in allocating memory space to hold an SQLDA structure

An SQLDA descriptor consists of a fixed-size header, followed by a variable number of entries called sqlvars, as shown in Figure 8-3. The content of the entries varies with the type of statement (FETCH, DESCRIBE, and so on), but in general, each entry contains a description of one host variable or one table column. Since each descriptor can contain a different number of entries, it is your responsibility to use the generic type definitions obtained from EXEC SQL INCLUDE SQLDA to allocate space for each descriptor needed by your particular application.

The header of the descriptor contains an "eye-catcher" field containing the characters "SQLDA" and three integers named sqldabc, sqln, and sqld. The sqldabc and sqln fields are set at the time that the descriptor is allocated, indicating the size of the descriptor in bytes and its total number of entries.

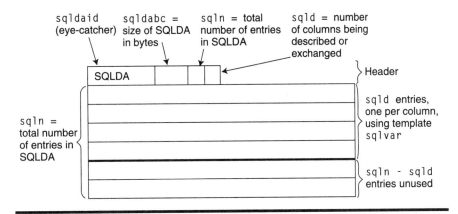

Figure 8-3: Overall Structure of an SQLDA Descriptor

These numbers are fixed for the life of the descriptor. The sqld field, on the other hand, indicates how many of the entries are currently in use to describe columns or host variables for a particular SQL statement. The value of sqld can change from one statement to another, but it must always remain less than or equal to sqln.

The content of the sqlvar entries depends on the usage of the descriptor, as follows:

1. If the descriptor is used in a PREPARE or DESCRIBE statement, each sqlvar entry describes one column of a query result. The sqlvar indicates the datatype of the column, its maximum length, and the name of the column (if any).

2. If the descriptor is used in an OPEN, FETCH, EXECUTE, or CALL statement, each sqlvar entry is used to exchange one data value with the database (an input value in the case of OPEN and EXECUTE, an output value in the case of FETCH, or a bidirectional value in the case of CALL). The sqlvar indicates the datatype of the value and the address and length of the buffer allocated by the host program to contain the value. It may also contain the address of the indicator variable that is used to represent null values.

The sqltype field of an sqlvar entry is used to indicate the datatype of the entry. (The typecodes used in this field are listed in Appendix C.)

The basic structures of the SQLDA and sqlvar, as described above, are the same for all products in the DB2 family. However, the new features of UDB

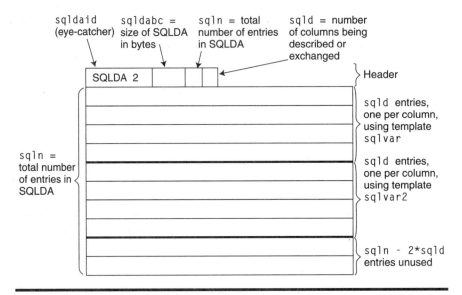

Figure 8-4: A Double-Size SQLDA Descriptor

have required some extensions to be made in the way that descriptors are used. These changes were necessary for the following reasons:

1. The length field in an `sqlvar` entry occupies only two bytes, which is not large enough to describe the length of a LOB-type value.

2. Some way is needed to describe the datatype of a column when that datatype is user-defined. Built-in datatypes can be indicated by predefined typecodes, but for user-defined (distinct) types, it is necessary to return the actual name of the datatype. This requires more space than is available in an `sqlvar` entry.

For these reasons, UDB relies on the concept of a "double-size" SQLDA, which is used whenever it is necessary to describe or exchange data that includes LOB types or distinct types. A double-size SQLDA contains *two* entries for each data value: an `sqlvar` entry and an `sqlvar2` entry. A double-size SQLDA can be distinguished from a single-size SQLDA because it contains the character "2" in byte 7 of its eye-catcher field, as shown in Figure 8-4. All the `sqlvar` entries come first, followed by all the `sqlvar2` entries. The `sqlvar2` entries are used to contain the information that will not fit into the

sqlvar entries: the lengths of LOB-type data and the datatype names of
distinct-type data. The sqln and sqld fields still indicate the total number of
entries in the descriptor and the number of columns being described, respectively. But the relationship between these two numbers is different: in a double-
size SQLDA, sqld cannot be more than half sqln.

The information pertaining to the nth column (or the nth data value) in a
double-size descriptor is found in two entries: entry number n (type sqlvar)
and entry number sqld + n (type sqlvar2). The second of these entries contains meaningful information only if the datatype of the column (or value) is
a LOB datatype or distinct type. The actual content of the sqlvar2 entry
depends on the usage of the descriptor, as follows:

1. If the descriptor is used in a PREPARE or DESCRIBE statement, each sqlvar2
entry describes the maximum length of the corresponding column (if it is a
LOB datatype) and/or the datatype of the column (if it is a distinct type). The
datatype is spelled out as a fully qualified name such as geometry.triangle.

2. If the descriptor is used in an OPEN, FETCH, EXECUTE, or CALL statement,
each LOB-type data value being exchanged has an sqlvar2 entry that contains two pieces of length information: the length of the buffer that holds the
value and a pointer to a buffer containing the actual length of the value itself.

The C declarations for the SQLDA, sqlvar, and sqlvar2 structures are
found in sqllib/include/sqlda.h and are given (with a few simplifica-
tions) below:

```
struct sqlda
{
    char          sqldaid[8];          /* Eye-catcher = 'SQLDA    '      */
    /***********************************************************************/
    /* The 7th byte has special meaning.  If it is '2', this means there */
    /* are twice as many sqlvars as there are host variables or columns. */
    /***********************************************************************/
    long          sqldabc;             /* SQLDA size in bytes=16+44*SQLN */
    short         sqln;                /* Number of SQLVAR elements      */
    short         sqld;                /* # of columns or host vars.     */
    struct sqlvar sqlvar[1];           /* First SQLVAR element           */
};
```

```
struct sqlvar                          /* Variable Description       */
{
    short          sqltype;            /* Typecode                   */
    short          sqllen;             /* Length of data value       */
    char           *sqldata;           /* Pointer to data value      */
    short          *sqlind;            /* Pointer to Null indicator  */
    struct sqlname sqlname;            /* Variable name              */
};

struct sqlvar2                         /* Variable Description       */
{
    union sql8bytelen  len;            /* 8-byte length, 4 bytes used now */
    char               *sqldatalen;    /* Pointer to 4-byte length buffer */
    struct sqldistinct_type sqldatatype_name;   /* Distinct type name    */
};

union sql8bytelen
{
    long           reserve1[2];     /* Reserved for future 8-byte lengths. */
    long           sqllonglen;      /* This is what is currently used       */
};

struct sqldistinct_type                /* Name of distinct type      */
{
    short          length;             /* Name length [1..27]        */
    char           data[27];           /* Name of distinct type      */
    char           reserved1[3];       /* Reserved                   */
};
```

8.3.4 Using an SQLDA in a PREPARE or DESCRIBE Statement

The SQLDA descriptor is used in PREPARE and DESCRIBE statements to investigate the "shape" of a query result—that is, the number of columns in the result set and the datatypes and names (if any) of the columns. In order to do this, you must first allocate a descriptor of the proper size. For this purpose, you can use the macro SQLDASIZE(n), which computes the size (in bytes) of an SQLDA structure containing n entries.

TABLE 8-2: Return Codes from PREPARE and DESCRIBE Statements

SQLCODE	SQLSTATE	Meaning
+236	01005	Your descriptor was too small, and the result set contains no LOBs or distinct types. The number of columns in the result set is returned in sqld. You must allocate a new descriptor containing at least this many entries and try again.
+237 +238 +239	01594 01005 01005	Your descriptor was too small, and the result set contains some LOBs and/or distinct types. The number of columns in the result set is returned in sqld. You must allocate a new descriptor containing at least twice this many entries and try again.

You should allocate a descriptor containing at least 2n entries, where n is the maximum number of columns in any result set that you expect to DESCRIBE. (If you are sure that no result set will ever contain a LOB datatype or a distinct type, you need only n entries rather than 2n.)

The following example allocates memory for a descriptor containing 50 entries and sets the values of the fields sqln (total number of entries) and sqldabc (total size in bytes).

```
short numEntries = 50;
short bytesNeeded = SQLDASIZE(numEntries);
struct sqlda *daptr;
daptr = (struct sqlda *)malloc(bytesNeeded);
daptr->sqln = numEntries;
daptr->sqldabc = bytesNeeded;
```

After you execute a PREPARE or DESCRIBE statement, you should examine the resulting SQLCODE (or SQLSTATE) to make sure that your descriptor was big enough to hold the result. If your descriptor was too small, you will get one of the return codes listed in Table 8-2.

The following code fragment illustrates the process of examining a descriptor after a DESCRIBE statement and reallocating a larger descriptor if necessary:

```
short entriesNeeded, bytesNeeded;
entriesNeeded = 0;
/* assume daptr points at an SQLDA structure */
EXEC SQL DESCRIBE s1 INTO :*daptr;
if (SQLCODE == 236)
    entriesNeeded = daptr->sqld;
if (SQLCODE == 237 || SQLCODE == 238 || SQLCODE == 239)
    entriesNeeded = 2 * daptr->sqld;
if (entriesNeeded > 0)
    {                   /* old SQLDA was too small */
    free(daptr);
    bytesNeeded = SQLDASIZE(entriesNeeded);
    daptr = (struct sqlda *)malloc(bytesNeeded);
    daptr->sqln = entriesNeeded;
    daptr->sqldabc = bytesNeeded;
    EXEC SQL DESCRIBE s1 INTO :*daptr;
    }
```

After your PREPARE or DESCRIBE statement has executed successfully, the seventh byte of the sqldaid field will contain the character "2" if the descriptor is double-size. The following macros have been defined (in sqlda.h) to make it easy to examine (and set) the character that indicates double-size:

GETSQLDOUBLED(daptr): Evaluates to 1 if daptr points to a double-size descriptor; otherwise, evaluates to 0.

SETSQLDOUBLED(daptr, newvalue): Sets the double-size indicator character of the given descriptor to a new value. To indicate a double-size descriptor, use SETSQLDOUBLED(daptr, SQLDOUBLED). To indicate a single-size descriptor, use SETSQLDOUBLED(daptr, SQLSINGLED).

The details of the descriptor structures returned by PREPARE and DESCRIBE are shown in Figure 8-5. The sqlvar entries indicate the names and datatypes of all the columns in the result set, using the typecodes listed in Appendix C. For every column that is a distinct type, the sqlvar2 entry contains the full name of the distinct type, and the `sqlvar` entry contains the typecode of the underlying base datatype. Since distinct types have the same representation as their underlying base datatype, the `sqltype` in the `sqlvar` entry can be used to indicate the proper type of variable for exchanging data with the distinct-type column.

The `sqllen` field of an `sqlvar` entry indicates the maximum length, in bytes, of the data value described by the entry, for all datatypes except Decimal and the LOB datatypes. For the Decimal datatype, the `sqllen` field contains the precision (first byte) and scale (second byte) of the data value. The precision and scale can be retrieved separately, as shown in the following example (assuming that `daptr` points to an SQLDA whose nth entry describes a Decimal value):

```
precision = ((char *)&(daptr->sqlvar[n].sqllen))[0];
scale     = ((char *)&(daptr->sqlvar[n].sqllen))[1];
```

For LOB datatypes, the `sqllen` field of `sqlvar` is set to zero, and the maximum length of the data value is indicated in the `len.sqllonglen` field of `sqlvar2`. Two macros have been provided (in `sqlda.h`) to help you examine (and set) the "long-length" information in an `sqlvar2` entry. Because of the alignment of the long-length data, you should use these macros rather than accessing the long-length field directly. The macros are as follows:

GETSQLDALONGLEN(daptr, n): Evaluates to the four-byte long-length field of the `sqlvar2` entry that corresponds to the nth column in the given descriptor.

SETSQLDALONGLEN(daptr, n, length): Sets the long-length field of the `sqlvar2` entry that corresponds to the nth column in the given descriptor. Use this macro to indicate the length of the data buffer you have allocated for input or output of a LOB-type value.

TIP: An easy way to get an SQLDA descriptor that you can use to insert or update rows in some table T is to PREPARE and DESCRIBE the statement SELECT * FROM t.

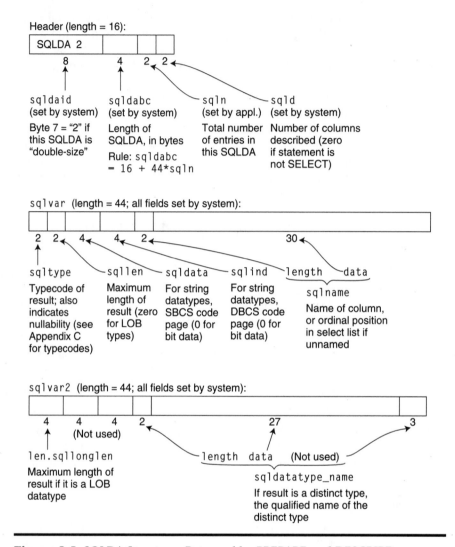

Figure 8-5: SQLDA Structures Returned by PREPARE and DESCRIBE Statements

8.3.5 Using an SQLDA in an OPEN, FETCH, EXECUTE, or CALL Statement

Another use of an SQLDA descriptor is for actual exchange of data between an application program and the database. In an OPEN or EXECUTE statement, the values being exchanged are input values that are being substituted for the parameter markers in a statement that was previously prepared. In a FETCH statement, the values being exchanged are output values that are being delivered into variables or buffers in the application program. These buffers might have been allocated on the basis of information returned by a previous PREPARE or DESCRIBE statement. In a CALL statement, data is being exchanged in both directions between a stored procedure and a client program. (Stored procedures are discussed in Chapter 9.)

The details of the SQLDA structures used in OPEN, FETCH, EXECUTE, and CALL statements are shown in Figure 8-6.

The `sqlname` field of the `sqlvar` structure has a specialized meaning in a CALL statement: a name consisting of four bytes of binary zeros indicates that the data value is a binary string and that no code page conversion should be done on the value when it is exchanged between a client program and a stored procedure. If an SQLDA is being used to exchange binary strings (such as Varchar FOR BIT DATA) in a CALL statement, the sixth byte of its `sqldaid` field should be set to a "+" character. (The use of a CALL statement to exchange data between a client program and a stored procedure is discussed in Section 9.2.1.)

As usual, the `sqlvar2` entries in the descriptor are used to carry information about LOB-type data values. When used in OPEN, FETCH, EXECUTE, and CALL statements, the `sqlvar2` entries contain two pieces of length information:

1. The length of the buffer allocated for input or output of the LOB-type value is carried in `sqlvar2.len`. This length information should be examined and set by the GETSQLDALONGLEN and SETSQLDALONGLEN macros described previously.

2. The actual length of an individual LOB-type value is carried in a four-byte buffer pointed to by `sqlvar2.sqldatalen`. This pointer allows you to manage the actual-length information for LOB-type data separately from the value itself. If the pointer is set to NULL, the actual-length information is carried in the first four bytes of the LOB-type value itself. The following macros have been provided (in `sqlda.h`) for getting and setting the actual-length pointer:

GETSQLDALENPTR(daptr, n): Returns the actual-length pointer from the `sqlvar2` entry that corresponds to the nth column in the given descriptor.

SETSQLDALENPTR(daptr, n, lenptr): Sets the actual-length pointer in the `sqlvar2` entry that corresponds to the nth column in the given descriptor.

Before a descriptor returned by a DESCRIBE statement can be used in a FETCH statement, the following information must be added to the descriptor for each value to be fetched:

- The address into which the data is to be fetched
- The length of the buffer allocated at this address to receive the data
- The address of the null indicator variable (if any)

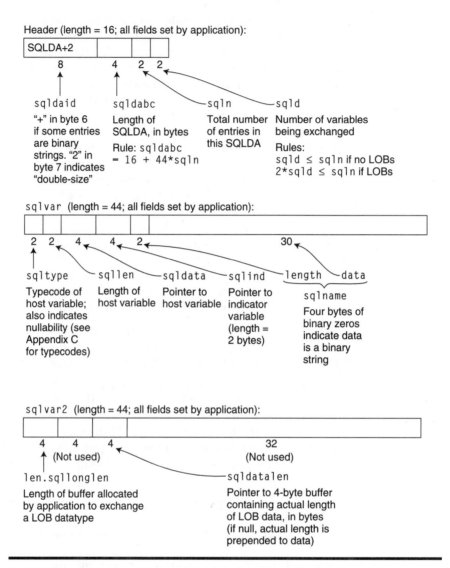

Figure 8-6: Use of an SQLDA Descriptor in OPEN, FETCH, EXECUTE, and CALL Statements

The task of preparing a descriptor for use in a FETCH statement consists of allocating buffers of the proper size and placing their addresses and lengths in the proper fields of the descriptor. For columns that permit null values (indicated by odd-numbered typecodes), a two-byte null indicator variable must be allocated as well as a buffer to receive the column value. The size of the buffer required for each column is indicated in the sqlvar.sqllen field for that column unless the datatype of the column is Decimal or a LOB datatype. Thus, the following code fragment will allocate buffers of the proper size for all columns except those containing Decimal or LOB-type data (assume that daptr points to a descriptor returned by a DESCRIBE statement):

```
for (i = 0; i < daptr->sqld; i++)
    {
    daptr->sqlvar[i].sqldata =
            (char *)malloc(daptr->sqlvar[i].sqllen);
    if (daptr->sqlvar[i].sqltype % 2 == 1)
        daptr->sqlvar[i].sqlind = (short *)malloc(2);
    }
```

TIP: Don't forget to set the sqlind pointer for all nullable columns. If you leave this pointer uninitialized, the system will attempt to store through it anyway, and your program will probably crash.

For some types of data, you have a certain amount of flexibility in the type of buffer that you use for data exchange. For example, if DESCRIBE returns a typecode of 448 (indicating Varchar) for a given column, you can leave the typecode as 448 and exchange the data in length-prefix form, or change the typecode to 460 and exchange the data in null-terminated form (be sure to allocate an extra byte for the null terminator).

LOB-type columns provide the greatest amount of flexibility in how data can be exchanged. For example, suppose that, after a DESCRIBE statement, daptr points to a descriptor in which the fifth entry has an sqltype code of 408, indicating a non-nullable Clob-type column. You can prepare to fetch the values in this column in any of the following ways:

1. Find the maximum length of the column by using the GETSQLDALONGLEN macro, allocate a memory buffer of at least this size, and place its address in the corresponding sqlvar.sqldata field. Use the SETSQLDALENPTR macro to indicate where you want the actual-length information to be delivered. Your code might look like this:

```
int n = 5;                             /* (use the actual column number) */
long maxLen;                           /* max. length of Clob column      */
long actLen;                           /* actual length of Clob data      */
char *buffPtr;                         /* points at buffer for data       */
sqlvar *var1Ptr;                       /* sqlvar entry for this column     */
var1Ptr = (struct sqlvar *) &(daptr->sqlvar[n]);
maxLen = GETSQLDALONGLEN(daptr, n);       /* get max. length of column   */
buffPtr = (char *)malloc(maxLen);         /* allocate data buffer        */
var1Ptr->sqldata = buffPtr;               /* set addr. of data buffer    */
SETSQLDALENPTR(daptr, n, &actLen);        /* set addr. of length buffer  */
```

Now this column is ready for FETCH. After each FETCH, the data will be in `*buffPtr` and its actual length will be in `actLen`.

2. Declare or dynamically allocate a Clob file-reference structure (struct `sql-file`, found in `sql.h`), and put its address in the `sqlvar.sqldata` pointer for the given column. Change `sqlvar.sqltype` from SQL_TYP_CLOB (408) to SQL_TYP_CLOB_FILE (808), indicating that the data should be delivered to a file. Fill in the file-reference structure with the name of the file where you want the Clob output to be delivered. Each FETCH statement will then replace (or append) the file with a new Clob value. Your code might look like this:

```
int n = 5;                              /* (use the actual column number) */
struct sqlfile fileRef;                 /* a file-reference structure     */
sqlvar *var1Ptr;                        /* sqlvar entry for this column    */
var1Ptr = (struct sqlvar *) &(daptr->sqlvar[n]);
strcpy(fileRef.name, "clobfile.txt");             /* initialize file ref    */
fileRef.name_length = strlen(fileRef.name);
fileRef.file_options = SQL_FILE_APPEND;           /* append data to file    */
var1Ptr->sqltype = SQL_TYP_CLOB_FILE;             /* requested output type  */
var1Ptr->sqldata = (char *)&fileRef;              /* addr. of file ref      */
var1Ptr->sqllen = SQL_LOBFILE_LEN;                /* size of file ref       */
```

Now this column is ready for FETCH. Each FETCH will append a new Clob to the output file named `clobfile.txt` and will return the new length of the file in `fileRef.data_length`.

3. Put the address of a Clob locator in the `sqlvar.sqldata` pointer for the given column. Change `sqlvar.sqltype` from SQL_TYP_CLOB (408) to SQL_TYP_CLOB_LOCATOR (964), indicating that you want to receive a locator rather than the actual data. After each FETCH, you will have a locator that you can use to manipulate the Clob-type data without actually retrieving the bits. Your code might look like this:

```
EXEC SQL BEGIN DECLARE SECTION;
    SQL TYPE IS CLOB_LOCATOR locator1;
EXEC SQL END DECLARE SECTION;
int n = 5;                              /* (use the actual column number) */
sqlvar *var1Ptr;                        /* sqlvar entry for this column    */
var1Ptr = (struct sqlvar *) &(daptr->sqlvar[n]);
var1Ptr->sqltype = SQL_TYP_CLOB_LOCATOR;       /* requested output type    */
var1Ptr->sqldata = (char *)&locator1;          /* addr. of locator buffer  */
var1Ptr->sqllen = sizeof(long);                /* length of locator buffer */
```

Now this column is ready for FETCH. After each FETCH, a new locator will be in `locator1`. After you have fetched a locator, you can use it to fetch part or all of the actual Clob value. One way to do this is by using a VALUES statement, as shown below. When you no longer need the locator, free it by using a FREE LOCATOR statement.

```
EXEC SQL BEGIN DECLARE SECTION;
    char clobValue[101];
EXEC SQL END DECLARE SECTION;
/* Fetch first 100 bytes of Clob */
EXEC SQL VALUES(substr(:locator1, 1, 100)) INTO :clobValue;
/* Free locator when no longer needed */
EXEC SQL FREE LOCATOR :locator1;
```

8.3.6 Example Program QUERY3

As an example of how to use an SQLDA descriptor, we will write an interactive query interface program using Embedded Dynamic SQL. The following program, QUERY3, is functionally equivalent to the CLI example program named QUERY1 in Section 8.1. It is revealing to compare these two programs side by side.

Remember that the purpose of our simple query interface example is to obtain an SQL statement from an interactive user, execute the statement, and display the results. As before, we will keep the program simple by handling only queries and by requiring that the result set be a single column of datatype Double or Clob.

Steps for Example Program QUERY3: A Query Interface Using Embedded Dynamic SQL

STEP 1: Declare variables. In Embedded Dynamic SQL, all variables used for database interactions must be declared in an SQL Declare Section.

STEP 2: Allocate an SQLDA descriptor for our queries. In this example, we require that all result sets have a single column, so we can predict the necessary size of the SQLDA in advance. Our SQLDA must contain two `sqlvar` entries, because two entries are needed to describe a single column of type Clob. If the number of columns in the result set were unknown, we would need to allocate a descriptor using the techniques described in Section 8.3.4. After allocating the SQLDA, we turn on its "doubled" flag and make it describe its own length by setting its `sqln` field to 2.

Code for Example Program QUERY3: A Query Interface Using Embedded Dynamic SQL

```c
#include <stdlib.h>
#include <string.h>
#include <stdio.h>
#include <sqlenv.h>

EXEC SQL INCLUDE SQLCA;

int main()
    {
    /*
    **   STEP 1: Declare variables
    */
    EXEC SQL BEGIN DECLARE SECTION;
        char dbname[9] = "testdb";    /* name of database              */
        char  qstring[100];           /* buffer for SQL query          */
        double answerDouble;          /* answer data (if type is DOUBLE) */
        SQL TYPE IS CLOB_LOCATOR
                    answerLocator;    /* answer locator (if type is CLOB) */
        char answerString[11];        /* answer buffer (if type is CLOB) */
        short nullindicator;          /* set to -1 if answer is null   */
        char  msgbuffer[500];         /* buffer for DB2 error message  */
    EXEC SQL END DECLARE SECTION;

    char *colnameptr;                 /* name of result column         */
    short colnamelen;                 /* actual length of column name  */
    short coltype;                    /* type of result column         */

    struct sqlda  *sqldaptr;          /* points to allocated sqlda     */

    /*
    **   STEP 2: Allocate an SQLDA containing two SQLVARs.
    **   (Remember, we need two SQLVARs to describe a single CLOB column.)
    */
    sqldaptr = (struct sqlda*) malloc( SQLDASIZE(2) );
    sqldaptr->sqln = 2;
    SETSQLDOUBLED(sqldaptr, SQLDOUBLED);
```

STEP 3: Connect to the database.

STEP 4: Establish a way for handling errors. In general, if an error is detected in processing a user's SQL statement, we want to display the error code and then prompt the user for another query. The WHENEVER statement causes this to happen by telling the system to go to the bottom of the query loop whenever an error is encountered. Unexpected errors in the SQL statements that we build into the program will be handled in the same way as user errors.

STEP 5: Prompt the user for an SQL statement and read it into the `qstring` buffer.

STEP 6: Prepare the query and get a description of the result set. The PREPARE and DESCRIBE statements could have been combined into a single PREPARE INTO statement. If the user's input was not a valid SQL statement, the program will automatically branch to the `nextquery` label. On the other hand, if the input was a valid SQL statement, we can learn something about it by examining the `sqld` field of the descriptor. If `sqld` is equal to zero, the statement was a valid statement but not a query, so we need to roll back any updates that might have been made to the database. If `sqld` is greater than zero, it indicates the number of columns in the result set. If this number is greater than one, we print an error message and prompt for the next query.

```
/*
**   STEP 3: Connect to database and check return code
**   (provide userid and password, if needed)
*/
EXEC SQL CONNECT TO :dbname;
if (SQLCODE < 0)
   {
   printf("Error in connecting to database\n");
   exit(1);
   }


/*
**   STEP 4: Establish a way for handling errors
*/
EXEC SQL WHENEVER SQLERROR GO TO nextquery;


/*
**   STEP 5: Get an SQL statement from the user
*/
printf("\nEnter a query, or empty string to quit:\n");
gets(qstring);

while (strlen(qstring)>0)
   {
   /*
   **   STEP 6: Prepare the query and get a description
   **   of the result set
   */
   EXEC SQL PREPARE Q1 FROM :qstring;

   EXEC SQL DESCRIBE Q1 into :*sqldaptr;

   if (sqldaptr->sqld == 0)
      {
      printf("Your statement was not a valid query.\n");
      printf("Any updates have been rolled back.\n");
      EXEC SQL ROLLBACK;
      }
   else if (sqldaptr->sqld > 1)
      printf("The result set has more than one column.\n");
```

STEP 7: Once we have established that the user's input was a valid single-column query, we can print the name of the column, which is found in the `sqlname` field of the first `sqlvar` entry in the descriptor.

STEP 8: In order to fetch the result set, it is necessary to open a cursor. The cursor will maintain a position in the result set as we fetch it, row by row. The explicit opening of a cursor is necessary in Embedded Dynamic SQL but not in CLI, since a CLI statement handle serves as an implicit cursor.

After opening the cursor, we branch according to the datatype of the result column, which is found in the `sqltype` field of the first `sqlvar` entry in the descriptor.

STEP 9: If the datatype of the result column is SQL_TYP_NFLOAT (nullable double-precision float), we need to fetch and display a column of floating-point numbers. The first step is to place the addresses of our Double-type answer buffer and indicator variable into the SQLDA descriptor. Then, each time we execute a FETCH statement, one answer value is fetched into the buffer. We continue fetching and displaying values (checking the indicator variable for nulls) until we receive an SQLCODE of 100, indicating that the end of the result set has been reached.

```
else   /* sqld is exactly 1 */
   {
   /*
   **   STEP 7: Print the column name
   */
   colnamelen = sqldaptr->sqlvar[0].sqlname.length;
   colnameptr = sqldaptr->sqlvar[0].sqlname.data;
   printf("%*.*s\n", colnamelen, colnamelen, colnameptr);
   printf("------------------\n");

   /*
   **   STEP 8: Open a cursor on the result set
   */
   EXEC SQL DECLARE C1 CURSOR FOR Q1;
   EXEC SQL OPEN C1;

   coltype = sqldaptr->sqlvar[0].sqltype;
   switch(coltype)
      {
      case SQL_TYP_NFLOAT:
         /*
         **   STEP 9: Fetch a column of Double-type answers
         **   and display them
         */
         sqldaptr->sqlvar[0].sqldata = (char *) &answerDouble;
         sqldaptr->sqlvar[0].sqllen = 8;
         sqldaptr->sqlvar[0].sqlind = &nullindicator;
         EXEC SQL FETCH C1 USING DESCRIPTOR :*sqldaptr;
         if (SQLCODE == 100)
            printf("Result set is empty.\n");
         else while (SQLCODE >= 0 && SQLCODE != 100)
            {
            if (nullindicator < 0) printf("(Null)\n");
            else printf("%f\n", answerDouble);
            EXEC SQL FETCH C1 USING DESCRIPTOR :*sqldaptr;
            }
         break;   /* end of DOUBLE case */
```

STEP 10: If the datatype of the result column is SQL_TYP_NCLOB (nullable Clob), we need to fetch and display a column of Clob-type data. As in the CLI version of this example program, we will fetch each Clob in the form of a locator, then use the locator to fetch the first 10 bytes of the actual Clob value. The first step is to place the address of our answerLocator variable into the descriptor, along with a code indicating that we wish to retrieve values in locator form. Each FETCH delivers another locator into our program variable.

STEP 11: Once we have fetched a locator, we can use it to fetch the first 10 characters (or any desired substring) of the Clob value, using a VALUES statement. After we are finished with each locator, we free it so that the database system does not need to maintain it until the end of the transaction.

Note that the VALUES and FREE LOCATOR statements are *static* SQL, not dynamic SQL, because we know at compile time exactly what they need to do.

STEP 12: This simple example has demonstrated the handling of two datatypes; obviously, it could be extended to handle other datatypes as well by adding more cases to the switch statement.

```
case SQL_TYP_NCLOB:          /* nullable CLOB */
   /*
   **   STEP 10: Fetch a column of Clob-type answers
   **   in Locator form
   */
   sqldaptr->sqlvar[0].sqltype = SQL_TYP_NCLOB_LOCATOR;
   sqldaptr->sqlvar[0].sqldata = (char *) &answerLocator;
   sqldaptr->sqlvar[0].sqllen = 4;
   sqldaptr->sqlvar[0].sqlind = &nullindicator;
   EXEC SQL FETCH C1 USING DESCRIPTOR :*sqldaptr;
   if (SQLCODE == 100)
      printf("Result set is empty.\n");
   else while (SQLCODE >= 0 && SQLCODE != 100)
      {
      if (nullindicator < 0) printf("(Null)\n");
      else
         {
         /*
         **   STEP 11: For each Clob, use its locator to fetch
         **   and display the first 10 characters of the answer.
         **   Don't forget to free each locator before fetching
         **   the next one.
         */
         EXEC SQL VALUES(substr(:answerLocator, 1, 10))
                   INTO :answerString;
         printf("%s ...\n", answerString);
         EXEC SQL FREE LOCATOR :answerLocator;
         }
      EXEC SQL FETCH C1 USING DESCRIPTOR :*sqldaptr;
      }
   break;    /* end of CLOB case */

default:
   /*
   **   STEP 12: Other datatypes could be added here
   */
   printf("Answer datatype %d is not DOUBLE or CLOB\n",
                                            coltype);
}       /* end of switch on coltype */
```

STEP 13: After fetching and displaying the result set, we close the cursor. The same cursor will be reopened to fetch the result of the next query.

STEP 14: This is the place to which control passes after a result set has been displayed or when an SQL error is encountered. At this point in the program, we display any error message that may be pending, and commit a transaction to release any locks that we may be holding. We then prompt the user to enter another SQL statement, and return to the top of the query loop.

STEP 15: When the user has indicated (by entering a null line) that there are no more queries to be processed, we disconnect from the database and exit from the program.

```
    /*
    **   STEP 13: Close the cursor
    */
    EXEC SQL CLOSE C1;

    }        /* end of processing a successful query */

nextquery:
    /*
    **   STEP 14: Print error codes, if any
    */
    if (SQLCODE < 0)
        {
        printf("Result of processing your SQL statement:\n");
        sqlaintp(msgbuffer, 500, 70, &sqlca);
        printf("Message: %s\n", msgbuffer);
        }

    /*
    ** Commit a transaction to release locks, and get the next query
    */
    EXEC SQL COMMIT;
    printf("\nEnter a query, or empty string to quit:\n");
    gets(qstring);
    }   /* end of while-loop that processes queries */

/*
**   STEP 15: Disconnect from database and exit
*/
printf("\nGoodbye, have a nice day.\n");
EXEC SQL CONNECT RESET;
return (0);

}    /* end of main */
```

Stored Procedures

Normally, when an application program is running on a client machine, each SQL statement is sent separately from the client to the server machine, and each result is returned separately. Sometimes, however, a piece of work can be identified that involves relatively heavy database activity but relatively little user interaction. In such a case, it may make sense to install this piece of work on the server machine in the form of a *stored procedure* that can be invoked by a single message from the client machine, thus reducing message traffic and improving application performance.

A complete stored-procedure application includes two parts: the stored procedure itself, which runs on the server machine, and the client program, which runs on the client machine. Stored-procedure applications have the restrictions that all input data must be passed from the client program to the stored procedure at invocation time, and result data can be returned to the client program only when the stored procedure is completed. No interactions between the client program and the stored procedure are permitted during execution of the stored procedure. For example, a client program might accumulate a collection of database updates and pass them to a stored procedure to be applied as a batch, with a return code indicating whether the entire batch was applied successfully or rolled back due to a failure.

You can write a stored procedure in any of the host programming languages supported by UDB: C, C++, COBOL, FORTRAN, REXX, or Java. The stored procedure must be compiled and installed on your server machine, much like a user-defined function; however, unlike a user-defined function, a stored procedure may contain SQL statements. The stored procedure can be invoked from a client program by means of a CALL statement. CALL can be used as a static SQL statement or can be invoked from a CLI program using functions such as SQLPrepare() and SQLExecute().

This chapter examines how a stored-procedure application might be implemented using the C programming language, and invoked from client programs using either static SQL or CLI. Information about writing stored procedures in other host languages can be found in the *Embedded SQL Programming Guide*. Several examples of stored procedures written in C are provided with the UDB system in the directory sqllib/samples/c.

9.1 THE SERVER SIDE

A stored procedure is simply an application program, installed on your server machine, that follows certain conventions for exchanging data with a client program. An SQLDA data structure (described in Section 8.3.3) is used both for passing input data to the stored procedure and for returning results. An SQLCA structure (described in Section 4.1.4) is used for returning codes and messages to the client program to indicate the success or failure of the stored procedure. This section discusses how to write stored procedures using the C host programming language.

When written according to UDB conventions, a stored procedure takes four parameters, but it really uses only two of them,[1] which are pointers to SQLDA and SQLCA structures. The declaration of such a stored procedure might look as follows:

```
SQL_API_RC SQL_API_FN procname(
        void          *dummy1,     /* not used        */
        void          *dummy2,     /* not used        */
        struct sqlda  *exchange_da, /* input and output */
        struct sqlca  *out_sqlca   /* output only      */
        );
```

In the example above, SQL_API_RC and SQL_API_FN are macros (defined in sqlsystm.h) that expand in a platform-dependent way to declare that the result type of the stored procedure is an integer. For example, under AIX, SQL_API_RC expands to the word "int" and SQL_API_FN expands to an empty string.

The parameter named exchange_da in the example above is a pointer to an SQLDA structure that is used to pass data in both directions between the client program and the stored procedure. When the stored procedure is invoked, the SQLDA contains a description (including datatypes, lengths, and buffer addresses) of all the data values to be exchanged in both directions. Input values are available to the stored procedure in the buffers pointed to by the SQLDA. The stored procedure returns values to the client program by copying them into the buffers pointed to by the SQLDA (of course, these values must conform to the datatypes and lengths indicated by the SQLDA) and by copying a set of return codes into the SQLCA structure provided by the out_sqlca parameter. The SQLCA and SQLDA structures are allocated by the client program.

The stored procedure does not connect to the database itself but relies on the database connection already established by the client. The stored procedure can

---

1. The two unused parameters are left over from an earlier stored procedure calling convention called DARI, which is still supported for compatability with earlier releases.

execute SQL statements but not statements such as CONNECT that would affect its database connection. When its job is done, the stored procedure must copy any information to be returned to the client program into the SQLDA and SQLCA structures passed to it as parameters. The stored procedure then returns one of two integer codes: `SQLZ_HOLD_PROC`, indicating that the procedure should be retained in memory to improve the performance of subsequent invocations, or `SQLZ_DISCONNECT_PROC`, indicating that no further invocations are expected and the procedure should be removed from memory. These return codes, which are defined in `sql.h`, affect only the handling of the stored procedure on the server machine and are not returned to the client program.

9.1.1 Example Program SERVER1: A Stored Procedure for a Bank

As an example, we will consider a stored procedure that might be used by a bank. Suppose that our bank has automatic teller machines distributed in many locations. Each teller machine has a list of accounts and is capable of functioning autonomously for a period of time, accepting deposit and withdrawal transactions against the accounts on its list. Periodically, each teller machine connects to the central database stored on the bank's server machine and invokes a stored procedure named SERVER1, which updates the central database to record a batch of deposits and withdrawals processed by the teller machine.

This example illustrates one way to solve a problem that often arises when dealing with stored procedures: finding a way to pass a large collection of input data to the stored procedure. In our example, the client program needs to pass a variable-length list of account numbers and net changes. We will accomplish this by packing the list of account numbers and net changes into a Clob and passing the Clob to the stored procedure. Even though the net changes are numbers, we convert them to character-string form before packing them into the Clob parameter. This technique avoids problems that might be caused by different numeric representations on the client and server platforms (sometimes called the "byte reversal problem").

In our simplified example, the stored procedure interacts only with the following table:

BANK.ACCOUNTS

ACCTNO   BALANCE

The code for the stored procedure is given in example SERVER1 and is explained in detail on the following pages.

Steps for Example Program SERVER1: Stored Procedure, Server Side

STEP 1: The stored procedure uses the INCLUDE SQLCA statement to get a local copy of an SQLCA structure that will capture the return codes of SQL statements executed inside the stored procedure. It also declares other host language variables that will be needed during execution. The stored procedure does not need to connect to a database, since it uses the database connection established by its client program.

STEP 2: The stored procedure unpacks its parameters from the SQLDA structure and interprets them as follows: The first entry of the SQLDA points to an integer that indicates the number of accounts to be updated. The second entry points to a Clob that is really a list of updates, each expressed as an account number and a net change. The account numbers and net changes are represented as 11-byte strings, packed within the Clob. To find the first of these strings, the stored procedure must skip over the 4-byte length field at the beginning of the Clob.

Code for Example Program SERVER1: Stored Procedure, Server Side

```c
#include <stdio.h>
#include <memory.h>
#include <sqlenv.h>

SQL_API_RC SQL_API_FN server1(
      void          *dummy1,            /* not used              */
      void          *dummy2,            /* not used              */
      struct sqlda *exchange_da,        /* for input and output  */
      struct sqlca *out_sqlca           /* sqlca for return codes */
      )
  {
  /*
  **   STEP 1: Declare a local SQLCA and some host variables
  */
  EXEC SQL INCLUDE SQLCA;

  EXEC SQL BEGIN DECLARE SECTION;
     char acctno[10];      /* account number to be updated       */
     long netchange;       /* net change in this account's balance */
  EXEC SQL END DECLARE SECTION;

  long n_updates;          /* total no. of accounts to update    */
  long counter;            /* how many accts updated so far      */
  char *account_data;      /* account changes packed inside CLOB */

  /*
  **   STEP 2: Interpret parameters.  The SQLDA structure named
  **   exchange_da has two SQLVAR entries, used as follows:
  **   1. (Integer) on input:  the number of accounts to be updated
  **               on output: no. of accounts processed successfully
  **   2. (Clob):   on input:  vector of (acct. no, net change) pairs.
  **                           Each value is represented as a
  **                           10-byte string.  Skip over the length
  **                           field in the first 4 bytes of the Clob.
  **               on output: set to null (don't return unnecessary data)
  */
  n_updates = *(long *)(exchange_da->sqlvar[0].sqldata);
  account_data = (char *)(exchange_da->sqlvar[1].sqldata + 4);
```

STEP 3: The stored procedure loops over the list of updates, extracting the account numbers and net changes and applying them to the database by an SQL UPDATE statement. The loop counts the number of updates that were successful and exits when the list is exhausted or an update fails.

STEP 4: After exiting from the loop, the stored procedure compares the number of successful updates with the total number of updates requested. If these numbers are equal, the stored procedure commits the transaction; otherwise, it rolls back all changes. The stored procedure runs in the same transaction as the client program that invoked it, so any commit or rollback executed by the stored procedure applies to updates performed by the client since the previous commit or rollback, as well as to updates performed by the stored procedure itself. If necessary, a stored procedure can execute a series of several transactions (however, a stored procedure can commit or rollback a transaction only if its client is using a Type 1 database connection).

STEP 5: The stored procedure sends the number of successful updates back to the client program by copying it into the first entry of the exchange SQLDA (since this SQLDA is used for both input and output, the original number of requested updates is overridden). This number enables the client program to find the first invalid update for diagnostic purposes. By convention, the client program knows that all changes were rolled back if any updates failed. The stored procedure also sets the null indicator of the second SQLDA entry to –128, which means that its data is used for input only and need not be copied back to the client program.

STEP 6: The stored procedure copies its local SQLCA into the one provided by the client program before returning. It then returns the code SQLZ_HOLD_PROC, which indicates that it expects to be called again and should be retained in main memory.

```
/*
**   STEP 3: Apply all the updates to the database
*/
for (counter = 0; counter < n_updates; counter++)
   {
   sscanf(account_data + (20 * counter), "%s", acctno);
   sscanf(account_data + (20 * counter) + 10, "%d", &netchange);

   EXEC SQL UPDATE bank.accounts
           SET balance = balance + :netchange
           WHERE acctno = :acctno;

   if (SQLCODE != 0) break;
   }

/*
**   STEP 4: If all updates were successful, commit work;
**   otherwise roll back
*/
if (counter == n_updates)
   EXEC SQL COMMIT;
 else
   EXEC SQL ROLLBACK;

/*
**   STEP 5: Copy counter into output SQLDA.  Set the second SQLDA
**   entry indicator to -128 (no need to return all the account data).
*/

*(long *)(exchange_da->sqlvar[0].sqldata) = counter;
*(short *)(exchange_da->sqlvar[1].sqlind) = -128;

/*
**   STEP 6: Copy local SQLCA into return SQLCA and return
*/
memcpy((char *)out_sqlca, (char *)&sqlca, sizeof(struct sqlca));
return (SQLZ_HOLD_PROC);
}
```

9.1.2 Rules for Implementing Stored Procedures

When writing the program that implements a stored procedure, you must observe the following rules:

1. A stored procedure must return to its caller (it must never call the `exit` function to terminate its process).

2. A stored procedure must not execute any SQL statements (such as CONNECT) that would change its database connection. The stored procedure must rely on the database connection established by the client program.

3. A stored procedure cannot execute an SQL COMMIT or ROLLBACK statement if it is called by a client program using a Type 2 database connection (distributed transaction).

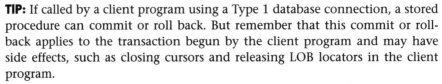

TIP: If called by a client program using a Type 1 database connection, a stored procedure can commit or roll back. But remember that this commit or rollback applies to the transaction begun by the client program and may have side effects, such as closing cursors and releasing LOB locators in the client program.

4. Since a stored procedure runs in background mode, it cannot display output on a screen using `printf`. It may, however, write into a file on the server machine. Since the stored procedure runs under a dummy userid, it can write into a file only if the file is authorized for writing by any user.

5. If a stored procedure sets the `sqlind` field of an SQLDA entry to –128, the data in that entry will not be returned to the client program. When using this technique, make sure that the client program provides a null indicator variable to receive the –128 code.

6. If your function implementation is written in C++, you should specify `extern "C"` as part of your function declaration in the implementation file. This will ensure that your function is made available for linking by the name you gave it rather than by a "mangled" name chosen by the C++ compiler. If possible, avoid using an overloaded C++ function name (otherwise, you will need to follow special procedures documented in the *Building Applications* manual for your platform).

7. Parameters of LOB datatypes (Blob, Clob, and Dbclob) can be exchanged only between UDB clients and UDB servers (not with servers on other platforms reached by the DRDA protocol).

8. If you pack binary data into a Blob, the data will be exchanged "as is" between client and server. If, for example, the representation of integers is different between the client and server platforms, the transformation from one representation to the other (such as byte reversal) is the responsibility of the stored procedure itself.

9. Stored procedures always interpret character strings using the database code page. If you pass parameters to a stored procedure using datatypes Char, Varchar, Long Varchar, Clob, Graphic, Vargraphic, Long Vargraphic, or Dbclob, the system will perform a transformation between the code page of the client application and that of the database. If the client application and the database are using different code pages, this transformation will damage any binary information packed inside the strings.[2]

10. When double-byte data (SQL datatype Graphic, Vargraphic, Long Vargraphic, or Dbclob) is exchanged with a stored procedure, it is always exchanged in multibyte format (not wide-character format). In other words, parameters and results of stored procedures always use the format specified by the precompiler option WCHARTYPE NOCONVERT. For more information about handling double-byte data inside stored procedures, see the *Embedded SQL Programming Guide*.

9.1.3 Installing a Stored Procedure

Before you can use a stored procedure, you must install it on a server machine. The installation process is similar to the process of "building" (precompiling, compiling, and binding) an application program, and also similar in some ways to the process of installing an external function. Before you can start the installation process, you must make sure that all the tables used by the stored procedure exist in the database in which the stored procedure will be installed. In our bank example, the table BANK.ACCOUNTS must be created before the stored procedure can be installed. The process of installing a stored procedure takes place on the server machine and varies with the platform on which the server is running. In general, the process consists of the following steps:

1. As in the case of an external function, you need to create a *module definition file* that lists all the entry points (functions) that are exported (made available for dynamic loading) by the file that implements your stored procedure. A single file can implement multiple stored procedures. The module definition file should be in the same directory as the stored procedure source file. The name and format of the module definition file required by your compiler are described in the *Building Applications* manual for your platform. Here are some examples:

---

2. However, you can inhibit code-page conversion for a given entry in an SQLDA by setting the seventh byte of the `sqldaid` field to the "+" character and setting the `sqlname` field of the given entry to four bytes of binary zeros.

- Suppose that stored procedures named `server1` and `server2` are implemented in a file named `stprocs.c`. If you are using the Microsoft Visual C++ compiler on Windows NT, you will need a module definition file named `stprocs.def`, with the following content:

```
LIBRARY stprocs
EXPORTS server1
        server2
```

- On AIX, the module definition file is called an *export file*. If you plan to compile and link the `stprocs.c` file on AIX using the IBM XLC compiler, you will need an export file named `stprocs.exp`, with the following content:

```
#! stprocs export file
server1
server2
```

TIP: The following steps must be repeated for every database in which your stored procedure will be used.

2. Connect to the database in which your stored procedure will be used, and then precompile, compile, and link the file that implements the stored procedure. UDB provides command files that can be used for this purpose with various platforms and compilers. They are found in the directories under `sqllib/samples` (for example, the files for building C and C++ applications are found in `sqllib/samples/c` and in `sqllib/samples/cpp`). Here are the names of some of these command files:

- `bldmsstp.bat` can be used with the Microsoft Visual C++ compiler on Windows NT.
- `bldvastp.bat` can be used with the IBM Visual Age C++ compiler on Windows and OS/2.
- `bldxlcsrv` can be used with the IBM XLC compiler on AIX.
- `bldcset` can be used with the IBM CSet++ compiler on AIX.

In general, these command files take four parameters: the name of the stored procedure, the name of the database in which it is to be installed, and the userid and password under which it is to be installed.

Before using one of these command files, you should read it and modify it as necessary, taking guidance from the comments in the file itself. For example, some of the files contain references to an error-checking utility program named `util` that is used in the UDB sample applications. If your stored procedure does not use this utility, you should delete references to `util.c` and `util.o` from the command file. Also, the `bldxlcsrv` and `bldcsetsrv` command files assume that the DB2 include and link libraries are installed in directories `/usr/lpp/db2_05_00/include` and `/usr/lpp/db2_05_00/lib`. If this is not the case, you should modify the compile and link commands to contain the correct locations of these libraries.

3. Place the executable file generated in Step 2 into the appropriate directory on the server machine. For example, after compiling and linking a source file named `stprocs.c`, the executable file generated on Windows or OS/2 is named `stprocs.dll`, and the executable file generated on AIX is simply named `stprocs`.

   The command file (such as `bldmsstp.bat`) that compiles and links your stored procedure will copy the resulting executable file to the default directory (`sqllib/function`). You need to explicitly copy the file yourself only if you want to install it in some directory other than the default directory. If your stored procedure is very well debugged and you wish to allow it to run in the same address space as the database engine for maximum performance, you can place its executable file into the directory `sqllib/function/unfenced`. This type of installation, called an *unfenced stored procedure*, exposes your database to possible damage caused by a faulty or malicious stored procedure. Before using an unfenced stored procedure, you should read the section "Working with Not-Fenced Stored Procedures" in the *Embedded SQL Programming Guide*.

   After the executable file has been copied to the appropriate directory, it should be made executable by any user. For example, under AIX, the `stprocss` file can be made executable by the following command:

   ```
   chmod a+x stprocs
   ```

   Remember that the process that executes the stored procedure will not be running under your userid, but under a dummy userid generated by the database system.

   TIP: Be very careful to protect the executable file that implements your stored procedure against unauthorized tampering. The database does not protect this file and will execute it whenever your stored procedure is invoked. If the file that implements your stored procedure is replaced by another executable file, it could potentially do something harmful.

4. If you wish other users to be able to use your stored procedure, grant to them the EXECUTE privilege on your stored procedure's package. The following example statement allows any user to execute the package created by precompiling the `stprocs.sqc` source file, which might implement `server1` and other stored procedures:

   ```
   GRANT EXECUTE ON PACKAGE stprocs TO PUBLIC;
   ```

5. "Register" your stored procedure by executing a CREATE PROCEDURE statement in the database where the procedure will be used. The syntax of this
statement is as follows:

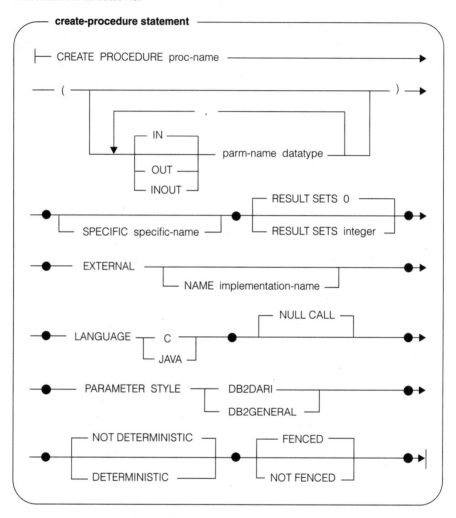

A CREATE PROCEDURE statement is similar to a CREATE FUNCTION statement in that it stores a description of the procedure in the system catalogs
named PROCEDURES and PROCPARMS. The details of CREATE PROCEDURE
are as follows:

- If no schema name is specified for the procedure, the default schema is equal
  to the current authid.

- Two procedures in the same schema may not have the same name and the
  same number of parameters, even if their parameter types are different.

- The CREATE PROCEDURE statement lists the names and datatypes of the parameters of the procedure. These parameters correspond to the arguments of the CALL statement that is used to invoke the procedure (see Section 9.2.1). The parameters also correspond to the individual SQLVAR entries inside the SQLDA structure that is passed to the implementing program (such as exchange_da in our example program). Since the entries in an SQLDA can be used for exchanging values in both directions between the stored procedure and the client program, each parameter is labeled IN (carries input to the stored procedure), OUT (carries results back to the client program), or INOUT (carries data in both directions).

- Like a user-defined function, a stored procedure can have a specific name that is useful mainly for DROP PROCEDURE and COMMENT ON PROCEDURE.

- In addition to returning data to the client program through its OUT and INOUT parameters, a stored procedure can return one or more *result sets* to the client program. Each result set is a set of rows, represented by a cursor that is left open by the stored procedure. If a stored procedure returns one or more result sets, this fact should be declared in the CREATE PROCEDURE statement. Result sets of stored procedures are discussed further in Section 9.2.3.

- The EXTERNAL clause tells UDB how to find the executable program that implements your stored procedure. The most complete form of an EXTERNAL clause gives the full path name of the executable file, followed by a "!", followed by the name of the proper entry point in that file. For example, the following clause tells the system that your function is implemented by the server1 entry point in the file /bank/bin/stprocs:

  EXTERNAL NAME '/bank/bin/stprocs!server1'

  If no path name is specified, the system looks for fenced procedures in the sqllib/function directory associated with your database, and for unfenced procedures in the sqllib/function/unfenced directory. Thus, if stprocs implements a fenced stored procedure and you have placed it in sqllib/function, you can shorten the phrase above as follows:

  EXTERNAL NAME 'stprocs!server1'

  In fact, if you specify no implementation name at all but only the keyword EXTERNAL, the system will use the procedure name as the implementation name, and will look for a file with this name in the default directory and invoke its default entry point.

TIP: Since the external name of your procedure is specified as a quoted string, it is case sensitive. The external name you specify must exactly match the name of your executable file and entry point, including upper- and lowercase.

- If your procedure is written in Java, you must specify LANGUAGE JAVA and PARAMETER STYLE DB2GENERAL (the convention for passing parameters to a Java procedure is described in Section 6.4.10).

- The implementation of a stored procedure is invoked even when the input parameters are null. You have no choice about this, but you can acknowledge it by specifying NULL CALL.

- If the result of your stored procedure is uniquely determined by its input parameters, you can make this fact known to the system by specifying DETERMINISTIC.

- If your stored procedure is trusted and you wish to run it in the same address space as the database manager, you may specify NOT FENCED. In order to create a NOT FENCED procedure, you must hold SYSADM or DBADM authority, or hold CREATE_NOT_FENCED authority on the database. UDB does not allow a NOT FENCED stored procedure to be written in REXX or to call CLI functions.

The following CREATE PROCEDURE statement might be used to register our example SERVER1 stored procedure:

```
CREATE PROCEDURE server1
  ( INOUT n_updates Integer,
    IN update_list Clob(8000) )
  EXTERNAL NAME 'stprocs!server1'
  LANGUAGE C
  DETERMINISTIC
  PARAMETER STYLE DB2DARI;
```

CREATE PROCEDURE is a new SQL statement, introduced for the first time in UDB Version 5. For compatibility with earlier versions of the product, you can still create a stored procedure simply by compiling and binding its implementation program, without executing a CREATE PROCEDURE statement. Such a procedure can be invoked by specifying its name in a CALL statement. However, even though it is not always required, it is a good practice to register your stored procedures by using CREATE PROCEDURE statements, for the following reasons:

- The CREATE PROCEDURE statement makes your stored procedures visible in the PROCEDURES catalog table, and via CLI catalog functions such as SQL-Procedures() and SQLProcedureColumns().

- The CREATE PROCEDURE statement gives you an opportunity to specify the mapping between a procedure name and a specific entry point in a specific implementation file. This gives you the flexibility to combine several stored procedures in the same implementation file, and to place the implementation file in a directory other than the default directory sqllib/function.

- A CREATE PROCEDURE statement is required if your procedure is written in the Java language.

9.1.4 Writing a Stored Procedure in Java

If you have a Java virtual machine on your server, you can use Java as the implementation language for some of your stored procedures. You must tell UDB where to find the Java virtual machine, and tell the Java virtual machine where to find the UDB class libraries that support Java stored procedures. This is done in two steps:

1. Set your CLASSPATH environment variable to include the paths `sqllib/function` and `sqllib/java/db2java.zip`.

2. Set the database manager configuration parameter named JDK11_PATH to the path name of the directory in which your Java virtual machine is installed. You can use the Control Center to set this configuration parameter, as described in Chapter 10.

To implement a stored procedure in Java, you need to create a Java class that extends (is a subclass of) the StoredProc class[3] provided in the UDB class library. The StoredProc class provides many methods, described in the *Embedded SQL Programming Guide,* that you will find helpful in writing your procedure. Your Java class can have several public methods, each of which implements a different stored procedure. Compile your Java class and install the resulting file in the `sqllib/function` directory.

The CREATE PROCEDURE statement for a Java stored procedure must specify the name of the class and method that implements the procedure, using the syntax EXTERNAL NAME `'classname!methodname'`. It must also specify LANGUAGE JAVA and PARAMETER STYLE DB2GENERAL. As the latter phrase suggests, Java stored procedures receive their parameters and return their results in a different way from other stored procedures. The main differences are as follows:

- Rather than receiving all its parameters packed inside an SQLDA structure, the Java method that implements a stored procedure has one parameter for each of the parameters of the stored procedure. Input parameters are converted from SQL datatypes into corresponding Java datatypes, as shown in Table 8-1. No parameters are needed for null indicators, because the `StoredProc` class provides an `isNull` method that can be used to test the nullness of any input parameter. A Java method can return a null value by simply not setting the value of an output parameter.

- The `StoredProc` class provides a collection of methods for setting the values of output parameters, using various Java datatypes. For example, a Java stored procedure might use the statement `set(5,x)` to set its output parameter number 5 to the value of variable x. This statement might invoke one of several

---

3. The full name of this class is `COM.ibm.db2.app.StoredProc`.

methods, depending on the datatype of variable x. In addition, **UDB** provides two classes named `COM.ibm.db2.app.Blob` and `COM.ibm.db2.app.Clob` that enable Java stored procedures to read and write their LOB-type parameters a few bytes at a time.

- A Java stored procedure can return an error code and message to the client program by throwing an exception of type `SQLException`, which is supported by the JDBC class library. The parameters of the `SQLException` constructor include an SQLCODE, an SQLSTATE, and a message. If a Java stored procedure throws an exception that is not an `SQLException`, the client program receives SQLCODE -4302 and SQLSTATE 38501.

A Java stored procedure does not acquire a database connection of its own, but uses the database connection acquired by the client program. The Java procedure gains access to this connection by calling the `getConnection()` method of the `StoredProc` class, which returns a `Connection` object representing the database connection of the client program.

UDB provides an example of a Java stored procedure in the `sqllib/samples/java` directory. Additional information about Java stored procedures and the class libraries that support them can be found in the *Embedded SQL Programming Guide*, and on the World Wide Web at `http://www.software.ibm.com/data/db2/java`.

9.1.5 Writing a Stored Procedure in BASIC

IBM's VisualAge for Basic provides support for creating **UDB** stored procedures and external functions, using the BASIC programming language. For each stored procedure or function written in BASIC, VisualAge for Basic automatically generates a "wrapper" program that enables the **UDB** server to invoke the procedure or function using C calling conventions.

As a development environment for creating stored procedures and external functions, VisualAge for Basic offers the following advantages:

- It provides a convenient language-oriented debugging environment that enables you to test your stored procedure on a client machine before installing it on a server.

- It provides graphical tools that simplify the process of installing a stored procedure on a server machine and registering it for use with a database.

- Since VisualAge for Basic does not use a precompiler, you do not need to manage two copies of your source program, one before precompilation and one after.

- BASIC is a relatively "safe" language in which to write a stored procedure, since it has no pointers and provides no direct access to system memory.

- VisualAge for Basic provides a level of integration between SQL and BASIC that is not available in other host languages. For example:

    A BASIC stored procedure does need an SQL Declare Section. Any BASIC variable of an appropriate type can be used in any SQL statement.

    There is a one-to-one correspondence between the parameters passed by the client program in a CALL statement and the parameters received by the stored procedure. In other words, there is no need for the stored procedure to "unpack" its parameters from an SQLDA structure.

    A stored procedure does not need to declare a local SQLCA structure and to copy its content into the parameter SQLCA before returning. The SQLCA structure passed to the stored procedure as a parameter serves double duty as a local SQLCA and is automatically returned to the client program on completion of the stored procedure.

    If the stored procedure is called from a client program that is also written using VisualAge for Basic, the client program can pass an array of values as a parameter to the stored procedure.

More information about VisualAge for Basic can be found in the following IBM publications:

GC26-8926 *VisualAge for Basic: Getting Started*
SC26-8692 *VisualAge for Basic Data Access Guide*
SC26-8963 *VisualAge for Basic Language Reference*

9.2 THE CLIENT SIDE

An application program running on a client machine can invoke a stored procedure on a server machine by means of an SQL CALL statement. The CALL statement passes input parameters from the client program to the stored procedure and returns output parameters to the client program after execution of the stored procedure.

9.2.1 The CALL Statement

The CALL statement names the procedure to be called and specifies its parameters. The parameters may be specified in the form of a list of host variables, which UDB will automatically pack into an SQLDA structure for exchange with the stored procedure. Alternatively, you can use the DESCRIPTOR syntax of the CALL statement to create your own SQLDA structure to be passed to the stored procedure.

Like any SQL statement, the CALL statement implicitly assigns return codes and messages to the SQLCA structure declared in the calling program. In the case of a CALL statement, the content of the SQLCA is determined by the SQLCA structure returned by the stored procedure (or, if the procedure is written in Java, by the exception, if any, that it throws).

The syntax of a CALL statement is as follows:

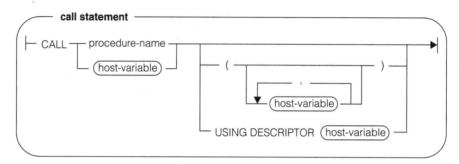

Although CALL is an SQL statement, it is subject to certain restrictions. It can be used in a host language program as a static SQL statement, and it can be invoked from a CLI program using the functions `SQLExecDirect()` or `SQLPrepare()` and `SQLExecute()`. However, a CALL statement cannot be executed from an interactive interface such as the Command Center or by using Embedded Dynamic SQL statements such as PREPARE and EXECUTE.

A CALL statement can specify the name of the stored procedure either directly or by specifying a host variable that contains the procedure name (the latter technique is useful if the procedure name contains lowercase characters). In either case, UDB must resolve the procedure name to a specific function or method in a specific library (the executable file that implements the stored procedure). This resolution process takes place as follows:[4]

1. If the procedure name is a simple name such as `proc1`:

   a. First, UDB searches the default directories (`sqllib/function` and `sqllib/function/unfenced`)[5] for a library with the given name containing a function with the same name. For example, `CALL proc1` would invoke the `proc1` function in the `proc1` library in one of the default directories.

---

4. These rules apply to stored procedure resolution on UDB. Other products in the DB2 family, such as DB2 for OS/390, use slightly different rules, described in the *SQL Reference*.
5. In OS/2, the default directory for fenced stored procedures is specified by the LIBPATH variable in CONFIG.SYS, and the default directory for unfenced stored procedures is `sqllib\dll\unfenced`.

b. If no library and function with the given name are found in the default directories, **UDB** searches the PROCEDURES catalog table for a stored procedure with the given name that was registered by a CREATE PROCEDURE statement. The chosen procedure must have the correct number of parameters, and its schema must be on the current function path. The library and function to be invoked are those specified in the EXTERNAL clause of the CREATE PROCEDURE statement. For example, given the CREATE PROCEDURE statement on page 564, CALL server1(:x, :y) would invoke the server1 function in the stprocs library in the sqllib/function directory.

TIP: Like any SQL identifier, a procedure name is folded to uppercase unless it is enclosed in double quotes. This rule applies to procedure names in CREATE PROCEDURE and CALL statements. However, an early implementation of the CALL statement failed to perform this folding. If you are having trouble calling a stored procedure that was registered by a CREATE PROCEDURE statement, try using an uppercase procedure name in your CALL statement.

2. If the procedure name contains a "!" character, the string to the left of the "!" identifies the library, and the string to the right of the "!" identifies the function within the library. The library may be identified by a full path name or by a filename in one of the default directories. Here are some examples:

CALL "myprocs!proc1" invokes the proc1 function in the myprocs library in one of the default directories.

CALL "d:\bank\bin\stprocs!server2" invokes the server2 function in the stprocs directory in the d:\bank\bin directory.

In a CALL statement, the arguments passed to the stored procedure must be host variables, not constants or expressions. The host variables may have null indicators. For example, the following statement is incorrect:

```
EXEC SQL CALL proc1(7, NULL);
```

The intent of the statement above is accomplished by the following correct statements:

```
x = 7;
xind = 0;
y = 0;
yind = -1;
EXEC SQL CALL proc1(:x :xind, :y :yind);
```

TIP: Make sure your client program and stored procedure agree on which of their exchanged variables have null indicators. If a stored procedure attempts to return a null value when no indicator variable has been provided, it will probably crash. When indicator variables are used, both the client program and the stored procedure should set their values explicitly.

If you use the DESCRIPTOR form of a CALL statement and provide your own SQLDA structure, and if one or more of the entries in your SQLDA contains binary data (such as Varchar FOR BIT DATA), you must set the sixth byte of the `sqldaid` field to the "+" character (rather than its normal blank character), and you must set the `sqlname` fields of the binary data entries to eight bytes of binary zeros. (The use of an SQLDA in CALL statements is described further in Section 8.3.5.)

There are no special requirements for installation of a client program that uses the CALL statement; you can simply precompile it, bind it to the database, and invoke it as you would any application program.

TIP: If you have trouble invoking a stored procedure, it is possible that your database manager is not properly configured. You can test for this problem by the command `db2 get database manager configuration`. The resulting display should identify your node as a "Database Server" and should list the values of the configuration parameters KEEPDARI as YES and MAXDARI as a positive number. The default values of KEEPDARI = YES, MAXDARI = 200 are acceptable. (You can display and set database manager configuration parameters by using the Control Center, as described in Chapter 10.)

CLIENT1A, shown below, is an example of a client program that exercises the SERVER1 stored procedure using an SQL CALL statement.

Example Program CLIENT1A: A Client Program Using CALL

```
#include <stdlib.h>
#include <stdio.h>
#include <sqlenv.h>

int main()
    {

    EXEC SQL BEGIN DECLARE SECTION;
        long n_updates_req;             /* no. of updates requested  */
        long n_updates;                 /* no. of successful updates */
```

```
    SQL TYPE IS CLOB(8000) update_list; /* list of update pairs      */
    char dbname[9] = "testdb";          /* name of database          */
    short indicator = 0;                /* indicator (not null)      */
EXEC SQL END DECLARE SECTION;

EXEC SQL INCLUDE SQLCA;                        /* local return code structure */

/*
**   Collect a series of account updates.
**   To exercise the stored procedure, we will make up five updates.
**   Each update consists of a pair of values: (acct. no., net change).
**   We pack each value into a 10-byte substring inside the Clob.
*/
n_updates = n_updates_req = 5;             /* five updates requested    */
update_list.length = 100;                  /* 10 values, 10 bytes each  */
strcpy(update_list.data, "CHK00001");      /* net change for account 1  */
strcpy(update_list.data+10, "+150");       /*     is +150               */
strcpy(update_list.data+20, "CHK00002");   /* net change for account 2  */
strcpy(update_list.data+30, "-75");        /*     is -75                */
strcpy(update_list.data+40, "CHK00003");   /* net change for account 3  */
strcpy(update_list.data+50, "-100");       /*     is -100               */
strcpy(update_list.data+60, "CHK00004");   /* net change for account 4  */
strcpy(update_list.data+70, "+90");        /*     is +90                */
strcpy(update_list.data+80, "CHK00005");   /* net change for account 5  */
strcpy(update_list.data+90, "-20");        /*     is -20                */

/*
**   Connect to the database.
*/
EXEC SQL CONNECT TO :dbname;
if (SQLCODE != 0)
    {
    printf("\nError in connecting to database.\n");
    printf("SQLCODE = %d, SQLSTATE = %5.5s\n", SQLCODE, sqlca.sqlstate);
    }

/*
**   Call the stored procedure, passing an Integer and a Clob
**   as host variables.  These host variables are automatically
**   packed into an SQLDA structure and used for both input and output.
*/
EXEC SQL CALL SERVER1(:n_updates, :update_list :indicator);
```

```
if (SQLCODE == 0)
    {
    /*
    **   The number of successful updates is returned in n_updates.
    **   Compare this to the number we requested.
    */
    if (n_updates == n_updates_req)
        {
        printf("\nStored procedure was successful.\n");
        printf("Number of accounts updated = %d\n", n_updates);
        }
    else
        {
        printf("\nError encountered after updating %d accounts.\n",
                n_updates);
        printf("All updates have been rolled back.\n");
        }
    }
else
    {
    printf("\nUnexpected error in stored procedure.\n");
    printf ("   SQLCODE = %d, SQLSTATE = %5.5s\n",
                                  SQLCODE, sqlca.sqlstate);
    }

EXEC SQL CONNECT RESET;

}       /* end of main */
```

9.2.2 Calling a Stored Procedure from a CLI Client

In Section 8.1, we discussed the advantages of using the Call Level Interface (CLI) to invoke SQL from a host language program. In a stored-procedure application, CLI can be used either in the stored procedure or in the client program, or in both.

CLIENT1B, shown below, is an example of a client program that was written using CLI and that invokes the SERVER1 stored procedure. Like CLIENT1A, it uses a CALL statement to invoke the stored procedure. The CALL statement is prepared for execution by the SQLPrepare() function; its parameters are bound to specific variables by the SQLBindParameter() function; and it is executed by the SQLExecute() function.

Example Program CLIENT1B: A CLI Client

```c
#include <sqlcli1.h>
#include <stdlib.h>
#include <string.h>
#include <stdio.h>

void errorExit(SQLHENV henv, SQLHDBC hdbc, SQLHSTMT hstmt, char *place);

int main()
   {
   SQLHENV henv;                      /* environment handle            */
   SQLHDBC hdbc;                      /* connection handle             */
   SQLHSTMT hstmt;                    /* statement handle              */

   SQLCHAR dbname[] = "testdb";       /* name of database              */
   char qstring[80];                  /* holds an SQL statement        */

   SQLINTEGER n_updates_req;          /* no. of updates requested      */
   SQLINTEGER n_updates;              /* no. of successful updates     */
   SQLINTEGER indicator1;             /* indicator variable for n_updates   */
   SQLINTEGER indicator2;             /* indicator variable for update_list */
   struct Clob                        /* list of update pairs, in a Clob    */
       {
       unsigned long length;
       char data[8000];
       } update_list;

   SQLRETURN rc;                      /* return code                   */

   /*
   ** Allocate environment, connection, and statement handles
   **  and establish a database connection.
   */
   SQLAllocHandle(SQL_HANDLE_ENV, SQL_NULL_HANDLE, &henv);
   SQLAllocHandle(SQL_HANDLE_DBC, henv, &hdbc);

   rc = SQLConnect(hdbc, dbname, SQL_NTS,
                         NULL, SQL_NTS,    /* allow userid to default   */
                         NULL, SQL_NTS);   /* allow password to default */
   if (rc != SQL_SUCCESS)
      errorExit(henv, hdbc, SQL_NULL_HSTMT, "Connecting to database");
```

```
SQLAllocHandle(SQL_HANDLE_STMT, hdbc, &hstmt);

/*
**   Collect a series of account updates.
**   To exercise the stored procedure, we will make up five updates.
**   Each update consists of a pair of values: (acct. no., net change).
**   We pack each value into a 10-byte substring inside the Clob.
*/
n_updates = n_updates_req = 5;              /* five updates requested   */
update_list.length = 100;                   /* 10 values, 10 bytes each */
strcpy(update_list.data, "CHK00001");       /* net change for account 1 */
strcpy(update_list.data+10, "+150");        /*     is +150              */
strcpy(update_list.data+20, "CHK00002");    /* net change for account 2 */
strcpy(update_list.data+30, "-75");         /*     is -75               */
strcpy(update_list.data+40, "CHK00003");    /* net change for account 3 */
strcpy(update_list.data+50, "-100");        /*     is -100              */
strcpy(update_list.data+60, "CHK00004");    /* net change for account 4 */
strcpy(update_list.data+70, "+90");         /*     is +90               */
strcpy(update_list.data+80, "CHK00005");    /* net change for account 5 */
strcpy(update_list.data+90, "-20");         /*     is -20               */

/*
**   Prepare a CALL statement with two parameter markers.
*/
strcpy (qstring, "CALL SERVER1(?, ?)");
rc = SQLPrepare(hstmt, (SQLCHAR *)qstring, SQL_NTS);
if (rc != SQL_SUCCESS)
   errorExit(henv, hdbc, hstmt, "Preparing CALL statement");

/*
**   Bind host variables to the parameter markers.
*/
SQLBindParameter(hstmt,
            1,                          /* first parameter marker    */
            SQL_PARAM_INPUT_OUTPUT,     /* used for input and output */
            SQL_C_LONG,                 /* datatype of host variable */
            SQL_INTEGER,                /* SQL datatype              */
            0,                          /* not used in this call     */
            0,                          /* not used in this call     */
            (SQLPOINTER)&n_updates,     /* address of host variable  */
            4,                          /* length of buffer          */
            &indicator1 );              /* null or length indicator  */
```

```
SQLBindParameter(hstmt,
                 2,                         /* second parameter marker     */
                 SQL_PARAM_INPUT,           /* used for input only         */
                 SQL_C_CHAR,                /* datatype of host variable   */
                 SQL_CLOB,                  /* SQL datatype                */
                 8000,                      /* max length of input data    */
                 0,                         /* not used in this call       */
                 (SQLPOINTER)update_list,   /* address of host variable    */
                 8000,                      /* length of buffer            */
                 &indicator2 );             /* null or length indicator    */

/*
**    Execute the CALL statement.
*/
indicator1 = 0;           /* length of an integer is implicit */
indicator2 = 104;         /* 4 bytes length, 100 bytes data    */

rc = SQLExecute(hstmt);
if (rc != SQL_SUCCESS && rc != SQL_SUCCESS_WITH_INFO)
    errorExit(henv, hdbc, hstmt, "Executing CALL statement");

/*
**    Check results.
**    The number of successful updates is returned in n_updates.
**    Compare this to the number we requested.
*/
if (n_updates == n_updates_req)
    {
    printf("\nStored procedure was successful.\n");
    printf("Number of accounts updated = %d\n", n_updates);
    }
else
    {
    printf("\nError encountered after updating %d accounts.\n",
            n_updates);
    printf("All updates have been rolled back.\n");
    }
/*
**    Clean up
*/
SQLFreeHandle(SQL_HANDLE_STMT, hstmt);    /* free statement handle    */
SQLDisconnect(hdbc);                      /* disconnect from database */
SQLFreeHandle(SQL_HANDLE_DBC, hdbc);      /* free connection handle   */
```

```
SQLFreeHandle(SQL_HANDLE_ENV, henv);        /* free environment handle  */
exit(rc);

}     /* end of main */

void errorExit(SQLHENV henv, SQLHDBC hdbc, SQLHSTMT hstmt, char *place)
   {
   SQLCHAR sqlstate[SQL_SQLSTATE_SIZE + 1];
   SQLINTEGER sqlcode;
   SQLSMALLINT msglength;
   SQLCHAR msgbuffer[SQL_MAX_MESSAGE_LENGTH + 1];
   SQLSMALLINT errno;

   printf ("\nSQL error at %s, transaction rolled back.\n", place);

   /*
   **   Retrieve error codes and messages.
   */
   errno = 1;
   while ( SQLGetDiagRec(SQL_HANDLE_STMT, hstmt, errno,
              sqlstate, &sqlcode, msgbuffer,
              SQL_MAX_MESSAGE_LENGTH+1, &msglength) == SQL_SUCCESS )
     {
     printf("   SQLCODE = %d, SQLSTATE = %s\n", sqlcode, sqlstate);
     printf("   MESSAGE: %s\n", msgbuffer);
     errno++;
     }

   /*
   **   Roll back and clean up.
   */
   SQLEndTran(SQL_HANDLE_DBC, hdbc, SQL_ROLLBACK);        /* rollback */
   SQLDisconnect(hdbc);                         /* disconnect from database */
   SQLFreeHandle(SQL_HANDLE_DBC, hdbc);   /* free connection handle   */
   SQLFreeHandle(SQL_HANDLE_ENV, henv);   /* free environment handle  */
   exit(-2);
   }
```

9.2.3 Result Sets

One useful feature of stored procedures is available only to client programs
that are written using CLI: the ability for the stored procedure to return result
sets. If a client program is written using static SQL, it can receive results from a

stored procedure only in the program variables or SQLDA structure that is passed via the CALL statement. But a client program written using CLI has another means of receiving results from a stored procedure, which can be used to retrieve one or more result sets, each containing many rows of data.

A stored procedure can return one or more result sets to a CLI client simply by opening a cursor on each result set and leaving the cursors open when it returns to the client program. If a CLI client invokes a stored procedure that leaves a cursor open, the client can retrieve the data associated with the open cursor by means of CLI functions such as `SQLNumResult-Cols()`, `SQLDescribeCol()`, `SQLBindCol()`, and `SQLFetch()`, using the statement handle that was used to execute the CALL statement that invoked the stored procedure. If more than one cursor was left open by the stored procedure, the first rows retrieved are the rows associated with the first cursor opened by the stored procedure. The end of the first result set is indicated by a return code of SQL_NO_DATA_FOUND from the `SQLFetch()` function. When a result set has been exhausted, the client can advance to the next result set (associated with the next cursor opened by the stored procedure) by calling the CLI function `SQLMoreResults()`. `SQLFetch()` and related functions can then be used to retrieve the rows in the next result set. After the last result set has been exhausted, further calls to `SQLMoreResults()` return the code SQL_NO_DATA_FOUND, indicating that no more result sets are available. In each result set, the client program can fetch only those rows that have not already been fetched by the stored procedure itself—for example, if a stored procedure opens a cursor and uses it to fetch the first five rows of the result set before returning to the client program, the client program can fetch the remainder of the rows in the result set, beginning with the sixth row.

Database Administration

T here's a lot more to database management than simply running queries and application programs. Databases need to be created, loaded with data, and configured for optimum performance on your hardware and for your mix of applications. You need to implement a plan for periodic backups to protect against loss of your valuable data. You may want to exercise some control over how your data is distributed on the physical devices attached to your machine. You may also want to monitor various internal database events, such as deadlocks, that may have an effect on the performance of your system.

Statistics need to be collected, so the optimizer will be able to make intelligent choices based on accurate estimates of the cost of various operations. You may wish to control the amount of time spent by the optimizer in choosing an access plan for each SQL statement. In fact, you may wish to find out exactly what access plan the optimizer has chosen for a given statement and how this plan would change if a different set of indexes were available or if the statistics of the tables involved were different.

This chapter is devoted to the various tasks that are involved in the administration of a database system and to the tools provided by UDB for accomplishing these tasks. Many of the tasks described in this chapter require one of the global authorities described in Section 2.8: System Administration (SYSADM), System Control (SYSCTRL), System Maintenance (SYSMAINT), or Database Administration (DBADM).

Database administration facilities are described in six UDB manuals with a combined length of more than 2,700 pages: *Administration Guide, Administration Getting Started, Command Reference, API Reference, System Monitor Guide and Reference,* and *Replication Guide and Reference.* This chapter provides an overall description of UDB administration facilities and some examples of their use, but for obvious reasons it cannot provide an exhaustive list of all the available options. After reading the overview in this chapter, you may wish to refer to the manuals listed above for more detailed information and syntax (see Appendix F for IBM publication numbers).

The previous chapters of this book have dealt primarily with SQL *statements.* This chapter, however, frequently discusses *commands.* The distinction between an SQL statement and a command is somewhat subtle. Both SQL statements and commands can be executed interactively in a Command Center or CLP session. In general, SQL statements operate on specific contents of the database, whereas commands operate on the global state of the database or the system. Also, in general, SQL statements are recognized by host language precompilers (when prefixed by EXEC SQL), whereas commands cannot be used in this way. This book follows the usage in the IBM product documentation regarding the distinction between SQL statements and commands.

This chapter contains several references to *configuration parameters*. There are two kinds of these parameters: *database manager configuration parameters* are settings that govern the behavior of the system as a whole, and *database configuration parameters* are settings that govern the behavior of a specific database. Each configuration parameter has a name and a value. The use of the Control Center to inspect and set configuration parameters is described in Section 10.3.

Most UDB administrative tasks can be accomplished in more than one way. This chapter focuses primarily on graphical database administration tools such as the Control Center, which in most cases provide the easiest way to get the job done. The Control Center has extensive online help that is available at every step of an administrative task. Most of the facilities that are available through the Control Center can also be invoked by commands (described in the *Command Reference*) and by application program interfaces (described in the *API Reference*).

10.1 DATABASES AND PHYSICAL SPACE

A *database* is a named collection of data containing various kinds of objects such as tables, indexes, views, and packages. A database is the scope for certain kinds of authorities, such as DBADM. It is also the unit to which an application program or interactive session can connect and within which SQL statements are executed. Each database contains a set of catalog tables that describes the content of the database. One of the first tasks in administering a UDB system is to create one or more databases. In order to understand the process of database creation, we first need to learn something about how UDB manages its physical storage.

10.1.1 Tablespaces and Bufferpools

The physical space within a database is organized into a collection of *tablespaces*. Each tablespace, in turn, consists of a collection of *containers*, each of which is either a directory in your machine's file system, a physical file, or a device such as a hard disk.

Each table is assigned to a tablespace, which contains the primary data for that table—however, a table may optionally keep its indexes in a second tablespace and its large objects in a third tablespace. More than one table may be assigned to the same tablespace. The system attempts to spread the data for each table uniformly across the containers of its tablespace. Figure 10-1 illustrates a database containing two tablespaces, of three and two containers, respectively. Tablespace 1 contains two tables, and Tablespace 2 contains three tables.

The unit of space allocation within a container is called an *extent*. As a table grows, it occupies new extents in all of the containers in its tablespace. For example, in Figure 10-1, Table 1 occupies extents in containers 1A, 1B, and 1C. All the extents in a tablespace have the same size, which you can specify when you create the tablespace (the default is controlled by a database configuration parameter named DFT_EXTENT_SZ). If you plan to store many small tables in a tablespace, you may wish to choose a small extent size to minimize wasted space, since each table will be stored in a separate extent.

By assigning tables to tablespaces and mapping tablespaces onto physical devices and directories, you can do a lot to optimize the performance of your database. For example, you can spread your data across multiple disk devices to take advantage of parallel input and output. You can use your fastest storage devices for your most frequently used tables and indexes and store less frequently used data on slower, less expensive devices. Since each tablespace can be independently backed up and restored, you can also cluster closely related tables in a tablespace so that they can be backed up as a unit. (Additional guidelines for assigning tables to tablespaces and mapping tablespaces onto physical storage devices can be found in the *Administration Guide*.)

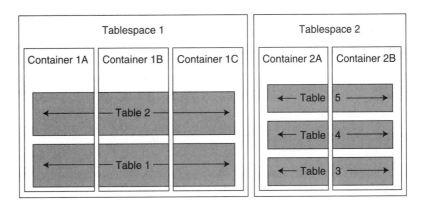

Figure 10-1: Organization of Physical Space into Tablespaces and Containers

UDB provides two different kinds of tablespaces, which are referred to by the terms *System Managed Space* (SMS) and *Database Managed Space* (DMS). An SMS tablespace uses the facilities of your operating system to manage physical space, whereas in a DMS tablespace, the physical space is managed directly by UDB. SMS tablespaces (the default) are easy to create and manage, and are well suited for many small and moderate-sized databases. DMS tablespaces provide an additional degree of control that can be helpful in large databases and high-performance applications, but they also require more sophistication on the part of the database administrator. A single database can contain both SMS and DMS tablespaces. Some of the differences between the two types of tablespaces are summarized in Table 10-1.

Each tablespace is associated with a *bufferpool*, which is an area of main system memory that is used for holding pages of data that have been fetched from the tablespace. UDB uses heuristic algorithms for prefetching pages that it thinks you are about to need into their respective bufferpools, and for moving pages from bufferpools back onto disk when it thinks they are no longer needed. By default, UDB provides one bufferpool named IBMDEFAULTBP, of an appropriate size for your platform, and uses it for all tablespaces. You can create and drop other bufferpools, and modify the sizes of bufferpools, by using the facilities of the Control Center (described in Section 10.3) or by using the SQL statements CREATE BUFFERPOOL, ALTER BUFFERPOOL, and DROP BUFFERPOOL.

TABLE 10-1: Properties of Tablespaces

System Managed Space (SMS)	Database Managed Space (DMS)
Each container is a directory in the filespace of your operating system. The space in this directory is not preallocated but grows as data is added to the tablespace. Data is stored in the form of files in the directory.	A container may be either a fixed-size, pre-allocated file, or a physical device such as a disk. In either case, all the storage for the container must be allocated when the container is created. If a container is a device, it must occupy the entire device (which may be a logical device).
Containers cannot be added to a tablespace after it is created.	Containers can be added to an existing tablespace, using the ALTER TABLESPACE statement.
All the data for a given table, including its indexes and large objects, must be stored in a single tablespace.	The primary data for a table can be stored in one tablespace, its indexes in a second tablespace, and its large objects (LOBs) in a third tablespace. This technique can improve the clustering of the table in physical storage.

Each tablespace is described by a row in the TABLESPACES catalog table. You can see a numbered list of all the tablespaces in your database by executing the following command:

```
LIST TABLESPACES;
```

To see a list of all the containers in a given tablespace, you can execute a LIST TABLESPACE CONTAINERS command, using one of the numbers in the list produced by the LIST TABLESPACES command, as in the following example:

```
LIST TABLESPACE CONTAINERS FOR 2;
```

Like bufferpools, tablespaces can be created, altered, and dropped by using the Control Center or by executing SQL statements. The SQL statements for managing tablespaces are listed below. In order to use any of these statements, you must have SYSADM or SYSCTRL authority.

CREATE TABLESPACE

In order to create an SMS tablespace, you need to specify the name of the tablespace and the path names of all its containers. Remember that each container in an SMS tablespace is a directory. If a relative path name is given, it is interpreted with respect to the local database directory of the database containing the tablespace (see Figure 10-2). If the last level of the path name does not exist, a directory with the given name is created.

In the following example, we create an SMS tablespace with three containers, implemented by directories on three different disks in an OS/2 or Windows NT file system. We then create a table in the new tablespace, causing the data in the table to be distributed among the three disks. Of course, before executing the CREATE TABLESPACE statement, our session must be connected to the database in which the tablespace is to be created.

```
CREATE TABLESPACE sms1 MANAGED BY SYSTEM
    USING ('d:\sms1', 'e:\sms1', 'f:\sms1');
CREATE TABLE accounts.receivable
    (custno  Char(6),
     amount  Money,
     dueDate Date,
     PRIMARY KEY(custno, dueDate))
    IN sms1;
```

When creating a DMS tablespace, it is necessary to specify not only the names of the files or devices that implement the containers, but also their sizes. The size of each file or device is specified as a number of 4K-byte pages, and the specified amount of space is allocated when the tablespace is created. In the following example, we create a DMS tablespace consisting of two containers, each implemented by a file of 10,000 pages.

```
CREATE TABLESPACE dms2 MANAGED BY DATABASE
    USING (FILE 'd:\dms2\dms2.dat' 10000,
             FILE 'e:\dms2\dms2.dat' 10000);
```

UDB recognizes two specialized kinds of tablespaces, called *temporary* and *long* tablespaces. A temporary tablespace provides space for the system to use for temporary results, such as a table that is materialized for sorting during the processing of a query. Every database must have at least one temporary tablespace. A tablespace can be designated as a temporary tablespace at the time of its creation by specifying CREATE TEMPORARY TABLESPACE.

A *long* tablespace is a tablespace that is dedicated to the storage of large objects. When a table is created, the CREATE TABLE statement can specify whether the table will store its large objects mixed with its other data in a regular tablespace or use a separate long tablespace for this purpose. Separating the large objects from the rest of the data can improve the clustering properties of the table and reduce the number of I/O operations needed to scan the table. A long tablespace must be a DMS tablespace and is designated at creation time by specifying CREATE LONG TABLESPACE. In the following example, we allocate a 50,000-page file to serve as a long tablespace and create a table that uses the long tablespace to store large objects.

```
CREATE LONG TABLESPACE longspace MANAGED BY DATABASE
    USING (FILE 'f:\longspace\space1.dat' 50000);
CREATE TABLE bridges
    (name        Varchar(32),
     latitude  Double,
     longitude Double,
     photo       Blob(1M))
    IN dms2 LONG IN longspace;
```

A CREATE TABLESPACE statement has the following optional parameters:

- EXTENTSIZE specifies the unit of space allocation inside the containers of the tablespace, in pages.

- PREFETCHSIZE specifies the number of pages to be fetched from the tablespace in advance of being referenced, in an attempt to anticipate page references and reduce waiting for I/O. Prefetching of pages is done automatically when the system is scanning a whole table, or whenever it detects a regular pattern of pages being fetched from disk into main memory.

- OVERHEAD is an estimate of the average latency time (in milliseconds) to begin a new I/O operation in the tablespace and is provided as information for the SQL optimizer.

- TRANSFERRATE is an estimate of the time required (in milliseconds) to read one 4K-byte page in the tablespace and is provided as information for the SQL optimizer.

- BUFFERPOOL names the bufferpool to be used for fetching pages from disk for this tablespace.

- IN NODEGROUP is an option that is meaningful only for parallel databases. It names the nodegroup on which the tablespace is stored. A nodegroup is a collection of nodes in a parallel system. Nodegroups are discussed in Section 10.2.2.

These optional parameters are discussed further in the *SQL Reference* and the *Administration Guide*. Each of them has a default value that is suitable for many applications.

ALTER TABLESPACE

After a tablespace has been created, the only alterations that can be made to it are as follows:

- The PREFETCHSIZE, OVERHEAD, TRANSFERRATE, and BUFFERPOOL properties of the tablespace can be changed, as in the following example:

```
ALTER TABLESPACE userspace1
    PREFETCHSIZE 64;
```

- New containers can be added to a DMS tablespace, as in the following example:

```
ALTER TABLESPACE longspace
    ADD (FILE 'f:\longspace\space2.dat' 50000);
```

When a new container is added to a tablespace, a background process automatically moves some extents from existing containers into the new container so that the data in the tablespace will be balanced across all its containers.

DROP TABLESPACE

Dropping a tablespace destroys all the objects (such as tables and indexes) that are completely contained in the tablespace. However, if a table spans multiple tablespaces (for example, it has data in one tablespace and indexes or large objects in another), none of the tablespaces containing parts of the table can be dropped until after the table has been dropped.

The following is an example of a statement that drops a tablespace:

```
DROP TABLESPACE dms2;
```

10.1.2 Creating and Dropping Databases

Now that we understand something about tablespaces, we are ready to discuss the process of creating a database. Each database resides in a directory on a server machine. The path name of this directory can be specified when the database is created (the default is controlled by the database manager configuration parameter DFTDBPATH). Multiple databases can be created in the same directory. All the databases residing in a given directory can be listed by the command LIST DATABASE DIRECTORY ON <path>.

The easiest way to create a database is to invoke the *Create Database* action of the Control Center, as described in Section 10.3. The Control Center will lead you through a dialog in which you can specify the characteristics of your new database. Alternatively, you can execute a CREATE DATABASE command using an interactive interface such as the Command Center. The simplest CREATE DATABASE command simply specifies the name of the database and allows all its characteristics to be chosen by default, as in the following example:

```
CREATE DATABASE mydata;
```

The following slightly more complex example creates a database in a specified directory and specifies that the database will be used for storing data using a Japanese character set (hence, it will be a double-byte database). A list of supported codesets and territories can be found in Appendix M of the *Administration Guide*.

```
CREATE DATABASE japan1
    ON 'D:\db\japan1'
    USING CODESET IBM-932 TERRITORY Ja_JP;
```

When you create a new database, UDB takes all the following actions:

- It creates physical directories to hold the database, under the specified database directory, and creates files to hold the database recovery log and handle other necessary bookkeeping details.

- It creates a set of tablespaces. The characteristics of these tablespaces can be specified in the CREATE DATABASE command or can be allowed to default. By default, a new database is created with three SMS tablespaces, named SYSCATSPACE (for catalog tables), USERSPACE1 (for user data), and TEMP-SPACE1 (for temporary storage). Additional tablespaces can be created later. Each database is required to have at least one temporary tablespace.

- In the SYSCATSPACE tablespace, it creates all the system catalog tables and their views and populates them to describe themselves. A new set of catalog tables and views for an empty database occupies about two megabytes of disk space.

- It sets the values of the database configuration parameters for the new database. Some of these configuration parameters (such as CODESET and TERRITORY) can be specified on the CREATE DATABASE command, while others receive default values.

- It binds a set of utility programs to the new database, creating packages for them so that they can be used in the new database.

- It grants DBADM authority to the user who created the database, and it grants the CONNECT, CREATETAB, and BINDADD database authorities to PUBLIC. This enables any user to connect to the new database, create tables in it, and bind application programs in it. If necessary, the holder of DBADM can later revoke these privileges from PUBLIC and replace them with more specific privileges granted to individual users.

Dropping a database is very simple if you hold SYSADM or SYSCTRL authority. You can accomplish the task by invoking the *Drop Database* action of the Control Center or by executing a DROP DATABASE command, as in the following example:

```
DROP DATABASE mydata;
```

A database cannot be dropped while any applications are connected to it. A database administrator can forcefully disconnect applications from a database by using the *Force Applications* action of the Control Center.

10.1.3 Where's the Data?

Figure 10-2 shows an example of how a UDB database might be implemented by a collection of physical files in the filespace of a server. The path name where the database resides is specified at database creation time. Under this directory is found another directory with the name of the UDB instance that created the database. The next directory in the hierarchy contains a node number (if the database is partitioned across several machines, each partition has a different node number). At the next level of the hierarchy is found one directory for each of the databases that share this database path. Each database is made up of tablespaces, which in turn are made up of containers. Tablespaces are not represented explicitly in Figure 10-2, since they do not map directly onto directories or files. For SMS tablespaces, each container is a directory. The location of the container directories is specified at tablespace creation time, and relative path names are interpreted with respect to the database directory. In an SMS container, each file holds data belonging to a different table or index. For example, the data belonging to a given table might be kept in a file named SQL00005.DAT in each of several container

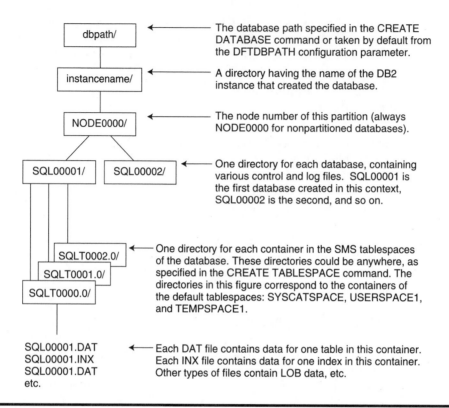

Figure 10-2: Physical Database Organization Using SMS Tablespaces

directories. Figure 10-2 shows the names of the container directories for the three default tablespaces named SYSCATSPACE, USERSPACE1, and TEMPSPACE1.

TIP: It is very important not to tamper with any of the files shown in Figure 10-2, since this might destroy the database. The database administrator should use the security facilities of the operating system to prevent users from tampering with database files.

10.2 PARALLEL DATABASES

Before going further into the details of UDB database administration, we need to discuss one of the most important new features introduced by UDB: support for parallel databases. A parallel database is a database in which multiple actions can take place at the same time, in order to get your job done faster or to accomplish more work per unit time.

Certain types of parallelism have been supported by DB2 for a long time. For example, at a given time, many users and applications can be connected to the same database and executing transactions. While it may seem that all the users are running simultaneously, the system is really distributing its time among the users in small slices, working for one user at a time. In a serial database system such as DB2 Version 2, each user is served by a single process, and the physical processor divides its time among these processes.

The new feature introduced by UDB is the ability for multiple processes, possibly utilizing multiple physical processors, to serve a given user simultaneously. By putting multiple processors to work on the same SQL statement, it is possible to scan large amounts of data very quickly and to dramatically reduce the time needed to process the statement.

One of the most important concepts in UDB parallelism is the concept of a *partition*. In a parallel system, a database can be split into several separate parts called partitions. Each table in the database may have some of its rows in each partition. It is helpful to visualize each partition as running on a separate machine, and this is usually the case, although it is possible for more than one partition to be assigned to the same machine. Each database partition has its own log and its own set of indexes.

UDB can apply two kinds of parallelism to the processing of an SQL statement. *Intra-partition parallelism* refers to simultaneous processes within a single partition, and *inter-partition parallelism* refers to simultaneous processes in multiple partitions. These two kinds of parallelism are independent of each other, and their relative importance depends on your hardware configuration. To avoid repeating these lengthy terms, I will abbreviate intra-partition parallelism as intraPP and inter-partition parallelism as interPP. The processing of a given SQL statement might involve intraPP, interPP, or both.

10.2.1 Intra-Partition Parallelism

IntraPP is often used on a symmetric multiprocessor (SMP) machine, in which multiple processors share common memory and disks, as shown in Figure 10-3. To exploit intraPP, the optimizer generates access plans that contain multiple *threads* that can be active simultaneously during processing of an SQL statement. Since (by definition) intraPP takes place within a single database partition, all

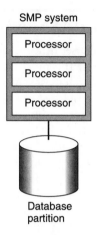

Figure 10-3: Intra-Partition Parallelism on a Symmetric Multiprocessor

the threads have access to all the data in the partition. The number of threads in an access plan, called the *degree* of the plan, may be more or less than the number of physical processors on the system. If there are more threads than processors, the processors distribute their time among the threads to keep them all active. It's even possible (but not very useful) to use intraPP on a machine that has only a single processor. IntraPP can be used with all versions of **UDB** (even the Personal Edition).

As an example of intraPP, consider the following SQL query, which searches for the salary of the highest-paid engineer:

```
SELECT max(salary)
FROM   emp
WHERE  job = 'Engineer';
```

If no JOB index exists, the optimizer might call for a scan over the whole EMP table, searching for engineers and keeping track of the highest salary encountered. To use intraPP with degree 4, the optimizer might generate a plan with four threads, each of which scans a different part of the table and finds the highest engineer's salary in its part. When all four parts of the scan are complete, one of the threads can compare the maximum salaries encountered by the four threads and select the global maximum to serve as the result of the query. If four real processors are available to execute the plan, it is likely that the query can be processed in about one-fourth the time required by a single-processor system. Even if the four threads are shared by two or three processors, a significant performance improvement can result.

IntraPP is completely transparent to SQL—it places no limitations on SQL statements and does not affect the result of any statement except by improving the performance of the system.

A UDB instance can be configured to exploit intraPP by a database manager configuration parameter named INTRA_PARALLEL. If INTRA_PARALLEL is set to YES, the optimizer generates plans containing multiple threads, and the run-time system executes these plans using multiple processors. Setting INTRA_PARALLEL to NO limits the system to single-thread plans and serial execution. The default value of INTRA_PARALLEL depends on the hardware platform on which your UDB instance is installed—it is YES for multiprocessor machines and NO for uniprocessors.

When an application program is bound, the DEGREE option of the PREP or BIND command can be used to limit the degree of the plans generated for the program. DEGREE can be set to an integer or to ANY, which places no limit on the degree chosen by the optimizer. The default value for DEGREE is controlled by a database configuration parameter named DFT_DEGREE, which in turn has a default value of 1.

The degree of the plan generated for a dynamic SQL statement can be limited by the special register named CURRENT DEGREE. Like the DEGREE bind-option, CURRENT DEGREE can be set to an integer or to ANY, and its default value is controlled by the DFT_DEGREE database configuration parameter.

When the system is executing a plan, the number of threads that are simultaneously active is limited by the degree of the plan, and can be further limited by a database manager configuration parameter named MAX_QUERYDEGREE, or by a SET RUNTIME DEGREE command.

TIP: Note that UDB will not exploit intraPP by default, even if your system has multiple processors. To take advantage of intraPP, you must explicitly specify a DEGREE bind-option, set the value of the CURRENT DEGREE register, or modify the DFT_DEGREE database configuration parameter.

10.2.2 Inter-Partition Parallelism

InterPP usually involves a collection of processors, each of which has its own main memory and disks that are not shared with other processors. This kind of hardware configuration is sometimes called a "shared-nothing" or "massively parallel" system. Because each processor is autonomous, shared-nothing systems are very flexible and can easily be scaled to handle very large databases by adding more processors. Each processor owns one partition of the database and can directly access data only in its own partition.

UDB with interPP is often used on a parallel hardware platform such as an IBM SP2, which contains many Risc System/6000 processors connected by a high-speed switch. Although the processors in an SP2 system are physically

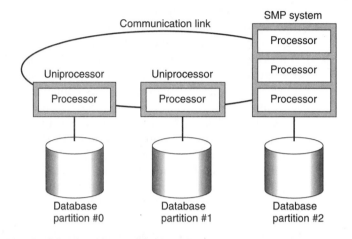

Figure 10-4: Inter-Partition Parallelism on Heterogeneous Platforms

inside the same box, each processor has its own main memory and its own disks. Alternatively, **UDB** with interPP can run on a collection of independent machines that are connected by a local-area or wide-area network. In this configuration, the participating machines may be similar to each other or may have individual differences. Some or all of the participating machines may be symmetric multiprocessors that provide intraPP of their own, as illustrated in Figure 10-4.

InterPP was first introduced in DB2 Parallel Edition for AIX, in which each of the separate partitions of the database was called a *node*. In **UDB**, the term *partition* is introduced, but some of the terminology from the original product is still in use. For example, a group of partitions is called a *nodegroup* and is operated on by commands such as ALTER NODEGROUP. To avoid confusion, remember that the terms *node* and *partition* are interchangeable.

In order to use **UDB** with interPP, you need to install **UDB** Enterprise-Extended Edition on each of the participating machines. In the sqllib directory on each machine, you must create a *node configuration file* named db2nodes.cfg, which lists the host name of each participating machine and assigns a *node number* between 0 and 999 to each machine. The following example illustrates the content of a simple node configuration file that assigns node numbers to six machines whose host names correspond to planets of the solar system (the node configuration file might be more complex if multiple nodes are assigned to the same machine or if a machine has more than one active TCP/IP interface):

```
0   mercury
1   venus
2   mars
3   jupiter
4   saturn
5   neptune
```

You can start or stop a parallel UDB system by executing a db2start or db2stop command on any participating machine—the command will propagate to all the machines listed in the node configuration file.

In UDB with interPP, each tablespace is assigned to a nodegroup, specified when the tablespace is created. A nodegroup is a collection of one or more of the nodes that are listed in your node configuration file. The rows of each table are distributed among the nodes in the nodegroup for its tablespace. Nodegroups are created and given names by statements such as the ones in the following example:

```
CREATE NODEGROUP group1 ON NODE ( 0 );
CREATE NODEGROUP group2 ON NODES (1, 3, 5);
CREATE NODEGROUP group3 ON ALL NODES;
```

You can obtain a list of all the nodes (partitions) and nodegroups defined on your system by using commands such as the following:

```
LIST NODES;
LIST NODEGROUPS SHOW DETAIL;
```

When a database is created, the following default nodegroups are created automatically:

- IBMDEFAULTGROUP, containing all the database partitions and serving as the nodegroup for the tablespace USERSPACE1

- IBMCATGROUP, containing only the partition at which the CREATE DATABASE command was executed, and serving as the nodegroup for the tablespace SYSCATSPACE. The partition in IBMCATGROUP is called the *catalog node* for the database, and it is the only partition in which the system catalog tables are stored.

- IBMTEMPGROUP, containing all the database partitions and serving as the nodegroup for the tablespace TEMPSPACE1

The tables in a multipartition nodegroup (called *partitioned tables*) must each have a *partitioning key* that determines how the rows of the table are distributed among the partitions. The partitioning key, specified at table creation time, consists of one or more columns, none of which may have a LOB datatype. When a row is inserted into a partitioned table, the value of the partitioning key is hashed into a value between 0 and 4,096. The resulting value is used as an index into the *partitioning map* for the nodegroup, an array of 4,096 entries that determines the node number of the partition on which the row will be stored, as shown in Figure 10-5. When a nodegroup is created, it is given a default partitioning map that contains an equal number of entries for each of the partitions in the nodegroup. As we will see in Section 10.7.6, the partitioning map of a nodegroup can be changed in order to compensate for *data skew* (a nonuniform distribution of partitioning key values).

For an application or user session that is connected to a parallel database, the node (partition) at which the CONNECT command was processed is called the *coordinator node*. Of course, several sessions can be connected to the same database, using the same or different coordinator nodes. The coordinator node for a session is responsible for communicating with the client and for distributing work to the other nodes as needed. The coordinator node uses a two-phase commit protocol to ensure that if any node fails during the course of a transaction, the transaction is rolled back at all participating nodes.

InterPP is almost completely transparent to SQL. The only rules and limitations imposed by a database with interPP are the following:

1. Each table whose tablespace is in a multinode nodegroup must have a partitioning key.

2. The columns of a partitioning key cannot be updated (if you want to update a value in one of these columns, you must delete the row and reinsert it with a new value).

3. If a partitioned table has a primary key, unique constraint, or unique index, the columns on which uniqueness is enforced must include the partitioning key columns of the table.

In a parallel database, it is the job of the optimizer (running on the coordinator node) to create a parallel plan for processing each SQL statement. The optimizer tries to split up the work in a way that uses as many processors as possible while minimizing the movement of data among the partitions. The parallel plan consists of a *subsection* for each partition that details the work to be done at that partition. The subsections are distributed by the coordinator node to the various partitions, which return their results to the coordinator node, where they are combined and delivered to the client.

You can greatly improve the performance of your applications by carefully planning how to partition your tables. One of the most powerful partitioning techniques is called *colocation*. Two tables are said to be *colocated* if their tablespaces are in the same nodegroup and if their partitioning keys have the

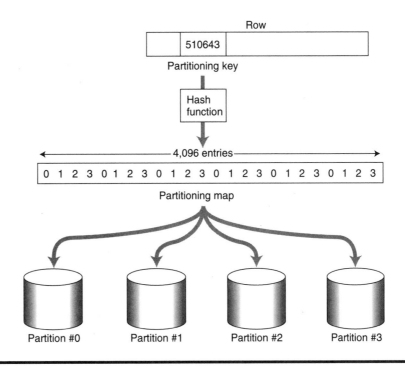

Figure 10-5: Use of a Partitioning Map to Assign a Row to a Partition

same datatype.[1] If you expect two tables to be equi-joined very frequently, you can improve the performance of the join by colocating the two tables, using their join columns as partitioning keys. In this case, the rows of the respective tables that will be joined to each other are always stored in the same partition, and each partition can perform part of the join independently.

If a join needs to be performed between two tables A and B that are not colocated, a significant amount of data will need to be moved among the partitions. Here are some of the strategies that the optimizer might consider:

- If an equi-join predicate includes the partitioning key of table A, the rows of table B might be moved to the partitions containing the matching rows of table A.

- If the tables are to be joined by an equi-join predicate that does not include the partitioning key of either table, the rows of both tables might be redistributed according to a temporary partitioning key based on their join columns.

---

1. Pairs of partitioning keys with certain combinations of datatypes, such as Real and Double or character strings of different lengths, are also compatible for purposes of colocation.

- If the join is not an equi-join, or if table B is very small, the system might choose to send all the rows of table B to every partition that includes any rows of table A.

Another technique for improving the performance of a partitioned database is called *buffered insert*, which is used by application programs that need to insert a large number of rows. It would be inefficient for each of these rows to be sent separately from the coordinator node to the partition where the row is to be stored. If the application was precompiled or bound with the option INSERT BUF, the coordinator node accumulates inserted rows in buffers rather than forwarding them immediately to their destination partitions. One 4K-byte buffer is used for each destination partition. When a buffer becomes full, or when another SQL statement such as UPDATE, DELETE, COMMIT, or ROLLBACK is encountered, all the rows in the buffer are sent together to the destination partition. One consequence of this strategy is that insertion errors may be reported asynchronously. For example, suppose that one of the inserted rows contains a unique key violation. The violation would not be discovered and reported until the buffer was transmitted to the destination partition. The error code would be returned to the SQL statement that caused the buffer to be transmitted, and this statement, together with all the insertions in the buffer, would be rolled back.

Additional information about optimizing the performance of a partitioned database can be found in the *Administration Guide*.

10.2.3 Reconfiguring a Parallel System

One of the advantages of a shared-nothing system architecture, such as that used for partitioned databases in UDB, is that it is relatively easy to reconfigure the system when necessary to adapt it to changing requirements. For example, in a UDB system with interPP, commands are available to redistribute data among the partitions, or to add a new partition or drop an existing partition. Since most of these commands were introduced in DB2 Parallel Edition Version 1, they use the term *node* rather than *partition*, and in order to be consistent with the command terminology, I will also use the term *node* in the remainder of this section.

Redistributing Data

Data can be redistributed among the nodes of a nodegroup by means of a REDISTRIBUTE NODEGROUP command, as in the following example:

```
REDISTRIBUTE NODEGROUP group1 UNIFORM;
```

The REDISTRIBUTE NODEGROUP command must be executed from the catalog node. It redistributes data according to a new partitioning map, which can come from any of the following sources:

1. It can be a *uniform* map that maps the same number of hash buckets onto each node (as in the example above).

2. It can be computed based on a user-provided *distribution file* that specifies how rows of data are distributed among the hash buckets. The distribution file must contain 4,096 non-negative integers that represent the relative number of rows that map into the 4,096 hash buckets. UDB automatically produces a new partitioning map that compensates for skewed data distribution, resulting in a uniform distribution of rows among the nodes.

3. It can be created manually or by using a utility such as the Splitter (discussed in Section 10.7.6).

The REDISTRIBUTE NODEGROUP command acquires an exclusive lock on each of the tables that has rows in the nodegroup, one at a time, and migrates all the rows of the table to their appropriate nodes according to the new partitioning map. It also invalidates all packages that operate on any of these tables. When the command is complete, it writes a file containing a completion message in the `sqllib/redist` directory.

TIP: After redistributing the data in a nodegroup, it's a good idea to rebind all the packages that were invalidated by the process, and to invoke the RUNSTATS command to gather the latest statistical information on all the affected tables.

Adding a Node

The process of adding a node to a UDB system consists of the following steps:

1. From any existing node, execute a START DATABASE MANAGER command with the ADDNODE option, specifying the node number and host name of the new node. For example, the following command adds a new node with node number 9, residing at port 0 of machine ZURBIE:

```
START DATABASE MANAGER NODENUM 9
    ADDNODE HOSTNAME zurbie PORT 0;
```

This command creates directories and files on the new node to support all the databases that exist in the current UDB instance. However, the new node does not become an effective part of the system until the next time the system is stopped.

2. Stop the UDB instance and restart it, using the following commands:

```
STOP DATABASE MANAGER;
START DATABASE MANAGER;
```

Stopping the system and restarting it causes the new node to be added to the db2nodes.cfg file, making it an effective part of the system. However, the new node is still not a member of any nodegroup.

3. For each nodegroup in which you wish the new node to participate, execute an ALTER NODEGROUP statement. For example, the following command makes node 9 a part of nodegroup GROUP1, and for each tablespace in this nodegroup, it creates a set of containers on node 9 that are similar to the existing containers on node 7:

```
ALTER NODEGROUP group1
    ADD NODE 9 LIKE NODE 7;
```

The new node is now a nodegroup member and has a set of containers for holding data, but it is still empty because it does not appear in any partitioning map.

4. For each nodegroup that includes the new node, execute a REDISTRIBUTE NODEGROUP command like this one:

```
REDISTRIBUTE NODEGROUP group1 UNIFORM;
```

As described in the previous section, this command causes data to migrate to the new node, rebalancing the content of all the nodes in the nodegroup. The new node is now fully in service.

Dropping a Node

The process of deleting a node from a UDB system consists of the following steps:

1. For each nodegroup in which the node is a member, execute an ALTER NODE-GROUP command to drop the node, as in the following example:

```
ALTER NODEGROUP group1 DROP NODE 9;
```

After execution of this command, the node is no longer a member of the nodegroup, but it still (temporarily) contains data that belongs to the nodegroup.

2. For each affected nodegroup, execute a REDISTRIBUTE NODEGROUP command like this one:

```
REDISTRIBUTE NODEGROUP group1 UNIFORM;
```

This command generates a new partitioning map that excludes the dropped node, and migrates all the data from the dropped node to other nodes in the nodegroup.

3. On the dropped node, run a DROP NODE VERIFY command to confirm that the node is no longer in use.

4. Stop the system with a command such as the following:

```
STOP DATABASE MANAGER DROP NODENUM 9;
```

The DROP NODENUM clause causes the node to be deleted from the db2nodes.cfg file. When the system is restarted, the node will no longer be a part of the system.

10.3 THE CONTROL CENTER

The Control Center is a graphical tool for administering UDB databases. It provides a convenient way to handle the day-to-day tasks of database administration, such as allocating physical space, creating tables and other objects, controlling user authorizations, and performing backup and recovery. You can run the Control Center on the machine where your database is located or on a different machine. In fact, you can use the Control Center to control several UDB databases on several different machines.

The Control Center is one of a collection of UDB tools that provide complementary features and consistent graphical user interfaces. Some of the other tools in the collection were discussed in Chapter 3: the Command Center, the Script Center, the Journal, and the Information Center. Each of these tools presents a set of icons that you can use to invoke any of the other tools.

To start the Control Center, double-click the Control Center icon on your desktop (it's inside the Administration Tools folder that was created when you installed DB2).

The Control Center runs on OS/2 and Windows machines, but not on AIX or other UNIX platforms. If your UDB system is installed on a UNIX machine, you can administer it remotely from a Control Center running on an OS/2 or Windows machine. Alternatively, you can forego the graphical interface and administer your database by typing commands at a text-oriented interface such as the CLP. Almost all the functions of the Control Center are available using text commands described in the *Command Reference*. In the future, IBM plans to supplement the Control Center with web-based database administration tools that allow you to administer your UDB system from a web browser on any platform—in fact, some of these web-based tools may be available by the time you are reading this book.

The Control Center views the world as a hierarchy of objects. The highest-level objects in the hierarchy are *systems*. A system is a machine, somewhere in the world, containing an installation of UDB. The Control Center maintains a list of systems that it knows about and records the information needed to communicate with each system (such as its network address, operating system, and communication protocol).

Within each system known to the Control Center, there may be one or more UDB *instances*. Each instance behaves like a separate installation of UDB (though, in fact, multiple instances on the same system may share some programs). The instances on a given system are kept physically separate and are administered separately (for example, each instance may have its own group of users with System Administration authority).

Each UDB instance may control one or more *databases*. Each database has a name and its own set of system catalog tables that describe the objects in the database. Each database has its own set of grantable authorities such as the authority to connect to the database and the authority to create tables in the database.

Systems, instances, and databases can be made known to the Control Center by entering the information manually or by invoking a Control Center feature called *Discovery* that automatically searches your local network for systems containing UDB installations, and discovers the instances and databases that exist on these systems.

Within each database are found many types of objects, including tables, views, indexes, triggers, and packages. The hierarchic relationship among systems, instances, databases, and other objects is illustrated in Figure 10-6, which shows two systems, one located in London and one in New York. Each of the systems contains two UDB instances, and each of these instances in turn manages two databases. All the objects in Figure 10-6 might be administered by one Control Center, running on the New York system, on the London system, or on a third system not shown in the figure.

The user interface of the Control Center is shown in Figure 10-7. The Control Center window is divided into two parts, which I will refer to as the *left panel* and *right panel*. The left panel shows the hierarchy of objects known to the Control Center, from systems down to small objects such as tables and views. Some of the entries in the hierarchy represent a general type of object (such as databases in general), and others represent a specific object (such as a specific database). Each entry in the hierarchy is connected to a small box containing a plus or minus sign. A plus sign indicates that more detail is available—clicking on the plus sign expands the entry to show its component parts, and changes the plus sign to a minus sign. An entry displayed with a minus sign is already fully expanded—clicking on the minus sign deletes the component parts from the display to save space. Left-clicking on any of the objects displayed in the left panel "selects" the object and causes its component parts to be displayed in the right panel. If you left-click on an entry that represents a general type of object, such as tables within a certain database, the individual tables in that database will appear in the right panel.

The Control Center display in Figure 10-7 shows two systems named cheddar and DON1. The DON1 system is expanded to show that it contains a single UDB instance named DB2, which is managing two databases named TESTDB and SAMPLE. The TESTDB database has also been expanded to show its compo-

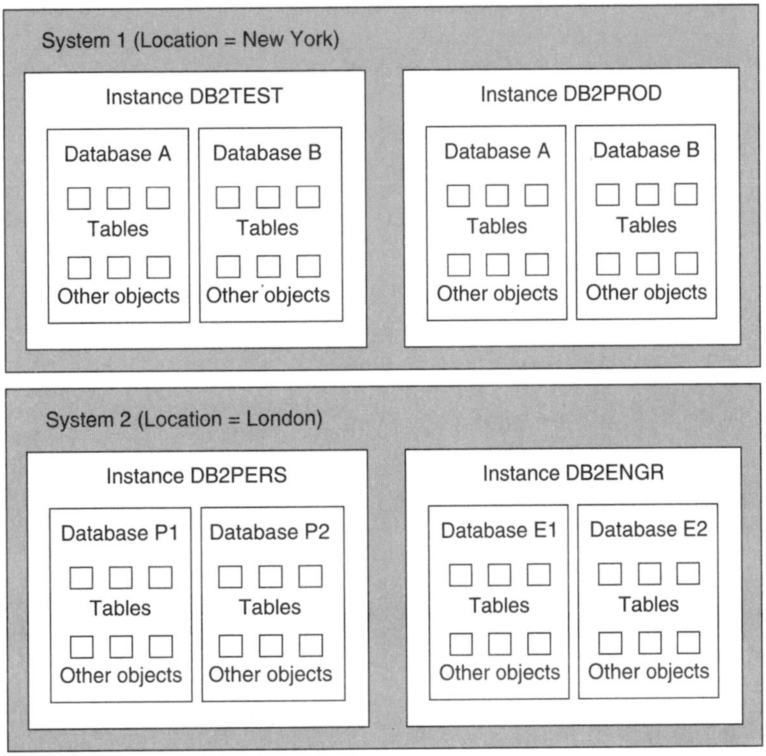

Figure 10-6: Hierarchic Relationship Among Systems, Instances, and Databases

nent parts, including the list of tables shown in the right panel. The SAMPLE database is displayed with a plus sign, indicating that it is not expanded.

You can right-click on any object in either the left or right panel of the Control Center to see a menu of actions that can be applied to that object. By invoking actions from the Control Center menus, you can perform most routine database administration tasks. For each action, the Control Center provides a convenient graphical interface that prompts you for the details of the actions, gives you online help, and checks your inputs for validity. Most of the actions that appear on Control Center menus are equivalent to commands or SQL statements that could be executed using a text-based interface such as the Command Center or CLP. Of course, to invoke a given action from the Control Center, you need the same level of authorization that you would need to execute the equivalent command or SQL statement.

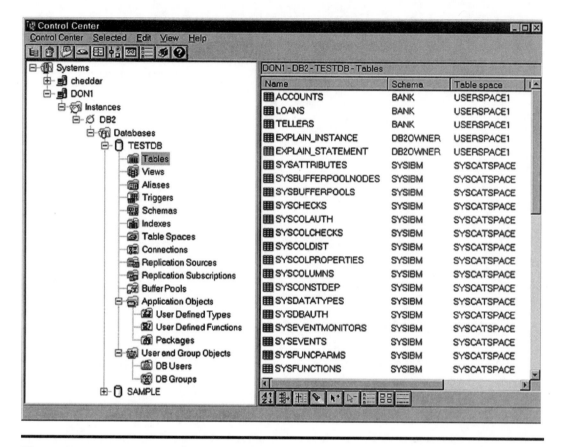

Figure 10-7: The Control Center Display

The actions supported by the Control Center for each type of object are described in the following sections.[2] In addition to the actions listed, two generic actions apply at several levels of the object hierarchy: *Refresh*, which updates the Control Center display to show the latest changes, and *Open New Control Center*, which opens a new Control Center window for operating on the selected object and its components.

---

2. The actions described in this section apply to single-partition databases. The actions that apply to multiple-partition databases are similar in concept but different in detail.

10.3.1 Systems (General)

The term *system* refers to a machine that the Control Center can communicate with to access a UDB instance. The Control Center maintains a list of known systems and supports the following action:

Add

This action adds a new system to the Control Center's list of known systems. When you invoke this action, a dialog box appears in which you can specify the name by which you will refer to the system, its network address, its operating system, and the protocol used to communicate with it (options include TCP/IP, APPC, IPX/SPX, and NetBIOS). Alternatively, you can click on the "Refresh" button in the dialog box to invoke the Discovery feature of the Control Center, which will search your local network for nearby machines containing UDB installations, and add them automatically to the list of known systems.
Equivalent command: CATALOG NODE
Authority required: SYSADM or SYSCTRL

10.3.2 Systems (Specific)

The following actions can be invoked on specific systems that are displayed in the Control Center hierarchy:

Change

This action can be used to add a comment to the Control Center's description of a system or to change its recorded characteristics such as its operating system or communication protocol. Of course, if the characteristics recorded by the Control Center for a given system are not correct, the Control Center will not be able to access the system.
Equivalent command: CATALOG NODE
Authority required: SYSADM or SYSCTRL

Remove

This action removes a system from the list of systems known to the Control Center.
Equivalent command: UNCATALOG NODE
Authority required: SYSADM or SYSCTRL

Generate Access Profile

This action generates a file that can be used on another machine to teach its UDB client how to communicate with the selected system (for a discussion of how to use an access profile on a client machine, see Section 10.4). A dialog box allows you to specify the name of the file to be generated.

10.3.3 Instances (General)

An *instance* behaves like a separate installation of UDB. A system may contain more than one instance. For example, a system might contain one instance for testing and a separate instance for production, or one instance for the personnel department and another instance for the engineering department. Since each instance is administered separately, the authority of each system administrator can be limited to a single instance.

Add

This action makes a new instance known to the Control Center. The easiest way to do this is by the Discovery feature of the Control Center. To use Discovery, click on "Instances" in the Control Center hierarchy below a specific system, invoke the Add action, and click on the "Refresh" button in the dialog box. The Control Center will automatically discover all the UDB instances that exist on the selected system. Alternatively, if you know the name and characteristics of a particular instance, you can fill them in manually.
Equivalent command: CATALOG NODE
Authority required: SYSADM or SYSCTRL

10.3.4 Instances (Specific)

The following actions are supported on a specific instance:

Start

Starts the instance. In a parallel database system, the instance is started on all participating machines. The instance must be started before an application or interactive session can connect to a database managed by the instance.
Equivalent command: START DATABASE MANAGER
Authority required: SYSADM, SYSCTRL, or SYSMAINT

Stop

Stops the instance. An instance cannot be stopped as long as any application or interactive session remains connected to one of its databases. A system administrator can forcibly disconnect applications from a database by using the *Force* action, described on page 606.

Equivalent command: STOP DATABASE MANAGER
Authority required: SYSADM, SYSCTRL, or SYSMAINT

Attach

This action prompts you for your userid and password, which are needed for certain other instance-level actions. *Attach* is not really necessary, since any action that requires a userid and password will prompt you for it anyway. However, the *Attach* action can be useful if you need to switch from one userid to another during a session.

Configure

A UDB instance is like a complex machine with many adjustments. All the adjustments have default settings that are appropriate for typical patterns of use. However, database administrators have the option of changing some of these adjustments in order to configure an instance for a particular hardware environment or mix of applications.

The adjustments that apply to a UDB instance are called *database manager configuration parameters*. When an instance is created, its database manager configuration parameters are set to default values. Some of these parameters deal with resource allocations, such as the amount of memory to be used for buffering messages between client and server. Other parameters record policy decisions such as the names of the groups that hold SYSADM, SYSCTRL, and SYSMAINT authority. Other parameters record how to find things, such as the default directory in which databases are to be created. Some of the parameters must be set to nondefault values in order to enable certain features of the system; for example, distributed transactions require the parameter named TM_DATABASE to be set to the name of the database to be used to coordinate the two-phase commit protocol.

When you invoke the *Configure* action for a selected instance, the Control Center shows you a list of all the configuration parameters that apply to that instance, grouped into categories such as Environment, Administration, and Performance. Within each category, all the configuration parameters are displayed in the form of a table containing the name, short description, and current value of each parameter (for some reason, the names of the parameters are in the last column of the table, labeled "DB2 Parameter"—you may need to scroll to the right to see them). Within a category, you can search for a specific parameter by using the "Find" feature (click on the button that looks like a flashlight). By interacting with a dialog box, you can change the values of the configuration parameters or reset them to their default values. The Control Center automatically checks your parameter settings for validity before it makes them effective. You can find a more complete description of the various configuration parameters in the *Administration Guide*.

Equivalent command: UPDATE DATABASE MANAGER CONFIGURATION
Authority required: SYSADM

TIP: Some configuration parameters do not become effective until the instance is restarted. You can restart the instance by using the *Stop* and *Start* actions.

Setup Communications

This action can be used to add a new communications protocol (for example, TCP/IP or NetBIOS) to an instance, enabling it to communicate with remote clients using this protocol.

List Applications

This action lists all applications that are currently connected to a database managed by the selected instance. For each application, you can see the authorization ID under which it is running, the database to which it is connected, and an Agent ID that you can use to forcibly disconnect the application from the database.
Equivalent command: LIST APPLICATIONS
Authority required: SYSADM, SYSCTRL, or SYSMAINT

Force Applications

This action can be used to forcibly disconnect a specific application by specifying one of the Agent IDs displayed by the List Applications action, or to forcibly disconnect all applications that are connected to databases managed by a given instance.
Equivalent command: FORCE APPLICATION
Authority required: SYSADM, SYSCTRL, or SYSMAINT

Change

This action can be used to add a comment to the Control Center's description of an instance, or to change its recorded characteristics such as its host name or communication protocol. Of course, if the characteristics recorded by the Control Center for a given instance are not correct, the Control Center will not be able to access the instance.
Equivalent command: CATALOG NODE
Authority required: SYSADM or SYSCTRL

Remove

This action removes an instance from the list of instances known to the Control Center.
Equivalent command: UNCATALOG NODE
Authority required: SYSADM or SYSCTRL

Snapshot Monitoring

The *snapshot monitor* is a tool that can be used to capture periodic "snapshots" of the state of the system, gathering information at various levels of detail. The information to be gathered by the snapshot monitor is controlled by an object called a *monitor profile.* By selecting a specific UDB instance in the Control Center and invoking the *Snapshot Monitoring* action, you can interact with the snapshot monitor in the following ways:

- Start the monitoring of information in the given instance
- Stop the monitoring of information in the given instance
- Display the information recently gathered for the given instance
- Display and modify the monitor profile for the given instance

(The snapshot monitor is described in Section 10.9.)
Equivalent commands: UPDATE MONITOR SWITCHES, GET SNAPSHOT
Authority required: SYSADM, SYSMAINT, or SYSCTRL

10.3.5 Databases (General)

The following actions are supported on databases in general:

Create

This action creates a new, empty database under a selected UDB instance. You are guided through the process of creating a database by a SmartGuide, which is a series of dialog boxes that prompt you for the characteristics of the new database, providing default values and helpful advice at every step of the process. You can specify details such as the tablespace to be used for system catalog tables, or you can accept default values for these details.
Equivalent command: CREATE DATABASE
Authority required: SYSADM or SYSCTRL

Create from Backup

This action creates a new database from a backup copy of another database that was made at some earlier time. The Control Center prompts you with a list of the backup images that are available and allows you to specify the name of the new database to be created.
Equivalent command: RESTORE DATABASE with INTO option
Authority required: SYSADM or SYSCTRL

Add

This action does not create a new database, but it makes an existing database known to the Control Center. For example, you might wish a particular database, managed by some remote UDB instance, to appear in your Control Center hierarchy. After the remote instance has been made known to the Control Center [see the *Add* action under Instances (General)], you can selectively add its databases to the hierarchy by this *Add* action. *Add* provides a convenient Discovery feature that automatically discovers all the databases managed by the remote instance and adds them all to the Control Center hierarchy. To use the Discovery feature, you simply click on the "Refresh" button in the *Add* dialog box.
Equivalent command: CATALOG DATABASE
Authority required: SYSADM or SYSCTRL

Show Monitor Summary

This action lists the databases that are currently being monitored by the snapshot monitor and summarizes the information gathered for each database in the most recent snapshot. (The snapshot monitor is described in Section 10.9.)

10.3.6 Databases (Specific)

The following actions are supported on a specific database:

Alter

This action displays the local name of the selected database, the name by which it is known on its host machine, and a comment. The only thing you can alter is the comment.

Drop

This action drops the selected database and destroys its content.
Equivalent command: DROP DATABASE
Authority required: SYSADM or SYSCTRL

Remove

This action removes the selected database from the list of databases known to the Control Center.
Equivalent command: UNCATALOG DATABASE
Authority required: SYSADM or SYSCTRL

Restart

This action can be used to restart a database after a failure such as a power out-age or software crash that leaves transactions in progress. Restart restores the database to a consistent state, in which all transactions that committed before the failure are made effective, and all transactions that were in progress at the time of the failure are rolled back.
Equivalent command: RESTART DATABASE
Authority required: None

Connect

This action establishes a connection with the selected database, which is nec-essary before performing certain actions on that database, such as creating tables. The *Connect* action prompts you for your userid and password. If you do not invoke *Connect*, any other action that requires a database connection will acquire one automatically, prompting you for your userid and password as needed. Establishing a database connection explicitly by using *Connect* helps the system to perform other actions more efficiently.
Equivalent SQL statement: CONNECT
Authority required: CONNECT authority on the selected database

Disconnect

This action is the inverse of Connect—it ends your connection to the selected database.
Equivalent SQL statement: DISCONNECT
Authority required: None

Authorities

This action displays a list of all the users and groups that have database-level authorities on the selected database. By interacting with a dialog box, you can grant and revoke additional database-level authorities.
Equivalent SQL statements: GRANT and REVOKE for database-level authorities
Authority required: DBADM

Configure

Like an instance, a database has many adjustments that can be set by database administrators. The adjustments that apply to a database are called *database configuration parameters*. The *Configure* action on a particular database causes a dialog box to appear that displays the current settings of the database configu-ration parameters, with a brief explanation of each parameter. The parameters are organized into groups such as Environment, Performance, Logs, and Recovery. Within each group, all the parameters are displayed in the form of a table containing the name, short description, and current value of each parameter (as in *Configure Instance*, the names of the parameters are in the last column of the table, labeled "DB2 Parameter," and you may need to scroll to the right to see them). By interacting with the dialog box, you can change the values of the configuration parameters or reset them to their default values. The Control Center automatically checks your parameter settings for validity before it makes them effective. You can find a more complete description of the various database configuration parameters in the *Administration Guide*.

The database configuration parameters named LOGRETAIN and USEREXIT, in the Logs group, are of particular interest. One of these parameters must be set to 1 in order to configure your database for forward recovery (discussed in Section 10.6). The default values for LOGRETAIN and USEREXIT are 0.
Equivalent command: UPDATE DATABASE CONFIGURATION
Authority required: SYSADM, SYSCTRL, or SYSMAINT

Configure Performance

This action invokes a SmartGuide that can help you to find a set of database configuration parameters that is appropriate for your database and its expected usage. The SmartGuide prompts you with a set of questions about your expected workload (for example, the relative priority of queries and transactions, and the expected number of transactions per minute). Based on your answers, it prepares a list of recommended values for the database configuration parameters. You can apply the suggested parameter values immediately or save them in a file and apply them later.

Backup

This action makes a backup copy of the selected database. The database can later be restored to its state at the time of the backup by the *Restore* action. The Backup action provides a SmartGuide that recommends a backup plan, based on your answers to questions about how your database will be used. The process of backing up and restoring a database is discussed in Section 10.6.
Equivalent command: BACKUP DATABASE
Authority required: SYSADM, SYSCTRL, or SYSMAINT

Restore

This action restores the content of the selected database from a previously saved backup copy. If your database is configured for forward recovery, you can also perform a *Rollforward* action, which reapplies the work of transactions that committed after the backup copy was made.
Equivalent command: RESTORE DATABASE
Authority required: SYSADM, SYSCTRL, or SYSMAINT

Restore to New

This action creates a new database from a backup copy of the selected database.
Equivalent command: RESTORE DATABASE with INTO option
Authority required: SYSADM or SYSCTRL

Rollforward

This action can be used after a *Restore* action to reapply database changes made by transactions that committed after the time when the backup copy was made. The Rollforward action requires that your database be configured for forward recovery.
Equivalent command: ROLLFORWARD DATABASE
Authority required: SYSADM, SYSCTRL, or SYSMAINT

Stop Rollforward

If your database is configured for forward recovery, a Restore action may leave the database in a state called *rollforward pending*. This state indicates that the database has been restored from a backup copy, but the system log contains some transactions that committed after the backup copy was made and that have not yet been reapplied. The *Stop Rollforward* action takes the database out of the rollforward pending state, making it available for use and effectively canceling the effects of the transactions that were not rolled forward.
Equivalent command: ROLLFORWARD DATABASE with STOP option
Authority required: SYSADM, SYSCTRL, or SYSMAINT

Show Explained Statements History

An *explained statement* is an SQL statement for which the UDB optimizer has generated an access plan and stored this plan in the database in a form that permits you to examine it. Explained statements can be created interactively by using the *Explain SQL* action (described below) or the *Create Access Plan* feature of the Command Center. If an application program is precompiled or bound with the option EXPLSNAP YES, all its static SQL statements are explained. The *Show Explained Statements History* action displays a list of all the explained statements in the database, including the date and time when each statement was optimized and the package (if any) in which it is contained. You can select one of the statements in the list and use the "Statement" menu to examine the original SQL statement and its access plan. The access plan is displayed in a graphical form that shows the sequence of operations used to process the SQL statement, and the expected cost of each operation, as shown in Figure 10-16.

Explain SQL

This action allows you to enter an SQL statement for which an access plan will be generated and displayed in graphical form. The access plan is also saved in the database so that it can be examined later using the *Show Explained Statements History* action, described above.

Snapshot Monitoring

By invoking this action for a specific database, you can interact with the snapshot monitor in the following ways:

- Start the monitoring of information for the given database
- Stop the monitoring of information for the given database
- Display the information recently gathered for the given database
- Display and modify the monitor profile that controls the gathering of information for the given database

(The snapshot monitor is described in Section 10.9.)
Equivalent commands: UPDATE MONITOR SWITCHES, GET SNAPSHOT
Authority required: SYSADM, SYSMAINT, or SYSCTRL

Monitor Events

An *event monitor* can be created by a database administrator to keep records on a specific type of event, such as a deadlock. By invoking the *Monitor Events* action for a specific database, you can display a summary of all the event monitors that have been created for that database, and you can interact with them in the following ways:

- Start or stop an individual event monitor
- Create a new event monitor
- Display the information gathered by an event monitor during a specific period of time

(Event monitors are described in Section 10.9.)
Equivalent commands: CREATE EVENT MONITOR, DROP EVENT MONITOR, SET EVENT MONITOR STATE
Authority required: SYSADM or DBADM

10.3.7 Objects Within Databases

The following objects are found within databases:

Tables

The *Create* action allows you to create a new table, using a SmartGuide that prompts you for the characteristics of the new table and provides defaults and guidance for each step in the process. Using the SmartGuide, you can specify the columns of the table, its primary and foreign keys, and the tablespaces in which it is stored. This action provides a graphical interface for the CREATE TABLE statement described in Section 7.2.1.

The Control Center also displays a list of the existing tables in your database. By selecting a specific table from the list, you can invoke any of the following actions:

1. *Alter.* This action allows you to add columns to the selected table, or to add and drop keys and constraints. It provides a graphical interface for the ALTER TABLE statement described in Section 7.2.2.

2. *Rename.* This action changes the name of the selected table, using the RENAME TABLE statement described in Section 2.6.3. You will not be allowed to rename the table if it is referenced in any views, triggers, or constraints.

3. *Drop.* This action drops the selected table, using the DROP TABLE statement described in Section 2.6.8.

4. *Copy.* This action makes a copy of the selected table, including its content, and gives a name to the new table. You can specify that the new table is to be created in a different database, or even on a different UDB instance than the original table. The new table has the same column names as the original table, but the primary key, foreign keys, and check constraints of the original table are not inherited by the new table.

5. *Privileges.* This action displays a list of all the users and groups that have privileges on the selected table. By interacting with a dialog box, you can grant and revoke additional privileges on the table. This action provides a graphical interface for the GRANT and REVOKE statements for table privileges, described in Section 2.8.7.

6. *Sample Content.* This action displays 200 sample rows from the selected table (not including any columns of large-object datatypes).

7. *Export.* This action invokes a utility program that extracts data from the database and saves it in a file, using one of several formats. The data to be exported need not come from a single table but can be computed by any SQL query, possibly containing a join or UNION of multiple tables and/or views. *Export* provides a graphical interface for the EXPORT command, which is described in Section 10.7.2.

8. *Import.* This action is the inverse of *Export.* It imports data into the database from files in one of several formats. The imported data can be used to update rows in an existing table, or to add new rows to a table, or to create a new table. The Import utility uses SQL INSERT statements, so all constraints and triggers remain active during the import process. *Import* provides a graphical interface for the IMPORT command, which is described in Section 10.7.3.

9. *Load.* This action invokes the Load utility program, which is a higher-performance alternative to *Import* for loading large amounts of data. Rather than inserting one row at a time, the Load utility constructs page images containing many rows and inserts them into the database a page at a time. During the loading process, triggers are not active, and check constraints and foreign key constraints are not enforced. If the table being loaded has some check or foreign key constraints, the Load utility leaves the table in Check Pending state. A table in Check Pending state cannot be accessed by SQL statements until its constraints are checked by the *Set Constraints* action. *Load* provides a graphical interface for the LOAD command, which is described in Section 10.7.4.

10. *Set Constraints.* This action can be used to suspend enforcement of the check constraints and foreign key constraints that apply to the selected table, or to "turn on" the enforcement of these constraints. While its constraints are suspended, the table is said to be in Check Pending state, and it is not available for access by normal SQL statements. When its constraints are reactivated, the table is put back into normal state, and any rows that violate a constraint are removed from the table and placed into a separate table called the *exception table.* *Set Constraints* provides a graphical interface for the SET CONSTRAINTS command, which is described in Section 10.7.5.

11. *Quiesce.* This action allows you to temporarily prevent other users from reading and/or updating the selected table and other tables in its tablespace. For example, you might want to prevent other users from updating a table while you are making a backup copy of the table by using the *Export* action. When you are ready to remove the restrictions on access to the table, invoke the *Quiesce* action again and select the "Quiesce Reset" option. The *Quiesce* action requires at least DBADM authority.

12. *Reorganize.* This action reorganizes the selected table on physical storage, eliminating fragmentation and making sure the table is stored efficiently. *Reorganize* can also be used to control the order in which the rows of a table are stored on disk pages. For example, if many queries search for employees by their jobcode, the number of pages accessed by these queries can be minimized by storing employees on disk pages, ordered by jobcode. *Reorganize* provides a graphical interface for the REORG command. Information about whether a table needs to be reorganized can be gathered by the REORGCHK command. REORG and REORGCHK are discussed further in Section 10.8.3.

13. *Run Statistics.* This action updates the statistical information that is recorded about the selected table and its indexes for use by the optimizer in creating access plans. To give the optimizer accurate information about a table, its statistics should be updated whenever a significant change occurs, such as loading or reorganizing the table, changing a large number of rows, or adding an index. *Run Statistics* allows you to specify the level of detail at which statistical information is gathered. As you might expect, gathering detailed statistics takes additional time and uses additional space in the system catalog tables but can potentially enable the optimizer to make better decisions. The kinds of statistics that UDB maintains on tables and indexes are described in Section 10.8.2.

14. *Define as Replication Source.* This action makes the selected table available as a source of data for replication. Once this step has been taken, you can define a "subscription" that automatically replicates all updates to this table into a target table, possibly in a different database on another system.

15. *Show Related Views.* This action shows a list of all the views whose definition contains a reference to the selected table.

16. *Snapshot Monitoring.* By invoking this action for a specific table, you can start or stop the monitoring of the table by the snapshot monitor. You can also display the information recently gathered on the table, and display or modify the monitor profile that controls the gathering of this information. (See Section 10.9.1 for more information about the snapshot monitor.)

Views

The *Create* action allows you to create a new view by providing a graphical interface for the CREATE VIEW statement described in Section 2.6.5. The Control Center also displays a list of existing views. By selecting a specific view from the list, you can invoke any of the following actions:

1. *Alter.* This action displays the definition of the view. The only thing about the definition that you can alter is the comment.

2. *Drop.* This action drops the view.

3. *Privileges.* This action displays a list of all the users and groups that have privileges on the selected view. By interacting with a dialog box, you can grant and revoke additional privileges. This action provides a graphical interface for the GRANT and REVOKE statements for view privileges, described in Section 2.8.7.

4. *Export.* This action allows you to export data from the view into an external file. It provides a graphical interface to the EXPORT command, described in Section 10.7.2.

5. *Sample Contents.* This action displays 200 sample rows from the selected view (not including any columns of large-object datatypes)

6. *Show Related Views.* This action shows a list of all the views whose definition contains a reference to the selected view.

Aliases

The *Create* action allows you to create a new alias by filling in a dialog box that is equivalent to a CREATE ALIAS statement, as described in Section 2.6.4. The Control Center also displays a list of existing aliases. By selecting a specific alias from the list, you can invoke any of the following actions:

1. *Alter.* This action displays the definition of the alias. The only thing about the definition that you can alter is the comment.

2. *Drop.* This action drops the alias.

Triggers

The *Create* action allows you to create a trigger by interacting with a dialog box that is equivalent to a CREATE TRIGGER statement, as described in Section 7.3.1. The Control Center also displays a list of existing triggers. By selecting a specific trigger from the list, you can invoke any of the following actions:

1. *Alter.* This action displays the definition of the trigger. The only thing about the definition that you can alter is the comment.

2. *Drop.* This action drops the trigger.

Schemas

The *Create* action allows you to create a schema by filling in a dialog box that is equivalent to a CREATE SCHEMA statement, as described in Section 2.6.7. The Control Center also displays a list of existing schemas. By selecting a specific schema from the list, you can invoke any of the following actions:

1. *Alter.* This action displays the name and owner of the schema, and a comment. The only thing about the alias that you can alter is the comment.

2. *Drop.* This action drops the schema. A schema cannot be dropped if it contains any tables or other objects.

3. *Privileges.* This action displays a list of all the users and groups that have privileges on the selected schema. By interacting with a dialog box, you can grant and revoke additional privileges on the schema. This action provides a graphical interface for the GRANT and REVOKE statements for schema privileges, described in Section 2.8.7.

Indexes

The *Create* action allows you to create an index by filling in a dialog box that allows you to specify the columns of the index key and whether the index has the UNIQUE property. This dialog box provides a graphical interface for the

CREATE INDEX statement, described in Section 2.6.6. The Control Center also displays a list of existing indexes, and allows you to invoke any of the following actions:

1. *Alter.* This action displays the definition of the index. The only thing about the definition that you can alter is the comment.

2. *Drop.* This action drops the index.

3. *Privileges.* This action displays a list of all the users and groups that have CONTROL privilege on the selected index. By interacting with a dialog box, you can grant and revoke CONTROL privilege to other users and groups. This action provides a graphical interface for the GRANT and REVOKE statements for index privileges, described in Section 2.8.7.

Tablespaces

The *Create* action allows you to create either a system-managed tablespace or a database-managed tablespace by interacting with a SmartGuide that guides you through the process. For either kind of tablespace, you can specify the set of containers where data is to be stored, and you can specify the performance characteristics of the physical devices used by the tablespace. This action provides a graphical interface for the CREATE TABLESPACE statement described in Section 10.1.1.

The *Show Monitor Summary* action lists the tablespaces that are currently being monitored by the snapshot monitor and summarizes the information gathered for each tablespace in the most recent snapshot. (The snapshot monitor is described in Section 10.9.1.)

The Control Center also displays a list of the existing tablespaces in your database. By selecting a specific tablespace from the list, you can invoke any of the following actions:

1. *Alter.* This action shows you a list of the containers in the selected tablespace. If the tablespace is a database-managed tablespace, you can also add new containers to it by interacting with a dialog box. You can also change performance-related characteristics of the tablespace, such as its bufferpool assignment and its PREFETCHSIZE and TRANSFERRATE. *Alter* provides a graphical interface to the ALTER TABLESPACE command, described in Section 10.1.1.

2. *Drop.* This action drops the tablespace and destroys all its contents.

3. *Backup.* This action makes a backup copy of the selected tablespace. In order to back up an individual tablespace (rather than a whole database), your system must be configured for forward recovery. *Backup* provides a graphical interface for the BACKUP command, described in Section 10.6.2.

4. *Restore.* This action restores the content of the selected tablespace from a previously saved backup copy. In order to restore an individual tablespace, your

database must be configured for forward recovery. The *Restore* action presents a dialog box in which you can choose the backup copy you wish to restore. *Restore* provides a graphical interface for the RESTORE command, described in Section 10.6.2.

5. *Rollforward.* This action can be used after a *Restore* action to reapply database changes made by transactions that committed after the time when the backup copy of the tablespace was made. *Rollforward* provides a graphical interface to the ROLLFORWARD command, described in Section 10.6.2.

6. *Snapshot Monitoring.* By invoking this action for a specific tablespace, you can start or stop the monitoring of the tablespace by the snapshot monitor. You can also display the information recently gathered on the table, and display or modify the monitor profile that controls the gathering of this information.

Connections

The *Show Monitor Summary* action lists the connections that are currently being monitored by the snapshot monitor in this database and summarizes the information gathered for each connection in the most recent snapshot. (The snapshot monitor is described in Section 10.9.1.)

Replication Sources

When you select *Replication Sources*, the Control Center displays a list of all the tables that are available as sources for data replication (see the *Define as Replication Source* action under *Tables*). You can select one or more of these tables and define a "subscription" for replicating updates to one or more target tables, possibly in a different database. The *Define Subscription* action causes a dialog box to appear, in which you can give the subscription a name, specify its source and target tables, and specify how often you wish updates to be propagated. You also need to specify the database in which the subscription definition is to be stored. The subscription then becomes an object in its own right and appears in the Control Center hierarchy under *Replication Subscriptions* for the database containing the source tables.

Replication Subscriptions

When you select *Replication Subscriptions* for a particular database, the Control Center displays a list of all the subscriptions whose source tables are in that database. Each of these subscriptions specifies how updates will be propagated from the source table to a target table, possibly in a different database. You can select one of the subscriptions and invoke any of the following actions:

1. *Change.* This action changes some part of the subscription, such as its frequency of propagating updates. The subscription definition is stored in a set of control tables, and the change to the subscription is represented in the form of some SQL statements that update the control tables. You can specify that these changes are to be made immediately *(Run SQL Now)* or saved and applied later *(Save to SQL File)*.

2. *Clone*. This action creates a new subscription similar to an existing one but with its target table in a different database.

3. *Activate*. This action causes a subscription to become active. Subscriptions are processed by a Capture program that runs on the source database and an Apply program that runs on the target database. These programs process only active subscriptions. Information about the Capture and Apply programs can be found in the *Replication Guide and Reference*.

4. *Deactivate*. This action causes the subscription to become inactive (no longer processed).

5. *Remove*. This action removes the subscription definition from the control tables in which it is stored.

Bufferpools

A bufferpool is an area of main memory into which database pages are read and held during processing. You can tune the performance of your system by controlling the number and size of its bufferpools, and the assignment of tablespaces to bufferpools.

The *Create* action allows you to create a new bufferpool and to specify its name and size. The Control Center also displays a list of existing bufferpools. By selecting a specific bufferpool from the list, you can invoke the following actions:

1. *Alter*. This action allows you to change the size of a bufferpool.

2. *Drop*. This action drops the bufferpool.

User-Defined Types

A list of user-defined distinct types can be found in the Control Center hierarchy under *Application Objects*. You can create a new distinct type by invoking the *Create* action. Each existing distinct type is displayed along with its source type. You can drop a distinct type by selecting it and invoking its *Drop* action.

User-Defined Functions

A list of user-defined functions can be found in the Control Center hierarchy under *Application Objects*. Each function is displayed with its fully qualified name and specific name, parameter types, and result type. You can drop one of these functions by selecting it and invoking its *Drop* action.

Packages

A list of packages that are bound in a given database can be found in the Control Center hierarchy under *Application Objects*. Each package is displayed along with information such as its authorization id, the time when it was bound, whether it is currently valid, and its isolation level. By selecting a specific package from the list, you can invoke the following actions:

1. *Show Explainable Statements.* This action lists all the SQL statements in the package for which an access plan is available for display. If the package was precompiled or bound with the option EXPLSNAP YES, all its static SQL statements are explained. You can select a statement and use the "Statements" menu to examine the original SQL statement and its access plan. The access plan is displayed in a graphical form that shows the sequence of operations used to process the statement, and the expected cost of each operation, as shown in Figure 10-16.

2. *Show Explained Statements History.* Like *Show Explainable Statements*, this action displays a list of all the explained SQL statements in the given package and allows you to examine their access plans in graphical form. However, rather than showing only the most recent access plan for each statement, this action lists each time that each statement was bound. By examining the access plans chosen for a given statement in multiple bindings, you can see the effects of changes such as adding an index to the database.

Users and Groups

The Control Center displays a list of all the users and groups who hold any kind of database privilege, including privileges on databases, tables, views, schemas, and indexes. By invoking the Add action, you can add a new user or group to the list. You can also select one of the users or groups on the list and invoke one of the following actions:

1. *Change.* This action displays all the privileges held by the selected user or group and allows you to revoke privileges or grant additional privileges, including the GRANT option. This action provides a graphical interface for the GRANT and REVOKE statements, described in Section 2.8.7.

2. *Remove.* This action revokes all privileges from the selected user or group.

10.4 THE CLIENT CONFIGURATION ASSISTANT

As described in Chapter 1, UDB is a client-server system in which the server manages the data, and the client provides the user interface. Whenever you interact with UDB, you are using a client, even if you happen to be using the same machine on which the server is installed. When you or one of your application programs needs to connect to a database, the client establishes the connection by communicating with the UDB server on which the database resides.

In order to handle requests for database connections, each UDB client maintains a list of databases to which it knows how to connect. Each database is identified by an *alias*, which serves as the local name of the database as seen by that client. The alias by which a database is known on a client may or may not be the same as the *native* name by which the database is known on its own server. The use of aliases is illustrated by Figure 10-8, which shows two UDB server systems named COMPANY3 and COLLEGE5. The COMPANY3 system has two UDB instances named ADMIN and ASSETS, which manage two databases each, and the COLLEGE5 system has one instance that also manages two databases. The client systems named CLIENT1 and CLIENT2 each need to access databases on both servers. In fact, CLIENT1 needs to access two databases, each of which has a native name of PEOPLE. In order to avoid confusion, CLIENT1 assigns the alias STAFF to the PEOPLE database at COMPANY3, and the alias FACULTY to the PEOPLE database at COLLEGE5.

TIP: Don't confuse database aliases, described in this section, with table aliases, described in Section 2.6.4.

For each database alias, a client needs to record the following information:

- The name of the system on which the database resides and the information needed to communicate with this system, such as its protocol and IP address
- The name of the UDB instance on the remote system where the database resides
- The native name of the database on the instance where it resides

All this information is stored by the client in two files, the *node directory* and the *database directory*. You can use the following commands to display the content of these directories at your client system:

```
LIST NODE DIRECTORY;
LIST DATABASE DIRECTORY;
```

A set of commands called the CATALOG commands are provided for updating the content of the node and database directories, as described in the *Command Reference*. But the easiest way to interact with these directories is by means of a graphical tool called the *Client Configuration Assistant* (CCA), which is supported on the Windows and OS/2 platforms. To start the CCA, simply click on its icon in the DB2 program group.

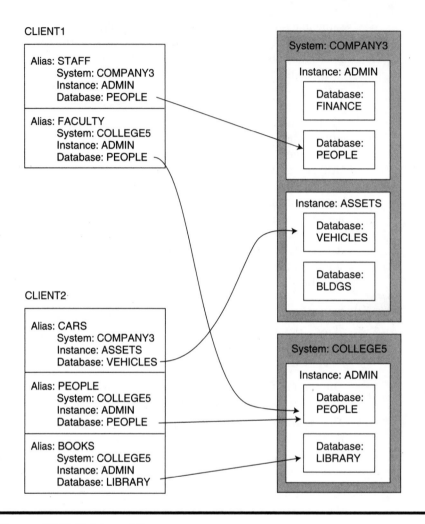

Figure 10-8: Database Aliases

Figure 10-9 shows how the main panel of the CCA might look for the CLIENT1 system in Figure 10-8. The CCA displays a list of all the aliases in its database directory. By selecting an alias, you can see the information recorded by the client about that database, and you can then click the *Delete* button to delete the alias or the *Properties* button to update its information.

To add a new alias to your client directories, click on the *Add* button of the CCA. You will be presented with a choice of the following ways in which a new alias can be defined:

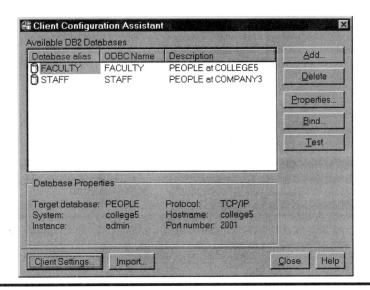

Figure 10-9: The Client Configuration Assistant

1. *Manually.* If you know all the information necessary to connect to the desired database, you can enter this information by hand.

2. *Access Profile.* If you have an access profile that was generated by the Control Center on some remote UDB system, you can add all the databases on that system to your client catalogs simply by giving the name of the access profile to the CCA.

3. *Search the Network.* This option invokes a powerful CCA feature called Discovery. Like the similar feature of the Control Center, the Discovery feature automatically searches your local network for UDB systems and displays its findings in the form of a hierarchy of systems, instances, and databases. Figure 10-10 shows a display in which the CCA has discovered four UDB systems, named CHEDDAR, DON1, NICO, and W4. The CHEDDAR and NICO entries in the display have been expanded to show their instances and databases. You can add one of these databases to your client directories by selecting the database, specifying an alias for it by clicking the *Alias* tab at the top of the window, and then clicking the *Done* button at the bottom of the window. Your client will then be able to connect to the selected database, referring to it by the alias you specified.

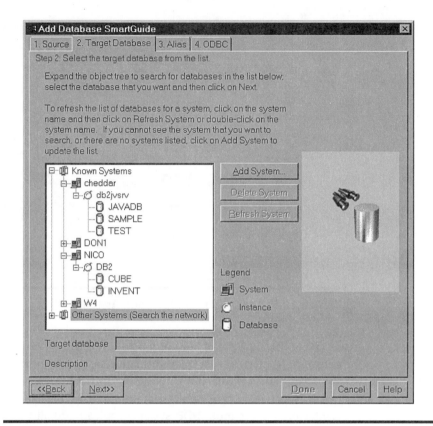

Figure 10-10: Using CCA Discovery to Search for New Databases

10.5 COMMANDS

As noted in the introduction to this chapter, the easiest way to accomplish most database administration tasks is by using the graphical interface of the Control Center. However, old-fashioned commands are still useful in certain situations, and we will discuss some of these commands in this section. Commands fall into two general categories: operating system–level commands, which can be invoked at the operating system command prompt, and UDB commands, which can be invoked during a session with an interactive UDB interface such as the Command Center.

TIP: On Windows NT, certain operating system–level commands cannot be executed in a normal command window but require a special DB2 command window. If you invoke one of these commands in a normal command window, you will get the message "Command line environment not initialized." You can create a DB2 command window by typing db2cmd in a normal command window, or by clicking *Start*, then *Programs*, then *DB2 for Windows NT*, then *Command Window*.

10.5.1 Managing Instances

As noted earlier, a given system may have multiple instances of UDB that are administered separately and used for different purposes, such as for testing and production or for manufacturing and sales. Each database belongs to a specific instance. The commands listed below are operating system–level commands that can be used to manage the UDB instances on your system.

db2icrt

Creates a new instance and gives it a name. The following example creates an instance named testdb2:

```
db2icrt testdb2
```

To create an instance on a UNIX system, you must hold root authority; on Windows NT or OS/2, you must be a member of the Administrators group. When you create an instance, your group becomes the holder of SYSADM authority for the instance.

db2idrop

Drops (destroys) an instance and all the databases that belong to it. This command requires the same level of authorization as db2icrt. The following example drops the instance named testdb2:

```
db2idrop testdb2
```

db2ilist

Lists all the instances that are available on your system. Example:

```
db2ilist
```

db2start

Starts the instance named in the DB2INSTANCE environment variable. Requires SYSADM, SYSCTRL, or SYSMAINT authority. An instance must be started before an application or interactive session can connect to any of its databases. If the given instance has multiple nodes, it is started on all nodes. Example:

```
db2start
```

db2stop

Stops the instance named in the DB2INSTANCE environment variable. Requires SYSADM, SYSCTRL, or SYSMAINT authority. On a multinode system, db2stop can be used to stop the current instance on an individual node or to drop a node from the system after all its data have migrated to other nodes. Example:

```
db2stop
```

An instance cannot be stopped as long as any application or interactive session remains connected to one of its databases. A system administrator can forcibly disconnect applications from an instance by invoking the *Force Applications* action in the Control Center.

10.5.2 The Profile Registry

During normal operations, the behavior of UDB is influenced by a collection of values that define its operating environment. Some of these values take the form of operating system environment variables. For example, DB2PATH specifies the directory in which UDB is installed, and DB2INSTANCE specifies the name of the UDB instance that is started by a db2start command. You can display and set the values of these environment variables using the facilities of your operating system (for example, in Windows NT, click on *Start*, then *Settings*, then *Control Panel*, then *System*, then *Environment*).

In addition to the operating system environment variables, UDB maintains its own collection of environment variables called the *profile registry*. For example, DB2OPTIONS controls the default behavior of the CLP, and DB2DBDFT specifies the default database for implicit connections in the absence of an explicit CONNECT command. A complete list of operating system environment variables and profile registry variables can be found in Appendix E of the *Administration Guide*.

Some variables in the profile registry can be set at more than one level—for example, at the instance level and also at a global level that applies to all instances. In general, a profile registry variable will be effective at the lowest level at which it is defined.

You can display and set the variables in the profile registry by using an operating system–level command named db2set, which requires SYSADM authority. The use of db2set is illustrated by the following examples:

db2set -all
Displays all the profile registry values that are currently defined. In the display, the values labeled [i] apply to the current instance, and the values labeled [g] apply globally (to all instances).

db2set -lr
Lists the names of all variables recognized by the profile registry, regardless of whether they are currently defined.

db2set -all *variable-name*
Displays the current value of the named variable, at all levels where it is defined. In the display, the values labeled [i] apply to the current instance, and the values labeled [g] apply globally (to all instances).

db2set *variable-name=new-value*
Sets the value of a profile registry variable for the current instance.

db2set -g *variable-name=new-value*
Sets the value of a profile registry variable globally (for all instances).

10.5.3 The Administration Server

The Control Center, Script Center, and other DB2 tools require the services of a database system, and for this purpose they use their own instance of UDB, called the Administration Server. The Administration Server is created automatically when you install UDB, and it is started automatically whenever you reboot your system. You should not have any need to interact directly with the Administration Server, or even to be aware of its existence, unless it dies unexpectedly for some reason. If this happens, your DB2 tools will stop working, and you will receive a message, "The DB2 Administration Server is not active." You can manually restart the Administration Server by using an operating system–level command named db2admin, as illustrated in the following examples:

db2admin start
Manually starts the Administration Server.

db2admin stop
Manually stops the Administration Server.

db2admin
Displays the instance name of the Administration Server on your system.

10.5.4 Other Operating System–Level Commands

This section describes some additional operating system–level commands that are supported by UDB. More details on these and other operating system–level commands can be found in the *Command Reference*. When executed on a server machine, these commands are directed to the instance named in the DB2INSTANCE environment variable.

db2batch

This command invokes a tool that is useful for performance measurement and benchmark testing. The db2batch tool reads an input file containing SQL statements, executes the statements, and generates an output file containing results and performance information. By embedding control statements in the input file, you can control the number of rows fetched in each result set, and the level of detail at which performance information is captured. You can simply measure the elapsed time for each SQL statement or gather much more detailed information such as the number of bufferpool reads and lock escalations that occurred during processing of each statement. By running db2batch repeatedly on a benchmark file while varying your database configuration parameters, you can observe the effect of the configuration parameters on system performance. The db2batch tool is described in detail in the *Administration Guide*. The following db2batch command executes the statements in the input file infile.sql against database testdb, capturing results and performance information in the file outfile.txt:

```
db2batch -d testdb -f infile.sql -r outfile.txt
```

db2bfd

This command is useful for examining the content of a bind file, produced by a PREP command with the BIND option, as discussed in Section 4.3. You can display the binding options for a bind file, as well as the SQL statements and host variable declarations in the application program from which the bind file was created. The following command displays the contents of the bind file named parts1.bnd, including its binding options, SQL statements, and host variable declarations:

```
db2bfd -b -s -v parts1.bnd
```

db2gov

This command invokes a utility called the DB2 Governor, which enables you to place limits on the resources consumed by certain users or applications. The

Governor periodically gathers statistics on the users and applications that are connected to a given database, and compares them with a set of rules in a configuration file. In the configuration file, for example, you can specify limits on the number of rows fetched or locks held by a user or application, or on the elapsed time of a transaction. If the Governor finds that an application has exceeded some limit, it can take a specified action such as reducing the application's priority or forcing it to disconnect from the database. The details of how to create a Governor configuration file are described in the *Administration Guide*. The following example command starts the Governor in database `testdb`, using the configuration file named `config.txt` and logging all actions in a logfile named `govlog.txt`:

```
db2gov start testdb config.txt govlog.txt
```

Once started, the Governor continues to run until it is stopped by a command such as the following:

```
db2gov stop testdb
```

db2rbind

The `db2rbind` command rebinds all the packages in a database. This might be useful after a reorganization of the database, in which statistics are updated and new indexes are created. Alternatively, the individual packages in the database can be rebound, either explicitly by REBIND commands or implicitly on their next use. The command in the following example rebinds all the packages in the `company` database and directs any error messages to a file named `rebind.log`:

```
db2rbind company /l rebind.log
```

db2sampl

This command creates a sample database, named SAMPLE, for experimentation. The sample database contains 12 tables that describe the employees, departments, and projects of a small company. (The tables in the sample database are described in Appendix E of the *SQL Reference*.) The command takes an optional parameter that specifies the location (path) where the database is to be created; if no path is specified, the location of the database is determined by the DFTDBPATH configuration parameter. Example:

```
db2sampl
```

10.5.5 UDB Commands

UDB supports a long list of commands that can be invoked from interactive interfaces such as the Command Center. We have already discussed many of these commands, such as the PREP and BIND commands discussed in Section 4.3 and the CREATE DATABASE command discussed in Section 10.1. Many of the actions available in the Control Center can also be invoked by commands. The complete syntax of all the commands can be found in the *Command Reference*. During an interactive session, you can see a list of all UDB commands by typing "?", and you can see the syntax of any command by typing "?" followed by the name of the command.

This section does not attempt to list all the commands supported by UDB. Instead, it lists a few commands that have not been discussed elsewhere and that provide some functionality in a particularly convenient form.

ACTIVATE

This command "starts up" a database and makes it ready to accept connections. This command is not really necessary, since the first connection to a database automatically causes the database to be activated. ACTIVATE can be used in advance of the first connection to avoid the brief delay associated with activating the database. When a database is no longer in use, a DEACTIVATE command can be used to release the system memory allocated to the database. Examples:

```
ACTIVATE DATABASE testdb;
DEACTIVATE DATABAE testdb;
```

ATTACH

This command can be executed on a client machine to specify the UDB instance to which instance-level commands such as CREATE DATABASE will be directed. Example:

```
ATTACH TO server3;
```

If an ATTACH command is executed without naming an instance, the command displays the name of the instance to which you are currently attached.

DESCRIBE

This command provides an easy way to list the column names and datatypes of a table or a query result. It can also be used to list all the indexes that exist for a given table. Examples:

```
DESCRIBE TABLE bank.accounts;
DESCRIBE SELECT avg(balance) FROM bank.accounts;
DESCRIBE INDEXES FOR TABLE bank.accounts;
```

GET

This command provides a quick way to get certain kinds of information about the system or about your current session. Examples:

GET AUTHORIZATIONS;
> Lists the authorities you hold.

GET CONNECTION STATE;
> Displays the database to which you are currently connected, if any.

GET DATABASE CONFIGURATION FOR testdb;
> Lists the values of the database configuration parameters for the named database. The easiest way to update these parameters is by using the Control Center.

GET DATABASE MANAGER CONFIGURATION;
> Lists the values of the database manager configuration parameters. Again, the easiest way to update these parameters is by using the Control Center.

LIST

This command provides a quick way to get some information about the database to which you are currently connected. Examples:

LIST NODEGROUPS;
> Lists the nodegroups in the current database.

LIST NODES;
> Lists the nodes in the current database.

LIST PACKAGES;
> Lists the packages that were bound by you in the current database, and their current state of validity.

LIST TABLES;
> Lists the tables in the current database whose schema name matches your userid.

LIST TABLES FOR SCHEMA research;
> Lists all the tables in the schema named RESEARCH.

LIST TABLESPACES;
> Lists the tablespaces in the current database.

RESET

This command provides a quick way to reset all the configuration parameters for the system or for a particular database to their default values. Examples:

```
RESET DATABASE MANAGER CONFIGURATION;
RESET DATABASE CONFIGURATION FOR testdb;
```

START DATABASE MANAGER

START DATABASE MANAGER is an alternative spelling of the db2start command. It can be either an operating system–level command or a UDB command. Example:

```
START DATABASE MANAGER;
```

STOP DATABASE MANAGER

STOP DATABASE MANAGER is an alternative spelling of the db2stop command. It can be either an operating system–level command or a UDB command. Example:

```
STOP DATABASE MANAGER;
```

10.6 MANAGING DATABASE RECOVERY

One of the most important tasks of a database management system is to protect against loss of data in the event of a hardware or software failure or a power interruption. UDB provides several facilities that can be used by a database administrator to protect databases and to recover from failures. These facilities can be used from the Control Center by selecting a database and invoking one of the recovery-related actions such as *Restart, Backup, Restore,* or *Rollforward,* or by executing a command that is equivalent to one of these actions. In this section, we will discuss the UDB recovery facilities in more detail.

One of the basic tools used for protecting against failures is the *backup*. A backup is a copy of a whole database or of some part of a database (one or more tablespaces). If the backup is made on some removable medium such as a tape or diskette, or if it is made on a different physical device from the one that stores the database, it can serve as a protection against failure of the database storage device. At any time, a backup can be used to restore the database to its state at the time the backup was taken. A database administrator should have a plan for backing up data regularly and for retaining multiple backup copies of critical data.

Another important tool for protecting data is the database *log*. A log is a set of files that record all the changes that are made to a database, including information about how the changes are organized into transactions and whether each transaction ended with a commit or a rollback (for a discussion of transactions, see Section 2.7.1). When each transaction is committed, all the log entries pertaining to that transaction are written onto disk so that they will survive a power failure and provide an independent record of the changes made by that transaction. The log is very important in restoring the database to a consistent state after a power or software failure. The system uses the log to ensure that all changes made to the database by committed transactions remain in effect—even if the updated page was in volatile memory at the time of the failure—and that all changes made to the database by transactions that were not committed before the time of the failure are rolled back. The log is also used when it is necessary to reapply the database changes made by a series of committed transactions, as in the case of forward recovery (described below).

The system log is maintained as a set of files in a directory whose path name is specified by the database configuration parameter named LOGPATH. The number of log files is controlled by the LOGPRIMARY configuration parameter, and the size of the log files is controlled by the LOGFILSIZ configuration parameter. To take advantage of I/O concurrency and to provide protection against media failure, it is wise to keep the log on a different physical device from the database itself.

10.6.1 Types of Recovery

UDB supports the following three types of recovery:

1. *Crash recovery.* Crash recovery is used immediately after a software failure or power outage. It restores the database to a transaction-consistent state in which updates are effective if and only if they were applied by committed transactions. Crash recovery is invoked by the RESTART command.

2. *Restore recovery.* This form of recovery is used to restore the content of a database from a backup that was taken at a previous time. Restore recovery involves the use of the BACKUP and RESTORE commands. It can be used by itself or in conjunction with forward recovery.

3. *Forward recovery.* After a database has been restored from a backup, forward recovery can be used to reapply changes that were made by transactions that committed after the backup was made. In this way, the database can be restored to a transaction-consistent state corresponding to any desired time between the time of the backup and the present. Forward recovery is invoked by the ROLLFORWARD command.

Crash recovery and restore recovery are always available on any database. Forward recovery, however, is available for a given database only if the database has been specifically enabled for this form of recovery. The decision of whether to enable forward recovery is an important one. The consequences of this decision are summarized in Table 10-2.

As a database administrator, you can enable forward recovery for your database by setting either the LOGRETAIN or the USEREXIT database configuration parameter to the value YES. Either of these configuration parameters causes the database log to be configured in such a way that it retains the entries needed for forward recovery.

If both LOGRETAIN and USEREXIT configuration parameters are set to NO (which is the default), the database log is treated as circular. That is, when the log reaches its maximum size, it wraps around and begins to reuse its own space, deleting its oldest entries. In this case, forward recovery is not enabled because there is no guarantee that all the entries needed for forward recovery can be found in the log.

TABLE 10-2: Consequences of Enabling Forward Recovery for a Database

If Forward Recovery Is *Not* Enabled	If Forward Recovery Is Enabled
After a failure, you can recover the database to its last transaction-consistent point before the failure.	Same. Recovery to a transaction-consistent point is always supported.
You can back up the database only at a time when no applications are connected to the database (this is called an *offline backup*).	You can back up the database while applications are connected to the database and transactions are in progress (this is called an *online backup*). Offline backups are also supported.
Each backup must contain the current state of an entire database.	A backup may contain the current state of a database or of one or more tablespaces. Thus tablespaces within a database can be independently backed up and restored. This gives you the flexibility to back up your more active tablespaces with greater frequency than your less active ones or to omit from your backup certain tablespaces containing large objects that can be reconstructed from another source.
You can restore the database to its state at the time of any available backup, but you cannot reapply transactions that occurred after the backup.	You can restore the database to its state at the time of any available backup; in addition, you can reapply subsequent committed transactions up to some desired time or up to the present.

If LOGRETAIN is set to YES, the log keeps growing by generating new files and retaining them indefinitely. In this case, you must provide some way to move old log files to an archive to prevent filling up your disk with log files.

If USEREXIT is set to YES, the log keeps growing by generating and retaining new files, but as each log file becomes full, a user-supplied program (called a *user exit*) is called, which can examine the log directory and move old log files to an archive if necessary. This is a way of automating the process of moving log files to an archive. (For more information about user exits, see Appendix J of the *Administration Guide*.)

When either the LOGRETAIN or USEREXIT configuration parameter is changed from NO to YES, the database is placed into a *Backup Pending* state in which it cannot be used until a full database backup has been taken. This backup provides a starting point for forward recovery if it should become necessary.

10.6.2 Recovery Commands

The commands for controlling database backup and recovery are described on the following pages and illustrated in Figure 10-11. Each of these commands is equivalent to a database action that can be invoked using the Control Center.

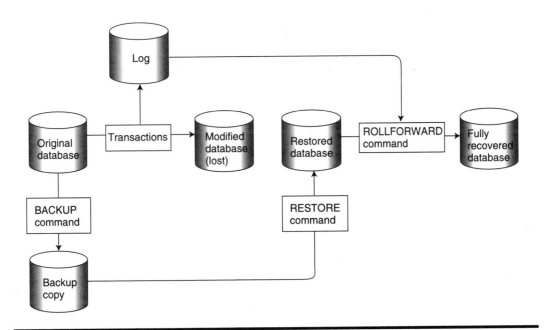

Figure 10-11: Database Backup and Recovery

RESTART

RESTART is the first command that should be issued against a database after a failure such as a power outage or a software crash while transactions are in progress. It establishes a database connection and uses the database log to restore the database to a transaction-consistent state. All database changes made by transactions that committed before the failure are made effective. All database changes made by transactions that rolled back before the failure, or by transactions that were in progress at the time of the failure, are rolled back.

The following is an example of a RESTART command:

```
RESTART DATABASE finance;
```

You can configure your database to automatically invoke a RESTART command when needed by setting the AUTORESTART database configuration parameter to ON. In this case, the RESTART command will be invoked automatically when the first application attempts to connect to your database after a failure.

A RESTART command affects only the node on which it is executed. If more than one node fails in a parallel database system, each node must be independently restarted.

If the database that is being restarted is a participant in some *distributed transactions* (transactions that connect to and modify multiple databases, possibly on different servers), it is possible that the status of a distributed transaction may be "in doubt" because a commit request was processed on some but not all servers. If in-doubt transactions are discovered by a RESTART command, you will receive a warning message. You can examine the in-doubt transactions and decide what to do about them by using the LIST INDOUBT TRANSACTIONS command (for details, see the *Administration Guide*).

BACKUP

The BACKUP command makes a copy of a database, in whole or in part, to one or more devices (often tapes) or directories on the server machine. Subject to the constraints in Table 10-2, the backup may be taken either online or offline and may apply either to the whole database or to a set of named tablespaces. In order to use the BACKUP command, you must have SYSADM, SYSCTRL, or SYSMAINT authority.

When using the BACKUP command, you can specify the following information:

- The name of the database to be backed up
- The names of the tablespaces to be backed up (default is the whole database)
- Whether the backup is offline or online (default is offline)
- The name of the devices or directories in which the backup files are to be created

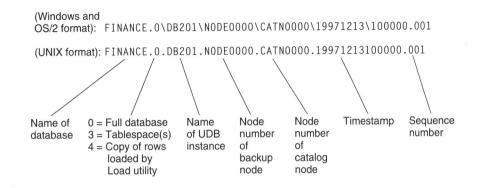

(Windows and
OS/2 format): `FINANCE.0\DB201\NODE0000\CATN0000\19971213\100000.001`

(UNIX format): `FINANCE.0.DB201.NODE0000.CATN0000.19971213100000.001`

| Name of database | 0 = Full database
3 = Tablespace(s)
4 = Copy of rows loaded by Load utility | Name of UDB instance | Node number of backup node | Node number of catalog node | Timestamp | Sequence number |

Figure 10-12: Structure of a Backup Filename

- Optionally, a userid and password against which to authorize the backup
- Optionally, some parameters for tuning the input/output process (such as the number and size of the buffers to be used)

A backup command generates one or more backup files in the named devices or directories. The generated files have names whose structure is shown in Figure 10-12.

On a parallel database system, you must back up each node independently. It is a good practice to back up all the nodes at the same time so that you will have a complete and consistent copy of the whole database.

Here are some examples of BACKUP commands:

- This command creates a full database backup of the FINANCE database to a named directory on the server.

  ```
  BACKUP DATABASE finance TO d:\backups;
  ```

- This command performs an online backup of a named tablespace in the FINANCE database. Applications can continue updating the database while the backup is being taken.

  ```
  BACKUP DATABASE finance
      TABLESPACE userspace1 ONLINE
      TO d:\backups;
  ```

TIP: If you add some containers to a tablespace, it is wise to perform a backup before continuing to use the database. This practice will help you to avoid some complexities that arise if you need to restore a tablespace to which containers have been added since the last backup was made. These complexities are discussed in the *Administration Guide*.

RESTORE

The RESTORE command restores the content of a database, using the content that was saved in a backup. It does not ordinarily restore the database configuration parameters, but can do so if these parameters have become lost or corrupted. RESTORE can also be used to create a new database and load it with the content saved in a whole-database backup. In order to use the RESTORE command, you must have SYSADM, SYSCTRL, or SYSMAINT authority.

The backup used in a RESTORE command may include the content of either the whole database or a set of tablespaces. Restoring a whole database must be done offline, but restoring tablespaces (other than the tablespace that contains the system catalog tables) can be done online, while applications are interacting with other tablespaces. On a parallel database system, you must invoke a RESTORE command separately on each node that is participating in the recovery.

When using a RESTORE command, you can specify the following information:

- The name of the database from which the backup was made.
- The name of the devices or directories on the server machine where the backup is stored.
- The date and time of the backup you want to use, if there is more than one backup in the designated location.
- If the RESTORE is directed to a target database that is different from the one that was backed up, the name and location of the target database. If the target database does not exist, it will be created. In this way, multiple independent copies of a database can be made.
- When restoring tablespaces, a list of the tablespaces to be restored and whether the RESTORE is to be done online or offline (default is offline).
- Optionally, a userid and password against which to authorize the RESTORE command.
- Optionally, some parameters for tuning the input/output process (such as the number and size of the buffers to be used).

By default, if forward recovery is enabled for your database, the RESTORE command will leave the database (or the tablespaces that were restored) in a state called *rollforward pending*. A database or tablespace in the rollforward pending state cannot be used until a ROLLFORWARD command has been applied to it, to reapply changes made by committed transactions. The rollforward pending state is mandatory if the RESTORE was done from an online backup or from a tablespace-level backup. However, if the RESTORE was done from a whole-database offline backup, the phrase WITHOUT ROLLING FOR-

WARD can be added to the RESTORE command, causing the database to avoid the rollforward pending state and to be usable immediately after the RESTORE is completed (in this case, changes made by transactions that committed after the time of the backup are lost).

Here are some examples of RESTORE commands:

- The following command restores the FINANCE database from a specified backup, identified by its directory and timestamp. If forward recovery is not enabled for the FINANCE database, the database will be restored to its state at the time of the backup and will be immediately usable. If forward recovery is enabled, the database will be left in the rollforward pending state and will not be usable until a ROLLFORWARD command has been executed on it. The phrase REPLACE EXISTING assures the system that you are aware that the existing content of this database will be deleted and replaced by the content of the backup.

  ```
  RESTORE DATABASE finance
      FROM d:\backups TAKEN AT 19971117160246
      REPLACE EXISTING;
  ```

- The following command is similar to the previous example except that it explicitly specifies that rollforward will not be done and that the database should be immediately usable:

  ```
  RESTORE DATABASE finance
      FROM d:\backups TAKEN AT 19971117160246
      REPLACE EXISTING
      WITHOUT ROLLING FORWARD;
  ```

- The following command uses the same backup as the previous examples, but this time it performs an online RESTORE on only one of the tablespaces in the FINANCE database. This kind of restore might be useful to restore a tablespace in which a media error has been encountered, without interrupting user access to the rest of the database. The restored tablespace is left in a rollforward pending state and will not be usable until a ROLLFORWARD command has been executed to resynchronize it with the other tablespaces in the database.

  ```
  RESTORE DATABASE finance
      TABLESPACE(userspace1) ONLINE
      FROM d:\backups TAKEN AT 19971117160246
      REPLACE EXISTING;
  ```

ROLLFORWARD

The ROLLFORWARD command is invoked after a RESTORE command to perform forward recovery on the database or on some of its tablespaces. It uses the log to reapply database changes made by transactions that committed after the time of the backup. In order to use the ROLLFORWARD command, you must have SYSADM, SYSCTRL, or SYSMAINT authority, and the database must be enabled for forward recovery.

A ROLLFORWARD command applies either to the whole database or to one or more tablespaces, whichever is in the rollforward pending state. A database or tablespace that is in the rollforward pending state cannot be used until a ROLLFORWARD has been successfully completed.

A ROLLFORWARD that applies to a whole database or to the tablespace that contains the system catalog tables (SYSCATSPACE) must be done offline. A ROLLFORWARD of tablespaces other than SYSCATSPACE can be done either online or offline.

A whole database can be rolled forward to any desired point in time between the time of the backup and the current time (end of logs). When a database is rolled forward to a designated time, the logs are used to reapply all changes made by transactions that committed before the designated time. Individual tablespaces can also be rolled forward to a designated time, with the following restrictions:

- SYSCATSPACE cannot be individually rolled forward to a designated time—it must be rolled all the way to the end of the logs.

- Tablespaces other than SYSCATSPACE can be individually rolled forward to a designated time, but only if no tables were created or dropped in the given tablespace after the designated time (since this would make the tablespace inconsistent with the system catalog tables).

- If a table has parts in more than one tablespace, all the tablespaces involved must be rolled forward together.

- If a table in a tablespace that is being rolled forward has a referential integrity relationship with a table in another tablespace, the table that is rolled forward will be left in a *check pending* state. The check pending state, described in Section 10.7.5, prevents the table from being used until its constraints have been checked.

On a multinode system, the ROLLFORWARD command must be executed only on the catalog node. By default, the command applies to all nodes listed in the db2nodes.cfg file, but it can also specify a subset of nodes to participate in the ROLLFORWARD. If you are recovering from a failure on an individual node, you can call for that node to roll forward to end of logs in order to resynchronize it with the other nodes. However, if you are rolling the database forward to a designated time, the ROLLFORWARD must apply to all nodes.

When using a ROLLFORWARD command, you can specify the following information:

- The name of the database to be rolled forward.
- The date and time to which you want the database to be rolled forward (default is end of logs). If rolling forward to end of logs on a multinode system, you can list the nodes that you wish to participate.
- When rolling forward tablespaces, a list of the tablespaces to participate and whether the process is to take place online or offline (default is offline).
- Optionally, a directory to search for archived log files, in addition to the regular log directory that is specified by the LOGPATH configuration parameter.
- Optionally, a userid and password against which to authorize the ROLLFORWARD command.

Here are some examples of ROLLFORWARD commands:

- This command rolls the FINANCE database forward to the current time. It might be used after restoring the database from a backup to reapply all transactions that were committed after the backup was taken. The phrase AND STOP is needed to take the database out of the rollforward pending state and make it available for use.

```
ROLLFORWARD DATABASE finance
    TO END OF LOGS AND STOP;
```

- This command rolls forward the FINANCE database, reapplying all transactions that were committed before a designated date and time.

```
ROLLFORWARD DATABASE finance
    TO 1997-12-25-10.30.59 AND STOP;
```

- This command rolls forward only certain tablespaces within the FINANCE database. The command is issued after a tablespace-level recovery, and it applies only to the specified tablespace (USERSPACE1). The command specifies that the forward recovery is to be conducted online and is to proceed all the way to the present time (end of logs).

```
ROLLFORWARD DATABASE finance
    TO END OF LOGS AND STOP
    TABLESPACE(USERSPACE1) ONLINE;
```

 TIP: Remember that if the database contains some columns of LOB datatypes that were created with the NOT LOGGED option, updates to these columns are not recorded in the log, and forward recovery does not apply to these columns. If, during forward recovery, an update to an unlogged column is encountered, the value of that column will be set to binary zeros.

10.6.3 Using the Journal for Recovery

In Section 3.1.3, we discussed the Journal, a graphical tool that keeps a record of significant events that take place in a UDB database. One of the panels of the Journal is the Recovery panel, which is shown in Figure 10-13. The Recovery panel shows a list of all the backup and recovery actions that have taken place in a given database. To restore the database using a given backup, simply select that backup on the Recovery panel, pull down the *Log* menu, and choose the *Restore* action. You will be presented with a SmartGuide in which you can graphically select all the options of the RESTORE command, such as the tablespaces to be restored and whether the RESTORE is to be followed by a ROLLFORWARD.

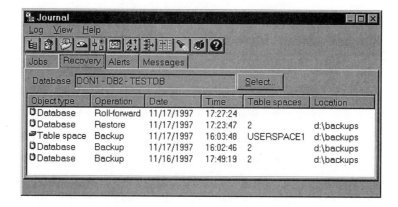

Figure 10-13: Recovery Panel of the Journal

10.7 MOVING DATA IN BULK

When a database is first created, it is often desirable to load it with data from some external source. Also, during operation of a database, a need sometimes arises to move a large bulk of data into or out of the database, exchanging it with some external source such as a set of files or another database. Of course, it would be possible to write a special-purpose application program to accomplish each of these data transfers, using SQL INSERT and/or SELECT statements embedded in some host programming language. UDB has saved you the trouble of writing many such specialized programs by providing a set of general-purpose utilities for moving data into and out of databases. These utilities can be summarized as follows:

1. *Export.* This utility extracts data from a database and saves it in a file, using one of several file formats. The data to be extracted is specified by an SQL query.

2. *Import.* This utility is the inverse of Export. It inserts data into a database table from an external file, using the same file formats supported by the Export utility. The Import utility inserts rows into the database table one at a time, using SQL INSERT statements. During the import, the table remains accessible to other applications. All constraints and triggers remain in effect during the import and are activated in the usual way as rows are inserted.

3. *Load.* This utility is a higher-performance alternative to Import. Rather than inserting rows into a table one at a time, the Load utility constructs page images containing many rows and inserts them into the database a page at a time. Indexes are constructed in a separate step after the bulk loading of data. During operation of the Load utility, the tablespace(s) that contain the table being loaded are not accessible to other applications. Also, during the loading of a table, constraints and triggers attached to that table are temporarily suspended. After the table is loaded, its constraints can be reactivated and applied to check the newly loaded data by means of a SET CONSTRAINTS statement.

TIP: Check constraints and foreign key constraints are enforced for loaded data at the end of the load process. However, there is no way to find and execute the set of triggers that would have been activated by the loaded data. Therefore, business rules that are implemented by triggers are not guaranteed to be enforced after a load. This is one of the advantages of implementing business rules by constraints rather than by triggers.

10.7.1 File Formats

Four standard file formats are available for use with the Export, Import, and Load utilities. These file formats can be summarized as follows:

1. *Delimited ASCII* (type DEL) files consist of streams of data values, ordered by row and by column within each row. Values are separated by column delimiters (by default, a comma), and rows are separated by row delimiters (by default, a newline character in UNIX and a carriage return/linefeed sequence in Windows and OS/2). Character-string values are enclosed in string delimiters (by default, a double quote). Null values are denoted by missing data (column delimiters separated by spaces or by nothing). When you export, import, or load a delimited ASCII file, you can override the default delimiters with your own delimiter characters. A delimited ASCII file contains data values, but it does not contain structural information such as table names and column names.

   The following example shows how four rows of data might be represented in a delimited ASCII file and illustrates the default formats for dates and times in delimited ASCII:

```
"Screwdriver", 5.10, 28, "Acme Tools", 19980115, "09.34.05"
"Hammer", 18.00, 8, "Tools Unlimited", 19980401, "09.34.05"
"Wrench", 24.50, 10, "Bob's House of Tools", 19971230, "21.34.05"
"Wrench, Adjustable", 32.29, 15, "Tools Unlimited", 19980215, "21.34.05"
```

2. *Nondelimited ASCII* (type ASC) files are similar to delimited ASCII files, except that the columns of data within each row are found in fixed positions and therefore do not need to be marked by delimiters. When using a nondelimited ASCII file, the Import and Load utilities must specify the exact format of the file (that is, the character positions assigned to each column of data).

   The following example shows how the four rows described above might be represented in a nondelimited ASCII file and illustrates the default formats for dates and times in nondelimited ASCII:

```
Screwdriver          5.10  28 Acme Tools            1998-01-15  09.34.05
Hammer              18.00   8 Tools Unlimited        1998-04-01  09.34.05
Wrench              24.50  10 Bob's House of Tools   1997-12-30  21.34.05
Wrench, Adjustable  32.29  15 Tools Unlimited        1998-02-15  21.34.05
```

 TIP: Note that the default representations of dates are different in delimited and nondelimited ASCII files.

3. *Integrated Exchange Format* (type IXF) files are the preferred format for transferring data between databases managed by UDB on the same platform or on

TABLE 10-3: Summary of Filetypes Supported by Export, Import, and Load

	Delimited ASCII (DEL)	Nondelimited ASCII (ASC)	Integrated Exchange Format (IXF)	Worksheet File (WSF)
Export	YES	NO	YES	YES
Import	YES	YES	YES	YES
Load	YES	YES	YES	NO

different platforms.[3] For example, an IXF file can be used to move data between a database running under Windows NT and a database running under AIX, automatically compensating for the different numeric formats used on these two platforms.

An IXF file is a binary file that contains not only data but a description of a table, including its column names, datatypes, and indexes. When a table is exported in IXF format, it can be recreated in another database, complete with its indexes and primary key. However, an IXF file does not contain information about foreign keys, constraints, or triggers.

4. *Worksheet* (type WSF) files are intended for interchange of data between UDB and certain versions of the Lotus 1-2-3 and Symphony products. WSF files can contain both column names and data. (More details about WSF files are included in the *DB2 Administration Guide*.)

Table 10-3 summarizes the filetypes that are supported by each of the three utilities for bulk movement of data.

10.7.2 Exporting Data

The Export utility extracts data from the database and saves it in a file using the DEL, IXF, or WSF format. The data to be exported need not come from a single table but can be computed by any SQL query, perhaps containing a join or UNION of multiple tables and/or views. In order to use the Export utility, you must hold SYSADM or DBADM authority, or CONTROL or SELECT privilege on each of the tables or views from which data is being exported.

---

3. UDB uses the personal computer (PC) version of the Integrated Exchange Format, which is not identical to the IXF format used on mainframes.

When exporting data into a DEL file, you can specify characters to be used for row, column, and string delimiters and for decimal points and plus signs. When exporting data into an IXF file, you can specify column names for the exported data. You can also specify a file in which messages will be saved that are generated during the export process; if no message file is specified, the messages are displayed on standard out.

The Export utility can be invoked from the Control Center by selecting a table to be exported, choosing the *Export* action, and answering the questions in the resulting dialog. Alternatively, you can execute an EXPORT command using an interactive interface such as the Command Center or CLP. The EXPORT command is explained in the *Command Reference*, and is illustrated by the following examples:

- This example exports the entire table named SHOP.TOOLS into a delimited ASCII file named TOOLS.DEL in the current directory. The phrase OF DEL indicates the type of file. Messages generated during the export are saved in a file named EXPORT.MSG in the current directory.

```
EXPORT TO tools.del OF DEL
    MESSAGES export.msg
    SELECT * FROM shop.tools;
```

- This example exports certain rows and columns of the SHOP.TOOLS table, specified by an SQL query, into an IXF file named TOOLS.IXF. The line beginning with METHOD N specifies new column names for the exported data.

```
EXPORT TO tools.ixf OF IXF
    METHOD N(toolname, price, acquired)
    MESSAGES export.msg
        SELECT name, price, adate
        FROM shop.tools
        WHERE adate >= '1998-01-01';
```

10.7.3 Importing Data

The Import utility inserts data into a database from a file using one of the four supported file formats. The data from the file is processed one row at a time, using SQL INSERT statements. Any constraints and triggers associated with the target table remain in effect during the import process. If insertion of a row fails (for example, because the row violates a constraint), the Import utility generates a message indicating the row number of the failing row, then proceeds to insert the remaining rows. At the conclusion of the import process, a message is generated summarizing the number of rows that were successfully inserted and the number of rows that failed. The Import utility then commits the transaction.

The Import utility must be invoked in one of the following modes:

INSERT: The target table must exist; new rows are inserted into the target table without affecting the existing content of the table.

INSERT_UPDATE: The target table must exist and have a primary key. New rows that match the primary key of an existing row cause that existing row to be updated. New rows that do not match a primary key of an existing row are inserted into the table.

REPLACE: The target table must exist. Its existing contents are deleted and replaced with the imported data.

CREATE (IXF files only): The target table must not exist. The target table (and its indexes, if any) are created from the table description contained in the IXF file. The data in the IXF file is then inserted into the new table.

REPLACE_CREATE (IXF files only): If the target table exists, its contents are deleted and replaced with the imported data, leaving the table definition unchanged. If the target table does not exist, it is created (including indexes) from the table description contained in the IXF file, and the data in the file is then inserted into the new table.

In order to use the Import utility, you must have authorities or privileges that are sufficient for what you are trying to do. To insert new rows into an existing table, you need INSERT privilege on that table. To replace the content of a table, you need CONTROL privilege on that table. To create a new table, you need CREATETAB privilege on the database and CREATEIN privilege on its schema. Of course, SYSADM or DBADM authority is sufficient to perform any of these operations.

When importing data from a delimited ASCII (DEL) file, you can specify characters to be used for row, column, and string delimiters and for decimal points and plus signs.

The Import utility can be invoked from the Control Center by selecting the table to be imported, choosing the *Import* action, and answering the questions in the resulting dialog. Alternatively, you can execute an IMPORT command using an interactive interface such as the Command Center or CLP. The IMPORT command is explained in the *Command Reference* and is illustrated by the following examples:

- In this example, the content of a delimited ASCII file is inserted into the existing table SHOP.TOOLS2.

```
IMPORT FROM tools.del OF DEL
    MESSAGES import.msg
    INSERT INTO shop.tools2;
```

- In this example, the content of a nondelimited ASCII file is used to replace the content of the existing table named SHOP.TOOLS3. When importing data from an ASC file, the user must specify the exact character positions in the file where each column of data is found. This is done by the line beginning with the phrase METHOD L.

```
IMPORT FROM tools.asc OF ASC
    METHOD L(1 20, 21 26, 29 30, 33 51, 54 63, 66 73)
    MESSAGES import.msg
    REPLACE INTO shop.tools3;
```

- In this example, the content of an IXF file is being used to create a new table named SHOP.TOOLS4. The IXF file contains a definition of the column names of the new table and specifies the indexes to be created on the new table.

```
IMPORT FROM tools.ixf OF IXF
    MESSAGES import.msg
    CREATE INTO shop.tools4;
```

- When data is being imported into a column whose datatype is one of the LOB datatypes (Blob, Clob, or Dbclob), the file being imported may contain either the actual LOB values or the names of files containing the LOB values. The latter case is indicated by the LOBSINFILE option of the IMPORT command, as shown in the following example. This example also illustrates INSERT_ UPDATE mode, in which data from the import file is used to update the values of existing rows that have a matching primary key.

```
IMPORT FROM pictures.ixf OF IXF
    MODIFIED BY LOBSINFILE
    MESSAGES import.msg
    INSERT_UPDATE INTO employees;
```

- The following command specifies that the Import utility should skip the first 300 rows in the import file and begin importing data starting with row 301. During the import process, a transaction will be committed after every 50 rows. This command illustrates how the importing of a large file might be restarted after a failure and how regular commit points can be used to protect against subsequent failures.

```
IMPORT FROM bigfile.ixf OF IXF
    COMMITCOUNT 50 RESTARTCOUNT 300
    MESSAGES import.msg
    INSERT INTO bigtable;
```

TIP: An easy way to create a new table with the same column names and datatypes as an existing table is to export the existing table into an IXF file with a WHERE clause that causes zero rows to be exported, then to invoke IMPORT on the IXF file with the CREATE option to create the new table. For example, the following combination of commands creates a new empty table named SHOP.NEWTOOLS that has the same column names and datatypes as the existing table named SHOP.TOOLS:

```
EXPORT TO toolsddl.ixf OF IXF
    SELECT *
    FROM shop.tools
    WHERE 1 < 0;
IMPORT FROM toolsddl.ixf OF IXF
    CREATE INTO shop.newtools;
```

10.7.4 Loading Data

The Load utility, like the Import utility, can load data into a table from a file; it can also load data from a pipe or from a device such as a tape. The main difference between Load and Import is that Load provides significantly higher performance for loading large quantities of data. This performance is accomplished partly by inserting data into the database one page at a time instead of one row at a time. In order to insert pages into the database, the Load utility must obtain exclusive access to the tablespace(s) being loaded; this processing is called *quiescing* the tablespaces. The Load utility also deactivates triggers and constraints for the table being loaded, for the duration of the load. To further enhance performance, the Load utility exploits parallelism of several kinds. For example, it uses parallel processes to write data into multiple tablespace containers, and it automatically makes use of multiple processors when running on a symmetric multiprocessor system.

In order to use the Load utility, you must hold SYSADM or DBADM authority. Before beginning a load, you should make the following preparations:

- If the table to be loaded does not exist, you must create it before invoking the Load utility. You may also create indexes before loading a table. The Load utility will collect index keys during the load process and will use these keys to construct the actual indexes after the data has been loaded. This is the most efficient way to create an index on a large table that is being newly loaded with data.

- If the table to be loaded has any uniqueness rules (such as a primary key, unique constraint, or unique index), you may choose to create an *exception table* to be used by the Load utility. After loading, any rows that are found to violate a uniqueness rule are removed from the loaded table and moved to the exception table.

The exception table can have any name you like, but it must have columns that exactly match (in name and datatype) the columns of the table being loaded. In addition, two more columns are recommended for the last two column positions of the exception table. The first of these "extra" columns, which should have datatype Timestamp, is used to indicate the time when the violation was discovered. The second "extra" column, which should have datatype Clob(32K), is used to indicate the name(s) of the constraint(s) that were violated by the exceptional row. If an exception table already exists for the table to be loaded (perhaps from a previous load), it would be wise to make sure the exception table is empty before the load begins.

TIP: If a column in the table to be loaded is declared NOT NULL, the corresponding column in the exception table must be declared NOT NULL also.

- If your database is configured for forward recovery, you must decide whether you want the Load utility to make an extra copy of all the data that is loaded. Forward recovery means that if a failure occurs and the database is restored from an earlier backup, the system is prepared to reapply any committed changes that took place after the time of the backup. In order to reapply the load process, the system needs an extra copy of the loaded data. You can ask the Load utility to create this extra copy by invoking it with the option COPY YES and specifying the name of the file or device where the copy is to be created. Alternatively, you can specify the NONRECOVERABLE option, in which case no copy is made of the loaded data, and the loaded table cannot participate in forward recovery.

  If your database is configured for forward recovery and you invoke the Load utility without specifying either COPY YES or NONRECOVERABLE, the table-space containing the loaded table will be left in a state called *Backup Pending*, in which its data is not accessible until a backup has been made. More details about forward recovery, backups, and the Backup Pending state can be found in Section 10.6.

- You must also decide whether you want the Load utility to collect statistics on the table being loaded, and/or on its indexes, and save these statistics in the system catalog tables. These statistics measure things like the distribution of values in the columns of the table, and they are useful to the optimizer in choosing access plans for queries against the table. You can use the Load utility to collect statistics only if you are loading the table from scratch, replacing any existing content. This is called *Replace Mode*, and is distinguished from *Insert Mode* in which the new rows are added to the table without affecting existing rows.

  To suppress the collection of statistics during loading, invoke the Load utility with the option STATISTICS NO. The default, which collects a limited set of statistics but not the most complete set, is called STATISTICS YES. The maximum set of statistics on the loaded table and all its indexes can be obtained by the option STATISTICS YES WITH DISTRIBUTION AND DETAILED INDEXES ALL. (Other intermediate options are described in the *Command Reference*.) If you do not gather statistics for a table during the loading process, you can gather them later using the *Run Statistics* action of the Control Center.

- You must make sure that enough temporary disk space is available for use by the Load utility for storing and sorting index keys. By default, the Load utility creates these temporary files in the `sqllib/tmp` directory of the current UDB instance, but you can specify a different directory or set of directories if you prefer.

The process of loading a table consists of the following phases:

1. The *load phase*. During this phase, data is loaded into the table, but indexes are not updated, triggers are suppressed, and constraints are not checked.

2. The *build phase*. During this phase, any indexes defined on the table are rebuilt.

3. The *delete phase*. During this phase, any rows that are found to violate a primary key, unique constraint, or unique index are deleted from the loaded table and moved to the exception table. If no exception table is provided, rows that violate uniqueness rules are discarded with a warning message. Only uniqueness rules are checked during this phase; foreign key and check constraints are still not checked.

 TIP: The Load utility always rebuilds existing indexes from scratch, whereas the Import utility updates existing indexes incrementally. Therefore, when adding a small number of rows to an existing large table with indexes defined, Import may give better performance than Load.

If the loaded table has any foreign key or check constraints, the Load utility leaves it in a special state called *Check Pending*. This means that constraints have not been checked for some of the data in the table. If the loaded table is a parent table in any referential integrity relationships, and if the load was done in Replace Mode, the child tables in these relationships are left in Check Pending state also. A table in Check Pending state cannot be accessed by SQL statements until some action has been taken to remove it from this special state. The usual way to remove a table from Check Pending state is by using the SET CONSTRAINTS statement (described in Section 10.7.5).

 TIP: When a table is loaded, its rows are placed into physical storage in the order in which they are read from the load file. This ordering is preserved even when data is being loaded into several partitions. It is a good practice to select an index that is expected to be used frequently and to load the rows of the table in the order of their key values in this index. The index you selected will then have the *clustering property*, which means that scanning the table using this index will result in the minimum number of I/O operations. Having an index with the clustering property can improve the performance of queries against a table. If you are unable to load the rows of a table in key-value order, you can create a clustering index later by reorganizing the table, using the *Reorganize* action of the Control Center.

The Load utility can be invoked from the Control Center by selecting the table to be loaded, choosing the *Load* action, and answering the questions in the resulting dialog. Alternatively, you can execute a LOAD command using an interactive interface such as the Command Center. Like IMPORT, LOAD can be invoked either in INSERT mode, which loads new rows into a table and leaves the existing rows unchanged, or in REPLACE mode, which deletes the existing content of the table and replaces it with the newly loaded data.

The LOAD utility allows you to specify the characters to be used for row, column, and string delimiters when loading data from a delimited ASCII (DEL) file. LOAD also supports several data conversion options that are convenient for loading data from various sources, including mainframe databases. These options include code-page conversions for character data, implicit decimal points for decimal data, and the ability to load numeric data by embedding binary or packed decimal data in an ASCII file.

The LOAD command is explained in the *Command Reference* and is illustrated by the following examples:

- In this example, LOAD is being used to insert the content of an IXF file into an existing table named SHOP.TOOLS. Messages generated during loading are saved in the file named LOAD.MSG, and rows that violate primary key or unique index constraints are diverted into an exception file named SHOP.BADTOOLS.

```
LOAD FROM tools.ixf OF IXF
  MESSAGES load.msg
  INSERT INTO shop.tools
  FOR EXCEPTION shop.badtools;
```

 TIP: After loading a table, if you attempt to use the table and receive the message "Tablespace access is not allowed" (SQLCODE –290, SQLSTATE 55039), it is probably because your database is configured for forward recovery and you neglected to specify COPY YES on your LOAD command. Your tablespace will not be accessible until you invoke a BACKUP command to back up the tablespace or the whole database.

- In this example, the Load utility is being used to replace the content of a table and to gather a complete set of statistics on the table and all its indexes. This example also makes an extra copy of all the newly loaded rows, for use in forward recovery. The copy file is placed in a directory specified by the LOAD command, and its name is determined by the convention for naming backup files (described in Figure 10-12).

```
LOAD FROM tools.ixf OF IXF
   MESSAGES load.msg
   REPLACE INTO shop.tools
   STATISTICS YES WITH DISTRIBUTION AND DETAILED INDEXES ALL
   COPY YES TO d:\backups;
```

 TIP: Remember that the STATISTICS option is valid only in REPLACE mode and that the COPY option is valid only if your database is configured for forward recovery.

- In this example, the Load utility is loading a table that includes a column of datatype Clob(10K). Rather than containing actual Clob values, the load file contains the names of the files that in turn contain the Clob values. The LOAD command uses the LOBSINFILE option and specifies the directory in which the Clob files can be found.

```
LOAD FROM students.del OF DEL
   LOBS FROM d:\students\resumes MODIFIED BY LOBSINFILE
   MESSAGES load.msg
   INSERT INTO college.students;
```

10.7.5 Check Pending State

The enforcement of check constraints and foreign key constraints is important to the integrity of the database, but it also carries a cost that must be paid whenever data is modified. For this reason, the Load utility suspends the checking of these kinds of constraints during the bulk loading of data. Whenever it loads data into a table that has check or foreign key constraints, the Load utility leaves that table in Check Pending state to indicate that it contains data against which some constraints have not been checked.

When a table is in Check Pending state, normal access to the table by SELECT, INSERT, UPDATE, and DELETE statements is not allowed. You are also not allowed to create an index on a table while it is in Check Pending state or to process such a table using the EXPORT, IMPORT, REORG, or REORGCHK commands.

You can find out whether a given table is in Check Pending state by looking at the STATUS column of the catalog table named TABLES. For a given table, a STATUS value of "N" indicates that the table is in normal state, and a STATUS value of "C" indicates that the table is in Check Pending state. A third status value, "X," applies only to views and indicates that the view is in an inoperative state. The following query might be used to find out whether the table named SHOP.TOOLS is in Check Pending state:

```
SELECT status
FROM syscat.tables
WHERE tabschema = 'SHOP'
AND tabname = 'TOOLS';
```

SET CONSTRAINTS

When a table is in Check Pending state, you can check its constraints and restore it to a normal state by using the *Set Constraints* action of the Control Center or by executing a SET CONSTRAINTS statement. When you do this, you need to specify what you want to happen if some rows are found in the table that violate one or more constraints. The best way to do this is by providing an *exception table* into which the offending rows will be moved. The exception table used by SET CONSTRAINTS has the same structure as the exception table used by the Load utility to hold rows that violate primary key and unique constraints. In fact, you may choose to use the same exception table for both a LOAD command and the SET CONSTRAINTS statement that follows it, thus collecting in a single place the rows that violate all kinds of constraints. If you invoke SET CONSTRAINTS without providing an exception table, and a row is found that violates a constraint, you will receive an error message and the table will be left in Check Pending state.

The use of the SET CONSTRAINTS statement is illustrated by the examples below. In order to use SET CONSTRAINTS, you must hold SYSADM or DBADM authority, or CONTROL privilege on the table(s) to which the statement applies. In addition, if your SET CONSTRAINTS statement inserts rows into an exception table, you must hold the necessary privilege to insert data into this table. The SET CONSTRAINTS process acquires and holds an exclusive lock on a table while its constraints are being checked.

- This example removes the SHOP.TOOLS table from Check Pending state, checks its contents against the existing check constraints and foreign key constraints, and turns on the enforcement of these constraints for future updates to the table. Since no exception table is specified, the table remains in Check Pending state if any rows are found that violate a constraint.

  ```
  SET CONSTRAINTS FOR shop.tools IMMEDIATE CHECKED;
  ```

- This example checks all the check constraints and foreign key constraints for the tables named SHOP.TOOLS and SHOP.PROJECTS and moves all the rows that are found to violate constraints out of these tables and into their respective exception tables. The SHOP.TOOLS and SHOP.PROJECTS tables are removed from Check Pending state and made available for normal processing, and enforcement of their constraints is resumed for future updates.

  ```
  SET CONSTRAINTS FOR shop.tools, shop.projects
     IMMEDIATE CHECKED
     FOR EXCEPTION IN shop.tools USE shop.badtools,
                  IN shop.projects USE shop.badprojects;
  ```

- This example places the table named SHOP.TOOLS into Check Pending state:

  `SET CONSTRAINTS FOR shop.tools OFF;`

TIP: You might choose to place a table into Check Pending state just before you execute an ALTER TABLE statement to add a new constraint to the table. If an ALTER TABLE statement is used to add a new constraint to a table that is in normal state and contains some rows that violate the new constraint, the ALTER TABLE statement will fail. But if such a table is put into Check Pending state, the ALTER TABLE statement will succeed. A SET CONSTRAINTS statement can then be used to turn on constraint checking, check the new constraint, and move any rows that violate the new constraint into an exception table.

- The SET CONSTRAINTS statement allows you to force a table to be taken out of Check Pending state without having its constraints checked. This is a dangerous thing to do, and presumably you will do it only if you have some independent means of ensuring that the table contains no data that violates constraints. (For example, you might have a program that examines a load file and checks it for violations before the table is loaded.) The command in the following example takes the SHOP.PROJECTS table out of Check Pending state without checking its constraints. After executing this command, the table will be available for normal access and its constraints will be enforced for future updates; however, the system cannot guarantee that all the rows of the table satisfy the existing constraints.

  `SET CONSTRAINTS FOR shop.projects ALL IMMEDIATE UNCHECKED;`

- When you force a table to be taken out of Check Pending state without checking its constraints, you are effectively assuming responsibility for whether its constraints are satisfied. For each table, the system records where the responsibility lies for guaranteeing that all constraints are satisfied. This information is recorded separately for foreign key constraints and for check constraints, in the CONST_CHECKED column of the TABLES catalog table. The first character of this column applies to foreign key constraints, and the second character applies to check constraints. The following encoding is used:

  "Y" means that constraints are enforced and guaranteed by the system.

  "N" means that the table is in Check Pending state and that constraints are not being checked.

  "U" means that the user has taken the table out of Check Pending state by a SET CONSTRAINTS statement with the UNCHECKED option. In this case, the system enforces constraints for new updates to the table, but the ultimate responsibility for ensuring that no rows of the table violate any constraints lies with the user. The table will remain in this state until it is put back into the Check Pending state.

The following query displays the Check Pending status of all the tables in the SHOP schema, including information about whether responsibility for guaranteeing constraints lies with the system or with the user:

```
SELECT tabname, status,
       substr(const_checked, 1, 1) AS fk_checked,
       substr(const_checked, 2, 1) AS cc_checked
FROM syscat.tables
WHERE tabschema = 'SHOP';
```

10.7.6 Loading a Partitioned Database

Loading data into a partitioned database presents some special challenges, because the data must first be split into several subsets based on the value of a partitioning key, and then each subset must be loaded into its respective partition. UDB provides two utility programs, called the *Splitter* and the *Autoloader*, to aid in this process.

Splitter

The Splitter is provided in the form of a program named db2split, found in sqllib/bin, that runs on all UDB platforms. Its job is to scan an input file containing data for a table, analyze the data according to a specified partitioning key, and prepare the data for loading into a nodegroup in a partitioned database. The input file can be in DEL or ASC format (described earlier), BIN format (containing binary numeric data), or PACK format (containing packed decimal data). Details of the input formats can be found in the *Administration Guide*.

The Splitter is controlled by a configuration file that specifies the names of the input and output data files, the partitioning key, the node numbers of the partitions in the nodegroup, and various other control parameters. The configuration file specifies one of the two following modes:

1. ANALYZE mode: In this mode, the Splitter scans the input file, analyzes its data distribution in the partitioning key columns, and generates an optimal partitioning map that can later be used to distribute the data uniformly among the partitions in the nodegroup. Before loading the data, you can install the generated partitioning map in the nodegroup to be loaded by means of a REDISTRIBUTE NODEGROUP command. (This step is optional, and you should note that a partitioning map that is optimal for one table may not be optimal for other tables in the same nodegroup.)

2. PARTITION mode: In this mode, the Splitter scans the input file and splits it into several load files, each containing data ready to be loaded into one of the

partitions of a nodegroup. The data is split by hashing the partitioning key of each row into one of 4,096 hash buckets, and then mapping the hash buckets into partitions using a partitioning map. The partitioning map is specified in the configuration file and might come from any of the following sources:

- It might have been generated by a previous run of the Splitter in ANALYZE mode.
- It might be a default partitioning map that distributes the hash buckets uniformly among the partitions.
- It might be the partitioning map that is currently in use in the nodegroup where the data will be loaded. This partitioning map can be retrieved from the system catalog tables named NODEGROUPS and PARTITIONMAPS, or by using a utility program named db2gpmap.
- It might have been constructed manually. A partitioning map is simply an array of 4,096 two-byte integers that indicate the node numbers associated with the 4,096 hash buckets.

The load files generated by the Splitter have name suffixes that identify the partitions where the data is to be loaded. When splitting data for a four-partition nodegroup, for example, the Splitter might generate files named LOADDATA.000, LOADDATA.001, LOADDATA.002, and LOADDATA.003. Each load file contains a header that records the partitioning map that was used to generate it. When loading the data from these files, the LOAD utility generates an error message if the current partitioning map of the nodegroup that is being loaded is not the same as the partitioning map by which the load files were generated.

A sample Splitter configuration file named db2split.cfg can be found in the sqllib/samples/splitter directory. Before using this sample, you will need to edit it, following the comments provided in the file, to customize it for your input and output. The following is an example of a command that invokes the Splitter under the control of the sample configuration file:

```
db2split -c db2split.cfg
```

Autoloader

The Autoloader is provided in the form of a program named db2autold, found in sqllib/misc, that runs only on **UDB** Enterprise-Extended Edition. It provides an easy-to-use interface with the same functionality as the Splitter and with some additional features as well. It can transfer its input data from a remote system via FTP, and after splitting the data it can actually load it into a designated nodegroup.

Like the Splitter, the Autoloader is controlled by a configuration file that specifies the input, the output, and the mode of operation. The Autoloader can be invoked in the following modes:

1. ANALYZE mode: This mode is similar to the ANALYZE mode of the Splitter. It scans an input data set and generates an optimal partitioning map for distributing the data among the partitions in a nodegroup.

2. SPLIT_ONLY mode: This mode is similar to the PARTITION mode of the Splitter. Using a given partitioning map, it splits an input data set into multiple load files ready for loading into the partitions of a nodegroup.

3. LOAD_ONLY mode: This mode actually loads the files generated by SPLIT_ONLY mode into the partitions of a nodegroup by invoking the Load utility on each of the partitions, using a LOAD command that is specified in the configuration file.

4. SPLIT_AND_LOAD mode: This mode combines the functionality of the SPLIT_ONLY and LOAD_ONLY modes. In this mode, the splitter output is piped directly to the Load utilities running on the various machines in the nodegroup. As a result, the split data does not need to be stored in intermediate files, and the total time for splitting and loading is minimized.

A sample Autoloader configuration file named `autoloader.cfg` can be found in the `sqllib/samples/autoloader` directory. Before using this sample, you will need to edit it, following the comments provided in the file, to customize it for your input and output. The following is an example of a command that invokes the Autoloader under the control of the sample configuration file:

```
db2autold -c autoloader.cfg
```

10.8 TUNING FOR PERFORMANCE

Since SQL is a nonprocedural language, a given SQL statement can often be executed in many different ways. For example, suppose that an SQL query joins two tables named SUPPLIERS and PARTS by matching values in their PARTNO columns. This query might be executed by scanning the SUPPLIERS table and for each row finding the matching rows in PARTS; or by scanning the PARTS table and for each row finding the matching rows in SUPPLIERS; or by sorting both tables into PARTNO order, then computing the join by merging the ordered tables. Each possible algorithm for execution of an SQL statement is called an *access plan*. The choice of an access plan is very important, because the execution time of an SQL statement can vary by several orders of magnitude, depending on which access plan is selected.

UDB contains an optimizer that automatically chooses an efficient access plan for each SQL statement. The optimizer is said to be *cost-based,* because it works by generating a list of access plans, comparing their costs based on built-in cost formulas, and selecting the plan with the least cost. The access plan that is most efficient for a given SQL statement depends on the tables that are accessed by the statement, the indexes that are maintained on these tables, and the statistical properties of the data in the tables. For example, if an SQL query contains a predicate on a column that has an index, and statistics show that this column has many distinct values, it probably makes sense to apply this predicate early in the access plan.

The UDB optimizer includes the following advanced features:

1. It applies *query rewrite algorithms* that can often change a query into a more efficient form. For example, subqueries are often transformed into joins that can be executed more efficiently. Predicates can sometimes be moved to new places in a query where they restrict the size of the result set more quickly, and additional predicates can sometimes be deduced from the predicates provided by the user.

2. It applies *merging algorithms* that can merge an SQL statement together with the view definitions, constraints, and triggers that are referenced or invoked by the statement. The result of this merging process is a single SQL statement that can be analyzed to find the global optimum access plan, rather than optimizing each view, constraint, and trigger separately.

3. Its cost formulas take into account a large collection of statistical information about the database, including distributions of data values within individual columns of tables. The optimizer also considers the physical characteristics of your machine and its storage media. Thus, the access plan selected for a given query might depend on whether your machine is limited by its CPU resources or by its I/O resources.

4. It can use either of two methods for determining the order in which several tables will be joined: *dynamic programming*, which is guaranteed to find the optimal join order, or *greedy join enumeration*, which devotes less time and memory space to the optimization process. Users are given control over the choice of join enumeration methods and other aspects of the optimizer performance.

In order to realize the full benefit of the UDB optimizer, users and database administrators have certain responsibilities. Since the optimizer's cost formulas depend on statistical information about the database, it is important that this statistical information be complete and accurate. The physical organization of data in storage also has an important effect on query-processing efficiency. For example, all the employees in a given department can be retrieved more efficiently if the employee table is organized in such a way that employees in the same department are clustered on a small set of physical pages. This section discusses the tools provided by UDB that allow users to control the optimization process, collect and maintain statistical information, and control the physical organization of data in tables.

10.8.1 Controlling the Optimizer

The UDB optimizer allows the user to control the trade-off between quality of access plan and resources devoted to the optimization process by selecting one of the following *optimization classes*:

Class 0: Minimum optimization.

Class 1: Optimization techniques roughly comparable to those of DB2 Version 1 for AIX and OS/2. Nonuniform distributions of data values in columns are not taken into consideration.

Class 2: Considers nonuniform value distributions in columns, but uses a relatively simple algorithm for planning joins, called "greedy join enumeration."

Class 3: Optimization techniques roughly comparable to those used by DB2 for OS/390. This is the lowest optimization class in which dynamic programming algorithms are used for planning joins.

Class 5: The default optimization class, using most of the techniques of the UDB optimizer. This class includes the optimization techniques that are felt to be most cost-effective for a typical mix of simple and complex SQL statements and employs heuristic rules to limit the amount of time spent on optimizing dynamic SQL statements.

Class 7: Similar to Class 5, but without the heuristic limits on optimization time for dynamic SQL statements.

Class 9: Full use of all the techniques of the UDB optimizer to produce the best possible access plan without regard to the resources used in the optimization process.

In general, higher optimization classes cause more time and memory to be used during optimization, potentially resulting in better performance when the SQL statement is executed. For example, dynamic programming is used only at Class 3 and above, and the full set of query rewrite rules is used only at Class 5 and above. Class 0 is recommended only for very simple statements operating on small tables in a dynamic query environment in which it is desired to keep optimization costs to a minimum. Class 9, on the other hand, is recommended only for use on specific "problem queries" that take a very long time to execute. Class 9 should be used in conjunction with Visual Explain (discussed in Section 10.8.4), which enables you to examine the details of the access plan selected by the optimizer. For most applications, Class 5 provides a good compromise between optimization cost and query performance.

If the optimizer finds that your system does not have enough memory to complete the optimization of a given SQL statement at a given optimization class, it will automatically fall back to a lower optimization class.

For static SQL statements used in an application program, the optimization class is controlled by the QUERYOPT parameter that was specified on the PREP or BIND command by which the program was bound. The following examples illustrate use of the QUERYOPT parameter on PREP and BIND commands:

```
PREP prog1.sqc QUERYOPT 1;
BIND prog1.bnd QUERYOPT 3;
```

For dynamic SQL statements, the optimization class is controlled by the content of a special register named CURRENT QUERY OPTIMIZATION. The following example illustrates the use of an SQL statement to set the value of the special register:

```
SET CURRENT QUERY OPTIMIZATION = 3;
```

The default value of the CURRENT QUERY OPTIMIZATION register, and the default optimization class for static SQL statements when no QUERYOPT parameter is specified, are controlled by a database configuration parameter named DFT_QUERYOPT, which in turn has a default value of 5.

10.8.2 Statistics

One of the areas in which UDB optimization technology is particularly advanced is in the completeness of its statistical information. Listed below are the catalog tables that contain statistical information used by the UDB optimizer. (For more information about catalog tables, see Appendix D.)

1. TABLES: This catalog table contains information about each table in the database, including the number of rows in the table, the number of physical pages occupied by the table, and the number of overflow records associated with the table. An overflow record is created when one of the rows of the table is updated in such a way that it no longer fits on its original page.

2. COLUMNS: This catalog table contains information about the data values stored in columns of tables. For each column on which information is gathered, COLUMNS records the number of different data values in the column, the second highest and second lowest values, and the average length of data values in the column. The second highest and second lowest values are recorded rather than the highest and lowest values, because the latter values are likely to be "outlying" values that do not reflect the distribution of values in the column.

Using the information in COLUMNS, the optimizer can make a crude estimate of the selectivity of a predicate on a given column. Better estimates can be made if more detailed information is gathered on the distribution of values in the column—and this is the purpose of the COLDIST catalog table.

3. COLDIST: This catalog table contains information about the distribution of data values in individual columns. This information is of two basic kinds: *frequent values* and *quantiles*.

For each column on which frequent-value information is gathered, COLDIST records the values that occur most frequently in the column and the number of times each of these values occurs. The number of frequent values recorded for each column is controlled by the NUM_FREQVALUES database configuration parameter, which defaults to 10.

For each column on which quantile information is gathered, COLDIST records a series of values that represent the distribution of data values in the column. For example, if five quantile values are collected, they represent the data values that equal or exceed 20%, 40%, 60%, 80%, and 100% of the data values in the column. The number of quantile values collected for each column is controlled by the NUM_QUANTILES database configuration parameter, which defaults to 20.

Column-distribution information is particularly important for those columns in which the data values are *skewed*, or nonuniformly distributed. For example, consider a company in which the lowest salary is $10,000 and the highest salary is $90,000. In the absence of column-distribution statistics, the optimizer assumes that salaries are distributed uniformly between these two extremes. But it may happen that most salaries in the company are concentrated in the range between $30,000 and $50,000. In that case, the predicate SALARY BETWEEN 70000 AND 80000 is much more selective than the predicate SALARY BETWEEN 30000 AND 40000. The selectivity of a predicate is very important to the optimizer, because it is an estimate of how useful the predicate is in narrowing the search space of a query. Column-distribution information enables the optimizer to make more accurate estimates of the selectivity of predicates on columns with skewed data distributions.

4. INDEXES: This catalog table contains information about each index in the database. An index is a treelike data structure associated with a specific set of columns in a specific table, called the *key columns* of the index. An index defined on multiple key columns can be used as if it were an index on any leading subset of its key columns—for example, an index defined on the COLOR, WEIGHT, and COST columns of the PARTS table can be used to find parts with a given color, a given color and weight, or a given color, weight, and cost.

Indexes are important to the UDB optimizer, because they provide two very useful properties: the *associative retrieval property* and the *ordering property*. The associative retrieval property means that an index can be used to quickly find rows that have a given key value. This property is useful for evaluating predicates on the key columns. The ordering property means that the index can be used to retrieve all the rows of a table in order of their key values. This property is useful for implementing ORDER BY and GROUP BY clauses and for certain kinds of join algorithms. An *index scan*, which retrieves all the rows of a table in order of the key values of a certain index, is one of the basic access methods used by the UDB optimizer.

The INDEXES catalog table can be used to record statistical information about an index in two levels of detail. The *basic index statistics* include the number of different values of the index key, considering both the full key and initial subsets of the key columns; the number of physical pages occupied by the index (used in estimating the cost of an index scan); and a measure of how well the index is *clustered*. The clustering measure indicates how well the actual rows of the table are clustered on physical pages according to the key values of the index and is used to predict the number of data pages that would be fetched during an index scan of a given table. The *detailed index statistics* provide a finer estimate of the number of page fetches required for an index scan, as a function of the size of the buffer in which pages are held during the scan.

5. FUNCTIONS: This catalog table contains information about the cost of executing a user-defined function. Both the CPU cost and the I/O cost of the function can be recorded. Since the system has no way to measure or estimate

these costs, they can only be supplied by a user who records them directly in the catalog table. If no information is available about the cost of executing a function, the system assumes a default cost.

6. TABLESPACES: This catalog table contains information about the performance of the physical storage media used in the database. Each tablespace may be stored on a device with different characteristics. For each tablespace, TABLESPACES records the time required to begin an I/O operation and the rate at which the device is capable of transferring data into main memory. These performance parameters are recorded at the time the tablespace is created (by a CREATE TABLESPACE statement) and can later be modified by an ALTER TABLESPACE statement.

Since the optimizer bases its choice of an access plan on the statistical information in the system catalog tables, it is very important that this information be current and accurate. On request, UDB will gather the latest statistics for a given table and its indexes and store them in the catalog tables described above. Statistics should be updated for a table whenever the table is loaded or reorganized; after a significant number of its rows have been inserted, updated, or deleted; or after a new column or index has been added to the table.

The easiest way to update the statistics for a table is by selecting the table on the Control Center display and invoking the *Run Statistics* action. In order to update the statistics for a table, you must hold SYSADM, SYSCTRL, SYS-MAINT, or DBADM authority, or the CONTROL privilege on the table. When you invoke *Run Statistics* for a table, you will be prompted for whether you wish the system to gather column distribution statistics and statistics for the table's indexes.

 TIP: After updating the statistics for a table and its indexes, you may wish to rebind your application programs that operate on the table to make sure that they are using the best access plan in light of the new statistics.

Manually Updating Statistics

Occasionally, you may wish to manually update the statistical information in the catalog tables with some values of your own choosing. For example, you may be investigating what access plans would be selected under various hypothetical circumstances.

In order to discuss how to modify statistics in the catalog tables, we must first discuss in greater depth the structure of the catalog tables themselves. The system maintains a set of base catalog tables in the SYSIBM schema. However, users ordinarily access catalog tables by means of *catalog views*. The following two sets of catalog views have been defined:

1. In the SYSCAT schema, a read-only view is provided for each catalog table. Users are advised to use the SYSCAT views rather than the underlying base catalog tables, because the SYSCAT views provide more consistent names. Throughout this book, when we use the term *catalog table* somewhat loosely, we are really referring to the catalog views in the SYSCAT schema.

2. In the SYSSTAT schema, updatable views are provided for certain catalog tables, namely, TABLES, COLUMNS, COLDIST, INDEXES, and FUNCTIONS. Each catalog view in SYSSTAT contains only the primary key columns and the statistical columns that users are allowed to update. Furthermore, the SYSSTAT views are defined in such a way that each user can see only those entries that they are authorized to update. You may update the statistical information for a table or index if you hold CONTROL privilege for that table or index or if you hold DBADM authority for the database. You may update the statistical information for a user-defined function if your userid matches the schema name of the function or if you hold DBADM authority.

The two sets of system catalog views are described in detail in Appendix D and illustrated in Figure D-1. To update statistical information in the system catalog tables, you can apply SQL UPDATE statements to the SYSSTAT catalog views. Any updates applied to these views immediately affect the base catalog tables and the SYSCAT views. Of course, changes to statistical information will not affect the access plan chosen for an application program until that program is rebound.

The SYSSTAT catalog views behave just like any updatable table, subject to the following special rules:

- You can modify catalog data only by means of UPDATE statements, not INSERT or DELETE statements.

- For most statistical columns, setting the column to the value –1 indicates that no statistical information is available. In this case, the optimizer will use a default value for the missing statistic.

- If the values that you use to update the catalog statistics are not reasonable, your update will be rejected. For example, you can update the cardinality of a table only to a positive number or to –1, which indicates that no statistics are available. If you attempt to set the cardinality of a table to –25 in SYSSTAT.TABLES, you will receive a message indicating that this value is inconsistent with the definition of the view.

The following examples illustrate manual updating of statistical information in the SYSTATS catalog views:

- This example modifies the statistics for the table named COMPANY.PARTS to make it appear that the table has 10,000 rows and occupies 250 pages of physical space.

```
UPDATE sysstat.tables
SET card = 10000, npages = 250, fpages = 250
WHERE tabschema = 'COMPANY' AND tabname = 'PARTS';
```

- This example modifies the statistics for the column named QONORDER in the COMPANY.PARTS table, asserting that this column contains 50 distinct values, with the second lowest value being 0 and the second highest value being 500.

```
UPDATE sysstat.columns
SET colcard = 50, low2key = '0', high2key = '500'
WHERE tabschema = 'COMPANY'
AND tabname = 'PARTS'
AND colname = 'QONORDER';
```

TIP: Some of the columns in the SYSSTAT catalog views, such as LOW2KEY and HIGH2KEY, contain values that are copied from columns of real database tables. For example, LOW2KEY and HIGH2KEY record the second lowest and second highest values for each column of data. Since the columns whose values are being recorded may be of any datatype, the LOW2KEY and HIGH2KEY columns contain a character-string representation of the values. A numeric value is represented by a character string containing the literal that would be used to represent that value in an SQL statement, such as '-29' or '3.25E-8'. When updating columns in the SYSSTAT views that represent column values, you must remember to represent each value in character-string form regardless of its datatype.

- This example modifies the statistics for the index named IPARTS1, asserting that the number of distinct key values in the index is 300.

```
UPDATE sysstat.indexes
SET firstkeycard = 300, fullkeycard = 300
WHERE indschema = 'COMPANY'
AND indname = 'IPARTS1';
```

TIP: When updating the key cardinality of a multicolumn index in SYSSTAT.INDEXES, remember to specify the cardinalities of all the initial subsets of the key columns. FIRSTKEYCARD counts the number of distinct values in the first key column only. FIRST2KEYCARD, FIRST3KEYCARD, and FIRST4KEYCARD count the number of distinct values in the first two, first three, and first four key columns. FULLKEYCARD counts the number of distinct values in the full key, including all its columns.

- This example modifies the statistics for a user-defined function in SYSSTAT.FUNCTIONS, asserting that the cost of executing the function is 50,000 machine instructions per invocation. Note that since the system does not automatically gather statistical information on functions, the only way to provide information about the cost of a function is by directly updating SYSSTAT.FUNCTIONS.

```
UPDATE sysstat.functions
SET insts_per_invoc = 5E4
WHERE funcschema = 'COMPANY'
AND specificname = 'PAYMENT001';
```

TIP: It is wise to identify a function by its specific name, which is always unique within a schema, rather than by its function name, which may not be unique.

Dumping Statistics: db2look

A tool named db2look is provided in the sqllib/misc directory for collecting statistical information from catalog tables and saving it in readable form in a file. In addition to statistical information, db2look can capture the SQL data definition statements needed to reproduce the tables and indexes in a given database. In this way, it is possible to create a "clone" of an existing database, including its statistics, for experimental purposes. For example, the following command creates a file named test.stats containing the data definition statements needed to recreate all the tables and indexes in the database testdb, and the SQL UPDATE statements needed to update the statistical catalog tables to duplicate the statistics of the original database:

```
db2look -d testdb -a -m -e -o test.stats
```

For more information about db2look, you can invoke its help text by typing the following on your operating system command line:

```
db2look -h
```

10.8.3 Reorganizing Tables

The units of physical storage that are transferred from disk to main memory during processing of an SQL statement are called *pages*. Each page consists of 4K bytes of data. All the rows of data in the database are assigned to physical pages, usually many rows to a page. The ideal organization for a database table is for its rows to be laid out on pages, ordered by their key values in some frequently used index. An index whose key corresponds to the physical ordering of rows in storage is said to have the *clustering property*. This is an important property to the optimizer, because a clustering index provides a way to scan over all the rows of a table while fetching the minimum number of pages from disk. When scanning by a clustering index, each page fetched will carry with it many rows with key values in the desired sequence.

Ideally, the rows of a table will nearly fill the pages on which they are stored, leaving a small amount of free space on each page for expansion. If there is too much free space on each page, the number of page fetches required to scan the table will be unnecessarily large. On the other hand, if there is not enough free space on each page, a row that is updated to have a longer value in some column may no longer fit on the page. When that happens, the row is moved to a new page and its position on the original page is filled by an *overflow record* that points to the new location of the row.

When a table is newly loaded, its physical organization can be nearly ideal, provided that the rows are loaded in the order defined by their key values in a clustering index. However, over a period of time, modifications to a table tend to cause its organization to depart from the ideal. If many rows are inserted into the table, they will degrade the clustering property of its clustering index. If many rows are deleted, there may be too much free space on the pages where rows are stored. If many rows are updated, the clustering property will be degraded, and some of the rows may be replaced by overflow records. The net result of all these changes is that the number of page fetches required to scan the table is increased.

The easiest way to restore a table to its optimal physical organization is by selecting the table on the Control Center display and invoking the *Reorganize* action. You will be prompted for the name of the index, if any, that you wish to have the clustering property for the table. After a table has been reorganized, its rows are packed on pages with the proper amount of free space, overflow records are eliminated, and if you specified a clustering index, the rows of the table are ordered in physical storage according to the key order of the clustering index. In order to reorganize a table, you must hold SYSADM, SYSCTRL, SYSMAINT, or DBADM authority or the CONTROL privilege on the table to be reorganized.

 TIP: After reorganizing a table, you should use the RUNSTATS command to collect a new set of statistics on the table and its indexes; then you should rebind any application programs that operate on the table to take advantage of its new organization.

REORGCHK

UDB provides a command called REORGCHK to help you decide when a table or set of tables needs to be reorganized. REORGCHK can generate a report on the organization status of a particular table, or all the tables owned by a given user, or all the tables in a database. In order to use REORGCHK, you must hold SYSADM or DBADM authority or CONTROL privilege on the tables to be checked.

A side effect of the REORGCHK command is to update the statistical information in the system catalog tables for each table that is checked (unless you specify by the phrase CURRENT STATISTICS that you want to continue using the current set of statistics).

The following examples illustrate use of the REORGCHK command:

- This example generates a report on the physical organization of the table named COMPANY.PARTS:

   REORGCHK ON TABLE company.parts;

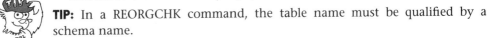

TIP: In a REORGCHK command, the table name must be qualified by a schema name.

- If you invoke REORGCHK without any operands, it generates a report on the physical organization of all the tables that you are permitted to reorganize. Example:

   REORGCHK;

For each table analyzed by REORGCHK, the generated report contains a line describing the table and a line describing each of its indexes.

For each table, three formulas are computed: F1, F2, and F3. Each of these formulas has a specified range of values for a table that is properly organized. F1 measures the number of overflow records in the table, F2 measures the amount of free space on the pages where the table is stored, and F3 measures the number of empty pages that would be fetched in a scan of the table. For each table, REORGCHK provides a three-character summary of the results of computing formulas F1, F2, and F3. For each formula, a hyphen indicates that the value is in the desired range, and an asterisk indicates that the value is outside the desired range. For example, a summary of "-**" for a given table would indicate that formula F1 is in the desired range but formulas F2 and F3 are not. A table with one or more asterisks in its summary report is a candidate to be reorganized.

For each index in the REORGCHK report, three formulas are also computed: F4, F5, and F6. F4 measures the clustering property of the index, F5 measures the amount of free space on index pages, and F6 measures whether the index has the appropriate number of levels. As in the case of tables, each index receives a three-character summary in the report, indicating by hyphens and asterisks which of the three formulas are within the desired range. For example, a summary of "*-*" for a given index would indicate that the index lacks the clustering property (measured by F4) and that formula F5 is in the desired range but formula F6 is not. If many indexes defined on a given table have asterisks in their summary reports, that table may be a candidate for reorganization. Remember, however, that in general only one index for a given table can have the clustering property.

Figure 10-14 shows the report generated by running REORGCHK on the sample database created by the db2sampl command. The only indication in this report that reorganization might be needed is an asterisk corresponding to the F2 formula for the EMP_ACT table.

Table statistics:

F1: 100*OVERFLOW/CARD < 5
F2: 100*TSIZE / ((FPAGES-1) * 4020) > 70
F3: 100*NPAGES/FPAGES > 80

CREATOR	NAME	CARD	OV	NP	FP	TSIZE	F1	F2	F3	REORG
CHAMBERL	DEPARTMENT	9	0	1	1	630	0	-	100	---
CHAMBERL	EMP_ACT	75	0	2	2	2700	0	67	100	-*-
CHAMBERL	EMP_PHOTO	12	0	1	1	84	0	-	100	---
CHAMBERL	EMP_RESUME	8	0	1	1	56	0	-	100	---
CHAMBERL	EMPLOYEE	32	0	2	2	2944	0	73	100	---
CHAMBERL	ORG	8	0	1	1	424	0	-	100	---
CHAMBERL	PROJECT	20	0	1	1	1380	0	-	100	---
CHAMBERL	STAFF	35	0	1	1	1505	0	-	100	---

Index statistics:

F4: CLUSTERRATIO or normalized CLUSTERFACTOR > 80
F5: 100*(KEYS*(ISIZE+10)+(CARD-KEYS)*4) / (NLEAF*4096) > 50
F6: 90*(4000/(ISIZE+10)**(NLEVELS-2))*4096/ (KEYS*(ISIZE+10)+(CARD-KEYS)*4)<100

CREATOR	NAME	CARD	LEAF	LVLS	ISIZE	KEYS	F4	F5	F6	REORG
Table: CHAMBERL.EMP_PHOTO										
SYSIBM	SQL970625163000290	12	1	1	20	12	100	-	-	---
Table: CHAMBERL.EMP_RESUME										
SYSIBM	SQL970625163008800	8	1	1	20	8	100	-	-	---

Figure 10-14: Example of a Report Generated by the REORGCHK Command

10.8.4 Explaining a Plan

Whenever a static SQL statement is bound or a dynamic SQL statement is prepared for execution, the UDB optimizer analyzes the statement and creates a plan for executing the statement. This plan may involve scanning one or more tables in the database, accessing a table through an index, or joining data from two tables using an algorithm such as a merge join or a nested loop join. In general, the plan for executing a statement can be represented in the form of a graph that shows how data flows from a source (one or more tables or indexes) to a destination (the result set of the SQL statement).

UDB provides a powerful facility called *Explain* that allows you to examine the plans that are created by the optimizer for executing your SQL statements. When you turn on the Explain facility, detailed information about access plans is captured and stored in a set of database tables called the *Explain tables*. You can then examine the Explain tables directly using SQL, or you can display the plans in graphical form using a feature of the Control Center called *Visual Explain*. By using Explain to examine access plans, you can gain insight into the performance of your SQL statements, and you can learn which indexes are actually being used by the system. This information can be valuable in tuning the performance of your system by dropping unnecessary indexes and creating new indexes to support frequently executed statements.

The Explain facility applies only to those types of SQL statements that have optimized plans: SELECT, INSERT, DELETE, UPDATE, and VALUES. Other SQL statements, such as CREATE and DROP, are executed in straightforward ways and do not require the services of the optimizer.

Before you can use Explain, you need to create the Explain tables that are used to capture the details of access plans. You can do this by connecting to the desired database and executing the CREATE TABLE statements in the file `sqllib/misc/EXPLAIN.DDL`. For example, you might create the Explain tables in a database named TESTDB by executing the following commands from the directory `sqllib/misc`:

```
db2 connect to testdb
db2 -tf EXPLAIN.DDL
```

By default, the schema name of the Explain tables is the same as your userid. (Thus, each user of the system gets a separate set of Explain tables.) For each statement optimized while the Explain facility is turned on, the Explain tables contain information about when and how the statement was optimized, the text of the statement, and the access plan selected by the optimizer. This information is stored in tables with the following names and contents (for a more detailed description of the Explain tables, see Appendix J of the *SQL Reference*):

EXPLAIN_INSTANCE: Each row represents a package in which one or more statements have been explained.

EXPLAIN_STATEMENT: Each row represents an SQL statement that has been explained. In this table, you can see the original text of the SQL statement and how this text was modified by merging constraints, triggers, and view definitions into the SQL statement. The columns of this table, which identify the package, statement number, and time of optimization, can be used as keys to access the other Explain tables to retrieve detailed information about the access plan for a given statement.

EXPLAIN_OBJECT: Each row represents one of the sources of data used by a plan, such as a permanent or temporary table or an index.

EXPLAIN_OPERATOR: Each row represents an operation, such as "Union" or "Merge Join," that was selected by the optimizer as part of a plan. In general, each operator has one or more input data flows and an output data flow.

EXPLAIN_ARGUMENT: The rows of this table contain detailed information about the individual operators in a plan, such as the columns to be used for sorting, and whether duplicate values are to be eliminated.

EXPLAIN_STREAM: Each row represents a flow of data between one operator and another or between an object and an operator.

EXPLAIN_PREDICATE: The rows in this table indicate how the predicates of the SQL statement are implemented by the operators in the plan.

TIP: The easiest way for several users to share a common set of Explain tables is for each user to create a set of aliases. For example, each user could create an alias named EXPLAIN_STATEMENT that resolves to the table SHARED.EXPLAIN_STATEMENT. Of course, each participating user must have INSERT and SELECT privileges on the shared Explain tables.

As noted above, there are two ways in which you can use the Explain facility to collect and display information about plans:

1. You can use the Explain facility to collect detailed plan information in the Explain tables, which you can then examine using SQL queries. This method is called *Tabular Explain*. Since Tabular Explain allows you to use the power of SQL to examine collections of plans, it is a good method to use when you need global information, such as finding all the plans that use a particular index.

2. You can use the Explain facility to collect plan information in a form called a *Visual Explain Snapshot*, which is stored in a Blob column in the EXPLAIN_ STATEMENT table. The snapshot information is in an internal format that can be displayed in graphical form by the Control Center. This method is the easiest way to visualize and understand the details of an individual plan.

UDB provides you with independent control over Tabular Explain and Visual Explain so that you can choose to capture either or both of these kinds of plan information. The controls are provided in the form of bind options named EXPLAIN and EXPLSNAP, and special registers named CURRENT EXPLAIN MODE and CURRENT EXPLAIN SNAPSHOT. The bind options, which can be used on PREP and BIND commands, control the capturing of Explain information during the binding of an application program. The special registers control the capturing of Explain information during processing of dynamic SQL statements. The possible values for the Explain-related bind options and special registers are shown in Table 10-4.

TABLE 10-4: Options for Controlling the Explain Facility

	Tabular Explain	Visual Explain
PREP and BIND options	EXPLAIN option. Values: NO: Do not capture Tabular Explain data for SQL statements in this program (this is the default). YES: Capture Tabular Explain data for static SQL statements in this program. ALL: Capture Tabular Explain data for both static and dynamic SQL statements in this program, regardless of the value of CURRENT EXPLAIN MODE.	EXPLSNAP option. Values: NO: Do not capture snapshot data for SQL statements in this program (this is the default). YES: Capture snapshot data for static SQL statements in this program. ALL: Capture snapshot data for both static and dynamic SQL statements in this program, regardless of the value of CURRENT EXPLAIN SNAPSHOT.
Special register	CURRENT EXPLAIN MODE. Values: NO: Do not capture Tabular Explain data for dynamic SQL statements (this is the default). YES: Capture Tabular Explain data for dynamic SQL statements and execute them. EXPLAIN: Capture Tabular Explain data for dynamic SQL statements but do not execute them.	CURRENT EXPLAIN SNAPSHOT. Values: NO: Do not capture snapshot data for dynamic SQL statements (this is the default). YES: Capture snapshot data for dynamic SQL statements and execute them. EXPLAIN: Capture snapshot data for dynamic SQL statements but do not execute them.

TIP: Don't forget to set the value of the Explain-related special registers back to NO after collecting the Explain information you need. Otherwise, the system will keep on collecting Explain information about all the dynamic SQL statements you execute, and this information will occupy a significant amount of space in your database.

As described in Chapter 3, the easiest way to see the access plan for an individual SQL statement is by using the Command Center. You can simply type the desired SQL statement in the Script panel of the Command Center and invoke the *Create Access Plan* menu item to see a Visual Explain graph that describes the access plan for the statement, as shown in Figure 3-3.

The easiest way to see the access plans that were selected by the optimizer for one of your application programs is by using the Control Center. Select the package for your program on the Control Center display and invoke the *Show*

Explainable Statements - PARTS1

Statement   Edit   View   Help

DON1 - DB2 - TESTDB - DB2OWNER.PARTS1

Statement ...	Section ...	Explain snapshot	Total cost	SQL text
39	1	Yes	25.18	SELECT partno, description, qon...
87	2	Yes	25.04	UPDATE parts SET qo...
99	3	Yes	25.29	SELECT min(price) into :H00008 ...
114	4	Yes	25.30	SELECT min(suppno) into :H0001...
124	5	Yes	25.03	INSERT INTO orders ...
128	6	Yes	25.04	UPDATE parts SET q...
161	7	Yes	50.50	SELECT p.partno, min(q.price) ...

Figure 10-15: List of Explainable Statements in a Package

Explainable Statements action. If your program was bound with the EXPLAIN or EXPLSNAP option turned on, you will see a list of the SQL statements in the program, as shown in Figure 10-15. You can then double-click on one of the statements (or select the statement and invoke *Show Access Plan* on the Statement menu) to see the Visual Explain graph for the statement, as shown in Figure 10-16.

10.9 MONITORING THE DATABASE

UDB provides a powerful tool called the *Database System Monitor* for use by system and database administrators. Using this tool, an administrator can acquire comprehensive information about the state of the database system and can collect information about events that occur over a period of time. This information can be useful for tuning performance and diagnosing problems. We have space here for only an overview of the Database System Monitor features; a more complete description of the monitor can be found in the *System Monitor Guide and Reference*.

The Database System Monitor really consists of two separate types of monitors with different but related purposes: a *snapshot monitor* and a set of *event monitors*. There is only one snapshot monitor, and you can easily turn it on to keep a record of various measurable quantities in the

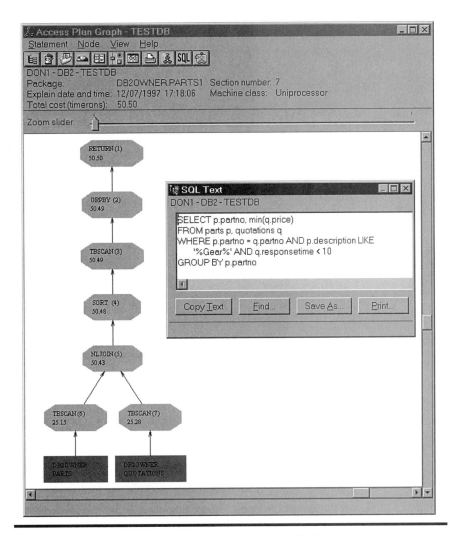

Figure 10-16: Visual Explain for a Statement in a Package

database system and how they change as a function of time. Event monitors, on the other hand, can be created by a database administrator to keep records on specific kinds of events that may occur, such as deadlocks. Each event monitor keeps records on a different set of events, and the event monitors can be independently started and stopped. Both types of monitor can be controlled using commands or application program interfaces, but the easiest way to control them is by means of the graphical user interface of the Control Center, as described in the following sections.

As a database administrator, you should be aware that the monitoring of each quantity or event has a small but cumulative effect on the performance of the system. A reasonable strategy might be to use targeted monitoring during periodic "tuneups" and to resolve specific problems, and otherwise to keep monitoring to a minimum.

10.9.1 The Snapshot Monitor

The purpose of the snapshot monitor is to provide information about the state of UDB and the data it controls, and to call attention to anomalous situations. This information is provided in the form of a series of *snapshots*, each of which represents the state of the system and its databases at a point in time. A database administrator can control the frequency of the snapshots and the amount of information that is collected in each snapshot.

The snapshot monitor has a large number of predefined *elements* that it knows how to measure. Some of these elements are counters, such as the number of times a deadlock has occurred. Others represent the current value of something, such as the number of applications that are connected to a database. Others represent a timestamp when something occurred, such as the time when the last transaction was completed. Still others represent the highest recorded value of something, such as the maximum size of the database heap.

The snapshot monitor provides database administrators with a great deal of flexibility in choosing the information to be gathered. An administrator can independently turn on or off the gathering of information about each of the following objects:

- A UDB instance
- A database
- Each tablespace within a database
- Each individual table within a database
- All the connections to a specific database

For each kind of object in the list above, several categories of measurements can be independently controlled. For example, within an individual database, an administrator can turn on or off the gathering of information about SQL statements, buffer pool activity, locks and deadlocks, and other categories. Within each category, the snapshot monitor collects several measurements. For example, if SQL statement monitoring is turned on for a given database, the snapshot monitor separately counts SELECT statements, data manipulation statements, data definition statements, COMMIT statements, dynamic statements, unsuccessful statements, and several other types of statements.

The behavior of the snapshot monitor is controlled by a *monitor profile*. A monitor profile specifies the interval between snapshots, the types of objects to be monitored, and the information categories to be turned on or off for each type of object. For the categories that are turned on, the monitor profile can specify an upper and lower alarm threshold for each measured element, and the action to be taken (such as an audible alarm or a pop-up message) when each element exceeds its upper or lower threshold. For example, an administrator might call for an alarm to be raised if the snapshot monitor detects more than ten rollbacks per second in a given database. A monitor profile also allows an administrator to define formulas computed from the measured elements, and to define upper and lower alarm thresholds for these formulas. UDB provides a default monitor profile, named db2smpv, in which the snapshot interval is 20 seconds and all the information categories are turned on. By copying this profile and modifying the copies, an administrator can create other named profiles for various purposes.

As shown in Figure 10-7, the Control Center displays a hierarchy in which some items represent a generic type of object (such as *Databases*), and other items represent a specific object (such as *TESTDB*). The generic items labeled *Databases, Tables, Tablespaces,* and *Connections* all provide an action named *Show Monitor Summary*. This action displays a summary of all the objects of the given type that are currently being monitored and the measurements collected for each object in the most recent snapshot. For example, Figure 10-17 shows a Monitor Summary for tables, including the most recent measurements for several tables.

The items in the Control Center hierarchy that represent a specific UDB instance, database, table, tablespace, or connection also support actions that control the snapshot monitor. For each specific object, *Start Monitoring* and

Name	Overflow Accesses	Rows Read per Second	Rows Written per Second
TESTDB.BANK.ACCOUNTS	0	379.82	189.91
TESTDB.BANK.LOANS	0	674.93	337.44
TESTDB.BANK.TELLERS	0	516.32	258.16

Figure 10-17: Snapshot Monitor Summary Display

Stop Monitoring cause the snapshot monitor to start and stop the gathering of information on the given object. *Show Monitor Profile* can be used to display and modify the monitor profile that specifies the information to be gathered on the given object. *Show Monitor Details* provides a more detailed display of the information gathered on the given object, including not only the most recent value of each measurement but also its average, maximum, and minimum value, and the upper and lower alarm thresholds defined for each measurement.

An example of a Monitor Detail display for a database is shown in Figure 10-18. Each row in the display describes some variable measured by the snapshot monitor. The icon at the left of each row indicates the status of the variable: a green box indicates a normal value, a red upward arrow indicates an upper-threshold alarm, and a red downward arrow indicates a lower-threshold alarm. For example, the first row of data in Figure 10-18 shows that an alarm will be raised when five deadlocks have occurred, but that the number of deadlocks is currently zero. By pulling down the *Database* menu at the top of the Monitor Detail display, an administrator can reset all the counters for the given database to zero.

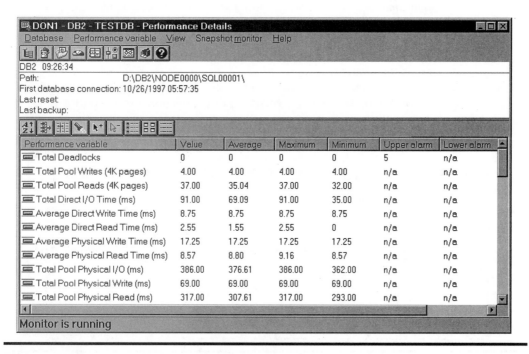

Figure 10-18: Snapshot Monitor Detail Display

By selecting one or more of the variables on the Monitor Detail display and then pulling down the *Performance Variable* menu, an administrator can display a graph of how the selected variable has been varying as a function of time during the last several snapshots. For example, the graph in Figure 10-19 shows how the number of committed SQL statements per second in a given database has been fluctuating during a period of several minutes.

When a monitored variable exceeds the upper or lower alarm threshold defined in its monitor profile, several things happen. If called for by the monitor profile, an audible alarm sounds and a window pops up with a message describing the event. The icon on the Control Center display that represents the object in which the anomalous measurement was made is displayed in red, indicating that the object is in Alert status. A description of the event is recorded and can be examined using the Journal tool, as described in Section 3.1.3. Another graphical tool, called the Alert Center, continuously displays a list of all the objects that are in Alert status. Figure 10-20 is an example of an Alert Center display in which the database named TESTDB is shown to be in Alert status. By

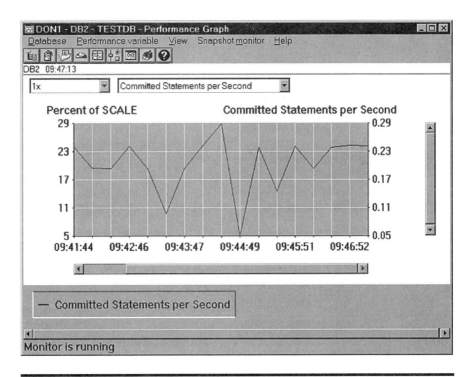

Figure 10-19: Snapshot Monitor Graphical Display

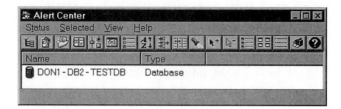

Figure 10-20: Alert Center Display

double-clicking on one of the objects shown in the Alert Center display, an administrator can go directly to the Snapshot Monitor Detail display (shown in Figure 10-18), where the reason for the Alert status can be seen.

10.9.2 Event Monitors

The purpose of an event monitor is to keep records on the occurrences of a specific type of event, directing these records into a file or pipe. Users can create multiple event monitors to monitor various types of events, and can activate and deactivate each event monitor independently. Event monitors differ from the snapshot monitor in the following ways:

1. Each event monitor is "customized" to monitor a particular type of event that is of interest to the user who created it.

2. Rather than delivering a "snapshot" of the state of the database system at a particular point in time, an event monitor delivers a stream of reports on events as they occur.

3. An event monitor is created in a particular database and monitors events only in that database (unlike the snapshot monitor, which can monitor events across databases).

In order to create and use an event monitor, you are required to have SYSADM or DBADM authority on the database in which events are to be monitored. Like the snapshot monitor, event monitors can be controlled using the Control Center. Each named database in the Control Center hierarchy provides an action called *Monitor Events*, which displays a summary of all the event monitors that have been defined in the given database, as shown in Figure 10-21. Each event monitor has a name and a status. *Started* means that the monitor is actively monitoring events and recording them in the directory shown in the Event Monitors display.

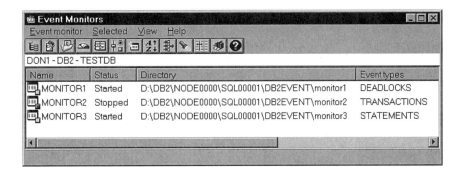

Figure 10-21: Summary of Event Monitors for a Given Database

While you are looking at the event monitor summary for a given database, you can create a new event monitor for that database by pulling down the *Event Monitor* menu and choosing the *Create* action. You will be presented with a window like the one shown in Figure 10-22, where you can specify the name of your event monitor, the type of event you wish it to monitor, and (optionally) the directory into which records of events are to be written. In addition to the general type of event to be monitored, you can specify a filter that restricts the events to those initiated by a particular user or application. For example, the window in Figure 10-22 is creating an event monitor named MONITOR4 that collects information on all SQL statements executed by the user GRUNDY.

The event monitor summary shown in Figure 10-21 also allows you to control a specific event monitor by selecting it on the display, then pulling down the *Selected* menu and choosing an action. In this way, you can start or stop the event monitor, remove its definition from the database, or view its results. If you choose the *View Event Monitor Files* action, you will see a list of the periods of time during which that event monitor has been running. By double-clicking on one of these periods, you can see a list of all the events recorded by the event monitor during that period. For example, Figure 10-23 shows a list of records on SQL statements executed by a given user. The records shown in Figure 10-23 might have been gathered by the event monitor created in Figure 10-22.

The format of the records generated by event monitors, and more information about how these records can be processed, can be found in the *System Monitor Guide and Reference*.

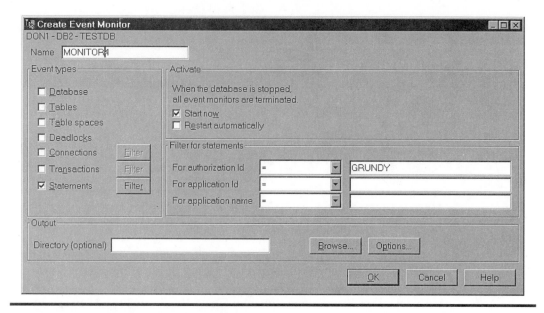

Figure 10-22: Creating an Event Monitor

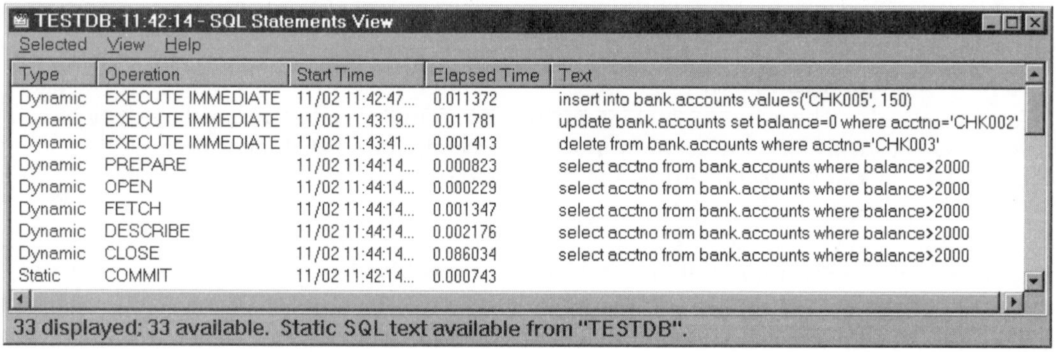

Figure 10-23: Output of an Event Monitor

Special Registers

Special registers contain values, maintained by the system, that describe and control the environment in which an SQL statement is executed. UDB maintains the following special registers:

CURRENT DATE (Datatype: Date)

This register contains the date on which the current statement is being executed. The date information is obtained from the operating system and cannot be manually set.

CURRENT DEGREE (Datatype: Char(5))

This register can be used to set a limit on the maximum degree of intra-partition parallelism to be used by dynamic SQL statements. Permissible values are string representations of integers between 1 and 32,767, or the word ANY, which allows UDB to choose its own degree of parallelism. The degree of intra-partition parallelism can also be limited by the MAX_QUERYDEGREE and INTRA_PARALLEL database manager configuration parameters.

The value of the CURRENT DEGREE register can be set by a statement such as the following:

```
SET CURRENT DEGREE = 'ANY';
```

The default value of the CURRENT DEGREE register is determined by the database configuration parameter named DFT_DEGREE, which in turn has a default value of 1.

CURRENT EXPLAIN MODE (Datatype: Char(8))

This register controls the gathering of Tabular Explain data for dynamic SQL statements. Tabular Explain data describes the access plan chosen by the optimizer for a given SQL statement. The data is stored in the form of special tables called Explain Tables, and can be retrieved by SQL statements. The format of the Explain Tables is described in the *Administration Guide*. For most purposes, the easiest way to study access plans is to gather Snapshot data rather than Tabular Explain data (see the CURRENT EXPLAIN SNAPSHOT special register).

The value of the CURRENT EXPLAIN MODE register can be set by a statement such as the following:

```
SET CURRENT EXPLAIN MODE = YES;
```

The valid values for CURRENT EXPLAIN MODE are as follows:

NO: Do not capture Tabular Explain data for dynamic SQL statements (this is the default).

YES: Capture Tabular Explain data for dynamic SQL statements and execute them.

EXPLAIN: Capture Tabular Explain data for dynamic SQL statements but do not execute them.

The CURRENT EXPLAIN MODE register applies to dynamic SQL statements only. Control over the gathering of Tabular Explain data for static SQL statements is provided by the EXPLAIN option of the PREP and BIND commands.

CURRENT EXPLAIN SNAPSHOT (Datatype: Char(8))

This register controls the gathering of Snapshot data for dynamic SQL statements. Snapshot data can be used by the Control Center to create a graphical display of an access plan, as described in Section 10.8.4. The value of the register can be given a value by a statement such as the following:

```
SET CURRENT EXPLAIN SNAPSHOT = YES;
```

The valid values for CURRENT EXPLAIN SNAPSHOT are as follows:

NO: Do not capture Snapshot data for dynamic SQL statements (this is the default).

YES: Capture Snapshot data for dynamic SQL statements and execute them.

EXPLAIN: Capture Snapshot data for dynamic SQL statements but do not execute them.

The CURRENT EXPLAIN SNAPSHOT register applies to dynamic SQL statements only. Control over the gathering of Snapshot data for static SQL statements is provided by the EXPLSNAP option of the PREP and BIND commands.

CURRENT FUNCTION PATH (Datatype: Varchar(254))

This register contains the list of schemas that will be searched to resolve the names of functions and datatypes used in dynamic SQL statements. The schema names are enclosed in double quotes and separated by commas. The value of the register can be set by the SET CURRENT FUNCTION PATH statement (described in Section 6.3.1). The default value is SYSIBM, followed by SYSFUN, followed by the current value of the USER special register.

CURRENT NODE (Datatype: Integer)

This register is useful in a parallel database system with multiple partitions. Its value is equal to the node number of the coordinator node for your application (the node to which your application is connected). If you are not connected to a partitioned database, the value of the register is zero.

CURRENT QUERY OPTIMIZATION (Datatype: Integer)

This register specifies the class of optimization techniques to be used in preparing dynamic SQL statements for execution (optimization of static SQL statements is controlled by the QUERYOPT bind option). The special register can be given a value by a statement such as the following:

```
SET CURRENT QUERY OPTIMIZATION = 5;
```

The valid values for CURRENT QUERY OPTIMIZATION are the integers 0, 1, 2, 3, 5, 7, and 9. (The meanings of these values are described in Section 10.8.1.) In general, higher values cause the optimizer to use more time and memory in choosing optimal access plans, potentially resulting in better plans and improved run-time performance. The extreme values 0 and 9 should be used with caution, since they may result in suboptimal plans or long optimization times, respectively. Level 5 is a good compromise for most applications. The default value for this special register is controlled by the database configuration parameter named DFT_QUERYOPT, which in turn has a default value of 5.

CURRENT SERVER (Datatype: Varchar(18))

This register contains the name of the database to which your application is currently connected. Database connections are controlled by the CONNECT statement (described in Section 2.7.2). If you are connected to a database using an alias, the value of CURRENT SERVER is the "native" name of the database on the server where it resides rather than the alias.

CURRENT TIME (Datatype: Time)

This register contains the time of day at which the current SQL statement is being executed. Multiple references to CURRENT TIME within the same SQL statement will all return the same value. The value of this register is obtained from the operating system and cannot be manually set.

CURRENT TIMESTAMP (Datatype: Timestamp)

This register contains a microsecond-level measure of the date and time at which execution of the current SQL statement began. Multiple references to CURRENT TIMESTAMP within the same SQL statement will all return the same value. The value of this register is obtained from the operating system and cannot be manually set.

CURRENT TIMEZONE (Datatype: Decimal(6,0))

This register contains the difference between Coordinated Universal Time (formerly known as Greenwich Mean Time) and the local time at your server, expressed as a six-digit decimal number representing hours (two digits), minutes (two digits), and seconds (two digits). For example, in California in the winter, the value of CURRENT TIMEZONE is –080000. The value of this register is obtained from the operating system and cannot be manually set.

USER (Datatype: Char(8))

This register contains the userid of the user who is connected to the database and executing the current application. This is the userid that is used for authorization checking of dynamic SQL statements, including statements executed using the CLP. Authorization checking of static SQL statements, on the other hand, is performed against the userid who bound the application, which is not in general the same as the content of the USER register. The value of USER is obtained from the operating system and cannot be manually set.

B Functions

S QL recognizes two types of functions: *scalar functions* and *column functions*. Scalar functions take one or more values as arguments and return a single result. Column functions take one column of values as an argument and return a single result. This appendix describes all the built-in functions of **UDB**. All the built-in column functions, and some of the built-in scalar functions, are in the SYSIBM schema. The remainder of the built-in scalar functions are in the SYSFUN schema. Both of these schemas are on the default function path, so all the built-in functions can be invoked by simple one-part names.

Operators such as + and || are an important special case of scalar functions. An infix operator such as x + y is treated as a call to the scalar function "+"(x,y), and a prefix operator such as -x is treated as a call to the scalar function "-"(x). This appendix describes the built-in operators of **UDB** as well as the built-in functions.

Each function is identified by its *signature*, which is the combination of its name and the datatypes of its parameters. The signatures of all the built-in functions are listed below, along with their return datatypes. In many cases, a family of functions will have the same name but different signatures. A function call is valid if the actual argument datatypes of the call match the formal parameter datatypes of the function or can be promoted to the formal parameter datatypes by moving to the right in one of the promotion hierarchies shown in Figure B-1.

In the function signatures that follow, it is often necessary to refer to a collection of related datatypes. The following symbols are used:

<any numeric datatype> includes Smallint, Integer, Decimal, Real, and Double

<any string datatype> includes Char, Varchar, Long Varchar, and Clob

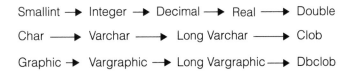

Figure B-1: Promotion Hierarchies for Function Parameters

<any DBCS datatype> includes Graphic, Vargraphic, Long Vargraphic, and Dbclob

<any built-in datatype> includes all datatypes except user-defined datatypes

<any short datatype> includes all datatypes except Long Varchar, Long Vargraphic, Blob, Clob, and Dbclob

<any datetime datatype> includes Time, Date, and Timestamp

<date string> means a Char or Varchar of a length of at least eight characters, containing a string representation of a date in one of the following formats: "1999-12-31" or "12/31/1999" or "31.12.1999"

<time string> means a Char or Varchar of length at least four characters, containing a string representation of a time in one of the following formats: "23:59" or "23:59:00" or "23.59" or "23.59.00" or "11:59 PM" or "11 PM"

<timestamp string> means a Char or Varchar of length 19 or 26 characters, containing a string representation of a timestamp in one of the following formats: "1999-12-31-23.59.00" or "1999-12-31-23.59.00.000000"

<date duration> means a Decimal(8,0) number representing a number of years, months, and days, expressed in format YYYYMMDD

<time duration> means a Decimal(6,0) number representing a number of hours, minutes, and seconds, expressed in format HHMMSS

<timestamp duration> means a Decimal(20,6) number representing a number of years, months, days, hours, minutes, seconds, and microseconds, expressed in format YYYYMMDDHHMMSS.nnnnnn

<same datatype> means that the return datatype of the function is the same as the datatype of its argument, with the following exception: if the argument datatype is Real, the result datatype is Double

<datatype of highest precedence> means the return datatype of the function is the same as the argument datatype that is farthest to the right in the promotion hierarchy in Figure B-1

B.1   COLUMN FUNCTIONS

Each of the following functions operates on a collection of values (a *column*) to produce a scalar result. In each of these functions (except the `grouping` function), the keyword DISTINCT may precede the argument to indicate that duplicate values are to be eliminated from the argument column before the function is applied. All column functions are found in the SYSIBM schema.

avg (*<any numeric datatype>*) → *<same datatype>*

Returns the average of the non-null values in the argument column. If the argument column contains no non-null values, the result is null. There are some exceptions to the result datatype rule: if the argument datatype is Smallint, the result datatype is Integer, and if the argument datatype is Real, the result datatype is Double.

count (*<any datatype>*) → Integer

count (*) → Integer

count_big (*<any datatype>*) → Decimal(31,0)

count_big (*) → Decimal(31,0)

Returns the number of non-null values in the argument column. The special form count(*) or count_big(*) is used for counting rows of a table, including rows that contain null values. The count_big function is provided for counts in which the result is too large to be expressed as an Integer.

grouping (*<any datatype>*) → Smallint

Used to distinguish regular null values from special nulls that represent "all values" generated during processing of "super-groups" as described in Section 5.6. The argument of the function should be a grouping expression. The function returns 1 only for special rows in which the argument expression has been merged into a higher-level group; otherwise, it returns 0.

max (*<any short datatype>*) → *<same datatype>*

Returns the maximum non-null value in the argument column. If the argument column contains no non-null values, the result is null.

min (*<any short datatype>*) → *<same datatype>*

Returns the minimum non-null value in the argument column. If the argument column contains no non-null values, the result is null.

stdev (*<any numeric datatype>*) → Double

Returns the standard deviation of a column of numbers (ignoring null values). If the argument column contains no non-null values, the result is null.

sum (*<any numeric datatype>*) → *<same datatype>*

Returns the sum of the non-null values in the argument column. If the argument column contains no non-null values, the result is null. Exceptions to the result datatype rule: if the argument datatype is Smallint, the result datatype is Integer. If the argument datatype is Real, the result datatype is Double. If the argument datatype is Decimal, the result datatype is Decimal with a precision of 31 digits.

variance (*<any numeric datatype>*) → Double

var (*<any numeric datatype>*) → Double

Returns the variance of a column of numbers (ignoring null values). If the argument column contains no non-null values, the result is null.

B.2   SCALAR FUNCTIONS

The following functions are called scalar functions because both their arguments and their result are scalar values. Some of these functions are built into the UDB implementation and reside in the SYSIBM schema. Others are external functions that are shipped with the system and reside in the SYSFUN schema. The schema in which each function resides is given in parentheses at the end of its description. The SYSIBM functions can in general be expected to have better performance than the SYSFUN functions. Since the default function path includes both the SYSIBM and SYSFUN schemas, you can make use of any of these functions without including a schema name in your function invocation.

abs (*<any numeric datatype>*) → *<same datatype>*

absval (*<any numeric datatype>*) → *<same datatype>*

Returns the absolute value of the argument. There is an exception to the rule that the result datatype is the same as the argument datatype: if the argument datatype is Decimal or Real, the result datatype is Double. (SYSFUN)

acos (Double) → Double

Returns the arccosine of the argument, as an angle expressed in radians. (SYSFUN)

ascii (*<any string datatype>*) → Integer

Returns the ASCII code of the first character of the argument string. (SYSFUN)

asin (Double) → Double

Returns the arcsine of the argument, as an angle expressed in radians. (SYSFUN)

atan (Double) → Double

Returns the arctangent of the argument, as an angle expressed in radians. (SYSFUN)

atan2 (Double x, Double y) → Double

Returns the arctangent of the point whose coordinates are x and y, as an angle expressed in radians. (SYSFUN)

blob (*<any string datatype>*) → Blob

blob (*<any string datatype>*, Integer n) → Blob(n)

blob (*<any DBCS datatype>*) → Blob

blob (*<any DBCS datatype>*, Integer n) → Blob(n)

blob (Blob) → Blob

blob (Blob, Integer *n*) → Blob(*n*)

Converts the first argument to a Blob datatype. The second argument, if specified, becomes the maximum length of the result (causing truncation if necessary). (SYSIBM)

ceil (*<any numeric datatype>*) → *<same datatype>*

ceiling (*<any numeric datatype>*) → *<same datatype>*

Returns the smallest integer greater than or equal to the argument. There is an exception to the rule that the return type is the same type as the argument type: if the argument type is Decimal or Real, the return type is Double. (SYSFUN)

char (Date) → Char(10)

char (Date, Keyword *k*) → Char(10)

char (Time) → Char(8)

char (Time, Keyword *k*) → Char(8)

char (Timestamp) → Char(26)

Returns a character-string representation of the argument. The keyword *k*, if present, governs the format of the string representation. Valid values for the keyword argument (which must not be enclosed in quotes) are ISO, USA, EUR, JIS, and LOCAL. (SYSIBM)

char (*<any string datatype>*) → Char( )

char (*<any string datatype>*, Integer *n*) → Char(*n*)

Converts the first argument to a fixed-length Char datatype. The second argument, if specified, becomes the length of the result (causing truncation or padding with blanks if necessary). The second argument, if present, must be between 0 and 254. (SYSIBM)

char (Smallint) → Char(6)

char (Integer) → Char(11)

char (Decimal) → Char( )

char (Decimal, Varchar) → Char( )

Returns a character-string representation of the first argument. If the first argument is Decimal and the second argument is Varchar, the second argument must be a single character and is used to represent the decimal point in the result string. (SYSIBM)

char (Double) → Char(24)

Returns a character-string representation of a double-precision floating-point value. (SYSFUN)

chr (Integer) → Char(1)

Returns the character whose ASCII code is equal to the argument. Returns null if the argument is not between 0 and 255. (SYSFUN)

clob (*<any string datatype>*) → Clob

clob (*<any string datatype>*, Integer *n*) → Clob(*n*)

Converts the first argument to a Clob datatype. The second argument, if specified, becomes the maximum length of the result (causing truncation if necessary). (SYSIBM)

coalesce (*<one or more arguments of compatible datatypes>*) → *<datatype of highest precedence>*

Returns the value of its first non-null argument, or null if all arguments are null. (See Section 6.6.2 for rules governing compatibility of argument datatypes.) coalesce and value are different names for the same function. (SYSIBM)

concat (*<any string datatype>*, *<any string datatype>*) → *<datatype of highest precedence>*

concat (*<any DBCS datatype>*, *<any DBCS datatype>*) → *<datatype of highest precedence>*

concat (Blob, Blob) → Blob

Returns the concatenation of the two arguments. Equivalent to concat or || used as an infix operator. If the result cannot be represented in the datatype of highest precedence, a suitable datatype is chosen. For example, if a concatenation of two fixed-length strings results in a string with a length greater than 254, the result datatype will be Varchar rather than Char. (SYSIBM)

cos (Double) → Double

Returns the cosine of an angle expressed in radians. (SYSFUN)

cot (Double) → Double

Returns the cotangent of an angle expressed in radians. (SYSFUN)

date (*<date string>*) → Date

Converts the argument from a string representation of a Date to an actual Date. The argument may be in any of the following formats (examples represent the last day of the year 1999): (SYSIBM)
"1999-12-31"
"12/31/1999"
"31.12.1999"
"1999365"

date (*<any numeric datatype>*) → Date

Converts the argument to an integer *n* by truncation. Returns the date that is *n* – 1 days after January 1, 0001. (SYSIBM)

date (Timestamp) → Date

date (*<timestamp string>*) → Date

Returns the date portion of the argument. (SYSIBM)

day (Date) → Integer

day (*<date string>*) → Integer

day (*<date duration>*) → Integer

day (Timestamp) → Integer

day (*<timestamp string>*) → Integer

day (*<timestamp duration>*) → Integer

Returns the day portion of the argument. (SYSIBM)

dayname (Date) → Varchar(100)

dayname (*<date string>*) → Varchar(100)

dayname (Timestamp) → Varchar(100)

dayname (*<timestamp string>*) → Varchar(100)

Returns the day of the week corresponding to the argument date, as a character string (Sunday, Monday, and so on). (SYSFUN)

dayofweek (Date) → Integer

dayofweek (*<date string>*) → Integer

dayofweek (Timestamp) → Integer

dayofweek (*<timestamp string>*) → Integer

Returns the day of the week corresponding to the argument date, as an integer (Sunday = 1, Monday = 2, and so on). (SYSFUN)

dayofyear (Date) → Integer

dayofyear (*<date string>*) → Integer

dayofyear (Timestamp) → Integer

dayofyear (*<timestamp string>*) → Integer

Returns the day of the year corresponding to the argument date, as an integer between 1 and 366. (SYSFUN)

days (Date) → Integer

days (*<date string>*) → Integer

days (Timestamp) → Integer

days (*<timestamp string>*) → Integer

Converts the argument to a date, then returns one more than the number of days between January 1, 0001 and this date. (SYSIBM)

dbclob (*<any DBCS datatype>*) → Dbclob

dbclob (*<any DBCS datatype>*, Integer *n*) → Dbclob(*n*)

Converts the first argument to a Dbclob datatype. The second argument, if specified, becomes the maximum length of the result (causing truncation if necessary). (SYSIBM)

decimal (*<any numeric datatype>*) → Decimal(15, 0)

decimal (*<any numeric datatype>*, Integer *p*) → Decimal(*p*, 0)

decimal (*<any numeric datatype>*, Integer *p*, Integer *s*) → Decimal(*p*, *s*)

Returns a decimal representation of the first argument, with the indicated precision and scale. The function name dec may be used as a synonym for decimal. (SYSIBM)

decimal (Varchar) → Decimal(15, 0)

decimal (Varchar, Integer *p*) → Decimal(*p*, 0)

decimal (Varchar, Integer *p*, Integer *s*) → Decimal(*p*, *s*)

decimal (Varchar, Integer *p*, Integer *s*, Varchar *d*) → Decimal(*p*, *s*)

The first argument is a character-string representation of a decimal number, which is converted to an actual decimal value with the indicated precision and scale. The fourth parameter, if present, is a single character that indicates how the decimal point is represented in the string input. The function name dec may be used as a synonym for decimal. (SYSIBM)

degrees (*<any numeric datatype>*) → Double

Converts the argument angle from radians to degrees. (SYSFUN)

difference (Varchar, Varchar) → Integer

Returns a measure of the difference between the sounds of two strings, as computed by the soundex function. The result is an integer between 0 and 4, where 4 represents the best sound match. (SYSFUN)

digits (Decimal) → Char( )

Returns a fixed-length character string representing the absolute value of the argument, not including its sign or decimal point. For example, digits(–123.45) is "12345." (SYSIBM)

double (*<any numeric datatype>*) → Double

double_precision (*<any numeric datatype>*) → Double

Converts the argument to a double-precision floating-point number. (SYSIBM)

double (Varchar) → Double

If the argument contains a valid representation of a floating-point value, this value is returned. (SYSFUN)

event_mon_state (Varchar) → Integer

The argument is the name of an Event Monitor (defined by a CREATE EVENT MONITOR statement). The function returns 1 if the named Event Monitor is active, 0 if it is inactive. (SYSIBM)

exp (Double x) → Double

Returns e^x, where x is the argument and e is the base of the natural logarithms. (SYSFUN)

float (*<any numeric datatype>*) → Double

Converts the argument to a double-precision floating-point number. (SYSIBM)

floor (*<any numeric datatype>*) → *<same datatype>*

Returns the largest integer less than or equal to the argument. There is an exception to the rule that the return type is the same type as the argument type: if the argument type is Decimal or Real, the return type is Double. (SYSFUN)

generate_unique ( ) → Char(13) FOR BIT DATA

Returns a value that is unique compared to any other execution of the same function. The value is based on the system clock and may be used as a unique key value when inserting rows into a table. The string returned by this function can be converted into a Universal Coordinated Time timestamp by passing it to the `timestamp` function. (SYSIBM)

graphic (*<any DBCS datatype>*) → Graphic

graphic (*<any DBCS datatype>*, Integer n) → Graphic(n)

Converts the argument to a fixed-length Graphic datatype, of the indicated length. If no length is specified, the length is derived from that of the argument. (SYSIBM)

hex (*<any built-in datatype>*) → Varchar

Returns a hexadecimal representation of the argument value. Each two bytes of the returned string represent one byte of the internal representation of the argument value. (SYSIBM)

hour (Time) → Integer

hour (*<time string>*) → Integer

hour (*<time duration>*) → Integer

hour (Timestamp) → Integer

hour (*<timestamp string>*) → Integer

hour (*<timestamp duration>*) → Integer

Returns the hour part of the argument. If the argument is a time, timestamp, or string, the result is an integer between 0 and 24. If the argument is a duration, the result is an integer between –99 and 99. (SYSIBM)

insert (Varchar x, Integer m, Integer n, Varchar y) → Varchar(4000)

insert (Clob(1M) x, Integer m, Integer n, Clob(1M) y) → Clob(1M)

insert (Blob(1M) x, Integer m, Integer n, Blob(1M) y) → Blob(1M)

The return string is computed by deleting from string x a substring of n characters beginning with character number m, and replacing the deleted substring by string y. (SYSFUN)

integer (*<any numeric datatype>*) → Integer

integer (Varchar) → Integer

Converts the argument to an integer, by truncation of the decimal part if necessary. If the argument is of datatype Varchar, it must be a character-string representation of an integer, such as "–123." The function name int may be used as a synonym for integer. (SYSIBM)

julian_day (Date) → Integer

julian_day (*<date string>*) → Integer

julian_day (Timestamp) → Integer

julian_day (*<timestamp string>*) → Integer

Returns the number of days between the beginning of the Julian calendar (January 1, 4712 B.C.) and the argument date. (SYSFUN)

lcase (Varchar) → Varchar(4000)

lcase (Clob(1M)) → Clob(1M)

Returns a copy of the argument string in which all the uppercase characters have been converted to lowercase. (SYSFUN)

left (Varchar *x*, Integer *n*) → Varchar(4000)

left (Clob(1M) *x*, Integer *n*) → Clob(1M)

left (Blob(1M) *x*, Integer *n*) → Blob(1M)

Returns the leftmost *n* characters of string *x*. (SYSFUN)

length (*<any built-in datatype>*) → Integer

Returns the length of the argument (not including a null indicator). For string-type arguments, returns the actual length (not the maximum length) in characters (for DBCS strings, each character is two bytes). For numeric or datetime arguments, returns the length in bytes of the internal representation. (SYSIBM)

ln (Double) → Double

Returns the natural logarithm of the argument. (SYSFUN)

locate (*<any string datatype>* *s1*, *<any string datatype>* *s2*) → Integer

locate (*<any string datatype>* *s1*, *<any string datatype>* *s2*, Integer *n*) → Integer

locate (Blob(1M) *s1*, Blob(1M) *s2*) → Integer

locate (Blob(1M) *s1*, Blob(1M) *s2*, Integer *n*) → Integer

Returns the starting position of the first occurrence of argument *s2* inside argument *s1*. The third argument, if any, indicates the position within *s1* where the search is to begin. If *s2* is not found within *s1*, 0 is returned. If any argument is a Clob, it is limited to a length of one megabyte. See `posstr` for a similar function. (SYSFUN)

log (Double) → Double

Returns the natural logarithm of the argument (same as `ln`). (SYSFUN)

log10 (Double) → Double

Returns the base-10 logarithm of the argument. (SYSFUN)

long_varchar (*<any string datatype>*) → Long Varchar

Converts the argument to the Long Varchar datatype, which has a maximum length of 32K characters. (SYSIBM)

long_vargraphic (*<any DBCS string datatype>*) → Long Vargraphic

Converts the argument to the Long Vargraphic datatype, which has a maximum length of 16K double-byte characters. (SYSIBM)

ltrim (Varchar) → Varchar(4000)

ltrim (Clob(1M)) → Clob(1M)

Returns a copy of the argument with leading blanks removed. (SYSFUN)

microsecond (Timestamp) → Integer

microsecond (*<timestamp string>*) → Integer

microsecond (*<timestamp duration>*) → Integer

Returns the microsecond part of the argument. (SYSIBM)

midnight_seconds (Time) → Integer

midnight_seconds (*<time string>*) → Integer

midnight_seconds (Timestamp) → Integer

midnight_seconds (*<timestamp string>*) → Integer

Returns the number of seconds between the argument time and the previous midnight. (SYSFUN)

minute (Time) → Integer

minute (*<time string>*) → Integer

minute (*<time duration>*) → Integer

minute (Timestamp) → Integer

minute (*<timestamp string>*) → Integer

minute (*<timestamp duration>*) → Integer

Returns the minute part of the argument. If the argument is a time, timestamp, or string, the result is an integer between 0 and 59. If the argument is a duration, the result is an integer between –99 and 99. (SYSIBM)

mod (Smallint *m*, Smallint *n*) → Smallint

mod (Integer *m*, Integer *n*) → Integer

Returns the remainder (modulus) of argument *m* divided by argument *n*. (SYSFUN)

month (Date) → Integer

month (*<date string>*) → Integer

month (*<date duration>*) → Integer

month (Timestamp) → Integer

month (*<timestamp string>*) → Integer

month (*<timestamp duration>*) → Integer

Returns the month part of the argument. If the argument is a date, timestamp, or string, the result is an integer between 1 and 12. If the argument is a duration, the result is an integer between –99 and 99. (SYSIBM)

monthname (Date) → Varchar(100)

monthname (*<date string>*) → Varchar(100)

monthname (Timestamp) → Varchar(100)

monthname (*<timestamp string>*) → Varchar(100)

Returns the name of the month part of the argument, as a mixed-case character string. (SYSFUN)

nodenumber (*<any datatype>*) → Integer

The argument must be the name of a column in some table that is referenced in the current SQL statement. For each row of the referenced table, nodenumber returns the number of the partition on which the row is stored, or zero if the database is not partitioned. (SYSIBM)

nullif (*<any datatype>, <any compatible datatype>*) → *<datatype of highest precedence>*

Returns null if the arguments are equal; otherwise, returns the first argument. (SYSIBM)

partition (*<any datatype>*) → Integer

The argument must be the name of a column in some table that is referenced in the current SQL statement. For each row of the referenced table, partition returns the partitioning map index that applies to the row (an integer between 0 and 4,095), or zero if the table has no partitioning key. (SYSIBM)

posstr (*<any string datatype>* s1, Varchar(4000) s2) → Integer

posstr (*<any DBCS datatype>* s1, Vargraphic(2000) s2) → Integer

posstr (Blob s1, Blob(4000) s2) → Integer

Returns the starting position of the first occurrence of argument s2 inside argument s1. If s2 is not found within s1, 0 is returned. See locate for a similar function. (SYSFUN)

power (Integer x, Integer n) → Integer

power (Double x, Double n) → Double

Returns the first argument raised to the power of the second argument, x^n. (SYSFUN)

quarter (Date) → Integer

quarter (*<date string>*) → Integer

quarter (Timestamp) → Integer

quarter (*<timestamp string>*) → Integer

Returns an integer between 1 and 4 representing the quarter of the year in which the argument occurs. (SYSFUN)

radians (Double) → Double

Converts the argument angle from degrees to radians. (SYSFUN)

raise_error (Varchar, Varchar) → *<void>*

Causes an error condition to be returned in the SQLCA. The first argument must be exactly 5 characters in length and becomes the SQLSTATE. The second argument is a message of up to 70 characters that is placed in the SQLERRMC field of the SQLCA. The SQLCODE is set to –438. The raise_error function returns no value but is considered to be compatible with the context in which it is used (often inside a CASE expression). (For a more complete discussion of raise_error, see Section 5.1.3.) (SYSIBM)

rand ( ) → Double

rand (Integer) → Double

Returns a random double-precision floating-point number between 0 and 1. The optional argument is used as a "seed" to begin a new random number sequence. (SYSFUN)

real (*<any numeric datatype>*) → Real

Converts the argument to a real (single-precision) number. (SYSIBM)

repeat (Varchar *x*, Integer *n*) → Varchar(4000)

repeat (Clob(1M) *x*, Integer *n*) → Clob(1M)

repeat (Blob(1M) *x*, Integer *n*) → Blob(1M)

Returns a string consisting of *n* repetitions of the string *x*. (SYSFUN)

replace (Varchar *x*, Varchar *y*, Varchar *z*) → Varchar(4000)

replace (Clob(1M) *x*, Clob(1M) *y*, Clob(1M) *z*) → Clob(1M)

replace (Blob(1M) *x*, Blob(1M) *y*, Blob(1M) *z*) → Blob(1M)

Returns a copy of the string *x*, with all occurrences of the string *y* replaced by string *z*. (SYSFUN)

right (Varchar *x*, Integer *n*) → Varchar(4000)

right (Clob(1M) *x*, Integer *n*) → Clob(1M)

right (Blob(1M) *x*, Integer *n*) → Blob(1M)

Returns the rightmost *n* characters of string *x*. (SYSFUN)

round (Integer *x*, Integer *n*) → Integer

round (Double *x*, Integer *n*) → Double

Rounds the argument *x* in such a way that its least significant digit is *n* digits to the right of the decimal point (if *n* is negative, the least significant digit is to the left of the decimal point). For example, round(12349, -2) is 12,350. For a related function, see truncate. (SYSFUN)

rtrim (Varchar) → Varchar(4000)

rtrim (Clob(1M)) → Clob(1M)

Returns a copy of the argument with trailing blanks removed. (SYSFUN)

second (Time) → Integer

second (*<time string>*) → Integer

second (*<time duration>*) → Integer

second (Timestamp) → Integer

second (*<timestamp string>*) → Integer

second (*<timestamp duration>*) → Integer

Returns the seconds part of the argument. If the argument is a time, timestamp, or string, the result is an integer between 0 and 59. If the argument is a duration, the result is an integer between –99 and 99. (SYSIBM)

sign (*<any numeric datatype>*) → *<same datatype>*

Returns +1 if the argument is positive, –1 if the argument is negative, 0 if the argument is zero. Exception to return type rule: if argument type is Decimal or Real, return type is Double. (SYSFUN)

sin (Double) → Double

Returns the sine of an angle expressed in radians. (SYSFUN)

smallint (*<any numeric datatype>*) → Integer

smallint (Varchar) → Integer

Converts the argument to a small integer, by truncation of the decimal part if necessary. If the argument is of datatype Varchar, it must be a character-string representation of an integer between –32,768 and +32,767. (SYSIBM)

soundex (Varchar) → Char(4)

Returns a four-character code that represents the sound of the words in the argument. For a related function, see difference. (SYSFUN)

space (Integer *n*) → Varchar(4000)

Returns a string consisting of *n* spaces. (SYSFUN)

sqrt (Double) → Double

Returns the square root of the argument. (SYSFUN)

substr (*<any string datatype> s*, Integer *m*, Integer *n*) → *<string datatype>*

substr (*<any string datatype> s*, Integer *m*) → *<string datatype>*

substr (*<any DBCS datatype> s*, Integer *m*, Integer *n*) → *<DBCS datatype>*

substr (*<any DBCS datatype> s*, Integer *m*) → *<DBCS datatype>*

substr (Blob *s*, Integer *m*, Integer *n*) → Blob

substr (Blob *s*, Integer *m*) → Blob

Returns a substring of string *s*, beginning at character *m* and containing *n* characters. If the third argument is omitted, the substring begins at character *m* and contains the remainder of string *s*. The argument *s* is padded with blanks if necessary to make a result string of length *n*. The result string is the same datatype as string *s*, with certain exceptions: if string *s* is a Varchar or Long Varchar and *n* is a constant less than 255, the result datatype is Char(*n*). Similarly, if string *s* is a Vargraphic or Long Vargraphic and *n* is a constant less than 128, the result datatype is Graphic(*n*). (SYSIBM)

table_name (Varchar *t*, Varchar *s*) → Varchar(18)

table_name (Varchar *t*) → Varchar(18)

This function is used to resolve aliases. If the name *t* (or the qualified name *s.t*) is an alias, it is resolved to a table or view. The unqualified name of the resolved table or view is returned. If *t* (or *s.t*) is not an alias, *t* is returned. (SYSIBM)

table_schema (Varchar *t*, Varchar *s*) → Char(8)

table_schema (Varchar *t*) → Char(8)

This function is used to resolve aliases. If the name *t* (or the qualified name *s.t*) is an alias, it is resolved to a table or view. The schema name of the resolved table or view is returned. If *t* (or *s.t*) is not an alias, the schema portion of the input name is returned (*s*, or if argument *s* is not present, the current authid). (SYSIBM)

tan (Double) → Double

Returns the tangent of an angle expressed in radians. (SYSFUN)

time (Time) → Time

time (*<time string>*) → Time

time (Timestamp) → Time

time (*<timestamp string>*) → Time

Returns the time portion of the argument. If the argument is a string representation of a Time or a Timestamp, it is converted to an actual Time. (SYSIBM)

timestamp (Timestamp) → Timestamp

timestamp (*<timestamp string>*) → Timestamp

Returns the Timestamp represented by the argument. If the argument is a string representing a Timestamp, it is converted to a real Timestamp. (SYSIBM)

timestamp (Date, Time) → Timestamp

timestamp (Date, *<time string>*) → Timestamp

timestamp (*<date string>*, Time) → Timestamp

timestamp (*<date string>*, *<time string>*) → Timestamp

Returns a Timestamp whose date part is taken from the first argument and whose time part is taken from the second argument. The microsecond part of the Timestamp is set to 0. (SYSIBM)

timestampdiff (Integer *u*, Char(22) *d*) → Integer

The first argument, *u*, indicates a time unit, as follows: 256 = years, 128 = quarters, 64 = months, 32 = weeks, 16 = days, 8 = hours, 4 = minutes, 2 = seconds, 1 = microseconds (symbolic constants for these units can be found in `sqllib/include/sqlcli1.h`). The second argument, *d*, is the result of subtracting two Timestamps and converting the result to character form. The function returns an integer representing an estimation of the interval *d* expressed in units *u*. For example, the number of days between Timestamps `t1` and `t2` can be found by `timestampdiff(16, char(t2-t1))`. (SYSFUN)

timestamp_iso (Date) → Timestamp

timestamp_iso (*<date string>*) → Timestamp

timestamp_iso (Time) → Timestamp

timestamp_iso (*<time string>*) → Timestamp

timestamp_iso (Timestamp) → Timestamp

timestamp_iso (*<timestamp string>*) → Timestamp

Converts the argument to a Timestamp. If the argument is a Date, inserts zeros into the time fields of the Timestamp. If the argument is a Time, inserts the current date into the date fields of the Timestamp. (SYSFUN)

translate (Char) → Char( )

translate (Varchar) → Varchar( )

Returns a copy of the argument string in which all lowercase characters have been translated to uppercase. For a similar function, see ucase. (SYSIBM)

translate (Char *s*, Varchar *t*, Varchar *f*) → Char

translate (Varchar *s*, Varchar *t*, Varchar *f*) → Varchar

translate (Graphic *s*, Vargraphic *t*, Vargraphic *f*) → Graphic

translate (Vargraphic *s*, Vargraphic *t*, Vargraphic *f*) → Vargraphic

translate (Char *s*, Varchar *t*, Varchar *f*, Varchar *p*) → Char

translate (Varchar *s*, Varchar *t*, Varchar *f*, Varchar *p*) → Varchar

translate (Graphic *s*, Vargraphic *t*, Vargraphic *f*, Vargraphic *p*) → Graphic

translate (Vargraphic *s*, Vargraphic *t*, Vargraphic *f*, Vargraphic *p*) → Vargraphic

Returns a copy of string *s*, in which some of the characters are translated to different characters. String *f* (the "from string") specifies the characters to be translated, and string *t* (the "to string") specifies the characters to which they are to be translated. Any character in *s* that is also found in *f* is replaced by the corresponding character in *t*. If string *t* is shorter than string *f*, it is padded to the same length by the "pad character," *p*, which must be a single character. If no pad character is specified, the pad character is assumed to be a single-byte or double-byte blank. (SYSIBM)

truncate (Integer *x*, Integer *n*) → Integer

truncate (Double *x*, Integer *n*) → Double

Truncates the argument *x* in such a way that its least significant digit is *n* digits to the right of the decimal point (if *n* is negative, the least significant digit is to the left of the decimal point). For example, truncate(12349, -2) is 12,340. truncate can be abbreviated as trunc. For a related function, see round. (SYSFUN)

ucase (Varchar) → Varchar(4000)

Returns a copy of the argument string in which all lowercase characters have been converted to uppercase. (SYSFUN)

value (*<one or more arguments of compatible datatypes>*) → *<datatype of highest precedence>*

Returns the value of its first non-null argument, or null if all arguments are null. (See Section 6.6.2 for rules governing the compatibility of argument datatypes.) value and coalesce are different names for the same function. (SYSIBM)

varchar (*<any string datatype>*) → Varchar( )

varchar (*<any string datatype>*, Integer *n*) → Varchar(*n*)

varchar (*<any datetime datatype>*) → Varchar( )

Returns a copy of the first argument converted to datatype Varchar. The second argument, if present, becomes the maximum length of the result string, causing truncation if necessary. (SYSIBM)

vargraphic (*<any DBCS datatype>*) → Vargraphic( )

vargraphic (*<any DBCS datatype>*, Integer *n*) → Vargraphic(*n*)

vargraphic (Varchar) → Vargraphic( )

Returns a copy of the first argument converted to datatype Vargraphic. The second argument, if present, becomes the maximum length of the result string, causing truncation if necessary. (SYSIBM)

week (Date) → Integer

week (*<date string>*) → Integer

week (Timestamp) → Integer

week (*<timestamp string>*) → Integer

Returns the week of the year in which the argument occurs, expressed as an integer between 1 and 54. Each week is considered to start on Sunday. (SYSFUN)

year (Date) → Integer

year (*<date string>*) → Integer

year (*<date duration>*) → Integer

year (Timestamp) → Integer

year (*<timestamp string>*) → Integer

year (*<timestamp duration>*) → Integer

Returns the year part of the argument. If the argument is a date, timestamp, or string, the result is an integer between 1 and 9999. If the argument is a duration, the result is an integer between –9999 and 9999. (SYSIBM)

B.3 OPERATORS

B.3.1 Prefix Operators

The following operators can be used as prefix operators (example: -x). These operators are resolved in the same way as unary functions. All these operators reside in the SYSIBM schema.

Operator	Operand Datatype	Result Datatype	Meaning
+	*<any numeric datatype>*	*<same datatype>*	Unary plus. Returns its operand.
−	*<any numeric datatype>*	*<same datatype>*	Unary minus. Returns the negation of its operand.

B.3.2 Infix Operators

The following operators can be used as infix operators (example: x + y). These operators are resolved in the same way as binary functions. All these operators reside in the SYSIBM schema.

Operator	First Operand Datatype	Second Operand Datatype	Result Datatype
+ (addition)	*<any numeric datatype>*	*<any numeric datatype>*	*<datatype of highest precedence>*
+	Date	*<date duration>*	Date
+	*<date duration>*	Date	Date
+	Time	*<time duration>*	Time
+	*<time duration>*	Time	Time
+	Timestamp	*<timestamp duration>*	Timestamp
+	*<timestamp duration>*	Timestamp	Timestamp
− (subtraction)	*<any numeric datatype>*	*<any numeric datatype>*	*<datatype of highest precedence>*
−	Date	Date	*<date duration>*
−	Date	*<date string>*	*<date duration>*
−	*<date string>*	Date	*<date duration>*
−	Date	*<date duration>*	Date

Operator	First Operand Datatype	Second Operand Datatype	Result Datatype
–	Time	Time	*<time duration>*
–	Time	*<time string>*	*<time duration>*
–	*<time string>*	Time	*<time duration>*
–	Time	*<time duration>*	Time
–	Timestamp	Timestamp	*<timestamp duration>*
–	Timestamp	*<timestamp string>*	*<timestamp duration>*
–	*<timestamp string>*	Timestamp	*<timestamp duration>*
–	Timestamp	*<timestamp duration>*	Timestamp
* (multiplication)	*<any numeric datatype>*	*<any numeric datatype>*	*<datatype of highest precedence>*
/ (division)	*<any numeric datatype>*	*<any numeric datatype>*	*<datatype of highest precedence>*
|| (concatenation)	*<string datatype>*	*<string datatype>*	*<datatype of highest precedence>*, or datatype in which result can be represented
||	*<DBCS datatype>*	*<DBCS datatype>*	*<datatype of highest precedence>*, or datatype in which result can be represented
||	Blob	Blob	Blob

Typecodes

ypecodes are used in the `sqltype` fields of SQLDA descriptors. When a DESCRIBE statement returns an SQLDA describing the results of a query, it uses typecodes to indicate the datatypes in the result set. Typecodes are also used to indicate datatypes whenever values are being exchanged between the application program and the database system via an SQLDA structure (for example, input values in an EXECUTE USING statement). A typecode identifies not just the datatype of the value as it is stored in the database, but also the host language datatype that is being used for input or output.

Each of the built-in SQL datatypes (Integer, Varchar, and so on) has one or more host language datatypes that can be used for exchange of that SQL datatype between applications and the database. Each of these combinations of an SQL datatype and a host language datatype is identified by a typecode.[1] Only a subset of these typecodes are returned by DESCRIBE statements. For example, typecode 460 will never be returned by DESCRIBE, because it denotes a datatype (null-terminated string) that is not used inside the database (though it is a valid host variable).

Typecodes are summarized in Table C-1. The symbolic names for the typecodes and the structures used in their C-language declarations are declared in `sqllib/include/sql.h`. These declarations may be overlaid on storage that is dynamically allocated for exchanging data with a dynamic SQL statement.

TABLE C-1: SQLDA Typecodes and the Datatypes They Represent

SQL Datatype	C-Language Datatype	Typecode If Not Nullable	Typecode If Nullable
Date	char[11]	SQL_TYP_DATE (384)	SQL_TYP_NDATE (385)
Time	char[9]	SQL_TYP_TIME (388)	SQL_TYP_NTIME (389)
Timestamp	char[27]	SQL_TYP_STAMP (392)	SQL_TYP_NSTAMP (393)
Null-terminated double-byte string	sqldbchar[n + 1] or wchar_t[n + 1]	SQL_TYP_CGSTR (400)	SQL_TYP_NCGSTR (401)

---

1. The Real and Double datatypes share the same typecode and are distinguished by the `sqllen` field in the SQLDA.

TABLE C-1 *(Continued)*

SQL Datatype	C-Language Datatype	Typecode If Not Nullable	Typecode If Nullable
Blob(n)	struct sqllob (defined in sql.h)	SQL_TYP_BLOB (404)	SQL_TYP_NBLOB (405)
Clob(n)	struct sqllob (defined in sql.h)	SQL_TYP_CLOB (408)	SQL_TYP_NCLOB (409)
Dbclob(n)	struct sqldbclob (defined in sql.h)	SQL_TYP_DBCLOB (412)	SQL_TYP_NDBCLOB (413)
Varchar(n)	struct sqlchar (defined in sql.h)	SQL_TYP_VARCHAR (448)	SQL_TYP_NVARCHAR (449)
Char(n)	char[n + 1]	SQL_TYP_CHAR (452)	SQL_TYP_NCHAR (453)
Long Varchar	struct sqlchar (defined in sql.h)	SQL_TYP_LONG (456)	SQL_TYP_NLONG (457)
Null- terminated character string	char[n + 1]	SQL_TYP_CSTR (460)	SQL_TYP_NCSTR (461)
Vargraphic(n)	struct sqlgraphic (defined in sql.h)	SQL_TYP_VARGRAPH (464)	SQL_TYP_NVARGRAPH (465)
Graphic(n)	sqldbchar[n + 1] or wchar_t[n + 1]	SQL_TYP_GRAPHIC (468)	SQL_TYP_NGRAPHIC (469)
Long Vargraphic	struct sqlgraphic (defined in sql.h)	SQL_TYP_LONGRAPH (472)	SQL_TYP_NLONGRAPH (473)
Real	float	SQL_TYP_FLOAT (480) (sqllen = 4)	SQL_TYP_NFLOAT (481) (sqllen = 4)
Double	double	SQL_TYP_FLOAT (480) (sqllen = 8)	SQL_TYP_NFLOAT (481) (sqllen = 8)
Decimal(p,s)	(no C equivalent)	SQL_TYP_DECIMAL (484)	SQL_TYP_NDECIMAL (485)
Integer	long	SQL_TYP_INTEGER (496)	SQL_TYP_NINTEGER (497)
Smallint	short	SQL_TYP_SMALL (500)	SQL_TYP_NSMALL (501)

TABLE C-1 *(Continued)*

SQL Datatype	C-Language Datatype	Typecode If Not Nullable	Typecode If Nullable
Blob File Reference	struct sqlfile (defined in sql.h)	SQL_TYP_BLOB_FILE (804)	SQL_TYP_NBLOB_FILE (805)
Clob File Reference	struct sqlfile (defined in sql.h)	SQL_TYP_CLOB_FILE (808)	SQL_TYP_NCLOB_FILE (809)
Dbclob File Reference	struct sqlfile (defined in sql.h)	SQL_TYP_DBCLOB_FILE (812)	SQL_TYP_NDBCLOB_FILE (813)
Blob Locator	long	SQL_TYP_BLOB_LOCATOR (960)	SQL_TYP_NBLOB_LOCATOR (961)
Clob Locator	long	SQL_TYP_CLOB_LOCATOR (964)	SQL_TYP_NCLOB_LOCATOR (965)
Dbclob Locator	long	SQL_TYP_DBCLOB_LOCATOR (968)	SQL_TYP_NDBCLOB_LOCATOR (969)

Definitions are given below for the structures referred to in the "C-Language Datatype" column of Table C-1.[2] In each of these definitions, data[n] represents an array of sufficient size to hold the data.

```
struct sqlchar          /* General-purpose VARCHAR   */
     {
     short               length;
     char                data[n];
     };

struct sqllob           /* General-purpose LOB       */
     {
     unsigned long       length;
     char                data[n];
     };
```

---

2. In sql.h, the definitions of these structures are written using macros and are somewhat more complex, partly for historical reasons and partly for platform independence. Simplified structure definitions are provided here for ease of explanation. See the sql.h and sqlsystm.h files in the sqllib/include directory for details.

```
struct sqlfile            /* File reference for LOBs    */
    {
    unsigned long     name_length;
    unsigned long     data_length;
    unsigned long     file_options;
    char              name[255];
    };
```

The following definitions apply when using the precompiler option WCHAR-TYPE NOCONVERT (the default):

```
struct sqlgraphic         /* General-purpose VARGRAPHIC */
    {
    short             length;
    sqldbchar         data[n];
    };


struct sqldbclob          /* General-purpose DBCLOB     */
    {
    unsigned long     length;
    sqldbchar         data[n];
    };
```

The following definitions apply when using the precompiler option WCHAR-TYPE CONVERT, which causes double-byte character data to be converted into wide-character (wchar_t) format. Wide-character format is used with the wide-character string library declared in wstring.h. The C functions named wcstombs() and mbstowcs() can be used to convert data between wide-character format and multibyte format.

```
struct sqlgraphic         /* General-purpose VARGRAPHIC */
    {
    short             length;
    wchar_t           data[n];
    };


struct sqldbclob          /* General-purpose DBCLOB     */
    {
    unsigned long     length;
    wchar_t           data[n];
    };
```

System Catalog Tables

The system catalog tables are maintained automatically by the UDB system. They contain *metadata*—that is, information about the data that is stored in the database. The base catalog tables are stored in the SYSIBM schema. For historical reasons, the names of these base catalog tables and their columns do not follow a consistent convention. For this reason, it is recommended that you interact with the catalog tables through two sets of *catalog views* that have been defined on them, which provide more consistent naming. Both sets of catalog views are documented in this appendix.

One set of catalog views is defined in the SYSCAT schema. Any user may read these views, but the views are not updatable. The term *catalog tables* is used loosely throughout this book to refer to the views in SYSCAT.

A second set of catalog views is defined in the SYSSTAT schema and is sometimes referred to as the *updatable catalog views*. The purpose of these views is to provide a means whereby authorized users can manually update statistics that are used for query optimization. It is not necessary for users to update these statistics manually, since the statistics are generated automatically by the RUNSTATS utility. However, manual update of the SYSTAT views provides a way for users to influence the system optimizer or to perform experiments on hypothetical databases.

Figure D-1 illustrates the relationship between the base catalog tables and the views that are defined on them, using the COLUMNS catalog as an example. Every catalog table in SYSIBM has a corresponding view in SYSCAT, and some catalog tables have a view in SYSSTAT as well. The name of the base catalog table underlying a catalog view is usually (but not always) the same as the name of the view with a "SYS" prefix added.

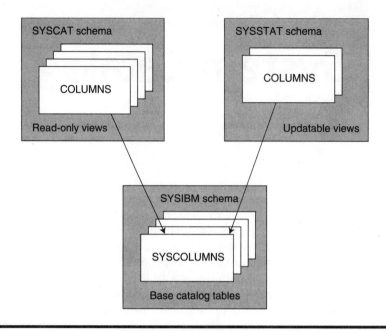

Figure D-1: Views of the System Catalog Tables

D.1 SYSCAT CATALOG VIEWS

All the following views are contained in the SYSCAT schema. None of these views are updatable. The catalog columns do not permit null values, except where noted.

D.1.1 BUFFERPOOLNODES

Each row represents a combination of a bufferpool and a node, in which the size of the bufferpool on that node is different from its default size for other nodes in the same nodegroup (as represented in the BUFFERPOOLS catalog table).

Column	Description
BUFFERPOOLID Integer	Internal bufferpool identifier.

Column	Description
NODENUM Smallint	Node number.
NPAGES Integer	Number of pages in this bufferpool on this node.

D.1.2 BUFFERPOOLS

Each row represents the configuration of a bufferpool on one nodegroup of a database, or on all nodes of a database.

Column	Description
BPNAME Varchar(18)	Name of the buffer pool.
BUFFERPOOLID Integer	Internal bufferpool identifier.
NGNAME Varchar(18)	Nodegroup name (if any).
NPAGES Integer	Default number of pages in this bufferpool on nodes in this nodegroup.
PAGESIZE Integer	Pagesize for this bufferpool on nodes in this nodegroup.
ESTORE Char(1)	Y = This bufferpool uses extended storage in this nodegroup. N = This bufferpool does not use extended storage in this nodegroup.

D.1.3 CHECKS

Each row represents a check constraint. Each check constraint applies to a specific table.

Column	Description
CONSTNAME Varchar(18)	Name of the check constraint. Constraint names (including all types of constraints) must be unique within a table. If no name is specified for a constraint when it is created, the system will generate a name automatically.
DEFINER Char(8)	Userid of the definer of the check constraint.

Column	Description
TABSCHEMA Char(8)	Qualified name of the table to which this constraint applies.
TABNAME Varchar(18)	
CREATE_TIME Timestamp	The time at which the constraint was defined. This timestamp is used in resolving functions that are used in this constraint. When the constraint is enforced, no function will be used that was created after the definition of the constraint.
FUNC_PATH Varchar(254)	The function path that was effective at the time the constraint was defined. This function path governs the resolution of functions used by the constraint.
TEXT Clob(32K)	The text of the CHECK clause of the check constraint, exactly as typed by the constraint definer.

D.1.4 COLAUTH

Each row represents a column-level privilege, indicating the type of the privilege and the column to which it applies.

Column	Description
GRANTOR Char(8)	Authid of user who granted the privilege.
GRANTEE Char(8)	Authid of user to whom the privilege was granted.
GRANTEETYPE Char(1)	G = Grantee is a group. U = Grantee is an individual user.
TABSCHEMA Char(8)	Qualified name of the table or view on which the privilege is held.
TABNAME Varchar(18)	
COLNAME Varchar(18)	Name of the column to which this privilege applies.
COLNO Smallint	Column number of this column within its table (starting with 0).
PRIVTYPE Char(1)	U = Update privilege. R = Reference privilege.

Column	Description
GRANTABLE Char(1)	N = Privilege is not grantable. G = Privilege is grantable.

D.1.5 COLCHECKS

Each row represents some column that is referenced by a check constraint. This catalog table is useful in finding the check constraints that apply to a given column.

Column	Description
CONSTNAME Varchar(18)	Name of the check constraint. Constraint names (including all types of constraints) must be unique within a table. If no name is specified for a constraint when it is created, the system will generate a name automatically.
TABSCHEMA Char(8)	Qualified name of the table containing the referenced column.
TABNAME Varchar(18)	
COLNAME Varchar(18)	Name of the column that is referenced by the check constraint.

D.1.6 COLDIST

This catalog table contains statistics used by the query optimizer. Each row describes either the nth most frequent value of some column or the nth quantile (cumulative distribution) value for some column. Statistics are kept for columns of real tables only (not views).

Column	Description
TABSCHEMA Char(8)	Qualified name of the table to which this row applies.
TABNAME Varchar(18)	
COLNAME Varchar(18)	Name of the column to which this row applies.

Column	Description
TYPE Char(1)	Indicates the type of data contained in this row. F = Frequent value. Q = Quantile value (for example, if five quantile values are maintained for a given column, 20% of the column values will be less than the first quantile value, 40% of the column values will be less than the second quantile value, and so on).
SEQNO Smallint	If TYPE = F, then n in this column identifies the nth most frequent value. If TYPE = Q, then n in this column identifies the nth quantile value.
COLVALUE Varchar(254) (allows nulls)	The data value, as a character literal, such as $1.23E - 4$. If the length of the literal is greater than 254 characters, it is truncated. A distinct-type value is represented as a value of the underlying base datatype. A null value in COLVALUE indicates that the value being described is null.
VALCOUNT Integer	If TYPE = F, then VALCOUNT is the number of occurrences of COLVALUE in the column. If TYPE = Q, then VALCOUNT is the number of rows whose value is less than or equal to COLVALUE.
DISTCOUNT Integer (allows nulls)	If TYPE = Q, this column records the number of distinct values that are less than or equal to COLVALUE (null if unknown). This information is collected only for columns that are the first key column of an index.

D.1.7 COLUMNS

Each row represents a column of a table or view. The columns of the catalog tables and views are listed in COLUMNS, along with the columns of user-defined tables and views.

Column	Description
TABSCHEMA Char(8)	The qualified name of the table or view containing this column.
TABNAME Varchar(18)	
COLNAME Varchar(18)	The name of the column.
COLNO Smallint	The ordinal position of this column among the columns in its table or view (first column = 0).

Column	Description
TYPESCHEMA Char(8)	Qualified name of the datatype of this column.
TYPENAME Varchar(18)	
LENGTH Integer	Maximum length of the data in this column. Zero if the datatype of the column is a distinct type. For double-byte string columns, LENGTH is expressed in characters (multiply by two to get the length in bytes).
SCALE Smallint	Scale if the column datatype is Decimal; zero otherwise.
DEFAULT Varchar(254) (allows nulls)	The default value of the column, expressed as a literal in character-string format. Quotes are used around strings that represent character values to distinguish them from special registers such as CURRENT DATE. The default value of a distinct type is represented as a casting expression such as SHOESIZE(8). If a column has no default, the value of DEFAULT is the null value. If a column has a default and the default is null, the value of DEFAULT is the unquoted string NULL.
NULLS Char(1)	Y = Column allows null values. N = Column does not allow null values.
CODEPAGE Smallint	Code page used to interpret values in this column. Zero for noncharacter datatypes.
LOGGED Char(1)	Applies only to columns whose datatype is Blob, Clob, Dbclob, or a distinct type based on one of the LOB datatypes (blank otherwise). Y = Column is logged. N = Column is not logged.
COMPACT Char(1)	Applies only to columns whose datatype is Blob, Clob, Dbclob, or a distinct type based on one of the LOB datatypes (blank otherwise). Y = Column is compacted to occupy minimum storage (may adversely affect update performance). N = Column is not compacted.
COLCARD Integer	Number of distinct values in the column (–1 if unknown).
HIGH2KEY Varchar(254)	Second highest data value in the column, represented as a literal in character-string format (zero-length string if unknown).
LOW2KEY Varchar(254)	Second lowest data value in the column, represented as a literal in character-string format (zero-length string if unknown).
AVGCOLLEN Integer	Average length of column values (–1 if unknown or if the datatype of the column is a long or LOB datatype).

Column	Description
KEYSEQ Smallint (allows nulls)	The ordinal position of this column within the primary key of its table, starting with 1 for the first column in the primary key (null if the column is not a part of the primary key).
PARTKEYSEQ Smallint (allows nulls)	The ordinal position of this column within the partitioning key for this table, starting with 1 for the first column in the key (zero or null if this column is not part of the partitioning key).
NQUANTILES Smallint	The number of quantile values recorded in the COLDIST catalog table for this column (–1 if no statistics are available for this column).
NMOSTFREQ Smallint	The number of most frequent values recorded in the COLDIST catalog table for this column (–1 if no statistics are available for this column).
REMARKS Varchar(254) (allows nulls)	Descriptive comment provided by user via COMMENT ON COLUMN statement.

D.1.8 CONSTDEP

Each row represents a dependency of a constraint on some other object. Each constraint applies to a specific table.

Column	Description
CONSTNAME Varchar(18)	Name of the constraint. Constraint names (including all types of constraints) must be unique within a table. If no name is specified for a constraint when it is created, the system will generate a name automatically.
TABSCHEMA Char(8)	Qualified name of the table to which the constraint applies.
TABNAME Varchar(18)	
BTYPE Char(1)	Type of the base object on which the constraint depends. Values: F = Function instance. I = Index.
BSCHEMA Char(8)	Qualified name of the base object on which the constraint depends. No dependencies are recorded on built-in functions, since these functions cannot be dropped.
BNAME Varchar(18)	

D.1.9 DATATYPES

Each row represents a datatype. Both built-in and user-defined datatypes are represented.

Column	Description
TYPESCHEMA Char(8)	Qualified name of the datatype. For built-in datatypes, the schema name is SYSIBM.
TYPENAME Varchar(18)	
DEFINER Char(8)	Userid under which the datatype was created.
SOURCESCHEMA Char(8) (allows nulls)	Qualified name of the source datatype for distinct types. Null for built-in datatypes.
SOURCENAME Varchar(18) (allows nulls)	
METATYPE Char(1)	S = System (built-in) datatype. T = Distinct (user-defined) datatype.
TYPEID Smallint	Internal datatype identifier.
SOURCETYPEID Smallint (allows nulls)	Internal datatype identifier of source datatype (null for built-in datatypes).
LENGTH Integer	Maximum length of the datatype. Zero for built-in parameterized datatypes such as Decimal and Varchar.
SCALE Smallint	Scale for distinct types based on the built-in Decimal datatype. Zero for all other datatypes (including Decimal itself).
CODEPAGE Smallint	For string datatypes and distinct types based on string datatypes, the code page used to interpret values of this datatype. Zero for all other datatypes.
CREATE_TIME Timestamp	Creation time of the datatype.
REMARKS Varchar(254) (allows nulls)	Descriptive comment supplied by a user via COMMENT ON DISTINCT TYPE statement.

D.1.10 DBAUTH

Each row represents a set of database-level authorities that have been granted by some grantor to some grantee, which may be an individual user or a group. All privileges granted by a given grantor to a given grantee are recorded in the same row of DBAUTH. All authorities apply to the database that contains the catalog table.

Column	Description
GRANTOR Char(8)	Userid of grantor of authority.
GRANTEE Char(8)	Receiver (holder) of authority. This name may identify an individual user or a group. Groups are defined and managed by the operating system.
GRANTEETYPE Char(1)	U = Grantee is an individual user. G = Grantee is a group.
DBADMAUTH Char(1)	Database Administration authority. Y = held, N = not held.
CREATETABAUTH Char(1)	Authority to create tables in the database. Y = held, N = not held.
BINDADDAUTH Char(1)	Authority to create (bind) packages in the database. Y = held, N = not held.
CONNECTAUTH Char(1)	Authority to connect to the database. Y = held, N = not held.
NOFENCEAUTH Char(1)	Authority to create nonfenced external functions in the database. Y = held, N = not held.
IMPLSCHEMAAUTH Char(1)	Authority to implicitly create a new schema by creating an object in a non-existing schema. Y = held, N = not held.

D.1.11 EVENTMONITORS

Each row represents an Event Monitor. Event Monitors are created by the CREATE EVENT MONITOR statement and controlled by the SET EVENT MONITOR STATE statement. Each Event Monitor monitors a set of events in the database and writes information about them into a given file or pipe.

Column	Description
EVMONNAME Varchar(18)	Name of Event Monitor. Since Event Monitor names are global in a database, they have no schema names.
DEFINER Char(8)	Userid of the user who defined the Event Monitor.
TARGET_TYPE Char(1)	The type of the target to which event data is written. F = File. P = Pipe.
TARGET Varchar(246)	The name of the target to which event data is written. If the target is a pipe, this column contains the name of the pipe. If the target is a file, this column contains the absolute path name of the directory into which the file will be written. The names of the files to be generated in this directory are 00000001.EVT, 00000002.EVT, and so on.
MAXFILES Integer (allows nulls)	Maximum number of event files that this Event Monitor will generate in the target directory. Null if there is no maximum or if the target type is not FILE.
MAXFILESIZE Integer (allows nulls)	Maximum size (in 4K pages) that each event file can reach before the Event Monitor creates a new file. Null if there is no maximum or if the target type is not FILE.
BUFFERSIZE Integer (allows nulls)	Size (in 4K pages) of the buffer used by the Event Monitor to accumulate event data before writing it into an event file. Null if the target type is not FILE.
IO_MODE Char(1) (allows nulls)	Indicates what happens if an event is detected when the buffer is full. B = Blocked; wait for buffer to be written to disk, then record event. (Prevents loss of data but may adversely affect system performance.) N = Not blocked. (Events may be lost during writing of buffer to disk. Less impact on system performance.) Null if target type is not FILE.
WRITE_MODE Char(1) (allows nulls)	Indicates how this monitor handles existing event data when the monitor is activated. Values: A = Append data to existing file. R = Replace existing file with new file. Null if target type is not FILE.
AUTOSTART Char(1)	Indicates whether the Event Monitor will be activated automatically when the server is started (by a DB2START command). Y = Yes, Event Monitor is activated automatically. N = No, Event Monitor is not activated until a SET EVENT MONITOR STATE command is executed.
NODENUM Smallint	The number of the node on which the event monitor runs and logs events.

Column	Description
MONSCOPE Char(1)	Monitoring scope: L = Local. G = Global.
REMARKS Varchar(254) (allows nulls)	Reserved for future use by the COMMENT statement to record a descriptive remark about the Event Monitor.

D.1.12 EVENTS

Each row represents an event that is being monitored by some Event Monitor.

Column	Description
EVMONNAME Varchar(18)	Name of Event Monitor that is monitoring this event. An Event Monitor may monitor more than one event. Since Event Monitor names are global in a database, they have no schema names.
TYPE Varchar(18)	The type of event being monitored. The possible values of this column are as follows: DATABASE, CONNECTIONS, TABLES, STATEMENTS, TRANSACTIONS, DEADLOCKS, TABLESPACES.
FILTER Clob(32K) (allows nulls)	The full text of the WHERE clause that defines the event that is being monitored, as it was typed in the CREATE EVENT MONITOR statement.

D.1.13 FUNCPARMS

Each row represents either a parameter or the result of a function that has an entry in the FUNCTIONS catalog table.

Column	Description
FUNCSCHEMA Char(8)	Qualified name of the function for which this row describes a parameter or result. Several function instances can have the same qualified name, if they have different signatures (this is called *overloading*).
FUNCNAME Varchar(18)	
SPECIFICNAME Varchar(18)	Specific name of the function for this row describes a parameter or result. The specific name of a function instance must be unique within its schema.

Column	Description
ROWTYPE Char(1)	Indicates what is described by this row. Values: P = A parameter of the function. R = The result of the function, before casting. C = The result of the function, after casting (for more details on casting, see the "CAST FROM" clause of the CREATE FUNCTION statement).
ORDINAL Smallint	If ROWTYPE = P, the ordinal position of this parameter among all the parameters of the function, starting with 1. If ROWTYPE = R and the function returns a table, the ordinal position of this column in the result table, starting with 1. Otherwise zero.
PARMNAME Varchar(18) (allows nulls)	Name of the parameter or result column, or null if no name exists.
TYPESCHEMA Char(8)	Qualified name of the datatype of the parameter or result.
TYPENAME Varchar(18)	
LENGTH Integer	Maximum length of the parameter or result. Zero if the parameter or result is a distinct type or has no well-defined maximum length.
SCALE Smallint	Scale of the parameter or result. Zero if the parameter or result is a distinct type or has no well-defined scale.
CODEPAGE Smallint	Code page used to interpret the parameter or result (zero if it is not a string datatype).
CAST_FUNCID Integer (allows nulls)	Internal function ID of function used to cast the argument (if this function is sourced on another function) or result (if ROWTYPE = C). Null otherwise.
AS_LOCATOR Char(1)	Y = Parameter or result is passed in the form of a locator. N = Not passed in the form of a locator.

D.1.14 FUNCTIONS

Contains a row for each user-defined function (including sourced and external functions, scalar and column functions). Also includes system-generated casting and comparison functions, but does not include built-in functions.

Column	Description
FUNCSCHEMA Char(8)	Qualified name of the function. Several function instances can have the same qualified name if they have different signatures (this is called *overloading*).
FUNCNAME Varchar(18)	
SPECIFICNAME Varchar(18)	Specific name of the function instance (must be unique within its schema). May be system-generated.
DEFINER Char(8)	Userid of the user who defined the function.
FUNCID Integer	Function identifier, assigned by the system for internal use.
RETURN_TYPE Smallint	Internal datatype identifier of result datatype of function. Can be joined with TYPEID column in DATATYPES catalog table.
ORIGIN Char(1)	Indicates how the function was created. E = User-defined, external function (written in a host language). U = User-defined, sourced function (sourced on another function). S = System-generated (for example, cast function of a distinct type).
TYPE Char(1)	S = Scalar function. C = Column function. T = Table function.
PARM_COUNT Smallint	Number of function parameters. See the FUNCPARMS catalog table for a description of the parameters.
PARM_SIGNATURE Varchar(180) for bit data	Concatenation of up to 90 parameter datatypes, in internal format. Used in function resolution and to guarantee uniqueness. Zero length if function takes no parameters.
CREATE_TIME Timestamp	Timestamp of function creation.
VARIANT Char(1)	Indicates whether two calls to the function with the same parameters will always yield the same result. Used in optimization of queries. Y = Variant (nondeterministic—results may differ). N = Invariant (deterministic—results are consistent). Blank if ORIGIN is not E.
SIDE_EFFECTS Char(1)	Indicates whether the function has side effects (any effect other than returning a result value). Used in optimization of queries. E = Function has side effects (hence number of invocations is important). N = No side effects. Blank if ORIGIN is not E.

Column	Description
FENCED Char(1)	Indicates whether the function is allowed to run in the same address as the database or is restricted (fenced) to a separate address space for safety. Y = Fenced N = Not fenced Blank if ORIGIN is not E.
NULLCALL Char(1)	Indicates whether the function should be invoked when one of its arguments is null. Y = Yes, invoke the function with null arguments. N = No, if any argument is null, the function is not invoked and the result is implicitly set to null. Blank if ORIGIN is not E.
CAST_FUNCTION Char(1)	Indicates whether the function is a cast function (meaning that it can be invoked by the notation CAST(type1 AS type2). Y = This is a cast function. N = Not a cast function.
ASSIGN_FUNCTION Char(1)	Indicates whether the function can be invoked implicitly by assigning a value to a target of a different datatype. For example, assigning an Integer to a column of distinct type Hatsize based on Integer might implicitly invoke the function hatsize(Integer). Y = Implicit assignment function. N = Not an implicit assignment function.
SCRATCHPAD Char(1)	Indicates whether this function has a scratchpad on which it can save information from one invocation to the next. Y = This function has a scratchpad. N = No scratchpad. Blank if ORIGIN is not E.
FINAL_CALL Char(1)	Indicates whether one extra call is made to this function at the end of processing an SQL statement (in addition to the calls for processing each row). Y = Final call is made. N = No final call. Blank if ORIGIN is not E.
PARALLELLIZABLE Char(1)	Y = The function can be executed in parallel on multiple nodes. N = The function cannot be executed in parallel.
CONTAINS_SQL Char(1)	Indicates whether an external function contains any SQL statements. N = Contains no SQL statements (no other value is supported in the current release).
DBINFO Char(1)	Y = Special environment parameter (DBINFO) is passed to the function. N = No DBINFO parameter is passed to the function.

Column	Description
RESULT_COLS Smallint	For a table function (TYPE = T), contains the number of columns in the result table; otherwise, contains 1.
LANGUAGE Char(8)	Implementation language of function body. Blank if ORIGIN is not E.
IMPLEMENTATION Varchar(254) (allows nulls)	If ORIGIN = E, contains the path name of the object code module that implements this function. If ORIGIN = U and the source function is built-in, this column contains the name and signature of the source function. Null otherwise.
PARM_STYLE Char(8)	Indicates the parameter style declared in the CREATE FUNCTION statement. Supported values are DB2SQL and DB2GENRL. Blank if ORIGIN is not E.
SOURCE_SCHEMA Char(8) (allows nulls)	If ORIGIN = U and the source function is a user-defined function, contains the specific name of the source function. If ORIGIN = U and the source function is built-in, SOURCE_SCHEMA is SYSIBM, and SOURCE_SPECIFIC is "N/A for built-in." Null if ORIGIN is not U.
SOURCE_SPECIFIC Varchar(18) (allows nulls)	
IOS_PER_INVOC Double	Estimated number of input/output operations per invocation of the function (used in query optimization). –1 if not known.
INSTS_PER_INVOC Double	Estimated number of CPU instructions per invocation of the function (used in query optimization). –1 if not known.
IOS_PER_ARGBYTE Double	Estimated average number of input/output operations per byte of each input parameter (used in query optimization). –1 if not known.
INSTS_PER_ARGBYTE Double	Estimated average number of CPU instructions per byte of each input parameter (used in query optimization). –1 if not known.
PERCENT_ARGBYTES Smallint	Estimated average percent of its input parameter bytes that the function will actually read (used in query optimization). –1 if not known.
INITIAL_IOS Double	Estimated number of "startup" input/output operations performed on the first invocation of the function in an SQL statement (used in query optimization). –1 if not known.
INITIAL_INSTS Double	Estimated number of "startup" CPU instructions executed on the first invocation of the function in an SQL statement (used in query optimization). –1 if not known.
CARDINALITY Integer	The predicted number of rows returned by a table function. –1 if not known or if the function is not a table function.
REMARKS Varchar(254) (allows nulls)	Descriptive comment supplied by a user via COMMENT ON FUNCTION statement.

D.1.15 INDEXAUTH

Each row represents a privilege held on an index.

Column	Description
GRANTOR Char(8)	Userid of the user who granted the privilege (or SYSTEM, if the privilege was granted by the system to the creator of the index).
GRANTEE Char(8)	Receiver (holder) of privilege.
GRANTEETYPE Char(1)	U = Grantee is an individual user. G = Grantee is a group.
INDSCHEMA Char(8)	Qualified name of index on which the privilege is held.
INDNAME Varchar(18)	
CONTROLAUTH Char(1)	Y = Control privilege is held (required to drop the index). N = Control privilege is not held.

D.1.16 INDEXES

Each row represents an index.

Column	Description
INDSCHEMA Char(8)	Qualified name of the index.
INDNAME Varchar(18)	
DEFINER Char(8)	Userid of the user who created the index.
TABSCHEMA Char(8)	Qualified name of the table to which the index applies.
TABNAME Varchar(18)	
COLNAMES Varchar(320)	List of names of the columns to which the index applies. Each column name is preceded by a "+" if the index is ascending on that column, or by a "−" if the index is descending on that column.

Column	Description
UNIQUERULE Char(1)	D = Index allows duplicate key values. U = Key values are required to be unique. P = Index is used to support a primary key (implies unique key values).
MADE_UNIQUE Char(1)	Y = Index was originally nonunique but was converted to a unique index by the system to support a unique or primary key constraint. If the key or constraint is dropped, the index will revert to its original nonunique status. N = The index remains as it was created.
COLCOUNT Smallint	The number of columns in the index key.
UNIQUE_COLCOUNT Smallint	The number of key columns necessary to guarantee uniqueness (–1 if the index allows duplicate key values). Rule: UNIQUE_COLCOUNT <= COLCOUNT.
INDEXTYPE Char(4)	REG = Regular index. CLUS = Clustering index (controls physical placement of newly inserted rows).
PCTFREE Smallint	Percentage of each index page to be reserved during initial construction of the index. This space is available for future inserts after the index is built.
IID Smallint	Internal identifier of the index.
NLEAF Integer	Number of leaf pages (lowest-level pages) occupied by the index. –1 if not known.
NLEVELS Smallint	Number of levels in the index (used in optimizer cost formulas). –1 if not known.
FIRSTKEYCARD Integer	Number of different values in the first key column of the index. –1 if not known.
FIRST2KEYCARD Integer	Number of different value combinations in the first two key columns of the index. –1 if not known.
FIRST3KEYCARD Integer	Number of different value combinations in the first three key columns of the index. –1 if not known.
FIRST4KEYCARD Integer	Number of different value combinations in the first four key columns of the index. –1 if not known.
FULLKEYCARD Integer	Number of different value combinations in the full index key. –1 if not known.
CLUSTERRATIO Smallint	A measure of how well the ordering of this index corresponds to the physical ordering of rows in storage (used in optimizer cost formulas). –1 if not known.
CLUSTERFACTOR Double	A finer measure of how well the index ordering corresponds to the physical ordering of rows in storage (used in optimizer cost formulas). –1 if not known.

Column	Description
SEQUENTIAL_PAGES Integer	Number of index leaf pages located on disk in index key order with few or no large gaps between them. −1 if not known.
DENSITY Integer	Ratio of SEQUENTIAL_PAGES to number of pages in the range of pages occupied by the index, expressed as a percent between 0 and 100. −1 if not known.
USER_DEFINED Smallint	A 1 indicates that this index was created by a user. An index can be physically destroyed only if USER_DEFINED and SYSTEM_REQUIRED are both 0.
SYSTEM_REQUIRED Smallint	A 1 indicates that this index is being used by the system to enforce a primary key or unique constraint. An index can be physically destroyed only if USER_DEFINED and SYSTEM_REQUIRED are both 0.
CREATE_TIME Timestamp	Time when the index was created.
STATS_TIME Timestamp (allows nulls)	The last time when any change was made to the recorded statistics for this index (for example, by the RUNSTATS utility). Null if no statistics are available for the index.
PAGE_FETCH_PAIRS Varchar(254) for bit data	A list of pairs of integers, represented in character form. Each pair represents the number of pages in a hypothetical buffer and the number of page fetches required to scan the index using that hypothetical buffer. (Zero-length string if no data is available.)
REMARKS Varchar(254) (allows nulls)	Descriptive comment supplied by a user via COMMENT ON INDEX statement.
TEXT Clob(32K) (allows nulls)	Reserved for future use.

D.1.17 KEYCOLUSE

Lists all columns that participate in a key defined by a unique, primary key, or foreign key constraint.

Column	Description
CONSTNAME Varchar(18)	Name of the constraint. Constraint names (including all types of constraints) are unique within a table.
TABSCHEMA Char(8)	Qualified name of the table containing the column.
TABNAME Varchar(18)	

Column	Description
COLNAME Varchar(18)	Name of the column.
COLSEQ Smallint	Ordinal position of the column within the key (first column = 1).

D.1.18 NODEGROUPDEF

Each row represents the participation of some node in a nodegroup.

Column	Description
NGNAME Varchar(18)	Name of the nodegroup.
NODENUM Smallint	Node number of a node in the nodegroup (an integer between 0 and 999, inclusive).
IN_USE Char(1)	Indicates the status of this node in this nodegroup. A = The node is newly added. Its containers have been created, but it is not yet in the partition map, pending completion of a Redistribute Nodegroup operation. D = The node will be dropped when Redistribute Nodegroup is completed. T = The node has been added without tablespaces. Containers must be explicitly specified for the node, and a Redistribute Nodegroup operation must be completed to add the node to the partition map. Y = The node is in the partition map.

D.1.19 NODEGROUPS

Each row represents a nodegroup.

Column	Description
NGNAME Varchar(18)	Name of the nodegroup.
DEFINER Char(8)	Authorization ID of the node group definer.
PMAP_ID Smallint	Identifier of the partition map for this nodegroup in the PARTITIONMAPS catalog table.

Column	Description
REBALANCE_PMAPID Smallint	Identifier of the partition map currently being used for redistribution of rows in this nodegroup (−1 if no Redistribute Nodegroup operation is in progress).
CREATE_TIME Timestamp	Creation time of the nodegroup.
REMARKS Varchar(254) (Allows nulls)	Descriptive comment supplied by a user via COMMENT ON NODE-GROUP statement.

D.1.20 PACKAGEAUTH

Each row represents a set of privileges on a package held by a user or by a group. A package represents the bound form of an application program.

Column	Description
GRANTOR Char(8)	Grantor of the privileges.
GRANTEE Char(8)	Receiver (holder) of the privileges.
GRANTEETYPE Char(1)	U = Grantee is an individual user. G = Grantee is a group.
PKGSCHEMA Char(8)	Qualified name of the package on which the privileges are held.
PKGNAME Char(8)	
CONTROLAUTH Char(1)	Indicates whether the control privilege (needed to drop the package) is held. Y = Privilege is held. N = Privilege is not held.
BINDAUTH Char(1)	Indicates whether the privilege to bind and rebind the package is held. Y = Privilege is held. N = Privilege is not held.
EXECUTEAUTH Char(1)	Indicates whether the privilege to execute the package is held. This privilege is required to successfully run the application program corresponding to this package. Y = Privilege is held. N = Privilege is not held.

D.1.21 PACKAGEDEP

Each row represents a dependency of a package on some object.

Column	Description
PKGSCHEMA Char(8)	Qualified name of the package.
PKGNAME Char(8)	
BINDER Char(8) (allows nulls)	User who bound the package.
BTYPE Char(1)	The type of the object on which the package depends. A = Alias. F = Function instance (user-defined functions only). I = Index. T = Table. V = View.
BSCHEMA Char(8)	Qualified name of the object on which the package depends. If a function instance on which the package depends is dropped, the package becomes "inoperative" and must be explicitly rebound. If any other kind of object (or privilege) on which the package depends is dropped, the system will automatically attempt to rebind the package on its next use.
BNAME Varchar(18)	
TABAUTH Smallint (allows nulls)	If BTYPE is T (table) or V (view), encodes the privileges that are required by this package (may include Select, Insert, Delete, and Update), using a combination of binary codes declared in sql.h.

D.1.22 PACKAGES

Each row describes a package that was created by binding some application program. The package is stored in the database and contains an optimized plan for executing each SQL statement in the program. This catalog table records some of the options that were specified on the PREP or BIND command that created the package. These options are used when the package is rebound, either implicitly or by an explicit REBIND command.

Column	Description
PKGSCHEMA Char(8)	Qualified name of the package.
PKGNAME Char(8)	

Column	Description
BOUNDBY Char(8)	Authorization ID used for authorization checking during binding of package (controlled by OWNER bind option; default = same as DEFINER).
DEFINER Char(8)	The userid of the user who actually bound the package.
DEFAULT_SCHEMA Char(8)	Default schema name used for unqualified names in static SQL statements (controlled by SCHEMA bind option; default = same as DEFINER).
VALID Char(1)	Indicates the status of the package. Y = Valid, ready for use. N = Not valid, but will be implicitly rebound on next use. The implicit rebind may restore the package to a valid state. X = Inoperative because some function instance used by the package no longer exists. An inoperative package will not be implicitly rebound; it can be restored to validity only by an explicit BIND or REBIND command.
UNIQUE_ID Char(8)	Time at which the package was originally created. This column serves as a timestamp to check for consistency between the application program and its package.
TOTAL_SECT Smallint	Number of sections in the package. Each section contains an optimized plan for executing one SQL statement.
FORMAT Char(1)	Format used by the package to represent dates and times. Codes: 0 = Derived from country code of database. 1 = USA. 2 = EUR. 3 = ISO. 4 = JIS. 5 = LOCAL.
ISOLATION Char(2) (allows nulls)	Isolation level of this package: RR = Repeatable Read. RS = Read Stability. CS = Cursor Stability. UR = Uncommitted Read.
BLOCKING Char(1) (allows nulls)	Cursor-blocking option. Controls whether rows of a query result are transmitted from server to client individually or in "blocks" for efficiency. N = No blocking used. B = Blocking used for fetch-only cursors. In ambiguous cases (no declaration of intent), cursors are assumed to be fetch-only. U = Blocking used for fetch-only cursors. In ambiguous cases (no declaration of intent), cursors are assumed to be updatable.
INSERT_BUF Char(1) (allows nulls)	Y = Inserts are buffered at coordinator node to reduce message passing in multinode systems (specified by INSERT bind option). N or null = Inserts are not buffered.

Column	Description
LANG_LEVEL Char(1) (allows nulls)	Records the LANGLEVEL option used when package was bound, which controls the interpretation of certain SQL features, including cursors: 0 = SAA1 (Systems Application Architecture). Cursors to be used in positioned updates must be declared FOR UPDATE. 1 = SQL92E (SQL92 Standard, Entry Level) or MIA (Multivendor Integration Architecture). Cursors to be used in positioned updates need not be declared FOR UPDATE.
FUNC_PATH Varchar(254)	The function path used when the package was last bound. The same function path is used on an implicit or explicit rebind of the package.
QUERYOPT Integer	Optimization class under which this package was bound. Values range from 0 to 9, indicating increasing levels of optimization.
EXPLAIN_LEVEL Char(1)	Explain level requested for this package. The Explain facility captures information about access plans in a form that can be displayed visually. (blank) = No Explain requested. P = Plan Selection level.
EXPLAIN_MODE Char(1)	Is the Tabular Explain facility active for this package? Y = Yes. N = No.
EXPLAIN_SNAPSHOT Char(1)	Is the Explain snapshot (Visual Explain) facility active for this package? Y = Yes. N = No.
SQLWARN Char(1)	Y = Positive values for SQLCODE, indicating warning conditions, are returned to the application program. N = Positive values for SQLCODE are suppressed and not returned to the application program.
SQLMATHWARN Char(1)	Specifies handling of arithmetic errors and retrieval conversion errors (controlled by database configuration parameter DFT_SQLMATHWARN at bind time). Y = Returns special null (indicator –2) and warning; processing continues. N = Treated as a hard error; statement is aborted.
EXPLICIT_BIND_TIME Timestamp	The time at which this package was last explicitly bound or rebound. When the package is implicitly rebound, no function instance will be selected that was created later than this time.
LAST_BIND_TIME Timestamp	Time at which the plan was last explicitly or implicitly bound or rebound. Used to check validity of EXPLAIN data.
CODEPAGE Smallint	Code page used by application program to interpret character-string data (–1 if not known).
DEGREE Char(5)	Indicates the limit on intra-partition parallelism specified at bind time. 1 = Package is limited to one thread of execution. ANY = No limit; degree determined by optimizer.

Column	Description
MULTINODE_PLANS Char(1)	Y = Package was bound in a parallel (multinode) environment. N = Package was bound in a serial (single-node) environment.
INTRA_PARALLEL Char(1)	Y = Some SQL statement in the package uses intra-partition parallelism. N = No SQL statement in the package uses intra-partition parallelism. F = Some SQL statement in the package can use intra-partition parallelism, but the package is currently bound for use on a nonparallel system.
REMARKS Varchar(254) (allows nulls)	Descriptive comment supplied by a user via COMMENT ON PACKAGE statement.

D.1.23 PARTITIONMAPS

Each row represents a partition map that is used to distribute the rows of a table among the nodes in a nodegroup by hashing the partitioning key of the table.

Column	Description
PMAP_ID Smallint	ID of partition map.
PARTITIONMAP Long Varchar for Bit Data	The actual partitioning map, a vector of 4,096 two-byte integers.

D.1.24 PROCEDURES

Each row represents a stored procedure.

Column	Description
PROCSCHEMA Char(8)	Qualified name of the stored procedure.
PROCNAME Varchar(18)	
SPECIFICNAME Varchar(18)	Specific name of the stored procedure (must be unique within its schema). May be system-generated.

Column	Description
PROCEDURE_ID Integer	Internal ID of the stored procedure.
DEFINER Char(8)	Userid under which the stored procedure was created.
PARM_COUNT Smallint	Number of parameters. See the PROCPARMS catalog table for a description of the parameters.

PARM_SIGNATURE
    Varchar(180)
    for bit data
	Concatenation of up to 90 parameter datatypes, in internal format. Zero length if procedure takes no parameters.

ORIGIN Char(1)	E = External.
CREATE_TIME Timestamp	Timestamp of procedure creation.
DETERMINISTIC Char(1)	Y = Results are deterministic (depend only on input). N = Results are nondeterministic (may vary for different calls with same input).
FENCED Char(1)	Indicates whether the procedure is allowed to run in the same address as the database or is restricted (fenced) to a separate address space for safety. Y = Fenced. N = Not fenced.
NULLCALL Char(1)	Indicates whether the procedure should be invoked when one of its arguments is null. Y = Yes, invoke the procedure with null arguments. (No other options are supported at present.)
LANGUAGE Char(8)	Implementation language of the procedure: C or JAVA.

IMPLEMENTATION
    Varchar(254)
    (allows nulls)
	Indicates where the implementation of the procedure can be found.
	Path/module/function when LANGUAGE = C.
	Class/method when LANGUAGE = JAVA.

PARM_STYLE Char(8)	DB2DARI (if LANGUAGE = C) or DB2GENRL (if LANGUAGE = JAVA).
RESULT_SETS Smallint	Number of result sets returned by the procedure.

REMARKS
    Varchar(254)
    (allows nulls)
	Descriptive comment supplied by a user via COMMENT ON PROCE-DURE statement.

D.1.25 PROCPARMS

Each row represents a parameter of a stored procedure.

Column	Description
PROCSCHEMA Char(8)	Qualified name of the procedure for which this row describes a parameter or result.
PROCNAME Varchar(18)	
SPECIFICNAME Varchar(18)	Specific name of the procedure.
ORDINAL Smallint	The ordinal position of this parameter among all the parameters of the procedure, starting with 1.
PARMNAME Varchar(18)	Name of the parameter.
TYPESCHEMA Char(8)	Qualified name of the datatype of the parameter.
TYPENAME Varchar(18)	
LENGTH Integer	Maximum length of the parameter. Zero if the parameter or result is a distinct type or has no well-defined maximum length.
SCALE Smallint	Scale of the parameter or result if its datatype is Decimal.
CODEPAGE Smallint	Code page of this parameter. Zero if the parameter is FOR BIT DATA or not a string type.
PARM_MODE Varchar(5)	IN = Input parameter. OUT = Output parameter. INOUT = Parameter used for both input and output.
AS_LOCATOR Char(1)	Always "N." Provides for possible future parameters passed in the form of locators.

D.1.26 REFERENCES

Each row represents a referential integrity (foreign key) constraint.

Column	Description
CONSTNAME Varchar(18)	Name of the constraint. Constraint names (including all types of constraints) must be unique within a table. If no name is specified for a constraint when it is created, the system will generate a name automatically.

Column	Description
TABSCHEMA Char(8)	Qualified name of child table.
TABNAME Varchar(18)	
DEFINER Char(8)	User who created the constraint.
REFKEYNAME Varchar(18)	Name of the primary or unique key constraint in the parent table.
REFTABSCHEMA Char(8)	Qualified name of parent table.
REFTABNAME Varchar(18)	
COLCOUNT Smallint	Number of columns in the foreign key (in the child table).
DELETERULE Char(1)	Indicates what happens when a row is deleted from the parent table. A = No Action; deletions from the parent table are not allowed if matching rows exist in the child table. C = Cascade; matching rows are deleted from the child table. N = Set Null; foreign key is set to null in matching rows of the child table. R = Restrict; deletions from the parent table are not allowed if matching rows exist in the child table.
UPDATERULE Char(1)	Indicates what happens when a primary key is updated in the parent table. R = Restrict; update not allowed if matching rows exist in child table. A = No Action; update not allowed if matching rows exist in child table.
CREATE_TIME Timestamp	Time at which the referential constraint was defined.
FK_COLNAMES Varchar(320)	List of column names that constitute the foreign key in the child table.
PK_COLNAMES Varchar(320)	List of column names that constitute the primary or unique key in the parent table.

D.1.27 SCHEMAAUTH

Each row represents a set of privileges held on a particular schema by a user or group of users. All schema privileges for a given schema, grantor, and grantee appear in a single row.

Column	Description
GRANTOR Char(8)	Authorization ID of the user who granted the privileges (or SYSIBM if privileges were granted by system).
GRANTEE Char(8)	Authorization ID of the user or group who holds the privileges.
GRANTEETYPE Char(1)	U = Grantee is an individual user. G = Grantee is a group.
SCHEMANAME Char(8)	Name of the schema.
ALTERINAUTH Char(1)	Indicates status of ALTERIN privilege: Y = Held but not grantable. G = Held and grantable. N = Not held.
CREATEINAUTH Char(1)	Indicates status of CREATEIN privilege: Y = Held but not grantable. G = Held and grantable. N = Not held.
DROPINAUTH Char(1)	Indicates status of DROPIN privilege: Y = Held but not grantable. G = Held and grantable. N = Not held.

D.1.28 SCHEMATA

Each row represents a schema.

Column	Description
SCHEMANAME Char(8)	Name of the schema.
OWNER Char(8)	The user who owns the schema.
DEFINER Char(8)	The user who created the schema (might be different from the owner, for example, if a schema was created by a database administrator for another user to own).
CREATE_TIME Timestamp	Timestamp indicating when the schema was created.
REMARKS Varchar(254) (allows nulls)	Descriptive comment supplied by a user via COMMENT ON SCHEMA statement.

D.1.29 STATEMENTS

Each row contains the text of an SQL statement used to generate one section of a package.

Column	Description
PKGSCHEMA Char(8)	Qualified name of the package.
PKGNAME Char(8)	
STMTNO Smallint	Line number of SQL statement within the source program.
SECTNO Smallint	Section number within the package.
SEQNO Smallint	Sequence number of this row. If the SQL statement occupies more than 3,600 bytes, it is stored in multiple rows, and the SEQNO column is used to number the rows used for a given SQL statement.
TEXT Varchar(3600)	The text of the SQL statement.

D.1.30 TABAUTH

Each row represents a set of privileges on a table or view, granted by a particular grantor to a particular grantee, which may be an individual user or a group. All the privileges granted by a given grantor to a given grantee on a given table or view are combined into a single row of TABAUTH.

Column	Description
GRANTOR Char(8)	Grantor of the privilege.
GRANTEE Char(8)	Receiver (holder) of the privilege.
GRANTEETYPE Char(1)	U = Grantee is an individual user. G = Grantee is a group.
TABSCHEMA Char(8)	Qualified name of the table or view to which the privilege applies.
TABNAME Varchar(18)	

Column	Description
CONTROLAUTH Char(1)	CONTROL privilege; needed to drop the table or view. Implies all other privileges. Y = Privilege is held. N = Not held.
ALTERAUTH Char(1)	ALTER privilege; needed to alter a table or to comment on a table or view. G = Privilege is held and grantable. Y = Held but not grantable. N = Not held.
DELETEAUTH Char(1)	DELETE privilege; needed to delete rows from a table or view. G = Privilege is held and grantable. Y = Held but not grantable. N = Not held.
INDEXAUTH Char(1)	INDEX privilege; needed to create an index on a table. G = Privilege is held and grantable. Y = Held but not grantable. N = Not held.
INSERTAUTH Char(1)	INSERT privilege; needed to insert rows into a table or view. G = Privilege is held and grantable. Y = Held but not grantable. N = Not held.
SELECTAUTH Char(1)	SELECT privilege; needed to read data from a table or view. G = Privilege is held and grantable. Y = Held but not grantable. N = Not held.
REFAUTH Char(1)	REFERENCE privilege; needed to create or drop a foreign key constraint that references this table as the parent table. G = Privilege is held and grantable. Y = Held but not grantable. N = Not held.
UPDATEAUTH Char(1)	UPDATE privilege; needed to update rows of the table or view. G = Privilege is held and grantable. Y = Held but not grantable. N = Not held.

D.1.31 TABCONST

Each row represents a constraint on a table. Includes check, unique, primary key, and foreign key constraints.

Column	Description
CONSTNAME Varchar(18)	Name of the constraint. Constraint names (including all types of constraints) must be unique within a table. If no name is specified for a constraint when it is created, the system will generate a name automatically.
TABSCHEMA Char(8)	Qualified name of the table to which the constraint applies.
TABNAME Varchar(18)	
DEFINER Char(8)	Userid under which the constraint was defined.
TYPE Char(1)	Type of the constraint. K = Check constraint. P = Primary key constraint. U = Unique constraint. F = Foreign key (referential integrity) constraint.
REMARKS Varchar(254) (allows nulls)	Descriptive comment supplied by a user via COMMENT ON CONSTRAINT statement.

D.1.32 TABLES

Each row represents a table, view, or alias. The system catalog tables and views are represented in TABLES, along with user-defined tables and views.

Column	Description
TABSCHEMA Char(8)	Qualified name of the table, view, or alias.
TABNAME Varchar(18)	
DEFINER Char(8)	Userid of the user who created the table, view, or alias.
TYPE Char(1)	Indicates the type of the object being described. T = Table. V = View. A = Alias.

Column	Description
STATUS Char(1)	Indicates whether the object is in a special status. N = Normal status. C = Check Pending status (applies to tables). X = Inoperative status (applies to views).
BASE_TABSCHEMA Char(8) (allows nulls)	If TYPE = A, these columns identify the table, view, or alias that is referenced by this alias; otherwise, they are NULL. The object referenced by an alias is not guaranteed to exist.
BASE_TABNAME Varchar(18) (allows nulls)	
CREATE_TIME Timestamp	Time of creation of the table, view, or alias.
STATS_TIME Timestamp (allows nulls)	Last time when any change was made to recorded statistics for this table. Null if no statistics are available.
COLCOUNT Smallint	The number of columns in the table or view.
TABLEID Smallint	Internal table identifier.
TBSPACEID Smallint	Internal identifier of the primary tablespace in which this table is stored. Zero for aliases and views.
CARD Integer	Number of rows in the table. −1 if unknown or if the object being described is not a table.
NPAGES Integer	Number of pages occupied by rows of this table. −1 if unknown or if the object being described is not a table.
FPAGES Integer	Total number of pages in the file used to store this table. −1 if unknown or if the object being described is not a table.
OVERFLOW Integer	The number of overflow records associated with this table. −1 if unknown or if the object being described is not a table.
TBSPACE Varchar(18) (allows nulls)	The name of the primary tablespace in which rows of the table are stored. Null for aliases and views.
INDEX_TBSPACE Varchar(18) (allows nulls)	The name of the tablespace that holds all the indexes created on this table. If this column is null, the indexes are created in the primary tablespace.
LONG_TBSPACE Varchar(18) (allows nulls)	The name of the tablespace that holds all large objects stored in this table (datatypes Long Varchar, Long Vargraphic, Blob, Clob, and Dbclob). If this column is null, the large objects are contained in the primary tablespace.

Column	Description
PARENTS Smallint (allows nulls)	The number of parent tables to which this table is related as a child table in a referential integrity constraint. Zero for aliases and views.
CHILDREN Smallint (allows nulls)	The number of child tables to which this table is related as a parent table in a referential integrity constraint. Zero for aliases and views.
SELFREFS Smallint (allows nulls)	The number of referential integrity constraints in which this table is related to itself as both parent and child. Zero for aliases and views.
KEYCOLUMNS Smallint (allows nulls)	The number of columns in the primary key of this table. Zero for aliases and views.
KEYINDEXID Smallint (allows nulls)	The internal identifier of the index that is used to enforce uniqueness of the primary key for this table. Zero for aliases and views.
KEYUNIQUE Smallint	Number of unique constraints that are defined on this table.
CHECKCOUNT Smallint	Number of check constraints that are defined on this table. Zero for aliases and views.
DATACAPTURE Char(1)	Y = Table participates in data replication. N = Does not participate in data replication.
CONST_CHECKED Char(32)	Indicates the status of the constraints that apply to this table. Byte 1 represents all referential integrity constraints, and byte 2 represents all check constraints. The other bytes are reserved. Status is encoded as follows: Y = Constraints are in normal status, checked and enforced by the system. U = Constraints are not checked by the system and may be violated, but access to the table is allowed. A table can be put into this status by the statement SET CONSTRAINTS FOR <table> IMMEDIATE UNCHECKED. N = Constraints are in Check Pending status (temporarily suspended, usually during loading of data). Constraints are not checked by the system, and normal access to the table is not allowed.
PMAP_ID Smallint (Allows nulls)	Identifier of the partition map used by this table. Null for aliases and views.
PARTITION_MODE Char(1)	Indicates how data is partitioned among nodes in a parallel system. H = Hashing. (blank) = No partitioning (also blank for views and aliases).

Column	Description
LOG_ATTRIBUTE Char(1)	0 = Table has normal logging. N = Table was created with "not logged initially" option, therefore cannot participate in referential integrity relationships.
PCTFREE Smallint	Percentage of space on each page that is reserved for future inserts. Can be changed by ALTER TABLE.
REMARKS Varchar(254) (allows nulls)	Descriptive comment provided by a user via the COMMENT ON TABLE or COMMENT ON ALIAS statement.

D.1.33 TABLESPACES

Each row represents a tablespace.

Column	Description
TBSPACE Varchar(18)	Name of the tablespace. Tablespaces have one-part names (not qualified by a schema name).
DEFINER Char(8)	User who defined the tablespace.
CREATE_TIME Timestamp	Time when the tablespace was created.
TBSPACEID Integer	Internal tablespace identifier.
TBSPACETYPE Char(1)	The type of the tablespace. S = System-managed space. D = Database-managed space.
DATATYPE Char(1)	The type of data that can be stored in the tablespace. A = All types of data. L = Long data only. T = Temporary tables only.
EXTENTSIZE Integer	The size of the extent used by this tablespace, in 4K pages. This many pages are written to one container in the tablespace before switching to the next container.
PREFETCHSIZE Integer	The number of 4K pages to be read when prefetch is performed in this tablespace.
OVERHEAD Double	The time required to begin an input/output operation, in milliseconds, averaged over the containers in this tablespace. Consists of a combination of controller overhead and disk seek and latency time.

Column	Description
TRANSFERRATE Double	Rate at which data can be read or written in this tablespace. Expressed in terms of milliseconds required to read one 4K page into a buffer, averaged over the containers in this tablespace.
PAGESIZE Integer	Size (in bytes) of pages in the tablespace.
NGNAME Varchar(18)	Name of the nodegroup for the tablespace.
BUFFERPOOLID Integer	ID of the bufferpool used by this tablespace (1 indicates default bufferpool).
REMARKS Varchar(254) (allows nulls)	Descriptive comment provided by a user via the COMMENT ON TABLESPACE statement.

D.1.34 TRIGDEP

Each row represents a dependency of a trigger on some other object. If an object that a trigger depends on is dropped, the trigger becomes inoperative.

Column	Description
TRIGSCHEMA Char(8)	The qualified name of the trigger.
TRIGNAME Varchar(18)	
BTYPE Char(1)	The type of the object that the trigger depends on. A = Alias. F = Function instance. T = Table. V = View.
BSCHEMA Char(8)	The qualified name of the object that the trigger depends on. If the object is a function instance, this is the specific name of the function instance.
BNAME Varchar(18)	
TABAUTH Smallint (allows nulls)	If BTYPE = T or V, this column encodes the operations that are performed by this trigger on the table or view. This is a means of recording a dependency of the trigger on the privileges required to perform these operations.

D.1.35 TRIGGERS

Each row represents a trigger.

Column	Description
TRIGSCHEMA Char(8)	The qualified name of the trigger.
TRIGNAME Varchar(18)	
DEFINER Char(8)	Authid under which the trigger was defined.
TABSCHEMA Char(8)	The qualified name of the table to which this trigger applies.
TABNAME Varchar(18)	
TRIGTIME Char(1)	The time when triggered actions are applied to the base table, relative to the event that activated the trigger. B = Trigger applied before event. A = Trigger applied after event.
TRIGEVENT Char(1)	The event that activates the trigger. I = Insert. D = Delete. U = Update.
GRANULARITY Char(1)	Indicates whether the trigger body is executed only once for the SQL statement that activates the trigger, or once for each row that is modified in the database. R = Row. S = Statement.
VALID Char(1)	Y = Trigger is valid. X = Trigger is inoperative. The definition of the trigger is retained in the catalog table, but in order to become valid the trigger must be recreated by a CREATE TRIGGER statement.
TEXT Clob(32K)	The full text of the CREATE TRIGGER statement, exactly as typed.
CREATE_TIME Timestamp	The time at which the trigger was created. This timestamp is used in resolving functions used by the trigger. No function will be selected that was created after the trigger was defined.
FUNC_PATH Varchar(254)	Records the function path at the time the trigger was defined. Used in resolving functions used by the trigger.
REMARKS Varchar(254) (allows nulls)	A descriptive comment supplied by a user via the COMMENT ON TRIGGER statement.

D.1.36 VIEWDEP

Each row represents a dependency of a view on some other object.

Column	Description
VIEWSCHEMA Char(8)	The qualified name of the view.
VIEWNAME Varchar(18)	
DEFINER Char(8) (allows nulls)	The user who created the view.
BTYPE Char(1)	The type of object that the view depends on. A = Alias. F = User-defined function instance. T = Table. V = View.
BSCHEMA Char(8)	The qualified name of the object that the view depends on.
BNAME Varchar(18)	
TABAUTH Smallint (allows nulls)	If BTYPE is T (table) or V (view), this column indicates which privileges on the underlying table or view are inherited by this view. Revocation of one of these underlying privileges from the definer of the view will cause loss of the same privilege on the view.

D.1.37 VIEWS

Each row represents a view.

Column	Description
VIEWSCHEMA Char(8)	The qualified name of the view.
VIEWNAME Varchar(18)	
DEFINER Char(8)	The user who created the view.
SEQNO Smallint	If the view definition is longer than 3,600 characters, it must be stored in fragments, one fragment per row. This column is a sequence number that permits the fragments to be reassembled into a complete view definition.

Column	Description
VIEWCHECK Char(1)	Indicates the check option that was specified when the view was created. The check option requires rows that are inserted or updated in the view to satisfy the view definition after the insertion or update. N = No check option. L = Local check option. C = Cascaded check option.
READONLY Char(1)	Indicates whether the view is inherently read-only because of its definition. Y = View is read-only. N = Rows of the view can be inserted, deleted, or updated by users with appropriate authorization.
VALID Char(1)	Indicates whether the view is currently in a valid state. Y = View is valid. X = View is inoperative; its definition is retained in the catalog table, but before it can be used it must be recreated by a CREATE VIEW statement.
FUNC_PATH Varchar(254)	The function path of the view creator at the time the view was defined. This path is used for resolving functions used inside the view definition. Function resolution for this view is also influenced by the CREATE_TIME timestamp in the TABLES entry that describes this view.
TEXT Varchar(3600)	The full text of the CREATE VIEW statement, exactly as typed. If the text is longer than 3,600 characters, it is stored in fragments, one per row.

D.2 SYSSTAT UPDATABLE CATALOG VIEWS

All the following catalog views are contained in the SYSSTAT schema. These views are defined in such a way that users see only those rows that they are authorized to update. Users with DBADM authority see all the updatable catalog rows, but other users see only those rows that pertain to objects that they own or for which they have CONTROL privilege.

The SYSSTAT catalog views can be updated by SQL statements, much like other tables. The views support only SQL UPDATE statements, not INSERT or DELETE statements. Furthermore, in each view, only certain columns are updatable. In the following descriptions, only the columns listed below the double line in each catalog are updatable.

Each of the updatable catalog views is defined with certain checks to ensure that the values assigned to its updatable columns are valid statistical values that can be used by the query optimizer. Catalog columns do not permit null values, except as noted.

D.2.1 COLDIST

This view contains statistics gathered about the distribution of data values in the columns of base tables, for use by the query optimizer. Each row describes either the *n*th most frequent value of some column, or the *n*th quantile (cumulative distribution) value for some column. Users of this view can see only statistics on those tables for which they hold CONTROL privilege (but users with DBADM authority can see statistics on all tables).

Column	Description
TABSCHEMA Char(8)	Qualified name of the table to which this row applies.
TABNAME Varchar(18)	
COLNAME Varchar(18)	Name of the column to which this row applies.
TYPE Char(1)	Indicates the type of data contained in this row. F = Frequent value. Q = Quantile value (for example, if five quantile values are maintained for a given column, 20% of the column values will be less than the first quantile value, 40% of the column values will be less than the second quantile value, and so on).
SEQNO Smallint	If TYPE = F, then *n* in this column identifies the *n*th most frequent value. If TYPE = Q, then *n* in this column identifies the *n*th quantile value.
COLVALUE Varchar(33) (allows nulls)	The data value, as a character literal, such as 1.23E − 4. If the length of the literal is greater than 33 characters, it is truncated. A distinct-type value is represented as a value of the underlying base datatype. A null value in COLVALUE indicates that the value being described is null.
VALCOUNT Integer	If TYPE = F, then VALCOUNT is the number of occurrences of COLVALUE in the column. If TYPE = Q, then VALCOUNT is the number of rows whose value is less than or equal to COLVALUE.
DISTCOUNT Integer (allows nulls)	If TYPE = Q, then DISTCOUNT is the number of distinct values in this column that are less than or equal to COLVALUE (null if unknown).

D.2.2 COLUMNS

This view contains information about the values stored in the columns of base tables. Users of this view can see only information on those tables for which they hold CONTROL privilege (but users with DBADM authority can see information on all tables).

Column	Description
TABSCHEMA Char(8)	The qualified name of the table or view containing this column.
TABNAME Varchar(18)	
COLNAME Varchar(18)	The name of the column.
COLCARD Integer	Number of distinct values in the column (–1 if unknown).
HIGH2KEY Varchar(33)	Second highest data value in the column, represented as a literal in character-string format (zero-length string if unknown).
LOW2KEY Varchar(33)	Second lowest data value in the column, represented as a literal in character-string format (zero-length string if unknown).
AVGCOLLEN Integer	Average length of column values (–1 if unknown or if the datatype of the column is a long or LOB datatype).

D.2.3 FUNCTIONS

This view contains information about the cost of executing user-defined functions. This information may be helpful to the optimizer in scheduling the execution of these functions. Information about functions is not provided by the RUNSTATS facility, so the estimates in FUNCTIONS are initialized to –1 (unknown) and remain unknown unless updated by the user. The system supplies default assumptions whenever function costs are unknown. A user of this view sees only information on those function instances whose schema name matches their userid (but a user with DBADM authority can see information on all function instances).

Column	Description
FUNCSCHEMA Char(8)	Qualified name of the function.
FUNCNAME Varchar(18)	
SPECIFICNAME Varchar(18)	Specific name of the function instance.

Column	Description
IOS_PER_INVOC Double	Estimated number of input/output operations per invocation of the function. −1 if not known (0 assumed).
INSTS_PER_INVOC Double	Estimated number of CPU instructions per invocation of the function. −1 if not known.
IOS_PER_ARGBYTE Double	Estimated average number of input/output operations per byte of each input parameter. −1 if not known (0 assumed).
INSTS_PER_ARGBYTE Double	Estimated average number of CPU instructions per byte of each input parameter. −1 if not known (0 assumed).
PERCENT_ARGBYTES Smallint	Estimated average percent of its input parameter bytes that the function will actually read. −1 if not known (100 assumed).
INITIAL_IOS Double	Estimated number of "startup" input/output operations performed on the first invocation of the function in an SQL statement. −1 if not known (0 assumed).
INITIAL_INSTS Double	Estimated number of "startup" CPU instructions executed on the first invocation of the function in an SQL statement. −1 if not known (0 assumed).
CARDINALITY Integer	The predicted number of rows returned by a table function. −1 if not known or if function is not a table function.

D.2.4 INDEXES

This view contains statistical information about indexes and their key values. Users of this view can see only information about those indexes for which they hold CONTROL privilege (but users with DBADM authority can see information on all indexes).

Column	Description
INDSCHEMA Char(8)	The qualified name of the index.
INDNAME Varchar(18)	
NLEAF Integer	Number of leaf pages (lowest-level pages) occupied by the index. −1 if not known.
NLEVELS Smallint	Number of levels in the index. −1 if not known.
FIRSTKEYCARD Integer	Number of different values in the first key column of the index. −1 if not known.

Column	Description
FIRST2KEYCARD Integer	Number of different value combinations in the first two key columns of the index. −1 if not known.
FIRST3KEYCARD Integer	Number of different value combinations in the first three key columns of the index. −1 if not known.
FIRST4KEYCARD Integer	Number of different value combinations in the first four key columns of the index. −1 if not known.
FULLKEYCARD Integer	Number of different values in the full index key. −1 if not known.
CLUSTERRATIO Smallint	A measure of how well the ordering of this index corresponds to the physical ordering of rows in storage. −1 if not known. Values may range from 0 to 100.
CLUSTERFACTOR Double	A finer measure of how well the index ordering corresponds to the physical ordering of rows in storage (used in optimizer cost formulas). −1 if not known. Values may range from 0 to 1.
SEQUENTIAL_PAGES Integer	Number of index leaf pages located on disk in index key order with few or no large gaps between them. −1 if not known.
DENSITY Integer	Ratio of SEQUENTIAL_PAGES to number of pages in the range of pages occupied by the index, expressed as a percent between 0 and 100. −1 if not known.
PAGE_FETCH_PAIRS Varchar(254) for bit data	A list of pairs of integers, represented in character form. Each pair represents the number of pages in a hypothetical buffer and the number of page fetches required to scan the index using that hypothetical buffer. (Zero-length string if no data available.)

D.2.5 TABLES

This view contains statistical information about the values stored in base (user) tables. Users of this view can see only information about tables for which they hold CONTROL privilege (but users with DBADM authority can see information on all base tables).

Column	Description
TABSCHEMA Char(8)	The qualified name of the table.
TABNAME Varchar(18)	

Column	Description
CARD Integer	Number of rows in the table (–1 if unknown).
NPAGES Integer	Number of pages occupied by rows of this table (–1 if unknown).
FPAGES Integer	Total number of pages in the file used to store this table (–1 if unknown).
OVERFLOW Integer	The number of overflow records associated with this table (–1 if unknown).

E

Syntax for Host Variable Declarations in C and C++

T his appendix summarizes the syntax that can be used for declaring host variables inside the SQL Declare Section of a C or C++ application program. In the syntax diagrams, items appearing in italics represent user-supplied names, lengths, and initial values. (Examples of host variable declarations, and an explanation of how they are used, can be found in Section 4.1.)

With each syntax diagram, a table is provided indicating the typecodes that correspond to the declarations in the diagram. Each datatype has two typecodes: an even typecode that indicates non-nullable data and an odd typecode that indicates nullable data. A host variable is considered nullable if it is used together with an indicator variable.

Some of the syntax diagrams in this appendix indicate that host variables can be declared as pointers. If a host variable is declared as a pointer, it must point to an object of a specific size, and it must be dereferenced each time it is used in an SQL statement. For example, the following code fragment declares host variables that are pointers to an integer and to an array of seven characters, respectively, and then uses these variables (properly dereferenced) in an SQL UPDATE statement:

```
EXEC SQL BEGIN DECLARE SECTION;
    long *p1;        /* pointer to long integer    */
    char (*p2)[7];   /* pointer to array of 7 chars */
EXEC SQL END DECLARE SECTION;

long newsalary = 25;
p1 = &newsalary;
p2 = (char(*)[7])"123456";  /* cast string to proper type */

EXEC SQL
    UPDATE emp SET salary = :*p1 WHERE empno = :*p2;
```

E.1 BASIC DATATYPES

Host variables for the basic SQL datatypes are declared in the SQL Declare Section, using pure C/C++ syntax, as shown in the following syntax diagrams.

E.1.1 Numeric Host Variables

Host variables for exchanging numeric data are declared as follows:

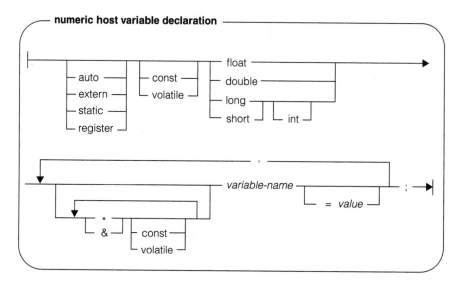

The SQL datatype of a numeric host variable is determined as shown in Table E-1.

TABLE E-1: SQL Datatypes Corresponding to Numeric Host Variables

If the declaration contains . . .	The SQL datatype is considered to be . . .	The SQLTYPE code for this datatype is . . . (not nullable/nullable)
float	Real	480/481 (length = 4)
double	Double	480/481 (length = 8)
long	Integer	496/497
short	Smallint	500/501

E.1.2 String Host Variables

Host variables for exchanging string data in null-terminated form are declared as follows:

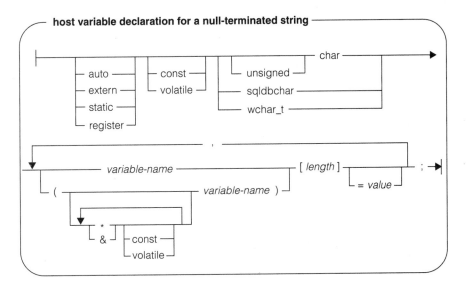

Notes:

- The precompiler permits a string-type variable to be declared without an explicit length, which implies a length of one character. To avoid confusion, I recommend always declaring an explicit length for string-type variables.

- Null-terminated variables should not be used to exchange data with columns declared FOR BIT DATA, since the data stored in these columns may contain binary zeros.

- If a variable is declared to be a pointer, it must point to an object of well-defined length. For example, char (*p)[20] is a pointer to a character string of length 20. Do not use the notation char *p to indicate a pointer to a string of indefinite length.

- Handling of double-byte strings is affected by the WCHARTYPE and LANG-LEVEL precompiler options. See the *DB2 Application Programming Guide* for details.

- To initialize a string variable of type wchar_t, use an L-type C literal such as L"double-byte data".

- The SQL datatype of the host variable is determined as shown in Table E-2.

TABLE E-2: SQL Datatypes Corresponding to Null-Terminated String Host Variables

If the declaration contains . . .	The SQL datatype is considered to be . . .	The SQLTYPE code for this datatype is . . . (not nullable/nullable)
char	Varchar (null-terminated)	460/461
sqldbchar or wchar_t	Vargraphic (null-terminated)	400/401

Host variables for exchanging string data in length-prefix form are declared as follows:

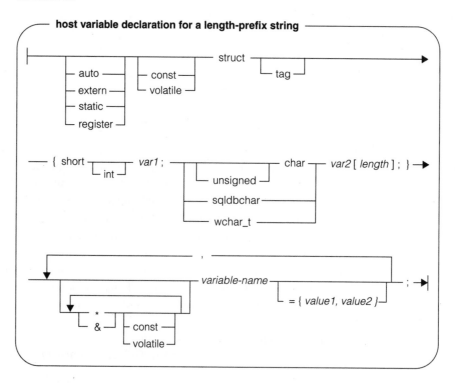

The SQL datatype of a length-prefix host variable is determined as shown in Table E-3.

TABLE E-3: SQL Datatypes Corresponding to Length-Prefix Host Variables

If the declaration contains . . .	The SQL datatype is considered to be . . .	The SQLTYPE code for this datatype is . . . (not nullable/nullable)
char, and length is 4,000 or less	Varchar	448/449
char, and length is between 4,001 and 32,700	Long Varchar	456/457
sqldbchar or wchar_t, and length is 2,000 or less	Vargraphic	464/465
sqldbchar or wchar_t, and length is between 2,001 and 16,350	Long Vargraphic	472/473

E.2 LARGE-OBJECT DATATYPES

UDB has three datatypes called LOB types for representing large objects. Host variables for exchanging data using these datatypes can be declared in the SQL Declare Section, using special syntax that is translated into C syntax by the SQL precompiler. (The LOB datatypes are discussed in Section 6.1.)

E.2.1 LOB Host Variables

Host variables for exchanging LOB data are declared as follows:

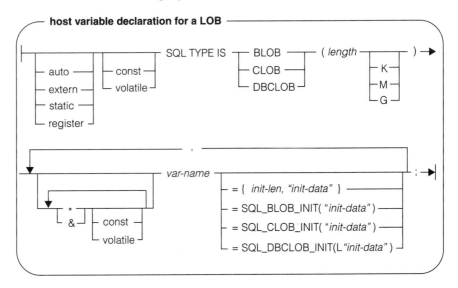

TABLE E-4: SQL Datatypes Corresponding to LOB Host Variables

SQL Datatype	SQLTYPE Code (not nullable/nullable)
Blob	404/405
Clob	408/409
Dbclob	412/413

Notes:

- SQL TYPE IS, BLOB, CLOB, DBCLOB, K, M, and G may be in mixed case.
- The maximum length of an initializing data string is 4,000 bytes.
- To initialize a Dbclob, use an L-type C literal such as L"double-byte data" if your program is precompiled with the option WCHARTYPE CONVERT.
- The syntax in the diagram above can be used to declare host variables of the types listed in Table E-4.

E.2.2 Locators and File References

Host variables for exchanging LOB data by means of locators or file references are declared as follows:

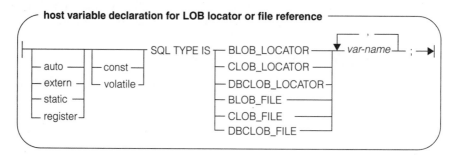

Notes:

- The SQL keywords in the declaration can be in mixed case.
- In a declaration of a LOB locator or file reference, the value of the LOB cannot be initialized. However, the *Embedded SQL Programming Guide* describes a variation of the syntax above that permits declaration of a pointer to a locator or file reference, and initialization of the pointer. This syntax has been omitted here for simplicity and clarity.
- The syntax in the diagram above can be used to declare host variables of the types listed in Table E-5.

TABLE E-5: SQL Datatypes Corresponding to Locator and File-Reference Host Variables

SQL Datatype	SQLTYPE Code (not nullable/nullable)
Blob Locator	960/961
Clob Locator	964/965
Dbclob Locator	968/969
Blob File Reference	804/805
Clob File Reference	808/809
Dbclob File Reference	812/813

F IBM Publications

The IBM documentation for the UDB product family consists of the publications listed below. When you purchase UDB, all the publications pertaining to your version of the product are included on the product CD, in PostScript format for printing and also in HTML form for viewing with a web browser. The publications can also be ordered individually from IBM using the form numbers in the tables below.

F.1 PLATFORM-INDEPENDENT PUBLICATIONS

The publications listed in Table F-1 describe aspects of UDB that apply across multiple platforms.

TABLE F-1: Platform-Independent Publications

Form Number	Title and Description
S10J-8154	*Administration Getting Started* Introduces basic concepts and tasks needed to administer a UDB database.
S10J-8157	*Administration Guide* Describes techniques and facilities used by UDB database administrators.
S10J-8167	*API Reference* Describes how to use application programming interfaces to perform database administration tasks.
S10J-8159	*CLI Guide and Reference* Describes how to develop application programs using the Call Level Interface.
S10J-8166	*Command Reference* Describes how to use system commands to perform database administration functions. Also describes how to use the Command Line Processor.
S10J-7888	*DB2 Connect Enterprise Edition Quick Beginnings* Provides basic information for installing, configuring, and using DB2 Connect Enterprise Edition and its clients.

TABLE F-1 *(Continued)*

Form Number	Title and Description
S10J-8162	*DB2 Connect Personal Edition Quick Beginnings* Provides basic information for installing, configuring, and using DB2 Connect Personal Edition.
S10J-8163	*DB2 Connect User's Guide* A general user's manual for DB2 Connect products.
S10J-8158	*Embedded SQL Programming Guide* Describes how to develop application programs using SQL statements embedded in a host programming language.
No form number (HTML only)	*Glossary* Provides definitions for terms used in UDB documentation.
No form number (HTML and PostScript only)	*Installing and Configuring DB2 Clients* Provides instructions for installing UDB client software: Client Application Enabler (CAE) and Software Developer's Kit (SDK).
S10J-8170	*Master Index* Provides a combined index for all the UDB publications.
S10J-8168	*Message Reference* Contains explanations for all messages and codes used in UDB.
S95H-0999	*Replication Guide and Reference* A general user's manual for the UDB data replication tools.
S10J-8155	*Road Map to DB2 Programming* Introduces various ways in which application programs can interact with UDB databases.
S10J-8156	*SQL Getting Started* Introduces the basic concepts of SQL.
S10J-8165	*SQL Reference* A complete reference manual for the SQL language as used in UDB.
S10J-8164	*System Monitor Guide and Reference* Describes how to use the system monitor to measure database activity, improve performance, and diagnose problems.
S10J-8169	*Troubleshooting Guide* Provides instructions for diagnosing and recovering from problems.

F.2 PLATFORM-SPECIFIC PUBLICATIONS

The publications listed in Table F-2 describe aspects of UDB that apply to a specific platform or group of platforms.

TABLE F-2: Platform-Specific Publications

Form Number	Title and Description
S10J-8161	*Building Applications for UNIX Environments* Provides step-by-step instructions for precompiling, compiling, and linking UDB application programs on AIX and other UNIX platforms.
S10J-8160	*Building Applications for Windows and OS/2 Environments* Provides step-by-step instructions for precompiling, compiling, and linking UDB application programs on Windows and OS/2 platforms.
S72H-9620	*DB2 Extended Enterprise Edition Quick Beginnings* Provides information on installing, configuring, and using UDB Extended Enterprise Edition on the AIX platform.
S10J-8150	*DB2 Personal Edition Quick Beginnings* Provides information on installing, configuring, and using UDB Personal Edition on OS/2, Windows 95, and Windows NT platforms.
S10J-8147	*Quick Beginnings for OS/2* Provides information on installing, configuring, and using UDB on the OS/2 platform.
S10J-8148	*Quick Beginnings for UNIX* Provides information on installing, configuring, and using UDB on AIX and other UNIX platforms.
S10J-8149	*Quick Beginnings for Windows NT* Provides information on installing, configuring, and using UDB on the Windows NT platform.

Index

Bold page numbers indicate a syntax diagram.

ABOUT THE AUTHOR

Don Chamberlin and Ray Boyce invented the SQL database language (originally called SEQUEL) in 1974. Don was also one of the managers of the System R project at IBM San Jose Research Laboratory, which produced the first implementation of SQL. For the development of SQL and System R, Don and several of his colleagues received the ACM Software System Award in 1988.

Don holds a B.S. from Harvey Mudd College and a Ph.D. from Stanford University. He has published numerous papers on database management, was named an ACM Fellow in 1994, and was elected to the National Academy of Engineering in 1997. He is also a member of the IBM Academy of Technology.

Don is a member of the research staff at IBM's Almaden Research Center, where he is working on object-relational features for future versions of DB2. He also teaches classes in computer engineering at Santa Clara University.